Windows™ Sockets Network Programming

Addison-Wesley Advanced Windows Series

Alan R. Feuer, Consulting Editor

The Addison-Wesley Advanced Windows Series focuses on programming for Windows 95 and Windows NT using the C and C++ programming languages. The series provides professional programmers with practical books that are technically sophisticated. Each book will cover in detail a specific aspect of Windows programming more deeply than the general reference manual, and will contain a testbed application that allows a programmer to experiment with the concepts covered in the text. The sample application, usable on its own, also provides a springboard for writing other applications.

Windows™ Sockets Network Programming

Bob Quinn
Dave Shute

ADDISON-WESLEY PUBLISHING COMPANY
Reading, Massachusetts · Menlo Park, California · New York · Don Mills, Ontario
Wokingham, England · Amsterdam · Bonn · Sydney · Singapore · Tokyo
Madrid · San Juan · Seoul · Milan · Mexico City · Taipei

The publisher offers discounts on this book when ordered in quantity for special sales.

For more information, please contact:

Corporate & Professional Publishing Group
Addison-Wesley Publishing Company
One Jacob Way
Reading, Massachusetts 01867

Text printed on recycled and acid-free paper

ISBN 0-201-63372-8

4 5 6 7 8 9 10 MA 00999897

Fouth printing, March 1997

To Sean, Melanie, Ann, and Rosemary — you're the greatest!

B.Q.

Contents

Foreword

In 1991 it was becoming apparent that Microsoft Windows was going to play a definitive role in the future of desktop computing. At the same time, if you listened closely, you could hear the first rumblings of the earth-shaking impact TCP/IP was going to have on the lives of many people. At the intersection of Microsoft Windows and TCP/IP, however, lay a problem. All the vendors of TCP/IP products for PCs had produced different programming interfaces for their own products. I was one of many programmers around the world sitting at my PC late at night telling myself *there must be a better way*.

That "better way" got started at a BOF ("Birds of a Feather") session at Interop in October 1991. In a room containing 30 or so of the brightest minds in the industry, the idea of creating a single, standard transport interface took shape. The key criteria were to keep it as close to the existing Berkeley Sockets API as possible and not to require a shoehorn to use the interface in a Windows message-based application. It's often tempting for technical people to want to do a perfect job and include everything in a technical design. One key decision we made as a group was to limit what we included in the interface to what the majority of programmers needed. Combined with the energy and willingness of competitive vendors to work together, this laid the foundation for the creation and success of the Windows Sockets API, or "WinSock" as it has become known.

Over the next 15 months, many people on the WinSock mailing list contributed to the development of the preliminary specification. Several interoperability sessions (WinSockathons) took place, and the result of this cooperative effort was the Windows Sockets version 1.1 API specification.

WinSock lies right at the heart of the explosion of interest in developing and using communications applications on Microsoft Windows PCs. The global community of developers who cooperated to define this programming standard is being joined by other programmers from all over the world who want to add communications capabilities to their software applications by using WinSock. In short, WinSock has become hugely popular and has been badly in need of a great book. Until now.

I'm honored to have been asked to write the foreword to this book. It fills a gaping hole by providing developers with the contextual framework and information detail needed to develop high-quality WinSock software. Whether you are new to WinSock or consider yourself a WinSock expert, you will learn things from this book. Bob and Dave draw on extensive, solid, pragmatic experience with WinSock. They give you an illuminating guided tour of what you need to know to develop robust WinSock-based software. In the same spirit of pragmatism exhibited by the WinSock Group, Bob and Dave have empathized with programmers in constructing this book. The first few chapters provide a solid background and framework within which to understand the details of WinSock, how it can best be used and exploited relative to your own programming requirements. For writing WinSock clients, servers, or intermediary DLL components, the following chapters are well structured and provide exactly the right level of detail and accessibility. Finally, as WinSock continues to thrive and progress, knowing where to go to get yet more information is important, so the appendices include pointers to other information sources.

Bob Quinn and Dave Shute have been immersed in WinSock since the beginning. They know it outside in, inside out, and probably dream about it in their sleep. I applaud them for their dreams and their efforts and wholeheartedly recommend this book.

Martin Hall
WinSock Group Chairman
CTO, Stardust Technologies, Inc.
May 1995

Preface

This book describes the Windows Sockets application programming interface (API), commonly known as "WinSock." This is intended to be a companion to the v1.1 Windows Sockets specification, not a replacement for it. The contents provide a roadmap for the specification, an orientation resource. The book describes and illustrates every aspect of the Windows Sockets specification, from top to bottom. It deals with optional features as well as many features in version 2.0 of the Windows Sockets specification.

The key focus of the text is to provide a "how to" guide for writing supportable and extensible network applications that will run efficiently over all Windows Sockets implementations. One of the most frustrating things to hear is, "It's impossible to write anything more than a basic 'hello world' that will execute over all WinSock implementations." This simply is not true. More often than not, when an application runs on one WinSock and fails on another, it is because the application developers made some incorrect assumptions. They assumed that WinSock could do something that the specification did not explicitly warrant. In other words, it may not have been the fault of the WinSock implementor, nor of the WinSock specification. You can avoid this type of application failure, and we show you how.

This book is for anyone who wants to know how to write a successful WinSock application. If you are writing a program from scratch, porting an existing one from Berkeley Sockets (or any other network API), writing a network DLL, or just updating an application that someone else wrote, then this book is for you. We deal with both 16-bit Windows platforms (Microsoft Windows 3.1 and Windows for Workgroups) and 32-bit platforms (Windows NT 3.1 and 3.5, and Windows 95). We also describe the other platforms that support the WinSock API: Platforms with Windows are adding Sockets.

Organization

The first half of the book contains a tutorial for network programming. We do not make any assumptions about what you already know. The second half is intended to be an in-depth reference, with detailed explanations and code examples. The appendices provide a quick reference.

After we describe Windows Sockets in general terms in Chapter 1, we provide an overview of network software architectures in Chapter 2. In

Chapter 3 we describe the protocols in the TCP/IP suite, with a focus on the services available to your network applications, and some of their pros and cons. We begin to provide some details about the WinSock programming interface in Chapter 4, as we describe the framework for all network applications in terms of the fundamental network function calls. Chapter 5 covers the different operation modes available, and Chapter 6 discusses the state machine implicit in every network application. That essentially ends the tutorial.

In Chapter 7 we present the source code for our largest application, an FTP client. Chapters 8, 9, and 10 are a catalog of detailed descriptions of all the WinSock function calls we have not discussed up to this point. Chapter 11 deals with the specifics of creating a dynamic link library to run over a WinSock DLL. Chapter 12 describes the issues and strategies involved with porting existing BSD Sockets source code to 16-bit and/or 32-bit Windows.

We start to wrap things up and tie up loose ends in Chapter 13, which details WinSock application debugging techniques and tools. Chapter 14 provides general advice and many specifics about traps and pitfalls to avoid in your WinSock applications. Chapter 15 describes the many different operating-system platforms that currently provide the WinSock API. Chapter 16 covers the optional features—some intentional, and some not—in the WinSock specification and tells you when and how to use them. Finally, Chapter 17 provides a detailed tour of all the new features in version 2.0 of the WinSock specification.

In Appendix A, we have illustrations and short descriptions of the headers for the protocols in the Internet suite (TCP/IP). Appendix B contains a quick reference for the entire WinSock API, including its functions, structures, and macros (including some that were forgotten). Appendix C provides a detailed WinSock error reference. Appendix D contains some mechanical details for compiling and linking applications, and Appendix E has network and bibliographical information sources.

Audience

Although we do not assume any prior knowledge of networks, protocols, or network programming with sockets or any other network API, it does not hurt to have some. This book is for novice and experienced network application developers alike. This text also includes extensive background and illustrative information not found in the v1.1 Windows Sockets specification, so even the most advanced WinSock application developer can benefit from reading it.

We do assume a knowledge of the C programming language and Microsoft Windows APIs (WinAPI or Win32).

Sample Applications

The sample applications in this book were created with Microsoft C version 1.51 (16-bit) and Microsoft C version 2.0 (32-bit). They are also compatible with Borland C version 4.0. Makefiles that support these platforms accompany the source code. The applications have been tested on almost all of the commercial and shareware versions of WinSock available, over Ethernet and PPP (point-to-point protocol), using both local and distant connections. If you find any problems with these applications, we'd like to hear about them. Please e-mail problem reports to bugs@sockets.com.

You can retrieve updates to the sample applications via the Internet:

```
http://www.sockets.com
ftp://ftp.sockets.com
```

Acknowledgments

Many thanks to many people for their help and participation in making this book possible. Thanks especially to the reader, who is the very reason for this book. May your Windows Sockets applications be great ones.

Thanks most of all to Bob Quinn. He wanted to give birth to this book; I only provided the hot water, towels, antiseptic, blankets, silver nitrate, topical anesthesia, and appropriate words.

Dave Shute Reading, MA
dks@world.std.com May 1995

There are far too many people that have helped in this endeavor for any acknowledgment list to do justice. Nonetheless, I want to mention a few people in particular. First and foremost, for their implicit contribution, is my family. It will be nice to spend time with them again. Second is my cowriter and friend, Dave Shute, whose red pencil is as pricelessly sharp as his wit.

I'm indebted to Larry Backman, Mike Khalandovsky, and John Keller at FTP Software, Inc., for their support and encouragement. Dave Barnard, Kerry Hannigan, and Helen Sylvester—FTP Software's crack SDK support staff—deserve a special note for their constant stream of challenges that did more to teach me about how to program—and how *not* to program—WinSock apps than anything else did.

My coadministrators in the WinSock 2.0 specification clarification functionality group, Paul Brooks and Vikas Garg, deserve a lot of credit for their untiring efforts to shed light into the dark corners of WinSock. In addition to clarifying many things in the spec, they also clarified some things in this book.

Other reviewers of note: Jim DeMarco, Fred Whiteside, Dave Andersen, Charlie Tai, Alun Jones, Eli Patashnik, and our consulting editor, Alan Feuer.

Thanks to the kind folks at Addison-Wesley: John Wait, Mike Hendrickson, Kim Dawley, Marty Rabinowitz, Simone Payment, and Katie Duffy.

Lastly, I want to thank Martin Hall for having initiated the Windows Sockets effort and his coauthors and contributors for helping him carry it through. The sure sign of a good idea is one that makes you think, "Why didn't I think of that!?" That's WinSock. It was a great idea, and its immediate success has confirmed this obvious fact.

Bob Quinn — Weston, Massachusetts
rcq@ftp.com — May 1995

1 Introduction to Windows Sockets

In This Chapter:

- What Is Windows Sockets?
- What Is Its History?
- What Are Its Benefits?
- What Is Its Future?
- Conclusion

Truth is a river that is always splitting up into arms that reunite. Islanded between the arms, the inhabitants argue for a lifetime as to which is the main river.

Cyril Connolly

Ask any network programmer about Windows Sockets, and most likely you will hear one of two very different reactions. The programmer will either angrily start listing the problems he or she has encountered, or enthusiastically start listing the gains he or she has made. The response depends on what question you ask. You'll get the former if you ask, "How do you like Windows Sockets?" You'll get the latter if you ask, "Would you give up Windows Sockets?"

Ask about life before Windows Sockets, and you are sure to hear about the *nightmare* that network programming used to be. Programmers universally talk with horror about what it was like to develop, package, and support a network application that could run over more than one TCP/IP software implementation in Microsoft Windows.[1] They remember that "dark time" when every TCP/IP vendor had its own network application programming interface (API).

[1] Windows is a trademark of Microsoft Corporation.

Version 1.1 of the Windows Sockets specification—better known as "WinSock"—has vastly improved network programming. It has established a single network API on which network software vendors were able to agree. True, it's not perfect: Varying interpretations have resulted in incompatibilities between WinSock implementations, and the specification allows optional support of some features that are not universally available. But these gray areas are on the fringes of the WinSock specification.

On the whole, the specification is complete and well defined and WinSock implementations are consistent. There are many success stories of applications that run well over all WinSock implementations. They include all types of applications: clients and servers that send and receive bulk or interactive data, using stream and datagram protocols. And they run on a variety of platforms, too: 16-bit Windows (Windows 3.x), 32-bit Windows (Windows NT and Windows 95), and others (OS/2, Sun workstations). The secret of their success is simple: They stay away from the fringes, the gray areas.

In this book we show you how to write a WinSock application that will run on any WinSock implementation. We highlight the gray areas and show you how to avoid them. We demonstrate defensive programming techniques so your application can deal with the vagaries of the network underneath the API, and the 16-bit and 32-bit Windows environments. We tell you what to do when your application encounters a network problem, so you will be able to help your customers when they call. In short, we tell you everything you need to know to write a successful WinSock application.

What Is Windows Sockets?

"Windows Sockets: An Open Interface for Network Programming under Microsoft Windows" is a specification that describes the WinSock network API. Version 1.1 is the current standard, released January 20, 1993. At this writing the provisional WinSock version 2.0 (revision 2.0.8, released May 19, 1995) is currently available, but there are no implementations available yet.

The specification is "open" in the same sense as other open systems: It was created in the spirit of cooperation, and it is freely available. WinSock resulted from a cooperative effort among a number of network software vendors. The specification, header file, and library are all you need to develop applications that use the WinSock API (assuming you have a C compiler and network stack), and these are publicly available (see Appendix D, "What You Need"). Anyone can create WinSock applications—or implement the API itself—without paying any licensing fees or royalties to its authors.

The Windows Sockets API (WSA) consists of a collection of function calls, data structures, and conventions. The WSA provides standard access to the network services of an underlying protocol stack to any Microsoft Windows application. You can create virtually any type of TCP/IP network application with the protocol services available through the Windows Sockets API. The API is comprehensive and flexible, yet because it insulates you from the low-level details of network processing, it's also clean and simple.

The Windows Sockets interface specification clearly defines the division of labor between the network application and the network protocol stack. It is a WinSock application's "job" to provide a good user interface and to format and parse data. It is the WinSock protocol stack's job to send and receive that data, using standard transport protocols, drivers, and network media. The application provides the content, and the stack provides the delivery.

Unlike many APIs, WinSock provides *binary compatibility* as well as source code compatibility. Consequently, programs require no changes at all when their executable version is moved from one network system vendor to another, or even between operating-system platforms.

The WinSock API is a kind of "programmatic plug" to the network. It is a standard network interface for applications in the same way a wall socket is a standard electric interface for appliances, or the phone jack is a standard

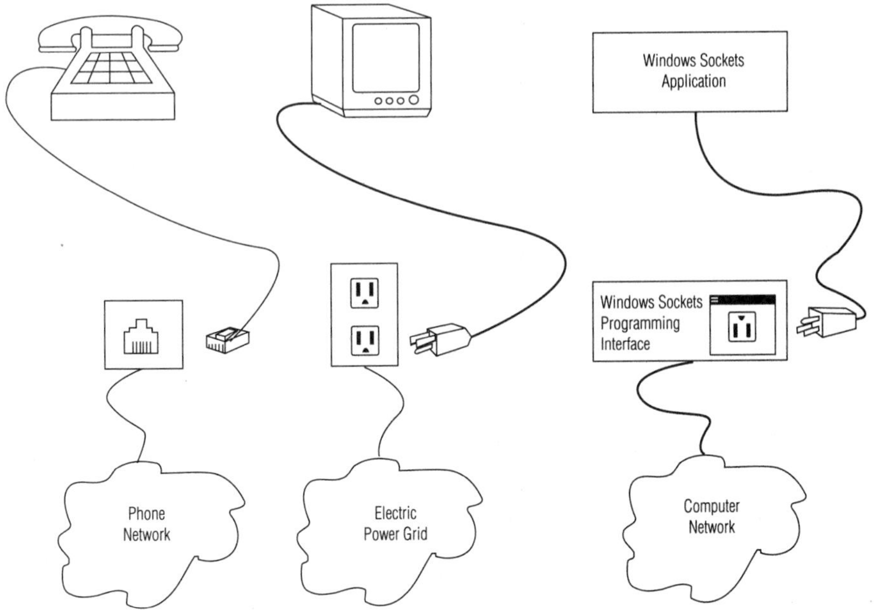

Figure 1-1 Standard applications using standard interfaces to access standard services.

system interface for telephones (see Figure 1-1). You can plug any appliance into any electric socket in any house, and it will work no matter how the power is generated—coal, water, nuclear fission—or what company generates it. You can plug any phone into any phone jack, and the phone will work no matter how the signal travels—copper, fiber, microwave—or what company sends it. You can now use any TCP/IP network application on any WinSock implementation, no matter what media it runs over—Ethernet, Token Ring, Serial Line—or what company provides the TCP/IP protocol stack. This means we now have universal network applications.

What Is Its History?

In the Fall of 1991, Martin Hall, of Stardust Technologies, organized an informal "birds-of-a-feather" gathering at InterOp, the flagship trade show of the TCP/IP networking industry. The purpose of the meeting was to investigate the possibility of creating a standard API for TCP/IP applications in Microsoft Windows. Representatives from PC-based TCP/IP protocol stack vendors and Windows network application developers were in attendance. Their conclusions were unanimous: A standard network API was essential to growth of the industry; the precedent of the Berkeley Sockets API was the model to build on; and the DLL technology was the most flexible vehicle. What began as an informal gathering became a formal working group.

The working group's charter required them to design an API that could better provide the basic network services necessary to create most client and server applications, and be provided by all network stack vendors. With Berkeley Sockets as its starting point, the group added APIs to fit the Windows message-based paradigm and deleted APIs that did not fit or were not commonly used. Expediency was a consideration in this process. In some cases, desirable APIs were excluded so that all network stack vendors could meet minimum requirements within the limits of their stack's functionality and architecture. The group also considered the need for portability between Windows systems (16-bit and 32-bit Windows).

In June of 1992, the working group released version 1.0 of the Windows Sockets API specification. Six months later, in January of 1993—after refining the API in working WinSock implementations—the group released version 1.1 of the specification, which is the current standard.

Windows Sockets now carries the endorsement of nearly all network software vendors, including Beame & Whiteside, DEC, Distinct, Frontier, FTP Software, Hewlett-Packard, Ipswitch, JSB Corporation, Microsoft, NetManage, Novell, Sun Microsystems, and Wollongong, to name just a few.

In the time since its release, a phenomenal number and variety of useful Windows Sockets applications have appeared, many of which are in the public domain. WinSock was instrumental in the success of the much-heralded Internet web browser Mosaic. Windows Sockets has come of age in the real world.

What Are Its Benefits?

This section examines the benefits Windows Sockets provides, as well as the beneficiaries. The benefits of the WinSock universal application interface are obvious. Life is simpler when one size fits all. When buying a new lamp, we take it for granted that the lamp will be compatible with the electricity provided by our local utility company. We can now take network service for granted the way we take electric service and phone service for granted. It's there and it works, and we don't have to give it a thought.

It Is an Open Standard

We all rely on a surprising number of formal and de facto standards in today's technology-rich world. This is especially true in the computer realm, where there are standard file formats, video graphics modes, and printer languages, to name just a few. Technology standards are more important than the technologies themselves, because the standards make technologies more accessible. The success of a technology depends in part on the need for that technology, but it also depends on how accessible it is.

Open standards make technology accessible and provide other benefits as well. The TCP/IP protocol suite is the ideal example of an open standard that has fostered the spread of technology. TCP/IP is responsible for the phenomenal growth of the Internet. Its success is due to its interoperability, which resulted from real-world testing and refinement by the many protocol stack and application developers involved in its development. This spirit of cooperation among competitors to develop a product that will benefit everyone is a hallmark of open standards. WinSock was developed in this spirit.

As an open standard, WinSock allows you to mix and match components from different vendors. It provides a well-defined interface, so that one vendor's product can interoperate with another's. It provides portability between platforms, and breeds healthy competition, since it allows comparison of products on a level playing field. It benefits both WinSock vendors and consumers. Everyone wins with WinSock.

It Provides Source Code Portability

The Windows Sockets API derives from the Berkeley Sockets API, as implemented in version 4.3 of the Berkeley Software Distribution (BSD4.3). Like its predecessor, Windows Sockets can provide access to different protocol suites, although version 1.1 of the Windows Sockets specification only focuses on TCP/IP. We also focus on TCP/IP in this book, although much of the material—like the API itself—is applicable to other protocols.

BSD Sockets is widely acknowledged as the standard programming interface for TCP/IP. TCP/IP was first widely supported on Berkeley UNIX machines, and the programming interface first provided was Berkeley Sockets. Not only has it been around for a while—since 1986, to be exact—it has been implemented on a number of different operating-system platforms. As a result, there are many programmers who know the Sockets API, and a lot of source code has been written for it. By building on this foundation, WinSock gives programmers a head start:

- Sockets application developers need only to complement their Sockets experience with Microsoft Windows application development techniques.
- Sockets application source code provides a working model of, or even ready-to-use, network code that needs only the addition of a graphical Microsoft Windows user interface.
- There are thousands of programs already written for Berkeley Sockets.

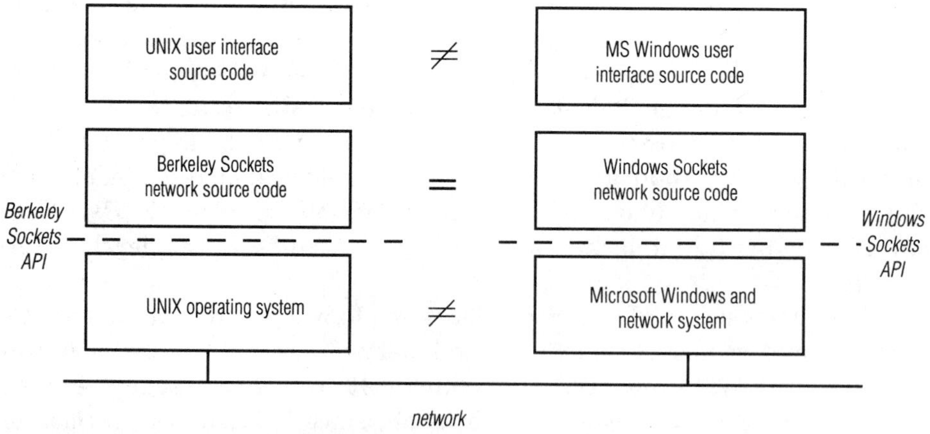

Figure 1-2 Network source code is portable from Berkeley Sockets to Windows Sockets.

You can bring much of your existing Berkeley Sockets application source code to Windows Sockets (see Figure 1-2). You will have to make substantial changes to adapt to the Microsoft Windows operating environment, especially in 16-bit Windows, but WinSock's BSD Sockets compatibility provides many advantages over starting an application from scratch.

For those already familiar with the Berkeley Sockets API, the learning curve for Windows Sockets is negligible. The shift from synchronous to asynchronous, message-based operation presents the highest hurdle you face. This shift—which represents a different way of thinking about program execution—exists for any application developer new to multitasking in the Windows environment. The concept of message-based operation is not specific to Windows Sockets applications alone, but to all Microsoft Windows applications.

The Windows Sockets API defines new asynchronous socket operation modes, but it also preserves existing synchronous modes. You can still create network applications that use the old network application models in which you wait for each network operation to complete (blocking) before proceeding to the next step, or poll (nonblocking) to detect operation completion. There are some significant caveats of which to be aware in 16-bit Windows, because it is not a "true multitasking" (preemptive) operating system (we highlight these for you throughout the book). Nonetheless, Windows Sockets' compatibility with Berkeley Sockets allows you to ease the transition to the Windows environment. This is especially true in the 32-bit Windows environments (NT and Windows 95), which provide preemptive multitasking similar to UNIX.

It Supports Dynamic Linking

Dynamic link libraries (DLLs) are a key feature of Microsoft Windows. They are libraries of executable procedures, with well-defined interfaces. As their name suggests, applications link with them dynamically at run time rather than statically at compile time. There are many advantages to this architecture:

- When multiple applications use a DLL simultaneously, they share code, which means there is only one copy of the DLL code in memory.
- The application is separate from the DLL, so you can change the DLL without changing the application (or vice versa).
- All DLLs that provide a compatible API also provide a compatible application binary interface (ABI).

The last advantage on the list is the most significant, because an ABI allows portability of executables, not just source code. This means that once you have compiled and linked your source code to create an executable program,

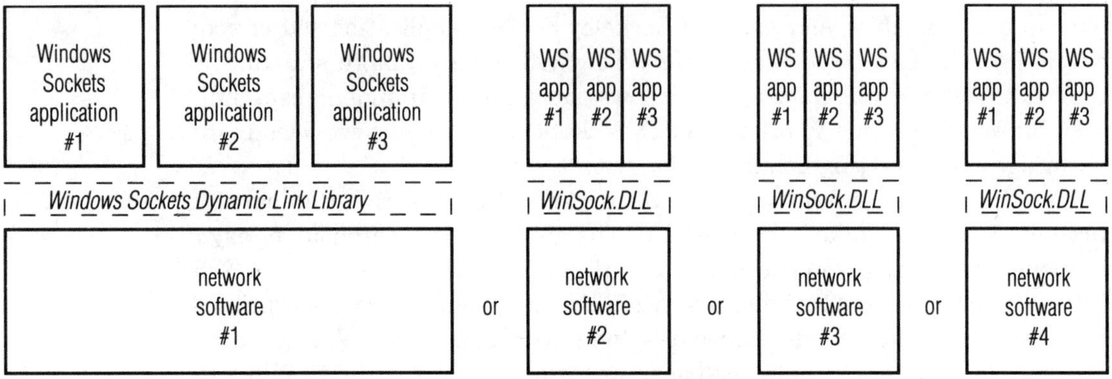

Figure 1-3 Any Windows Sockets-compatible application will run unchanged over any network protocol stack that has a Windows Sockets-compliant interface.

it will run over the Windows Sockets ABI—the WinSock.DLL dynamic link library file—from any vendor (see Figure 1-3). You will not have to recompile or relink your source code to execute your application over different vendors' WinSock.DLL. Conversely, you could also update your executable without changing the WinSock DLL. Binary portability gives you the ultimate in flexibility and convenience.

Benefits Summary

Windows Sockets spread a wealth of benefits to everyone creating, selling, using, and managing network protocol and application software. Everyone wins:

- Users get new and improved applications, since developers now have more time to dedicate to features, rather than to network API idiosyncrasies.
- Users can choose stacks based on price and performance rather than on what applications are available.
- Users can choose from a wider variety of applications.
- Network applications can run over protocol stacks they may not have supported otherwise.
- Network vendors broaden their base of third-party applications.
- Network vendors enjoy an efficiency of time, effort, and expense in maintenance of a single API.
- Network vendors and administrators have a clear and simple upgrade path provided by the dynamic link library support.

- Network software administrators, retailers, and distributors can stock a single version of a network application.

What Is Its Future?

The Windows Sockets specification is a living document. Its evolution has always been anticipated. Version 1.1 has proven itself in the many successful implementations and applications in use today. Its successor—Windows Sockets version 2.0, called WinSock 2—adds many useful new features that ensure WinSock's continued success well into the future.

The WinSock 2 API preserves the version 1.1 API in its entirety, so existing applications can still run without modification. It also adds many new features and clarifies ambiguities in version 1.1. In Chapter 17 we describe WinSock 2 in detail, but here's a brief summary of some of its more significant new features:

- It defines generic APIs that allow for creation of protocol-independent network applications. Such applications could use indiscriminately and without modification any of the protocols currently installed on a machine (e.g., TCP/IP, DECNet, OSI, SPX/IPX).
- It prescribes a new architecture for simultaneous execution of multiple name services and transport protocols.
- It defines TCP/IP extensions—such as raw sockets, interface list, out-of-band (OOB) setting (RFC 793 or 1122), IP header socket options, time-to-live setting, and multicast support—many of which are Berkeley sockets compatible.
- It adds support for quality-of-service specifications (QOS), which enhance support of link-layer protocols like ATM and ISDN, and address the special needs of new media for use in mobile computing.
- It provides "scatter and gather" to allow writing to and reading directly from multiple buffers during network I/O.
- It adds socket groups for priority assignment to benefit multimedia applications, so one data stream can take precedence over another during bandwidth shortages.
- It endorses asynchronous I/O and event objects (Win32 API concepts).
- It provides APIs for socket sharing (simultaneous access of a socket between different tasks).

- It provides for connect and disconnect data and conditional acceptance of incoming connections.
- It defines protocol-independent APIs for multipoint and multicast support.

Obviously, WinSock version 2.0 is a big step from version 1.1. This further development of the specification enhances its current status by making it more useful and expanding its scope. The many new functions WinSock 2 adds provide more flexibility and power to the API, but they also complicate it. Fortunately, the core API version 1.1 supports remain intact.

We concentrate on version 1.1 of the WinSock API in this book, giving details of a few useful new WinSock 2 additions in Chapter 17. Some of these features are also available as optional features in some version 1.1 WinSock implementations. With the solid understanding of version 1.1 concepts and usage this book provides, you will be equipped to take advantage of the additional features in WinSock 2 implementations.

Conclusion

Windows Sockets is an indispensable part of the network application development landscape. It is not perfect—there are still some troublesome differences between implementations—but it is possible to create applications that avoid the problems these differences create. The key is to use defensive programming techniques and avoid the ambiguous areas of the specification.

In this book we show you what to do, and what not to do, in order to create a Windows Sockets application that can run successfully on any WinSock implementation. We examine the requirements for the development of a WinSock application in either the 16-bit or 32-bit Windows environment (or both).

The original promise of WinSock—the ability to create universal applications—is very nearly fulfilled already. The current API will remain while the Windows Sockets specification expands to fulfill new promises. The WinSock API promises to meet the needs of new network media and other protocols, not to mention hitherto unimagined network applications.

Computers are going mobile, and so will WinSock. The network pipes are getting bigger because bandwidth is expanding, and WinSock will help to utilize this bandwidth effectively. The Internet is begging for applications to make navigation, search, and retrieval easier, and WinSock is the perfect platform to help such applications spread and evolve. We've only scratched the surface of network multimedia delivery. As we discover more, WinSock will be there. WinSock is a tool that makes technology accessible. It is a facilitator and a catalyst, and it is here for the long haul.

2 Windows Sockets Concepts

In This Chapter:

- The OSI Network Model
- The WinSock Network Model
- OSI Layers in WinSock
- Modular Boxes
- Services and Protocols
- Protocols and APIs

All talk, as the Chinese masters of old say,
is at best a finger pointing at the moon.
The finger is not the moon and cannot
pull the moon down.

Heinrich Dumoulin

The Open Systems Interconnect (OSI) network reference model presents a high-level view of all network systems. It reduces the complex subject of networking to its essential components and shows how these components fit together in a common framework. Using the framework, we can define and illustrate network concepts and terminology. We also use it as the basis for our own WinSock network model.

In this chapter we provide a brief overview of the OSI network model, define a few common network terms and concepts, and describe our WinSock network model. We spend most of the chapter analyzing a hypothetical network application in terms of the OSI model and our WinSock model. We use network terms and concepts to describe the services you get from Windows Sockets and define what you must implement yourself to create a network application. We show you the differences between services and protocols, as well as protocols and programming interfaces, so that there is no confusion about how the pieces fit together in your application and the network system.

We use the concepts and terminology defined in this chapter throughout the rest of the book. The purpose of this chapter is to establish a common language we'll use to describe and illustrate the mechanics, design, implementation, and debugging of WinSock applications. If nothing else, this chapter provides a view of how a Windows Sockets application—and the WinSock API itself—fit in the big picture of the networking world.

The OSI Network Model

The primary intent of this chapter is to define and illustrate concepts that we use throughout the book. Some of these are concepts of our own, such as the WinSock model, but most of them are well established in the network industry. The fundamental concept from which almost all the others derive is the OSI network model. Many readers will have encountered this model already, but to avoid making any assumptions—and to emphasize its significance—we'll provide a brief overview of the OSI network model first.

The International Standards Organization (ISO) established a subcommittee in 1977 to design a standard network architecture. The subcommittee's goal was to identify and define a set of generic functions that could handle all

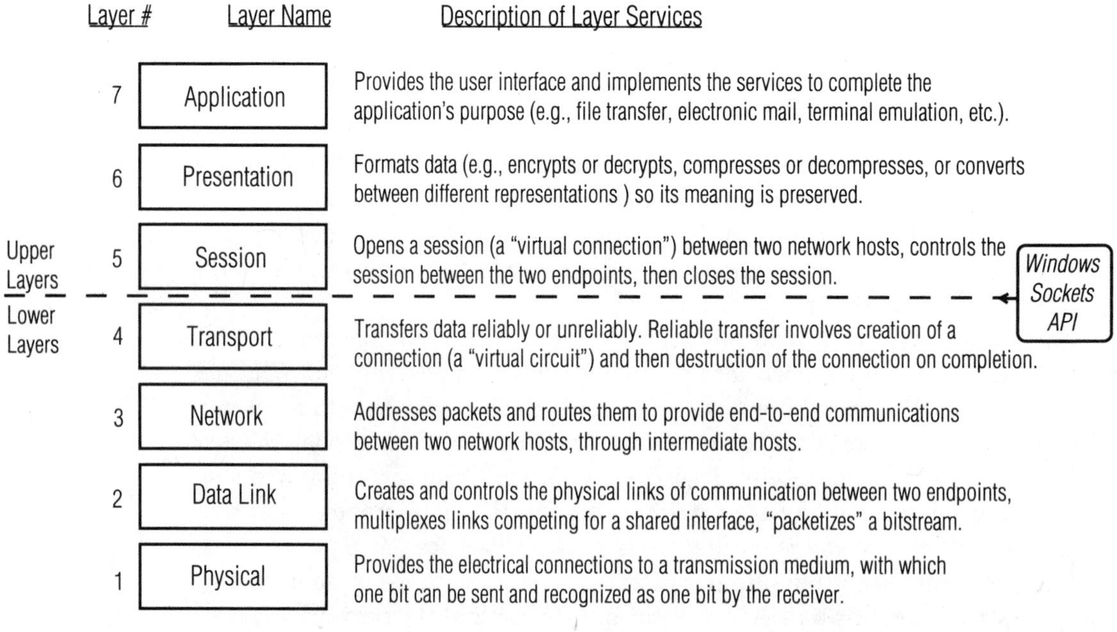

Figure 2-1 Open Systems Interconnect (OSI) Network Reference Model.

possible network communications between computers. They created the Open Systems Interconnect (OSI) network reference model as a result. Figure 2-1 displays the components and organization of the OSI model.

Many in the networking industry use the term "protocol stack" as a synonym for "protocol suite," a collection of related protocols. Protocol stack alludes to the "stack" of boxes represented in the OSI reference model. The metaphor of the stack illustrates the hierarchy in the model; the layers below support the layers above with the services they provide. In our Windows Sockets model we refer to all the lower layers as the **network system**, and we call the upper layers the WinSock **application**.

Services and Interfaces

The OSI model identifies a hierarchy of seven layers. Each layer has a functional role—a collection of related **services**—characterized by the OSI layer name. Each layer accesses the services of the next layer down by using its **interface**. A layer's interface, represented by the top line of each box in Figure 2-1, provides a collection of well-defined **function calls** to make its services available.

In the OSI model the work flows downward. The upper layers depend on the lower layers to do the dirty work, to implement their ideas. Each layer passes its work orders downward through the interface of the layer below. How the lower layers perform the service is not of concern to the upper layers. They are only concerned that the job is done.

To illustrate, consider your phone service. You use a phone to dial, connect, and talk with someone easily, and without knowing much about how the phone operates. The phone's keypad, mouthpiece, and earpiece are all you interact with; they are the top layer's interface. You do not see the lower layers at work, nor do you need to know anything about how they work in order to use them.

Among other things, the low layers translate sounds into electrical current. These analog electric signals may be converted to digital form, or into light pulses on a fiber optic cable, before they are converted back again to sound on the other end. Your call may be routed and rerouted through different phone offices and trunk lines while you converse. These lower-layer activities and their technologies are completely transparent to you. Similarly, the implementation details of the lower-layers in the OSI network model are transparent to the upper layers in a network system as two network applications converse.

About the only time a lower layer is not transparent to the upper layers is when a failure occurs. Failures "bubble up" through the OSI layers. There is a chain reaction as one service request failure causes the one above it to fail. Eventually, the uppermost layer reports an error condition. Part of the trick of debugging a problem is in determining which lower layer has had a problem.

The WinSock Network Model

We superimpose a structure on the OSI network model to define our WinSock network model. We refer to the upper layers in the OSI network model as a WinSock application, the lower layers form the network system, and the WinSock application programming interface (API) sits between the two. These three components comprise our WinSock network model.

WinSock application: *Provides upper-layer functionality (OSI layers 5–7)*

Network system: *Provides lower-layer functionality (OSI layers 1–4)*

WinSock API: *Allows upper layers access to lower-layer services*

Typically, a WinSock application is a single executable application program, complete with a user interface. It might also be an intermediate dynamic link library (DLL) with a higher-level API and applications of its own. For that matter, it might be a stack of DLLs, with an application on top. We'll illustrate these different WinSock application configurations later in this chapter, after we've described the services each OSI layer provides. In our WinSock model, we consider anything that accesses a WinSock DLL as a WinSock application.

A network system typically has a modular architecture as illustrated in Figure 2-2, although other configurations are possible. Our WinSock model includes any network system that provides an API that complies with the Windows Sockets specification (version 1.1).

The WinSock API (WSA) provides access to the network system, and WinSock applications use the system's services to send and receive information. In Figure 2-2, the dashed line that represents the location of the WSA also indicates the division of labor between the network system and the WinSock application. The line also coincides with the division in the OSI network model between the "lower layers" and "upper layers."

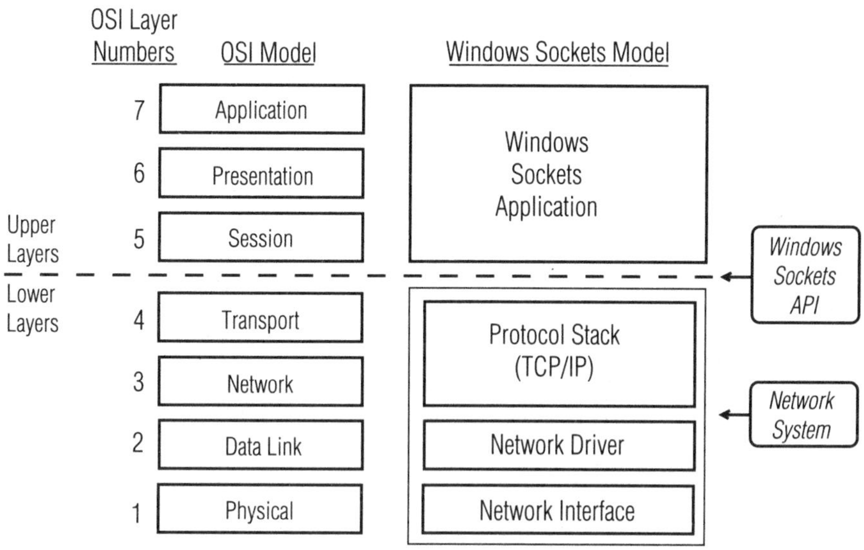

Figure 2-2 The WinSock model compared to the OSI network model.

Information and Data

WinSock applications provide information services to computer users. They let users transfer information between computers—and people—quickly and easily. **Information** is by definition "cooked," or loaded with meaning and always complete. This contrasts with **data**, which is "raw," has little meaning, and is possibly incomplete. Data comprises information, but not all data is informative. Information has structure and meaning, and data has neither. Data is an arbitrary collection of octets (bytes).

Each layer deals with its own information, and anything it receives from a layer above is considered formless and meaningless data. The network system layer in our WinSock network model simply sends and receives data, as requested by a WinSock application layer. This data is meaningful to a WinSock application, but not to a network system. When a WinSock application sends a block of information that has a specific length, format, and meaning, the network system may fragment that data arbitrarily and reassemble it at the other end before delivery. It may treat the data as a stream of bytes and require the application to reassemble the block after delivery. How the data is treated depends on the transport services requested, but in any case the network system delivers data without regard to content or meaning.

Application Protocols

An **application protocol** defines the rules governing communication between network applications. These rules describe an application's information and how it is used by the applications sending and receiving the information. Two applications must have an application protocol in order to communicate, because it defines what the applications expect of each other. Application protocols can range from simple to complex. As you might imagine, more complex information services require more complex application protocols.

A network system also uses established protocols to exchange application data with other network systems, but Windows Sockets applications never "see" the network-system information exchange. The Windows Sockets API shields applications from the "lower-layer" protocols, which is to an application's advantage. That way the application does not have to implement the complicated details of network and transport protocols (like the TCP/IP protocol suite) nor deal with the different network drivers, or network hardware, or packet formats. If it did, you would have to rewrite your application for every network card, or at least for every network media (Ethernet, Serial line, Token Ring, etc.).

Windows Sockets lets you deal with what you want to in your application: your information service, as implemented by your application protocol. The (hidden) network system takes care of all the other details for you. The network system delivers specific services, and you do not need to worry about how it does it.

OSI Layers in WinSock

Our WinSock network model is essentially a simplified version of the OSI network model. However, the individual OSI functionality layers still exist within the WinSock model at a conceptual level. Now we will describe the functional roles of each OSI layer—the services they provide—and describe their interfaces as we relate them to our WinSock model. We use a hypothetical electronic mail program as a sample network application to illustrate what each layer does in practical terms. We start at the uppermost layer—the application layer—and work our way down.

Application Layer

The top layer, layer 7, interacts with the user. It provides the user interface that takes user commands and presents information to the user. Windows uses the keyboard, mouse, and screen to provide for standard input and output, but other interfaces are available. Hardware devices like joysticks, soundcards, microphones, and video cameras are examples of other user interfaces that some applications use.

A Windows Sockets application's application layer deals with user input (commands) and application output (responses). The application layer's services define the application's purpose. For instance, if the application is an electronic mail program, the user reads and writes mail using the application layer. The e-mail application layer might provide other nonnetwork features, such as collecting e-mail addresses in an address book or archiving messages sent and received in a database.

In addition to providing the user interface and incidental features, the application layer does most of the information processing. It implements the mechanisms for dealing with the application-specific information. In our electronic mail example, the application layer creates the headers for outgoing mail messages and parses those of incoming mail messages. Mail messages are the application's unit of information.

Each mail message has a header and a body (see Figure 2-3). The message header has a few well-defined fields such as destination, sender, sender location, date, carbon copy list, and so forth. The message body has some information fields within it also, which define multimedia inserts. The application-layer mechanism in our electronic mail program parses the header information of an outgoing message to determine where to send it. It also parses the multimedia inserts in the body of an incoming message to display graphics, or play sounds or video clips for the user.

message header
message body
To: jd@schleppco.com (Joe D. Veloper)
From: hu@anycorp.com (Hap P. User)
Subject: Your awesome mail program
Hi Joe!
I love your mail program! It has all the features I want, it's easy to use, and I haven't encountered a single problem yet. Thank you for a quality product.
Regards,
Hap

Figure 2-3 Sample e-mail application: The application layer provides a user interface to allow writing mail message and defines mail message (header) format.

After a user creates an e-mail message with our sample program, the application layer calls the presentation layer for further processing. Our sample application can compress or encrypt a message if the user asks for these services. Otherwise, it may bypass the presentation layer and call the session layer to mail the message (and receive any incoming messages). There are no standard interfaces for the presentation layer.

Presentation Layer

An application's presentation layer, layer 6, formats information it has received from the application layer. If an application does any type of data conversion, it does it in its presentation layer. Some examples of common presentation-layer functions are compression, encryption, screen formatting, and translation (e.g., ASCII to EBCDIC). The presentation layer is optional. It may not exist in an application, if the application does not need any data formatting services.

Our sample mail application uses the presentation layer to encrypt our outgoing mail message and also to decrypt incoming mail messages that need it (see Figure 2-4). When our sample e-mail application finishes processing the outgoing mail message, its presentation layer calls the session layer to send the data. There are no standard programming interfaces for the session layer.

Session Layer

The session layer, layer 5, establishes, controls, and then closes a "high-level" connection called a **session.** A session is different from a "low-level" transport-layer (layer 4) connection. A session is a "virtual connection," which means it can exist over a connectionless transport protocol, or even when network communications have stopped. An application maintains the state of its communications in the session layer, and this state can simulate a connection, even when one does not exist.

An application that transfers large files could benefit from session-layer services, especially on an unreliable network system. The session layer establishes a session with the remote host and begins transfer of the file. At preestablished intervals, the receiver sends a "synch message" back to the sender to indicate how much data it received successfully. Both the sender and receiver store the message. If the transport connection fails, the virtual connection still exists. When the session layer gets a new transport connection, the file transfer begins again at the last "synch point" rather than at the beginning of the file. The session layer ends the session (the virtual connection) when the file transfer completes.

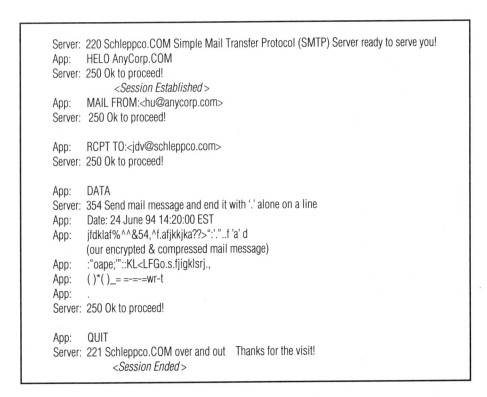

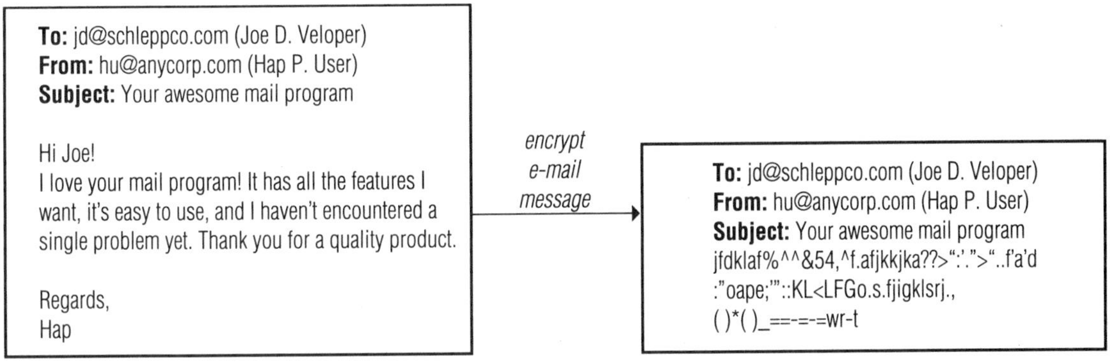

Figure 2-4 Sample e-mail application: The presentation layer allows a user to encrypt an outgoing message.

```
Server: 220 Schleppco.COM Simple Mail Transfer Protocol (SMTP) Server ready to serve you!
App:    HELO AnyCorp.COM
Server: 250 Ok to proceed!
                <Session Established>
App:    MAIL FROM:<hu@anycorp.com>
Server: 250 Ok to proceed!

App:    RCPT TO:<jdv@schleppco.com>
Server: 250 Ok to proceed!

App:    DATA
Server: 354 Send mail message and end it with '.' alone on a line
App:    Date: 24 June 94 14:20:00 EST
App:    jfdklaf%^^&54,^f.afjkkjka??>":'."..f 'a' d
        (our encrypted & compressed mail message)
App:    :"oape;'"::KL<LFGo.s.fjigklsrj.,
App:    ( )*( )_= =-=-=wr-t
App:    .
Server: 250 Ok to proceed!

App:    QUIT
Server: 221 Schleppco.COM over and out   Thanks for the visit!
                <Session Ended>
```

Figure 2-5 Sample application ("App"): The session layer establishes a "session" with the mail server ("Server") using SMTP (RFC 821) conventions. In this example App just sends a message and ends the session.

Our sample e-mail application uses the session layer to create a session with an electronic mail server, send mail messages, and then close the session. Each session lasts as long as there are messages to send. The session layer maintains a record of what messages it sent successfully, to avoid resending them.

The session layer uses the services of the transport layer to create, control, and close sessions. The sample session dialog illustrated in Figure 2-5 does not show the transport API functions used to establish the connection before the SMTP 220 "ready for mail" message from the server. Our sample application uses other transport functions to send commands and data (e.g., "MAIL FROM" followed by sender's user id), to receive responses (numeric, followed by text), and finally, to close the session. All these commands and responses are part of our application's session layer protocol (which implements the Simple Mail Transport Protocol, as defined by Postel in RFC 821).

The transport API used to connect with the SMTP server, to send and receive the session commands and responses, and then to disconnect is a standard interface: It is the Windows Sockets API!

Transport Layer

The transport layer, layer 4, provides the services that we typically associate with networking: "end-to-end" transfer of data (source to destination). The OSI model describes this transfer as reliable, but unreliable variations are also available. Reliable transfer requires a connection; unreliable transfer is connectionless. These two types of transfers are important to understand, so we discuss them in detail in the next chapter. For now it is enough to know that the transport layer provides both types of data transfer and the Windows Sockets API provides access to both.

Our sample e-mail application uses reliable, connection-oriented stream transport (we describe what this means in Chapter 3, "TCP/IP Protocol Services"). As Figure 2-6 shows, the session layer requests creation of a connection when it creates a session. It sends and receives data contained in the mail messages using the `send()` and `recv()` functions. The session layer closes the transport connection when it closes the session. The transport layer interfaces with the network layer to package, address, and send the data it receives from the session layer. For reliable data transfer the transport layer manages acknowledgments of data receipt, data sequence numbers, buffering, flow control, and retransmissions.

The transport layer uses the network-layer interface. In many cases the network interface is unavailable to an application because it is hidden in the protocol stack software. A Windows Sockets implementation can optionally

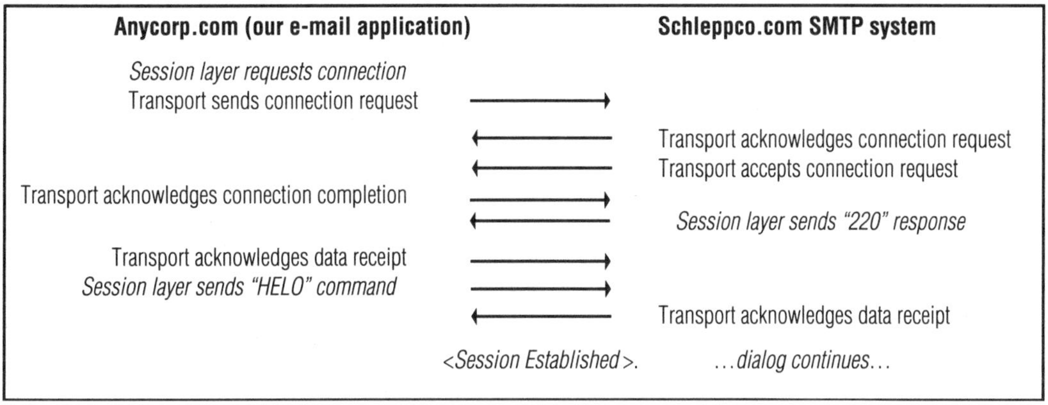

Figure 2-6 Sample application: The transport layer does the "low-level" work to establish a connection and acknowledge data in response to session-layer requests.

provide the network layer API with SOCK_RAW sockets. Although the Windows Sockets specification does not define this API, Berkeley Sockets v4.3 SOCK_RAW API is the de facto standard.

The SOCK_RAW capability is useful for some specialized applications that need low-level access to network protocols (to manipulate the contents of the IP header, for example) for network administration tasks. It is mostly used to access low-level protocols that provide simple services (like sending an ICMP Echo Request, to check if a TCP/IP host is "alive"). However, most applications do not need SOCK_RAW, so you should avoid it. It will only make your applications less portable (i.e., it won't run over all WinSock implementations, as we describe in Chapter 16, "Optional Features").

Network Layer

The network layer, layer 3, routes, fragments, and reassembles packets of data (see Figure 2-7). Its primary purpose is addressing, which includes the routing service that allows a packet to make its way through an internetwork of bridges and routers. With the fragmentation service the network layer breaks large packets into smaller chunks for transmission on networks that cannot handle the original, larger packets. The receiving network layer recreates the original (large) packet by reassembling the individual fragments in their original order (we'll illustrate how this works with IP in the next chapter).

Although our e-mail application uses the network-layer services, the Windows Sockets API insulates the application from its interface as well as its mechanical details. The network layer routes packets it receives from the

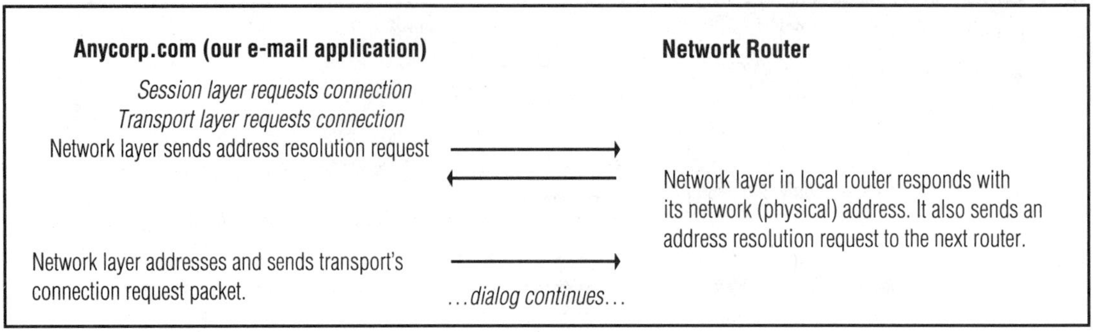

Figure 2-7 At the network layer, each router between Anycorp.com and Schleppco.com does "next hop" address resolution to establish a route so transport-layer control and data packets can be "routed."

transport layer on the e-mail application's behalf. After addressing a packet, the network layer interfaces with the data link layer to send it.

There are many proprietary data link interfaces, but fortunately standard interfaces are predominant. There are three data link interface standards for PC's: the Open Device Interface (ODI) from Novell, the Packet Driver interface from FTP Software, and the Network Device Interface Specification (NDIS) from Microsoft and 3COM. The major advantage to these three interface specifications is that they are capable of managing service requests from a number of different network layers simultaneously. So, for example, you could have a WinSock DLL that supports both the IPX/SPX and TCP/IP protocol suites running over a single network interface card.

Data Link Layer

The data link layer, layer 2, is also known as the *network driver layer*. It controls the network interface hardware and manages competing requests if two or more network layers are using the network interface simultaneously. It creates and prefixes the media access control (MAC) header on the packet it receives from the network layer, before sending the packet to the physical layer for transmission (see Figure 2-8). Conversely, it strips the MAC header off an incoming packet before passing it up to the network layer (just as any OSI layer removes its information before passing incoming data "up" to the layer above).

Again, our sample e-mail application uses the data link layer services, but it does so completely transparently. Our sample e-mail application does not interact with the data link layer, so our application does not do anything different when the network driver or media changes.

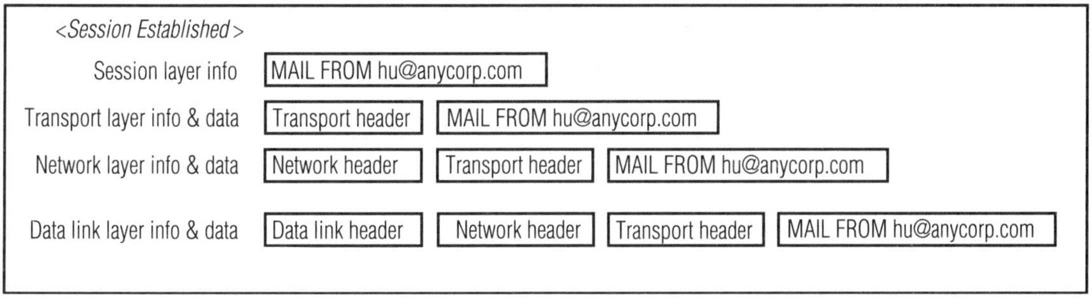

Figure 2-8 The data link layer adds network-media-specific (e.g., Ethernet or Token Ring) information to each outgoing packet. This figure illustrates how each layer adds information to the data the session layer originally asked to be sent

The data link layer uses a proprietary interface to "talk to" the network interface card at the physical layer. The interface for each network card can vary greatly. Device drivers—the software that interacts with the hardware—is as "low level" as software gets. Writing drivers is a task that is not for the faint of heart. Even the network interface card manufacturers often hire outside firms to write drivers for their products. Fortunately, drivers that work well are widely available for most cards, so you will probably never have to face that challenge.

Physical Layer

The physical layer, layer 1, is the hardware, the network interface card itself. This layer "talks" directly with the physical network media. It creates (and detects) messages on the media using the prescribed method (e.g., electrical

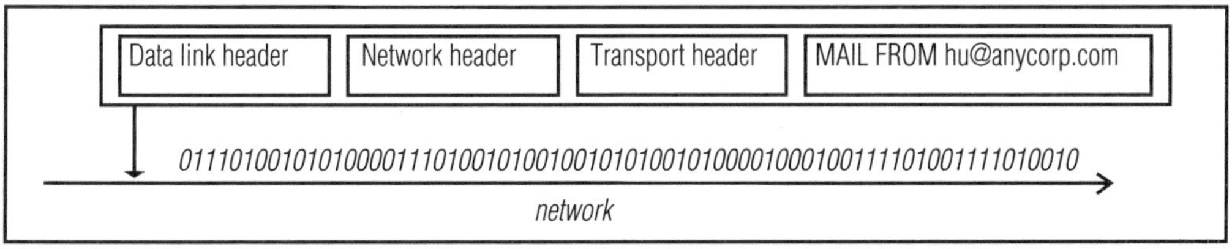

Figure 2-9 The physical layer sends data link data in binary form according to the physical requirements of the network media (e.g., on Ethernet, they are electrical signals within specified voltage levels that signify "on" or "off").

voltage levels, radio signals, or light pulses). Its primary purpose is to send data in one-bit streams and make sure it is received.

This layer is where the information from our sample e-mail application, transferred as data between the lower layers, is finally sent onto the network bit by bit as shown in Figure 2-9. The physical layer does a lot of work to send a single e-mail message, but it operates quickly and, unless there is a failure, the details involved are completely transparent to the application.

Modular Boxes

The boxes in the OSI model, and in our Windows Sockets model, imply a modular architecture that allows for mixing and matching network components. Each layer hides its services' implementation details, so the contents of each box can change. Though the internals change, the services and interface remain the same.

Since the Windows Sockets architecture supports dynamic linking, and most protocol stacks support the standard network driver interfaces, this modularity is a reality. You can change the version or vendor of a WinSock DLL, or change the driver and media, without affecting a Windows Sockets application at all.

Version 1.1 of the Windows Sockets specification focuses on the TCP/IP protocol stack, but—like its model, Berkeley Sockets—it is flexible enough to handle other protocol suites as well. In fact, Windows Sockets on NT provides support for Appletalk, DECnet, and Novell's SPX/IPX. Since most network drivers can handle multiple protocol stacks simultaneously, Windows Sockets can provide access to a number of different protocol stacks running at the same time over a single network interface card. NT's Windows Sockets does this also.

Version 2.0 of the Windows Sockets specification (WinSock 2) embraces the architecture that Windows NT uses to support multiple protocols from multiple vendors simultaneously. As we describe in Chapter 17, WinSock 2 formally supports the Open Systems Interconnect (OSI) protocol in addition to SPX/IPX, DECnet, and Appletalk. The sketch of how the pieces are put together in WinSock2 is similar to Figure 2-10. One significant difference is that the "proprietary stack APIs" is instead a single standardized Service Provider API (SPI).

Figure 2-10 illustrates many key points we have mentioned in this chapter:

- You can combine layers. Many protocol stacks combine the transport and network layers, for instance, and as a result the network layer does not have a distinct API.

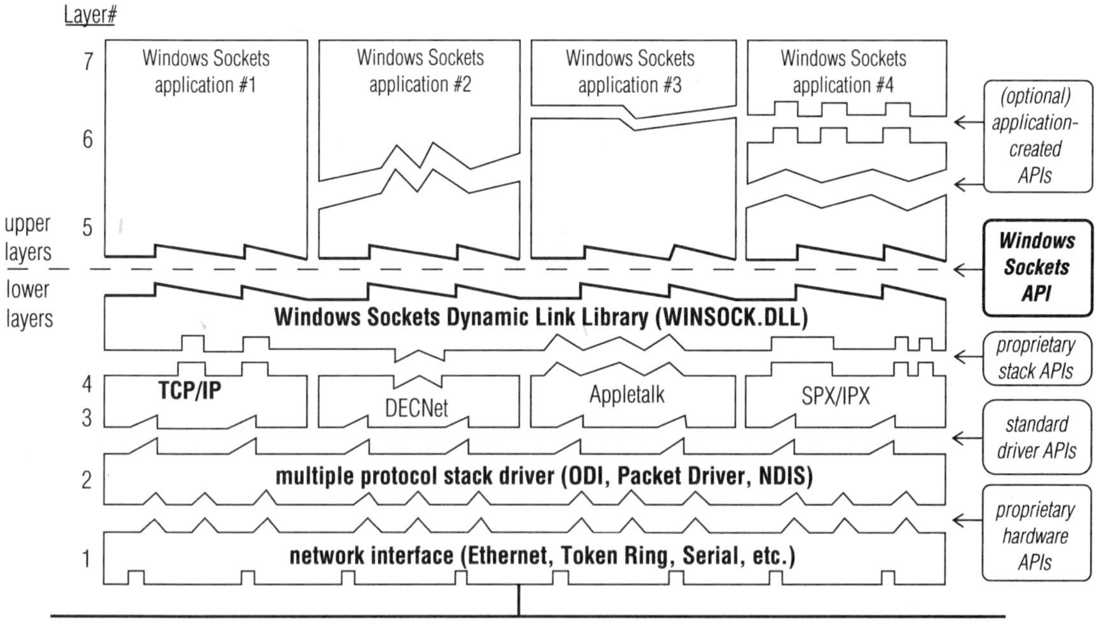

Figure 2-10 Windows Sockets applications, WINSOCK.DLL, protocol stacks, and drivers.

- Some layers are optional. Many applications do not need a presentation or session layer, for example.
- The Windows Sockets API (WSA) is uniform even if the API for the underlying stack is not. The WSA insulates the Windows Sockets application from a protocol stack's proprietary interface and a stack's "low-level" implementation details.
- Windows Sockets is protocol independent, so it can adapt to many different protocol suites (version 1.1 of the Windows Sockets specification focuses on TCP/IP, but version 2.0 provides for others).
- Windows Sockets is network media independent, so any Windows Sockets application can run over any network media that the network system supports.
- Windows Sockets can support a number of different protocol suites simultaneously, although the v1.1 Windows Sockets architecture does not allow more than one WinSock DLL to be in use at a time (so a single DLL must provide support for all the protocol suites). WinSock 2 provides a more flexible architecture to support multiple vendors and protocols simultaneously.

Services and Protocols

In Figure 2-11 we show how a Windows Sockets application and network system on one computer relate to those on another computer. We include the router to make the illustration more realistic. By definition, an "internetwork" always has at least one router. You use a router to connect different network medias: Ethernet to Token Ring, FDDI to X.25, Serial Line to wireless, and so on. A router provides network-layer services—addressing and fragmentation—to amend for media differences (different addressing and packet sizes). Routers are transparent to Windows Sockets applications. Failure of a router is like failure of any lower layer; if failure is detected, an error may be reported by the Windows Sockets API.

The arrows in Figure 2-11 denote the conversation between **peer layers**. Peer layers "talk" to each other using the same **protocol**, which is a precise set of rules for communication between peer layers. The rules describe requests and responses appropriate to the current state. In other words, a protocol defines the context-sensitive syntax and semantics of each layer's information.

The "conversation" between two peer layers is logically independent of the conversations between other peer layers. The protocol implements that layer's services and occurs in response to the requests of the layer above and, of course, ultimately of the application user.

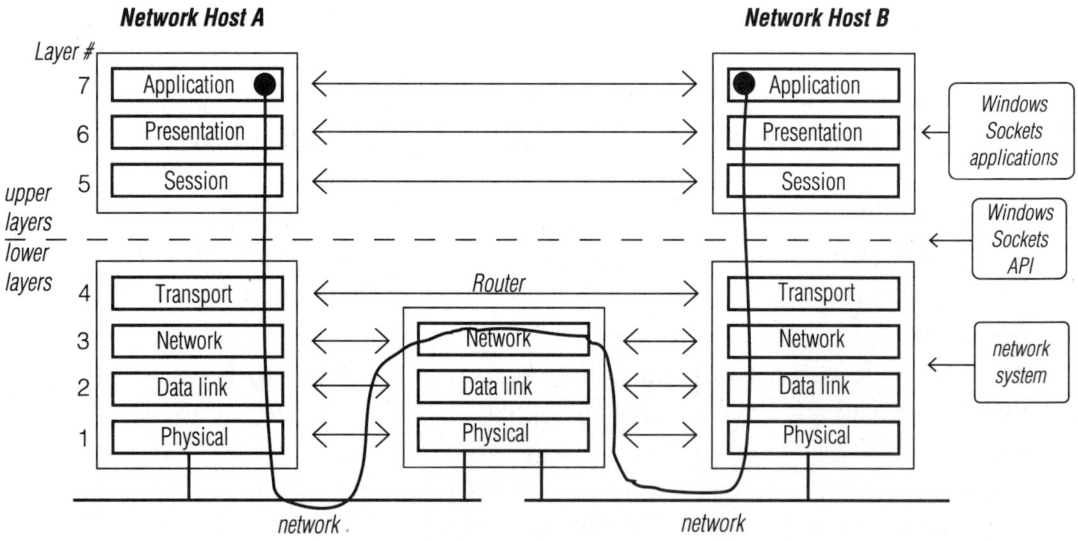

Figure 2-11 Compound OSI network model illustrating (conceptual) communication between peer layers. The freeform line shows the route application data actually follows.

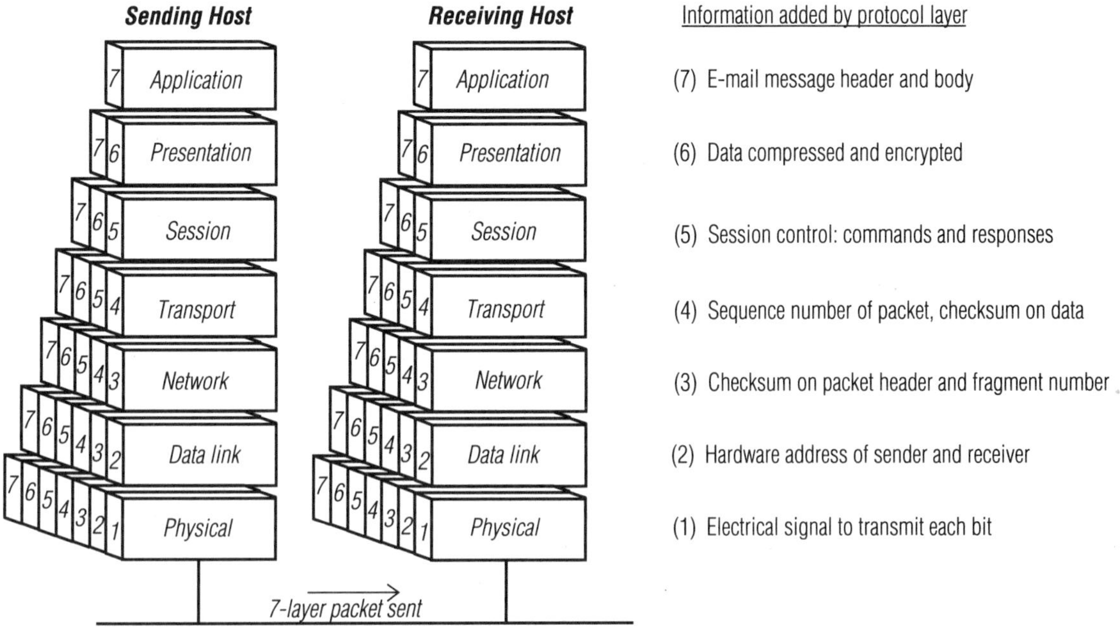

Figure 2-12 Compound OSI model that describes the type of information peer protocols communicate in our sample e-mail application network.

The peer-layer dialogs illustrated in Figure 2-11 are only conceptual, not the actual data path. Figure 2-12 illustrates how an application passes its information to the layer below, which adds its own information and passes it down to the next layer. Each layer's information accumulates on the way down the stack. Think of an envelope, put into another envelope, and into another, and so on. We hinted at this information encapsulation earlier in this chapter when we defined each OSI layer. As our sample e-mail application's information went down the stack, each layer added information. Figure 2-8 shows an outgoing data packet getting larger as each of the lower layers adds its protocol header. The packet containing the protocol information for all seven layers traverses the network until it reaches the destination host.

On the receiving end, each layer removes its information—takes it out of its envelope—interprets it, and responds according to protocol. It then passes the remaining data up to the next layer. The application layer, at the top, receives only the application-layer information.

Referring again to our sample e-mail application, here's an incomplete sketch to give you an idea of what happens on the receiving end (at our e-mail application's peer). Assume that we've established an e-mail session and the application is sending the body of a compressed and encrypted e-mail message:

Physical layer: Assembles a packet from bits received and passes it to the data link layer.

Data link layer: Checks the hardware address in packet (if there is one), to be sure this is the correct destination (packet ignored, if not). Removes media header and passes remaining data up to the network layer.

Network layer: Checks header for integrity (IP has a header checksum). Checks the network layer address, to be sure this is the correct destination (packet ignored, if not). Removes network header and passes remaining data up to the transport layer.

Transport layer: Checks data for integrity (TCP, UDP, and ICMP all have checksum fields in the header). Checks if other header information—like source and destination port numbers—matches a current active socket and also that the header information is appropriate for its current state (packet is ignored, and an error response might be generated, if not). If all is well, the transport layer passes remaining data (if any) up to the session layer. The transport layer might also send a response back to its peer (e.g., an acknowledgment of data received).

Session layer: The Simple Mail Transport Protocol (SMTP) prescribes that an e-mail message body ends with <CRLF>.<CRLF> (a single period on a line by itself), so the session layer in our e-mail peer scans the text received from the transport layer for this 5-byte sequence. If the character sequence is found, the session layer responds by sending a "250 Ok to proceed!" message back to the peer (by making a request to the transport layer). It also gives all data received "up" to the presentation layer.

Presentation layer: Decrypts and decompresses the message and gives translated data "up" to the application layer.

Application layer: Notifies the user that there's a message to read and displays it when requested.

Protocols and APIs

The Windows Sockets API is protocol independent. The differences in the APIs used to access various protocol stacks invoke the different address requirements of each protocol suite. There are also subtle differences in the transport services available, but these differences are mostly transparent to an application.

The reason for stressing Windows Sockets' protocol independence is the very common error of confusing an API with the protocol suite it supports. An API provides access to the services in a protocol stack, but the protocol suite does not determine the API's identity and structure. Different protocols provide the same services. Conversely, a protocol suite can make its services available through any API. Windows Sockets is not the first and will not be the last API for TCP/IP, for example.

So, if you ever hear the question, "If I have a program written using the Transport Layer Interface (TLI) on an AT&T System V UNIX system, can it talk to a program written using Windows Sockets?" the answer is an emphatic "yes!" As long as both the TLI and Windows Sockets applications are using the same protocol stack (TCP/IP, DECNet, or whatever), it will work fine.

If you have two networked computer systems and you want them to talk to each other, the only time you need the same API is if you are planning to use the same source code. You always need the same protocol-suite support on both.

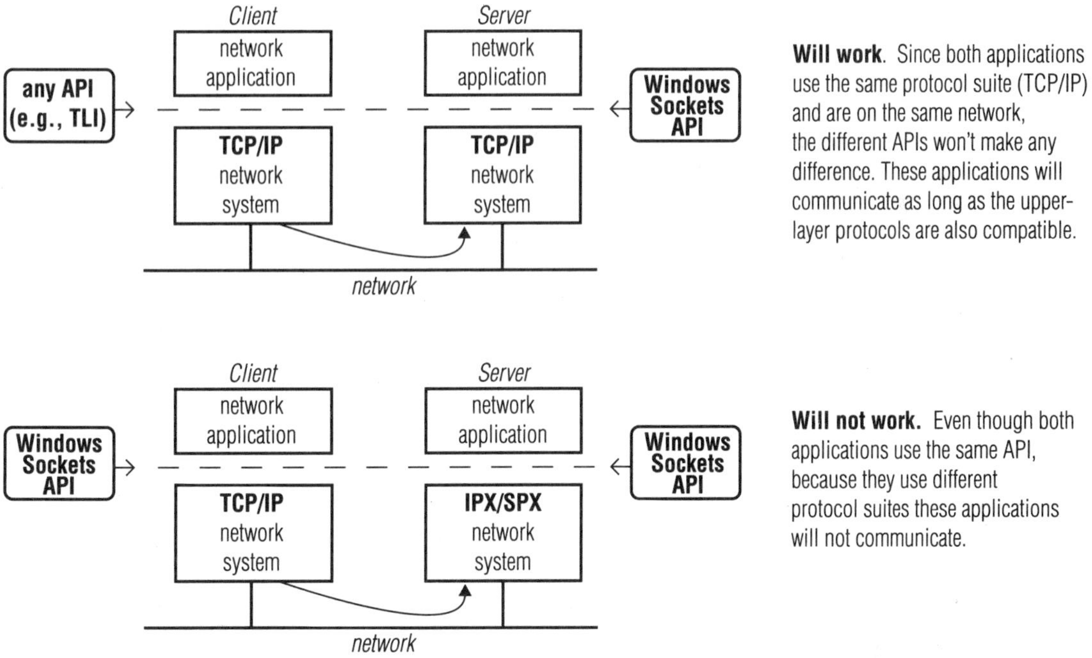

Figure 2-13 APIs need not be the same, but protocols must.

3 TCP/IP Protocol Services

In This Chapter:

- What Is TCP/IP?
- What Is Its History?
- Transport Services
- Network Services
- Support Protocols and Services
- What Is Its Future?

Details are all there are.

Maezumi

Windows Sockets, like its predecessor, Berkeley Sockets, is protocol independent. The generic design of the Windows Sockets API (WSA) allows access to the services of most network protocols. Version 1.1 of the Windows Sockets specification focuses on the TCP/IP protocol suite, but the Windows Sockets DLLs for Windows NT and Windows 95 also support the Appletalk and SPX/IPX protocols.

Because of the focus on TCP/IP in version 1.1 of the WinSock specification, and since most WinSock applications currently use the Internet protocols, we dedicate this chapter to the protocols that make up the TCP/IP suite. In particular, we concentrate on the services TCP/IP protocols provide. We describe enough about the protocols to help you design your Windows Sockets applications. We show you *what* the TCP/IP protocols do, not *how* they do it.

Windows Sockets insulates you from the low-level protocols, so you do not have to deal with them. About the only times you do need to know such low-level details are when using some idiosyncratic protocol feature or having a network-system problem. For that reason, we wait until Chapter 13, "Debugging," to discuss protocol mechanics (and we provide a description in Appendix B).

What Is TCP/IP?

TCP/IP is an acronym for Transmission Control Protocol/Internet Protocol and refers to two of the primary protocols in what is also known as the Internet Suite. The TCP/IP protocols provide for network connection between any computer systems, across varying network media, and under possibly adverse conditions.

> A basic objective of the Internet design is to tolerate a wide range of network characteristics—e.g., bandwidth, delay, packet loss, packet reordering, and maximum packet size. Another objective is robustness against failures of individual networks, gateways, and hosts, using whatever bandwidth is still available. Finally, the goal is full "open system interconnection" : an Internet host must be able to interoperate robustly and effectively with any other Internet host, across diverse Internet paths.[1]

The strength of TCP/IP is its compatibility with nearly any lower-layer network infrastructure. The fact that its protocols are based on open standards enhances its standing.

The services provided by the Internet protocols are equivalent to the session, presentation, transport, and network layers in the OSI network reference model. As we described in the last chapter, the network and transport layers address and send data—reliably or not—anywhere on a heterogeneous network. The session layer synchronizes communication between application endpoints, and the presentation layer prepares application information.

Figure 3-1 illustrates the TCP/IP protocol suite as it relates to the OSI model and to our Windows Sockets model. As you can see, TCP and IP are not the only protocols in the TCP/IP suite. Notice also that the data link and physical layers are *not* part of the Internet suite; independence from the lower layers is what allows TCP/IP to run over any network driver and media (Ethernet, Token Ring, FDDI, etc.). The application layer is *not* included in the TCP/IP suite either, since user interfaces vary widely between network applications and operating-system platforms.

These are the services provided by each of the protocols named in Figure 3-1:

Session and Presentation Layers:

File Transfer Protocol (FTP): file transfer

Simple Mail Transport Protocol (SMTP): electronic mail service

[1] "Hosts Requirements," RFC 1122, page 8.

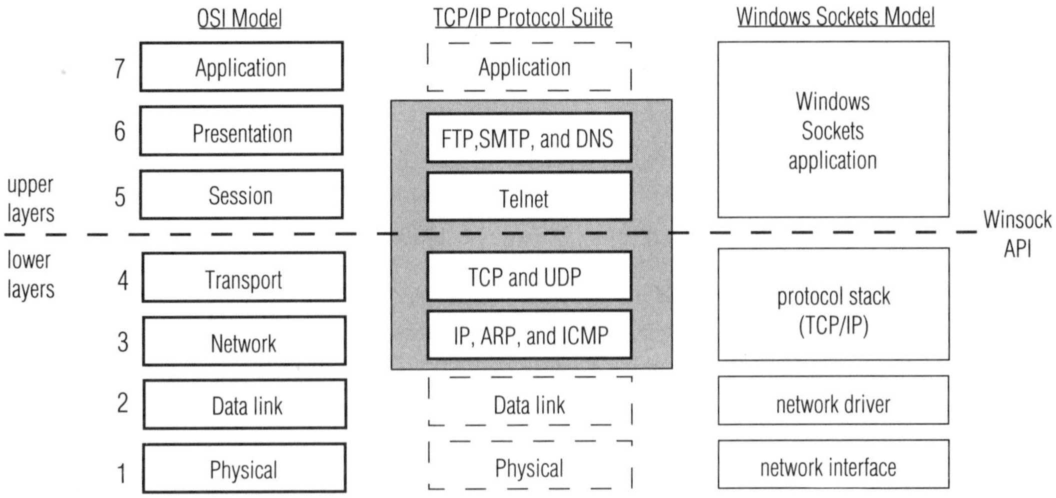

Figure 3-1 The TCP/IP protocol suite compared to the OSI model and Windows Sockets model.

Telnet: terminal negotiation for remote login

Domain Name Services (DNS): host name to IP address mapping

Transport Layer:

User Datagram Protocol (UDP): connectionless data transport

Transmission Control Protocol (TCP): reliable data transport

Network Layer:

Internet Protocol (IP): hardware-independent addressing, routing, fragmentation, and reassembly of packets

Address Resolution Protocol (ARP): IP address to hardware address mapping

Internet Control Message Protocol (ICMP): error and control messages

The application (upper-layer) protocols like Telnet, FTP, and SMTP are important to the interoperability provided by the TCP/IP protocol suite. They provide common application protocols for common network services. There are many other protocols we could list—like archie, gopher, talk, veronica, and wais—but those three have always been considered a part of TCP/IP, since they provide the most basic network application services: e-mail, file transfer, and remote login.

The WinSock API provides access to the services of the transport and network protocols: the network system. The higher-layer protocols are not available through the WinSock API, but must be implemented by the WinSock application. The Domain Name Service (DNS) Protocol is one notable exception. DNS is a "support protocol" that allows an application to reference host names as well as host addresses (if an application knows a host name, it can get an address, and vice versa). This convenient—if not essential—service is available through the WinSock API. We describe its services in a little more detail later in this chapter and show you how to access these services in Chapter 8, "Host Names and Addresses" (where we describe WinSock functions like `gethostbyname()`, `WSAAsyncGetHostByName()`, etc.).

We saw SMTP in action in our sample application in Chapter 2. We show you FTP and Telnet in later chapters and sample programs, but we do not discuss these application protocols more here. Instead, we concentrate on the services the transport and network protocols provide. These are the heart and soul of the Internet network system.

What Is Its History?

The Department of Defense Advanced Research Projects Agency (DARPA) originally developed the TCP/IP network system. The intent was to satisfy the U.S. military's need for a standard data communications system that could deliver data reliably and quickly even under rapidly changing and potentially adverse conditions. TCP/IP evolved into its current set of specifications through field testing and adjustment under real-world conditions. As a result, TCP/IP implementations delivered a robust, flexible, high-performance networking capability. The U.S. government made the specifications available to the public: an open system. The rest—as they say—is history.

Most computer systems now provide TCP/IP. There are IP-capable routers to connect virtually any network media. TCP/IP is the glue that holds the Internet together, and the Internet spans the globe. In order to ensure interoperability, the governing body of the Internet—the Internet Activities Board (IAB)—uses a mechanism called "Request for Comments" (RFC). These are documents that describe in detail the required and allowed behavior of standard protocol implementations.

Since many RFCs define high-level application protocols, it is not uncommon for you to keep an RFC as a constant reference during the design, implementation, and debugging of standard applications. Other than that, you might need to reference an RFC when you encounter an unusual problem at the transport or network layer. As a rule, though, you need not reference them.

The Requests for Comments relevant to the protocols we mentioned above are as follows (note that these RFC numbers do change as the standards are updated and old RFCs sometimes become obsolete). Notice that RFC 1122, referred to as "Host Requirements," is relevant to many TCP/IP protocols; it is essentially a clarification document for existing TCP/IP RFCs.

Session and Presentation Layers:

Domain Name Services (DNS): RFCs 1034 and 1035

File Transfer Protocol (FTP): RFC 959

Simple Mail Transfer Protocol (SMTP): RFC 821

Telnet: RFCs 854, 855, and others

Transport Layer:

User Datagram Protocol (UDP): RFCs 768 and 1122

Transmission Control Protocol (TCP): RFCs 793 and 1122

Network Layer:

Address Resolution Protocol (ARP): RFCs 826, 1042, and 1122

Internet Protocol (IP): RFCs 791 and 1122

Internet Control Message Protocol (ICMP): RFCs 792 and 1122

Transport Services

Windows Sockets provides direct access to the transport layer, OSI layer 4, which provides the most important and visible services in the OSI model. Your choice of transport services is a fundamental design decision based on the purpose and requirements of your network application. The two service types available are connection-oriented and connectionless, and UDP and TCP—the two primary protocols in the TCP/IP protocol suite—provide these two types of service.

Connectionless Services: UDP

Connectionless transport, also called **datagram service**, is unreliable. But don't confuse "reliability" with "quality." This service is unreliable because it neither guarantees delivery nor preserves the packet sequence. If a datagram does not reach its destination or it is damaged along the way, the service will not notify you of failure. If an application sends datagram A and then datagram B, datagram B may be received before A (see Figure 3-2).

The datagram service is analogous to postal delivery. Usually we do not consider the postal service as unreliable, but first-class mail service does not guarantee delivery or preserve sequence either. But most first-class deliveries make it to their destination without a problem (and we typically do not care about the order of arrival).

The connectionless transport service is simple, and its simplicity is often to its advantage. It has low overhead, so it provides efficiency that can result in performance benefits, and it is easy to use. Although datagram service is unreliable, datagram applications need not be unreliable. Any datagram application can implement the services that provide reliability.

An application receiving data can send acknowledgments for each datagram received. An application sending data can retransmit a datagram if an acknowledgment is not received within a timeout period. Each packet can contain a sequence number or timestamp so a receiver can resequence data

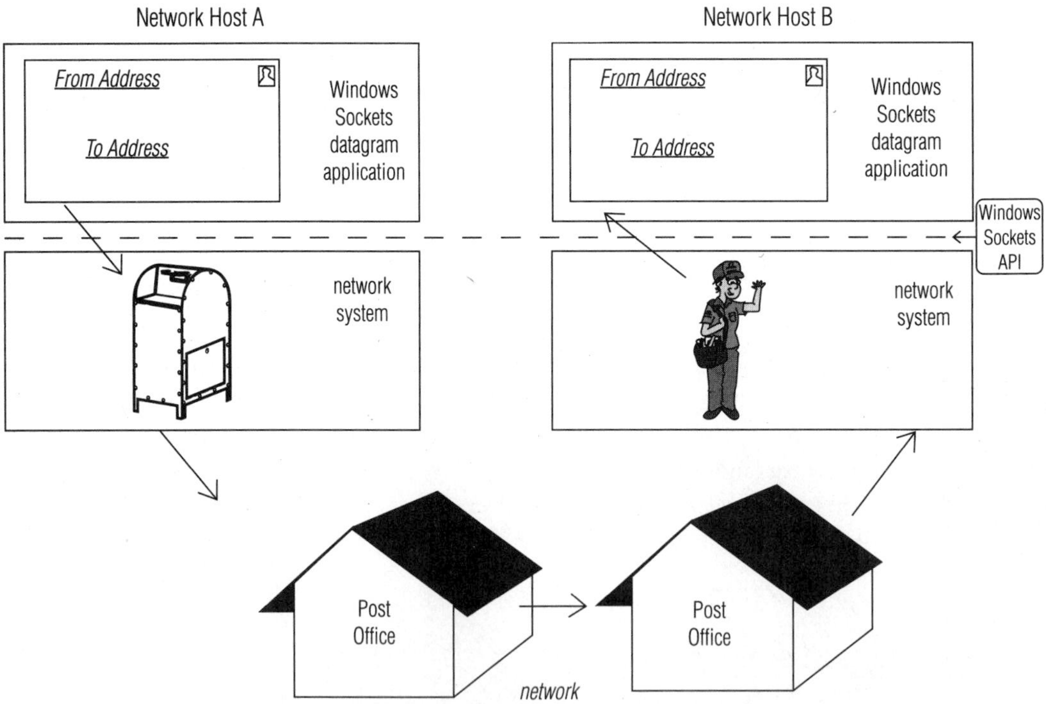

Figure 3-2 When an application sends a datagram, the datagram service will not indicate whether it arrived. If an application sends two, either one may arrive before the other.

when needed and detect and discard duplicate data that arrives. Adding these features to the basic service to increase its reliability is not unlike requesting a receipt from the postal service by sending registered mail.

The datagram service is ideal for applications with short transactions in which the overhead of creating and destroying a connection would be more work than the data transfer itself. It is also perfect for an application that implicitly provides acknowledgment. For example, an application that sends a query to a database server expects a reply. If the reply arrives and is complete, the application is done. If the reply does not arrive within a timeout period, the application can resend the query (or take other action, such as displaying an error message for the user).

Some applications trade reliability for higher capacity. They use connectionless services to achieve high data throughput, especially if they can tolerate data loss. These applications sequence data and provide synchronization between the sender and receiver at the application level. A few examples of such applications are those sending video or audio or receiving samples from real-time data-collection devices.

Oddly enough, there are a few applications that would be unreliable if they used a "reliable" service. For instance, a real-time audio and video application does not want to wait as data is retransmitted, or allow the transport flow-control mechanisms to disrupt the "natural" data flow.

Since the datagram service is connectionless (i.e., not "tied" to a single remote host), it is also capable of multicasting or broadcasting. Some applications need to communicate with many hosts simultaneously, using a single address. Connection-oriented protocols cannot provide this service.

The User Datagram Protocol (UDP) is the primary datagram protocol in the TCP/IP suite. Internet Control Message Protocol (ICMP) is another datagram transport protocol. You access ICMP using SOCK_RAW sockets—an optional feature of the Windows Sockets API—so ICMP is not generally available.

UDP, like any datagram protocol, transmits and receives discrete packets. In other words, if you transmit a certain number of bytes in a single send operation, you can receive that same number of bytes on a single receive operation. The packet boundary is preserved as the data traverses the network. UDP also uses the TCP/IP standard checksum algorithm—the ones' complement sum of 16-bit words—to do a cursory verification of data received (the UDP checksumming is an optional feature of TCP/IP protocol stacks, but most have it enabled).

What UDP does *not* provide is the guarantee of delivery. When a TCP/IP implementation receives a UDP datagram, it does not return an acknowledgment to verify receipt. UDP also does *not* preserve transmission sequence. As we discussed, though, it is possible to implement reliability and sequencing within a Windows Sockets application that uses UDP.

Connection-oriented Services: TCP

Unlike connectionless transport, **connection-based transport**, also called **stream service**, is reliable. A connection is a virtual circuit. The circuit is "virtual" because it appears that it is hardwired, although it is not. A virtual circuit provides reliable data transfer by automatically (transparent to an application) acknowledging data received, retransmitting data if an acknowledgment is not received, preserving data sequence, and avoiding duplication of data.

The connection-oriented data-transfer service is directly analogous to telephone service. When you dial a phone number, sometimes you get a busy signal that rejects your connection attempt. If you get a ring signal and someone answers, you've established a connection. This virtual circuit exists

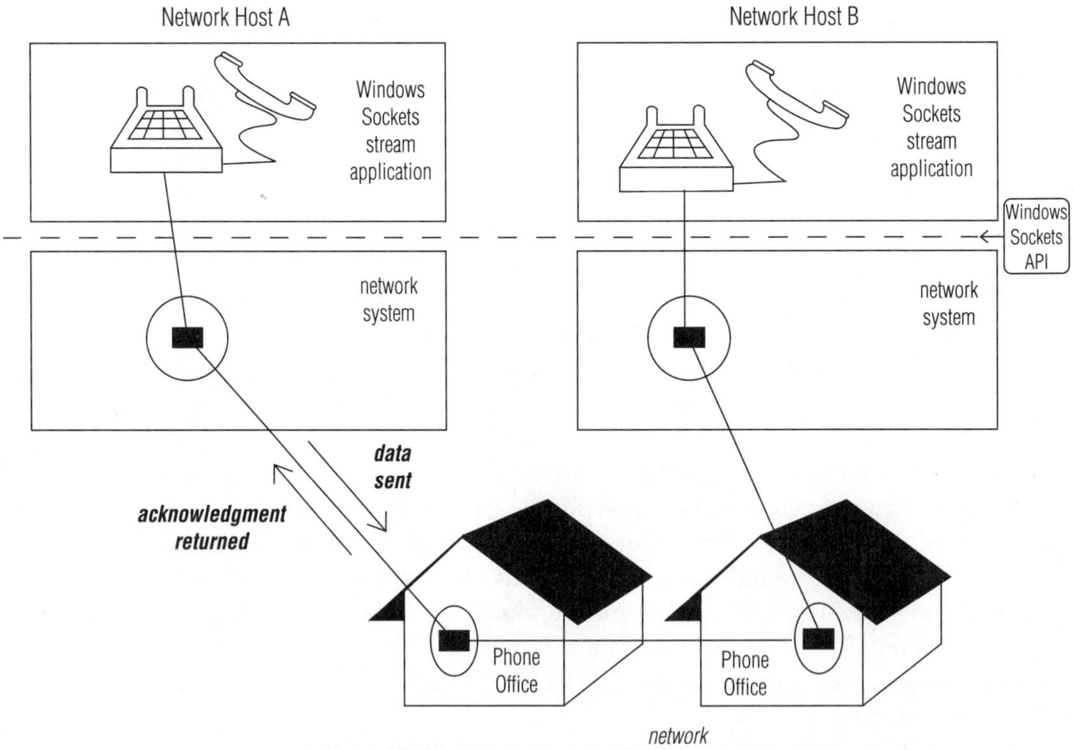

Figure 3-3 Stream services maintain a virtual circuit, and all data transferred is acknowledged.

without noticeable interruption until you hang up the phone. When you speak, you get immediate feedback that indicates the person at the other end heard and understood what you said. These things all have analogs on a transport connection.

The connection-oriented service is not as simple as the connectionless ones. There is overhead involved in creating and releasing a virtual circuit, and with data acknowledgment, retransmission, and sequencing. But the reliable data transport is invaluable to applications that cannot afford to lose any data and do not want to implement reliability themselves. It is also usually easier to use stream service.

The component services that combine to provide reliable data delivery are:

- acknowledged delivery
- error detection
- retransmission after acknowledgment timeout
- preservation of data sequence
- nonduplication of data
- flow control

The Transmission Control Protocol (TCP) provides all of these services in its connection-oriented data-transport protocol. It guarantees data delivery without making any assumptions about network reliability. TCP provides reliable transport by providing a number of subservices: data acknowledgment, data sequencing, data retransmission, and deletion of duplicate data. TCP also provides flow control and out-of-band data transmission.

What TCP does *not* do is preserve packet boundaries. TCP provides a stream, which means it puts as much or as little data in each packet as it needs. Thus, if a sending application transmits a certain number of bytes in a single send operation, the receiver will *not* necessarily get all the transmitted bytes in a single receive operation. The receiver may need to buffer data as needed and do more than one receive operation, because the data may be delivered in separate packets. We will describe some common problems this can cause for applications that are not properly designed in Chapter 13, "Debugging."

Deciding on a Transport: UDP versus TCP

Network application developers must choose between using connection-oriented or connectionless transport protocols for data delivery. It is important to know as much about the service capabilities and limitations of the available transport protocols, since deciding on a transport is one of the most significant decisions you will face in the design of your Windows Sockets application. First you decide on the services you want your application to provide to the user, and then you decide which transport protocol is best suited to the task.

Application developers too often assume the network packet and computational overhead involved with TCP will adversely affect data throughput, so they opt for the simplicity of UDP. Then they attempt to ensure reliability by implementing the mechanisms within their application. The final result is that they do more work and they incur more computational overhead in their application with UDP than they would have if they had used TCP. "Those that ignore TCP, are doomed to reinvent it."[2]

The rule of thumb: *Use TCP, unless you have a good reason not to.*

Experience proves that for TCP the price–performance ratio of computational and network overhead to network throughput is negligible. The most significant reason to use TCP is that your program will be easier to write. In the previous section we gave a few examples of applications for which connectionless protocols would be appropriate; here are some of their characteristics:

- They use broadcast or multicast services.
- Real-time data—like audio and video—is sensitive to delays, so it cannot tolerate data retransmission or congestion-control mechanisms like TCP slow-start and the Nagle algorithm.
- They require short transactions that provide implicit acknowledgment and tolerate duplicate datagrams.

Sometimes you can avoid the question of which protocol to use by designing your application to use two sockets: one for each protocol. For example, the UNIX "talk" application uses UDP to send an initial query to get the port to which to connect. This query can be sent as a broadcast to discover which host(s) is running the talk server. When a positive response is received, the UDP packet returned contains the TCP port number to which to connect for the talk connection.

[2] A favorite quip of James Van Bokkelen, co-founder of FTP Software, author of RFCs 1091 and 1173, and contributor to other RFCs, including 1122 and 1123.

Network Services

IP Services

The services of the Internet Protocol (IP) are the key to internetworking. IP provides packet addressing, routing, fragmentation, and reassembly. Packet addressing allows transmission of packets from one IP host to another, and routing means the selection of a path for transmission. Since all IP datagrams can be rerouted dynamically, this allows for load balancing throughout the network and a high degree of fault tolerance for data transport. Fragmentation and reassembly of packets allow transmission of large IP packets through "small packet" networks, and it is this capability that allows interconnection of different network media, the linchpin of the TCP/IP protocol suite.

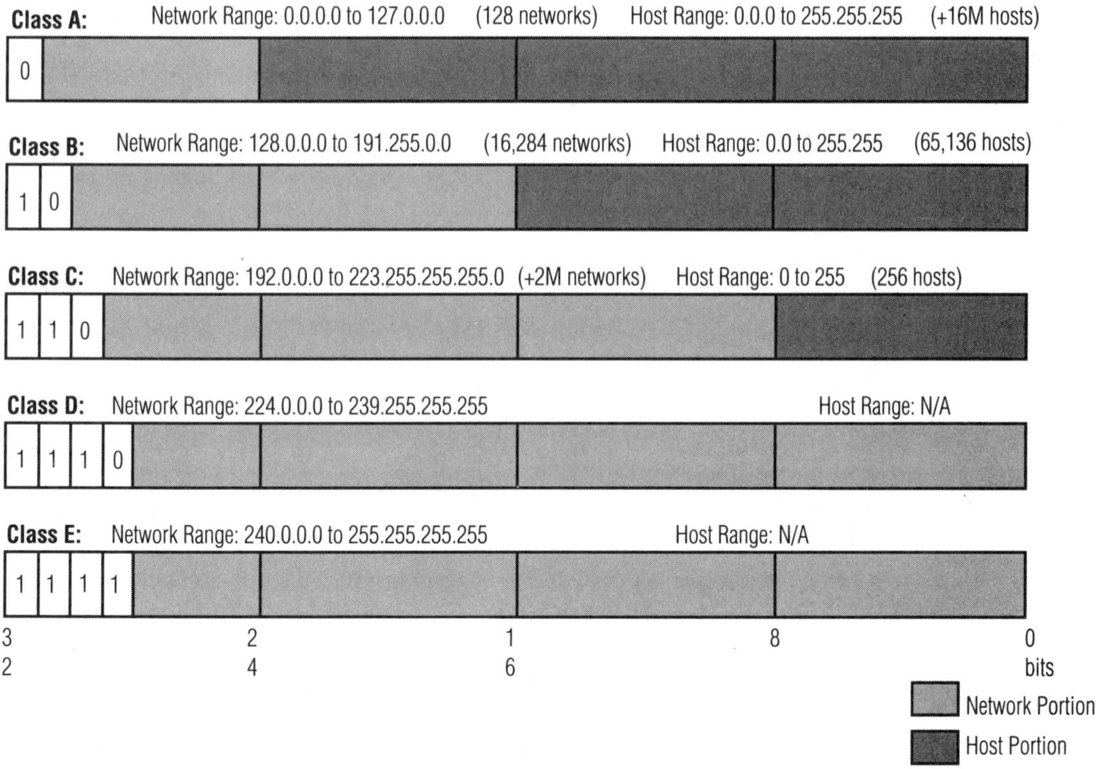

Figure 3-4 Internet Protocol address classes illustrating the bit encoding, network and host portions, and address ranges.

Most of these services are completely transparent to a Windows Sockets application, however. The WinSock application sending a packet cannot affect packet routing or fragmentation. Intermediate routers along the network path between communicating hosts handle packet routing and fragment them as needed. Then the receiving TCP/IP protocol stack takes care of any necessary packet reassembly, so by the time an application receives its data, the job is done.

The one Internet Protocol service that *every* Windows Sockets applications uses is addressing. For a network application using TCP/IP to contact another network host, it must use a valid IP address. We'll see how the network system uses addresses when we examine Windows Sockets application mechanics in Chapter 4, "Network Application Mechanics."

The size of an IP address as it appears in an IP packet is four bytes. You reference the four-byte IP address in your application as a string in the "dotted-decimal" notation. The values of the four high-order bits differentiate between five address classes: A, B, C, D, and E (see Figure 3-4). Every IP address is made up of a network address portion and a host address portion, and the class of an IP address determines the size of each of these portions.[3]

Many network sites use "subnet bits" to increase the size of the network portions of A and B class addresses, to be more like C. Having more subnets—each separated by a router—with fewer hosts on each makes it easier to isolate problems. The range of addresses in Class D is for multicast addresses, which can be received by many hosts simultaneously like packets sent to broadcast addresses, but without the disadvantages of broadcasts. We describe multicasting and its unique application potential in Chapter 16. Except for one address, Class E is reserved for future use.

There are a few special addresses and ranges worth noting:

- The default broadcast address is 255.255.255.255. This is called a "limited broadcast" because routers will *never* forward any packets sent to this address. A "directed broadcast" address is the network portion of an address, with the host portion of the address set to broadcast (e.g., 128.127.255.255). These direct a broadcast packet to a specific subnet (although routers may be configured so they do not forward directed broadcast packets). To receive packets from either address, you need to call the Windows Sockets `setsockopt()` function with the SO_BROADCAST option, as we describe in Chapter 9. You must use a UDP

[3] RFC 1519 describes "Classless Inter-Domain Routing," but use of CIDR is generally avoided because having a large number of hosts on a subnet defeats the purpose of subnetting.

(SOCK_DGRAM) socket to send or receive broadcasts; since TCP is connection-oriented, by definition a TCP socket can only send to and receive from a single host.

- The "Hosts Requirements" RFC 1122 specifies that any network address with the network number 127 is a "loopback" (e.g., 127.0.0.1). However, interprocess communication (IPC) between Windows Sockets applications running on the same host is not guaranteed by the Windows Sockets specification. It is more efficient and reliable to use an IPC mechanism designed specifically for Windows, like dynamic data exchange (DDE) or object linking and embedding (OLE).
- Do not use the loopback address to test network applications on a single PC, either. To get dependable results, always use networked computers to test applications.

ICMP Services

The Internet Control Message Protocol (ICMP) would seem to be a transport protocol since it runs over IP, but it's considered a network layer protocol along with IP. Practically speaking it is a "support protocol" that does not transport data. Instead, as its name implies, it delivers control, error, and informational messages between Internet hosts.

There are many types of ICMP messages (we show them all in Appendix A, "TCP/IP Protocol Headers"). A few do not affect an application at all. Many ICMP messages affect an application's operation quite visibly. If one is received for a UDP or TCP socket you are using, it generates an error in your application (an asynchronous message and/or the failure of a Windows Sockets function). The error value from the `WSAGetLastError()` function can hint at the type of ICMP message you received. One such example is the WSAHOSTUNREACH error, which indicates receipt of the ICMP "host unreachable" error message.

The "redirect" and "source quench" are control messages that provide direct packet rerouting and flow-control services. A "redirect" message has an invisible effect on a network application (it reroutes packets) and cannot be detected by any feature of the Windows Sockets API. It is a low-level control message between TCP/IP protocol stacks, and there is no reason for an application to know about it. The "source quench" message is designed to notify a UDP application that it is sending datagrams too quickly, although there is not a specific error for source quench defined in the Windows Sockets API.

The ICMP "echo request" and "echo reply" control messages provide the most frequently used diagnostic tool in the Internet suite. The ubiquitous *ping* program uses this pair of messages: It sends an echo request to an IP address, then reads the echo reply a TCP/IP stack is obliged to return. This simple query and response effectively checks base-level communications between two TCP/IP hosts. With "ping" you can verify that

- Your local stack and network hardware can transmit and receive.
- The remote host IP address you used is valid.
- A packet can be routed to the remote host and back.
- The remote host has a working network interface and TCP/IP stack.

In Berkeley Sockets, an application can access the ICMP protocol using SOCK_RAW type sockets. Although ICMP is a required part of every TCP/IP implementation, support of SOCK_RAW is optional in version 1.1 of the Windows Sockets API. In Chapter 16, "Optional Features," we show you a sample application derived from the Berkeley ping program, although this application will not run on every vendor's Windows Sockets implementation.

Support Protocols and Services

So-called support protocols do not move application data, and many of their services are unavailable through the Windows Sockets API, but they are essential to the TCP/IP protocol suite and to your applications. We call them "support protocols" because without them the other Internet protocols could not do their job. There are quite a few support protocols, but the most well known and frequently used among them are the Internet Control Message Protocol (ICMP), Domain Name Services (DNS), and Address Resolution Protocol (ARP).

Domain Name Service (DNS)

The Domain Name Service, implemented by the domain protocol, provides the most common version of host name resolution service. It allows a TCP/IP host to retrieve the IP address of another host from a server, when all that is known of the host is its name. The converse service is also provided (with an IP address, you can retrieve the host name). Although the domain protocol itself is transparent, an application accesses its services directly by the functions that do host name resolution: `gethostbyname()`, `gethostbyaddr()`, `WSAAsyncGetHostByName()`, and `WSAAsyncGetHostByAddr()`. We describe how to use these functions in Chapter 8, "Host Names and Addresses."

Address Resolution Protocol (ARP)

Most network interfaces have a unique address burned into read-only memory (ROM) by the manufacturer. These addresses appear in the "source" field of every packet sent by the network interface in the media access control (MAC) link-layer header. This address must also appear in the "destination" field of every MAC packet an interface is to receive (except broadcast and multicast packets). Address resolution is the process of mapping of an interface's IP address to its hardware address.

A TCP/IP stack must retrieve the hardware address of the destination IP host (or the first router along the path to the other host) before an IP packet can be sent. So, whenever a Windows Sockets application initiates contact with another TCP/IP host over a medium that supports ARP, an ARP request is sent and an ARP reply is expected in return. When address resolution succeeds, it is completely transparent to the application. The hardware address of an interface is not available to a Windows Sockets application, because it is not needed. It is the TCP/IP stack's job to take care of that low-level detail.

However, if address resolution fails, then the function call your Windows Sockets application made will fail. For TCP you will get an error; for UDP you may not. We cover the details of the address resolution process in Chapter 13, "Debugging," because it is a very useful diagnostic tool. For now we will just say that if the remote host is *off* the local network and unavailable, you will likely get an ICMP error message in response. This ICMP message is likely to cause a Windows Sockets function failure with WSAEHOSTUNREACH error value. If you try to connect to a host *on* the local network that does not respond to an ARP request, you will not get an ICMP message, but the connection attempt will fail with a WSAETIMEDOUT error.

Finally, just to state the obvious, note that you will not see the address resolution process occurring on serial lines. Using the Serial Line Internet Protocol (SLIP) and Point-to-Point Protocol (PPP), ARP is unnecessary. Serial interfaces neither have nor need hardware addresses since there is only one interface at the other end of the point-to-point serial line connection. They do have IP addresses, though.

Other Support Protocols

There are many other support protocols we could mention. Some, like the Reverse Address Resolution Protocol (RARP), are below the API and are transparent (RARP does the opposite of ARP: Given a hardware address, it provides the IP address for it, which is useful for bootstrapping a diskless network host). Some, like the Router Information Protocol (RIP), Gateway-to-Gateway

Protocol (GGP), and Exterior Gateway Protocols (EGP), provide secondary support of packet routing and may be transparent to your TCP/IP stack itself. The Internet Group Management Protocol (IGMP) is essential to support of multicasting (as we describe in Chapter 16, "Optional Features"). As with all Internet protocols, there are RFCs that describe and define these protocols.

What Is Its Future?

Under the umbrella of the Internet Society (ISOC) and Internet Architecture Board (IAB), the Internet Engineering Task Force (IETF) shepherds the Internet standards as it plans for the expansion of the Internet. As the Internet grows at the amazing rate of about 10 percent *per month*, the TCP/IP protocols continue to spread and the demands on them increase.

The most apparent strain on the TCP/IP protocol suite is on the address space. Each 32-bit IP address must be unique for each interface on the Internet, and version 4 of the Internet Protocol cannot sustain the current growth rate through the year 2000 (Class B addresses may be gone by the end of 1995). The IETF is currently examining several proposed strategies for extending the address space to accommodate continued growth. In addition to increasing the size of the address space, these strategies in "IP next generation" (IPng) support new services for anticipated needs. These new services provide for better mobile communications, switching between different network carriers, and new messaging services for audio and video transmissions. It remains to be seen what type of recoding of existing TCP/IP applications these changes will require. Version 2.0 of the WinSock specification is designed to accommodate many of these future network application demands.

Many of the high-level application protocols, such as those for electronic mail and network management, are seeing significant changes already (unrelated to IPng). The Multipurpose Internet Mail Extensions (MIME) is already supported in many Windows Sockets electronic mail applications. The MIME protocol is backward compatible to the existing Simple Mail Transport Protocol (SMTP), with extensions to support embedding and transmission of binary files, including graphics, sound, and video.

The TCP/IP protocol suite is still as dynamic as it has always been. Part of the reason it has such wide appeal is because it responds to the needs of network users. The reason it is so responsive is because network users maintain it. It is and always will be an open standard: by the users and for the users.

4 Network Application Mechanics

In This Chapter:

- Client-Server Model
- Network Program Sketch
- Open a Socket
- Name the Socket
- Associate with Another Socket
- Send and Receive between Sockets
- Close the Socket
- Client and Server Sketches

Whole sight; or all the rest is desolation.

John Fowles

You can create an endless variety of network applications with the Windows Sockets API. Despite the many differences between application services and application protocols you can implement, all network programs reduce to a single simple network programming model. If you can get a firm grasp of this model, you will have a good understanding of the mechanics behind any network application.

In this chapter we introduce you to this network application model, focusing in particular on the universal attributes of TCP and UDP applications. This chapter describes the framework that is the superstructure for all network applications.

There are many details we do not cover here. We defer the details of how an application locates network services and finds network addresses and the specifics of how best to design your application based on the services you want to provide. But after reading this chapter, you should have a good idea of how to put a network application together and how it works.

Client—Server Model

Every network application has a communications endpoint. There are two types of endpoints: clients and servers. By definition, a client sends the first packet, and a server receives it (see Figure 4-1). This is not the extent of their functionality, but we characterize each end by the role it plays during this initial communication.

It is possible for two network applications to begin simultaneously, but it is impractical to require it. It is very difficult to start two programs at the same instant, and the nature of a network–with varying traffic loads and the like–makes the arrival of packets at each end unpredictable. For these reasons, we design each pair of network applications to perform complementary network operations in sequence, rather than simultaneously. The server application executes first and waits to receive; the client executes second and sends the first network packet.

After initial contact, either the client or the server is capable of sending and receiving data. We use this initial contact to characterize their relationship only for the purposes of definition. The services these applications provide can reverse this relationship any time after their first communication between each other.

Client and Server Association

We type sockets by the protocol they support. For two sockets to communicate as client and server, they must have the same socket types. Either both sockets must be stream (TCP) or both must be datagram (UDP).

Client applications must be able to locate and identify a server's socket. A server application names its socket to establish its identity, so clients can reference it. A **socket name** (for TCP/IP) consists of the *IP address* and *port number*, as well as the *protocol*. A client can use the Windows Sockets service name functions to find out a standard server's port number, and a server's IP address is easy to find with Windows Sockets host name resolution functions if you know the server's host name (we show you how to retrieve port numbers and resolve host names in Chapter 8, "Host Names and Addresses"). However, if you do not know the host name or IP address of your server, the name or address of an appropriate server can be hard to come by. Some new resource location protocols allow a client to retrieve server IP addresses from a central database, but for the most part you must know the server's name or address before you can run a client.

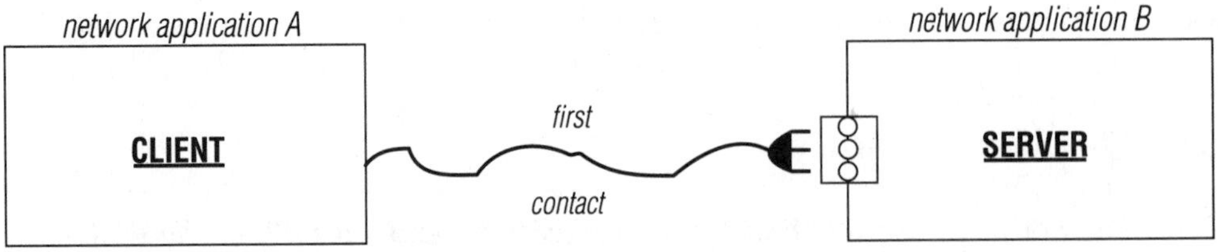

Figure 4-1 A client initiates communications to a server.

When the client socket successfully contacts a server socket, their two names combine to form an **association**. When one socket bonds with another to form an association, the association establishes the identity of both sockets. At that point, each socket is uniquely identified by the combination of its own name and that of its peer. This association has five elements:

- protocol (same for both client and server sockets)
- client IP address
- client port number
- server IP address
- server port number

For stream (TCP)–a connection-oriented protocol–the life of an association corresponds directly to the creation and destruction of the TCP virtual circuit between a client and a server. Since datagram (UDP) sockets are connectionless, the protocol does not clearly define the life of a UDP association. In theory, each datagram packet transmitted creates and destroys an association. But most UDP applications use the same association for the life of the socket.

As we will see, the idea of an association is fundamental to more than Windows Sockets programming. This concept is relevant to network communications in general. The information in an association identifies and guides each packet through the network, from one network application to its peer application.

Network Program Sketch

All network application programs–clients and servers–boil down to five simple steps:

- Open a socket.
- Name the socket.
- Associate with another socket.
- Send and receive between sockets.
- Close the socket.

If the sequence of steps seems familiar, it's no coincidence. The sequence of steps involved in network I/O is analogous to those used in file I/O. Network I/O is actually a descendant of file I/O:

File I/O	*Network I/O*
open a file	open a socket
	name the socket
	associate with another socket
read and write	send and receive between sockets
close the file	close the socket

In the chart above, the first operation of opening a file corresponds to three operations on a socket (open, name, and associate). A file already has an identity when you open it; it already has a name and a system device associated with it. Unlike files, when a socket is opened, it has an incomplete identity. To complete its identity, a network application must assign it a name and associate it with another socket. One significant similarity between opening a socket and a file is that both operations return a handle, an arbitrary descriptor with which to access the opened resource. The handle hides the details of what it represents. Although you can sometimes use a socket handle like a file handle, it makes your source code nonportable since file handles and socket handles are not equivalent on all operating platforms (we discuss this issue in Chapter 15, "Platforms").

The socket send and receive operations are very similar in concept to the file read and write operations. To execute these operations, you always use the descriptor to reference the open resource (file or socket). When you close a file or a socket, you release its descriptor back to the system for reuse. A file's name persists, even after you close the file, but when you close a socket you destroy its name. If a socket handle is 'dup'licated, the name is destroyed on the *last* close (more on this in Chapter 15, "Platforms").

It is not important to remember the details about how files relate to sockets. Remember that socket operations are similar to file operations. This will orient you as we detail each step involved in the network sketch.

Open a Socket

A **socket** is an endpoint of communication, created in software, and equivalent to a computer's network (hardware) interface. It allows a network application to "plug into" the network. Not physically, but metaphorically. Typically you have only one physical network interface on a computer, but the number of sockets you can have is far more. Many (software) sockets can use a single network interface simultaneously. There is a one-for-many correspondence between a network interface and sockets, as Figure 4-2 illustrates.

socket( )

Both clients and servers require a socket to access the network. To open a socket you call the `socket()` function (see Figure 4-3):

```
SOCKET PASCAL¹ FAR socket (int af,        /* protocol suite */
                   int type,              /* protocol type */
                   int protocol);         /* protocol name */
```

af: "address family," otherwise known as the socket domain

type: socket type

protocol: the protocol to use

Opening a socket returns a **descriptor**. A socket descriptor is similar to a file descriptor, as we mentioned, and to a Windows handle. They are all opaque identifiers. You use a file handle to access an open file and a Windows

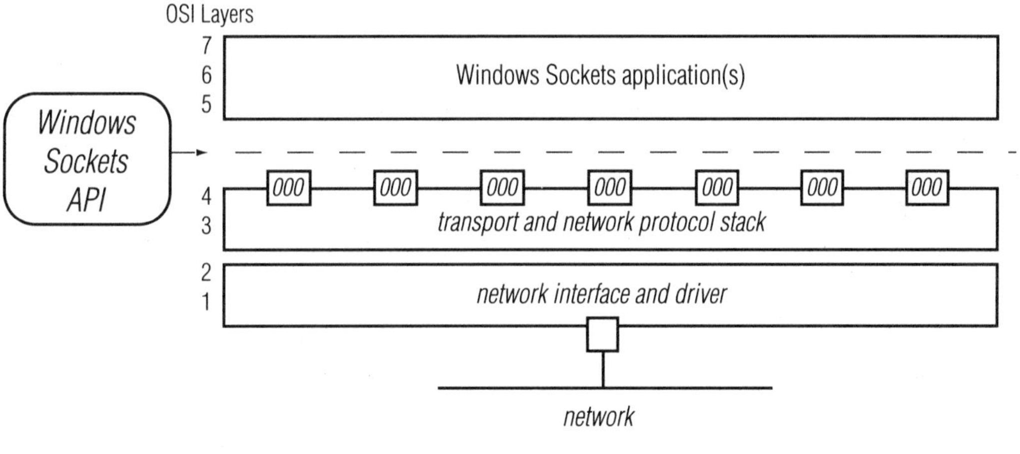

Figure 4-2 A network system may have only one network interface, but the Windows Sockets API can offer many sockets.

[1] A "PASCAL" function type in a C function declaration may look strange to newcomers to Windows programming. It denotes the Pascal calling convention and pushes arguments on the stack in the same order as they appear in a function prototype (left to right). Many Windows functions are type PASCAL, although it is not a requirement. PASCAL functions produce smaller and more efficient code, since the calling function need not adjust the stack after the function returns (the callee pops them off). The downside is that PASCAL functions cannot do variable argument lists. Also note that using PASCAL means function names will be put in uppercase by the linker.

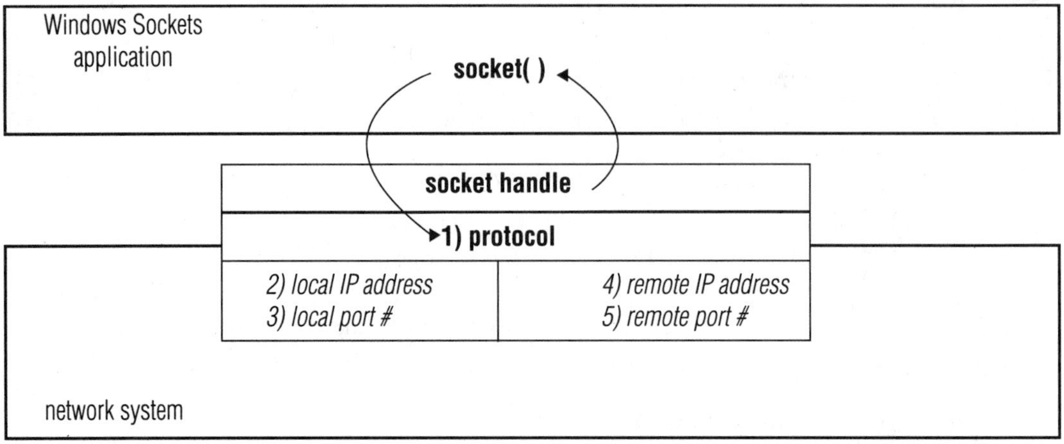

Figure 4-3 The socket() function requests a socket of a certain type, characterized by its protocol. It returns a socket handle.

handle to access an object (like a window or device context). Similarly, you use a socket descriptor to access an open socket, your network object.

You should never anticipate any particular value for a socket descriptor. The Windows Sockets specification does not determine their values, so they may be different for different implementations. The only illegal value is defined by the WinSock macro INVALID_SOCKET. A socket descriptor is an unsigned integer, but you should treat the data type–like its value–as an unknown (we deal with the 16-bit versus 32-bit integer issue in Chapter 15, "Platforms"). The rule of thumb is: Use the descriptor, but do not look too closely at it.

The *af* parameter (address family) indicates the protocol suite in use. Version 1.1 of the WinSock specification defines PF_INET as the only valid value; it denotes the Internet address family or protocol family (TCP/IP). At the time of this writing, Windows NT version 3.51 also supports other protocols like IPX/SPX (AF_IPX) and Appletalk (AF_APPLETALK), but we will not discuss them any further in this chapter.

The *type* parameter often implicitly indicates the *protocol* within an address family. For example, in the TCP/IP address family the protocol for the SOCK_DGRAM socket type is always UDP, and the protocol for the SOCK_STREAM socket type is always TCP. In these cases, the socket function ignores the value for *protocol*, but it is good practice to set the value to 0.

There is a third socket type, SOCK_RAW, which version 1.1 of the Windows Sockets specification acknowledges but does not require. You use SOCK_RAW sockets for protocols other than TCP and UDP. For example, this is how you access the Internet Control Message Protocol (ICMP). Unlike the SOCK_STREAM or SOCK_DGRAM socket types, when you select the socket type SOCK_RAW there are no defaults. You must always specify the protocol value (as we describe in Chapter 16).

You can hardcode the value for the *protocol* parameter in your program or retrieve it by calling either the `getprotobyname()` or `WSAAsyncGetProtoByName()`[2] functions. You rarely need these functions, so we will not discuss them just yet (we describe these and other support routines in Chapter 9).

The `socket()` function returns a socket descriptor when it succeeds and the value INVALID_SOCKET when it fails. After the `socket()` function fails–as after almost any Windows Sockets function fails–you should call `WSAGetLastError()` to retrieve the error value that suggests why it failed. Do not call `WSAGetLastError()` if the `socket()` function succeeds. A successful call to any function does *not* reset the error value (it still has the value of the last error that occurred on any socket used in this program).

As a final note, remember that for two sockets to communicate as client and server they must both have the same socket types. Both sockets must be SOCK_STREAM (TCP) or both must be SOCK_DGRAM (UDP). It is impossible for a TCP client socket to connect to a UDP server socket.

Name the Socket

A client must be able to locate and identify the server's socket. The server application must name its socket to provide for this. If a server application does not name its socket, the protocol stack will reject a client's attempt to communicate. A socket name is not just a label like "Fred," but consists of the socket attributes. There are three attributes that make up a socket name: protocol, port number, and address. So a server must assign these three attributes to a socket, and a client must reference them for the server and client to communicate.

sockaddr Structure

To name its socket, the server initializes the socket address structure and calls the `bind()` function. The socket structure and `bind()` function assign location and identity attributes to a socket. We will defer discussion of the `bind()` function briefly, while we take a closer look at the data structure it uses:

```
struct sockaddr {
   u_short      sa_family;      /* address family */
   char         sa_data[14];    /* undefined */
};
```

[2] The function name prefix "WSA" denotes a Windows Sockets API function.

sa_family: address family

sa_data: address structure data area defined according to address family value

This is the generic socket address structure. You will never use the socket structure in this form, because the *sa_data* field is not well defined. As Figure 4-4 shows, you always use a redefinition of the socket structure, specific to the current address family (protocol suite). Although `sockaddr` is not formally declared as a tagged union, you use it as one. The value in the *sa_family* field is the tag that defines the interpretation of the *sa_data* area.

sockaddr_in Structure

For the TCP/IP address family (PF_INET), you will always reference the fields in the `sockaddr_in` structure and never those of the generic `sockaddr` structure. Here is the definition of the Internet protocol address family structure:

```
struct sockaddr_in {
   short       sin_family;        /* address family (PF_INET) */
   u_short     sin_port;          /* port (service) number */
   struct      in_addr sin_addr;  /* IP address (32-bit) */
   char        sin_zero[8];       /* <unused filler> */
};
```

sin_family: address family

sin_port: 16-bit port number in network order

sin_addr: 32-bit Internet address in network order

Notice that the *sin_family* field corresponds to the *sa_family* field in the generic `sockaddr` structure. The dummy field *sin_zero* ensures that the `sockaddr_in` structure is the same size as the `sockaddr` structure.

Now let's look at where the values for the `sockaddr_in` structure's fields come from and what they mean.

Port Numbers

The value of the *sin_port* field is the port number. This unsigned 16-bit value identifies the network application protocol (e.g., the service) supported by the server. When you are initializing this value in your application, you should adhere to the existing conventions, as defined in the "Assigned Numbers"

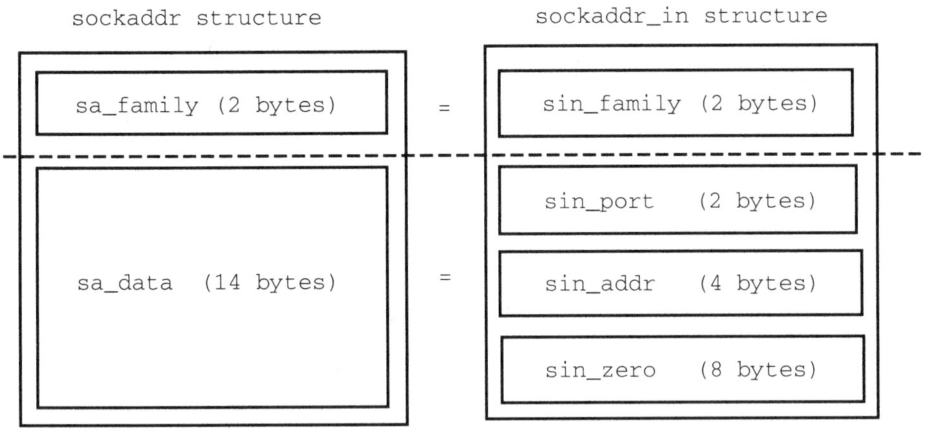

Figure 4-4 You always use the specific structure, not the generic one. So, a TCP program always references the sin_port and sin_addr fields, but never sa_data.

RFC, which is updated regularly by the Internet Assigned Numbers Authority (IANA). At the time of this writing, the latest revision was RFC 1700, released in October 1994:

0–1023:	Reserved for well-known services (e.g., FTP)
1024:	Reserved by IANA
1025–5000:	Typical range for user-defined services

As you can see, the conventional port number range for nonstandard, so-called user-defined services is 1025—5000. Many services in this range have actually become de facto standards or assigned by IANA. You can use a value above 5000, but there are many servers using those higher values also. It may help to check the services database on the system you are writing your server for, or the latest Assigned Numbers RFC, to avoid possible conflicts with existing server applications.

An alternative to hardcoding the port number in your application is to get it from the services database. The functions `getservbyname()` and `WSAAsyncGetServByName()` allow you to retrieve these port numbers from the services database by referencing the service name. For example, if your server supports the standard TCP/IP File Transfer Protocol (as defined in RFC 959), you could call `getservbyname()` and request the port number for the FTP service. It would likely return the value 21 (0x15), which you would assign to the *sin_port* field. We discuss these database functions for service and protocol resolution and other supporting functions in more detail in Chapter 10, "Support Routines."

Local IP Address

The value in the *sin_addr* field in the `sockaddr_in` structure is for an IP address. Depending on the function, it might refer to either a local IP address or a remote IP address. For a call to the `bind()` function, *sin_addr* always refers to the local IP address. In other words, you initialize *sin_addr* with the interface address for the same host on which you are calling `bind()`.

On most systems, you should simply use the address INADDR_ANY to request the stack to assign the local IP address automatically. You might want to assign a specific IP address if you have a "multihomed host" (more than one network interface card and IP address in the system), but even then you can use INADDR_ANY to allow the network system to assign the appropriate network interface.

What's in a Socket Name?

As we have said, there are three attributes to a socket name:

- protocol
- port number
- IP address

Now that we have described these components of a socket name, we will show you how to finish assigning them to a socket. You specify the protocol when you open the socket with a call to the `socket()` function, and now you specify the port number and IP address by initializing the `sockaddr_in` structure and calling `bind()`.

bind( )

The `bind()` function names the local socket with the values in the `sockaddr_in` structure. Here is the `bind()` function prototype:

```
int PASCAL FAR bind (SOCKET s,          /* an unbound socket */
   struct sockaddr FAR *addr,           /* local port and IP addr */
   int namelen);                        /* addr structure length */
```

s: socket handle

addr: pointer to a socket address structure (always a `sockaddr_in` data structure for TCP/IP)

namelen: length of socket structure pointed to by *addr* (size of (struct `sockaddr`))

Notice that a pointer to the `bind()` function prototype references the generic socket structure `sockaddr`. In your function call to `bind()`, it is standard operating procedure to cast the pointer to your TCP/IP-specific `sockaddr_in` structure to the generic `sockaddr` structure. You will see this in sample programs we present later.

The `bind()` function returns zero on success and SOCKET_ERROR when it fails. The most common error that `WSAGetLastError()` returns after `bind()` fails is WSAEADDRINUSE (10048). This occurs when this or another application has already bound to the same socket name (the same port number and local IP address combination). You can set the option SO_REUSEADDR with the `setsockopt()` function to prevent this error, but use of this option can be problematic so we do not recommend it (see Chapter 9, "Socket Information and Control"). It is best to assume that each socket name must be unique, since this will avoid possible conflicts that cause `bind()` to fail.

Client Socket Name Is Optional

A server must name its socket to allow the client to find it on the network. A client is not required to name its socket, but neither is it restricted from naming it. If a client application deems it necessary to name its socket, it can do so by calling `bind()`, as shown in Figure 4-5, for the server. *This is not recommended*, however. Naming a client socket with a specific port number can cause conflicts when you run more than one client simultaneously or sequentially (`bind()` will fail with WSAEADDRINUSE (10048)). Fortunately, network application protocols that require a client to explicitly name its socket are rare.

One way or another, every socket needs a fully qualified name. When you do not *explicitly* name a client socket with `bind()`, the protocol stack *implicitly* names it for you. The stack assigns the local IP address and picks an arbitrary port number within the user-defined services range. The major advantage to implicit naming is that the protocol stack always assigns a unique port number to avoid conflicts with other sockets. On a TCP socket, the protocol stack implicitly names the socket when you call `connect()`. On a UDP socket, it implicitly names with `connect()` or `sendto()`.

It is also possible to call `bind()` with a port number value of zero. In effect, this requests the network system to assign the next available port

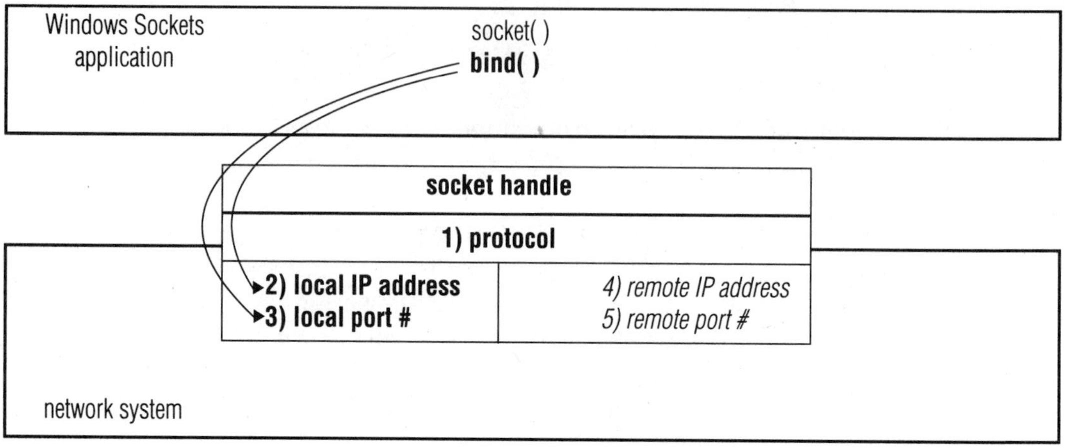

Figure 4-5 The `bind()` function assigns the local IP address and port number, to explicitly name the local socket.

number. You can retrieve the port number that the system assigns by calling `getsockname()` after `bind()` returns.

You can name a local socket only once. So, if you call `bind()`, then `connect()` or `sendto()` will not implicitly name a socket. Conversely, after you call `connect()` or `sendto()`, `bind()` will fail with the WSAEINVAL (10022) error that says "socket already bound to an address" (i.e., is already named).

Associate with Another Socket

So far, we have opened sockets in both the server and client, and named the socket–at least in the server. Now the server needs to prepare its socket to receive, and the client needs to send. When the client is successful, it will create an *association* between the client and server sockets.

As mentioned earlier, and as Figure 4-6 shows, there are five elements in a socket association:

- protocol (same for both client and server sockets)
- client IP address
- client port number
- server IP address
- server port number

The combination of the two socket names creates an association. There are three steps involved in combining the two socket names:

- Server prepares for an association.
- Client initiates the association.
- Server completes the association.

As you have probably guessed, the details of each of these steps are different for different socket types (different protocols). We detail each ahead.

Every association is unique on any (inter)network. This is always true. The association is what makes each network packet unique. It guides each packet as it travels over the network. The protocol stack at each end of an association maintains this information and inserts it in every network (IP) and transport header

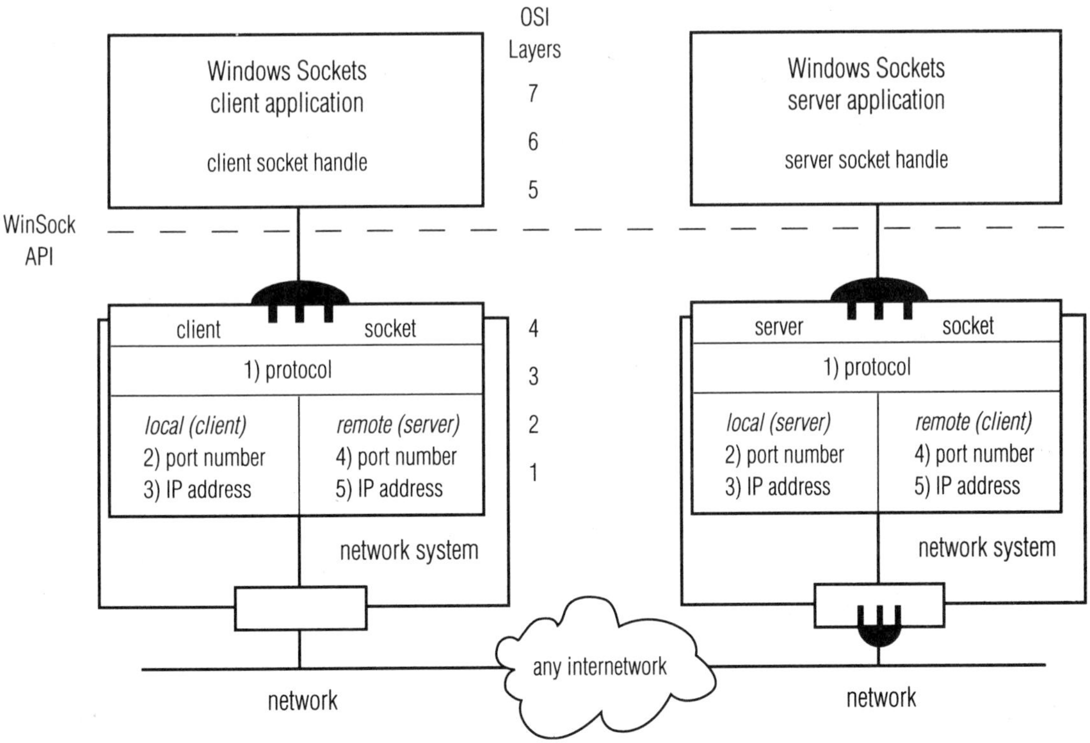

Figure 4-6 After the association is completed, the client and server know the socket name of their peer. The combination of the two socket names defines the association.

(TCP or UDP) sent between the client and server. The protocol stack receiving a packet uses the association elements to identify the socket it belongs to. We will describe this process in more detail later, when we discuss receiving data.

How a Server Prepares for an Association

A **datagram (UDP) server** does not do anything to prepare to associate with a client, since it creates an association when it receives data. So, in a server application you call any one of the functions `WSAAsyncSelect()`, `recv()`, `recvfrom()`, or `select()` to prepare a UDP server to receive data. We will describe these functions shortly, when we describe sending and receiving between sockets.

For a **stream (TCP) server**, there are additional steps required to make its named socket available to a client. See the `listen()` function.

listen( )

A TCP server must prepare to accept a connection attempt from a TCP client by calling the `listen()` function:

```
int PASCAL FAR listen(SOCKET s, /* a named, unconnected socket */
                      int backlog); /* pending connect queue length */
```

s: socket handle to a named socket (bind() called), but not yet connected

backlog: length of the pending connection queue (not the same as the number of accepted connections)

The `backlog` parameter is the number of incoming connection requests you want the stack to queue while you process connection(s) your server has already accepted. By Berkeley Sockets convention, this number is always greater than or equal to 1 and less than or equal to 5. We will describe this in more detail when we analyze source code examples in later chapters.

The `listen()` function returns zero on success or SOCKET_ERROR if it fails. The `listen()` function does not fail often. The most likely error from `WSAGetLastError()` after it does fail is WSAEMFILE (10024), which suggests you are out of socket descriptors. When this occurs, it may help to change your program to reduce the value for backlog you have requested.

After you call `listen()` on a TCP socket, another function call is necessary to prepare to detect the incoming connection request from a client. There are three ways to do this: You can call `accept()`, or `select()`, or `WSAAsyncSelect()`. Using `accept()` is the easiest but not the most efficient. You would typically use the `select()` function in more complex server applications (handling multiple sockets). `WSAAsyncSelect()` is the function of choice for any Windows Sockets application.

The `select()` and `WSAAsyncSelect()` functions are complex and deserve some detailed explanation. We will postpone their detailed discussion until later. For now, suffice it to say that if you use `select()` you should check for writability. If you use `WSAAsyncSelect()`, you need to request the FD_ACCEPT event for `WSAAsyncSelect()`, to prepare to detect an incoming connection.

How a Client Initiates an Association

For a **datagram (UDP) client**, there are two different ways to initiate an association. The first method is preferable if your application sends to different remote hosts from the same socket during execution. This method involves sending with the `sendto()` function. The advantage to using `sendto()` is that you can change the target of each datagram you send. It has a `sockaddr` structure as a parameter, so you can change the remote socket name each time you call it.

The second method for initiating an association takes several steps. You initialize the socket structure, call the `connect()` function to establish the remote target, and then call `send()`. You typically use this method when the UDP socket will be sending to the same remote address for the life of the socket, although this is not a requirement. This also implicitly sets a filter for the datagrams on that socket, so you `recv()` only datagrams from the named destination address. If you need to send to another host, you can call `connect()` again to change your target "on the fly," although you should disconnect first (by connecting to INADDR_ANY).

We discuss the `connect()` function next. We'll cover the `send()` and `sendto()` functions when we describe sending and receiving between sockets.

connect( )

Since a **stream (TCP) client** is connection-oriented, to create an association it must initiate a connection. You do this by calling the `connect()` function, which initiates creation of a virtual circuit on a TCP socket or sets a default socket name for a UDP socket.

```
int PASCAL FAR connect (SOCKET s,    /* an unconnected socket */
struct sockaddr FAR *addr,           /* remote port and IP addr */
int namelen);                        /* addr structure length */
```

s: socket handle

addr: pointer to a socket address structure (always a `sockaddr_in` structure for TCP/IP)

namelen: length of structure pointed to by *addr* (size of (struct `sockaddr`))

The parameters for `connect()` are the same as those for `bind()`. Before calling `connect()` you must initialize the socket address structure. This is also similar to `bind()`, but with a distinct difference. For `connect()` you initialize the values for `sin_port` and `sin_addr` with the *remote* socket name, not the local socket name as for `bind()`. The `connect()` function requires the socket name of the server with which the client is attempting to associate.

The `connect()` function returns zero on success or SOCKET_ERROR on failure. For a TCP socket, the most common error from `WSAGetLastError()` after `connect()` fails is probably WSAECONNREFUSED (10061). There are only a few cases that cause this error: The server is not running, you initialized *sin_port* incorrectly on the client (or server), or you went to the wrong IP address. Calling `connect()` on a UDP socket does not access the network. The most likely error for a UDP socket is WSAEADDRINUSE (10048). This occurs when you call `connect()` more than once on the same local socket and reference the same remote socket name.

Note: It is possible to call `connect()` on a TCP socket with the same or different destination socket name after an initial attempt fails. However, we recommend you call `closesocket()` and `socket()` to get a new socket before attempting another connection, since many WinSocks do not allow a reconnection after a `connect()` failure.

As we mentioned earlier, the `connect()` function implicitly names a local socket if you have not already called `bind()` (which explicitly names it). If you have not named a socket yet, `connect()` will automatically assign an unused port number in the user-defined range and assign an appropriate local interface address (see Figure 4-7). It is not necessary for most clients to call `bind()`, because of this implicit port assignment.

How a Server Completes an Association

For a **datagram (UDP) server**, completing an association is as simple as it is for a UDP client to initiate one. The server simply reads the data the client sent to it, using either the `recv()` or `recvfrom()` function.

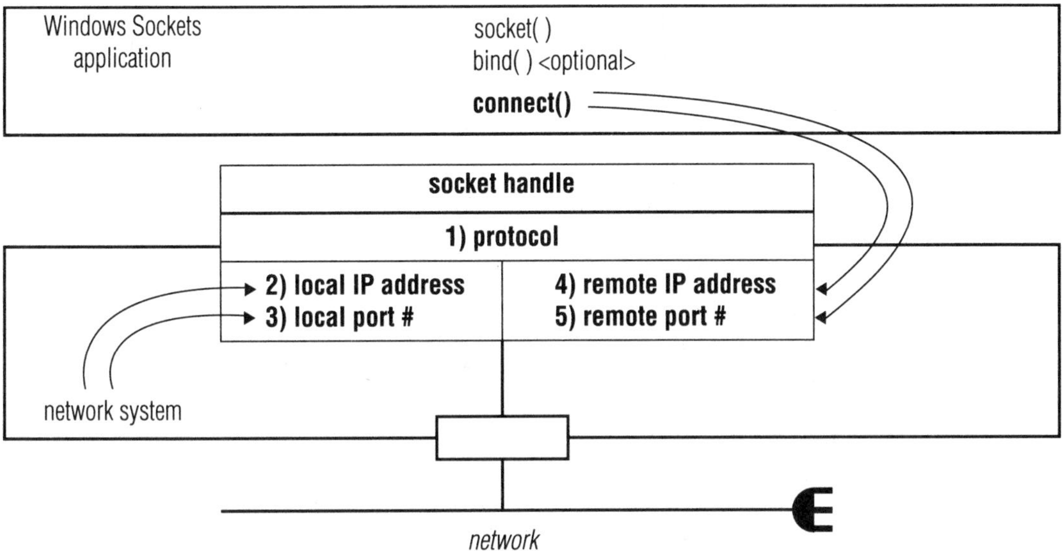

Figure 4-7 The `connect()` function assigns the remote IP address and port number and will also implicitly name the local socket, if not yet explicitly named. It also initiates communication to the server socket over the network.

To read data from a client, the server must detect it. You can do this with `recv()` or `recvfrom()`, both of which read data into application buffers as it arrives. There are also ways to detect incoming data without actually reading it. You can use the MSG_PEEK flag with `recv()` or `recvfrom()`, or call the function `ioctlsocket()` or `select()`. The recommended method is to detect incoming data by calling `WSAAsyncSelect()` to request notification of the FD_READ event.

We discuss all of this in more detail in the later section about sending and receiving data between sockets.

A **stream (TCP) server** detects an incoming connection attempt when `accept()` succeeds, or when `select()` indicates writability (`writefds` flag set) on the listening socket, or when it receives a `WSAAsyncSelect()` FD_ACCEPT Windows message. If you used the `accept()` function to detect the incoming connection, then you have already completed the association when `accept()` succeeds. If you used either `select()` or `WSAAsyncSelect()`, you now need to complete the association by calling the `accept()` function.

accept( )

The `accept()` function returns a new socket for a newly created connection after accepting a pending connection request from a listening socket.

```
SOCKET PASCAL FAR accept (SOCKET s,   /* a listening socket */
       struct sockaddr FAR *addr,     /* name of incoming socket */
       int FAR *addrlen);             /* length of sockaddr */
```

s: socket handle

addr: pointer to socket address structure (always a `sockaddr_in` for TCP/IP)

addrlen: length of socket structure that *addr* points to (size of (struct `sockaddr`))

The `accept()` function has the same parameters as both `connect()` and `bind()`. Unlike these functions, however, you do not initialize the socket structure before you call `accept()`. Instead, the contents of the `sockaddr_in` structure are filled in by the `accept()` function itself. When `accept()` succeeds, it provides the name of the remote socket that just connected (see Figure 4-8). In other words, the `sin_port` field contains the port number of the client and `sin_addr` contains the client's IP address. Thus, when it succeeds, `accept()` returns a valid socket. It returns INVALID_SOCKET when it fails. This function rarely fails, however.

Although the value of the socket descriptor returned should not matter to your application at all, it is noteworthy that the *accept() function returns a new socket*. The listening socket referenced in the call to `accept()` still listens for new connections after `accept()` returns. Keep this in mind, because this means server applications have more than one socket to close.

Send and Receive between Sockets

At this point, we have established an association between the client and server sockets. In other words, the client found the server and the server recognized the client. The two sockets are now peers, and you can send data in either direction.

Sending Data on a "Connected" Socket

send( )

An application can send data using the `send()` function on a TCP or UDP socket:

```
int PASCAL FAR send (SOCKET s,    /* associated socket */
```

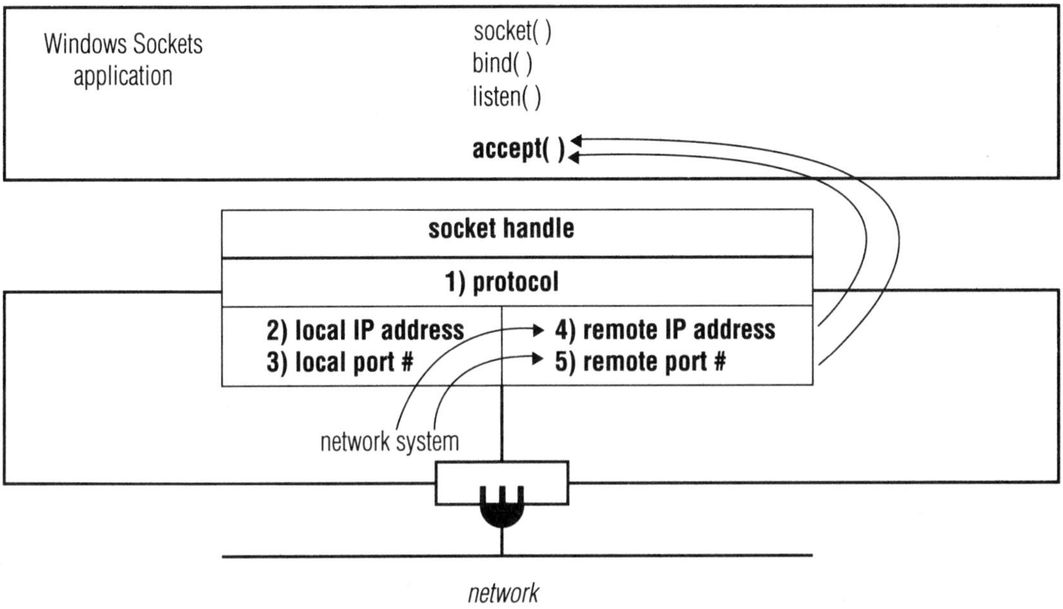

Figure 4-8 The `accept()` function receives the remote IP address and port number (remote socket name) from the client that just connected.

```
    const char FAR *buf,        /* buffer with outgoing data */
    int len,                    /* bytes to send */
    int flags);                 /* option flags */
```

s: socket handle

buf: pointer to a buffer that contains application data to send

len: length of data (in bytes) to send

flags: flags to affect the send (MSG_OOB, MSG_DONTROUTE)

With a **datagram (UDP) socket**, you can use `send()` only if you have called the `connect()` function to establish an association. The `send()` function takes its target socket name from the association, which is why a socket is "valid" only if it has an association established. If you do not call `connect()` first, `send()` will fail and `WSAGetLastError()` will return the WSAENOTCONN error.

As mentioned earlier, calling `connect()` is preferable on a UDP socket when you use only one target address for the life of the socket. However, it's not limited to a single target for the life of the socket, since you can call `connect()` multiple times to set different target socket names. We recommend you call `connect()` with INADDR_ANY as the destination address before trying to connect to a new address, since some WinSocks require this type of disconnection before they will allow a new connection.

If you know your application will send datagrams to a number of different addresses, then you should use the `sendto()` function instead of `send()`. We describe the `sendto()` function in the next section.

With a **stream (TCP) socket**, you can use the `send()` function only if you have called `connect()` successfully. You must have a virtual circuit established to call `send()`. If you do not call `connect()` first, `send()` will fail and `WSAGetLastError()` will return the WSAENOTCONN error.

The *buf* parameter is a pointer to a buffer in your application. It should point to the first byte of the data you want to send. You set the value of the `len` parameter to the number of bytes you want to send from the buffer. For UDP sockets, this value cannot exceed the maximum datagram size limit returned from `WSAStartup()` during program initialization (we describe `WSAStartup()` and the information it returns in Chapter 10, "Support Routines"). For TCP sockets you can use any value, but there is no guarantee the function will send all the requested data in one call.

The `flags` parameter is for options. Typically, the value for `flags` should be 0. There are only two supported by the v1.1 WSA specification, MSG_DONTROUTE and MSG_OOB. These options are used in specialized applications, so we will defer discussion of them.

The `send()` function returns the number of bytes sent on success and SOCKET_ERROR on failure. There are several things to note about a successful case. On a TCP socket, the operation is *successful even if it sent less than the number of bytes you requested*. This is because TCP is a stream, so it does not preserve boundaries within the data. This will occur whether you have a blocking or nonblocking TCP socket. It is the application's responsibility to know how much data it needs to send, keep track of how much it sent, and retry the operation until it sends all it needs to. On a UDP socket, the function will fail if the datagram is too large, and `WSAGetLastError()` will return the WSAEMSGSIZE (10040) error.

Also, a successful return from `send()` does not necessarily mean that the data has appeared on the network yet. It means only that the *protocol stack had room to buffer* the data. The protocol stack may delay transmission to comply with protocol conventions. For example, the Nagle algorithm, which is used to reduce trivial network traffic, delays TCP transmissions until either a full TCP segment (a full packet) is queued or all outstanding data (all data sent) is acknowledged (we discuss the Nagle algorithm in Chapter 9, "Socket Information and Control," when we describe the TCP_NODELAY socket option).

Sending Data on an "Unconnected" Socket

sendto( )

```
int PASCAL FAR sendto (SOCKET s,   /* a valid socket */
        const char FAR *buf,       /* buffer with outgoing data */
        int len,                   /* bytes to send */
        int flags,                 /* option flags */
        struct sockaddr FAR *to,   /* remote socket name */
        int tolen);                /* length of sockaddr */
```

s: socket handle

buf: pointer to buffer to receive data

len: length of data (in bytes) to send

flags: flags to affect behavior of send function (MSG_OOB, MSG_DONTROUTE)

to: pointer to socket structure (always a `sockaddr_in` for TCP/IP) that contains destination address and port number (socket name)

tolen: length of socket structure pointed to by *to* (size of (struct `sockaddr`))

For **datagram (UDP) sockets**, the `sendto()` function is almost identical to `send()`, except for two key differences: the "state" of the socket it allows, and where it gets the target (destination) socket name. As far as the `sendto()` function is concerned, any UDP socket is a "valid socket"; nothing is required to prepare a UDP socket to use `sendto()`. However, we recommend you call `bind()` or `connect()` before attempting `sendto()` because some WinSock implementations require you to name the local socket before you can send.

The `sendto()` function uses the socket named in the sockaddr *to* parameter as the target on a UDP socket. Even if you have `connect()`ed a UDP socket, you can `sendto()` a different destination address at any time. Of course, you must initialize the *to* parameter with the remote socket name before calling `sendto()` on a UDP socket.

For **stream (TCP) sockets**, the `send()` and `sendto()` functions are *exactly* the same. The *to* parameter is superfluous on a TCP socket. The `sendto()` function requires a connected TCP socket and always uses the remote socket as the target. In other words, on a TCP socket `sendto()` ignores the *to* parameter.

Receiving Data

An application can receive data using either the `recv()` or `recvfrom()` function. Much of what we said about `send()` and `sendto()` is also true for their counterparts, `recv()` and `recvfrom()`. You will notice that the parameters for each pair of functions are the same, and they have the same socket "state" requirements. They also return the number of bytes received when successful or SOCKET_ERROR on failure. There are some significant differences, however, as we note below.

To simply detect the availability of data (without reference to how much is pending), you can use `select()` or `WSAAsyncSelect()`. To use `select()`, you use the FD_SET macro to set the `readfds` parameter with your socket descriptor value. Using `WSAAsyncSelect()` to notify your application of the FD_READ event is the recommended method. We'll provide a detailed discussion of these flexible and powerful functions in Chapter 6, "Socket States."

recv( )

```
int PASCAL FAR recv (SOCKET s,      /* associated socket */
        char FAR *buf,              /* buffer with outgoing data */
        int len,                    /* bytes to send */
        int flags);                 /* option flags */
```

s: socket handle

buf: pointer to buffer to receive data

len: length of data (in bytes) to send

flags: flags to affect behavior of send function (MSG_PEEK, MSG_OOB)

Similar to `send()`, the `recv()` function can only be used on a connected socket. Whereas `send()` uses the destination socket for `connect()` as the default destination, `recv()` uses it to filter datagrams it receives. The `recv()` function reads only those datagrams that have the default address and port number as the source (the protocol stack discards all datagrams received from other addresses or ports).

recvfrom( )

```
int PASCAL FAR recvfrom (SOCKET s,   /* a valid socket */
        char FAR *buf,               /* buffer with outgoing data */
        int len,                     /* bytes to send */
```

```
int flags,                    /* option flags */
struct sockaddr FAR *from,   /* remote socket name */
int fromlen);                 /* length of sockaddr */
```

s: socket handle

buf: pointer to buffer to receive data

len: length of data (in bytes) to send

flags: flags to affect behavior of send function (MSG_PEEK, MSG_OOB)

from: pointer to socket structure (always a `sockaddr_in` for TCP/IP) that contains source address and port number (socket name)

fromlen: length of socket structure pointed to by *from* (size of (struct `sockaddr`))

Of course, one key difference between `sendto()` and `recvfrom()` is the content of the sockaddr parameter (the *to* and *from* parameters, respectively). After `recvfrom()` succeeds, the `sockaddr_in` structure pointed to by the *from* parameter contains the name of the source socket–the port number and address–that sent the data. Note: This means you cannot determine the source address or port of datagrams you receive by initializing *from* before you call `recvfrom()`.

The `flags` parameter values for `recv()` and `recvfrom()` can be MSG_OOB and MSG_PEEK. Many applications use the MSG_PEEK flag to find out how much data is available for reading. The MSG_PEEK flag will even allow an application to look at data received without removing it from the protocol stack's buffers. One other way to find out how much data is available for reading is to use the `ioctlsocket()` function with the FIONREAD option (although this does not also let you "peek" at the data). We describe MSG_PEEK, MSG_OOB, and FIONREAD in Chapter 6, "Socket States."

Association as Socket Demultiplexer

We pointed out earlier how unimportant the value or data type of a socket descriptor is to a network application. It is also significant to note that a socket descriptor is local to the system that created it. The socket descriptor never appears in packets sent between a client and a server. So how does each system know to which socket to direct an incoming packet?

The 5-tuple that defines each association–protocol, local port, local IP address, remote port, remote IP address–appears in every packet that passes between the associated sockets. The IP header contains both IP addresses, and each TCP or UDP header contains both ports. When the protocol stack receives a packet from a remote host, it uses the association information (the two socket names) to direct its data to the proper socket (see Figure 4-9). The association information contained in each packet

- allows a packet to reach its destination
- identifies the socket it belongs to once it arrives
- allows the receiver to know the name of the socket that sent the data

Close the Socket

Closing a socket would seem to be the simplest operation, but this is far from true–at least not for a connected TCP socket.

closesocket( )

```
int PASCAL FAR closesocket (SOCKET s);      /* a valid socket */
```

s: socket handle

The `closesocket()` function returns zero on success or SOCKET_ERROR on failure. Failure is unlikely. After the `closesocket()` function returns, any function call that references that socket descriptor will fail with a WSAENOTSOCK (10038) error.

For datagram (UDP) sockets, the `closesocket()` function does no more than return the socket resources to the protocol stack. It always returns immediately. For stream (TCP) sockets, the `closesocket()` function does quite a bit more, because TCP is a connection-oriented protocol. Along with returning socket resources to the protocol stack, `closesocket()` attempts to close the connection, if one exists. There are a number of ways you can do this, too.

By default, the `closesocket()` function is nonblocking (it returns immediately, whether it succeeds or fails). There is a socket option SO_LINGER, used with the function `setsockopt()`, that allows you to set a timeout for `closesocket()` on a stream socket. If you use `setsockopt()` SO_LINGER to set a timeout value for `closesocket()`, then it does not return until it completes or times out with a blocking socket or fails with WSAEWOULDBLOCK with a nonblocking socket (see Chapter 5 for a definition of blocking and nonblocking). During this time the WinSock DLL calls

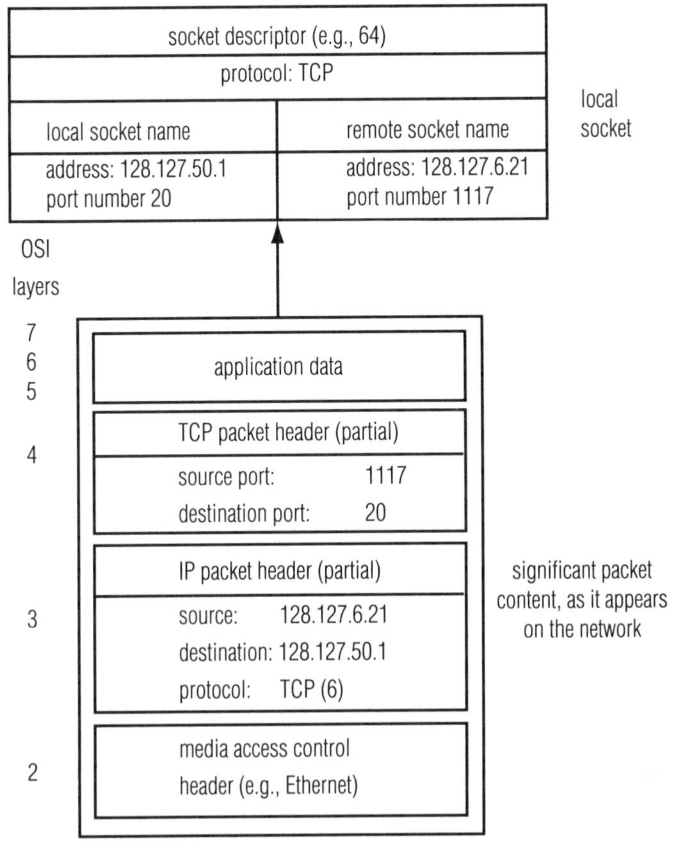

Figure 4-9 The protocol stack uses both the local and remote socket names to fully identify a socket. Every packet contains both local and remote socket names.

the current blocking hook function. When `closesocket()` times out, it aborts the connection (sends a TCP reset). See the section on the SO_LINGER socket option in Chapter 9, "Socket Information and Control," for a more detailed discussion.

shutdown( )

Before you call the `closesocket()` function, you should do a "partial close" of a TCP connection. This is the primary purpose of the `shutdown()` function; it does not release any system resources used by a socket. We recommend its use on a TCP connection. You can use `shutdown()` on a UDP socket, but it is not recommended.

```
int PASCAL FAR shutdown (SOCKET s,     /* a valid socket */
       int how);                      /* flag describing shutdown */
```

s: socket handle

how: flag that indicates the behavior

The *how* parameter is a bit flag that describes how the socket will be shut down. There are three acceptable values for the *how* parameter:

0: receives are disallowed (lower layer protocols are not affected)

1: sends are disallowed (a TCP FIN is sent to remote socket)

2: sends and receives are disallowed (a TCP FIN is sent to remote socket)

Disallowing receives with *how=0* does not affect the lower-layer protocols, so it is *not recommended*. It causes more problems than it solves. A TCP socket stops receiving (closes its TCP protocol window) when incoming data fills its buffers. After `shutdown()` *how=0*, a closed TCP window is likely and it will not be opened again. The application will not be emptying the stack's buffers by calling `recv()` or `recvfrom()`. On a UDP socket, calling `shutdown()` *how=0* also causes problems. The protocol stack can legally discard incoming UDP packets for which it does not have buffer space and it does not return an ICMP error back to the sender. The net effect in both cases is that the sender does not get a clear indication of the receiver's intention to stop receiving. The result of this is not consistently predictable.

Disallowing sends with *how=1* has no effect on a UDP socket. On a TCP socket, it initiates a graceful close (sends a TCP FIN packet) that in effect tells the other side you are done sending but does not disallow the other side from continuing to send. *This is the recommended method* of shutting down a TCP connection when the other side might still have data to send. After calling `shutdown()` *how=1*, you would want to call `recv()` until there is no more data, then call `closesocket()` to complete the close. There are some TCP/IP stacks that will not complete a TCP close (i.e., ACKnowledge your TCP FIN, and respond with a TCP FIN) unless they receive an acknowledgment for all the data they have queued to send. If you do a partial close, and read all data, you can be sure `closesocket()` will complete a graceful close on systems like this. See the `CloseConn()` function in the sample WinSockx library in Chapter 7 for an example.

Disallowing sends and receives with *how=2* initiates a graceful close of a TCP connection but does not allow any further receives. If you use this, you cannot use the defensive programming strategy detailed above for *how=1*.

Therefore, *how=2* is not an optimal choice. However, there have been some Windows Sockets implementations that will not `closesocket()` properly unless you call `shutdown()` *how=2* first, so this call may be inevitable.

Client and Server Sketches

It is not possible to make a single network client and server pair of network programs that you can use for either datagram or stream sockets, without some modification. This is not surprising, given the differences between the connection-oriented and connectionless paradigms. Thus, what we will do here is sketch the generic program designs for TCP and UDP. We need to stress that these are just sketches. You would use many other supporting functions–some of which we have mentioned in this chapter–in a complete Windows Sockets application. The following examples are the "bare-bones" superstructures for all Windows Sockets Network applications, so it is worthwhile to present them.

Connection-oriented (TCP) Network Applications

Client	*Server*
`socket()`	`socket()`
initialize `sockaddr_in` structure	initialize `sockaddr_in` structure
with server (remote) socket name	with server (local) socket name
	`bind()`
	`listen()`
`connect()------------------------>`	
	`accept()`
<association created, either side can send or receive>	
`send()--------------------------->`	`recv()`
`recv()<-------------------------`	`send()`
`closesocket()`	`closesocket()` (connected socket)
	`closesocket()` (listening socket)

Connectionless (UDP) Network Applications

Set the Remote Socket Name Once

Client	*Server*
`socket()`	`socket()`
initialize `sockaddr_in` structure	initialize `sockaddr_in` structure
with server (remote) socket name	with server (local) socket name
	`bind()`
`connect()`	
`send()------------------------>`	`recv()`
<association created, either side can send or receive>	
`recv()<-------------------------`	`send()`
`closesocket()`	`closesocket()`

Set the Remote Socket Name Each Datagram

Client	*Server*
`socket()`	`socket()`
initialize `sockaddr_in` structure	initialize `sockaddr_in` structure
with server (remote) socket name	with server (local) socket name
	`bind()`
`sendto()------------------------->`	`recvfrom()`
`recvfrom()<-----------------------`	`sendto()`
`closesocket()`	`closesocket()`

Note: In this example, if the client application also called `bind()`, then the two hosts would be "peers." By definition, a peer is both a client and a server (a peer can initiate or receive initial communications).

Also note: of course, a client or server can use either the `connect()/recv()` or `sendto()/recvform()` regardless of what APIs the peer application uses to send and receive.

5 Operation Modes

In This Chapter:

- What Are Operation Modes?
- Blocking Mode
- Nonblocking Mode
- Asynchronous Mode
- Performance Differences
- Platform Differences

Time is the longest distance between two places.

Tennessee Williams

Most Windows Sockets functions initiate network operations that involve communication with another network host. The communication usually takes time to complete: sometimes a lot, sometimes a little. Whether your application waits for network operation to complete and how it detects operation completion characterizes the operation mode your application uses. In turn, your application's operation mode determines its design and capabilities as much as its role as a client or server.

In this chapter we describe the three operating modes available in the Windows Sockets API: blocking, nonblocking, and asynchronous. We illustrate these terms and highlight their advantages and disadvantages. We look at them in terms of their resulting code complexity, application flexibility, and system overhead.

Code complexity is a relative term. The three operation modes each have their own coding paradigms. Apparent simplicity or complexity can be deceiving. We show you functionally similar code for each operation mode and point out where they are simple and where they are complex.

Application flexibility relates to how well operation modes provide for specific application requirements. Some examples of application capabilities influenced by operation mode are simultaneous processing of multiple sockets, fast and efficient throughput of bulk data, and interactive data handling.

Code complexity and application flexibility affect your application, but in the nonpreemptive 16-bit Windows environment system overhead affects other applications running simultaneously. For example, if your application transfers large amounts of data at times, it is surprisingly easy to "hog the system." At these times users may not be able to control your application or run other applications simultaneously. We describe ways to avoid such asocial behavior.

We wrap up the chapter with a brief discussion of threaded operation. Threads are platform dependent: They are only available in 32-bit Windows (Windows NT and Windows 95), not in 16-bit Windows (Windows 3.x). Threads make it easier to avoid some of the operation-mode limitations resulting from the nonpreemptive 16-bit Windows. But because threads are not available in 16-bit Windows—which will probably remain the predominant Windows platform for a while to come—threads are not a universal solution.

What Are Operation Modes?

Windows Sockets has three distinct operation modes. The best way to describe them is to illustrate by analogy. They compare nicely to the three "operation modes" you have to choose from when trying to reach someone by telephone. Imagine calling a phone number and getting an answer, but finding out the person you want to speak with is not available immediately. In this case your choices are

- wait on hold until the person comes to the phone
- hang up and call back later
- leave a message to have the person call you back.

These three possible actions correspond exactly to the three operation modes of Windows Sockets functions: *blocking*, *nonblocking*, and *asynchronous* (see Figure 5-1). The considerations are similar also.

Wait on Hold: Blocking

If you wait on hold until the person comes to the phone, you will probably not do much else. You might be able to divide your attention as you wait—doing desk work or chatting with someone—but you cannot use your phone. This is similar to a blocking operation: It yields to do some other things, but you cannot do more than one network operation.

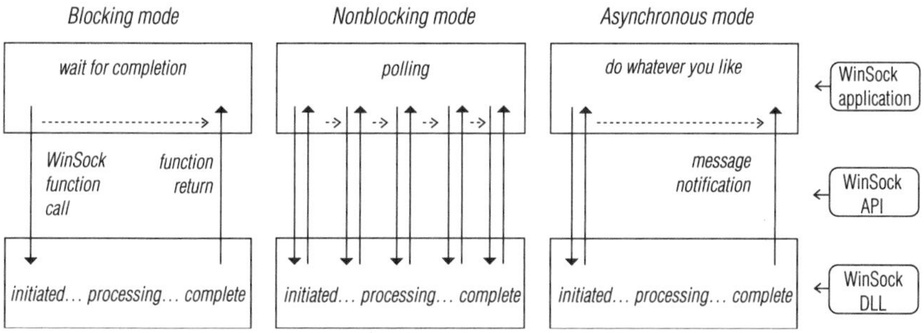

Figure 5-1 WinSock applications using different operation modes to detect network operation completion.

In **blocking operation mode**, a Windows Sockets function returns only when the operation completes. It may succeed or it may fail, but either way you know that the operation completed before the function returned. There are limitations to what applications you can create, but if your application demands are modest you can create simple sequential network code.

However, the nonpreemptive 16-bit Windows environment complicates things. While the WinSock DLL processes a blocking call, it yields to other Windows applications. As a result, your application must be able to handle messages while a blocking call is outstanding. Since you cannot make any other WinSock function calls within a task (or thread) when a blocking call is outstanding, the messages you receive when a blocking operation is pending can be problematic if they usually initiate network operations. Your code needs to deal with these reentrant messages appropriately while in the blocking context.

Call Again Later: Nonblocking

If you hang up and call again later, then you need to figure out when and how often to call. You do not want to call back constantly, since that would waste your time and energy. It is better to space the calls so you are free to do what you like in between. That way you are not tied to the phone and you can use the phone to make other calls if you like. This is similar to a nonblocking operation: You need to "poll" to complete an operation, but you do not want to poll too often or you can waste system resources.

In **nonblocking operation mode**, a Windows Sockets function returns immediately. In some cases the return value indicates success, but in others it indicates failure. But failure of a function in nonblocking operation mode is not necessarily a bad thing. The error value (returned by a call to

`WSAGetLastError()` after the function fails) may be WSAEWOULDBLOCK, which literally means that "the function would have blocked if it had to wait until operation completion before it returned."

Depending on the function, WSAEWOULDBLOCK indicates either that the WinSock DLL has started the operation, but it is not complete at this time (i.e., the operation is pending), or that the WinSock DLL tried but could not satisfy the operation request at this time. In the first case, the operation will eventually complete, and there are various ways to detect completion (which we describe in Chapter 6, "Sockets States"). In the latter case, the "would block" error indicates you need to retry the call.

The problem with nonblocking mode is that an application needs to retry functions over and over—*polling*—to complete an operation, or detect its completion. This incurs significant system overhead if you poll too often, or adversely affects application performance—such as data throughput—if you do not poll often enough. Besides that, it complicates the code.

Request a Callback: Asynchronous

If you request that the person call you back, then you transfer the effort and responsibility to the person you called. You can do whatever you like as you wait for the callback, including using the phone to make other calls. It is okay if your phone is busy when the person calls back, because it is his or her responsibility to try again. This is similar to asynchronous operation: The WinSock DLL sends you a message when the event for which you requested a callback occurs.

Asynchronous operation mode is nonblocking since you return from the call before the operation completes. But unlike regular nonblocking operation mode, the WSAEWOULDBLOCK means that the WinSock DLL will send a message (i.e., "call you back") to notify you either when a pending operation completes or when to retry an operation.

Asynchronous operation mode is the mode of choice. You get efficient and "friendly" Windows operation with fast data throughput. The asynchronous source code is not compatible with Berkeley Sockets, but its simplicity and efficiency offset its lack of portability.

Blocking Mode

A blocking function waits until the requested network operation completes—successfully or not—before it returns. Upon completion, the function's return value indicates success or failure of the operation. When you get a socket descriptor from the `socket()` function call, it will use blocking mode by default. Having a blocking socket affects the way many WinSock functions operate. Other WinSock functions always operate in blocking mode. In this section we describe blocking sockets and blocking functions.

Blocking Sockets

As just stated, a socket returned from the `socket()` function operates in blocking mode by default. This means that calls to some WinSock functions that reference that socket handle will block until the resulting operation completes. Here is a list of all the functions that block when an application references a blocking socket in the socket handle input parameter:

Function Name	*Blocks until...*
accept()	the application receives a connection request
closesocket()	the close operation completes (only stream sockets block, and only when `setsockopt()` SO_LINGER is set with a nonzero timeout)
connect()	the connect operation completes (and only with a stream socket)
recv() and recvfrom()	the network system receives data for this socket
send() and sendto	buffers are available in network system for outgoing data (and only with a stream socket)

Use of a blocking socket means your network code is simpler, because its actions are sequential. Upon return from a function call you know the requested operation is complete (successfully or not). But do not be fooled. Because of the message reentrancy issue in nonpreemptive 16-bit Windows, blocking operations are more complicated than they seem. This problem is related to the "fake blocking" required by cooperative multitasking, as we describe in a moment.

Blocking Functions

Some functions always block, whether or not the socket passed to it is a blocking socket. Most of the functions that always block do not even take a socket as an input parameter.

Function Name	*Description*
select( )	detects readability, writability, and errors on sets of sockets
gethostbyname( )	retrieves host information for a host name
gethostbyaddr( )	retrieves host information for a host address
getprotobyname( )	retrieves the protocol number for a protocol name
getprotobynumber( )	retrieves the protocol name for a protocol number
getservbyname( )	retrieves service information for a service name
getservbyport( )	retrieves service information for a port number

The `select( )` function is the only function that references a socket. It actually references many sockets simultaneously, as it takes three sets of sockets as input arguments. It operates in blocking mode whether or not any of the sockets in the sets are in blocking mode. It does not perform any network I/O, but it does examine the current state of each socket in each set. We describe `select( )` in detail in Chapter 6, "Socket States."

The `gethostbyname( )` and `gethostbyaddr( )` functions are the only ones in this list likely to generate any network I/O. These functions often use a remote server to resolve the host name or address—using DNS for TCP/IP, for instance—so they may take a while to return from a blocking operation. The Windows Sockets specification does not stipulate how a WinSock DLL should resolve host names and addresses, however, so alternately they could reference a host file on the local system (and return quickly). We discuss these implementation variations in Chapter 8, "Host Names and Addresses."

The Windows Sockets specification also does not determine how the WinSock DLL should provide protocols and services resolution for the functions `getprotobyname( )`, `getservbyport( )`, and similar ones. Most WinSock implementations perform protocols and services resolution by referencing "database" files of local services and protocols, so they typically return quickly. This is also how Berkeley Sockets operates. We describe these functions and their implementations in Chapter 10, "Support Routines."

Blocking Is Fake

Everyone would agree that Microsoft Windows' most useful feature is its support of multitasking. Ironically, few would say that multitasking is Windows' most impressive feature.

The problem is that Windows 3.1 (16-bit Windows) does not support "real" multitasking. It supports "cooperative" multitasking, which means that it is easy for an "unfriendly program" to adversely affect the rest of the system. This is not true for Windows NT or Windows 95, which have preemptive, 32-bit operating systems.

Cooperative multitasking posed a problem for WinSock DLL designers because the API they were emulating, Berkeley Sockets, has roots firmly embedded in UNIX. Berkeley Sockets assumes that the operating system is capable of preempting any application that tries to monopolize system resources. In Berkeley tasks cannot affect each other, so it is okay if sockets operate in blocking mode. If an application wants to sit idle and wait for a network operation to complete, there is no problem.

In 16-bit Windows, a blocking operation is actually **fake blocking**. Fake blocking means that although your application waits for the network operation to complete, the WinSock DLL yields as you wait. A WinSock DLL fake blocks by calling a **blocking hook** function as it waits for an operation to complete.

There is a default blocking hook function in every WinSock DLL in 16-bit Windows. In 32-bit Windows, WinSock does not use a blocking hook function by default, but an application can install one with `WSASetBlockingHook( )` if needed (see Chapter 10, "Support Routines," for more information).

Typically, the default blocking hook function is the same one defined in the Windows Sockets specification (see the `WSASetBlockingHook( )` documentation). It calls the WinAPI functions `PeekMessage( )`, `DispatchMessage( )`, and `TranslateMessage( )` in a fashion similar to a Windows application message loop. This default blocking hook processes Windows messages and implicitly yields to other processes in the system. Its purpose is to yield and check for interruption—from `WSACancelBlockingCall( )`—as it waits for operation completion. By yielding, the default blocking hook function allows other applications to operate simultaneously, which is beneficial. But it also allows your application to receive messages as you wait for a blocking operation to complete. That is not as advantageous.

The messages your application receives while a blocking operation is outstanding are called **reentrant messages**. They sneak in the back door, while your application waits at the front door for the blocking operation to complete. Reentrant messages can wreak havoc if your application does not consider the possibility of the blocking context when it processes messages. For example, if your application tries to do another network operation in response to a message, the function will fail with WSAEINPROGRESS if there is a blocking operation pending. Your application should be able to handle this error gracefully.

The potential for reentrant messages is a fact of life in 16-bit Windows. Any WinSock application that uses blocking operation mode in 16-bit Windows must be able to handle these reentrant messages gracefully. In addition to handling the WSAEINPROGRESS error without aborting your application, you can attempt to avoid the error by checking for the blocking context with `WSAIsBlocking( )`, as we show you in a moment.

Blocking Hook Functions

It is possible for an application to replace the default blocking hook function with one of its own. The Windows Sockets `WSASetBlockingHook( )` function is designed for this purpose. Its counterpart, `WSAUnhookBlockingHook( )`, puts the default blocking hook function back in place (we describe these functions in detail in Chapter 10, "Support Routines").

Beware: The `WSASetBlockingHook( )` function is not as versatile as you might think. It is available for applications that need to perform some legitimate operations, such as extra keyboard processing, as they block. If you install a blocking hook function that yields to other processes exclusively, or does not yield at all, then your application will not work over all WinSock DLLs. As we describe in Chapter 11, "DLLs over WinSock," it is possible to write a blocking hook function that avoids reentrant messages. Unfortunately, because some WinSock architectures rely on Windows messages, such a blocking hook function will not always work.

The Windows Sockets specification does not prescribe WinSock DLL architecture. There is no mandate that a WinSock DLL must allow a blocking hook that avoids reentrant messages. As a result, some WinSock DLLs use Windows messages internally. If your blocking hook prevents receipt of messages, then these DLLs fail. Blocking operations never complete when these blocking hooks stop message traffic.

Consequently, if you want your application to work on all Windows Sockets implementations, you must always have a blocking hook function that yields properly. There is at least one technique that uses Windows subclassing to yield and avoid reentrant messages, as we demonstrate in the sample DLL in Chapter 11. However, this technique prohibits user interaction with your application during blocking operations, so it is less than optimal. Ideally, applications that use blocking sockets in 16-bit Windows should avoid problems caused by reentrant messages by managing the blocking context, as we describe next.

The Blocking Context

The Windows Sockets specification stipulates that while a blocking operation is outstanding in each (16-bit) task or (32-bit) thread, no other network operation is possible. This is called the **blocking context**, and during this time all other WinSock calls, other than `WSACancelBlockingCall( )`, will fail with WSAEINPROGRESS.

If you use blocking operation mode anywhere in your application, there is always a chance that your application could encounter the blocking context when you want to make another call to WinSock. There are a number of things you can do to avoid problems with this blocking context:

- React to the WSAEINPROGRESS error gracefully if you make a WinSock call.
- Detect the blocking context with `WSAIsBlocking( )` to avoid a WinSock call.
- Maintain application state to detect blocking context and avoid a WinSock call.

React to WSAEINPROGRESS Gracefully

Whenever you initiate network operations in an application that uses blocking operation mode, you need to expect WinSock functions to fail with the WSAEINPROGRESS error. This failure occurs when there is a pending blocking operation. Any WinSock function—whether or not it initiates another blocking operation—can fail with WSAEINPROGRESS if there is an outstanding blocking function. The only exceptions are the functions `WSACancelBlockingCall( )`, which we look at shortly, and `WSAIsBlocking( )`, which we look at next.

The WSAEINPROGRESS error should never be fatal to your application. You should always expect the error and be able to handle it gracefully (i.e., without aborting the application). With every WinSock function call, you need to ask yourself what to do if you encounter this error. Sometimes you will want to retry the failed operation at some other time, and other times you can skip it. Your actions when a WinSock function fails with WSAEINPROGRESS depend entirely on your application design. Ideally, you will avoid the error. We show you how to avoid it with our other two strategies for handling the blocking context.

Detect with WSAIsBlocking( )

The `WSAIsBlocking( )` function is specifically designed to detect the blocking context.

```
BOOL PASCAL FAR WSAIsBlocking(void);     /* TRUE if blocking */
```

`WSAIsBlocking()` does not take any parameters; the current task or thread is the implicit input parameter. It simply returns TRUE if there is a blocking operation outstanding, and FALSE if not. When it returns TRUE, you know to avoid WinSock function calls, since they will fail with the WSAEINPROGRESS error.

The `WSAIsBlocking()` function works well for reporting the blocking context, and this is perfectly adequate for most applications to avoid having to react to the WSAEINPROGRESS error. But applications may have other contexts they do not want interrupted. They may perform a series of network or nonnetwork operations—some of which may yield—and may want to prevent reentrancy in that context. A more generalized way to monitor application context is for the application to keep track of itself.

Maintain Application State

Another way for an application to avoid the WSAEINPROGRESS error, as well as to avoid interrupting other contexts, is to maintain a variable that indicates the current application state. This strategy involves setting a variable to indicate an operation currently underway and checking that state variable before initiating new operations. In this way you can be sure your application is in a proper state to perform an operation before you attempt it. In effect, this makes your application "self-aware."

It is extra work to maintain application state, but an application that is self-aware can avoid many problems that can occur in a multitasking environment. It ensures that your application does everything in the proper sequence and proper context. You can avoid WSAEINPROGRESS, as well as other errors, by maintaining application state. For instance, if you indicate in a state variable that the `connect()` function succeeded, then you know that `send()` function will not fail with WSAENOTCONN.

Cancelling Blocking Operations

There are many reasons to cancel a pending blocking operation: for instance, to allow users to back out when they make a mistake or when they are tired of waiting. It is possible to allow an application user to cancel these or any other blocking operation at any point, or use a Windows timer to implement a timeout of your own (more on blocking operation timeouts in a moment). The `WSACancelBlockingCall()` function allows you to force completion of a pending blocking operation by forcing failure. The `WSACancelBlockingCall()` is an escape hatch for any blocking operation.

```
int PASCAL FAR WSACancelBlockingCall (void);    /* 0 on success */
```

Similar to `WSAIsBlocking( )`, `WSACancelBlockingCall( )` does not take any parameters; the task or thread is the implicit parameter. `WSACancelBlockingCall( )` cancels the pending blocking operation or fails if no operation is pending. On failure, it returns SOCKET_ERROR and `WSAGetLastError( )` returns the WSAEINVAL error. But `WSACancelBlockingCall( )` is not as simple as it seems.

Cancellation Occurs Later

Beware: `WSACancelBlockingCall( )` always returns immediately. It does not wait until the pending blocking operation is cancelled, so the blocking operation is still pending upon return from `WSACancelBlockingCall( )`.

The blocking operation cancellation completes when the interrupted function fails with the WSAEINTR error ("interrupted system call"). At times there may be a significant delay between the call to `WSACancelBlockingCall( )` and the WSAEINTR failure, as the Windows scheduler reverts control to the blocking routine. Of course, in 16-bit Windows you need to yield nicely as you wait for the cancellation to take effect. Note: Even if you yield between calls, you cannot loop on `WSAIsBlocking( )` as you wait for cancellation (or cancellation will not complete).

To handle cancellation, all blocking function calls must be prepared to handle the WSAEINTR error appropriately. Your application design determines what is appropriate handling. For most, and especially for stream sockets, it means closing the socket since further socket use is limited.

Further Socket Use Is Limited

The WinSock specification warns that cancellation of some blocking socket calls can leave a socket in an indeterminate state. The `accept( )` and `select( )` functions are the only exceptions noted; so cancelling them should be okay at any point. Cancellation of other blocking functions may compromise the integrity of a data stream (a connected TCP socket). If this happens, subsequent function calls will fail with the WSAECONNABORTED error.

After cancellation of blocking functions other than `accept( )` and `select( )`, the only network function guaranteed to work is `closesocket( )`. And `closesocket( )` is only guaranteed if you abort the connection—set a 0 timeout with `setsockopt( )` SO_LINGER—rather than attempt a graceful close (see Chapter 9, "Socket Information and Control," for more information on setsockopt( ) SO_LINGER). This possibility limits the general usefulness of WSACancelBlockingCall( ).

Cancellation May Fail

Notice in the following code example that we set a state variable before cancelling the blocking operation to record the cancellation request. Because of the delay between calling WSACancelBlockingCall( ) and the cancellation, the pending blocking operation may actually complete before it is cancelled. In this case a function would return indicating success, rather than failing with WSAEINTR as it should.

If you record the state before attempting to cancel a blocking operation, you can proceed with an application cancellation even if the cancellation fails (i.e., if the blocking function returns successfully). Otherwise, an application might proceed as though the cancellation were never done. This could be a potentially disastrous—or simply annoying—outcome, which might require another cancellation attempt.

Code Example

Here is an example of how an application cancels a blocking operation:

```
/*  user has requested blocking operation cancellation,
 *  or we've had a timeout on a blocking operation and
 *  we want the application to cancel it. */
< set a state variable to indicate user cancellation >
if (WSAIsBlocking( ))  {
      /* cancel the blocking call */
      WSACancelBlockingCall( );
}
```

Then any blocking function must be able to handle the WSAEINTR error returned when cancellation takes effect, as we illustrate here with the recv( ) call:

```
nRet = recv (s, (LPSTR)achInBuf, cbInLen, 0);
 if (nRet == SOCKET_ERROR) {
    /* recv( ) function failed, get the WinSock error */
    nWSAerror = WSAGetLastError( );

    /* if blocking call cancelled then abort connection */
```

```
        if (nWSAerror == WSAEINTR) {
              <set SO_LINGER timeout=0 and close connection>
        } else {
              /* recv( ) failed with unexpected error */
              <report WinSock error to user>
        }
        return;   /* quit function */
    } else if (nRet == 0) {
          /* remote system closed stream connection */
          <connection closed>
    } else {
          /* recv( ) returned successfully */
          <check amount received and process>
          <check state for user cancellation>
    }
```

Timeouts on Blocking Operations

Blocking functions do not return until their operation completes. So what happens if their operation never completes? The WinSock DLL and protocol stack will automatically time-out some operations, you can set the timeout for others, and there are a couple of generally useful timeout strategies for blocking operations. We describe each of the following types of timeouts next:

- automatic timeouts
- user-settable timeouts
- application timeouts
- TCP keep-alive timeouts

Automatic Timeouts

Some functions, such as `connect( )`, `send( )`, and `gethostbyname( )`, will time-out automatically. The timeouts for `connect( )` and `send( )` affect non-blocking operations as well as blocking operations. The application does not have any control over the timeout period for these functions, however. The network system alone determines when their timeout occurs. These network-system timeouts are related to the timeouts implemented for the protocols in use (e.g., ARP timeout, TCP SYN or ACK timeouts, or DNS query timeouts). The WinSock API does not provide a way to detect or change these network-system timeout values.

User-Settable Timeouts

Other functions, such as `select()` and `closesocket()`, allow an application to determine a timeout value. We will leave `select()`—which does not do I/O, but detects socket state—for detailed discussion in Chapter 6, "Socket States." As for `closesocket()`, keep in mind that it does not block by default, even with a blocking socket. The SO_DONTLINGER option is the default for `closesocket()`, so it will block only if you have a blocking socket and set a nonzero timeout by calling `setsockopt()` to enable the SO_LINGER option. In general, your application should not set a nonzero timeout for `closesocket()`. As we explain in Chapter 9, "Socket Information and Control," there is seldom a need to override the default timeout a stack sets for a TCP connection.

Application Timeouts

Some functions, such as `recv()`, `recvfrom()`, or `accept()`, can block forever. These functions have no time limit, so it is possible that `recv()` or `recvfrom()` will never return if no data is received (actually, 32-bit WinSock supports a SO_RCVTIMEO option; see Chapter 15, "Platforms," for more information) and that `accept()` will not return if no connection requests are received. For these functions you would need to implement a timeout mechanism in your 16-bit Windows application by using a Windows timer followed by a call to `WSACancelBlockingCall()`. Do not do this casually, however, since `WSACancelBlockingCall()` has many limitations. Your application will be better off if you avoid the need to cancel these blocking calls by waiting to call them until you know they can be satisfied. We will describe how to do this in Chapter 6, "Sockets States."

TCP Keep-Alive Timeouts

Another way to enable a timeout on a stream socket is by setting the `setsockopt()` SO_KEEPALIVE option. This causes the protocol stack to send TCP "keep-alive" packets periodically. The receiver is obliged to reflect the keep-alive packet back to the sender as an acknowledgment of receipt. If the reflection is not received, any subsequent or pending I/O operation will fail with the WSAETIMEDOUT error.

As good as SO_KEEPALIVE sounds, there is no standard for the transmission period of keep-alives and their use is generally discouraged. The prevailing opinion is that they waste bandwidth and there are better methods available at the application level. For more information on `setsockopt()` SO_KEEPALIVE, see Chapter 9, "Socket Information and Control."

No Receive Minimum

The *len* input parameter to the `recv( )` or `recvfrom( )` function specifies the length of the buffer for incoming data (see Chapter 4, "Network Application Mechanics" for specifics). In effect, *len* specifies an upper limit on the number of incoming data bytes that `recv( )` or `recvfrom( )` can copy into the incoming buffer. However, you must not assume that the length field is also the minimum number of bytes WinSock must copy before returning from a blocking `recv( )` or `recvfrom( )`. This is a common error that can make your application appear to lose data.

A blocking `recv( )` or `recvfrom( )` returns after the network system copies *any number of bytes* into the incoming buffer. It will copy no more than the *len* field specifies, but it may copy less. Your application should always compare the return value from your `recv( )` and `recvfrom( )` calls with the number of bytes you expected to receive. You may need to receive again to get all the data you expected.

Code Example

Here is a pseudocode that illustrates a simple application that uses blocking mode. This is a stream client application that connects to a server, sends a fixed-length string to an echo server, reads the string back, and then closes the connection.

Notice we use two variables to keep track of state in this example. We have one global variable that keeps track of application state and prevents the user from initiating the test twice, so we should never encounter a WSAEINPROGRESS error. The other state variable is *nRet,* which indicates a previous error condition. We do not show handling of WSAEINTR for interrupted blocking calls, simply because we do not do anything special for them (we display an error message and abort the connection, just as we do with other fatal errors).

We also do not compare the number of bytes returned from `send( )` or `recv( )` with the number in the *len* field in this example either. However, we should. In a real application we would have receive and send loops similar to those in the nonblocking code example that appears later in this chapter.

```
SOCKET s;
SOCKADDR_IN stDstAddr;     /* destination socket structure */
static char szDstAddr = "128.127.50.7";
static char achOutBuf[] =
```

```
    "This is a jest of the emergency comedy system";
static char achInBuf[BUFSIZE];
int nBytesToXfer;
int nRet;

void block_example( ) {
  s  = socket(PF_INET, SOCK_STREAM, 0);  /* get a stream socket */
  if (s == INVALID SOCKET) {
      <report WinSock error to user>
      goto jest_end;
  }
  /* initialize destination socket address structure */
  stDstAddr.sin_family = PF_INET;
  stDstAddr.sin_port = htons(IPPORT_ECHO);
  stDstAddr.sin_addr = inet_addr (szDstAddr);
  /* connect to server */
  nRet = connect(s, (LPSOCKADDR)&stDstAddr, sizeof(SOCKADDR));
  if (nRet == SOCKET_ERROR) {          /* connect failed */
      <report WinSock error to user>
      goto jest_end;
  }
  nBytesToXfer = _fstrlen(achOutBuf); /* we're connected! */
  nRet = send(s,                    /* send the string */
        (LPSTR)&achOutBuf,
        nBytesToXfer, 0);
  if (nRet == SOCKET_ERROR) {
      <report WinSock error to user>
      goto jest_end;
  }
  nRet = recv(s,              .     /* read the string back */
        (LPSTR)&achInBuf,
        nBytesToXfer, 0);
  if (nRet == SOCKET_ERROR) {
      <handle error>
  } else if (nRet == 0) {          /* remote closed connection */
      <report unexpected condition to user>
  }

jest_end:
   if (nRet == SOCKET_ERROR) { /* if we had an error before this */
       LINGER stLinger;    /* we should abort the connection */
```

```
        stLinger.l_onoff = TRUE;/* by setting 0 close timeout */
        stLinger.l_linger = 0;
        nRet = setsockopt(s, SOL_SOCKET, SO_LINGER,
              (LPSTR)&stLinger, sizeof(LINGER));
        if (nRet == SOCKET_ERROR) {
             <report WinSock error to user>
         }
    }
  nRet = closesocket(s);     /* close connection and socket */
  if (nRet == SOCKET_ERROR) {
      <handle error>
  }
  return;
}  /* end block_example( ) */
```

In the active window procedure in both server and client applications that use code like this, we would need to handle reentrant messages. This code allows a user to cancel a test (by pressing a cancel button), and we would wait until our test completion if we receive a request to close from Windows. We would also do something similar to handle a WM_CLOSE command.

```
     #define IN_PROGRESS     1
     #define DESTROY_PENDING 2
     int nAppState;    /* application state (a global variable) */
    ...
     switch (msg) {
         ...
         case WM_COMMAND:
             switch (wParam) {
                 case IDOK:    /* user wants to start sample app */
                       if (nAppState & IN_PROGRESS) {
                             <tell user test is in progress>
                       } else {
                            nAppState |= IN_PROGRESS; /* set state */
                            block_example( );          /* do test */
                            nAppState &= ~IN_PROGRESS;/* unset state*/
                             if (nAppState & DESTROY_PENDING)
                                   PostQuitMessage(0);
                             break;
                      }
                case IDCANCEL:    /* user cancel request */
```

```
                    if (WSAIsBlocking( )) {
                          WSACancelBlockingCall( );
                          break;
                    }
          }
          break;
      case WM_DESTROY:
          /* wait until proper completion to quit */
          if (nAppState & IN_PROGRESS) {
              nAppState |= DESTROY_PENDING;
              if (WSAIsBlocking( ))
                    WSACancelBlockingCall( );
          } else {
              PostQuitMessage(0);
          }
          break;
  ...
  } /* end switch(msg) */
  return (0L);
```

Nonblocking Mode

A nonblocking function call returns immediately whether or not the relevant network operation has completed. Unlike blocking calls, nonblocking calls do not wait for the operation to complete before returning to the calling application. As we have seen, the network code in applications that use blocking mode is relatively simple, but it is complicated by the need to handle reentrant messages. Blocking mode also limits the ability of an application to service multiple sockets simultaneously, since only one blocking operation can be pending in a task. An application that uses nonblocking mode does not have a blocking context to contend with. Functions return immediately, before an operation completes. This makes it easier to have multiple sockets with simultaneous pending operations.

However, along with the control and flexibility that nonblocking operation mode provides comes responsibility. You need to yield explicitly so that your user can command your application at all times and other applications are not impacted. Yet, you do not want to yield so much that your application's performance is adversely affected. This is a tricky balancing act that makes it difficult to create purely nonblocking applications. Most nonblocking applications are hybrids that use nonblocking sockets and the blocking select( ) function to multiplex multiple sockets efficiently (we describe the select( ) function in detail in Chapter 6, "Socket States").

How Do You Make a Socket Nonblocking?

A socket handle returned from a socket( ) call will block on I/O operations by default. An application can make a socket nonblocking implicitly or explicitly.

If you call WSAAsyncSelect( ), you automatically make a socket nonblocking. But as we show you shortly, using WSAAsyncSelect( ) is synonymous with using asynchronous operation mode. In this mode you interact with the socket differently than you do in traditional nonblocking operation mode.

To explicitly make your socket nonblocking, call ioctlsocket( ) with the FIONBIO command (we describe ioctlsocket( ) in detail in Chapter 9, "Socket Information and Control"). Here is a pseudocode example of how to do this:

```
u_long argp = 1L;  /* nonzero enables nonblocking mode */
int nRet;
SOCKET s;
...
/* get a datagram socket (blocking by default) */
s = socket(PF_INET, SOCK_DGRAM, 0);
if (s == INVALID_SOCKET) {
      <display WinSock error to user>
}
/* make the socket nonblocking */
nRet = ioctlsocket (s, FIONBIO, (u_long FAR*)&argp);
if (nRet == SOCKET_ERROR) {
      <display WinSock error to user>
}
```

Note: As we describe in Chapter 9, if your application needs to change *back* to blocking from nonblocking with ioctlsocket( ) FIONBIO, then you should reexamine your application design.

Success and Failure Are Not Absolutes!

"Success and failure are not absolutes!" is the credo for nonblocking operation mode. Nonblocking function calls can fail with error codes that indicate success or indicate the current socket state. Other function calls may appear to have succeeded, without having completed the requested operation. This behavior may seem confusing, but you can deal with it easily.

WSAEWOULDBLOCK Error

If a function fails and `WSAGetLastError( )` indicates the error is WSAEWOULDBLOCK, then *the function call did not fail*—at least not fatally.

Depending on the function, this error means either that the WinSock DLL has initiated the operation or that you should try to call the function again later. Here is a list of the functions that can return the WSAEWOULDBLOCK error; notice that these are the same functions that can block if you pass a blocking socket (refer to the list in the earlier "Blocking Mode" section).

Function Name	*"Failure" with WSAEWOULDBLOCK error means...*
accept( )	The application has yet to receive a connection request, so try again later.
closesocket( )	`setsockopt( )` SO_LINGER called with nonzero timeout on a nonblocking stream socket. On some WinSocks the close operation may be in process, and on others you may need to retry. We recommend not setting a nonzero timeout with SO_LINGER on a nonblocking socket to avoid this ambiguity (see Chapter 9 for more details).
connect( )	WinSock DLL has initiated the connect operation on a stream socket, so check later to detect completion.
recv( ) and recvfrom( )	No data was received by network system for this socket, so try again later.
send( ) and sendto	No buffers are available in network system for outgoing data on a stream socket, so try again later (datagram would fail silently).

The `WSAAsyncGetXByY( )` asynchronous database functions that do host name, protocol, and service resolution can also fail with WSAEWOULDBLOCK. When this is the case, it indicates that network-system resources are currently unavailable, so the application should try calling the function again later.

Partial Success

Even if a nonblocking socket function returns indicating success, it may not mean it did exactly what you asked. For example, the `send( )`, `sendto( )`, `recv( )`, and `recvfrom( )` functions may return a value less than the value in the length input parameter you passed. We saw earlier that a blocking `recv( )` or `recvfrom( )` could return indicating it transferred less data than an application may have expected. This is more likely to occur with nonblocking sockets than blocking sockets. It occurs on sends as well as receives. It occurs frequently with stream sockets, since packet boundaries are not preserved.

As a result, it is very important to check the return value from these functions. Do not just check for success or failure. Compare the value returned to the length you requested to transfer. You may have to adjust your buffer pointer and length and retry the operation to transfer the remainder. As you might imagine, the larger the "length" value, the more likely this is to occur (generally, you are safe if you do not specify a length above the default TCP maximum segment size of 536).

Polling Instead of Blocking

Our definition of "operation mode" includes the method an application uses to detect when to begin an operation, as well as how to detect operation completion after a function fails with WSAEWOULDBLOCK. There are a few functions whose primary purpose is to provide an efficient method of detecting when to initiate an operation, or when an operation has completed. We describe these functions, especially `WSAAsyncSelect( )` and `select( )`, in detail in Chapter 6, "Socket States." Another way to detect these socket states is to poll with a nonblocking socket.

Explicit Yielding

As we have mentioned so often already, Windows 3.1 (16-bit Windows) is a cooperative multitasking operating system. Because of this, it is essential to yield frequently to avoid impacting the system. If you create an application that sends or receives bulk data without yielding explicitly, you will notice an effect on the rest of the system. Your application and others will be unresponsive. Drop-down menus will not appear. Commands will not function. The system will appear to be hung as each data transfer takes place.

We do not see this problem in the blocking version, because while an operation (fake) blocks the WinSock DLL yields to other tasks. Blocking operations yield implicitly in Windows Sockets. This seems odd: Blocking operations do not block the system, but nonblocking operations can. A few solutions are available. One is to create a hybrid application that uses nonblocking sockets for everything except detecting the current socket state; for that you use the blocking `select()` function. Another option is to create your own blocking hook function that yields on demand, although it can cause problems with nesting if not done properly.

Code Example

Here is a pseudocode example that uses a nonblocking socket and the polling operation to accomplish exactly the same thing as the pseudocode for a blocking socket we saw earlier. It illustrates the Windows Sockets code in a simple stream client application that connects to a server, sends a fixed-length string, reads it back, then closes the connection (like connecting to an echo server).

Notice that we poll on `recv()` to detect connection completion. This method is compatible with Berkeley Sockets, but we do not recommend that you use it. It is inefficient and leaves margin for problems since it is so dependent on specific error values. We recommend you use `select()` readfds to detect connection completion, or better yet the asynchronous FD_CONNECT notification (see Chapter 6, "Socket States," for more information).

Also note that we do not yield in our loops in this example, which is extremely asocial in the 16-bit Windows environment. We do loop to make sure that we have sent and received all the data requested, unlike the earlier blocking example where we did a single send and receive operation.

```
#define TIMEOUT 30000
SOCKET s;
SOCKADDR_IN stDstAddr
int nRet, nWSAerror;
static char achOutBuf [] =
      "This is a jest of the emergency comedy system";
static char achInBuf [BUFSIZE];
BOOL bInProgress;
int nBytesToXfer, nBytesXferred;
u_long lGiveupTime;

<assume we already got a stream socket, and made it nonblocking>

/* initialize destination socket address structure */
stDstAddr.sin_family = PF_INET;
stDstAddr.sin_port = htons(IPPORT_ECHO);
```

```
stDstAddr.sin_addr = inet_addr (szDstAddr);
/* connect to server */
nRet =  connect(s, (LPSOCKADDR)&stDstAddr, sizeof(SOCKADDR));
if ((nRet == SOCKET_ERROR) &&         /* connect( ) failed */
     (WSAGetLastError() != WSAEWOULDBLOCK)) {
       <report (only) fatal WinSock error to user>
       goto jest_end;
}
/*---- begin: not recommended, for demonstration only ----*/
do {
       /* peek for data to detect connection completion */
       nRet = recv (s, (LPSTR) achInBuf, 1, MSG_PEEK);
       if (nRet == SOCKET_ERROR) {
              nWSAerror = WSAGetLastError( );
              if ((nWSAerror == WSAECONNREFUSED) ||
                   (nWSAerror == WSAETIMEDOUT)) {
                     <report fatal connect WinSock error to user>
                     goto jest_end;
              }
       } else {
              break;    /* connected (with data pending)! */
       }
} while (nWSAerror != WSAEWOULDBLOCK)  /* end of connect loop */
/*---- end: not recommended, for demonstration only ---- */

nBytesXferred = 0;
nBytesToXfer = _fstrlen((LPSTR)achOutBuf);
for (lGiveupTime = GetTickCount( ) + TIMEOUT;
              (nBytesXferred < nBytesToXfer)&&
              (GetTickCount( ) < lGiveupTime);) {
       nRet = send(s,              /* send string */
              (LPSTR)&(achOutBuf [nBytesXferred]),
              nBytesToXfer-nBytesXferred, 0);
       if (nRet == SOCKET_ERROR) {
              nWSAerror = WSAGetLastError( );
              if (nWSAerror != WSAEWOULDBLOCK) {
                 <report (only) fatal WinSock error to user>
                 goto jest_end;
              }
       } else {
```

```
    nBytesXferred += nRet; /* tally bytes sent (so far) */
        nWSAerror = 0;          /* reset error value */
      }
} /* end of send( ) loop */

if (nWSAerror != 0) {/* if error, we max'd on retry attempts */
      <report error>    /* do not receive if we did not send */
      goto jest_end;
}
nBytesXferred = 0;
for (lGiveupTime = GetTickCount( ) + TIMEOUT;
      (nBytesXferred < nBytesToXfer)&&
      (GetTickCount( ) < lGiveupTime);) {
      nRet = recv(s,                         /* receive string */
                        (LPSTR)&(achInBuf [nBytesXferred]),
             BUF_SIZE-nBytesXferred,
             0);
      if (nRet == SOCKET_ERROR) {
             nWSAerror = WSAGetLastError( );
        if (nWSAerror != WSAEWOULDBLOCK) {
               <report error>    /* fatal error */
               goto jest_end;
           }
    } else if (nRet == 0) {         /* closed by remote host */
             <report error>
             goto jest_end;
    } else{
           nBytesXferred += nRet;     /* tally bytes received */
           nWSAerror = 0;             /* reset error value */
    }
} /* end of recv( ) loop */

if (nWSAerror != 0) {     /* if error, we max'd on retries */
      <report error>
}

jest_end:
   nRet = closesocket(s);     /* close connection and socket */
    <check return value>
```

We are polling (looping) to detect the connection completion. Notice how we expect various errors as we call `recv()` in the loop. The errors change as the status changes, finally indicating success (or failure) when the connect operation completes. As mentioned earlier, this is here for demonstration only; we do not recommend that you try this at home.

We are also polling (looping) to send the data. We retry the send as many times as needed, in case we do not send as much as we want to on one send. The code can pick up where we left off and will send no more than we want. We retry if we get a "would block" error, which occurs when the network system cannot buffer our outbound data. Notice that we also have a 30-second timeout to limit how long we are willing to retry our send, in case the network-system buffers never become available.

Finally, we are polling (looping) to receive the data in much the same way we polled to send data. The one difference is that we are prepared to have `recv()` return a 0, which would indicate the remote host closed the connection.

This code will work as you see it (with details like error handling filled in), but it does not scale well. In other words, you would not want to use this sample code to send and receive large amounts of data. Its biggest problem is that it does not yield, as mentioned a moment ago.

Asynchronous Mode

Berkeley Sockets has an asynchronous operation mode. It involves using the `signal()` function to register an application function for the network system to "upcall" when certain events occur. The way the Windows Sockets API implements asynchronous operation mode is much different, however. In fact, Windows Sockets' asynchronous operation mode is one of the most blatant departures from Berkeley Sockets. This is because it takes advantage of the Windows architecture.

Windows are objects. Objects are opaque; their internal details are hidden. Objects communicate with each other by passing messages. Messages arrive asynchronously, and objects respond to messages. The Windows Sockets asynchronous operation mode uses Windows messages instead of upcalls, so the asynchronous operation mode is a Windows natural. Windows is a message-driven environment, and Windows Sockets' asynchronous operation mode is message driven to take advantage of the environment.

As we have seen so far, applications that operate in purely nonblocking mode tend to monopolize system resources. It is difficult to create a "friendly" Windows application that uses nonblocking operations exclusively. We also saw how deceptive simple blocking applications are and how they tend to limit support of multiple sockets in a single task. But on the bright side, blocking applications are "friendly" in Windows by yielding properly.

Now we will show you how you can gain the benefits of nonblocking operation without impacting the system performance. We will show you how to write simple code that does not have backdoors that can lead to trouble. With asynchronous operation your application "off-loads" work to let the WinSock DLL handle it and utilizes the message-driven architecture of Windows rather than simply coping with it. Asynchronous operation cannot provide the best data throughput, but it does very well, and there are strategies for improving its performance, as we demonstrate in our sample FTP client application in Chapter 7.

What Are the Asynchronous Functions?

There are a number of different asynchronous functions. A few perform so-called database routines to retrieve host names and the like, but the most significant of all is the general-purpose `WSAAsyncSelect( )`, which detects socket state.

We describe all of these asynchronous functions in detail in other chapters. The host name resolution functions are in Chapter 8, "Host Names and Addresses"; the protocol and services functions are in Chapter 10, "Support Routines"; and `WSAAsyncSelect( )` is in Chapter 6, "Socket States." We provide a brief overview of these functions here to introduce asynchronous operation mode.

Function Name	*Description*
`WSAAsyncGetHostByAddr( )`	retrieves host information for a host address
`WSAAsyncGetHostByName( )`	retrieves host information for a host name
`WSAAsyncGetProtoByName( )`	retrieves the protocol number for a protocol name
`WSAAsyncGetProtoByNumber( )`	retrieves the protocol name for a protocol number
`WSAAsyncGetServByName( )`	retrieves service information for a service name
`WSAAsyncGetServByPort( )`	retrieves service information for a port number
`WSAAsyncSelect( )`	requests the WinSock DLL to notify the application of one or more "events," such as connection completion, outgoing buffer availability, and data arrival

WSAAsyncGetXByY( )

`WSAAsyncGetXByY( )` is not an actual function name but denotes the asynchronous database functions, all of which look and act the same. Here is the prototype for `WSAAsyncGetHostByName( )`, probably the most frequently used of these functions; the prototypes for the others are similar:

```
HANDLE PASCAL FAR WSAAsyncGetHostByName (
    HWND hWnd,              /* handle of window to rcv msg */
    unsigned int wMsg,      /* msg to be received */
    char FAR *name;         /* host name to resolve */
    char FAR *buf;          /* buffer for results */
    int buflen);            /* length of buffer */
```

The asynchronous database functions—for host name, protocol, and services resolution—take a window handle, a message, and a buffer as input parameters, in addition to the object they need to resolve. They return immediately, before the requested operation completes. The return value is a handle that uniquely identifies that query (so they can match up the response), or 0 if there is an error in placing the request.

When the WinSock DLL completes the resolution for the application, it copies the resulting information into the buffer the application provided. At that point, or when the WinSock DLL determines that it cannot complete the resolution, it posts a message to the application. The message posted is the message the application requested when it made the query. The *wParam* argument contains the query handle returned from the `WSAAsyncGetXByY( )` function call. The upper word in *lParam* contains an error value (if the query failed), and the lower word in *lParam* has the buffer length of a successful response. Use the "message cracker" macros WSAGETASYNCERROR( ) and WSAGETASYNCBUFLEN( ) to extract the error value and buffer length, respectively, to ensure portability between 16-bit and 32-bit WinSock.

In summary, here is what occurs for the asynchronous host name, protocol, and services "database functions":

- The application makes a request to be notified of the resolution event.
- The function returns a query handle, or 0 if it cannot handle the query.
- The WinSock DLL then posts a message to the application when the query operation completes, and the message indicates resolution success or failure.

WSAAsyncSelect( )

`WSAAsyncSelect( )` is different from the `WSAAsyncGetXByY( )` functions. It is less specialized than they are. An application calls `WSAAsyncSelect( )` to request notification of up to a half-dozen different network events, or errors. Two of the events—FD_CONNECT and FD_CLOSE—indicate operation completion, and the others indicate when an application can make a particular function call with reasonable assurance of success. In addition to requesting asynchronous notification for one or more events, `WSAAsyncSelect( )` also automatically makes the socket nonblocking, and no handle is returned (the socket is the handle). We describe `WSAAsyncSelect( )` in more detail in Chapter 6, "Socket States."

Cancelling Asynchronous Operations

You can cancel an asynchronous operation initiated by any of the `WSAAsyncGetXByY( )` functions with a call to `WSACancelAsyncRequest( )`. Notice that this does *not* affect asynchronous operations initiated by the `WSAAsyncSelect( )` function.

```
/* returns 0 on success, or SOCKET_ERROR on failure */
int PASCAL FAR WSACancelAsyncRequest
    (HANDLE hAsyncTaskHandle);  /* asynch operation to cancel */
```

hAsyncTaskHandle: the handle of the asynchronous operation to be cancelled, which was originally returned from a call to `WSAAsyncGetXByY( )`

The return value indicates 0 on success, or SOCKET_ERROR on failure. The common errors are WSAEINVAL ("handle invalid") and WSAEALREADY ("asynch operation already cancelled"). As the Windows Sockets specification notes, there is little distinction between these two errors, so "a Windows Sockets application should treat the two errors as equivalent."[1]

Unlike a blocking operation, WinSock does not have an asynchronous equivalent of `WSAIsBlocking( )` to detect an outstanding asynchronous operation. Also, if an application calls `WSACleanup( )` while an asynchronous operation is pending, the asynchronous operation is cancelled (and no notification is sent).

[1] Section 4.3.8 of v1.1 Windows Sockets specification

Code Example

Here is some pseudocode to describe the same application that we looked at in the previous blocking and nonblocking pseudocode examples. This also will connect, send a fixed-length string, read the fixed-length string back, and then close the connection.

```
SOCKET s;
int nRet;
static char achOutBuf[] =
       "This is a jest of the emergency comedy system";
static char achInBuf[BUFSIZE];
BOOL bInProgress;
int nBytesToXfer, nBytesXferred;

s  = socket(...);               /* get a stream socket */
      < check whether 's' is INVALID_SOCKET>
/* request notification for connect, read, write, and close events
 *  (and automatically make socket nonblocking) */
nRet = WSAAsyncSelect(s, hWnd, IDM_ASYNC,
      FD_READ | FD_WRITE | FD_CONNECT | FD_CLOSE);
if (nRet == SOCKET_ERROR) {
      < handle error >
}
      <initialize sockaddr structure>
nRet = connect(s,...);          /* try to "connect" to a server */
if (nRet == SOCKET_ERROR) {     /* error! */
    if (WSAGetLastError() != WSAEWOULDBLOCK) {
        <handle error>
    }
}
```

And here is the section of a window procedure that handles the asynchronous notification messages that WinSock posts when an asynchronous event occurs:

```
int nAsyncEvent, nAsyncError;
switch (msg) {
  ...
  CASE IDM_ASYNC {
    int nAsyncEvent = WSAGETSELECTEVENT(lparam);
```

```
int nAsyncError = WSAGETSELECTERROR(lparam);
if (nAsyncError) {
<handle error>
}
switch (nAsyncEvent) {
  case FD_CONNECT
      < we could do initialization here, if we needed it>
      break;
  case FD_WRITE
    /* this event occurs when we're initially connected
     * and subsequently whenever send( ) fails with an
     * WSAEWOULDBLOCK error */
    nRet = send(s,              /* send string */
          (LPSTR)&(achOutBuf[nBytesXferred]),
           nBytesToXfer-nBytesXferred, 0);
    if (nRet == SOCKET_ERROR) {
          nWSAerror = WSAGetLastError( );
          if (nWSAerror != WSAEWOULDBLOCK) {
            <handle error>         /* fatal error */
        }
    } else{
        nBytesXferred += nRet; /* tally bytes sent */
    }
    /* all bytes are sent, now close the connection */
          <call shutdown (how=1)>
          <loop on recv( ) until *any* error occurs>
    break;
case FD_CLOSE
    /* we received a <FIN> in response to the "half-close"
     * we did with shutdown(how=1). Now close socket
     * and return other network-system resources */
    nRet = closesocket(s);
    if (nRet == SOCKET_ERROR) {
          if (WSAGetLastError( ) != WSAEWOULDBLOCK) {
                <handle error>
        }
    }
    break;
case FD_READ:
       nRet = recv(s,              /* receive string */
             (LPSTR)&(achInBuf[nBytesXferred]),
```

```
                BUF_SIZE-nBytesXferred,
                0);
             if (nRet == SOCKET_ERROR) {
              nWSAerror = WSAGetLastError( );
              if (nWSAerror != WSAEWOULDBLOCK) {
                  <handle error>    /* fatal error */
              }
          } else {
              nBytesXferred += nRet; /* tally bytes recv'd */
          }
          break;
      }
    }
    ...
}
```

Parts of this code are the same as the earlier nonblocking example. But overall, this is very different. Although asynchronous operation mode uses nonblocking sockets, we do not have polling loops here. If we need to retry a send because an outgoing buffer is unavailable (so `send()` fails with WSAEWOULDBLOCK), the retry occurs automatically when the WinSock DLL subsequently posts an FD_WRITE message. If we do not read all the available data with a `recv( )`, the WinSock DLL notifies the application with an FD_READ message.

Not only is the code simpler, but unlike the nonblocking example, this

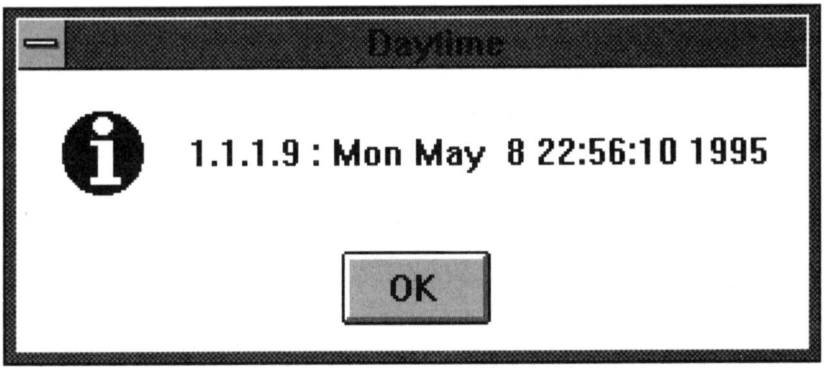

Figure 5-2 AU_Time application showing the response from a "daytime" server.

code scales well. This application also yields automatically as it processes messages.

AU_Time Application

Here is an example of an application that uses asynchronous operation mode with a UDP socket to implement a combination client *and* server for the daytime service. Daytime is a simple service that provides a human-readable string containing the current date and time. As a client, our application simply sends a message to the daytime port, reads the response, and displays it. As a server, it responds to datagrams it receives by sending a formatted date/time string back to the sender.

It does not do much, but it illustrates the basics of asynchronous operation using `WSAAsyncSelect()` and FD_READ notification messages. The screen capture in Figure 5-2 shows our main window and menu, along with the message box we display upon receipt of the date and time from a "daytime" server. In this case the client just received a response from the daytime server running on IP address 1.1.1.9.

The menu selections do the following:

- *File:* provides the standard *Exit* command to leave the program
- *Open:* gets a SOCK_DGRAM socket, registers for FD_READ notification with `WSAAsyncSelect()`, and binds to the daytime port
- *Sendto*: prompts for a destination host name or address, resolves the destination, and sends an arbitrary datagram to the daytime port
- *Options:* allows the user to enable or disable broadcasts, which effects a call to `setsockopt()` SO_BROADCAST (see Chapter 9, "Socket Information and Control," for more information about this socket option)
- *Help:* provides the standard About command to display application information in the "About" dialog box

```
/*---------------------------------------------------------------------
 *
 * Program: Asynch UDP Time Client and Server
 *
 * file name: au_time.c
 *
 * copyright by Bob Quinn, 1995
 *
```

```
 *  Description:
 *    Client and server application that uses and provides "daytime"
 *    service as described by RFC 867. Using UDP, this simple
 *    service responds to an empty datagram received on port 13
 *    by returning the current date and time as an ASCII
 *    character string.
 *
 ---------------------------------*/
#include "..\wsa_xtra.h" /* see Chapter 7 */
#include <windows.h>
#include <windowsx.h>

#include <winsock.h>
#include <string.h> /* for _fmemcpy( ) & _fmemset( ) */
#include <time.h>
#include "resource.h"
#include "..\winsockx.h"  /* see Chapter 7 */

/* timeout id and period (in milliseconds) */
#define TIMEOUT_ID     1
#define TIMEOUT_PERIOD 30000

#define BUF_SIZE 1024
#define ERR_SIZE 512

/*-------- global variables --------*/
WSADATA stWSAData;  /* WinSock DLL Info */

char szAppName[] = "AU_Time";

BOOL bReceiving = FALSE;           /* state flag */
SOCKET hSock = INVALID_SOCKET;     /* socket handle */
char szHost[MAXHOST_NAME] = {0}; /* remote host (name or address) */
SOCKADDR_IN stLclName;  /* local socket name (address and port) */
SOCKADDR_IN stRmtName;  /* remote socket name (address and port) */

char achInBuf  [BUF_SIZE];  /* input buffer */
char achOutBuf [BUF_SIZE];  /* output buffer */

BOOL bBroadcast = FALSE;    /* broadcast-enabled flag */
HWND hwndMain;         /* main window handle */
HINSTANCE hInst;       /* instance handle */
```

```
/*-------- function prototypes --------*/
LONG FAR PASCAL WndProc (HWND,UINT,WPARAM,LPARAM);
BOOL FAR PASCAL AboutDlgProc (HWND,UINT,UINT,LONG);
BOOL FAR PASCAL DestDlgProc  (HWND,UINT,UINT,LONG);

/*-------------------------------------------------------------------
 *
 *  Function: WinMain( )
 *
 *  Description:
 *     Initialize and start message loop
 *
 */
int PASCAL WinMain
  (HANDLE hInstance,
   HANDLE hPrevInstance,
   LPSTR  lpszCmdLine,
   int    nCmdShow)
{
    MSG msg;
    int nRet;
    WNDCLASS  wndclass;

    lpszCmdLine = lpszCmdLine; /* avoid warning */

    hInst = hInstance;    /* save instance handle */

    if (!hPrevInstance) {
      /* register window class */
      wndclass.style          = CS_HREDRAW | CS_VREDRAW;
      wndclass.lpfnWndProc    = WndProc;
      wndclass.cbClsExtra     = 0;
      wndclass.cbWndExtra     = 0;
      wndclass.hInstance      = hInstance;
      wndclass.hIcon          = LoadIcon(hInst,
                                 MAKEINTRESOURCE(AU_TIME));
      wndclass.hCursor        = LoadCursor(NULL,IDC_ARROW);
      wndclass.hbrBackground  = COLOR_WINDOW+1;
      wndclass.lpszMenuName   = MAKEINTRESOURCE(AU_TIME);
      wndclass.lpszClassName  = szAppName;
```

```
  if (!RegisterClass (&wndclass)) {
    return (0);
  }
}

hwndMain = CreateWindow(
    szAppName,
    "Daytime Client & Server",
    WS_OVERLAPPEDWINDOW,
    CW_USEDEFAULT,
    CW_USEDEFAULT,
    400,
    200,
    NULL,
    NULL,
    hInstance,
    NULL
);

if (!hwndMain)    /* quit now if class registration failed */
    return 0;
/*--------initialize WinSock DLL--------*/
nRet = WSAStartup(WSA_VERSION, &stWSAData);
/* WSAStartup( ) returns error value if failed (0 on success) */
if (nRet != 0) {
  WSAperror(nRet, "WSAStartup( )");
  /* No sense continuing if we cannot use WinSock */
} else {

  ShowWindow(hwndMain, nCmdShow);    /* display our window */
  UpdateWindow(hwndMain);

  while (GetMessage (&msg, NULL, 0, 0)) {  /* main message loop */
    TranslateMessage(&msg);
    DispatchMessage (&msg);
  }

  /*--------release WinSock DLL--------*/
  nRet = WSACleanup( );
  if (nRet == SOCKET_ERROR)
```

```
        WSAperror(WSAGetLastError( ), "WSACleanup( )");
    }
    /* return resource explicitly */
    UnregisterClass(szAppName, hInstance);

    return msg.wParam;
} /* end WinMain( ) */
/*-------------------------------------------------------------------
 *
 * Function: WndProc( )
 *
 * Description:
 *    Process application messages for our main window
 */
LONG FAR PASCAL  WndProc
  (HWND hwnd,
   UINT msg,
   WPARAM wParam,
   LPARAM lParam)
{
    FARPROC lpfnProc;
    int nAddrSize = sizeof(SOCKADDR);
    WORD WSAEvent, WSAErr;
    HMENU hMenu;
    int nRet;

    switch (msg) {
      case WSA_ASYNC:
        /* We received a WSAAsyncSelect( ) FD_ notification message
         *  Parse the message to extract FD_ event value and error
         *  value (if there is one).
         */
        WSAEvent = WSAGETSELECTEVENT (lParam);
        WSAErr   = WSAGETSELECTERROR (lParam);
        if (WSAErr) {
          /* error in asynch notification message: display to user */
          WSAperror(WSAErr,"FD_READ");
         /* fall-through to call reenabling function for this event */
        }
        switch (WSAEvent) {
          case FD_READ:
```

```
  /* receive the available data */
 nRet = recvfrom (hSock, (char FAR *)achInBuf, BUF_SIZE, 0,
    (struct sockaddr *) &stRmtName, &nAddrSize);

 /* display error if receive failed (but do not repeat error
   *  if input message contained an error) */
  if ((nRet == SOCKET_ERROR) && (!WSAErr)) {
    WSAperror(WSAErr,"recvfrom( )");
    break;
  }

  if (bReceiving) {
    /*---------------------
     * CLIENT:
     * if we sent a request, display the response */
    achInBuf[nRet-2] = 0; /* remove CR/LF */
    /* display the data received, and who it came from */
    wsprintf ((LPSTR)achOutBuf, "%s : %s",
      inet_ntoa(stRmtName.sin_addr), (LPSTR)achInBuf);
    MessageBox (hwnd, (LPSTR)achOutBuf,
      "Daytime", MB_OK | MB_ICONASTERISK);

    /* remove the timeout alert */
    KillTimer (hwnd, TIMEOUT_ID);

    /* reset the socket state */
    bReceiving = FALSE;
  } else {
    /*------------------------------------------------
     * SERVER:
     *  send time to host we received request from */
    time_t stTime;
    time (&stTime);
    wsprintf (achOutBuf, "%s", ctime(&stTime));
   nRet = sendto (hSock, achOutBuf, strlen(achOutBuf), 0,
        (LPSOCKADDR)&stRmtName, sizeof(SOCKADDR));
    if (nRet == SOCKET_ERROR)
      WSAperror(WSAGetLastError( ), "sendto( )");
  }
  break;
default:
```

```
          break;
      } /* end switch(WSAEvent) */
      break;
    case WM_COMMAND:
      switch (wParam) {
```

The "Open" menu command sends the IDM_OPEN message to AU_TIME.

```
        case IDM_OPEN:
          /* if we already have a socket open, then close it first */
          if (hSock != INVALID_SOCKET) {
            nRet = closesocket(hSock);
            hSock = INVALID_SOCKET;
          }
          if (nRet == SOCKET_ERROR)
            WSAperror(WSAGetLastError( ), "socket( )");

          /* get a UDP socket */
              hSock = socket (AF_INET, SOCK_DGRAM, 0);
              if (hSock == INVALID_SOCKET)  {
            WSAperror(WSAGetLastError( ), "socket( )");
          } else {
            int okay = TRUE;

            /* request async notification for data arrival */
           nRet = WSAAsyncSelect(hSock, hwnd, WSA_ASYNC, FD_READ);
            if (nRet == SOCKET_ERROR) {
              WSAperror(WSAGetLastError( ), "WSAAsyncSelect( )");
              okay = FALSE;
            }

            /* name the socket, to receive requests as a server */
            stLclName.sin_family = PF_INET;
            stLclName.sin_port    = htons(IPPORT_DAYTIME);
            stLclName.sin_addr.s_addr = INADDR_ANY;
            nRet = bind(hSock,(LPSOCKADDR)&stLclName,
              sizeof(struct sockaddr));
            if (nRet == SOCKET_ERROR) {
              WSAperror(WSAGetLastError( ), "bind( )");
              okay = FALSE;
            }
```

```
      if (ok) {
        wsprintf ((LPSTR)achOutBuf,
          "Socket %d, named and registered for FD_READ",
          hSock);
        MessageBox (hwnd, (LPSTR)achOutBuf,
         "Ready to Send or Receive", MB_OK | MB_ICONASTERISK);
      }
    }
    break;
```

The "Sendto" menu command sends the IDM_SENDTO message to AU_TIME.

```
  case IDM_SENDTO:
    /* create dialog box to prompt for destination host */
    lpfnProc = MakeProcInstance((FARPROC)DestDlgProc,hInst);
    nRet = DialogBox (hInst, "DESTINATIONDLG",
      hwndMain, lpfnProc);
    FreeProcInstance((FARPROC) lpfnProc);

   /* check destination address and resolve it if necessary */
    stRmtName.sin_addr.s_addr = GetAddr((LPSTR)szHost);
    if (stRmtName.sin_addr.s_addr == INADDR_ANY) {
      if (nRet != -1)
       /* tell user to enter a host (unless they cancelled) */
       MessageBox (hwnd, "Need a destination host to send to",
          "Cannot connect!", MB_OK | MB_ICONASTERISK);
    } else {
      /* set timer so we can give up after waiting a while */
      if (!SetTimer (hwnd, TIMEOUT_ID, TIMEOUT_PERIOD, NULL))
        MessageBox (hwnd, "SetTimer failed", "Error",
          MB_OK | MB_ICONASTERISK);

      /* set socket state to indicate we're waiting
       * for a response as a client */
      bReceiving = TRUE;

      /* send a dummy datagram to daytime port to
       *  request daytime response */
      stRmtName.sin_family = PF_INET;
```

```
          stRmtName.sin_port    = htons (IPPORT_DAYTIME);
          nRet = sendto(hSock, (char FAR *)achOutBuf, 1, 0,
                      (LPSOCKADDR)&stRmtName, sizeof(SOCKADDR));
          if (nRet == SOCKET_ERROR)
            WSAperror(WSAGetLastError( ),"sendto( )");
        }
        break;
```

The "Options" menu command allows the user to enable or disable broadcasts, which sends an IDM_BROADCAST message to AU_TIME.

```
      case IDM_BROADCAST:
      /* call setsockopt( ) SO_BROADCAST to enable or disable */
        hMenu = GetMenu(hwnd);
        bBroadcast = !CheckMenuItem (hMenu, IDM_BROADCAST,
            (bBroadcast ? MF_UNCHECKED : MF_CHECKED));
        nRet = setsockopt(hSock, SOL_SOCKET, SO_BROADCAST,
            (LPSTR)&bBroadcast, sizeof(BOOL));
        if (nRet == SOCKET_ERROR)
          WSAperror (WSAGetLastError( ), "setsockopt( )");
        break;

      case IDM_ABOUT:
        lpfnProc = MakeProcInstance((FARPROC)DlgAbout,hInst);
        DialogBox (hInst, "AboutBox", hwnd, lpfnProc);
        FreeProcInstance((FARPROC) lpfnProc);
        break;

      case IDM_EXIT:
        PostMessage(hwnd, WM_CLOSE, 0, 0L);
        break;

      default:
          return (DefWindowProc(hwnd, msg, wParam, lParam));
    } /* end case WM_COMMAND: */
    break;

  case WM_TIMER:
    /* timeout occurred */
    bReceiving = FALSE;           /* reset state */
```

```
        KillTimer (hwnd, TIMEOUT_ID);  /* release timer */
        MessageBox (hwnd, "No response from daytime server",
           "Timeout", MB_OK | MB_ICONASTERISK);
        break;

      case WM_QUERYENDSESSION:
      case WM_CLOSE:
        /* close the socket before we leave */
        if (!SendMessage(hwnd, WM_COMMAND, IDM_CLOSE, 1L))
          DestroyWindow(hwnd);
        /* release timer (if it's active) */
        if (bReceiving)
          KillTimer(hwndMain, TIMEOUT_ID);
        break;

      case WM_CREATE:
        /* center dialog box */
        CenterWnd (hwnd, NULL, TRUE);
        break;

      case WM_DESTROY:
        PostQuitMessage(0);
        break;

    default:
        return (DefWindowProc(hwnd, msg, wParam, lParam));
  } /* end switch (msg) */

  return 0;
} /* end WndProc( ) */

/*-----------------------------------------------------------------
 *
 * Function: DestDlgProc( )
 *
 * Description:
 *  Prompt user for a destination host
 */
BOOL FAR PASCAL  DestDlgProc (
  HWND hDlg,
```

```
  UINT msg,
  UINT wParam,
  LPARAM lParam)
{
  static int wRet, nOptName, nOptVal, nOptLen, nOptIDC, nLevel, WSAerr;
  static HANDLE hwnd, hInst;
  static struct linger stLinger;

   switch (msg) {
     case WM_INITDIALOG:

       /* get parameters passed */
       if (lParam) {
          hInst = LOWORD(lParam);
          hwnd  = HIWORD(lParam);
       }

       /* set display values */
       SetDlgItemText (hDlg, IDC_DESTADDR, szHost);
       SetFocus (GetDlgItem (hDlg, IDC_COMBO1));

       /* center dialog box */
       CenterWnd (hDlg, hwndMain, TRUE);

       return FALSE;

     case WM_COMMAND:
       switch (wParam) {

        case IDOK:
          GetDlgItemText (hDlg, IDC_DESTADDR, szHost, MAXHOST NAME);
          EndDialog (hDlg, TRUE);

        case IDCANCEL:
          EndDialog (hDlg, -1);
          break;
     }
     return(TRUE);
   }
   return(FALSE);

} /* end DestDlgProc( ) */
```

Performance Differences

Most network applications perform bulk data transfers between hosts at some point during execution. It is not surprising that one of the primary goals of most network application developers is to maximize data throughput. Some application designs are inherently more efficient than others, but the operation mode(s) used in an application probably affects data transfer and transaction time more than anything else. There is no universally correct answer, and any one you use should undergo analysis and fine-tuning. But we can make some generalities:

- Nonblocking is the fastest, but it incurs the most overhead and so is the least "friendly."
- Asynchronous operation transfers data quickly yet remains "friendly."
- Blocking mode is the "friendliest" but is relatively slow.

We recommend using asynchronous operation whenever possible. It requires some extra effort to keep track of application state, but applications are simple and elegant in design overall, they are capable of fast data transfer, they are good neighbors in the 16-bit cooperative multitasking environment, and they operate well in 32-bit environments as well. See the sample FTP client application in Chapter 7 for a good example of an asynchronous application capable of speedy data transfer.

Platform Differences

Microsoft Windows 3.x (16-bit Windows) is just one of the platforms that support the Windows Sockets API. The API itself does not change between platforms, but some of the operating-system features of these various platforms allow for different Windows Sockets application designs and have different execution characteristics. We make a complete survey in Chapter 15, "Platforms," but here we mention a couple of significant differences.

The two environments we are most interested in are Windows NT and Windows 95.

Blocking Is Real

Both Windows NT and Windows 95 are preemptive, "real multitasking" operating systems. As a result, applications cannot possibly monopolize system resources. The operating system prevents one application from starving other applications of CPU time. There is no such thing as an "unfriendly application."

In this environment, the blocking function is truly blocking. This means that if an application (or thread) is blocking, no default blocking hook function is processing messages behind the scenes, and there is no possibility of an application's being "reentered" by a message it receives while a blocking operation is pending. As a result, the `WSAIsBlocking()` and `WSACancelBlockingCall()` functions are useless, since you never have an opportunity to use them. However, you can install your own custom blocking hook function with `WSASetBlockingHook()`, and it will be called as a blocking operation executes. You would also use `WSAUnhookBlockingHook()` to uninstall your custom blocking hook function, as in 16-bit Windows.

Threaded Applications

Both Windows NT and Windows 95 support threads. In a sense, a **thread** is a child process, since there must be a parent process to create a thread. But once created, a thread executes independently of its parent.

A "threaded application" is simply one that has threads. A single application may have multiple threads executing in blocking mode simultaneously without affecting each other adversely. Threads offer special possibilities; since they can share the same socket, you could have one that sends, while another receives.

- An advantage of threads is that you can create an application that handles many sockets simultaneously and uses blocking sockets. They provide many application possibilities and lend themselves to server design in particular (although you should be careful; they do not scale well due to the system overhead they incur).
- A disadvantage of threads is that any program using them is not as portable to 16-bit Windows. (Win32s, the Win32 API emulator for 16-bit Windows, does not support threads.)

We do not provide any examples of threaded applications in this text. Although they do have value for many applications, asynchronous operation mode provides as many benefits, and portability, too.

Other Things Hold True

Windows NT and Windows 95 are, of course, Windows environments with the same message-driven architecture as (16-bit) Windows 3.1. Hence, they support asynchronous operation mode, so any asynchronous applications can run without change.

Applications written to use nonblocking operation mode function on preemptive systems also. The preemptive system relieves applications of some of their responsibilities, since they will automatically preempt applications that have tight polling loops that would lockup on any 16-bit Windows system. However, such tight polling loops should be avoided because they are CPU intensive (i.e., they waste resources).

6 Socket States

In This Chapter:

- What Are the Socket States?
- What Are the Methods of Detection?
- WSAAsyncSelect( )
- select( )
- Peeking at Data
- Out-of-Band Data
- The Listening State

I have a simple philosophy: Fill what's empty.
Empty what's full. Scratch where it itches.

Alice Roosevelt Longworth

In the previous two chapters we described the framework for all network applications and the modes in which they operate. In this chapter we show you the engine of every network application, the driving force of an application's execution. Regardless of the socket type, operation mode, or type of application, the changes in socket state are what propel a network application. To operate efficiently your application needs to detect transitions in socket state efficiently.

For example, some nonblocking function calls initiate an operation, then return before the requested operation has completed. In order to proceed, an application needs to detect when that operation has completed. An application also needs to know when it can make service requests and expect the network system to satisfy them. There are different ways to detect operation completion and to determine when best to make network service requests. The methods you choose will make a big difference in how well your application will perform and how well other applications run simultaneously.

In this chapter we describe the various methods for detecting the current socket state and transitions to new states. We focus on how concise and flexible these methods are. Efficiency is our top concern, however, because the detection methods you use will have a profound effect on the performance of your application and the rest of the system.

What Are the Socket States?

The current socket state qualifies which network operations would succeed immediately, which operations would block, and which ones would fail (as well as the WinSock error value with which it would fail). Sockets have a finite number of possible states, and the WinSock API clearly defines the conditions—the network events and application function calls—that initiate transitions between them. Different socket types—datagram and stream sockets—have different states and different transitions.

Datagram Socket States

We can illustrate the datagram socket states and the progression between them with a **state diagram**. The state diagram in Figure 6-1 illustrates all the states you can detect programatically. It also shows the transitions that occur when an application makes WinSock function calls, or receives packets from a remote host. The states outside of the dotted box are mutually exclusive of each other, but the ones inside are not. In other words, a socket could have data pending on it *and* have a shortage of buffers for outgoing data, but it could not be "open" and "closed" at the same time.

As Table 6-1 shows, datagram sockets have only a few states, and because they are connectionless they can reach some states implicitly. For instance, a datagram socket is **writable** as soon as it is opened, and it is **readable** as soon as it is **named**. As a result, your application can begin sending data immediately after the `socket( )` call, or receiving immediately after you name it explicitly with `bind( )` or implicitly with `sendto( )`. It is not necessary to establish an association with a remote socket to send or

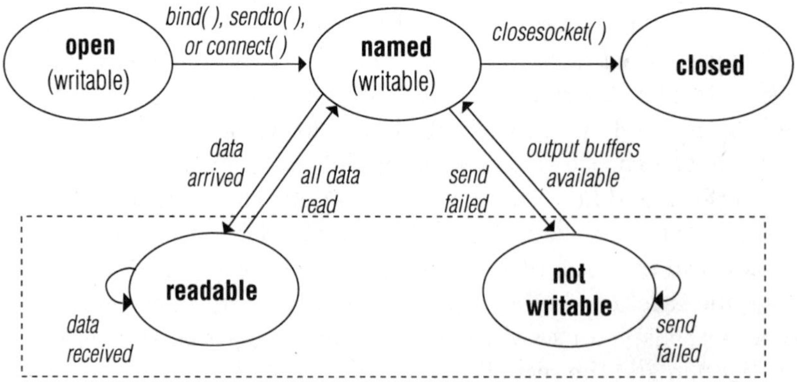

Figure 6-1 State diagram of datagram socket.

Table 6-1 Datagram socket states

Datagram Socket State	*Description*
open (writable)	socket returned from `socket( )` call, but not yet named (naming can occur explicitly with `bind( )`, or implicitly with either `sendto( )` or `connect( )`)
named (writable)	socket named (bound to a local address and port number), and it may also have an "association" with another host, because datagram sockets are "connectionless." It is possible to send data.
readable	data received by network system and ready to be read by application (with calls to `recv( )` and `recvfrom( )`)
not-writable	network system does not have enough buffers available to accommodate outgoing data (so `send( )` and `sendto( )` fail with WSAEWOULDBLOCK)
closed	socket handle is invalid (application has called `closesocket( )`)

receive, although you can also call `connect( )` to implicitly name the socket and set the default destination address for `send( )`.

Because a datagram socket is connectionless, it is unlikely to reach the **not-writable** state. Data transmission on a datagram socket is "unreliable," so the network system does not have to buffer outgoing data for possible retransmission. This means there is less likelihood that the network system will run out of buffers, although it could if there were too much incoming data or if other network applications were sharing the network system buffers at the same time. It also means the network system is not required to report an error if it cannot send application data. A network system can legally drop outgoing datagrams without sending them or reporting an error when no buffers are available. This makes it even less likely that a datagram socket will ever reach the not-writable state.

An application does not need to do much to detect state on a datagram socket. About the only state most datagram applications need to detect and act upon is the **readable** state.

Stream Socket States

Just as we did for datagram sockets, we can also illustrate the stream socket states and the progression between them in a state diagram. Figure 6-2 illustrates the stream socket states we can detect programmatically and the

WinSock function calls and network events that initiate state transitions. The states in the dotted box in Figure 6-2 are inclusive—they could all occur simultaneously—and those outside the box are mutually exclusive of each other. In other words, it is possible for an application to be **not-writable** and **readable** at the same time (and vice versa) since incoming and outgoing data often use the same buffers.

It should not come as a surprise that the state diagram for a connection-oriented stream socket in Figure 6-2 is more complex than the one for a datagram socket (as Table 6-2 details), a few states—**readable, writable,** and **closed**—are the same, but the **open** state has a different meaning. Unlike a datagram socket, the **not-writable** state is relatively common on a stream socket since the network system buffers outgoing data (for retransmission). The other states—**connection pending, close pending,** and **OOB data readable**—are unique to stream sockets.

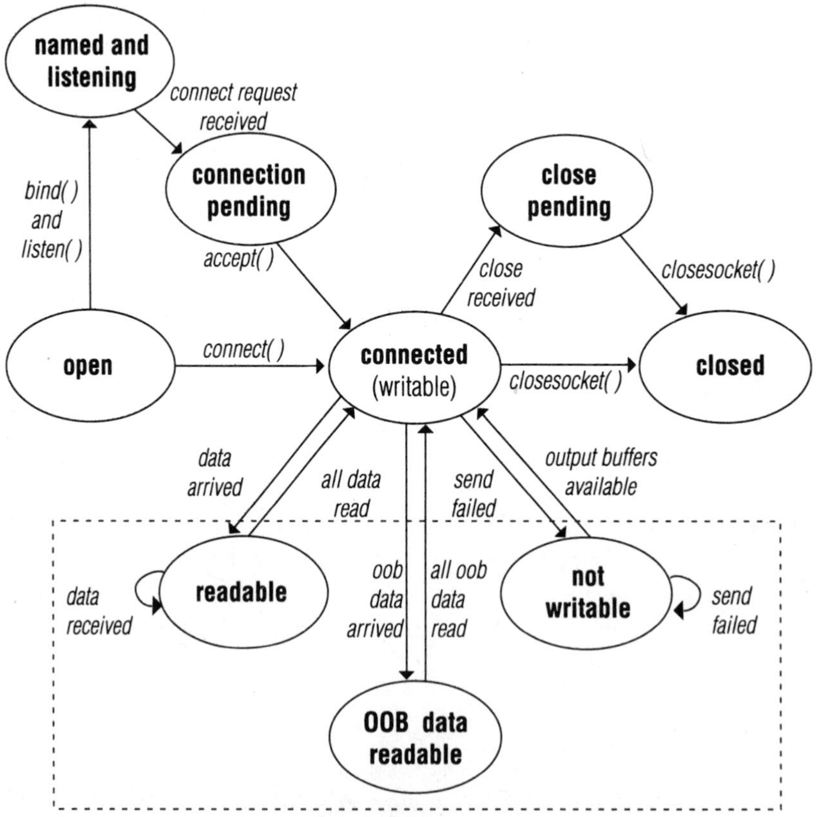

Figure 6-2 State diagram of stream socket.

Table 6-2 Stream socket states

Stream Socket State	*Description*
open	socket returned from `socket( )` call, but not yet named (naming can occur explicitly with `bind( )` or implicitly with `connect( )`)
named and listening	socket named (bound to a local network address and port number) and ready to accept incoming connection requests
connect pending	incoming connection request received by network system, waiting for application to "accept" the connection
connected (writable)	association (virtual circuit) established between local and remote sockets, so sending and receiving data is possible (a connected socket is always named too)
readable	data received by network system and ready to be read by application (with calls to `recv( )` or `recvfrom( )`)
OOB data readable	"out-of-band" data received by network system and ready to be read by application (with calls to `recv( )` or `recvfrom( )`)
not-writable	network system does not have enough buffers available to accommodate outgoing data (so `send( )` or `sendto( )` fail with WSAEWOULDBLOCK)
close pending	virtual circuit (at least half) closed. For TCP it means the network system received a TCP <FIN> or <RST> from the remote host (it may still be writable after a <FIN>)
closed	socket handle is invalid (application has called `closesocket( )`)

There is one technical inaccuracy in Figure 6-2. The **close-pending** state is typically still writable after an application receives a graceful close from the remote host. To simplify the illustration, we did not include this detail.

What Are the Methods of Detection?

There are a number of different ways to detect the various socket states and transitions between them. There are three basic methods of socket state detection:

- function call success or failure (and error value)
- synchronous detection (`select( )`, `ioctlsocket( )`, `getsockopt( )` and I/O flags)
- asynchronous notification (`WSAAsyncSelect( )`)

Using asynchronous notification of socket states and transitions is by far the most efficient and results in simple and elegant code. We describe this and the other methods of state detection in the rest of this chapter. Table 6-3 lists the detection methods for specific socket states.

Function Call Success or Failure

It is possible to infer the current state of a socket from the success or failure —and error value—of most functions. On a blocking socket, this works fine since functions return when the network operation is complete. However, this is not an effective or efficient way to monitor socket state with nonblocking sockets. For them, it is the "brute force" method and is crude and prone to error. The problem is that you cannot assume that specific error values will consistently indicate specific socket states.

About the only notable exception to this rule is the WSAEWOULDBLOCK error. It reliably indicates the state for which you are testing is *not* true. For example, as we describe in Chapter 5, "Operation Modes," it is possible to detect when a nonblocking socket is readable by polling `recv( )` or `recvfrom( )`. With a nonblocking socket, these functions "fail" with WSAEWOULDBLOCK when no data is available for reading (with or without the MSG_PEEK flag). However, as we also point out in Chapter 5, polling on a nonblocking socket is very inefficient. Also, if you do not yield as you poll in 16-bit Windows, you can easily monopolize the system as you wait for operations to complete.

The bottom line is that application dependence on return values from functions to detect state is only acceptable on blocking sockets (although whether or not blocking sockets themselves are acceptable is debatable). On nonblocking sockets, you should avoid polling since that method depends on specific error values, and you should not depend on specific error values to detect socket state. There are better methods available that utilize WinSock functions specifically designed for socket state detection.

Table 6-3 Socket state detection methods

Socket State	*Detection Methods*
open	• `socket( )` function succeeds • any function that takes a socket parameter would fail with WSAENOTSOCK if an application passed an invalid socket handle
named	• `getsockname( )` returns a valid port number in sockaddr (a socket must be connected to return the full local socket name, which includes the local address)
listening*	• on blocking socket, `accept( )` blocks (until connect request received) • on nonblocking socket, `accept( )` fails with WSAEWOULDBLOCK • `getsockopt( )` SO_ACCEPTCONN indicates TRUE for optval
connection pending*	• `accept( )` on listening socket succeeds • `select( )` readfds set for socket • `WSAAsyncSelect( )` FD_ACCEPT message received by application
connected	• `connect( )` fails with WSAEISCONN error on nonblocking socket • `send( )` or `sendto( )`, `recv( )` or `recvfrom( )` succeed • `select( )` writefds set for socket • `WSAAsyncSelect( )` FD_CONNECT message received by application
writable	• `send( )` or `sendto( )` succeeds • `select( )` writefds set for socket • `WSAAsyncSelect( )` FD_WRITE message received by application
readable*	• `recv( )` or `recvfrom( )` succeeds (with or without MSG_PEEK flag set) • `ioctlsocket( )` FIONREAD succeeds • `select( )` readfds set for socket • `WSAAsyncSelect( )` FD_READ message received by application
OOB data readable*	• `ioctlsocket( )` SIOCATMARK succeeds (if SO_OOBINLINE is enabled) • `select( )` exceptfds set on socket (if SO_OOBINLINE is disabled) • `WSAAsyncSelect( )` FD_OOB message received by application
not-writable	• `send( )` or `sendto( )` fails with WSAEWOULDBLOCK (i.e., not "writable") • `select( )` writefds not set for socket

continued on next page

Table 6-3 Continued

Socket State	*Detection Methods*
close pending*	• `recv( )` returns 0 • `select( )` readfds set for socket • `WSAAsyncSelect( )` FD_CLOSE message received by application
closed	• any function that takes a socket parameter would fail with WSAENOTSOCK if an application passed a closed (invalid) socket

* state valid for stream sockets only

Function Name	*Description*
getsockopt() SO_ACCEPTCONN	detects the listening state on a TCP socket
ioctlsocket() FIONREAD	detects readable socket state
ioctlsocket() SIOCATMARK	detects inline out-of-band data readable state
recv() or recvfrom() MSG_PEEK	detects readable socket state
select() readfds, writefds, exceptfds	detects readable, writable, and OOB data states

Synchronous Detection

Synchronous detection means calling a blocking or nonblocking function that indicates the current state of a socket by the return value from the function call. Windows Sockets has a number of functions, commands, options, and I/O flags specifically designed to detect the socket state.We describe these synchronous socket detection methods in more detail later in this chapter.

Asynchronous Detection

Asynchronous detection means the WinSock DLL detects a socket state at any time after an application calls the asynchronous socket state detection function. The WinSock DLL notifies the application of the current state or a state transition by posting a message. Only one function provides this type of asynchronous detection and notification of socket state:

Function Name	*Description*
WSAAsyncSelect()	detects and provides asynchronous notification for socket states: connected, readable, writable, not-writable, connection pending, OOB data readable, close pending

WSAAsyncSelect( )

A call to `WSAAsyncSelect( )` requests the WinSock DLL to notify an application of the current socket state and of any subsequent changes to the socket state. `WSAAsyncSelect( )` is the most versatile state detection and reporting function. It can detect and report more socket states than any other function. `WSAAsyncSelect( )` also allows you to create an efficient application that can effectively multiplex any number of sockets simultaneously. It lends itself to elegant application design that takes full advantage of the message-driven architecture of any Microsoft Windows environment.

```
HANDLE PASCAL FAR WSAAsyncSelect
   (SOCKET s,   /* socket that needs event notification */
   HWND hWnd,   /* handle of window to receive event message */
   unsigned int wMsg,   /* message to post when event occurs */
   long lEvent);        /* bit flags of network events to report */
```

s: socket handle for any valid socket

hWnd: handle of window to receive asynchronous notification message

wMsg: message for WinSock DLL to post. Notice that you get the same message for all the events in *lEvent*

lEvent: event(s) for which you want WinSock DLL to post notification. A socket event is equivalent to the current socket state or a transition to a new state. You can use a bitwise-OR operand to combine any number of events. The valid events are FD_READ, FD_WRITE, FD_OOB, FD_ACCEPT, FD_CONNECT, and FD_CLOSE.

`WSAAsyncSelect( )` always returns immediately. On failure it returns SOCKET_ERROR, and you call `WSAGetLastError( )` to get the cause of the failure. There are only a few possible errors, none of which indicates the current socket state. Either the WinSock DLL is not initialized, the network is unavailable, a blocking operation is pending, or you passed an invalid parameter such as an invalid window handle.

On success `WSAAsyncSelect( )` returns zero. This indicates that

- The socket is now nonblocking.
- If any of the requested events match the current socket state, the WinSock DLL will post a message for each one.
- If any of the requested events match the socket state at any time henceforth, the WinSock DLL will post a message for each one (as long as the application has called the "reenabling function" for that event).
- If this socket creates any new sockets with `accept( )`, the WinSock DLL will also monitor and post notification for the same events on those new sockets.

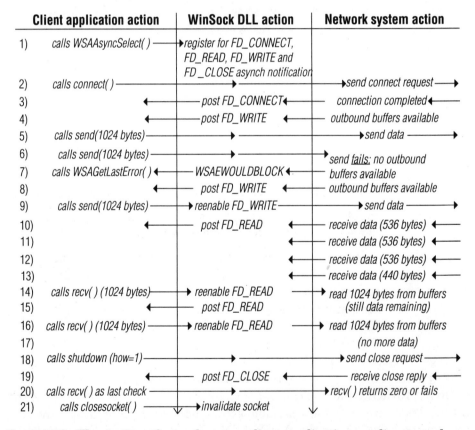

	Client application action	WinSock DLL action	Network system action
1)	*calls WSAAsyncSelect( )* →	*register for FD_CONNECT, FD_READ, FD_WRITE and FD_CLOSE asynch notification*	
2)	*calls connect( )* →	→	*send connect request* →
3)	←	*post FD_CONNECT* ←	*connection completed* ←
4)	←	*post FD_WRITE* ←	*outbound buffers available*
5)	*calls send(1024 bytes)* →	→	*send data* →
6)	*calls send(1024 bytes)* →	→	*send fails: no outbound*
7)	*calls WSAGetLastError( )* ←	*WSAEWOULDBLOCK* ←	*buffers available*
8)	←	*post FD_WRITE* ←	*outbound buffers available*
9)	*calls send(1024 bytes)* →	*reenable FD_WRITE* →	*send data* →
10)	←	*post FD_READ* ←	*receive data (536 bytes)* ←
11)		←	*receive data (536 bytes)* ←
12)		←	*receive data (536 bytes)* ←
13)		←	*receive data (440 bytes)* ←
14)	*calls recv( ) (1024 bytes)* →	*reenable FD_READ* →	*read 1024 bytes from buffers*
15)	←	*post FD_READ*	*(still data remaining)*
16)	*calls recv( ) (1024 bytes)* →	*reenable FD_READ* →	*read 1024 bytes from buffers*
17)			*(no more data)*
18)	*calls shutdown (how=1)* →	→	*send close request* →
19)	←	*post FD_CLOSE* ←	*receive close reply* ←
20)	*calls recv( ) as last check* →	→	*recv( ) returns zero or fails*
21)	*calls closesocket( )* →	*invalidate socket*	

Figure 6-3 Illustration of asynchronous client application sending to and receiving from echo server.

`WSAAsyncSelect( )` state detection for the named events remains in effect until you invalidate the socket handle with `closesocket( )`, or call `WSAAsyncSelect( )` with a different *lEvent* value (a zero *lEvent* value cancels all notification). You cannot change the socket from nonblocking with `ioctlsocket( )` FIONBIO while `WSAAsyncSelect( )` is in effect, and the socket is still nonblocking after cancellation.

How Does WSAAsyncSelect( ) Work?

Many people are initially intimidated by the apparent complexity of `WSAAsyncSelect( )`. However, it is really quite simple—and your application will be, too—once you understand how it works. Basically, you tell `WSAAsyncSelect( )` what you want to know about, and the WinSock DLL tells you everything you need to know when you need to know it. Of course, there is more to it than just that, but those are the essentials of `WSAAsyncSelect( )`.

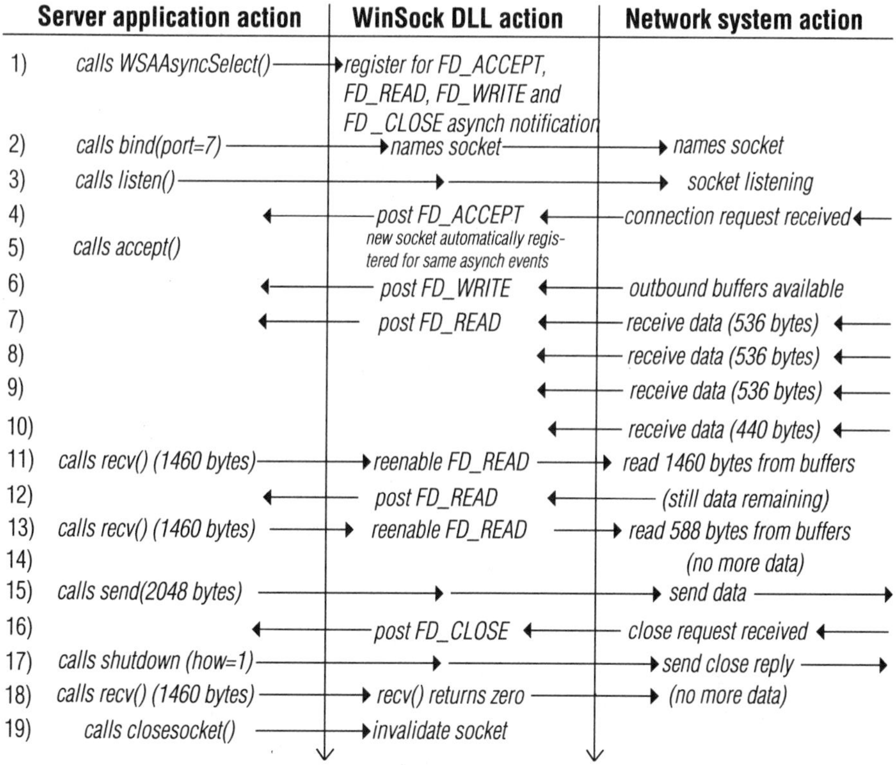

Figure 6-4 Illustration of asynchronous TCP echo server application receiving from and sending to client.

The simplest way to explain `WSAAsyncSelect( )` is to show it in action. Figure 6-3 illustrates a TCP client application that requests notification for FD_CONNECT, FD_READ, FD_WRITE, and FD_CLOSE asynchronous events. The client then connects to an echo server, sends data, reads it back, and closes the connection gracefully. Figure 6-4 illustrates the TCP echo server application to which the client connects. The server registers for most of the same asynchronous events but uses FD_ACCEPT instead of FD_CONNECT.

Of course, the client and server need not both operate in asynchronous mode to interact. Any client and server can use different operation modes. We use an asynchronous notification on both for illustrative purposes.

Table 6-4 `WSAAsyncSelect( )` asynchronous event notification messages

Event Name	*When It Occurs (Socket State)*	*Practical Meaning*	*Reenable Function(s)*
FD_ACCEPT*	**connection pending:** connection request received	`accept( )` likely to succeed	`accept( )`
FD_CLOSE*	**close pending:** connection close received (graceful close or abort)	remote done sending data (though data may remain); `closesocket( )` will complete immediately	<none>
FD_CONNECT	**connected:** connection now established	association established, so sending and receiving possible on socket	<none>
FD_OOB*	"oob data readability": out-of-band data with ready to read	`recv( )` with MSG_OOB flag will return OOB data	`recv( )` or `recvfrom( )` MSG_OOB flag*
FD_READ	**readable:** data received by network system is ready for application to read	`recv( )` or `recvfrom( )` likely to succeed	`recv( )` or `recvfrom( )`
FD_WRITE	**writable:** send is possible (network system buffers available for outgoing data)	`send( )` or `sendto( )` likely to succeed	`send( )` or `sendto( )`

* event valid for stream sockets only

What Are the WSAAsyncSelect( ) Events?

The *lEvent* argument for the `WSAAsyncSelect( )` function contains the asynchronous events of interest to your application. Table 6-4 lists those six events, each of which is equivalent to a socket state. The WINSOCK.H file contains macros for the bitflag values of each:

> FD_ACCEPT, FD_CLOSE, FD_CONNECT, FD_OOB, FD_READ, and FD_WRITE.

You can request notification for any number of events at once, regardless of the current state of the socket. You use the bitwise-OR operand to combine these macro values. All events receive the same message (as we describe shortly, the *lParam* contains the event value to differentiate each message). For example, the following function call enables asynchronous notification for the socket states **connected, readable, writable,** and **close pending**:

```
nRet = WSAAsyncSelect(s, hWnd, IDM_ASYNC,
      FD_READ | FD_WRITE | FD_CONNECT | FD_CLOSE);
if (nRet == SOCKET_ERROR) {
      < handle error >
}
```

When a call to `WSAAsyncSelect( )` succeeds, the WinSock DLL checks the current state of the socket immediately. It then posts a notification message for each requested event that matches the current socket state. So, for example, if we made the call above with a TCP socket after establishing a connection, and data had already arrived, the WinSock DLL would immediately post FD_CONNECT, FD_WRITE, and FD_READ notification messages to our application window.

Avoid Windows of Misopportunity

Although you can call `WSAAsyncSelect( )` any time—as in our example—and you can call it any number of times during the execution of an application, we recommend against it. The best thing to do is to register for all the events you need on a socket immediately after you open the socket (i.e., upon return from the `socket( )` function). There is no reason to do otherwise since the notification remains in effect for the life of the socket, and `accept( )`'d sockets inherit asynchronous notification registration. Actually, there is some danger in calling `WSAAsyncSelect( )` at any other time or too often in your application.

The problem in calling `WSAAsyncSelect( )` at any time other than immediately after creation (before any network I/O) is the potential for a race condition as a WinSock DLL registers for asynchronous notification. An event may occur just after the WinSock DLL attempts to detect it but before WinSock registers for notification. The window of misopportunity is small, but it exists. So the rule of thumb is always call `WSAAsyncSelect( )` to register for asynchronous notification of events before the events can occur. For example, always register for FD_CONNECT before you call `connect( )`, not after.

The potential for problems calling `WSAAsyncSelect( )` more than once is also slight, but it is also easy to avoid. There may be messages en route when you call `WSAAsyncSelect( )` to change or cancel notification. Your application may get confused if it is not prepared for them. Your application may also be confused by the apparent extra messages the WinSock DLL posts as it notifies you of the current socket state each time you call `WSAAsyncSelect( )`.

Calling `WSAAsyncSelect( )` once just after you create the socket and register for all the events of interest avoids the potential for these problems. Your application code will be simpler too.

What Are Reenabling Functions?

The documentation for `WSAAsyncSelect( )` in the WinSock specification refers to events as "level-triggered" and "edge-triggered." In a sense, these terms refer to detection of the current socket state and state transitions, respectively. However, by this definition all events are both level-triggered and edge-triggered since `WSAAsyncSelect( )` may detect any event when first called (the current "level") or when the event occurs any time after that point (the "edge"). A better way to differentiate the events is to note which ones have reenabling functions and which ones do not.

Events have reenabling functions so that the WinSock DLL can avoid flooding an application with notification messages. After the WinSock DLL posts a notification message, it does not post another one until the application calls the reenabling function. In Figures 6-3 and 6-4 you can see an illustration of how the reenabling function works with the FD_READ event. WinSock posts an FD_READ message when data first arrives (the "edge") but does not post again as more data arrives. After the application calls `recv( )`—the FD_READ reenabling function—the WinSock DLL posts another FD_READ message because the socket is still readable (there is still some data "level"). Figure 6-5 illustrates the reenabling algorithm for FD_READ and other events in a state diagram.

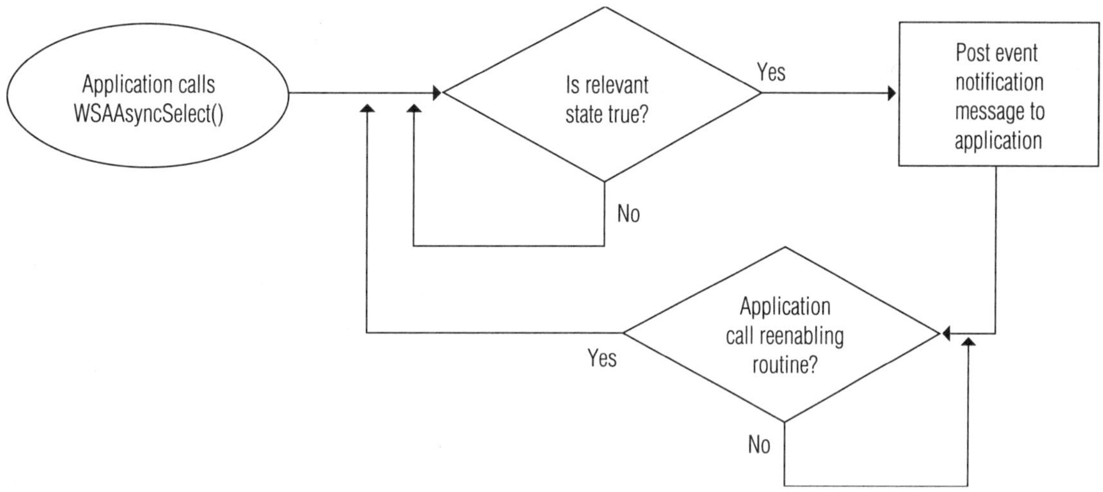

Figure 6-5 Flowchart of `WSAAsyncSelect()` "level-triggering" event notification algorithm in a WinSock DLL.

Table 6-4 shows that all events have reenabling functions except FD_CONNECT and FD_CLOSE. This makes sense since these events can occur only once per call to `WSAAsyncSelect( )` on a stream socket, and FD_CONNECT occurs only once per call to `connect( )` on a datagram socket (FD_CLOSE does not occur at all).

What Is in a Notification Message?

The WinSock DLL notifies your application by posting the message in *wMsg* to the window handle in *hWnd* with all the information you need:

- the *s* socket handle (in *wParam*)
- the event value (in the low word of *lParam*)
- a WinSock error value, if there is one (in the high word of *lParam*)

From this information you can always tell on which socket a specific event occurred. The WinSock DLL posts one message per event (per socket) and only one event per message. To ensure portability between different Windows environments (specifically, 16-bit and 32-bit), you should always use the `WSAGETSELECTEVENT( )` macro to remove the event value from *lParam*.

Any message may contain an error. The WinSock specification defines specific subsets of errors that each event may report, but the standard caveat of error handling to *expect anything* holds true, as always. In your message handler routine, you should always check for an error before you do anything else. Use the WSAGETSELECTERROR( ) macro to remove the error value from *lParam*. (Note: You should *not* call `WSAGetLastError( )` after receiving an event notification message, since this error value will often differ from the one in a message.)

When an error value is nonzero, you can use a normal error handler to display or log the error. Depending on the socket type and context, you may also choose to close the socket, but this is not always necessary. For instance, on datagram sockets transient error conditions are commonplace in an application that is sending to different addresses.

It is important to note that even when a message contains an error, you must still call the reenabling function to reenable notification for that event (if you expect to receive notification again). The call to the reenabling function is likely to fail with the same error as the one reported (although not necessarily), so you may want to ignore it if you have already reported it once. Note that the reenabling function may actually succeed. Be prepared for anything.

Be Prepared for Failure

Although receiving notification for an event, such as FD_READ, FD_WRITE, FD_OOB, or FD_ACCEPT, gives you a reasonable likelihood of success when you make the appropriate function call, there is no guarantee of success. As the WinSock specification says, "A robust application must be prepared for the possibility that it may receive a message and issue a Windows Sockets API call which returns WSAEWOULDBLOCK immediately."[1]

The problem is simple. Between the time a WinSock DLL posts an asynch notification message to your application and the time your application acts upon it, things can change. Your DLL may be servicing many sockets simultaneously, so it might simply be busy when you make the function call in response to the asynch message.

When this occurs, it is easy to handle a WSAEWOULDBLOCK gracefully: Just return from the window procedure quietly. The WinSock DLL is required to post another notification message, since you called the reenabling function and the state did not change since the DLL posted the first message. By simply handling "would block" errors gracefully, your application can avoid some potentially serious problems.

[1] v1.1 Windows Sockets specification Section 4.3.7, page 90, second paragraph under "Comments"

Looping in Response

Asynchronous notification has an inherent latency between the event and the arrival of the event notification message. As a result, polling on a nonblocking socket to detect state transitions, and sometimes even blocking mode, can be faster than using asynchronous notification. However, there is a way to reduce the effect of notification latency to increase performance.

The only event adversely affected by this latency is FD_READ. You can offset the effect by calling `recv( )` or `recvfrom( )` more than once in response to each FD_READ message. This will generate extra FD_READ messages each time you call and data still remains. The extra messages will enhance the effect of the looping reads, and together you can increase your data throughput substantially. The WinSock specification suggests that you disable `WSAAsyncSelect( )` before looping to avoid the extra messages. As we noted earlier, however, calling `WSAAsyncSelect( )` multiple times can generate extra messages, too. It is also unnecessary.

To loop safely calling `recv( )` and `recvfrom( )` in FD_READ, you should

- limit the number of times you loop (eight times or less is a good number)
- handle the WSAEWOULDBLOCK error gracefully (as noted earlier, you should do this anyway)

Although it is not necessary, for added security you can increase your message queue with `SetMessageQueue( )`. However, this must be done very early in your application since the `SetMessageQueue( )` function replaces the existing message queue with a new one and discards all queued messages in the process.

Cancelling Asynchronous Notification

There are two ways to cancel `WSAAsyncSelect( )` asynchronous notification:

- Call `WSAAsyncSelect( )` with a NULL value for the *lEvent* parameter.
- Close the socket by calling `closesocket( )`.

Note that in both cases asynchronous notification messages may still remain in the message queue. Your application should anticipate them and either avoid normal processing when they arrive (i.e., don't call any WinSock functions in response to them) or be prepared to handle the function failure that may result (e.g., failure with the WSAENOTSOCK error after a call to `closesocket( )`). Since a socket is invalid after an application calls `closesocket( )`, the WinSock

DLL will not post any new messages to the application for that socket. This includes the FD_CLOSE notification message.

Note also that the `WSACancelAsyncRequest( )` is *not* relevant to `WSAAsyncSelect( )` asynchronous operations. As we note in Chapter 5, "Operation Modes," `WSACancelAsyncRequest( )` cancels asynchronous operations for the `WSAAsyncGetXByY( )` collection of "database" functions.

Event Descriptions

At this point, we have already described everything there is to know about `WSAAsyncSelect( )`. If you feel comfortable, you can skip this section. The following detailed descriptions of each event (in alphabetical order) are designed to provide a single location of information about each event, to allow for easy reference.

FD_ACCEPT Event

The FD_ACCEPT event notifies an application of the **connection pending** state (arrival of an incoming connection request). It indicates that a call to `accept( )` should succeed immediately, and `accept( )` is the reenabling function for FD_ACCEPT. FD_ACCEPT is valid only for stream sockets, and it can occur only on a socket in the listening state (i.e., after you have called `bind( )` and `listen( )`).

Specifically, a WinSock DLL will post an FD_ACCEPT message

- when you call `WSAAsyncSelect( )`, if there is currently a connection request available to accept
- when a connection request arrives, if FD_ACCEPT was not already posted
- after you call `accept( )`, if there is another connection request available to accept

The WinSock DLL posts an FD_ACCEPT message to your application when another application—typically one running on a remote host—makes a connection request to the port number and IP address on which your socket is listening. When your application receives an FD_ACCEPT message, you must call `accept( )` to get the socket handle for the new connection. Note that the socket returned from `accept( )` inherits all the properties of the listening socket. This means it will be nonblocking and automatically registered to receive the same notification messages as the application specified when it referenced the listening socket in a call to `WSAAsyncSelect( )`.

FD_CLOSE Event

The FD_CLOSE event notifies an application of the **close pending** state. FD_CLOSE is valid only for stream sockets, and it can occur only after a connection was established with a call to either `connect( )` or `accept( )`. The WinSock DLL posts FD_CLOSE to an application when the remote host in a virtual circuit aborts the connection or closes it gracefully. In a graceful close, the remote host may be responding to a close request that the local host sent.

Specifically, a WinSock DLL will post an FD_CLOSE message

- when you call `WSAAsyncSelect( )`, if the socket connection has been closed (gracefully or abortively) by the remote system
- after the remote system initiated graceful close
- after the local system initiates graceful close with `shutdown( )` and the remote system has responded with "End of Data" notification (e.g., TCP FIN)
- when the remote system aborts connection (e.g., sent TCP RST), and *lParam* will contain the WSAECONNRESET error value

Note that although receipt of FD_CLOSE means the remote end is done sending data, it does not mean that you have finished reading all the data available. The version 1.1 WinSock specification is ambiguous about this, so you may still have data buffered for reading at this point. As a result, as illustrated in Figures 6-3 and 6-4 and our code example, you should always call `recv( )` upon receipt of FD_CLOSE to check for any remaining data. When `recv( )` returns 0 or fails (with any error), you can be sure that no data remains. Version 2.0 of WinSock repairs this ambiguity, but you should still call `recv( )` to retain compatibility with v1.1 and ensure your application will receive all the data sent.

Version 1.1 of the Windows Sockets specification also contains an error. It says, "In TCP terms, this means that the FD_CLOSE is posted when the connection goes into FIN_WAIT or CLOSE_WAIT states," which is *incorrect*. Version 2.0 of WinSock correctly references the TIME_WAIT state instead of FIN_WAIT. In other words, the WinSock DLL posts an FD_CLOSE when the network system receives a TCP packet with the FIN bit set from the remote host (in a graceful disconnect). Also, since the FD_CLOSE message can contain a WSAECONNRESET error, a WinSock DLL will post an FD_CLOSE after receipt of a TCP packet with the RST bit set (in an abortive disconnect).

FD_CONNECT Event

The FD_CONNECT event notifies an application of the **connected** state (i.e., when an outgoing connection request has completed). FD_CONNECT is valid for both datagram and stream sockets, and it can occur only in a client application after you have called `connect( )`.

Specifically, the WinSock DLL will post an FD_CONNECT message

- when you call `WSAAsyncSelect( )`, if there is currently a connection established
- after you call `connect( )`, when connection is established (even when `connect( )` succeeds immediately, as is typical with a datagram socket)

Typically, an application registers for FD_CONNECT notification if it needs to execute a one-time-only initialization procedure. You should register for FD_WRITE instead of FD_CONNECT if you want to start sending data when the socket is writable. If your application registers for both FD_CONNECT and FD_WRITE events, you will always receive the FD_CONNECT message first.

FD_OOB Event

The FD_OOB event notifies an application of the **out-of-band data readable** state (also known as "OOB data"). This means that `recv( )` or `recvfrom( )` with MSG_OOB flag should succeed (these are the reenabling functions for FD_OOB).

Specifically, the WinSock DLL will post an FD_OOB message

- when you call `WSAAsyncSelect( )`, if there is OOB data currently available to receive with the MSG_OOB flag
- when OOB data arrives, if FD_OOB was not already posted
- after you call `recv( )` or `recvfrom( )` with MSG_OOB flag, if OOB data is still available to receive

Note that the FD_OOB event is valid only for stream sockets and only when the SO_OOBINLINE socket option is disabled (which it is, by default). You can check whether SO_OOBINLINE is currently enabled or disabled with a call to `getsockopt( )` SO_OOBINLINE (see Chapter 9, "Socket Information and Control"). When SO_OOBINLINE is enabled, OOB data is treated as normal data, and so WinSock will not post FD_OOB notification to your application. Instead, it will post FD_READ, as it does for normal data.

When your application receives an FD_OOB message, you can call `recv( )` or `recvfrom( )` with *flag* set to MSG_OOB to read the urgent data. With TCP, "out-of-band data" is equivalent to "urgent data," and there is never more than *one byte* of OOB data. This byte is removed from the stream and can be read only with the MSG_OOB flag.

There are problems with OOB data as implemented on stream sockets using TCP "urgent data." We describe these problems in the "Out-of-Band Data" section later in this chapter. As a rule, do not use out-of-band data in your application if you can avoid it. It has too many problems, and there is too much confusion about proper implementation, so differences exist between WinSock implementations.

FD_READ Event

The FD_READ event notifies an application of the **readable** state (data arrival). It indicates that `recv( )` or `recvfrom( )` should succeed immediately, and `recv( )` and `recvfrom( )` are the reenabling functions for the FD_READ event. FD_READ is valid for both stream and datagram sockets.

Specifically, the WinSock DLL will post an FD_READ message

- when you call `WSAAsyncSelect( )`, if there is data currently available to receive
- when data arrives, if FD_READ was not already posted
- after you call `recv( )` or `recvfrom( )` (with or without MSG_PEEK), if data is still available to receive

Note: When `setsockopt( )` SO_OOBINLINE is enabled, data includes both normal data and out-of-band (OOB) data in the instances noted above.

When your application receives an FD_READ message, you should always call `recv( )` or `recvfrom( )` to read the data from the network system (whether or not the FD_READ message contained an error). If any data remains after you call `recv()` or `recvfrom( )`, the WinSock DLL will post another FD_READ message.

If your application receives data in bulk at any time during execution, you may want to call `recv( )` or `recvfrom( )` multiple times for each FD_READ message to increase data throughput. By doing so, you can offset the latency between data arrival and the receipt of FD_READ messages. We describe this technique in the "Looping in Response" section earlier in this chapter. We also use it in the asynchronous notification code example to follow.

FD_WRITE Event

The FD_WRITE event notifies an application of the **writable** state (the availability of buffers for outgoing data). It indicates that `send( )` or `sendto( )` should succeed immediately, and `send( )` and `sendto( )` are the reenabling functions for the FD_WRITE event.

Specifically, the WinSock DLL will post an FD_WRITE message

- when you call `WSAAsyncSelect( )`, if a `send( )` or `sendto( )` is likely to succeed
- after you call `connect( )` or `accept( )`, when connection was established
- after `send( )` or `sendto( )` fails with WSAEWOULDBLOCK, when `send( )` or `sendto( )` is likely to succeed

Note that if an application registers for both FD_CONNECT and FD_WRITE, the WinSock DLL will always post the FD_CONNECT message first.

FD_WRITE is valid for both stream and datagram sockets, but because datagram sockets do not buffer outgoing data and are unreliable, you will rarely encounter an FD_WRITE message on a datagram socket. On the other hand, these may occur frequently on a stream socket sending bulk data (particularly on a slow link), since stream sockets buffer all outgoing data for possible retransmission.

Your application could use the first FD_WRITE notification to initiate a data transfer if your application is designed to send data before receiving any. You will only get subsequent FD_WRITE messages if a call to `send( )` or `sendto( )` fails with the WSAEWOULDBLOCK error. In this event, you can resume the data transfer where it left off by using the same buffer pointer referenced when the send function failed.

AS_Echo Application

AS_Echo is a server application that shows `WSAAsyncSelect( )` in action with FD_ACCEPT, FD_READ, FD_WRITE, and FD_CLOSE enabled on a TCP socket. This application has no user interface to control network operations, but it is completely driven by the network events and the changes in state that they signal. AS_Echo accepts a connection request after receiving FD_ACCEPT notification, reads data after receiving an FD_READ message, and immediately writes the data back. If a `send( )` fails with a WSAEWOULDBLOCK error, it waits until FD_WRITE notification to resume writing again. It closes a connection in response to an FD_CLOSE message.

AS_Echo provides the standard TCP echo service as defined by RFC 862. It would work nicely with the client applications shown in the code examples in Chapter 5, "Operation Modes." It can also support any number of connections simultaneously.

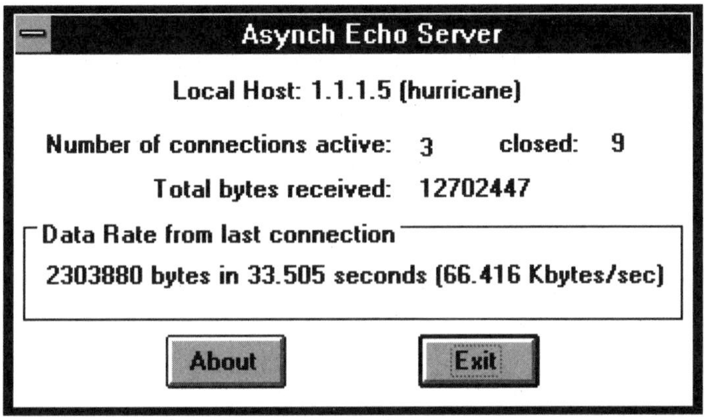

The screen capture above shows what the AS_Echo application looks like in operation. It displays the following items:

- Local Host: the IP address and host name of the machine on which the AS_Echo server application is running
- Number of connections active: the current number of echo clients being serviced (we update this count as we accept a new connection)
- closed: the number of clients that have disconnected (we update this count as we close an existing connection)
- Total bytes received: the total number of bytes received from all clients that have come and gone (we update this byte counter dynamically as we receive data)
- Data Rate from last connection: shows the statistics from the connection that just closed, including total number of bytes received and sent, the time it took, and the resulting data transfer rate in kilobytes per second

The data rate displayed here is not bad, but it is not great either. The server is capable of much faster rates. This sample was run between two hosts with 8-bit Ethernet cards, and most important, the client applications were designed to operate synchronously: They send more data only after they receive previous data, which makes them slow.

In any case, reading and writing bulk data simultaneously tends to reduce the data rate. As evidenced by the fast transfers we get from the sample FTP client in Chapter 7, simplex (one-way) bulk data is capable of much faster rates than duplex (two-way) bulk data.

AS_Echo also creates a logfile each time it executes. Here are the last few lines from AS_ECHO.LOG for the execution shown in the preceding screen capture. When we exited the server, three connections were still active; they were aborted and their final stats were discarded:

```
>>> socket: 66 connected from 1.1.1.9
>>> socket: 68 connected from 1.1.1.7
<<< socket: 66 disconnected from 1.1.1.9
2122840 bytes in 32.681 seconds (62.512 Kbytes/sec)
<<< socket: 68 disconnected from 1.1.1.7
623420 bytes in 10.436 seconds (57.632 Kbytes/sec)
>>> socket: 70 connected from 1.1.1.3
<<< socket: 70 disconnected from 1.1.1.3
2303880 bytes in 33.505 seconds (66.416 Kbytes/sec)
Final Totals: Bytes Received: 13964819, Connections: 9
```

AS_Echo handles multiple connections simultaneously by maintaining a "database" of connections. Upon receipt of an FD_ACCEPT notification message, it calls `accept( )`: if it succeeds, it creates a connection data record and puts it in a linked list. Each record contains all the vital information we need for each connection, such as socket handle, remote socket name, connection state, data statistics, and I/O buffer. The record remains for the life of the connection. When the connection goes away, AS_Echo frees the connection structure memory.

```
/*---------------------------------------------------------------------
 *
 * Program: Asynch Echo Server (TCP)
 *
 * filename: as_echo.c
 *
 * copyright by Bob Quinn, 1995
 *
 *  Description:  Server application that implements echo protocol as
 *    described by RFC 862. This application demonstrates simultaneous
 *    multiple user support using asynchronous operation mode.
```

```
 *
 ---------------------------------------------------------------*/
#define STRICT
#include "..\wsa_xtra.h"  /* see sample library section of Chapter 7 */
#include <windows.h>
#include <windowsx.h>

#include <winsock.h>
#include "resource.h"
#include <string.h>
#include <stdlib.h>
#include <time.h>
#include <stdio.h>
#include <dos.h>
#include <direct.h>
#include "..\winsockx.h"  /* see sample library section of Chapter 7 */

/*---------------- global data ------------*/
char szAppName[] = "as_echo";

SOCKET hLstnSock=INVALID_SOCKET; /* listening socket */
SOCKADDR_IN stLclName;          /* local address and port number */
char szHost_name[MAXHOST_NAME]={0};/* local host name */
int  iActiveConns;              /* number of active connections */
long lByteCount;                /* total bytes read */
int  iTotalConns;               /* connections closed so far */

typedef struct stConnData {
  SOCKET hSock;                 /* connection socket */
  SOCKADDR_IN stRmtName;        /* remote host address and port */
  LONG lStartTime;              /* time of connect */
  BOOL bReadPending;            /* deferred read flag */
  int  iBytesRcvd;              /* data currently buffered */
  int  iBytesSent;              /* data sent from buffer */
  long lByteCount;              /* total bytes received */
  char achIOBuf  [INPUT_SIZE];  /* network I/O data buffer */
  struct stConnData FAR*lpstNext;/* pointer to next record */
} CONNDATA, *PCONNDATA, FAR *LPCONNDATA;
LPCONNDATA lpstConnHead = 0;    /* head of the list */

char szLogFile[] = "as_echo.log";/* connection log file */
```

```
HFILE hLogFile=HFILE_ERROR;
BOOL  bReAsync=TRUE;

/*------------ function prototypes ------------*/
int WINAPI WinMain (HINSTANCE, HINSTANCE, LPSTR, int);
BOOL CALLBACK Dlg_Main (HWND, UINT, UINT, LPARAM);
BOOL CALLBACK Dlg_About (HWND, UINT, UINT, LPARAM);
BOOL InitLstnSock(int, PSOCKADDR_IN, HWND, u_int);
SOCKET AcceptConn(SOCKET, PSOCKADDR_IN);
long SendData(SOCKET, LPSTR, int);
int RecvData(SOCKET, LPSTR, int);
void DoStats (long, long, LPCONNDATA);
LPCONNDATA NewConn (SOCKET, PSOCKADDR_IN);
LPCONNDATA FindConn (SOCKET);
void RemoveConn (LPCONNDATA);

/*--------------------------------------------------------------------
 *  Function: WinMain()
 *
 *  Description:
 *      Initialize and start message loop
 *
 */
int WINAPI WinMain
  (HINSTANCE hInstance,
   HINSTANCE hPrevInstance,
   LPSTR  lpszCmdLine,
   int    nCmdShow)
{
    int nRet;

    lpszCmdLine   = lpszCmdLine;    /* avoid warning */
    hPrevInstance = hPrevInstance;
    nCmdShow      = nCmdShow;

    hInst = hInstance;  /* save instance handle */

    /*-------------initialize WinSock DLL-------------*/
    nRet = WSAStartup(WSA_VERSION, &stWSAData);
    /* WSAStartup()returns error value if failed (0 on success) */
```

```
    if (nRet != 0) {
      WSAperror(nRet, "WSAStartup()");
      /* no sense continuing if we can't use WinSock */
    } else {

      DialogBox (hInst, MAKEINTRESOURCE(AS_ECHO), NULL, Dlg_Main);
      /*--------------release WinSock DLL--------------*/
      nRet = WSACleanup();
      if (nRet == SOCKET_ERROR)
        WSAperror(WSAGetLastError(), "WSACleanup()");
    }

    return(0);
} /* end WinMain()*/

/*-------------------------------------------------------------------
*
 * Function: Dlg_Main()
 *
 * Description:
 *    process windows message
 */
BOOL CALLBACK Dlg_Main
  (HWND hDlg,
   UINT msg,
   UINT wParam,
   LPARAM lParam)
{
    LPCONNDATA lpstConn;              /* work pointer */
    WORD WSAEvent, WSAErr;
    SOCKADDR_IN stRmtName;
    SOCKET hSock;
    struct hostent *lpHost;
    BOOL bRet = FALSE;
    int  nRet, cbRcvd, cbSent;

    switch (msg) {
      case WSA_ASYNC:
        /*--------------------
         * async notification message handlers
         *--------------------*/
```

```
    hSock = (SOCKET)wParam;                      /* socket */
    WSAEvent = WSAGETSELECTEVENT (lParam);  /* extract event */
    WSAErr   = WSAGETSELECTERROR (lParam);  /* extract error */
    lpstConn = FindConn(hSock);             /* find socket struct */

    /* close connection on error (don't show error) */
    if (WSAErr && (hSock != hLstnSock))  {
      PostMessage (hWinMain, WSA_ASYNC,
          (WPARAM)hSock, WSAMAKESELECTREPLY(FD_CLOSE,0));
      break;
    }
    switch (WSAEvent) {
  case FD_READ:
        if (lpstConn) {
          /* read data from socket and write it back */
          cbRcvd = lpstConn->iBytesRcvd;
          if ((INPUT_SIZE - cbRcvd) > 0) {
            lpstConn->bReadPending = FALSE;
            nRet = RecvData(hSock,
              (LPSTR)&(lpstConn->achIOBuf[cbRcvd]),
              INPUT_SIZE-cbRcvd);
            lpstConn->iBytesRcvd += nRet;
            lpstConn->lByteCount += nRet;
            lByteCount += nRet;
            _ltoa(lByteCount, achTempBuf, 10);
            SetDlgItemText(hWinMain, IDC_BYTE_TOTAL, achTempBuf);
          } else {
            /* no buffer space now, so defer the net read */
            lpstConn->bReadPending = TRUE;
          }
        }
        /* fall through to write data back to client */
```

In response to FD_READ notification, we call our own `RecvData( )` function, tally the data received, and update the on-screen statistics.

```
      case FD_WRITE:
        /* send data (may not be any to send initially) */
        if (lpstConn && lpstConn->iBytesRcvd) {
          cbSent = lpstConn->iBytesSent;
          lpstConn->iBytesSent += SendData(hSock,
```

```
      (LPSTR)&(lpstConn->achIOBuf[cbSent]),
      lpstConn->iBytesRcvd - cbSent);

  /* if we sent everything we received, reset counters */
   if (lpstConn->iBytesSent == lpstConn->iBytesRcvd) {
      lpstConn->iBytesSent = 0;
      lpstConn->iBytesRcvd = 0;
   }

   /* if there's a read pending, then do it */
   if (lpstConn->bReadPending) {
      PostMessage (hWinMain, WSA_ASYNC,
        (WPARAM)hSock, WSAMAKESELECTREPLY(FD_READ,0));
   }
 }
 break;
```

We use FD_WRITE only after a previous `send( )` failed with WSAEWOULDBLOCK.

```
case FD_ACCEPT:
  /* accept the incoming data connection request */
  hSock = AcceptConn(hLstnSock, &stRmtName);
  if (hSock != INVALID_SOCKET) {
    /* get a new socket structure */
    lpstConn = NewConn(hSock, &stRmtName);
    if (!lpstConn) {
      /* from sample library in Chapter 7 */
     CloseConn(hSock, (LPSTR)0, INPUT_SIZE, hWinMain);
    } else {
      iActiveConns++;
      SetDlgItemInt(hWinMain, IDC_CONN_ACTIVE,
        iActiveConns, FALSE);
    }
  }
  break;
```

All connections originate in response to an FD_ACCEPT notification of an incoming connection request. We accept the connection, initialize a new connection record for it, and update our on-screen connection count.

```
case FD_CLOSE:                   /* data connection closed */
  if (hSock != hLstnSock) {
    /* read any remaining data and close connection */
    CloseConn(hSock, (LPSTR)0, INPUT_SIZE, hWinMain);
    if (lpstConn) {
      DoStats(lpstConn->lByteCount,
        lpstConn->lStartTime, lpstConn);
      RemoveConn(lpstConn);
      iTotalConns++;
      SetDlgItemInt(hWinMain, IDC_CONN_TOTAL,
        iTotalConns, FALSE);
      iActiveConns--;
      SetDlgItemInt(hWinMain, IDC_CONN_ACTIVE,
        iActiveConns, FALSE);
    }
  }
  break;
```

When a client closes the connection, we get an FD_CLOSE notification. Whether or not the client closes gracefully or aborts, we call our standard close routine, which does a `shutdown( )` how=1, loops on `recv( )` until it returns zero or an error, then calls `closesocket( )`.

```
      default:
        break;
    } /* end switch(WSAEvent) */
    break;

case WM_COMMAND:
    switch (wParam) {

      case IDC_ABOUT:
        DialogBox (hInst, MAKEINTRESOURCE(IDD_ABOUT),
             hDlg, Dlg_About);
        break;

      case WM_DESTROY:
      case IDC_EXIT:
        /* close listening socket */
        if (hLstnSock != INVALID_SOCKET)
          closesocket(hLstnSock);
```

```
        /* close all active connections */
        for (lpstConn = lpstConnHead;
             lpstConn;
             lpstConn=lpstConn->lpstNext) {
          CloseConn(lpstConn->hSock, (LPSTR)0,
             INPUT_SIZE, hWinMain);
          RemoveConn(lpstConn);
        }
        /* write final stats, and close logfile */
        if (hLogFile != HFILE_ERROR) {
          wsprintf (achTempBuf,
            "Final Totals: Bytes Received: %lu, Connections: %d\n",
            lByteCount, iTotalConns);
          _lwrite (hLogFile, achTempBuf, strlen(achTempBuf));
          _lclose (hLogFile);
        }
        EndDialog(hDlg, msg);
        bRet = TRUE;
        break;

      default:
         break;
    } /* end case WM_COMMAND: */
    break;

case WM_INITDIALOG:
  hWinMain = hDlg;      /* save our main window handle */

  /* get a socket listening */
  hLstnSock = InitLstnSock (IPPORT_ECHO,
      &stLclName, hWinMain, WSA_ASYNC);

  /* get our local info for display */
  stLclName.sin_addr.s_addr = GetHostID ();
  gethostname (szHost name, MAXHOST_NAME);
  wsprintf(achTempBuf, "Local Host: %s (%s)",
      inet_ntoa(stLclName.sin_addr),
      szHost_name[0] ? (LPSTR)szHost_name : (LPSTR)"<unknown>");
  SetDlgItemText (hWinMain, IDC_LOCAL_HOST, achTempBuf);

  /* assign an icon to dialog box */
```

```
#ifndef WIN32
        SetClassWord(hDlg,GCW_HICON,
          (WORD)LoadIcon(hInst,MAKEINTRESOURCE(AS_ECHO)));
#else
        SetClassLong (hDlg, GCL_HICON, (LONG)
          LoadIcon((HINSTANCE) GetWindowLong(hDlg, GWL_HINSTANCE),
          __TEXT("AS_ECHO")));
#endif

        /* open logfile, if logging enabled */
        hLogFile = _lcreat (szLogFile, 0);
        if (hLogFile == HFILE_ERROR) {
          MessageBox (hWinMain, "Unable to open logfile",
            "File Error", MB_OK | MB_ICONASTERISK);
        }
        /* center dialog box */
        CenterWnd (hDlg, NULL, TRUE);
        break;

      default:
        break;
  } /* end switch (msg) */

  return (bRet);
} /* end Dlg_Main()*/

/*---------------------------------------------------------------
 * Function: InitLstnSock()
 *
 * Description: Get a stream socket, and start listening for
 *  incoming connection requests.
 */
BOOL InitLstnSock(int iLstnPort, PSOCKADDR_IN pstSockName,
  HWND hWnd, u_int nAsyncMsg)
{
  int nRet;
  SOCKET hLstnSock;
  int nLen = SOCKADDR_LEN;

  /* get a TCP socket to use for data connection listen */
  hLstnSock = socket (AF_INET, SOCK_STREAM, 0);
```

```
  if (hLstnSock == INVALID_SOCKET)  {
    WSAperror(WSAGetLastError(), "socket()");
  } else {
    /* request async notification for most events */
    nRet = WSAAsyncSelect(hLstnSock, hWnd, nAsyncMsg,
           (FD_ACCEPT | FD_READ | FD_WRITE | FD_CLOSE));
    if (nRet == SOCKET_ERROR) {
      WSAperror(WSAGetLastError(), "WSAAsyncSelect()");
    } else {

      /* name the local socket with bind()*/
      pstSockName->sin_family = PF_INET;
      pstSockName->sin_port   = htons(iLstnPort);
      nRet = bind(hLstnSock,(LPSOCKADDR)pstSockName,SOCKADDR_LEN);
      if (nRet == SOCKET_ERROR) {
          WSAperror(WSAGetLastError(), "bind()");
      } else {

        /* listen for incoming connection requests */
        nRet = listen(hLstnSock, 5);
        if (nRet == SOCKET_ERROR) {
          WSAperror(WSAGetLastError(), "listen()");
        }
      }
    }
    /* if we had an error, then we have a problem. Clean up */
    if (nRet == SOCKET_ERROR) {
        closesocket(hLstnSock);
        hLstnSock = INVALID_SOCKET;
    }
  }
  return (hLstnSock);
} /* end InitLstnSock()*/

/*--------------------------------------------------------------
 * Function: AcceptConn()
 *
 * Description: In response to FD_ACCEPT, call accept() to
 *  respond to connection request and establish connection
 */
SOCKET AcceptConn(SOCKET hLstnSock, PSOCKADDR_IN pstName)
```

```
{
  SOCKET hNewSock;
  int nRet, nLen = SOCKADDR_LEN;

  hNewSock = accept (hLstnSock, (LPSOCKADDR)pstName, (LPINT)&nLen);
  if (hNewSock == SOCKET_ERROR) {
    int WSAErr = WSAGetLastError();
    if (WSAErr != WSAEWOULDBLOCK)
      WSAperror (WSAErr, "accept");
  } else if (bReAsync) {
    /* This SHOULD be unnecessary, since all new sockets are supposed
     *  to inherit properties of the listening socket (like all the
     *  asynch events registered) but some WinSocks don't do this.
     * Request async notification for most events */
    nRet = WSAAsyncSelect(hNewSock, hWinMain, WSA_ASYNC,
           (FD_READ | FD_WRITE | FD_CLOSE));
    if (nRet == SOCKET_ERROR) {
      WSAperror(WSAGetLastError(), "WSAAsyncSelect()");
    }
    /* try to get lots of buffer space */
    GetBuf(hNewSock, INPUT_SIZE, SO_RCVBUF);
    GetBuf(hNewSock, INPUT_SIZE, SO_SNDBUF);
  }
  return (hNewSock);
} /* end AcceptConn()*/

/*-------------------------------------------------------------
 * Function: SendData()
 *
 * Description: Send data from buffer provided
 */
long SendData(SOCKET hSock, LPSTR lpOutBuf, int cbTotalToSend)
{
  int cbTotalSent  = 0;
  int cbLeftToSend = cbTotalToSend;
  int nRet, WSAErr;

  /* send as much data as we can */
  while (cbLeftToSend > 0) {
    /* send data to client */
    nRet = send (hSock, lpOutBuf+cbTotalSent,
```

```
      cbLeftToSend < MTU_SIZE ? cbLeftToSend : MTU_SIZE, 0);

    if (nRet == SOCKET_ERROR) {
      WSAErr = WSAGetLastError();
      /* display significant errors */
      if (WSAErr != WSAEWOULDBLOCK) {
        WSAperror(WSAErr, (LPSTR)"send()");
      }
      break;
    } else {
      /* update byte counter, and display */
      cbTotalSent += nRet;
    }
    /* calculate what's left to send */
    cbLeftToSend = cbTotalToSend - cbTotalSent;
  }
  return (cbTotalSent);
} /* end SendData()*/

/*-------------------------------------------------------------
 * Function: RecvData()
 *
 * Description: Receive data into buffer provided
 */
int RecvData(SOCKET hSock, LPSTR lpInBuf, int cbTotalToRecv)
{
  int cbTotalRcvd = 0;
  int cbLeftToRecv = cbTotalToRecv;
  int nRet=0, WSAErr;

  /* read as much as we can buffer from client */
  while (cbLeftToRecv > 0) {

    nRet = recv (hSock,lpInBuf+cbTotalRcvd, cbLeftToRecv, 0);
    if (nRet == SOCKET_ERROR) {
      WSAErr = WSAGetLastError();
      /* display significant errors */
      if (WSAErr != WSAEWOULDBLOCK)
        WSAperror(WSAErr, (LPSTR)"recv()");
      /* exit recv()loop on any error */
      break;
    } else if (nRet == 0) { /* other side closed socket */
```

```
        /* quit if server closed connection */
        break;
      } else {
        /* update byte counter */
        cbTotalRcvd += nRet;
      }
      cbLeftToRecv = cbTotalToRecv - cbTotalRcvd;
    }
    return (cbTotalRcvd);
  } /* end RecvData()*/

  /*---------------------------------------------------------------
   * Function: DoStats()
   *
   * Description: Display data transfer rate
   */
  void DoStats (long lByteCount, long lStartTime, LPCONNDATA lpstConn) {
    LONG dByteRate;
    LONG lMSecs;

    /* calculate data transfer rate, and display */
    lMSecs = (LONG) GetTickCount()- lStartTime;
    if (lMSecs <= 55)
      lMSecs = 27;  /* about half of 55Msec PC clock resolution */

    if (lByteCount > 0L) {
      if (lpstConn) {
        wsprintf (achTempBuf,
        "<<< socket: %d disconnected from %s\n",
          lpstConn->hSock,
          inet_ntoa(lpstConn->stRmtName.sin_addr));
        _lwrite(hLogFile, achTempBuf, strlen(achTempBuf));
      }
      dByteRate = (lByteCount/lMSecs); /* data rate (bytes/Msec) */
      wsprintf (achTempBuf,
        "%ld bytes in %ld.%ld seconds (%ld.%ld Kbytes/sec)\n",
        lByteCount,
        lMSecs/1000, lMSecs%1000,
        (dByteRate*1000)/1024, (dByteRate*1000)%1024);
      SetDlgItemText (hWinMain, IDC_DATA_RATE, achTempBuf);
      if (hLogFile != HFILE_ERROR)
```

```
      _lwrite (hLogFile, achTempBuf, strlen(achTempBuf));
  }
} /* end DoStats()*/

/*----------------------------------------------------------------
 * Function: NewConn()
 *
 * Description: Create a new socket structure and put in list
 */
LPCONNDATA NewConn (SOCKET hSock, PSOCKADDR_IN pstRmtName) {
  int nAddrSize = sizeof(SOCKADDR);
  LPCONNDATA lpstConnTmp, lpstConn = (LPCONNDATA)0;
  HLOCAL hSockData;
  /* allocate memory for the new socket structure */
  hSockData = LocalAlloc (LMEM_ZEROINIT, sizeof(SOCKDATA));

  if (hSockData != 0) {
    /* lock it down and link it into the list */
    lpstConn = LocalLock(hSockData);

    if (!lpstConnHead) {
      lpstConnHead = lpstConn;
    } else {
      for (lpstConnTmp = lpstConnHead;
           lpstConnTmp && lpstConnTmp->lpstNext;
           lpstConnTmp = lpstConnTmp->lpstNext);
      lpstConnTmp->lpstNext = lpstConn;
    }

    /* initialize socket structure */
    lpstConn->hSock = hSock;
    _fmemcpy ((LPSTR)&(lpstConn->stRmtName),
              (LPSTR)pstRmtName, sizeof(SOCKADDR));
    lpstConn->lStartTime = GetTickCount();

    /* log the new connection */
    if (hLogFile != HFILE_ERROR) {
      wsprintf(achTempBuf,
        ">>> socket: %d connected from %s\n", hSock,
        inet_ntoa(lpstConn->stRmtName.sin_addr));
      _lwrite(hLogFile, achTempBuf, strlen(achTempBuf));
```

```
    }
  } else {
    MessageBox (hWinMain, "Unable allocate memory for connection",
      "LocalAlloc()Error", MB_OK | MB_ICONASTERISK);
  }
  return (lpstConn);
} /* end NewConn()*/

/*-----------------------------------------------------------------
 * Function: FindConn()
 *
 * Description: Find socket structure for connection
 */
LPCONNDATA FindConn (SOCKET hSock) {
  LPCONNDATA lpstConnTmp;

  for (lpstConnTmp = lpstConnHead;
       lpstConnTmp;
       lpstConnTmp = lpstConnTmp->lpstNext) {
    if (lpstConnTmp->hSock == hSock)
      break;
  }
  return (lpstConnTmp);
} /* end FindConn()*/

/*-----------------------------------------------------------------
 * Function: RemoveConn()
 *
 * Description: Free the memory for socket structure
 */
void RemoveConn (LPCONNDATA lpstConn) {
  LPCONNDATA lpstConnTmp;
  HLOCAL hSock;

  if (lpstConn == lpstConnHead) {
    lpstConnHead = lpstConn->lpstNext;
  } else {
    for (lpstConnTmp = lpstConnHead;
         lpstConnTmp;
         lpstConnTmp = lpstConnTmp->lpstNext) {
```

```
      if (lpstConnTmp->lpstNext == lpstConn)
        lpstConnTmp->lpstNext = lpstConn->lpstNext;
    }
  }
  hSock = LocalHandle(lpstConn);
  LocalUnlock (hSock);
  LocalFree (hSock);
} /* end RemoveConn()*/
```

We use the three functions above—`NewConn( )`, `FindConn( )`, and `RemoveConn( )`—to create, search, and maintain our linked list of connection structures. The dynamic nature of this list allows the server application to support any number of connections, which can come and go in any order. It is a very flexible design.

select( )

The `select( )` function is the synchronous counterpart of `WSAAsyncSelect( )`. As the name indicates, the WinSock authors modeled `WSAAsyncSelect( )` after `select( )` and added capabilities as they adapted it to the message-driven environment.

Like `WSAAsyncSelect( )`, `select( )` is a general-purpose state detection and reporting function. It can detect all the states that `WSAAsyncSelect( )` can detect, although it does not provide the same fine resolution. In order to determine some socket states, you must interpret the results of a call to `select()` in the context of the current socket state.

Unlike `WSAAsyncSelect( )`, `select( )` takes sets of sockets as input parameters each time you call it, and it blocks. It is a "socket multiplexer," which means it allows you to detect the socket state of more than one socket simultaneously. These may be any combination of datagram or stream sockets, in blocking or nonblocking modes.

The `select( )` function operates synchronously, which means the results come when the function returns. It is a Berkeley Sockets–compatible function, so its use offers the advantage of source code portability. Notice that the type name "fd_set" reveals the BSD heritage where a socket is equivalent to a file handle. An "fd_set" refers to a "file descriptor set" in Berkeley. This is unlike WinSock, where sockets are not necessarily equivalent to file handles. Another significant difference is that the fd_sets in WinSock are opaque data structures instead of a set of bit flags. You must use the WinSock macros to manipulate them.

```
/* returns # sockets ready, 0 on timeout, or SOCKET_ERROR */
int PASCAL FAR select
    (int nfds,      /* not used, included for compatibility */
    fd_set FAR *readfds,  /* sockets to check for readability */
    fd_set FAR *writefds, /* sockets to check for writability */
    fd_set FAR *exceptfds,/* sockets to check for exceptions */
    struct timeval FAR *timeout); /* time to block, or NULL */
```

nfds: WinSock ignores this value. It was retained for compatibility with the Berkeley Sockets prototype (where this value is the upper limit on the number of socket descriptors in each `fd_set` to check).

readfds: set of socket descriptors you want to check for the **readable** state. It may also indicate **close pending**.

writefds: set of socket descriptors you want to check for the **writable** state. It may also indicate the **connected** state.

exceptfds: set of socket descriptors you want to check for the **out-of-band data readable** state or an error condition

timeout: pointer to `timeval` structure that contains timeout for `select( )` NULL pointer blocks indefinitely and timeout of zero returns immediately (nonblocking)

The `select( )` function blocks when the *timeout* value (in the `timeval` structure) is nonzero. It will return immediately—that is, act as a nonblocking function—if the *timeout* value is zero. This does not mean *timeout* is a NULL pointer. If it is, then `select( )` blocks indefinitely. When it blocks, `select( )` acts like any other blocking function: The WinSock DLL calls the current blocking hook function; `WSAIsBlocking( )` returns true; and all other functions, except `WSACancelBlockingCall( ),` fail with WSAEINPROGRESS.

On timeout, `select( )` returns zero. The contents of the readfds, writefds, or exceptfds input/output argument structures are indeterminate. You should always reinitialize these arguments before you call `select( )` again.

On failure, `select( )` returns SOCKET_ERROR. There are only a few possible errors, none of which reports the socket state of any of the sockets in the input arguments. The most significant errors are WSAEINTR and WSAEINPROGRESS, which are relevant to any applications that use blocking operations, as we describe in Chapter 5, "Operation Modes."

On success, `select( )` returns the number of sockets whose current state matches a designated state(s). So, for example, if you put three different sockets in readfds, writefds, and exceptfds socket sets and `select( )` returns the value 2, then you have to figure out which two sockets have which socket state. Since each fd_set can indicate multiple states, they are overloaded with meaning. In addition to the work you must do to determine which fd_set contains which socket(s) upon return from `select( )`, you also need to infer which state they indicate. You can do so by keeping track of the current state of each socket in your application.

Obviously, using `select( )` involves more work than `WSAAsyncSelect( )`: more work for you in coding—which increases the potential for bugs—and more work for the system during execution.

How Do You Use select( )?

Here is a short description of the steps to follow in order to use the `select( )` function. This description reflects what the code example at the end of this section does.

1. With the FD_ZERO( ) macro, initialize each readfds, writefds, or exceptfds fd_set that you need to check.
2. With the FD_SET( ) macro, add each socket you want to check to each fd_set of interest.
3. Initialize the *timeout* timeval structure to the timeout period you want, or use a NULL pointer if you want `select( )` to block indefinitely.
4. Call `select( )`.
5. If `select( )` returns a value other than zero (which indicates a timeout) or SOCKET_ERROR (which indicates failure), then that is the number of sockets that have reached one of the designated states. Check each fd_set and socket with the FD_ISSET( ) macro until you find as many matches as the count returned from `select( )`.
6. Infer the socket state of each socket you find (based either on fd_set or on the socket state variable you maintain, or by an I/O call to WinSock), service the sockets appropriately, and return to step 1.

Notice that you need to reinitialize all fd_sets *every time* you call `select( )`. This is essential since `select( )` modifies the contents of each fd_set to report the results. You should initialize the fd_sets whether or not the `select( )` call succeeds. Unlike Berkeley Sockets, WinSock does *not* guarantee the fd_sets will remain unmodified if `select( )` fails.

select( ) Macros

As mentioned already, the fd_set input parameters are opaque data constructs. Just as the data type of a socket handle is of no concern to you as a WinSock application developer, it is the same with a set of sockets. For the sake of portability of your application, you should *not* try to manipulate the sets directly. The WinSock header file provides a collection of macros that do the "dirty work" for you and guarantee portability. Here is a list of them with a brief description of each:

- FD_CLR(): removes a socket handle from an fd_set
- FD_ISSET(): checks if a socket handle is a member of an fd_set
- FD_SET(): adds a socket handle to the fd_set
- FD_ZERO(): clears all contents of the fd_set

We will provide a prototype of each here. This is inappropriate since they are macros and not function calls, but it conveys the way to use them effectively since they take input parameters, and one of them has a boolean return value.

FD_CLR( )

```
void FD_CLR (
     SOCKET s,                  /* handle of socket to remove */
     fd_set FAR *fdset)        /* socket set to remove it from */
```

s: handle of socket to remove from the socket set

fd_set: pointer to socket set from which to remove the socket

Use the FD_CLR( ) macro to remove a socket from a socket set. This macro is usually not needed.

FD_ISSET( )

```
BOOL FD_ISSET (
     SOCKET s,                  /* handle of socket to check for */
     fd_set FAR *fdset)          /* socket set in which to look */
```

s: handle of socket for which you are looking in the socket set

fd_set: pointer to socket set in which you are looking for the socket

FD_ISSET( ) returns TRUE if *s* is in the *fd_set*. You use FD_ISSET( ) after a call to `select( )` succeeds to detect whether a socket is present in a socket set.

A successful call to `select( )` returns the number of sockets in each of the socket sets readfds, writefds, or exceptfds you provided that match the states they indicate. You need to use FD_ISSET( ) on each socket set with each socket until you detect the same number of matches as the number `select( )` returned.

FD_SET( )

```
void FD_SET (
    SOCKET s,                /* handle of socket to add to set */
    fd_set FAR *fdset)       /* socket set into which to add it*/
```

s: handle of socket you want to add to socket set

fd_set: pointer to socket set into which to add the socket

FD_SET( ) simply adds a socket handle to a socket set. Because `select( )` uses the fd_sets to provide results upon return as well as for input parameters, you must add the sockets you want to the fd_set(s) before every call to `select( )`.

FD_ZERO( )

```
void FD_ZERO (
     fd_set FAR *fdset) /* socket set to zero out */
```

fd_set: pointer to socket set to initialize with zeroes.

The FD_ZERO( ) macro initializes an fd_set to the NULL set (no sockets). You should use this on every fd_set you use as an input parameter, before you initialize a fd_set with the socket descriptor(s) of interest.

select( ) Input Parameters

The *readfds*, *writefds*, and *exceptfds* input parameters each point to a set of socket descriptors for `select( )` to examine. Each fd_set is equivalent to one or more socket states or state transitions. For example, one or more socket sets can indicate the following states on one or more of its sockets:

- *readfds:* indicates **readable** or **close pending** socket states
- *writefds:* indicates **writable** or **connected** socket states

- *exceptfds:* indicates **out-of-band data readable** socket state, or an error

Each socket set can contain the same or different socket handles. `select( )` (detected with FD_ISSET( )) alters the contents of each fd_set to provide the function results. A NULL value for any fd_set indicates you do not want to check the state(s) on any socket(s).

When an fd_set contains a socket upon return from `select( )`, the state it indicates depends on the socket state beforehand. Since `select( )` is a synchronous function, it is not difficult to keep track of which state it might indicate. Even if you do not know, trying an appropriate I/O function with the socket can give you an indication of the socket state.

readfds

If a socket is in the listening state and *readfds* is set, then it indicates the presence of an incoming connection request. In other words, a call to `accept( )` should succeed immediately on that socket.

If a socket is connected and *readfds* is set for a socket, then it indicates that the socket is **readable** (there is data available to receive). In other words, when *readfds* is set on that socket, `recv( )` or `recvfrom( )` should succeed immediately. This includes out-of-band data, if the socket option SO_OOBINLINE is enabled. However, SO_OOBINLINE is disabled by default.

If the remote end has closed a connection (on a stream socket), then *readfds* indicates the **close pending** state. The subsequent call to `recv( )` or `recvfrom( )` will return zero if the remote end closed the connection gracefully, or fail with WSAECONNRESET if it aborted the connection.

writefds

If a socket has a connection pending after calling `connect( )` with a non-blocking socket and *writefds* is set, then it indicates the **connected** state (i.e., the outgoing connection attempt has completed successfully).

In all other cases, when *writefds* is set for a socket, then it indicates that the socket is **writable**. In this case either `send( )` or `sendto( )` should complete immediately and with success.

exceptfds

The *exceptfds* indicates an exceptional condition: the **out-of-band data readable** state or an error condition.

If a socket has the SO_OOBINLINE socket option disabled (the default setting), then you may have "out-of-band" data available for reading. You can receive it by calling `recv( )` or `recvfrom( )` with *flag* set to MSG_OOB. In general, you should avoid using OOB data in your application. See the "Out-of-Band Data" section in this chapter for more information.

When *exceptfds* indicates an error condition, it typically indicates only one of two errors: failure of a nonblocking `connect( )` or TCP keep-alive timeout, but a robust application should be prepared to handle any error. For information on TCP keep-alives, look at the SO_KEEPALIVE socket option in Chapter 9, "Socket Information and Control."

Ideally, you should be able to retrieve the error that an *exceptfds* indicates for a socket with a call to `getsockopt( )` SO_ERROR. Unfortunately, support of the SO_ERROR socket option is not consistent in all WinSock implementations, so you may need an alternate method for error retrieval if it fails.

You cannot rely on the return from `WSAGetLastError( )`, since it simply reports the last error on the socket resulting from a function failure previous to your call to `select( )`. The only viable alternative is to call an I/O function (like `send( )` or `recv( )`) and watch it fail, and *then* call `WSAGetLastError( )` to find out why. This is not foolproof, since it may cause a different error than `select( )` detected, but it is as accurate as possible without `getsockopt( )` SO_ERROR support.

timeval Structure

If you want `select( )` to block until one or more of the conditions are met on the specified sockets, then you need to set a nonzero timeout value. In that case, you need to initialize the timeval structure with the amount of time you want `select( )` to block. The increments are seconds and microseconds. Here's what the timeval structure looks like:

```
struct timeval {
      long tv_sec;          /* seconds */
      long tv_usec;         /* milliseconds */
}
```

tv_sec: seconds for timeout

tv_usec: microseconds for timeout (limited to minimum of 51 *milli*seconds on IBM PC-compatible systems)

With a NULL pointer to the timeval structure, `select( )` blocks indefinitely until a relevant event occurs on one or more of the sockets in each socket set.

With a nonzero timeout value, `select( )` blocks for the time specified. `select( )` returns zero to indicate a timeout if none of the relevant events occurs on the sockets in each socket set.

With a timeout value of zero, `select( )` operates as a nonblocking function that returns immediately whether or not it succeeds. In this case the WinSock DLL does not call the blocking hook function. If none of the states is true for the socket sets provided, `select( )` returns a 0 value, as it does in the event of any other timeout.

Note that the timeval structure is defined as a constant, so WinSock does not modify its contents in any way. This differs from Berkeley Sockets, where the contents of *timeout* is indeterminate upon return from `select( )`. Either way, the hopeful macros `timerisset` and `timercmp` are useless. The `timerclear` macro is useful, however, when you want to initialize the contents of a timeval structure to zero.

Also note that the system clock in an IBM PC-compatible system only provides 51 *milli*second resolution (that's 51 thousandths of a second). As a result, the shortest timeout you can hope to get is 51,000 microseconds (a microsecond is a millionth of a second).

Don't Use select( ) as a Timer

In Berkeley Sockets, it is not uncommon to use `select( )` as a timer. To do so, you specify NULL sets for the *readfds*, *writefds*, and *exceptfds* input parameters with a nonzero *timeout* value. Although the Windows Sockets specification does not say you *cannot* do this, it does not say you can either. Hence, this is an optional feature of Windows Sockets implementations.

A call to `select( )` with NULL fd_sets may fail (with the WSAEINVAL error). For this reason, and because the WinAPI provides timer functions, we recommend that you avoid trying to use this side-effect "feature" of `select( )`.

Beware of Timeout Zero

It is possible to make `select( )` a nonblocking function by specifying a zero timeout value in the timeval structure you point to in the timeout input parameter. This is okay to do occasionally from your application, but it suffers the same dangers that any nonblocking function does if not used properly.

If you call `select( )` with a zero timeout in a tight loop (in 16-bit Windows) without yielding, your application will starve other applications of CPU time. In other words, your application will not be "friendly." Not only will other applications suffer, but your application users won't be happy either; they won't be able to raise any response from your application's commands.

It is usually better to set a (positive) timeout value to let your application yield automatically (by calling the blocking hook function).

Code Example

The following pseudocode example illustrates how to use `select( )` in an application. It is rather simple since we are checking a single socket only, not multiple sockets, and we are not checking for the writable state:

```
#define BUF_SIZE  1460
SOCKET hSock;      /* socket handle */
fd_set stReadFDS; /* select()  "file descriptor set" structures */
fd_set stXcptFDS;
struct timeval stTimeOut;  /* for select()timeout (none) */
char   achInBuf[BUF_SIZE]; /* input buffer */
int     nRet ;             /* work variable */

/* now wait for "readability", or an error (exception) */

/* clear all sockets from FDS structure, then put our socket
 *  into the socket descriptor set */
FD_ZERO(&stReadFDS);
FD_ZERO(&stXcptFDS);
FD_SET(hSock, &stReadFDS);
FD_SET(hSock, &stXcptFDS);

/* initialize the timeout value to 1 second */
stTimeOut.tv_sec  = 1;
stTimeOut.tv_usec = 0;

/* call select() to check for readability until timeout */
nRet = select(-1, &stReadFDS, NULL, &stXcptFDS, &stTimeOut);

if (wRet == SOCKET_ERROR) {
      <report error to user>        /* select() failed */
      goto AppExit;
} else if (nRet != 0) {
      /* check for exception first */
      if (FD_ISSET (hSock, &stXcptFDS)) {
            <check for OOB data, or getsockopt() SO_ERROR>
            goto AppExit;
```

```
        }
        if (!(FD_ISSET (hSock, &stReadFDS))) {
              /* This should never happen!!!  If select returned
               *  a positive value, something should be set in
               *  either our exception or our read socket set  */
              goto AppExit;    /* bail! */
        }
}
/* if we're here we know our socket was in fdread socket
 *  set, so we should be able to recv() data from it  */
nRet = recv(hSock, achInBuf, BUF_SIZE, 0);
if (nRet == SOCKET_ERROR) {
  <report error to user>
} else {
  <process data we just read into input buffer>
  return (0);           /* success */
}

AppExit:
return (SOCKET_ERROR);  /* failure */
```

If we had checked multiple sockets, we would have needed to save the descriptors we were checking before we called `select( )`. We could store them in an array of socket, for instance, although if each fd_set had a different collection of sockets we would need an array for each fd_set we wanted to keep track of.

Upon a successful return from `select( )`, we would then need a loop—or a loop within a loop if we had separate arrays—to check for each socket in each fd_set. We would loop until FD_ISSET uncovered as many matches as `select( )` indicated in its return value.

Notice again the tedious coding required to use `select( )`. But more important, consider the work a processor must do. You can imagine that in a polling loop servicing multiple sockets simultaneously this apparent inefficiency would reduce application performance, and overall system performance. `WSAAsyncSelect( )` is far more efficient, and the code involved is simple and elegant.

Peeking at Data

Most applications need to detect data arrival, the **readable** socket state. For some applications, however, knowing that there is data to read is not enough.

They need to know *how much data* is available, or they may even need to *look at the data,* before they remove it from the incoming data queue.

Both operations are possible in Windows Sockets. In both cases, you use Berkeley Sockets–compatible function calls. For detecting how much data is available, use `ioctlsocket( )` with the FIONREAD command. To copy incoming data into an application buffer for examination without removing it from the network system buffers, you use `recv( )` or `recvfrom( )` with the MSG_PEEK flag.

We do not recommend the use of either FIONREAD or MSG_PEEK. Any "peek read" operation is inherently inefficient, and if you use them improperly they can cause your application to fail. Your application may fail even if you code correctly, since some WinSock implementations do not support the MSG_PEEK flag.

Your application will work faster, and it will be more portable and more robust and reliable if you simply use `recv( )` and `recvfrom( )` to read data directly into your own application buffers for processing, rather than trying to examine it while it is in the network-system buffers.

ioctlsocket( ) FIONREAD Command

The `ioctlsocket( )` function can detect "readability" on a socket with the FIONREAD command and provide the number of bytes pending for `recv( )` or `recvfrom( )`. To detect pending data with `ioctlsocket( )`, the *cmd* input parameter must have the value FIONREAD.

It always returns immediately whether or not data is pending, with a blocking or a nonblocking socket. If `ioctlsocket( )` returns a value of zero to indicate success, the buffer that *argp* points to will contain the number of bytes that can be read atomically (i.e., in a single call to `recv( )` or `recvfrom( )`) from socket *s*. If no data is available, it returns zero in *argp*.

For a datagram socket this value is the number of bytes *in the first datagram* available for reading. It is *not* a total number of bytes for all pending datagrams.

For a stream socket this value is typically the total number of bytes queued for reading on the socket. But beware, because this is *not* guaranteed. It is a data stream, which means message boundaries are not preserved. It also means you cannot reliably impose message boundaries by trying to wait until a certain number of bytes arrives. You cannot assume that the number of bytes sent will exactly correspond to the number of bytes `ioctlsocket( )` FIONREAD will show at the receiving end.

The value that `ioctlsocket()` FIONREAD reports may be less than the full amount buffered if your data straddles a network-system buffer boundary. If your application does not call `recv( )` or `recvfrom( )` to remove data from the buffer in this case, it will fail. The data you expect has been received, but `ioctlsocket( )` FIONREAD will never report the full amount. This is a deadlock situation that illustrates one of the many potential problems with peeking at data.

For more information on the `ioctlsocket( )`, refer to Chapter 9, "Socket Information and Control."

recv( ) with MSG_PEEK Flag

You can use `recv( )` or `recvfrom( )` with the MSG_PEEK flag to detect data availability and copy the data into an application buffer without dequeueing it from a network-system buffer (for more information on `recv( )` and `recvfrom( )`, see Chapter 4, "Network Application Mechanics").

When you put MSG_PEEK in the *flags* input parameter, `recv( )` or `recvfrom( )` will return the number of bytes pending for read without removing the data from the network-system buffers. If you provide a valid pointer to a buffer, you can also use it to "peek" at the data by copying it into the application buffer. This can help if your application needs to see the data before it knows what to do with it. Since the data remains in the network-system buffer, a subsequent call to `recv( )` or `recvfrom( )` will yield the same data (or possibly more on a nonblocking socket).

Note that the MSG_PEEK flag can be combined with the MSG_OOB flag (using a bitwise-OR operand) to combine their functionality.

Beware: If you use the MSG_PEEK flag on a socket that is registered for FD_READ notification and there is data available, the WinSock DLL will post an FD_READ message. In other words, `recv( )` and `recvfrom( )` operate as reenabling functions even when you use the MSG_PEEK flag. The message generated will be extra (i.e., there may be an FD_READ message for which there is no data to receive). But the `recv( )` call in your FD_READ message handler can gracefully recover from a failure with a WSAEWOULDBLOCK error, as it should anyway, this will not cause a problem.

Nonetheless, we discourage the use of MSG_PEEK. It is inefficient since it causes the network system to copy data into your buffers twice: once to peek and another time for real. It decreases data throughput since it leaves data in the system buffers, which may prevent the arrival of new data. It is unreliable since some WinSock implementations do not support it. And it is unnecessary anyway, since your application can always create a buffer into which to read data for examination; if you have to copy the data from there into another buffer, this is not a big deal. Do not use MSG_PEEK; your application will be better for it.

Out-of-Band Data

Some applications need to send high-priority data that can "jump the queue" at the receiving end so that the receiving application can give it immediate attention. This is the purpose of *out-of-band data* (also known as *OOB data*), available on stream sockets.

Some standard application protocols use out-of-band data, like Telnet and Rlogin. For instance, when the remote end is sending a large amount of data, the receiver may send a signal "out-of-band" to ask sender to stop sending. The application protocol for some network database applications use OOB data to cancel pending queries. In general, though, applications don't use the out-of-band data facility. As we'll see shortly, there are some good reasons to avoid it.

WinSock has a number of mechanisms for dealing with OOB data, some of which behave differently according to how the SO_OOBINLINE socket option is currently set:

- MSG_OOB I/O flag sends and receives out-of-band data.
- `setsockopt( )` SO_OOBINLINE option enables and disables "inline" receipt of out-of-band data (it is disabled by default). See Chapter 9, "Socket Information and Control," for information on SO_OOBINLINE.
- FD_OOB `WSAAsyncSelect( )` message provides asynchronous notification of out-of-band data arrival (when SO_OOBINLINE is disabled).
- `select( )` *exceptfds* provides synchronous notification of out-of-band data arrival (when SO_OOBINLINE is disabled).
- `ioctlsocket( )` SIOCATMARK command detects the location of out-of-band data in a data stream (when SO_OOBINLINE is *enabled*).

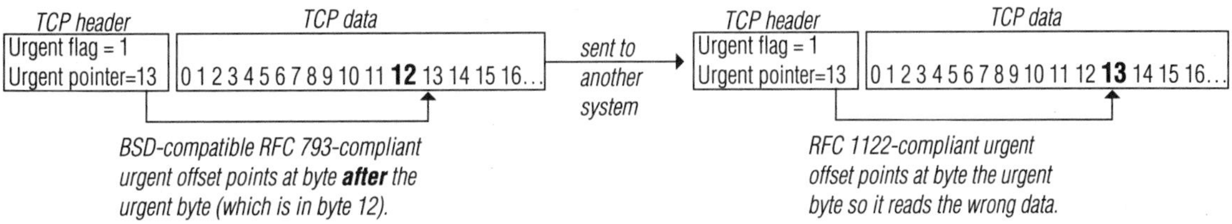

Figure 6-6 Illustrates how an application can read the wrong urgent data if it is sent from a system with an incompatible urgent data pointer interpretation.

Earlier in this chapter we describe both `WSAAsyncSelect( )` FD_OOB notification and `select( )`'s *exceptfds*. In the remainder of this section we highlight some OOB data issues, describe `ioctlsocket( )` SIOCATMARK, and illustrate how to use it in an application.

TCP Limitations

For TCP, "out-of-band" data is always sent "in-band" within the normal data stream as "urgent data," and there is only *one byte*. TCP does not have an independent transmission channel for urgent data, so the concept of out-of-band transmission is an abstraction. It is out-of-band only to the extent that the TCP header marks it so the receiving end can identify its location for special handling. The urgent byte is removed from the data stream if SO_OOBINLINE is disabled, and you read it by calling `recv( )` or `recvfrom( )` with *flag* set to MSG_OOB.

The use of a logically independent transmission channel sounds feasible, but it does not work well in practice. There are problems with OOB data as provided by TCP, because it tries to use the same data stream for both normal and OOB data.

Apart from the logistical problem of OOB data within a data stream, Section 2.2.3 in the v1.1 WinSock specification highlights another significant reason to avoid out-of-band data. The original TCP specification (RFC 793) conflicts with the "Hosts Requirements" (RFC 1122) as to how a TCP packet's urgent pointer should indicate the location of urgent data within the packet. RFC 793 says the urgent pointer indicates the byte *after* the last urgent data byte, whereas RFC 1122 says it points to the *last* urgent data byte itself. If the sender and the receiver do not agree, then the receiver reads the wrong OOB data (as illustrated in Figure 6-6).

You can avoid this problem in your application if your urgent data is unique. In this case you'll know when the data you're reading is not urgent data, so you can adjust your buffer pointer back or forward one byte to find the correct data. If your urgent data is not unique or if you do not know the value, then you will need to read the bytes on either side of the urgent data to try to determine which byte is really the end of the urgent data the sender intended your application to receive. For either method, you'll want SO_OOBINLINE enabled to preserve the urgent data context (e.g., the bytes on either side of the byte you read).

However, OOB data with TCP has other problems that do not have viable solutions. If more than one TCP packet arrives indicating urgent data, the receiving network system may preserve only the last urgent byte or marker. The Windows Sockets specification does not require a network system to preserve earlier OOB data. As a result, if your application does not read urgent data before subsequent urgent data arrives, then the earlier urgent data will be lost. Actually, with SO_OOBINLINE enabled, only the marker is lost (the data remains in the stream). But with SO_OOBINLINE disabled, the single byte of urgent data will be overwritten.

The bottom line is that using out-of-band data in an application is problematic. You should avoid creating an application that relies on out-of-band data transmission on a stream socket that uses TCP. Ultimately, the only way to avoid problems with transmission of high-priority data is to send it on a separate socket, independent of your data. This is similar to how the FTP application protocol works (as specified by RFC 959). It reserves a "control connection" for sending commands and responses "out-of-band," and it establishes a separate connection each time a command requires data transfer. See the sample client FTP application in Chapter 7 for an illustration of how this operates.

ioctlsocket( ) SIOCATMARK Command

With SO_OOBINLINE enabled, an application needs to check for out-of-band data arrival with the `ioctlsocket( )` function's SIOCATMARK command.

To detect pending out-of-band data with `ioctlsocket( )`, the *cmd* input parameter must have the value SIOCATMARK. If `ioctlsocket( )` returns a value of zero to indicate success, the buffer that *argp* points to will contain FALSE if there *is* out-of-band data to be read, or TRUE if there is *not* any out-of-band data to be read.

Confusing? Yes! Even more so considering that although `ioctlsocket( )` is supposed to be the equivalent of Berkeley Socket's `ioctl( )` function, these SIOCATMARK results are exactly the opposite of Berkeley's.

The overhead involved with using SIOCATMARK to detect out-of-band data is considerable too. With SO_OOBINLINE enabled, you cannot use `select( )` or `WSAAsyncSelect( )` to detect out-of-band data arrival. The only alternative is to poll with `ioctlsocket( )` SIOCATMARK between each call to `recv( )` or `recvfrom( )`.

Code Example

The following pseudocode shows how to poll for out-of-band data in a `recv( )` loop. It assumes that `hSock` is a TCP socket and that you called `setsockopt( )` to enable SO_OOBINLINE (which is disabled, by default). There is *much* confusion about how this works, *especially* among WinSock providers. We do not recommend its use.

```
#define BUF_SIZE 1460
char achInBuf[BUF_SIZE];
char cOOBData;
u_long lOobUnFlag = FALSE;
SOCKET hSock;  /* must be a TCP socket w/ SO_OOBINLINE enabled */
int nRet, I;
/* check for OOB data preceding mark */
nRet = ioctlsocket (hSock, SIOCATMARK, &lOobUnFlag);
if (wRet == SOCKET_ERROR) {
      <report error to user>
      goto RecvDataExit;
}
while (!lOobUnFlag) { /* if FALSE, we have OOB pending! */

      /* With OOB pending, call recv( ) to read data up to the
       *  OOB mark (indicated when SIOCATMARK is TRUE again).
       *  In this example, as is common, we do not preserve
       *  the data preceding the OOB data mark. */
      nRet = recv (hSock, BUF_SIZE, achInBuf, 0);
      if (nRet == SOCKET_ERROR) {
            if (WSAGetLastError != WSAEWOULDBLOCK) {
            <report error to user>
            goto RecvDataExit;
      } else {
            return (0);  /* no non-OOB bytes read */
      }
}

< no OOB Data pending, so go about normal business >
<     of reading and processing normal data        >
return (0);  /* success */

RecvDataExit:
  return (SOCKET_ERROR);  /* failure */
```

The Listening State

The getsockopt( ) SO_ACCEPTCONN is an odd duck. Unlike almost all the other options, it does not indicate the status of a socket option that setsockopt( ) controls; you cannot use SO_ACCEPTCONN with the `setsockopt( )` function. Rather, it indicates the socket state. Upon return, the contents of the *optval* buffer is TRUE if a stream socket is in the listening state (see Chapter 9, "Socket Information and Control" for more information on the `getsockopt( )` function).

This option has very limited usefulness, since you already know if a socket is listening if the `listen( )` function succeeds. However, there is one case (rare indeed) when you might want to use SO_ACCEPTCONN. If your server does not call `accept( )` immediately upon detection of a connection request (perhaps because it can only service one socket at a time), then the queue for connection requests waiting to be accepted could perhaps be filled.

In this instance, you could use the SO_ACCEPTCONN option to check whether the listening socket is (still) listening. If not, then you can infer that your pending connection queue is full and that your server is rejecting connection requests. Although, if your server cannot `accept( )` any of the pending connections, there is not much you can do to remedy the problem. So what's the use? The bottom line is that few (if any) applications use `getsockopt( )` SO_ACCEPTCONN.

7 Sample Application and Library

In This Chapter:

- Sample FTP Client
- Sample Library
- WinSock x.h

People love chopping wood. In this activity one immediately sees results.

Albert Einstein

You can learn a lot by reading about WinSock, but the only way to become proficient is to use it. In other words, you need to write a WinSock application, or two or three, before you can call yourself a WinSock programmer. Similarly, a book that teaches about WinSock cannot teach entirely by description. The book must contain working code samples to illustrate concepts concretely. Ideally, the examples should demonstrate a *useful* application of the concepts described. That is the purpose of this chapter.

This chapter presents the source code for a complete WinSock application that demonstrates many of the concepts presented throughout the book and provides practical code that you can build upon in your own applications. We have a client WinSock application that implements the File Transfer Protocol (FTP), as described by RFC 959. It uses the asynchronous operation mode to provide file transfer to and from an FTP server application.

This chapter also includes the source code to the functions we use in our FTP client, and in other samples throughout the book. Most of these functions simplify common procedures that use a number of WinSock function calls. Others are API add-ons that frequently come in handy. We provide a short description of each as well as pointers to where they are used in our code examples.

Sample FTP Client

Sharing data is the fundamental motivation for networking computers. It is not surprising that a major portion of Internet traffic is file transfer protocol (FTP). File transfer is a relatively crude way to share data, compared to the elegance of something like Sun's Network File System (NFS), which creates virtual drives. But despite its simplicity, FTP is an effective way to share data between heterogeneous network hosts.

As we described in Chapter 3, FTP is considered part and parcel of the TCP/IP suite. Jonathan B. Postel and Joyce K. Reynolds describe the FTP in RFC 959. They provide a lucid description of a simple and generic, yet rich and powerful, application protocol for sending and receiving files between network hosts.

Our implementation of the FTP protocol in our sample client application gives us the chance to demonstrate many of the points we describe in the book. This sample illustrates

- bulk data transfer on a TCP socket in asynchronous operation mode
- reading variable length records on a TCP socket
- an application state machine
- TCP client WinSock function sequences
- TCP server WinSock function sequences

File Transfer Protocol Overview

There are four essential elements to the file transfer protocol:

- **Control connection:** An FTP client establishes a control connection to an FTP server, and uses it to send and receive all FTP commands and replies.

- **Data connection:** Some FTP commands cause the client and server to establish a separate data connection to transfer bulk data. They close the connection when they complete the transfer.

- **FTP commands:** An FTP client sends commands to an FTP server on the control connection. Each command begins with a three- or four-letter code. Some commands also send arguments.

- **FTP replies:** An FTP server responds to the initial control connection from the client and to all subsequent FTP commands. Each reply begins with a three-digit code that indicates the status of the request. Commands have subsets of possible reply codes, and many of them vary.

The File Transfer Protocol has quite a few developer-friendly characteristics. All FTP commands and replies are sent in Telnet ASCII text, which is convenient for debugging with a network analyzer and reading output at either end of an FTP connection. Having a separate command and data stream simplifies things at the receiving end and speeds data transfers by avoiding overhead. The subset of possible replies for each command makes it possible to anticipate every outcome for each command. The FTP command and response dialog provides an orderly execution flow.

Control Connection

An FTP client establishes a TCP connection to an FTP server by connecting to the well-known port for FTP service (port 21). This initial connection between FTP client and server is called the "control connection." The client uses this connection to send all FTP commands to the server and to read all replies. Some replies may span many lines, but they are always ASCII data and never in bulk.

For bulk data, as in data files or detailed file directory listings, the FTP protocol establishes a separate "data connection" that exists for the duration of the data transfer (the close by the sending end signifies the end of file).

Data Connection

Only three commands initiate the creation of a data connection between an FTP client and server: STOR (send a file), RETR (receive a file), and LIST (receive an extended file directory). Typically, the FTP client uses the PORT command to send the local socket name (IP address and port number) to the FTP server, and the server connects back to that address and port. The client then acts as a server to accept the data connection from the server, and the data transfer begins as soon as the connection is established.

The side sending data typically initiates the close of a data connection when the data transfer is complete; receipt of the TCP <FIN> indicates end of file on the receiving side. In other words, for a STOR command the client initiates the close, and for RETR or LIST commands the server initiates the close.

FTP Commands

All FTP commands (and replies) are in network virtual terminal (NVT) ASCII text (as defined by RFC 854), and they all end with ASCII carriage-return and line-feed characters (character values 0x0A and 0x0D, respectively). Although the commands are typically upper case, RFC 959 says they should not be case sensitive, so they may be upper, lower, or mixed case. Our FTP client always sends them in upper case.

The following list contains the subset of FTP commands our sample application uses.

FTP Commands	*Description*
ABOR	Cancel any pending commands
CWD {directory}	Change current directory
DELE {filename}	Delete the specified file
LIST [[path][fileset]]	Get a detailed file directory list (uses ASCII)
PASS {password}	Send a user password (follows USER command)
PORT {socket name}	Client tells server what address to connect to for data
PWD	Get current directory
QUIT	Logout from FTP server (close control connection)
RETR {filename}	Get (receive) the specified file (uses data type set)
STOR {filename}	Put (send) the specified file (uses data type set)
TYPE {data type}	Change data type (e.g., 'I' for binary, 'A' for ASCII)
USER {username}	Send a user name to initiate login sequence

To find out the commands an FTP server supports, you can send the FTP "HELP" command, and an FTP server will reply with a list of commands. A server will also reply with the syntax of a command or a short description if you send the HELP command with another command as an argument. The following sample dialog shows the command list sent in reply to the HELP command and the responses to the "HELP ABOR" and "HELP LIST" command queries:

```
HELP
214- The following commands are recognized (* =>'s unimplemented).
   USER    PORT    STOR    MSAM*   RNTO    NLST    MKD     CDUP
   PASS    PASV    APPE    MRSQ*   ABOR    SITE    XMKD    XCUP
   ACCT*   TYPE    MLFL*   MRCP*   DELE    SYST    RMD     STOU
   SMNT*   STRU    MAIL*   ALLO    CWD     STAT    XRMD    SIZE
   REIN*   MODE    MSND*   REST    XCWD    HELP    PWD     MDTM
   QUIT    RETR    MSOM*   RNFR    LIST    NOOP    XPWD
214 Direct comments to ftp-bugs@elvis.sockets.com.
HELP ABOR
```

```
214 Syntax: ABOR (abort operation)
HELP LIST
214 Syntax: LIST [ <sp> path-name ]
```

FTP Replies

RFC 959 defines a subset of possible server replies for each FTP command. Each reply begins with a three-digit ASCII number sequence that qualifies success or failure of the command request. For most purposes, the first digit is sufficient to tell you what you need to know. There are five possible values for the first digit, and five possible meanings:

1xx: *Positive preliminary reply*, "We're okay so far, but we're not done yet."

2xx: *Positive completion reply,* "We're done, and we succeeded."

3xx: *Positive intermediate reply,* "We're okay so far, but you need to do this...."

4xx: *Transfer negative reply,* "We failed, but maybe you can try again later."

5xx: *Permanent negative completion reply,* "We failed. Don't try that again."

Here's another sample dialog to illustrate the protocol between an FTP client and server. You may notice that the textual description that follows each reply value does not match the reply text recommended by RFC 959. This is often the case on FTP servers, although the meaning is the same.

```
220 elvis.sockets.com FTP server (Version 5.60) ready.
USER bq
331 Password required for rcq.
PASS elvis lives
230 User rcq logged in.
PWD
257 "/lusers/bq" is current directory.
PORT 127,128,50,69,4,110
200 PORT command successful.
TYPE A
200 Type set to A.
LIST
150 Opening ASCII mode data connection for /bin/ls.
226 Transfer complete.
QUIT
```

In the above dialog we received the 220 reply after we established the control connection. The first 2 indicates success, and the second 2 indicates the reply is connection related. Together with the third digit, 0, the 220 reply means that the FTP server is ready to receive commands.

The first command we send is USER, which requires one argument: a valid user name. The first digit of the reply, 3, indicates we need to provide more information; the second digit, 3, indicates this reply is authentication related; and together with the third, 1, the reply means "user name is okay, but also needs a password." So we send a password.

The PASS command requires the password as an argument. We get the 230 reply, which indicates a successful login with authentication.

Our FTP client application also sends a PWD command after we log into the FTP server to "print the current working directory." The 2 reply indicates success, and the 5 indicates that the command and reply are file system related. The reply text contains the current working directory we requested, delimited by double quotes.

The next thing our log shows is that the application user requested a long remote file directory (which includes file attributes along with the file names). This request requires three FTP commands to complete: PORT, TYPE, and LIST. The PORT command tells the FTP server to which address and port to connect. The TYPE command tells the server what type of data to send (the A indicates ASCII). The LIST command uses a data connection to transfer the file directory information back to the client.

When the LIST data is transferred successfully and the server has initiated the close of the data connection, the server then sends the 226 reply to indicate that the data transfer is complete. It is possible to receive this reply before you have read all the data from the data connection. As we will see when we examine the source code later, you must not assume any coordination between the data and control sockets.

FTP Finite State Machine

Each element of the file transfer protocol is well defined, and transactions are orderly. Commands are kept separate from data, each command has a finite number of possible responses, and each reply is easily deciphered. Commands are also kept separate from one another on the control connection, since RFC 959 stipulates that

> the communication between the user and server is intended to be an alternating dialogue. As such, the user issues an FTP command and the server responds with a prompt primary reply. The user should wait for this initial primary success or failure response before sending further commands.

In other words, there can only be one command pending at any point in time. Commands should not overlap.

This finite number of well-defined elements in the file transfer protocol, and its sequential nature, allow for orderly and precise communication between an FTP client and server application. They also make FTP well suited for representation and implementation as a finite state machine. We can illustrate each FTP command and reply transaction as a simple machine.

Figure 7-1 illustrates the finite state machine for FTP transactions in its simplest form, since it focuses on individual FTP transactions on the control connection. A more complete finite state machine includes the TCP connection states for both the control and data connections, as illustrated by Figure 7-2.

We used these state machines to guide the design of our FTP client application. Our functions closely correspond with the vectors between states in our finite state machine. Here is a numbered list of our primary functions (the numbers correspond to those in Figure 7-2):

Function Name	*Description*
1) InitCtrlConn( ):	Initiate the control connection to the FTP server
2a) QueueFtpCmd( ):	Format an FTP command, and place into internal send queue
2b) SendFtpCmd( ):	Send the next FTP command in our internal send queue
3a) RecvFtpRply( ):	Read the reply from the FTP server
3b) ProcessFtpRply( ):	Determine what the reply means and what to do next
4) InitDataConn( ):	Initialize passive data connection for FTP server to connect to
5) AcceptDataConn( ):	Accept the connection request from the FTP server
6a) SendData( ):	Send data on a data connection
6b) RecvData( ):	Receive data from a data connection
7) EndData( ):	Clean up a data connection and display transfer statistics
8) CloseConn( ):	Close a connection (control or data)

The most important characteristic of our sample application is that it keeps track of the application state. Our application is self-aware, meaning that at any point during execution we can determine what we can and cannot do. This allows us to avoid making WinSock calls that will fail out of the proper context, and we can notify users when they try something inappropriate.

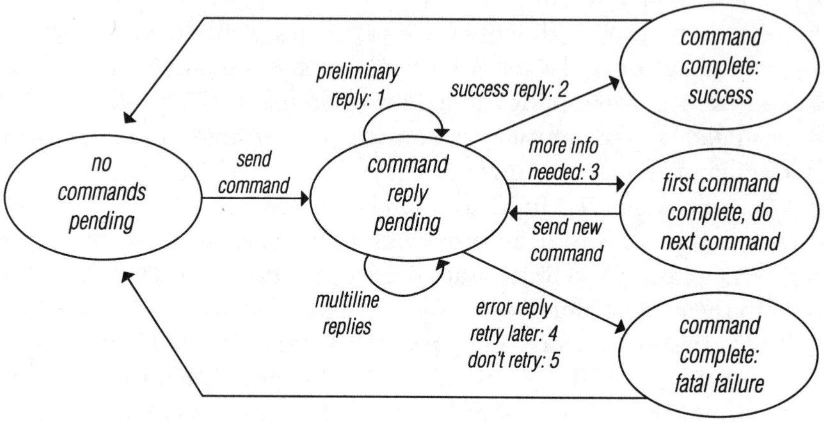

Figure 7-1 Simple finite state machine for FTP commands and replies.

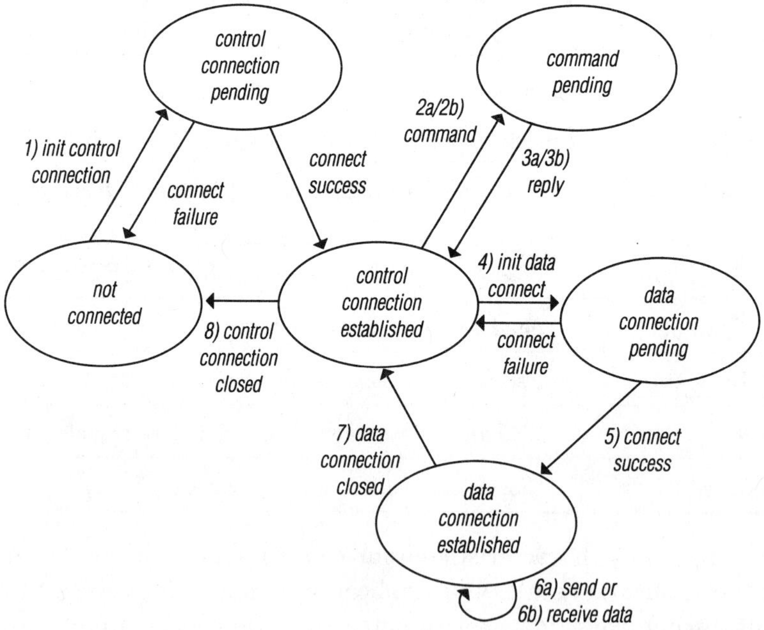

Figure 7-2 Finite state machine for FTP connections, commands, and replies.

Keeping track of application state is important in any application, but it is most important in applications that use asynchronous operation mode as ours does. It is also more difficult to do in asynchronous mode, but it need not complicate an application. As we point out in our description of our FTP client application source code, we keep track of application state by updating and monitoring the connection status, socket values, and pending commands.

AC_FTP Application

Here is the source code for our sample FTP client application. This is a no-frills implementation that concentrates on the network code at the expense of a user interface. It uses asynchronous operation mode on TCP sockets and shows how to establish a connection actively (as a client for the control connection) as well as passively (as a server for the data connections). We have inserted short descriptions at key locations throughout the source code to point out and describe significant features in the application design and implementation.

```
/*---------------------------------------------------------------------
 *
 * Program: Asynch Ftp Client (TCP)
 *
 * filename: ac_ftp.h
 *
 * copyright by Bob Quinn, 1995
 *
 *  Description: Common declarations
 --------------------------------------------------------------------- */
#include <winsock.h>

#define CMD_SIZE    128
#define RPLY_SIZE   MTU_SIZE
#define MAXNULPUT   1048576

/* FTP commands that take arguments (subset) */
#define CWD  1
#define DELE 2
#define PASS 3
#define PORT 4
#define RETR 5
#define STOR 6
#define TYPE 7
#define USER 8
```

```
/* FTP commands without arguments (subset) */
#define ABOR 9
#define LIST 10
#define PWD  11
#define QUIT 12

/* FTP command strings */
extern LPSTR aszFtpCmd[13];

/*----------- application states ----------- */
#define NOT_CONNECTED     0
#define CTRLCONNECTED     2
#define DATACONNECTED     4

/*----------- global variables ----------- */

extern char szAppName[];

extern BOOL nAppState;              /* application state */

extern BOOL bToNul;                 /* get to NUL device file */
extern BOOL bFromNul;               /* put from NUL device file */
extern BOOL bIOBeep;                /* beep on FD_READ, FD_WRITE */
extern BOOL bDebug;                 /* debug output to WinDebug */
extern BOOL bReAsync;               /* call WSAAsyncSelect after accept */
extern BOOL bLogFile;               /* write cmds and replies to logfile */

extern SOCKET hCtrlSock;            /* FTP control socket */
extern SOCKET hLstnSock;            /* listening data socket */
extern SOCKET hDataSock;            /* connected data socket */

extern char szHost[MAXHOSTNAME];    /* remote host name or address */
extern char szUser[MAXUSERNAME];    /* user ID */
extern char szPWrd[MAXPASSWORD];    /* user password */

extern SOCKADDR_IN stCLclName;      /* control socket name (local) */
extern SOCKADDR_IN stCRmtName;      /*                     (remote) */
extern SOCKADDR_IN stDLclName;      /* data socket name (local client) */
extern SOCKADDR_IN stDRmtName;      /*                  (remote server) */

extern char achInBuf  [INPUT_SIZE];/* network input data buffer */
```

```
extern char achOutBuf [INPUT_SIZE];/* network output buffer */
extern char szFtpRply [RPLY_SIZE]; /* FTP reply (input) buffer */
extern char szDataFile[MAXFILENAME];/* file name */
extern char szFtpCmd  [CMD_SIZE];  /* FTP command buffer */
extern char achRplyBuf[BUF_SIZE];  /* reply display buffer */

typedef struct stFtpCmd {
  int   nFtpCmd;                   /* FTP command value */
  char  szFtpParm[CMD_SIZE];       /* FTP parameter string */
} FTPCMD;

#define MAX_CMDS 4
/* first one (index=0) is awaiting a reply
 * second (index=1) is next to be sent, etc. */
extern FTPCMD astFtpCmd[MAX_CMDS]; /* FTP command queue */
extern int nQLen;                  /* number entries in FTP cmd queue */

extern int nFtpRplyCode;           /* FTP reply code from server */
extern int iNextRply;              /* index to next reply string */
extern int iLastRply;

extern HFILE hDataFile;            /* file handle for open data file */
extern LONG lStartTime;            /* start time for data transfer */
extern LONG lByteCount;

extern char szLogFile[];           /* FTP command and reply log file */
extern HFILE hLogFile;

/*------------ function prototypes ----------- */
BOOL CALLBACK Dlg_Main    (HWND,UINT,UINT,LPARAM); /* dialog procedures */
BOOL CALLBACK Dlg_Login   (HWND,UINT,UINT,LPARAM);
BOOL CALLBACK Dlg_File    (HWND,UINT,UINT,LPARAM);
BOOL CALLBACK Dlg_Options(HWND,UINT,UINT,LPARAM);
BOOL CALLBACK Dlg_About   (HWND,UINT,UINT,LPARAM);

SOCKET InitCtrlConn(PSOCKADDR_IN, HWND, u_int);  /* control connection */
BOOL QueueFtpCmd(int, LPSTR);
int  SendFtpCmd(void);
void AbortFtpCmd(void);
int  RecvFtpRply(SOCKET, LPSTR, int);
void ProcessFtpRply(LPSTR, int);
```

```
SOCKET InitDataConn(PSOCKADDR_IN, HWND, u_int);  /* data connection */
SOCKET AcceptDataConn(SOCKET, PSOCKADDR_IN);
long SendData(SOCKET*, HFILE, int);
int  RecvData(SOCKET, HFILE, LPSTR, int);
void EndData(void);
int  CloseConn(SOCKET*, LPSTR, int, HWND);

void not_connected(void);                        /* utility functions */
HFILE CreateLclFile(LPSTR);
/* eof ac_ftp.h */


/*---------------------------------------------------------------------
 *
 * Program: Asynch Ftp Client (TCP)
 *
 * filename: ac_ftp.c
 *
 * copyright by Bob Quinn, 1995
 *
 *  Description:
 *    Client application that uses "file transfer protocol" (FTP)
 *    service as described by RFC 959.  This application demonstrates
 *    bulk data transfer techniques and reading variable length records
 *    from a byte stream (TCP socket).  The user interface is minimized
 *    in order to emphasize the network code.
 *
 --------------------------------------------------------------------- */
#define STRICT
#include "..\wsa_xtra.h"   /* see sample library section in chapter */
#include <windows.h>
#include <windowsx.h>

#include <string.h>    /* for _fmemcpy() and _fmemset() */
#include <winsock.h>
#include "resource.h"
#include <time.h>
#include <stdio.h>
#include <dos.h>
#include <direct.h>
#ifdef _WIN32
```

```
#include <io.h>         /* for Microsoft 32bit find file structure */
#else
#include <direct.h>     /* for Microsoft 16bit find file structure */
#endif
#include "..\winsockx.h"   /* see sample library section in chapter */

#include "ac_ftp.h"

/* FTP commmand strings (indexed by our command macro values) */
LPSTR aszFtpCmd[] = {
  "",     "CWD", "DELE", "PASS","PORT","RETR","STOR",
  "TYPE","USER","ABOR","LIST","PWD",  "QUIT"
};
char szAppName[] = "AC_FTP";

BOOL nAppState=NOT_CONNECTED;     /* application state */

BOOL bToNul   =FALSE;             /* get to NUL device file */
BOOL bFromNul=FALSE;              /* put from NUL device file */
BOOL bIOBeep =FALSE;              /* beep on FD_READ, FD_WRITE */
BOOL bDebug   =FALSE;             /* debug output to WinDebug */
BOOL bReAsync=TRUE;               /* call WSAAsyncSelect after accept() */
BOOL bLogFile=TRUE;               /* write cmds and replies to logfile */

SOCKET hCtrlSock=INVALID_SOCKET; /* FTP control socket */
SOCKET hLstnSock=INVALID_SOCKET; /* listening data socket */
SOCKET hDataSock=INVALID_SOCKET; /* connected data socket */

char szHost[MAXHOSTNAME]={0};     /* remote host name or address */
char szUser[MAXUSERNAME]={0};     /* user ID */
char szPWrd[MAXPASSWORD]={0};     /* user password */

SOCKADDR_IN stCLclName;           /* control socket name (local client) */
SOCKADDR_IN stCRmtName;           /*                    (remote server) */
SOCKADDR_IN stDLclName;           /* data socket name (local client) */
SOCKADDR_IN stDRmtName;           /*                 (remote server) */

char achInBuf  [INPUT_SIZE];      /* network input data buffer */
char achOutBuf [INPUT_SIZE];      /* network output buffer */
char szFtpRply [RPLY_SIZE]={0};   /* FTP reply (input) buffer */
char szDataFile[MAXFILENAME]={0};/* file name */
```

```
char szFtpCmd  [CMD_SIZE]={0};   /* FTP command buffer */
char achRplyBuf[BUF_SIZE];       /* reply display buffer */

/* first one (index=0) is awaiting a reply
 * second (index=1) is next to be sent, etc. */
FTPCMD astFtpCmd[MAX_CMDS];      /* FTP command queue */
int nQLen;                       /* Number of entries in FTP cmd queue */

int nFtpRplyCode;                /* FTP reply code from server */
int iNextRply;                   /* index to next reply string */
int iLastRply;

HFILE hDataFile=HFILE_ERROR;     /* file handle for open data file */
LONG lStartTime;                 /* start time for data transfer */
LONG lByteCount;

char szLogFile[] = "ac_ftp.log"; /* FTP command and reply log file */
HFILE hLogFile=HFILE_ERROR;

/*---------------------------------------------------------------
 *  Function: WinMain()
 *
 *  Description: Initialize and start message loop
 */
int WINAPI WinMain
  (HINSTANCE hInstance,
   HINSTANCE hPrevInstance,
   LPSTR  lpszCmdLine,
   int    nCmdShow)
{
    MSG msg;
    int nRet;

    lpszCmdLine   = lpszCmdLine;   /* avoid warning */
    hPrevInstance = hPrevInstance;
    nCmdShow      = nCmdShow;

    hInst = hInstance; /* save instance handle */

    /*-----------initialize WinSock DLL----------- */
    nRet = WSAStartup(WSA_VERSION, &stWSAData);
```

```
    /* WSAStartup() returns error value if failed (0 on success) */
    if (nRet != 0) {
      WSAperror(nRet, "WSAStartup()");
      /* no sense continuing if we can't use WinSock */
    } else {

      DialogBox (hInst, MAKEINTRESOURCE(AC_FTP), NULL, Dlg_Main);

      /*-----------release WinSock DLL---------- */
      nRet = WSACleanup();
      if (nRet == SOCKET_ERROR)
        WSAperror(WSAGetLastError(), "WSACleanup()");
    }

    return msg.wParam;
} /* end WinMain() */
```

We initialize the WinSock DLL in `WinMain()` with `WSAStartup()` and call `WSACleanup()` before we exit. This is convenient since `WinMain()` is the entry and exit point for the application.

Our application will not run at all if a WinSock DLL is not available, if it is not compatible with version 1.1 of the WinSock specification, or if the TCP/IP protocol stack was not initialized properly. We wouldn't want it to run in this case anyway, since it would not be able to do anything. If `WSAStartup()` fails, we display a message box that contains a short description of the error returned.

Notice that we use a dialog box as our main window. We do this to minimize extraneous user interface code in our application.

```
/*--------------------------------------------------------------------
 *
 * Function: Dlg_Main()
 *
 * Description: Do all the message processing for the main dialog box
 */
BOOL CALLBACK Dlg_Main
  (HWND hDlg,
   UINT msg,
   UINT wParam,
   LPARAM lParam)
```

```
{
    int nAddrSize = sizeof(SOCKADDR);
    WORD WSAEvent, WSAErr;
    SOCKET hSock;
    BOOL bOk, bRet = FALSE;
    int  nRet;
    LONG lRet;

    switch (msg) {
      case WSA_ASYNC+1:
        /*-----------------------------------------------
         * data socket async notification message handlers
         *----------------------------------------------- */
        hSock = (SOCKET)wParam;                   /* socket */
        WSAEvent = WSAGETSELECTEVENT (lParam);  /* extract event */
        WSAErr   = WSAGETSELECTERROR (lParam);  /* extract error */
        /* if error, display to user (listen socket should not have
         *  an error, but some WinSocks incorrectly post it) */
        if ((WSAErr) && (hSock == hDataSock))  {
          int i,j;
          for (i=0, j=WSAEvent; j; i++, j>>=1); /*convert bit to index */
            WSAperror(WSAErr,aszWSAEvent[i]);
          /* fall-through to call reenabling function for this event */
        }
        switch (WSAEvent) {
          case FD_READ:
            if (bIOBeep)
              MessageBeep(0xFFFF);
            if (hDataSock != INVALID_SOCKET) {
              /* receive file data or directory list */
              RecvData(hDataSock, hDataFile, achInBuf, INPUT_SIZE);
            }
            break;
          case FD_ACCEPT:
            if (hLstnSock != INVALID_SOCKET) {
              /* accept the incoming data connection request */
              hDataSock =
                AcceptDataConn(hLstnSock, &stDRmtName);
              nAppState |= DATACONNECTED;
              /* close the listening socket */
              closesocket(hLstnSock);
```

```
        hLstnSock = INVALID_SOCKET;
        lStartTime = GetTickCount();
        /* data transfer should begin with FD_WRITE or FD_READ.
         * Fall-through to jumpstart sends since FD_WRITE is not
         * always implemented correctly */
      }
    case FD_WRITE:
       /* send file data */
      if (astFtpCmd[0].nFtpCmd == STOR) {
        lRet = SendData(&hDataSock, hDataFile, MTU_SIZE);
      }
      break;
    case FD_CLOSE:                    /* data connection closed */
      if (hSock == hDataSock) {
        /* read remaining data into buffer and close connection */
        CloseConn(&hDataSock,
          (astFtpCmd[0].nFtpCmd != STOR) ? achInBuf : (LPSTR)0,
          INPUT_SIZE, hDlg);
        EndData ();
      }
      break;
    default:
       break;
  } /* end switch(WSAEvent) */
  break;
```

Now we are in our main dialog procedure. The preceding section handles the asynchronous notification messages for a data connection established to handle a PORT command followed by either a LIST, STOR, or RETR command. This is one of the most significant sections in the application, since it handles the data connection responsible for bulk data transfer. Notice that we have our data message handler up front in our window procedure to maximize code efficiency. In effect, this also maximizes our data throughput, since the data transfer is asynchronous message-driven.

When we receive an asynchronous event notification message, we always parse the event notification information and check for an error value first. Any error reported in an asynchronous message from a TCP socket is fatal, so it is not necessary to "fall through" and service the event as we do here. We could simply close the socket when we receive an error, but instead we close the socket when the reenabling function fails. After an error is received, the WinSock function call we make is likely to fail with an error message that is redundant of the one we just displayed. We let it fail with the I/O command just to show what happens.

The FD_ACCEPT event is always the first event to occur on a data connection. This signals receipt of a connection request from the FTP server in response to the PORT command the client sent. We accept the incoming connection and save the connected socket before we close the listening socket. We close the listening socket because our FTP client—like most—listens on a different port number each time we need to establish a data connection, so we only need to handle a single connection each time we listen. If we had a server application that handled more than one connection simultaneously, or in a series, we would not close the listening socket.

The last thing we do in response to the FD_ACCEPT event notification is to get the current time by calling `GetTickCount()`. The next time we get the time is when we close the data connection and call the `EndData()` function, after the data transfer completes. The difference between the start and end times is the **transfer time**, which is limited by the PC clock to a resolution of fifty-five milliseconds. More on this later.

Actually, calling `GetTickCount()` is not the last thing we do after an FD_ACCEPT. In addition, we "fall through" and call `SendData()` as we would normally do only in response to receipt of an FD_WRITE message. Many WinSocks have incorrectly implemented the FD_WRITE notification and therefore do not post an FD_WRITE message when a connection is first established. We fall through to call `SendData( )` after an FD_ACCEPT to make up for this deficiency. We may end up with an extra FD_WRITE message on WinSocks to implement FD_WRITE correctly, but we handle it gracefully in `SendData()`.

We do not call the `SendData()` function anywhere else in our application. If and when a call to `send()` fails with WSAEWOULDBLOCK due to buffer shortage, the WinSock is required to post an FD_WRITE notification when `send()` can be called again (i.e., when buffer space is available). Fortunately, WinSocks are very good about reliably posting FD_WRITE for this event.

We always call our `RecvData()` function in response to an FD_READ. As you will see when we describe the `RecvData()` function, we often do multiple calls to `recv()` in response to a single FD_READ message. This generates extra FD_READ messages whenever there is more data pending after a call to `recv()`. The downside of this is that we may make extra calls to `recv()` that will fail with WSAEWOULDBLOCK since we have already read the data. But we expect these failures, as the specification says we should, and handle them gracefully (by ignoring them).

The benefits of performing multiple calls to `recv()` in response to a single FD_READ message far outweigh the negative aspects. This allows us to remove data from the network system buffers quickly, which increases the data flow. In other words, this speeds up the data transfer rate. Alternately, we could disable asynchronous notification before we call `recv()`, and reenable it again afterwards as the WinSock specification recommends, but experience has shown this is unnecessary. The only place this multiple read method has been a problem is in the TCP/IP stack shipped with version 3.1 of Windows NT. It failed to reenable FD_READ notification after a multiple call to `recv()`. However, this stack version has been superceded by newer versions that do not suffer from this debilitating bug.

The FD_CLOSE event is the last thing to occur after a RETR command. In an FTP file transfer in the (default) stream mode that we use, the sending side always initiates the close of the data connection. As a result, we do not need to service the FD_CLOSE notification when we send a file (with the LIST or STOR command), since we may have already closed the connection. This is why we check to see if the socket matches our data socket. Another reason we check for a valid data socket is that some WinSocks mistakenly post an FD_CLOSE message after closing a listening socket.

We register for asynchronous notification of FD_ACCEPT, FD_READ, FD_WRITE, and FD_CLOSE on a socket before we call `bind()` and `listen()` in our `InitDataConn()` function. Although unnecessary, we reregister for these events in our `AcceptDataConn()` function called when FD_ACCEPT received, as we explain later.

```
case WSA_ASYNC:
        /*---------------------------------------------------------
         * control socket async notification message handlers
         *--------------------------------------------------------- */
        WSAEvent = WSAGETSELECTEVENT (lParam);  /* extract event */
        WSAErr   = WSAGETSELECTERROR (lParam);  /* extract error */
        if (WSAErr) { /* if error, display to user */
          int i,j;
          for (i=0, j=WSAEvent; j; i++, j>>=1); /* convert bit to index */
          WSAperror(WSAErr,aszWSAEvent[i]);
          /* fall-through to call reenabling function for this event */
        }
        hSock = (SOCKET)wParam;
        switch (WSAEvent) {
          case FD_READ:
             if (!iNextRply) {
                /* receive reply from server */
                iLastRply = RecvFtpRply(hCtrlSock,szFtpRply,RPLY_SIZE);
```

```
    }
    if (iLastRply && (iLastRply != SOCKET_ERROR)) {
        /* display the reply message */
        GetDlgItemText (hWinMain, IDC_REPLY, achRplyBuf,
          RPLY_SIZE-strlen(szFtpRply));
        wsprintf (achTempBuf, "%s%s", szFtpRply, achRplyBuf);
        SetDlgItemText (hWinMain, IDC_REPLY, achTempBuf);

        /* save index to next reply (if there is one) */
        nRet = strlen(szFtpRply);
        if (iLastRply > nRet+2) {
          iNextRply = nRet+3;
          /* adjust if reply only had LF (no CR) */
          if (szFtpRply[nRet+2])
            iNextRply = nRet+2;
        }
    }
    /* figure out what to do with reply based on last command */
    ProcessFtpRply (szFtpRply, RPLY_SIZE);
    break;
  case FD_WRITE:
    /* send command to server */
    if (astFtpCmd[1].nFtpCmd)
      SendFtpCmd();
    break;
  case FD_CONNECT:
    /* control connected at TCP level */
    nAppState = CTRLCONNECTED;
    wsprintf(achTempBuf, "Server: %s", szHost);
    SetDlgItemText (hDlg, IDC_SERVER, achTempBuf);
    SetDlgItemText (hDlg, IDC_STATUS, "Status: connected");
    break;
  case FD_CLOSE:
    if (nAppState & CTRLCONNECTED) {
      nAppState = NOT_CONNECTED;        /*reset app state */
      AbortFtpCmd();
      if (hCtrlSock != INVALID_SOCKET) /*close control socket */
        CloseConn(&hCtrlSock, (PSTR)0, 0, hDlg);
      SetDlgItemText (hDlg,IDC_SERVER,"Server: none");
      SetDlgItemText (hDlg,IDC_STATUS,"Status: not connected");
    }
```

```
        break;
      default:
        break;
    } /* end switch(WSAEvent) */
    break;
```

The section just shown handles the asynchronous notification messages for our control connection. Notice that we use different message values for control and data sockets (we use WSA_ASYNC for the control connection and WSA_ASYNC+1 for the data connection). We need to handle the events differently for data and control sockets, and using different messages allows us to keep their code separate and simple.

As with data events, the first thing we do with asynchronous event notifications on our control connection is check for error values and report them. We fall through to the resulting handler and subsequently close the socket when the resulting WinSock function calls fail. Again, we could have alternately closed the connection up front after an error, since TCP errors are always fatal. The only exception to this rule is after a connection attempt fails, but many WinSocks do not allow another `connect()` attempt after any failures, so you should always get a new socket before retrying.

Unlike the data connection, which accepts a connection passively, the control socket actively initiates a TCP connection in our `InitCtrlConn()` function. As a result, we handle the FD_CONNECT event we receive after the connection operation completes (successfully or not). If the connect attempt fails, the FD_CONNECT event will contain an error value that indicates why the attempt failed. When the connect attempt succeeds, we simply update our application status variable and display a message to the user.

The FD_READ event occurs when we receive replies from the server. We call our `RecvFtpRply()` function to read the reply, then `ProcessFtpRply()` to parse the reply and take appropriate action. The code between these two function calls manages our buffers so we can pick up where we left off in previous reads after we encounter partial reads. We expect partial reads on the TCP socket since a data stream does not preserve message boundaries, so we may receive a reply in more than one packet. This does not happen often, however, since replies are generally small in size.

In response to an FD_WRITE event, we call our `SendFtpCmd()` function. This would occur only if a previous attempt to `send()` an FTP command failed with WSAEWOULDBLOCK.

We initiate closing procedures when we receive an FD_CLOSE notification. Since this may be an unexpected closure by the server side, or due to a connection failure between our client and server, we cannot reliably predict the context. As a result, we attempt to close any outstanding data connections or listening sockets and any open data file. We then change the application status and notify the user.

```
case WM_COMMAND:
 switch (wParam) {
   case IDC_CONNECT:
      /* if we already have a socket, tell user to close it */
      if (nAppState & CTRLCONNECTED) {
          MessageBox (hDlg,"Close the active connection first",
             "Can't Connect", MB_OK | MB_ICONASTERISK);
      } else {

        /* prompt user for server and login user information */
        bOk = DialogBox (hInst, MAKEINTRESOURCE(IDD_SERVER),
               hDlg, Dlg_Login);

        if (bOk) {
          /* check destination address and resolve if necessary */
          stCRmtName.sin_addr.s_addr = GetAddr(szHost);
          if (stCRmtName.sin_addr.s_addr == INADDR_ANY) {

            /* tell user to enter a host */
            wsprintf(achTempBuf,
              "Sorry, server %s is invalid.  Try again", szHost);
            MessageBox (hDlg, achTempBuf,
              "Can't connect!", MB_OK | MB_ICONASTERISK);
          } else {

            /* initiate connect attempt to server */
            hCtrlSock =
              InitCtrlConn(&stCRmtName, hDlg, WSA_ASYNC);
          }
        }
      }
      break;

    case IDC_CLOSE:
      if (nAppState & CTRLCONNECTED) {
        /* set application state so nothing else is processed */
        nAppState = NOT_CONNECTED;
```

```
    /* if we're listening, stop now */
    if (hLstnSock != INVALID_SOCKET) {
      closesocket(hLstnSock);
      hLstnSock = INVALID_SOCKET;
    }
    /* if there is a data connection, then abort it */
    if (hDataSock != INVALID_SOCKET)
      QueueFtpCmd (ABOR, 0);
    /* quit the control connection */
    if (hCtrlSock != INVALID_SOCKET)
      QueueFtpCmd (QUIT, 0);
    SetDlgItemText (hDlg,IDC_SERVER,"Server: none");
    SetDlgItemText (hDlg,IDC_STATUS,"Status: not connected");
  }
  break;

case IDC_RETR:
  /* prompt for name of remote file to get */
  if (nAppState & CTRLCONNECTED) {
    bOk = DialogBox (hInst, MAKEINTRESOURCE(IDD_FILENAME),
      hDlg, Dlg_File);

    if (bOk && szDataFile[0]) {
      if (!bToNul) {
        /* if user provided a file name, open same name
         *  here for write.  Truncate the file name to
         *  8 chars plus 3, if necessary */
        hDataFile = CreateLclFile (szDataFile);
      }
      if (hDataFile != HFILE_ERROR || bToNul) {
        /* tell the server where to connect back to us */
        hLstnSock =
          InitDataConn(&stDLclName, hDlg, WSA_ASYNC+1);
        if (hLstnSock != INVALID_SOCKET) {
           /* queue PORT, TYPE, and RETR cmds */
          if (QueueFtpCmd(PORT, 0)) {
            if (QueueFtpCmd (TYPE, "I"))
              QueueFtpCmd(RETR, szDataFile);
          }
        }
```

```
      }
    }
  } else
    not_connected();
  break;

case IDC_STOR:
  /* prompt for name of local file to send */
  if (nAppState & CTRLCONNECTED) {
    bOk = DialogBox (hInst, MAKEINTRESOURCE(IDD_FILENAME),
      hDlg, Dlg_File);

    if (bOk && szDataFile[0]) {
      if (!bFromNul) {
        /* if user provided file name, try to open it */
        hDataFile = _lopen(szDataFile, 0);
        if (hDataFile == HFILE_ERROR) {
          wsprintf(achTempBuf,
            "Unable to open file: %s", szDataFile);
          MessageBox (hWinMain,
            (LPSTR)achTempBuf,"File Error",
            MB_OK | MB_ICONASTERISK);
        }
      }
      if (hDataFile != HFILE_ERROR || bFromNul) {
        /* tell the server where to connect back to us */
        hLstnSock =
          InitDataConn(&stDLclName, hDlg, WSA_ASYNC+1);
        if (hLstnSock != INVALID_SOCKET) {
          /* queue PORT, TYPE, and STOR cmds */
          if (QueueFtpCmd (PORT, 0)) {
            if (QueueFtpCmd (TYPE, "I"))
              QueueFtpCmd (STOR, szDataFile);
          }
        }
      }
    }
  } else
    not_connected();
  break;
```

```
case IDC_ABOR:
  if (hCtrlSock != INVALID_SOCKET)
    /* abort the pending FTP command */
    QueueFtpCmd (ABOR, 0);
  break;

case IDC_LCWD:
  /* prompt for directory, and move to it on local system */
  bOk = DialogBox (hInst, MAKEINTRESOURCE(IDD_FILENAME),
          hDlg, Dlg_File);

  if (bOk && szDataFile[0]) {
    if (!(_chdir (szDataFile))) {
      getcwd (szDataFile, MAXFILENAME-1);
      SetDlgItemText (hDlg, IDC_LPWD, szDataFile);
    }
  }
  break;

case IDC_LDEL:
  /* prompt for file name, and delete it from local system */
  bOk = DialogBox (hInst, MAKEINTRESOURCE(IDD_FILENAME),
          hDlg, Dlg_File);

  if (bOk && szDataFile[0]) {
    /* if user provided file name, then delete it */
    remove (szDataFile);
  }
  break;

case IDC_LDIR:
  /* get local file directory, and display in notepad */
  if (GetLclDir(szTempFile)) {
    wsprintf (achTempBuf, "notepad %s", szTempFile);
    WinExec (achTempBuf, SW_SHOW);
  }
  break;

case IDC_RCWD:
  /* prompt for directory, and move to it on remote system */
  if (nAppState & CTRLCONNECTED) {
```

```
      szDataFile[0] = 0;
      bOk = DialogBox (hInst, MAKEINTRESOURCE(IDD_FILENAME),
        hDlg, Dlg_File);

      if (bOk && szDataFile[0]) {
        QueueFtpCmd (CWD, szDataFile);
      }
    } else
      not_connected();
    break;

  case IDC_RDEL:
    /* prompt for file name, and delete it from remote system */
    if (nAppState & CTRLCONNECTED) {
      szDataFile[0] = 0;
      bOk = DialogBox (hInst, MAKEINTRESOURCE(IDD_FILENAME),
        hDlg, Dlg_File);

      if (bOk && szDataFile[0]) {
        /* if user provided file name, send command to delete */
        QueueFtpCmd (DELE, szDataFile);
      }
    } else
      not_connected();
    break;

  case IDC_RDIR:
    /* get remote file directory, and display in notepad */
    if (nAppState & CTRLCONNECTED) {
      hDataFile = CreateLclFile (szTempFile);
      if (hDataFile != HFILE_ERROR) {
        /* prepare to receive connection from server */
        hLstnSock =
          InitDataConn(&stDLclName, hDlg, WSA_ASYNC+1);
        if (hLstnSock != INVALID_SOCKET) {

          /* queue PORT, TYPE, and LIST cmds */
          if (QueueFtpCmd (PORT, 0))
            if (QueueFtpCmd (TYPE, "A"))
              QueueFtpCmd (LIST, 0);
```

```
        }
      }
    } else
      not_connected();
    break;
```

The main dialog procedure in the preceding code contains handlers for each of our most significant dialog controls. All of them are button controls that either perform an operation locally or queue one or more FTP commands for the server. The following list briefly describes what each button does (look at the screen capture that appears later for reference):

IDC_LDIR:	Get the local file directory, and display in notepad
IDC_LDEL:	Delete a local file
IDC_LCWD:	Prompt for a directory name, then change directory on the local system
IDC_CONNECT:	Prompt for server host and login information, resolve the destination host address, and initiate connection
IDC_RDIR:	Initialize a data connection, and queue the PORT and LIST command sequence to server to get a detailed file directory listing from the server
IDC_RDEL:	Prompt for file name, then queue DELE command to server to delete a file
IDC_RCWD:	Prompt for directory name, then queue CWD command to change directory
IDC_STOR:	Prompt for file name, then initialize a data connection, and queue PORT, TYPE, and STOR command sequence to send file
IDC_RETR:	Prompt for file name, then initialize a data connection, and queue PORT, TYPE, and RETR command sequence to receive file
IDC_ABOR:	Send ABOR command (closes data connection and clears command queue)
IDC_CLOSE:	Close the control connection to server, and clean up

Notice that in the handlers for most controls that initiate network access to the server, we check the current application state before doing anything. When users are not already connected, we tell them that they need to establish a connection: when they try to connect with an already active connection, we tell them to close the active connection first. This is the minimum we should do to attempt to be user-friendly in this UI-sparse sample application. It is important not to leave users wondering if the application did what they asked it to, and to tell them why not if the application did not perform as expected.

```
            case IDC_OPTIONS:
              DialogBox (hInst, MAKEINTRESOURCE(IDD_OPTIONS),
                  hDlg, Dlg_Options);
              break;

            case IDABOUT:
              DialogBox (hInst, MAKEINTRESOURCE(IDD_ABOUT),
                  hDlg, Dlg_About);
              break;

            case WM_DESTROY:
            case IDC_EXIT:
              SendMessage (hDlg, WM_COMMAND, IDC_CLOSE, 0L);
              if (hLogFile != HFILE_ERROR)
                _lclose(hLogFile);
              EndDialog(hDlg, msg);
              bRet = TRUE;
              break;

            default:
               break;
          } /* end case WM_COMMAND: */
          break;

      case WM_INITDIALOG:
        hWinMain = hDlg;    /* save our main window handle */

        /* assign an icon to dialog box */
#ifdef WIN32
        SetClassLong (hDlg, GCL_HICON, (LONG)
           LoadIcon((HINSTANCE) GetWindowLong(hDlg, GWL_HINSTANCE),
           __TEXT("AC_FTP")));
```

```
#else
         SetClassWord(hDlg,GCW_HICON,(WORD)
           LoadIcon(hInst, MAKEINTRESOURCE(AC_FTP)));
#endif

        /* initialize FTP command structure array */
        memset (astFtpCmd, 0, (sizeof(struct stFtpCmd))*MAX_CMDS);

        /* display current working directory */
        getcwd (szDataFile, MAXFILENAME-1);
        SetDlgItemText (hDlg, IDC_LPWD, szDataFile);

        /* open logfile, if logging enabled */
        if (bLogFile) {
          hLogFile = _lcreat (szLogFile, 0);
          if (hLogFile == HFILE_ERROR) {
            MessageBox (hWinMain, "Unable to open logfile",
              "File Error", MB_OK | MB_ICONASTERISK);
            bLogFile = FALSE;
          }
        }
        /* center dialog box */
        CenterWnd (hDlg, NULL, TRUE);
        break;

      default:
        break;
  } /* end switch (msg) */

  return (bRet);
} /* end Dlg_Main() */
```

The remainder of our main dialog procedure contains mundane dialog handlers to initialize our dialog, display the *About* box, and exit the application. Notice that we get the local directory and open a logfile (if enabled) when we initialize our main dialog box, and close it before we exit. We also send an IDC_CLOSE message before we exit to shut down open sockets and close any open data file.

```
/*---------------------------------------------------------------------
 * Function: Dlg_Login
 *
```

```
 * Description: Prompt for destination host, user name, and password
 */
BOOL CALLBACK Dlg_Login (
  HWND hDlg,
  UINT msg,
  UINT wParam,
  LPARAM lParam)
{
   BOOL bRet = FALSE;
   lParam = lParam;  /* avoid warning */

   switch (msg) {
     case WM_INITDIALOG:
       SetDlgItemText (hDlg, IDC_SERVER, szHost);
       SetDlgItemText (hDlg, IDC_USERNAME, szUser);
       SetDlgItemText (hDlg, IDC_PASSWORD, szPWrd);
       CenterWnd (hDlg, hWinMain, TRUE);
       break;
     case WM_COMMAND:
       switch (wParam) {
         case IDOK:
           GetDlgItemText (hDlg, IDC_SERVER, szHost, MAXHOSTNAME);
           GetDlgItemText (hDlg, IDC_USERNAME, szUser, MAXUSERNAME);
           GetDlgItemText (hDlg, IDC_PASSWORD, szPWrd, MAXPASSWORD);
           EndDialog (hDlg, TRUE);
           bRet = TRUE;
           break;
         case IDCANCEL:
           EndDialog (hDlg, FALSE);
           bRet = FALSE;
           break;
         default:
           break;
       }
   }
   return(bRet);
} /* end Dlg_Login */
```

The `Dlg_Login()` dialog procedure is self-explanatory. It is invoked when a user pushes the IDC_CONNECT button control as long as an active connection does not exist already. We prompt the user for an FTP server host (host name or address) and login information (user name and password). We use this information in our `InitCtrlConn()` function to establish the control connection to the FTP server.

```
/*---------------------------------------------------------------
 * Function: Dlg_File()
 *
 * Description: Prompt for a file name (also used for directory names)
 */
BOOL CALLBACK Dlg_File (
  HWND hDlg,
  UINT msg,
  UINT wParam,
  LPARAM lParam)
{
   BOOL bRet = FALSE;
   lParam = lParam;  /* avoid warning */

   switch (msg) {
     case WM_INITDIALOG:
       CenterWnd (hDlg, hWinMain, TRUE);
       break;
     case WM_COMMAND:
       switch (wParam) {
         case IDOK:
           GetDlgItemText (hDlg, IDC_FILE, szDataFile, MAXFILENAME);
           EndDialog (hDlg, TRUE);
           bRet = TRUE;
           break;
         case IDCANCEL:
           EndDialog (hDlg, FALSE);
           bRet = FALSE;
           break;
       }
   }
   return(bRet);
} /* end Dlg_File() */
```

We invoke our file dialog box from a number of places in our main dialog procedure to prompt for a file or directory name. Each of the following buttons invokes this dialog box:

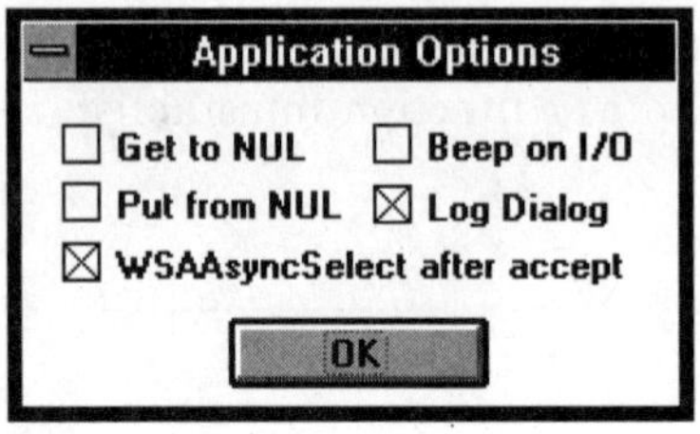

Control ID	*Prompts for*
IDC_LDIR	local directory name
IDC_RDIR	remote directory name
IDC_STOR	name of local file to send
IDC_RETR	name of remote file to receive
IDC_LDEL	name of local file to delete
IDC_RDEL	name of remote file to delete

```
/*-----------------------------------------------------------------------
 * Function: Dlg_Options()
 *
 * Description: Allow user to change a number of run-time parameters
 *  that affect the operation, to allow experimentation and debugging.
 */
BOOL CALLBACK Dlg_Options (
  HWND hDlg,
  UINT msg,
  UINT wParam,
  LPARAM lParam)
{
   BOOL bRet = FALSE;
   lParam = lParam;  /* avoid warning */

   switch (msg) {
     case WM_INITDIALOG:
       CheckDlgButton (hDlg, IDC_TO_NUL,  bToNul);
       CheckDlgButton (hDlg, IDC_FROM_NUL,bFromNul);
       CheckDlgButton (hDlg, IDC_LOGFILE, bLogFile);
       CheckDlgButton (hDlg, IDC_IOBEEP,  bIOBeep);
       CheckDlgButton (hDlg, IDC_REASYNC, bReAsync);
       CenterWnd (hDlg, hWinMain, TRUE);
       break;
```

```
    case WM_COMMAND:
      switch (wParam) {
        case IDC_TO_NUL:
          bToNul = !bToNul;
          break;
        case IDC_FROM_NUL:
          bFromNul = !bFromNul;
          break;
        case IDC_LOGFILE:
          bLogFile = !bLogFile;
          break;
        case IDC_IOBEEP:
          bIOBeep = !bIOBeep;
          break;
        case IDC_REASYNC:
          bReAsync = !bReAsync;
          break;
        case IDOK:
          if (bLogFile && hLogFile == HFILE_ERROR) {
            bLogFile = FALSE;
          } else if (!bLogFile && hLogFile != HFILE_ERROR) {
            _lclose(hLogFile);
            hLogFile = HFILE_ERROR;
          } else if (bLogFile && hLogFile == HFILE_ERROR) {
            hLogFile = _lcreat (szLogFile, 0);
            if (hLogFile == HFILE_ERROR) {
              MessageBox (hWinMain, "Unable to open logfile",
                "File Error", MB_OK | MB_ICONASTERISK);
              bLogFile = FALSE;
            }
          }
          EndDialog (hDlg, TRUE);
          bRet = TRUE;
          break;
      }
  }
  return(bRet);
} /* end Dlg_Options() */
```

The Options dialog box allows the user to change the settings for a number of run-time variables that affect the way the FTP client operates. This allows some experimentation, benchmarking of data rates, evaluation of WinSock implementations, and debugging.

```
┌─────────────────────────────────────┐
│ ─   │    Application Options         │
├─────────────────────────────────────┤
│  ☐ Get to NUL    ☐ Beep on I/O       │
│  ☐ Put from NUL  ☒ Log Dialog        │
│  ☒ WSAAsyncSelect after accept       │
│              ┌──────┐                │
│              │  OK  │                │
│              └──────┘                │
└─────────────────────────────────────┘
```

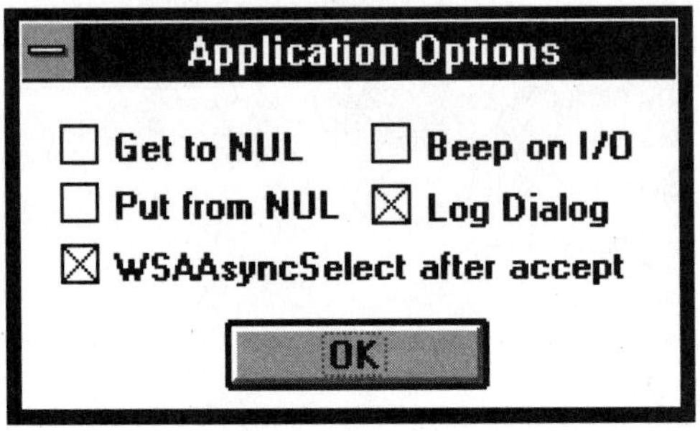

Option Name	Description
Get to NUL	When you get a file (receive), it goes to NUL device rather than a disk file. This allows you to benchmark data receives without the effect that writing to disk can have.
Put from NUL	When you put a file (send), it writes arbitrary data from memory (and automatically stops sending after sending 1 megabyte), for benchmarking purposes.
Beep on I/O	Beeps when receiving data when an FD_READ event occurs, and beeps on sending data for debugging and warm fuzzy feelings.
Log Dialog	Writes control connection dialog and data transfer statistics to the logfile named AC_FTP.LOG.
WSAAsyncSelect after accept:	WSAAsyncSelect after accept: Enables or disables a call to WSAAsyncSelect() after a return from accept() since some WinSocks don't allow newly accepted sockets to inherit listening socket attributes.

```
/*-----------------------------------------------------------------
 * Function: not_connected()
 *
 * Description: Tell the user that the client needs a connection
 */
void not_connected(void) {
  MessageBox (hDlgMain, "You need to connect to an FTP Server",
    "Not Connected", MB_OK | MB_ICONASTERISK);
}
```

The simple `not_connected( )` function above needs little explanation. We call it from a number of places in our main dialog procedure when the user tries to issue an FTP command, without being currently connected to an FTP server.

```
/*---------------------------------------------------------------
 * Function: InitCtrlConn( )
 *
 * Description: Get a TCP socket, register for async notification,
 *   and then connect to FTP server
 */
SOCKET InitCtrlConn(PSOCKADDR_IN pstName, HWND hDlg, u_int nAsyncMsg)
{
  int nRet;
  SOCKET hCtrlSock;

  /* get a TCP socket for control connection */
  hCtrlSock = socket (AF_INET, SOCK_STREAM, 0);
  if (hCtrlSock == INVALID_SOCKET)  {
    WSAperror(WSAGetLastError(), "socket()");
  } else {

    /* request async notification for most events */
    nRet = WSAAsyncSelect(hCtrlSock, hDlg, nAsyncMsg,
           (FD_CONNECT | FD_READ | FD_WRITE | FD_CLOSE));
    if (nRet == SOCKET_ERROR) {
      WSAperror(WSAGetLastError(), "WSAAsyncSelect()");
      closesocket(hCtrlSock);
      hCtrlSock = INVALID_SOCKET;
    } else {

      /* initiate nonblocking connect to server */
      pstName->sin_family = PF_INET;
      pstName->sin_port   = htons(IPPORT_FTP);
      nRet = connect(hCtrlSock,(LPSOCKADDR)pstName,SOCKADDR_LEN);
      if (nRet == SOCKET_ERROR) {
           int WSAErr = WSAGetLastError();

           /* anything but "would block" error is bad */
```

```
          if (WSAErr != WSAEWOULDBLOCK) {
            /* report error and clean up */
            WSAperror(WSAErr, "connect()");
            closesocket(hCtrlSock);
            hCtrlSock = INVALID_SOCKET;
          }
      }
    }
  }
  return (hCtrlSock);
} /* end InitCtrlConn() */
```

We call the `InitCtrlConn()` function from the main dialog procedure after the user presses the IDC_CONNECT button. This function performs the series of WinSock calls found in most TCP client applications for initiating a connection: We get a socket with `socket()`, name the remote socket to which to connect in a `sockaddr_in` structure, and initiate the connection with `connect()`.

The one significant variation from the client framework we describe in Chapter 4 is our call to `WSAAsyncSelect()`. We use this to register for asynchronous notification when the connection completes, when data arrives or outgoing buffers are available for sending, and when the connection closes.

As always, we check the return value of every function call. The only error we anticipate and dismiss is WSAEWOULDBLOCK from the `connect()` call. We expect this error to occur, because the call to `WSAAsyncSelect()` makes the socket nonblocking. Since the TCP connect operation requires a number of network transactions, it often "fails" with an WSAEWOULDBLOCK error to indicate the connect operation is pending. We count on the FD_CONNECT asynchronous notification to notify us when the connect operation completes (successfully or not).

```
/*---------------------------------------------------------------
 * Function: SendFtpCmd()
 *
 * Description: Format and send an FTP command to the server
 */
int SendFtpCmd(void)
{
  int nRet, nLen, nBytesSent = 0;
  int nFtpCmd = astFtpCmd[1].nFtpCmd;

  /* create a command string (if we don't already have one) */
```

```
 if (szFtpCmd[0] == 0) {

   switch (nFtpCmd) {
     case PORT:
       wsprintf (szFtpCmd, "PORT %d,%d,%d,%d,%d,%d\r\n",
         stDLclName.sin_addr.S_un.S_un_b.s_b1,  /* local addr */
         stDLclName.sin_addr.S_un.S_un_b.s_b2,
         stDLclName.sin_addr.S_un.S_un_b.s_b3,
         stDLclName.sin_addr.S_un.S_un_b.s_b4,
         stDLclName.sin_port & 0xFF,            /* local port */
        (stDLclName.sin_port & 0xFF00)>>8);
       break;
     case CWD:
     case DELE:
     case PASS:
     case RETR:
     case STOR:
     case TYPE:
     case USER:
       /* FTP commmand and parameter */
       wsprintf (szFtpCmd, "%s %s\r\n",
         aszFtpCmd[nFtpCmd], &(astFtpCmd[1].szFtpParm));
       break;
     case ABOR:
     case LIST:
     case PWD:
     case QUIT:
       /* solitary FTP command string (no parameter) */
       wsprintf (szFtpCmd, "%s\r\n", aszFtpCmd[nFtpCmd]);
       break;
     default:
       return (0);  /* we have a bogus command! */
   }
 }
 nLen = strlen(szFtpCmd);

 if (hCtrlSock != INVALID_SOCKET) {
   /* send the FTP command to control socket */
   while (nBytesSent < nLen) {
     nRet = send(hCtrlSock, (LPSTR)szFtpCmd, nLen-nBytesSent, 0);
     if (nRet == SOCKET_ERROR) {
```

```
        int WSAErr = WSAGetLastError();

        /* if "would block" error, we'll pick up again with async
         *  FD_WRITE notification, but any other error is bad news */
        if (WSAErr != WSAEWOULDBLOCK)
          WSAperror(WSAErr, "SendFtpCmd()");
        break;
      }
      nBytesSent += nRet;
    }
  }
  /* if we sent it all, update our status and move everything up
   *  in command queue */
  if (nBytesSent == nLen) {
    int i;

    if (nFtpCmd == PASS)                    /* hide password */
      memset (szFtpCmd+5, 'x', 10);

    if (bLogFile)                            /* log command */
      _lwrite (hLogFile, szFtpCmd, strlen(szFtpCmd));

    GetDlgItemText (hWinMain, IDC_REPLY,  /* display command */
      achRplyBuf, RPLY_SIZE-strlen(szFtpCmd));
    wsprintf (achTempBuf, "%s%s", szFtpCmd, achRplyBuf);
    SetDlgItemText (hWinMain, IDC_REPLY, achTempBuf);

    szFtpCmd[0] = 0;  /* disable FTP command string */

    /* move everything up in the command queue */
    for (i=0; i < nQLen; i++) {
      astFtpCmd[i].nFtpCmd = astFtpCmd[i+1].nFtpCmd;
      astFtpCmd[i+1].nFtpCmd = 0;         /* reset old command */
      if (*(astFtpCmd[i+1].szFtpParm)) {
       memcpy(astFtpCmd[i].
              szFtpParm,astFtpCmd[i+1].szFtpParm, CMD_SIZE);
        *(astFtpCmd[i+1].szFtpParm) = 0; /* terminate old string */
      } else {
        *(astFtpCmd[i].szFtpParm) = 0;    /* terminate unused string */
      }
    }
```

```
    nQLen--;          /* decrement the queue length */

    switch (nFtpCmd) {
      case (USER):
        SetDlgItemText (hWinMain, IDC_STATUS,"Status: connecting");
        break;
      case (STOR):
        SetDlgItemText (hWinMain, IDC_STATUS,"Status: sending a file");
        break;
      case (RETR):
        SetDlgItemText (hWinMain, IDC_STATUS,
          "Status: receiving a file");
        break;
      case (LIST):
        SetDlgItemText (hWinMain, IDC_STATUS,
          "Status: receiving directory");
        break;
      case (QUIT):
        SetDlgItemText (hWinMain, IDC_SERVER, "Server: none");
        SetDlgItemText (hWinMain, IDC_STATUS, "Status: not connected");
        break;
    }
  }
  return (nBytesSent);
} /* end SendFtpCmd() */
```

The `SendFtpCmd()` function sends the next command from our FTP command queue. We call `SendFtpCmd()` from `QueueFtpCmd()`, `ProcessFtpCmd()`, and the FD_WRITE event handler for our control connection socket (in our main dialog procedure). We call this function only when a command is not currently pending, unless the command to send is the ABOR command. ABOR is the exception because it is designed specifically to interrupt and cancel a pending FTP command.

There are essentially three sections in `SendFtpCmd()`:

- Assemble a command string, if we do not already have one.
- Call on WinSock to send the command string.
- Update status for the user, and adjust our command queue.

We always refer to manifest constant values to keep track of FTP commands requested and queued. We use these manifest constant values as indices into a table of strings when we need to send the actual command, since commands are all in NVT ASCII text. The command assembly section copies this string into the command buffer in our FTP command queue structure, along with the requisite carriage-return and line-feed end-of-line character sequence. For some commands we also insert a parameter, and for the PORT command we need to insert six parameters to send the local socket name to the server.

It usually does not take more than one call to `send()` to send our command string, since command strings are always shorter than the smallest MSS for TCP. But we loop on the `send()` to be sure, since TCP is a data stream, which means there is no guarantee that a single call will suffice. As always, we check for an error and break out of the loop if the send operation fails. We ignore the WSAEWOULDBLOCK error since the FD_WRITE will pick up where we left off when outgoing buffers are available again. We report any other error to the user.

If we sent the entire command string, we show the user the command string sent. We then move everything up in our application queue so the pending command is in the first location in our queue/array (index 0) and the next command to send is in the second location (index 1). We then decrement our queue length. Finally, we update the application status to inform the user if we have done anything significant.

```
/*---------------------------------------------------------------
 * Function: QueueFtpCmd()
 *
 * Description: Put FTP command in command queue for sending after we
 *  receive responses to pending commands or now if nothing is pending
 */
BOOL QueueFtpCmd(int nFtpCmd, LPSTR szFtpParm) {

  if ((nFtpCmd == ABOR) || (nFtpCmd == QUIT)) {
    AbortFtpCmd();
    if (hCtrlSock != INVALID_SOCKET)
      SetDlgItemText (hWinMain, IDC_STATUS,"Status: connected");
  } else if (nQLen == MAX_CMDS) {
    /* notify users if they can't fit in the queue */
    MessageBox (hWinMain, "Ftp command queue is full, try again later",
       "Can't Queue Command", MB_OK | MB_ICONASTERISK);
    return (FALSE);            /* not queued */
  }
```

```
  nQLen++;  /* increment FTP command counter */

  /* save command vitals */
  astFtpCmd[nQLen].nFtpCmd = nFtpCmd;
  if (szFtpParm)
    lstrcpy (astFtpCmd[nQLen].szFtpParm, szFtpParm);

  if (!(astFtpCmd[0].nFtpCmd) && astFtpCmd[1].nFtpCmd) {
    /* if nothing pending reply, then send the next command */
    SendFtpCmd();
  }
  return (TRUE);    /* queued! */
} /* end QueueFtpCmd() */
```

The `QueueFtpCmd()` function queues the command passed as an argument, along with its argument (if it has one). The only commands that are not queued are ABOR and QUIT, which clear the current queue. If another command is not already pending, we call `SendFtpCmd()` to assemble the command string and send it to the server.

```
/*---------------------------------------------------------------
 * Function: AbortFtpCmd()
 *
 * Description: Clean up routine to abort a pending FTP command and
 *  clear the command queue
 */
void AbortFtpCmd(void) {
  int i;

  if (hLstnSock != INVALID_SOCKET){/* close listen socket */
    closesocket(hLstnSock);
    hLstnSock = INVALID_SOCKET;
  }
  if (hDataSock != INVALID_SOCKET){ /* close data socket */
    CloseConn(&hDataSock,
      (astFtpCmd[0].nFtpCmd != STOR) ? achInBuf : (PSTR)0,
      INPUT_SIZE, hWinMain);
    EndData();
  }
  for (i=0;i<MAX_CMDS;i++)       {    /* clear command queue */
    astFtpCmd[i].nFtpCmd = 0;
```

```
  nQLen = 0;
} /* end AbortFtpCmd() */
```

`AbortFtpCmd()` is a cleanup routine that aborts a pending command, closes its data sockets (both the listening socket and connected socket), and clears the command queue. We call this from a number of places throughout the application, including in response to user commands.

```
/*---------------------------------------------------------------
 * Function: RecvFtpRply()
 *
 * Description: Read the FTP reply from server (and log it)
 */
int RecvFtpRply(SOCKET hCtrlSock, LPSTR szFtpRply, int nLen)
{
  int nRet=0;

  if (hCtrlSock != INVALID_SOCKET) {
    memset(szFtpRply,0,nLen);    /* init receive buffer */

    /* read as much as we can */
    nRet = recv(hCtrlSock,(LPSTR)szFtpRply,nLen,0);

    if (nRet == SOCKET_ERROR) {
      int WSAErr = WSAGetLastError();
      if (WSAErr != WSAEWOULDBLOCK) {
        WSAperror (WSAErr, "RecvFtpRply()");
      }
    } else if (bLogFile)    /* log reply */
      _lwrite (hLogFile, szFtpRply, nRet);
  }
  return (nRet);
} /* end RecvFtpReply() */
```

`RecvFtpRply()` is called from the FD_READ event handler for our control connection socket in our main dialog procedure. All we do here is read whatever we can in a single call to `recv()`.

We could have had a loop on `recv()` here as we do in our `RecvData()` function, but we are not as concerned about data throughput on the control connection as we are on the data connection. Consequently, we rely on further FD_READ notification if we do not read all the pending data at once.

Most replies are less than the minimum MSS anyway, so multiple calls to `recv()` are not needed often, although some multiple-line replies do require multiple reads.

As always, we check the return value for an error condition. The only acceptable error value is WSAEWOULDBLOCK, so we report all others to the user. As the WinSock specification notes, robust applications should expect to encounter a WSAEWOULDBLOCK error even after FD_READ notification. We can expect to get another FD_READ notification when the `recv()` call is again likely to succeed.

```
/*---------------------------------------------------------------
 * Function: ProcessFtpRply()
 *
 * Description: Figure out what happened, and what to do next
 */
void ProcessFtpRply (LPSTR szRply, int nBufLen)
{
  LPSTR szFtpRply;
  int nPendingFtpCmd, i;

  /* skip continuation lines (denoted by a dash after reply code
   * or with a blank reply code and no dash) */
  szFtpRply = szRply;
  while ((*(szFtpRply+3) == '-') ||
        ((*(szFtpRply)==' ')&&
         (*(szFtpRply+1)==' ')&&(*(szFtpRply+2)==' '))) {
    /* find end of reply line */
    for (i=0;*szFtpRply!=0x0a &&
             *szFtpRply &&
             i<nBufLen-3; szFtpRply++,i++);
    szFtpRply++;        /* go to beginning of next reply */
    if (!(*szFtpRply)) /* quit if end of string */
      return;
  }

  *szFtpCmd  = 0;                    /* disable old command string */
  nPendingFtpCmd = astFtpCmd[0].nFtpCmd; /* save last FTP cmd */
  if ((*szFtpRply != '1') &&
      (nPendingFtpCmd != LIST) &&
      (nPendingFtpCmd != STOR) &&
      (nPendingFtpCmd != RETR))
```

```
  /* for any but preliminary reply, clear old command */
  astFtpCmd[0].nFtpCmd = 0;

/* first digit in 3-digit FTP reply code is the most significant */
switch (*szFtpRply) {
  case ('1'):  /* positive preliminary reply */
    break;
  case ('2'):  /* positive completion reply */
    switch(nPendingFtpCmd) {
      case 0:
        /* check for "220 Service ready for new user" reply, and
         *  send user command to log in if login message found */
        if ((*(szFtpRply+1)=='2') && (*(szFtpRply+2)=='0'))
          QueueFtpCmd(USER, szUser);
        break;
      case CWD:
      case USER:
      case PASS:
        /* We're logged in!  Get remote working directory */
        QueueFtpCmd(PWD, 0);
        break;
      case PWD:
        /* display remote working directory */
        SetDlgItemText (hWinMain, IDC_RPWD, &szFtpRply[4]);
        break;
      case TYPE:
      case PORT:
        /* send next command (it's already queued) */
        SendFtpCmd();
        break;
      case ABOR:
        /* close the data socket */
        if (hDataSock != INVALID_SOCKET)
          CloseConn(&hDataSock, (PSTR)0, 0, hWinMain);
        break;
      case QUIT:
        /* close the control socket */
        if (hCtrlSock != INVALID_SOCKET)
          CloseConn(&hCtrlSock, (PSTR)0, 0, hWinMain);
        break;
      default:
```

```
            break; /* nothing to do after most replies */
        }
        break;
      case ('3'):  /* positive intermediate reply */
        if (nPendingFtpCmd == USER)
          QueueFtpCmd(PASS, szPWrd);
        break;
      case ('4'):  /* transient negative completion reply */
      case ('5'):  /* permanent negative completion reply */
        /* if port failed, forget about queued commands */
        if (nPendingFtpCmd != ABOR)
          QueueFtpCmd(ABOR, 0);
        break;
  }
} /* end ProcessFtpRply() */
```

After we read a reply from the server with `RecvFtpRply()`, we use `ProcessFtpRply()` to decipher it and take any appropriate action. First we ignore any continuation lines in multiline FTP replies. We can easily detect these since they have a dash after the reply code (in the fourth character position of the reply string). We leave these strings in our reply buffer for later display.

Next we disable the pending command to indicate that we have successfully received a reply so we can send any pending commands. Notice that we do not clear the pending command if we receive a preliminary reply code or have a LIST or RETR command pending. A preliminary reply value means that the command is still pending, and we do not clear it if either LIST or RETR is pending, because these commands are receiving on data connections.

We do not reset the pending command for commands that are receiving on data connections, because the reply arrives from the control connection, which operates entirely independent of the data connection. As a result, it is possible to receive a reply that indicates a successful data transfer completion after a LIST or RETR command, before we have read all the data sent. If we tried to close the connection at this point, we could lose data. Instead, we wait for the end-of-file indication that the FD_CLOSE event notification represents before we close our end of the data connection (the `EndData()` function resets the pending command for LIST, RETR, and STOR).

At the heart of `ProcessFtpRply()`, we expend a minimal effort processing the replies by concentrating on the first digit in the reply code, and the pending command. As we described earlier, the value of the first digit is all we need to determine whether our command succeeded, failed, is underway, or needs more information. The pending command determines what our next action should be. In most instances we do not have much to do.

```
/*---------------------------------------------------------------
 * Function: InitDataConn()
 *
 * Description: Set up a listening socket for a data connection
 */
SOCKET InitDataConn(PSOCKADDR_IN lpstName, HWND hDlg, u_int nAsyncMsg)
{
  int nRet;
  SOCKET hLstnSock;
  int nLen = SOCKADDR_LEN;

  /* get a TCP socket to use for data connection listen */
  hLstnSock = socket (AF_INET, SOCK_STREAM, 0);
  if (hLstnSock == INVALID_SOCKET)  {
    WSAperror(WSAGetLastError(), "socket()");
  } else {
    /* request async notification for most events */
    nRet = WSAAsyncSelect(hLstnSock, hDlg, nAsyncMsg,
           (FD_ACCEPT | FD_READ | FD_WRITE | FD_CLOSE));
    if (nRet == SOCKET_ERROR) {
      WSAperror(WSAGetLastError(), "WSAAsyncSelect()");
    } else {

      /* name the local socket with bind( ) */
      lpstName->sin_family = PF_INET;
      lpstName->sin_port   = 0;  /* any port will do */
      nRet = bind(hLstnSock,(LPSOCKADDR)lpstName,SOCKADDR_LEN);
      if (nRet == SOCKET_ERROR) {
          WSAperror(WSAGetLastError(), "bind()");
      } else {

        /* get local port number assigned by bind() */
        nRet = getsockname(hLstnSock,(LPSOCKADDR)lpstName,
             (int FAR *)&nLen);
        if (nRet == SOCKET_ERROR) {
            WSAperror(WSAGetLastError(), "getsockname()");
        } else {
```

```
            /* listen for incoming connection requests */
            nRet = listen(hLstnSock, 5);
            if (nRet == SOCKET_ERROR) {
                 WSAperror(WSAGetLastError(), "listen()");
            }
          }
        }
      }
      /* if we haven't had an error but we still don't know the local
       *  IP address, then we need to try to get it before we return */
      if (!lpstName->sin_addr.s_addr) {
        lpstName->sin_addr.s_addr = GetHostID( );
        if (!lpstName->sin_addr.s_addr) {
          MessageBox (hDlg, "Can't get local IP address",
            "InitDataConn( ) Failed", MB_OK | MB_ICONASTERISK);
          nRet = SOCKET_ERROR;
        }
      }
      /* If we had an error or we still don't know our IP address,
       *  then we have a problem.  Clean up */
      if (nRet == SOCKET_ERROR) {
           closesocket(hLstnSock);
           hLstnSock = INVALID_SOCKET;
      }
    }
    return (hLstnSock);
} /* end InitDataConn() */
```

Our `InitDataConn()` function initializes the data connection for a LIST, RETR, or STOR command. Note that our FTP client prepares to accept the data connection passively from the server. Hence, although this procedure is part of a client application, it actually performs like a server for the data connection.

Just as we describe in Chapter 4, the procedure for accepting a connection involves getting a socket, naming it, and then listening for an incoming connection request. One important distinction to notice here is that we do not assign a specific port number before naming the socket. Instead, we assign a port value of zero and allow the WinSock to assign an arbitrary port number for us. We then call `getsockname()` to discover the port number we were given. Later we send this port number to the server in the PORT command so the server knows where to connect. The FTP protocol does this to allow back-to-back data connections within the same client or simultaneous data connections in FTP clients running concurrently. If we tried to use the same port number every time, we would have a problem with duplicate socket names (and encounter the WSAEADDRINUSE error).

Notice also that we do not rely on `getsockname()` to return our local IP address along with the port number assigned. Unfortunately, some WinSocks do not return the local IP address from `getsockname()` after `bind()`, so we use our `GetHostID()` library function to get our local IP address. That makes it possible for us not to get the right IP address if we have more than one network interface, but we have to have something to put into the PORT command as our local address.

```
/*---------------------------------------------------------------
 * Function: AcceptDataConn()
 *
 * Description: Accept an incoming data connection
 */
SOCKET AcceptDataConn(SOCKET hLstnSock, PSOCKADDR_IN pstName)
{
  SOCKET hDataSock;
  int nRet, nLen = SOCKADDR_LEN, nOptval;

  hDataSock = accept (hLstnSock, (LPSOCKADDR)pstName, (LPINT)&nLen);
  if (hDataSock == SOCKET_ERROR) {
    int WSAErr = WSAGetLastError();
    if (WSAErr != WSAEWOULDBLOCK)
      WSAperror (WSAErr, "accept");
  } else if (bReAsync) {
    /* This SHOULD be unnecessary, since all new sockets are supposed
     *  to inherit properties of the listening socket (like all the
     *  asynch events) registered but some WinSocks don't do this.
     * Request async notification for most events */
    nRet = WSAAsyncSelect(hDataSock, hWinMain, WSA_ASYNC+1,
           (FD_READ | FD_WRITE | FD_CLOSE));
    if (nRet == SOCKET_ERROR) {
      WSAperror(WSAGetLastError(), "WSAAsyncSelect()");
    }
    /* try to get lots of buffer space */
    nOptval = astFtpCmd[0].nFtpCmd==STOR ? SO_SNDBUF : SO_RCVBUF;
    GetBuf(hDataSock, INPUT_SIZE*2, nOptval);
  }
```

```
  return (hDataSock);
} /* end AcceptData() */
```

We call the `AcceptDataConn()` function in response to an FD_ACCEPT event on our data socket. We call `accept()` to accept the incoming connection request from the server and save the socket handle returned. As with any asynchronous event, we are prepared for a WSAEWOULDBLOCK failure. This is unlikely, but if it occurs we would expect the WinSock to notify us of the FD_ACCEPT event again since we have called `accept()` (which is the reenabling function for the FD_ACCEPT event).

Notice that we reenable asynchronous events on the newly connected data socket. As our comments indicate, this should be unnecessary. We have an application option to disable this extra call for testing, but we do for added security since some WinSocks do not pass on socket attributes to accepted sockets.

Before we leave, we call our `GetBuf()` library function to try to request a large send or receive buffer from the WinSock. As we describe later in this chapter, the `GetBuf()` function calls `setsockopt()` with SO_SNDBUF (for a STOR command) or SO_RCVBUF (for a LIST or RETR command). These options are not required of every WinSock implementation, so they may fail. We also may not get as much buffer space as we request. Nonetheless, this is worth the effort because having larger network buffers can significantly increase our data throughput potential.

```
/*---------------------------------------------------------------
 * Function: SendData()
 *
 * Description: Open data file, read, and send
 */
long SendData(SOCKET *hDataSock, HFILE hDataFile, int len)
{
  static int cbReadFromFile;          /* bytes read from file */
  static int cbSentToServer;          /* number of buffered bytes sent */
  static HFILE hLastFile;             /* handle of last file sent */
  long cbTotalSent = 0;               /* total bytes sent */
  int nRet, WSAErr, cbBytesToSend;

  /* reset our counters when we access a new file */
  if (hLastFile != hDataFile) {
    cbReadFromFile = 0;
    cbSentToServer = 0;
    hLastFile = hDataFile;
```

```
}

/* read data from file, and send it */
do {
  if (bIOBeep)
    MessageBeep(0xFFFF);

  /* calculate what's left to send */
  cbBytesToSend = cbReadFromFile - cbSentToServer;
  if (cbBytesToSend <= 0) {

    /* read data from input file, if we need it */
    if (!bFromNul) {
      cbReadFromFile = _lread(hDataFile, achOutBuf, INPUT_SIZE);
      if (cbReadFromFile == HFILE_ERROR) {
        MessageBox (hWinMain, "Error reading data file",
          "SendData( ) Failed", MB_OK | MB_ICONASTERISK);
        break;
      } else if (!cbReadFromFile){
        /* EOF: no more data to send */
        CloseConn(hDataSock, (PSTR)0, 0, hWinMain);
        EndData( );
        break;
      } else {
        cbBytesToSend = cbReadFromFile; /* send as much as we read */
      }
    } else {
      /* just send whatever's in memory (up to our max) */
      if (lByteCount < MAXNULPUT) {
        cbBytesToSend = INPUT_SIZE;
      } else {
        CloseConn(hDataSock, (PSTR)0, 0, hWinMain);
        EndData();
      }
    }
    cbSentToServer = 0;  /* reset tally */
  }
  /* send data to server */
  nRet = send (*hDataSock, &(achOutBuf[cbSentToServer]),
             ((len < cbBytesToSend) ? len : cbBytesToSend), 0);
```

```
    if (nRet == SOCKET_ERROR) {
      WSAErr = WSAGetLastError();
      /* display significant errors */
      if (WSAErr != WSAEWOULDBLOCK)
        WSAperror(WSAErr, (LPSTR)"send()");
    } else {
      /* update byte counter, and display */
      lByteCount += nRet;
      _ltoa(lByteCount, achTempBuf, 10);
      SetDlgItemText(hWinMain, IDC_DATA_RATE, achTempBuf);
      cbSentToServer += nRet;/* tally bytes sent since last file read */
      cbTotalSent    += nRet;/* tally total bytes sent since started */
    }
  } while (nRet != SOCKET_ERROR);

  return (cbTotalSent);
} /* end SendData() */
```

The `SendData()` function is a data pump we use to send data on a data connection for a STOR command. It is one giant loop that reads from our open input data file and sends it. Because reading the data file from disk can incur significant system overhead and slow things down, we try to read large amounts each time we access the data file. We are conservative in the amount of data we send to try to minimize the overhead we might incur from fragmentation and reassembly. We describe the rationale behind the small sends in more detail in Chapter 14, "Dos and Don'ts."

We are always prepared for `send()` to fail with WSAEWOULDBLOCK. In this case, the WinSock would post an FD_WRITE event notification message to us when the system buffers are freed, so we can resume sending again. As we saw earlier, our FD_WRITE handler simply calls `SendData( )`, and our static variables in `SendData()` allow us to pick up where we left off without sending too much or too little data.

```
/*---------------------------------------------------------------
 * Function: RecvData()
 *
 * Description: Receive data from net and write to open data file
 */
int RecvData(SOCKET hDataSock, HFILE hDataFile, LPSTR achInBuf, int len)
{
```

```
  static HFILE hLastFile;          /* handle of last file sent */
  static int cbBytesBuffered;      /* total bytes received */
  int cbBytesRcvd = 0;
  int nRet=0, WSAErr;

   if (hDataFile != hLastFile) {
      hLastFile = hDataFile;
      cbBytesBuffered = 0;
   }

  /* read as much as we can from server */
    while (cbBytesBuffered < len) {

      nRet = recv (hDataSock,&(achInBuf[cbBytesBuffered]),
        len-cbBytesBuffered, 0);

      if (nRet == SOCKET_ERROR) {
        WSAErr = WSAGetLastError();
        /* display significant errors */
        if (WSAErr != WSAEWOULDBLOCK)
          WSAperror(WSAErr, (LPSTR)"recv()");
        /* exit recv() loop on any error */
          goto recv_end;
      } else if (nRet == 0) { /* other side closed socket */
        /* quit if server closed connection */
        goto recv_end;

      } else {
        /* update byte counter, and display */
        lByteCount += nRet;
        _ltoa(lByteCount, achTempBuf, 10);
        SetDlgItemText(hWinMain, IDC_DATA_RATE, achTempBuf);
        cbBytesRcvd += nRet;      /* tally bytes read */
        cbBytesBuffered += nRet;
      }
    }
recv_end:
  if (!bToNul &&
      ((cbBytesBuffered > (len-MTU_SIZE)) ||
       ((nRet == SOCKET_ERROR) &&
        WSAGetLastError() != WSAEWOULDBLOCK) ||
```

```
        (nRet == 0))) {
      /* if we have a lot buffered, write to data file */
      nRet = _lwrite(hDataFile, achInBuf, cbBytesBuffered);
      if (nRet == HFILE_ERROR)
        MessageBox (hWinMain, "Can't write to local file",
          "RecvData( ) Failed", MB_OK | MB_ICONASTERISK);
      cbBytesBuffered = 0;
    } else if (bToNul)
      cbBytesBuffered = 0;
  return (cbBytesRcvd);
} /* end RecvData() */
```

The `RecvData()` function reads as much data as possible from the data connection each time it is called, although it is called in response to a single FD_READ event notification message. Our repeated calls to `recv()` generate extra FD_READ messages if data still remains, but as we described earlier the advantages of such a strategy far outweigh the disadvantages. Simply put, reading data as we find it is faster than waiting to be told it is there.

All it takes to allow `RecvData()` to handle the extra FD_READ messages is handling the WSAEWOULDBLOCK error gracefully. Since any robust application should be prepared to do this anyway, this does not represent any extra effort.

To increase our speed slightly, we could have kept a counter of the number of our extra calls to `recv()` (the number of times we looped). In our FD_READ handler, we could then ignore that number of FD_READ messages after checking for errors rather than calling `RecvData()` and having it fail with WSAEWOULDBLOCK. The increase in speed is not significant, however, since constantly calling `RecvData()` helps to offset the delay between data arrival and message notification.

Notice that we try to minimize the significant system overhead involved with disk access by postponing writes to disk until we have a large amount of data buffered. Just in case something is left over when we receive an FD_CLOSE notification from the server to signal end of file, we finish reading data and writing to our data file in the `CloseConn()` function when we close the data connection.

```
/*-----------------------------------------------------------
 * Function: EndData()
 *
 * Description:  Close up the data connection
 */
void EndData (void) {
```

```
  LONG dByteRate;
  LONG lMSecs;

  /* calculate data transfer rate, and display */
  lMSecs = (LONG) GetTickCount() - lStartTime;
  if (lMSecs <= 55)
    lMSecs = 27;  /* about half of 55Msec PC clock resolution */

  /* socket check should not be necessary, but some WinSocks
   *  mistakenly post FD_CLOSE to listen socket after close */
  nAppState &= ~(DATACONNECTED);
  SetDlgItemText (hWinMain, IDC_STATUS, "Status: connected");

  if (lByteCount > 0L) {
    dByteRate = (lByteCount/lMSecs); /* data rate (bytes/Msec) */
    wsprintf (achTempBuf,
      "%ld bytes %s in %ld.%ld seconds (%ld.%ld Kbytes/sec)",
      lByteCount,
      ((astFtpCmd[0].nFtpCmd==STOR) ? "sent":"received"),
      lMSecs/1000, lMSecs%1000,
      (dByteRate*1000)/1024, (dByteRate*1000)%1024);
    SetDlgItemText (hWinMain, IDC_DATA_RATE, achTempBuf);
    if (hLogFile != HFILE_ERROR)
      _lwrite (hLogFile, achTempBuf, strlen(achTempBuf));
  }
  lStartTime = 0L;
  if (hDataFile != HFILE_ERROR) {
    _lclose (hDataFile);
    hDataFile = HFILE_ERROR;
    if (astFtpCmd[0].nFtpCmd == LIST) {
      wsprintf (achTempBuf, "notepad %s", szTempFile);
      WinExec (achTempBuf, SW_SHOW);
    }
  }
  astFtpCmd[0].nFtpCmd = 0;  /* reset pending command */
} /* end EndData() */
```

We call `EndData()` after we close a data connection with `CloseConn()`. Its main purpose is to record the data transfer end time, find the difference from the start time, calculate using the total byte count, and display it. Because the PC clock resolution is not better than 55 milliseconds, the resulting data rate is inaccurate for small amounts on fast network interfaces. But overall, the calculation is pretty dependable.

We also use this location to display the data file we just received if the last command was a LIST command (so the data file contains a detailed remote file directory). And we reset the pending command here too (rather than in `ProcessFtpCmd()`, as we do for other commands).

```
/*---------------------------------------------------------------
 * Function: CloseConn()
 *
 * Description: Standard way to close TCP connection gracefully
 */
int CloseConn(SOCKET *hSock, LPSTR achInBuf, int len, HWND hWnd)
{
  char achDiscard[BUF_SIZE];
  int nRet;

  if (*hSock != INVALID_SOCKET) {
    /* disable asynchronous notification if window handle provided */
    if (hWnd) {
      nRet = WSAAsyncSelect(*hSock, hWnd, 0, 0);
      if (nRet == SOCKET_ERROR)
        WSAperror (WSAGetLastError(), "CloseConn() WSAAsyncSelect()");
    }

    /* half-close the connection to close neatly (we don't check for
     *  an error since some WinSocks fail shutdown() how=1 with
     *  WSAEINVAL after they receive a TCP <RST>) */
    shutdown (*hSock, 1);

    /* read remaining data (until EOF or error) */
    nRet = 1;
    while (nRet && (nRet != SOCKET_ERROR)) {
      if (achInBuf)
        nRet = RecvData(*hSock, hDataFile, achInBuf, len);
      else
        nRet = recv (*hSock, (LPSTR)achDiscard, BUF_SIZE, 0);
    }
    /* close the socket, and ignore any error
     *  (since we can't do much about them anyway) */
    closesocket (*hSock);
```

```
    *hSock = INVALID_SOCKET;  /* we always invalidate socket */
  }
  return (nRet);
} /* end CloseConn() */
```

We use the `CloseConn()` function to close either a data connection or control connection. This demonstrates the recommended way to close a TCP connection gracefully by doing a "half-close" with `shutdown()`, reading any remaining data, and then calling `closesocket()` to release socket resources. This function could be part of our standard library, except for the call to our `RecvData()` function. We call `RecvData()` when we are receiving a file—after a LIST or RETR command—since we want to be sure to read and store any remaining data to our data file.

The way we call `WSAAsyncSelect()`is not necessary. We do so to avoid receiving an FD_CLOSE message, since we do not need that notification. There is really nothing that can prevent socket closure before you exit this function. So any reference to the socket handle after you exit from `CloseConn()` would fail with the WSAENOTSOCK error.

AC_FTP in Operation

The following screen capture shows our FTP client in action. This display shows the results immediately after the user sent a file named *winsock.htm* by pressing the "Send" button. As the FTP Protocol Dialog window shows, this action caused the FTP client to send the STOR command with its filename argument.

The FTP Protocol Dialog window also shows that the transfer completed successfully. The other replies indicate that the client sent the TYPE I (binary, not ASCII) and PORT commands before it sent the STOR command. Other replies are from the PWD, PASS, and USER commands used to log into the FTP server.

The Remote Working Directory window shows the reply to the PWD command, with the numeric reply prefix removed. It also contains the button controls that allow a user to get the file directory of the current remote directory, change the remote directory, or delete a file from the remote system.

Button Text	*Control ID*	*FTP Command*	*Description*
DIR	IDC_RDIR	LIST	Get remote file directory, and display in notepad
CWD	IDC_CWD	CWD	Change remote directory, and update window
DEL	IDC_DEL	DELE	Delete a file from the remote system

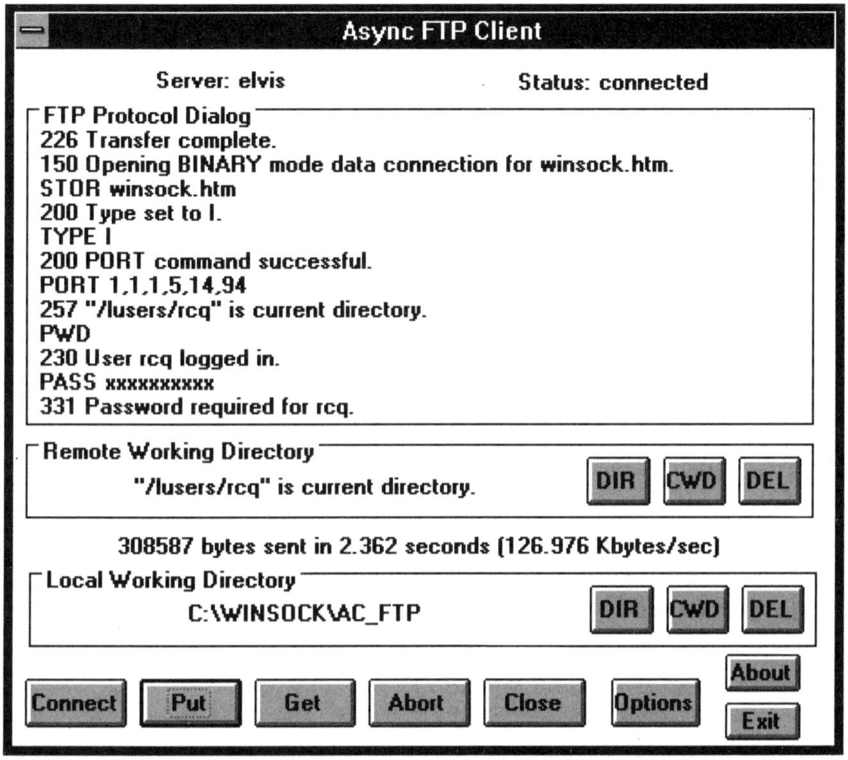

The Local Working Directory window provides the same information and functionality as the Remote Working Directory window, but it deals with the local file system rather than the remote system. As a result, its DIR, CWD, and DEL buttons do not initiate any FTP commands or network access.

The client displays data transfer statistics in the space between the Local Working Directory and Remote Working Directory windows. They show the number of bytes sent or received, the time it took, and the resulting data rate. In this example, the transfer was between two systems with 8-bit Ethernet interface cards on the same subnet. Your mileage will vary based on the many variables that affect the transfer rate: the network media, network interfaces, drivers, WinSocks. Overall, this application provides very fast transfer rates.

The buttons at the bottom provide the primary functionality for our FTP client application.

Button Text	*Control ID*	*FTP Commands*	*Description*
Connect	IDC_CONNECT	USER, PORT, PWD	Log in and get remote directory
Put	IDC_STOR	PORT, TYPE, STOR	Send a file
Get	IDC_RETR	PORT, TYPE, RETR	Receive a file
Abort	IDC_ABOR	ABOR	Abort any pending FTP command
Close	IDC_CLOSE	ABOR, QUIT	Close the control connection
Options	IDC_OPTIONS	not applicable	Invokes options dialog box

The About and Exit buttons are self-explanatory.

Sample Library

Our sample library is called WINSOCKX.LIB and contains a number of functions that one or more of the sample applications in this book use. Most of the library routines perform network operations of some kind by calling WinSock, but some perform nonnetwork operations such as window manipulation, creating files, and retrieving file directories.

The library functions that call WinSock provide high-level functionality commonly needed in many WinSock applications. They combine WinSock function calls to perform operations that many WinSock applications commonly implement. In a sense, they provide extensions to the WinSock API. They make it easier to use by hiding some of the low-level details.

In this section we provide a description of each function and give pointers to where the source code is located in the book. A few functions do not perform any network operations: They center a window or get a file directory. We provide their source code here.

Here are the functions in our sample library:

Function Name	*Description*
CenterWnd( )	Moves window to center of parent window
CloseConn( )	Standard TCP close routine: shutdown(how=1)/recv( )/closesocket( )
CreateLclFile( )	Creates a file on local system with file name provided

Dlg_About( )	Displays contents of the WSAData structure in application "about" box
GetAddr( )	Returns the address value for a hostname or address string
GetBuf( )	Gets the largest possible send or receive buffer up to limit provided
GetHostID( )	Gets the local IP address (may be default address on multi-homed hosts)
GetLclDir( )	Gets the file directory for the current working directory of local system and writes it to a file with file details (date, time, size)
GetPort( )	Gets a port number in network order from service name or port number string
WSAErrStr( )	Copies short error description for a WinSock error value into a buffer
WSAperror( )	Displays WinSock Error value, macro text, and short description

CenterWnd( )

The `CenterWnd()` library routine is not network related. This function is as mundane as they get. It simply centers *hWnd* passed in the first argument relative to the parent window *hParentWnd* passed in the second argument. The third argument, *bPaint*, is the repaint flag we pass to `MoveWindow()`.

We call `CenterWnd()` in all our sample applications as we process WM_CREATE or WM_INITDIALOG messages when the window is first created.

```
/*-----------------------------------------------------------
 * Function: CenterWnd()
 *
 * Description: Center window relative to the parent window
 */
void CenterWnd(HWND hWnd, HWND hParentWnd, BOOL bPaint) {
  RECT rc2, rc1;
  RECT FAR *lprc;
  int nWidth, nHeight, cxCenter, cyCenter;

  if (!hParentWnd)  /* if we have no parent, use desktop! */
    hParentWnd = GetDesktopWindow();
```

```
  GetWindowRect (hParentWnd, &rc2);
  lprc = (RECT FAR *)&rc2;

  cxCenter = lprc->left+((lprc->right-lprc->left)/2);
  cyCenter = lprc->top+((lprc->bottom-lprc->top)/2);

  GetWindowRect (hWnd, &rc1);
  nWidth  = rc1.right-rc1.left;
  nHeight = rc1.bottom-rc1.top;

  MoveWindow (hWnd,
   cxCenter-(nWidth/2),
   cyCenter-(nHeight/2),
   nWidth, nHeight,
   bPaint);
  return;
} /* end CenterWnd() */
```

CloseConn( )

The `CloseConn()` function contains the preferred routine for closing any TCP connection gracefully.

- It ensures that no data is lost by premature closure if `WSACleanup()` is called immediately following return from `closesocket()`.
- It aids closure with remote TCP/IP hosts that will not complete a close unless all data sent has been acknowledged.
- It allows an application to close a socket in response to FD_CLOSE notification and still read remaining data before closure.

We use this function in our sample echo server in Chapter 5 and reference it from a number of other places throughout the book. We highly recommend that you use this method to close your TCP sockets.

```
/*---------------------------------------------------------------
 * Function: CloseConn()
 *
 * Description: Close a TCP connection gracefully and ensure
 *  no data loss on WinSocks that post FD_CLOSE when data is
 *  still available to read
 */
```

```
int CloseConn(SOCKET hSock, LPSTR achInBuf, int len, HWND hWnd)
{
  int nRet;
  char achDiscard[BUF_SIZE];
  int cbBytesToDo=len, cbBytesDone=0;

  if (hSock != INVALID_SOCKET) {
    /* disable asynchronous notification if window handle provided */
    if (hWnd) {
      nRet = WSAAsyncSelect(hSock, hWnd, 0, 0);
      if (nRet == SOCKET_ERROR)
        WSAperror (WSAGetLastError(), "CloseConn() WSAAsyncSelect()");
    }

    /* half-close the connection to close neatly */
    nRet = shutdown (hSock, 1);

    /* read remaining data (until EOF or error) */
    for (nRet=1; (nRet && (nRet != SOCKET_ERROR));) {
      if (achInBuf) {
        nRet = recv (hSock,
                     &achInBuf[cbBytesDone],
                     cbBytesTodo, 0);
        if (nRet && (nRet != SOCKET_ERROR)) {
          cbBytesToDo -= nRet;
          cbBytesDone += nRet;
        }
      } else {
        /* no buffer provided, so discard any data */
        nRet = recv (hSock, achDiscard, BUF_SIZE, 0);
      }
    }
    /* close the socket, and ignore any error
     *  (since we can't do much about them anyway) */
    closesocket (hSock);
  }
  return (nRet);
} /* end CloseConn() */
```

CreateLclFile( )

The `CreateLclFile()` function is not network related. It calls `_lcreat(0)` to create the *szFileName* file passed to it. If the attempt fails—typically because the file name is illegal or the file already exists—then it notifies the user with a message and invokes the IDD_FILENAME dialog to prompt for a new file name.

Obviously, this is not a very flexible "library" routine since it requires this specific dialog named IDD_FILENAME. We use this routine in our sample FTP client application to create the local file for display of file directory, or while executing a RETR command (i.e., while getting a file from the server).

```
/*-------------------------------------------------------------------
 * Function: CreateLclFile()
 *
 * Description: Try to create a file on local system, and if it
 *  fails notify user and prompt for new local file name
 */
HFILE CreateLclFile (LPSTR szFileName) {
  HFILE hFile;
  char szRmtFile[MAXFILENAME];

  hFile = _lcreat (szFileName, 0);  /* create the file */

  strcpy (szRmtFile, szFileName);   /* save remote file name */
  while (hFile == HFILE_ERROR) {
    wsprintf(achTempBuf,
      "Unable to create file %s.  Change the name.", szFileName);
    MessageBox (hWinMain, achTempBuf,
      "File Error", MB_OK | MB_ICONASTERISK);
    if (!DialogBox (hInst, MAKEINTRESOURCE(IDD_FILENAME),
      hWinMain, Dlg_File)) {
      /* no new file name provided, so quit */
      break;
    } else {
      /* try to create new file name */
      hFile = _lcreat (szFileName, 0);
    }
  }
  strcpy (szFileName, szRmtFile);  /* replace remote file name */

  return (hFile);
} /* end CreateLclFile() */
```

Dlg_About( )

The `DlgAbout()` library routine is not network related. It is the dialog procedure we used for the "About box" in all of our sample applications. It displays the program name, icon, copyright notice, and compile time and date. It also displays most of the information about the WinSock DLL in use from the WSAData structure that `WSAStartup()` fills in.

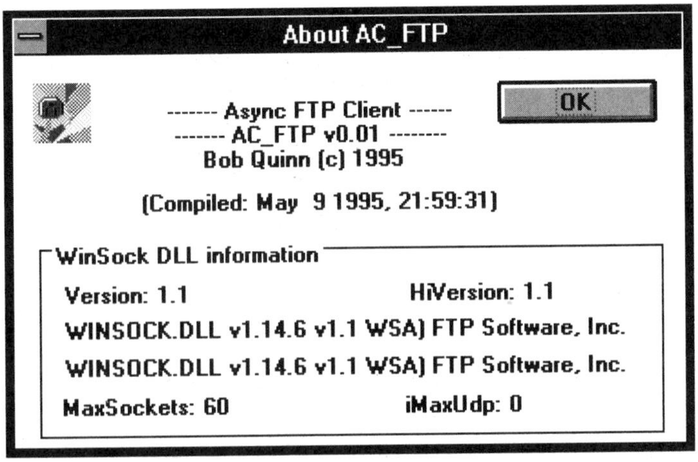

Obviously, this assumes that a previous call to `WSAStartup( )` was successful. It also assumes that the application used a WSAData structure named `stWSAData`.

```
/*-------------------------------------------------------------------
 * Function: Dlg_About()
 *
 * Description: Displays application vitals, and WinSock DLL information
 */
BOOL CALLBACK Dlg_About (
        HWND hDlg,
        UINT msg,
        UINT wParam,
        LPARAM lParam)
{
        char achDataBuf[WSADESCRIPTION_LEN+1];

        lParam = lParam;        /* avoid warning */
```

```
    switch (msg) {
        case WM_INITDIALOG:
                wsprintf (achDataBuf, "(Compiled: %s, %s)\n",
                    (LPSTR)__DATE__, (LPSTR)__TIME__);
            SetDlgItemText (hDlg, IDC_COMPILEDATE, (LPCSTR)achDataBuf);
            wsprintf (achDataBuf,
                "Version: %d.%d",
                LOBYTE(stWSAData.wVersion),  /* major version */
                HIBYTE(stWSAData.wVersion)); /* minor version */
            SetDlgItemText (hDlg, IDS_DLLVER, (LPCSTR)achDataBuf);
            wsprintf (achDataBuf,
                "HiVersion: %d.%d",
                LOBYTE(stWSAData.wVersion),  /* major version */
                HIBYTE(stWSAData.wVersion)); /* minor version */
            SetDlgItemText (hDlg, IDS_DLLHIVER, achDataBuf);
            SetDlgItemText (hDlg, IDS_DESCRIP,
              (LPCSTR)(stWSAData.szDescription));
            SetDlgItemText (hDlg, IDS_STATUS,
              (LPCSTR)(stWSAData.szSystemStatus));
            wsprintf (achDataBuf,
                "MaxSockets: %u", stWSAData.iMaxSockets);
            SetDlgItemText (hDlg, IDS_MAXSOCKS, (LPCSTR)achDataBuf);
            wsprintf (achDataBuf,
                "iMaxUdp: %u", stWSAData.iMaxUdpDg);
            SetDlgItemText (hDlg, IDS_MAXUDP, (LPCSTR)achDataBuf);

            /* center dialog box */
            CenterWnd (hDlg, hDlgMain, TRUE);

            return FALSE;

              case WM_COMMAND:
              switch (wParam) {
                  case IDOK:
                      EndDialog (hDlg, 0);
                      return TRUE;
              }
              break;
    }
    return FALSE;
} /* end Dlg_About() */
```

GetAddr( )

The `GetAddr()` function takes a host string *szHost* as input and returns an IP address. The *szHost* string may be an address in standard IP address string format known as the "dotted-decimal notation" (e.g., "128.127.50.77"), or it may be a host name.

GetBuf( ) first attempts to translate the host into a numeric IP address in network order, with `inet_addr()`. If this fails, `GetAddr()` checks to make sure you did not pass the limited broadcast address string "255.255.255.255" since that would make `inet_addr()` appear to fail—as it returns the value for SOCKET_ERROR (–1)—when it actually succeeds (the numeric value for this address is 0xFFFF).

If `inet_addr()` fails (for real), then `GetAddr()` calls `gethostbyname()` to resolve the string as a host name. This introduces a weakness in this function, since `gethostbyname()` operates in blocking mode. It would be possible to make a better version that used `WSAAsyncGetHostByName()` to use asynchronous notification upon completion, but the application would have to parse the asynchronous notification message (as we describe in Chapter 8).

We use `GetAddr()` in most of our sample applications to simplify processing of a destination input by a user. It is very convenient.

```
/*-----------------------------------------------------------
 * Function: GetAddr()
 *
 * Description: Given a string, it will return an IP address.
 *   First it tries to convert the string directly.
 *   If that fails, it tries to resolve it as a host name.
 *
 * WARNING: gethostbyname() is a blocking function
 */
u_long GetAddr (LPSTR szHost) {
  LPHOSTENT lpstHost;
  u_long lAddr = INADDR_ANY;

  /* check that we have a string */
  if (*szHost) {

    /* check for a dotted-IP address string */
    lAddr = inet_addr (szHost);

    /* if not an address, then try to resolve it as a host name */
```

```
      if ((lAddr == INADDR_NONE) &&
          (_fstrcmp (szHost, "255.255.255.255"))) {

        lpstHost = gethostbyname(szHost);
        if (lpstHost) {  /* success */
          lAddr = *((u_long FAR *) (lpstHost->h_addr));
        } else {
          lAddr = INADDR_ANY;    /* failure */
        }
      }
    }
    return (lAddr);
} /* end GetAddr() */
```

GetBuf( )

The `GetBuf()` function attempts to get as much send or receive buffer space from the network system as possible. It references the socket passed in *hSock* to call `setsockopt()` and set either SO_SNDBUF or SO_RCVBUF (the value of the *nOptVal* argument). It attempts to request the size in the *nBigBufSize* argument, but if that fails with an error (typically WSAENOBUFS) then it reduces the request amount by half and retries the request.

It stops retrying when the requested size is less than the MTU_SIZE (as defined in WINSOCKX.H, shown ahead), so this routine is good for increasing the buffer size, not for *reducing* the buffer size. We also do not retry if the call to `getsockopt()` shows less than the amount we requested. This would be the case if `setsockopt()` failed silently (i.e., it did not fulfill our request at all, but did not fail with SOCKET_ERROR) or only allocated part of the amount requested. For more information on `setsockopt()` and `getsockopt()`, see Chapter 9.

`GetBuf()` is useful for applications that do bulk data transfers. It returns the amount actually assigned (assuming `getsockopt()` succeeds). We use it in our sample FTP client application and in our echo server application (in Chapter 6). As we describe in Chapter 14, the idea behind increasing network buffer space is to decrease bottlenecks that can limit data transfer rates. The network-system buffers are the first part of the "data pipe" between the local application and the one on the remote machine it is communicating with. Increasing the network buffer space can have a dramatic effect on data throughput.

```
/*-----------------------------------------------------------
 * Function: GetBuf()
```

```
 *
 * Description: Get as much send or receive buffer space as
 *   WinSock allows starting with the amount requested
 */
int GetBuf (SOCKET hSock, int nBigBufSize, int nOptval) {
  int nRet, nTrySize, nFinalSize=0;

  for (nTrySize=nBigBufSize;
    nTrySize>MTU_SIZE;
    nTrySize>>=1) {
    nRet = setsockopt(hSock, SOL_SOCKET, nOptval,
      (char FAR*)&nTrySize, sizeof(int));
    if (nRet == SOCKET_ERROR) {
      int WSAErr = WSAGetLastError();
      if ((WSAErr==WSAENOPROTOOPT) || (WSAErr==WSAEINVAL))
        break;
    } else {
      nRet = sizeof(int);
      getsockopt(hSock, SOL_SOCKET, nOptval,
        (char FAR*)&nFinalSize, &nRet);
      break;
    }
  }
  return (nFinalSize);
} /* end GetBuf() */
```

GetHostID( )

Our `GetHostID()` function is analogous to the Berkeley `gethostid()` function missing from the WinSock API. Our function strives greatly to make up for this deficiency in WinSock, since there is no completely reliable method of retrieving a local IP address. It is as close to 100 percent reliable as possible with v1.1-compliant WinSocks (in WinSock 2, it is much easier to retrieve the local address).

First we try to use `gethostname()` to retrieve the local system's host name, and then we use `gethostbyname()` to resolve it. If that fails (either because `gethostname()` fails or returns a NULL string), or if we cannot resolve it with `gethostbyname()`, then we get a UDP socket, "connect" it to a nonexistent address and port (which does not generate any network traffic), and call `getsockname()` to try and discover the local address.

Fortunately, most applications do not need to know the local address. The UNIX "talk" protocol is one example of an application protocol with a legitimate need to know the local IP address (it sends it to the remote host). We use this function in our FTP client to get the local address to send to the server and in our echo server (in Chapter 6) to display the local host information.

```
/*-------------------------------------------------------------
 * Function: GetHostID()
 *
 * Description:  Get the Local IP address using the following algorithm:
 *    - get local host name with gethostname()
 *    - attempt to resolve local host name with gethostbyname()
 *    If that fails:
 *    - get a UDP socket
 *    - connect UDP socket to arbitrary address and port
 *    - use getsockname() to get local address
 */
LONG GetHostID () {
    char szLclHost [MAXHOSTNAME];
    LPHOSTENT lpstHostent;
    SOCKADDR_IN stLclAddr;
    SOCKADDR_IN stRmtAddr;
    int nAddrSize = sizeof(SOCKADDR);
    SOCKET hSock;
    int nRet;

    /* init local address (to zero) */
    stLclAddr.sin_addr.s_addr = INADDR_ANY;

    /* get the local host name */
    nRet = gethostname(szLclHost, MAXHOSTNAME);
    if (nRet != SOCKET_ERROR) {
      /* resolve host name for local address */
      lpstHostent = gethostbyname((LPSTR)szLclHost);
      if (lpstHostent)
        stLclAddr.sin_addr.s_addr =
           *((u_long FAR*) (lpstHostent->h_addr));
    }

    /* if still not resolved, then try second strategy */
    if (stLclAddr.sin_addr.s_addr == INADDR_ANY) {
      /* get a UDP socket */
```

```
      hSock = socket(AF_INET, SOCK_DGRAM, 0);
      if (hSock != INVALID_SOCKET)  {
        /* connect to arbitrary port and address (NOT loopback) */
        stRmtAddr.sin_family = AF_INET;
        stRmtAddr.sin_port   = htons(IPPORT_ECHO);
        stRmtAddr.sin_addr.s_addr = inet_addr("128.127.50.1");
        nRet = connect(hSock,
                       (LPSOCKADDR)&stRmtAddr,
                       sizeof(SOCKADDR));
        if (nRet != SOCKET_ERROR) {
          /* get local address */
          getsockname(hSock,
                      (LPSOCKADDR)&stLclAddr,
                      (int FAR*)&nAddrSize);
        }
        closesocket(hSock);   /* we're done with the socket */
      }
    }
    return (stLclAddr.sin_addr.s_addr);
} /* GetHostID() */
```

GetLclDir( )

`GetLclDir()` is not a network-related library function. It queries the local operating system for a file directory for the fileset *szTempFile* and writes the result to a temporary disk file. We use this function in our sample FTP client application. It is not very flexible as a library routine since it assumes you want the directory written to a disk file and uses the file name from the variable `szTempFile`.

```
/*---------------------------------------------------------------
 * Function: GetLclDir()
 *
 * Description: Get the local file directory and write to
 *   temporary file for later display
 */
BOOL GetLclDir(LPSTR szTempFile)
{
#ifdef WIN32
  struct _finddata_t stFile; /* Microsoft's 32bit find file structure */
```

```
#else
  struct _find_t stFile;      /* Microsoft's 16bit find file structure */
#endif
  HFILE hTempFile;
  int nNext;

  hTempFile = CreateLclFile (szTempFile);

  if (hTempFile != HFILE_ERROR) {
#ifdef WIN32
    nNext =_findfirst("*.*", &stFile);
    while (!nNext)  {
      wsprintf(achTempBuf, " %-12s %.24s  %9ld\n",
               stFile.name, ctime( &( stFile.time_write ) ), stFile.size );
      _lwrite(hTempFile, achTempBuf, strlen(achTempBuf));
      nNext = _findnext(nNext, &stFile);
    }
#else
    nNext = _dos_findfirst("*.*",0,&stFile);
    while (!nNext)  {
      unsigned month, day, year, hour, second, minute;
      month  =  (stFile.wr_date >>5)   & 0xF;
      day    =   stFile.wr_date & 0x1F;
      year   = ((stFile.wr_date >> 9)  & 0x7F) + 80;
      hour   =  (stFile.wr_time >> 11) & 0x1F;
      minute =  (stFile.wr_time >> 5)  & 0x3F;
      second =  (stFile.wr_time & 0x1F) << 1;
      wsprintf(achTempBuf,
        "%s\t\t%ld bytes \t%d-%d-%d \t%.2d:%.2d:%.2d\r\n",
        stFile.name, stFile.size,
        month, day, year, hour, minute, second);
      _lwrite(hTempFile, achTempBuf, strlen(achTempBuf));
      nNext = _dos_findnext(&stFile);
    }
#endif
    _lclose (hTempFile);
    return (TRUE);
  }
  return (FALSE);
} /* end GetLclDir() */
```

GetPort( )

The `GetPort()` library routine takes a string as an input argument and returns a port number in network order. It is analogous to the `GetAddr()` library routine described earlier. First it attempts to convert the string to a number with the standard C run-time library "ASCII to integer" `atoi()` function. If this fails, it treats the string as a service name and calls the `getservbyname()` function to resolve it.

`GetPort()` is convenient in applications that allow a user to select a port number or service. It allows simple processing of the input.

```
/*-----------------------------------------------------------------
 * Function: GetPort()
 *
 * Description: Returns a port number (in network order) from a
 *  string.  May involve converting from ASCII to integer, or
 *  resolving as service name.
 *
 * NOTE: This function is limited since it assumes the service
 *  name will not begin with an integer, although it *is* possible.
 */
u_short GetPort (LPSTR szService)
{
  u_short nPort = 0;  /* port 0 is invalid */
  LPSERVENT lpServent;
  char c;

  c = *szService;
  if ((c>='1') && (c<='9')) {
    /* convert ASCII to integer, and put in network order */
    nPort = htons((u_short)atoi (szService));
  } else {
    /* resolve service name to a port number */
    lpServent = getservbyname((LPSTR)szService, (LPSTR)"tcp");
    if (!lpServent) {
      WSAperror (WSAGetLastError( ), "getservbyname( )");
    } else {
      nPort = lpServent->s_port;
    }
  }
  return (nPort);
} /* end GetPort( ) */
```

WSAErrStr( )

The `WSAErrStr()` library routine returns a brief error string that describes the error value passed in *WSAErr*. It copies the string into the buffer in *lpErrBuf*. We use this function primarily from our `WSAperror()` function described below, but you could call it directly from your own error handler. It assumes that the string resources for all the WinSock error strings are available in the application. We describe these strings along with `WSAGetLastError()` in Chapter 10, "Support Routines." "Most of the strings are derived from the strings that the Berkeley Sockets `perror()` function prints for equivalent error values.

```
/*-------------------------------------------------------------
 * Function: GetWSAErrStr()
 *
 * Description: Given a WinSock error value, return error string
 */
int GetWSAErrStr (int WSAErr, LPSTR lpErrBuf) {
    int err_len=0;
    HANDLE hInst;
    HWND hwnd;

    hwnd  = GetActiveWindow();
    hInst = GetWindowWord(hwnd, GWW_HINSTANCE);

    if (WSAErr == 0)            /* if error passed is 0, use the */
      WSAErr = WSABASEERR;      /*  base resource file number */

    if (WSAErr >= WSABASEERR)  /* valid Error code? */
       /* get error string from the table in the resource file */
      err_len = LoadString(hInst, WSAErr, lpErrBuf, ERR_SIZE/2);

    return (err_len);
}  /* end GetWSAErrStr() */
```

WSAperror( )

The Windows Sockets API dces not include a counterpart of the Berkeley Sockets `perror()` function. BSD's global *errno* variable is the implicit input parameter to the `perror()` function; `perror()` prints a short textual description of the error to the `stderr` device in Berkeley UNIX.

In Windows, the `stderr` stream does not exist. As we mentioned already, the *errno* variable does not exist in Windows Sockets either, but the `WSAGetLastError()` function is a close match. Using a simple message box, and a resource file to store strings with error values for resource IDs, we have created our own `perror()` function equivalent. We call it `WSAperror()`.

Notice that `WSAperror()` does not call `WSAGetLastError()` automatically but takes the error value as an input argument. This makes `WSAperror()` flexible enough to handle errors applications received in asynchronous notification messages.

The following screen capture is an example of the message box output after our asynchronous FTP client application attempted to connect to a host that was not available.

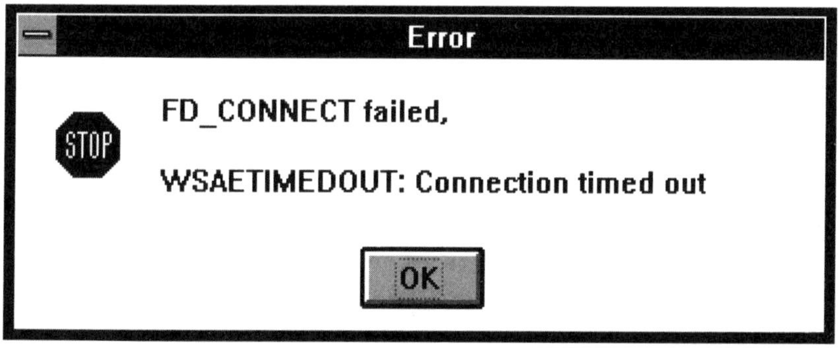


```
/*-------------------------------------------------------------
 * Function: WSAperror()
 *
 * Description: Displays the input parameter string (typically the
 *  name of the function that failed), and a string description that
 *  corresponds to the WinSock error value input parameter.
 */
void WSAperror (int WSAErr, LPSTR szFuncName)
{
    static char achErrBuf [ERR_SIZE];     /* buffer for errors */
    static char achErrMsg [ERR_SIZE/2];

    WSAErrStr (WSAErr, achErrMsg);

       wsprintf (achErrBuf, "%s failed,%-40c\n\n%s",
         szFuncName,' ',achErrMsg);

       /* display error message as is (even if incomplete) */
```

```
    MessageBox (GetActiveWindow, achErrBuf, "Error",
                     MB_OK | MB_ICONHAND);
    return;
}  /* end WSAperror() */
```

Here are the relevant contents of the resource file that contains the short descriptions of each error value. For more details on each error, refer to Appendix C, "Error Reference." For all but the error values that are particular to the Windows Sockets API itself, the following text is quoted directly from the Berkeley Sockets error descriptions (which you can see on a BSD UNIX system by typing "man errno"):

```
STRINGTABLE DISCARDABLE
BEGIN
    WSABASEERR        "[0] No Error"
    WSAEINTR          "WSAEINTR: Interrupted system call"
    WSAEBADF          "WSAEBADF: Bad file number"
    WSAEACCES         "WSACCESS: Permission denied"
    WSAEFAULT         "WSAEFAULT: Bad address"
    WSAEINVAL         "WSAEINVAL: Invalid argument"
    WSAEMFILE         "WSAEMFILE: Too many open files"
    WSAEWOULDBLOCK    "WSAEWOULDBLOCK: Operation would block"
    WSAEINPROGRESS    "WSAEINPROGRESS: Operation now in progress"
    WSAEALREADY       "WSAEALREADY: Operation already in progress"
    WSAENOTSOCK       "WSAENOTSOCK: Socket operation on non-socket"
    WSAEDESTADDRREQ "WSAEDESTADDRREQ: Destination address required"
    WSAEMSGSIZE       "WSAEMSGSIZE: Message too long"
    WSAEPROTOTYPE     "WSAEPROTOTYPE: Protocol wrong type for socket"
    WSAENOPROTOOPT    "WSAENOPROTOOPT: Bad protocol option"
    WSAEPROTONOSUPPORT "WSAEPROTONOSUPPORT: Protocol not supported"
    WSAESOCKTNOSUPPORT "WSAESOCKTNOSUPPORT: Socket type not supported"
    WSAEOPNOTSUPP     "WSAEOPNOTSUPP: Operation not supported on socket"
    WSAEPFNOSUPPORT "WSAEPFNNOSUPPORT: Protocol family not supported"
    WSAEAFNOSUPPORT
     "WSAEAFNNOSUPPORT: Address family not supported by protocol family"
    WSAEADDRINUSE     "WSAEADDRINUSE: Address already in use"
    WSAEADDRNOTAVAIL "WSAEADDRNOTAVAIL: Can't assign requested address"
    WSAENETDOWN       "WSAENETDOWN: Network is down"
    WSAENETUNREACH    "WSAENETUNREACH: Network is unreachable"
```

```
    WSAENETRESET      "WSAENETRESET: Net dropped connection or reset"
    WSAECONNABORTED "WSAECONNABORTED: Software caused connection abort"
    WSAECONNRESET     "WSAECONNRESET: Connection reset by peer"
    WSAENOBUFS        "WSAENOBUFS: No buffer space available"
    WSAEISCONN        "WSAEISCONN: Socket is already connected"
    WSAENOTCONN       "WSAENOTCONN: Socket is not connected"
    WSAESHUTDOWN      "WSAESHUTDOWN: Can't send after socket shutdown"
    WSAETOOMANYREFS "WSAETOOMANYREFS: Too many references, can't splice"
    WSAETIMEDOUT      "WSAETIMEDOUT: Connection timed out"
    WSAECONNREFUSED "WSAECONNREFUSED: Connection refused"
    WSAELOOP          "WSAELOOP: Too many levels of symbolic links"
    WSAENAMETOOLONG "WSAENAMETOOLONG: File name too long"
    WSAEHOSTDOWN      "WSAEHOSTDOWN: Host is down"
    WSAEHOSTUNREACH "WSAEHOSTUNREACH: No Route to Host"
    WSAENOTEMPTY      "WSAENOTEMPTY: Directory not empty"
    WSAEPROCLIM       "WSAEPROCLIM: Too many processes"
    WSAEUSERS         "WSAEUSERS: Too many users"
    WSAEDQUOT         "WSAEDQUOT: Disc Quota Exceeded"
    WSAESTALE         "WSAESTALE: Stale NFS file handle"
    WSAEREMOTE        "WSAEREMOTE: Too many levels of remote in path"
    WSASYSNOTREADY    "WSASYSNOTREADY: Network SubSystem is unavailable"
    WSAVERNOTSUPPORTED
      "WSAVERNOTSUPPORTED: WINSOCK DLL Version out of range"
    WSANOTINITIALISED
      "WSANOTINITIALISED: Successful WSASTARTUP not yet performed"
    WSAHOST_NOT_FOUND
      "WSAHOST_NOT_FOUND: Host not found"
    WSATRY_AGAIN        "WSATRY_AGAIN: Non-Authoritative Host not found"
    WSANO_RECOVERY
      "WSANO_RECOVERY: Non-Recoverable errors: FORMERR, REFUSED, NOTIMP"
    WSANO_DATA
      "WSANO_DATA: Valid name, no data record of requested type"
END
```

WinSockx.h

This header file accompanies the WinSockx sample library. It defines a number of common manifest constant values, contains redefinitions for Win32, externs some global variables defined in globals.c, and prototypes the functions in our WinSockx library.

```
/*---------------------------------------------------------------------
 * filename: winsockx.h
 *
 * copyright by Bob Quinn, 1995
 *
 *  Description: Specifics to our winsockx.lib library (macros,
 *   externals, and prototypes)
 *
 -------------------------------------------------------------------- */
#include <windows.h>

#define MTU_SIZE    1460
#define INPUT_SIZE  8192
#define BUF_SIZE    1024
#define ERR_SIZE    512

#define MAXUSERNAME  64
#define MAXPASSWORD  32
#define MAXFILENAME  64

/* our asynch notification message */
#define WSA_ASYNC WM_USER+1

extern WSADATA stWSAData;    /* WinSock DLL Info */

extern char *aszWSAEvent[7];     /* for error messages */
extern char achTempBuf[BUF_SIZE];/* screen I/O data buffer and such */
extern char szTempFile[10];      /* temporary work file name */

extern HWND hWinMain;           /* main window (or dialog) handle */
extern HINSTANCE hInst;         /* instance handle */


/*---- library function prototypes ---- */
void    CenterWnd(HWND, HWND, BOOL);
int CloseConn(SOCKET, LPSTR, int, HWND);
HFILE   CreateLclFile (LPSTR);
BOOL CALLBACK Dlg_About (HWND, UINT, UINT, LPARAM);
u_long  GetAddr(LPSTR);
int     GetBuf(SOCKET, int, int);
```

```
LONG     GetHostID(void);
BOOL     GetLclDir(LPSTR szTempFile);
u_short GetPort (LPSTR);
void     WSAperror (int, LPSTR);
int      WSAErrStr (int, LPSTR);
```

Globals.c

These are declarations of global variables used throughout our library.

```
/*---------------------------------------------------------------------
 * filename: globals.c
 *
 * copyright by Bob Quinn, 1995
 *
 *  Description: Globals used by winsockx library and common to
 *   its users
 *
 --------------------------------------------------------------------- */
#include <winsock.h>
#include "..\winsockx.h"
#include "..\wsa_xtra.h"

WSADATA stWSAData;              /* WinSock DLL info */

char *aszWSAEvent[] = {         /* for error messages */
  "unknown FD_ event",
  "FD_READ",
  "FD_WRITE",
  "FD_OOB",
  "FD_ACCEPT",
  "FD_CONNECT",
  "FD_CLOSE"
};

char achTempBuf [BUF_SIZE]={0};  /* screen I/O data buffer and such */
char szTempFile []="delete.me";  /* temporary work file */

HWND hWinMain;                   /* main window (dialog) handle */
HINSTANCE hInst;                 /* instance handle */
```

WSA_Xtra.h

These are some things that the standard WinSock.H file forgot, got wrong, or left optional.

```
/*
 * Filename: wsa_xtra.h
 *
 * Description:
 *   - macros WinSock v1.1 forgot
 *   - fixes one broken macro in v1.1
 *   - structures for optional features
 */
#ifndef _WSA_XTRA_
#define _WSA_XTRA_

#include <winsock.h>

/* fix of broken macro in v1.1 WinSock.H */
#undef  IPROTO_GGP
#define IPROTO_GGP  3
#ifndef IPROTO_IGMP
#define IPROTO_IGMP 2
#endif

/* to avoid word size sensitivity */
#ifndef WIN32
#define EXPORT __export
#else
#define EXPORT
#endif

#define MAXHOSTNAME   255   /* maximum length of a DNS host name */
#define MAXADDRSTR    16    /* maximum length of an IP address string */

/* handy in many places */
#define SOCKADDR_LEN sizeof(struct sockaddr)

/* WinSock version information (use WSA_VERSION for WSAStartup( )) */
#ifndef MAKEWORD
#define MAKEWORD(l,h) ((WORD)(((BYTE)(l))|(((WORD)(BYTE)(h))<<8)))
```

```
#endif
#define WSA_MAJOR_VERSION 1
#define WSA_MINOR_VERSION 1
#define WSA_VERSION MAKEWORD(WSA_MAJOR_VERSION, WSA_MINOR_VERSION)

/* for UNIX compatibility */
#define bcopy(s,d,n)    _fmemcpy((d),(s),(n))
#define bcmp(s1,s2,n)   _fmemcmp((s1),(s2),(n))
#define bzero(s,n)      _fmemset(((s),0,(n))

#define IP_TTL     4  /* level=IPPROTO_IP option, Time To Live */
#define MAX_TTL    255       /* maximum IP "Time To Live" value */

/* ICMP types */
#define ICMP_ECHOREPLY  0     /* ICMP type: echo reply */
#define ICMP_ECHOREQ    8     /* ICMP type: echo request */

/* definition of ICMP header as per RFC 792 */
typedef struct icmp_hdr {
       u_char  icmp_type;            /* type of message */
       u_char  icmp_code;            /* type sub code */
       u_short  icmp_cksum;          /* ones complement cksum */
       u_short  icmp_id;             /* identifier */
       u_short  icmp_seq;            /* sequence number */
       char  icmp_data[1];    /* data */
} ICMP_HDR, *PICMPHDR, FAR *LPICMPHDR;
#define ICMP_HDR_LEN  sizeof(ICMP_HDR)

/* definition of IP header version 4 as per RFC 791 */
#define      IPVERSION    4
typedef struct ip_hdr {
       u_char ip_hl;               /* header length */
       u_char ip_v;            /* version */
       u_char ip_tos;              /* type of service */
       short  ip_len;          /* total length */
       u_short ip_id;              /* identification */
       short  ip_off;          /* fragment offset field */
       u_char ip_ttl;              /* time to live */
       u_char ip_p;            /* protocol */
       u_short ip_cksum;             /* checksum */
       struct in_addr ip_src;        /* source address */
```

```
       struct  in_addr ip_dst;        /* destination address */
} IP_HDR, *PIP_HDR, *LPIP_HDR;
#define IP_HDR_LEN sizeof(IP_HDR)

#ifndef WSA_MULTICAST
/*
 * The following constants are from the BSD /include/netinet/in.h
 *  header file.  They DO NOT match the values defined by Steve Deering
 *  of Stanford University <deering@pescadero.Stanford.EDU> (WinNT v3.5
 *  did use Deering's values, however, which are 2-6 ...offset 7)
 *
 *  The use of these multicast options is described in "IP Multicast
 *  Extensions for 4.3BSD UNIX-related systems (MULTICAST 1.2 Release)."
 *  It describes the extensions to BSD, SunOS, and Ultrix to support
 *  multicasting, as specified by RFC 1054 (since superceded by
 *  RFC 1112).
 */
#define DEERING_OFFSET      7   /* subtract this bias for NT options */

#define IP_MULTICAST_IF     9   /* set/get    IP multicast interface */
#define IP_MULTICAST_TTL    10  /* set/get    IP multicast timetolive */
#define IP_MULTICAST_LOOP   11  /* set/get    IP multicast loopback */
#define IP_ADD_MEMBERSHIP   12  /* add  (set) IP group membership */
#define IP_DROP_MEMBERSHIP  13  /* drop (set) IP group membership */

#define IP_DEFAULT_MULTICAST_TTL     1
#define IP_DEFAULT_MULTICAST_LOOP    1
#define IP_MAX_MEMBERSHIPS           20

/* the structure used to add and drop multicast addresses (the
 *  imr_interface field is ignored since we only support one interface)
 */
typedef struct ip_mreq {
       struct in_addr imr_multiaddr; /* multicast group to join */
       struct in_addr imr_interface; /* interface to join on */
}IP_MREQ;
#endif

#endif /* _WSA_XTRA_ */
```

8 Host Names and Addresses

In This Chapter:

- Hostname and Address Resolution
- Host Table, DNS, and NIS
- Local Host Information
- Addresses and Formatting
- Protocol and Address Families

The ability to simplify means to eliminate the unnecessary so that the necessary may speak.

Hans Hofman

Given the choice between using a host name or a network address, most people will choose to use a host name. A host name is easier to remember, since it is not just a label but also a mnemonic. For example, the host name *www.sockets.com* means more than an address like 128.127.50.66. This host name describes the type of software (application protocol) you need to access it, the type of information you will find there, and the type of site it is. It's a **com**mercial site that offers **sockets** application development information that you can access with **w**orld **w**ide **w**eb browsers (which use http). Other host names can convey other types of information, too. And some host names do not convey anything but are easy to remember because they are attractive and "catchy."

The only problem is that an application needs a network address to allow one application to communicate with an application on another host. As a result, a client application needs to resolve a host name into the corresponding network address to contact the server. We call this translation process *hostname resolution*. WinSock has a pair of functions that perform this process for you.

In this chapter we describe the two WinSock hostname resolution functions and show you how to use them. We also describe the WinSock functions to translate from a network address back to a host name, which we call *address resolution*. We reveal a little about the underlying host database and the mechanisms involved with hostname and address resolution, since it helps to know what types of problems can occur. We also describe the surprisingly complex process of retrieving the network address for a local host. In the final section, we describe the WinSock functions that translate network addresses between numeric and textual forms.

Hostname and Address Resolution

When someone uses a client application, they need to designate another network host to communicate with, a destination. They might have the network address for that host, but more often they will have a host name. Since network operations all reference an address, not a host name, the client application needs to answer the question, "What is the network address that corresponds to this host name?" The process of answering this question is called *hostname resolution*.

A server application accepts connection requests from client applications. A server typically accepts a connection from any network host, without regard to its address or host name. But there may be times—perhaps for security reasons—when a server needs to translate a network address back to its host name. As mentioned, we call this process *address resolution*. It is essentially a mirror process of name resolution whereby you use a network address to resolve the host name.

The WinSock API has one pair of functions for name resolution and another pair for address resolution operations. One function in each pair blocks until the operation completes, and the other notifies the application asynchronously upon completion. All of the hostname and address resolution functions retrieve complete list information about a host when resolution succeeds. The functions that perform hostname resolution are `gethostbyname( )` and `WSAAsyncGetHostByName( )`. The functions that do address resolution are `gethostbyaddr( )` and `WSAAsyncGetHostByAddr( )`. These functions are similar to the other so-called database functions that provide protocol and service resolution, as we describe in Chapter 10, "Support Routines."

Windows Sockets offers a choice between operation modes because hostname or address resolution requests can take some time to process. The WinSock specification does not prescribe the mechanisms behind these processes, so they may involve reading a local host database or requesting information from any number of remote host database systems (we describe more about these different mechanisms in the "Host Table, DNS, and NIS" section later in this chapter). Resolution can occur instantaneously, or it can take a minute or more. You have a choice between resolution operation modes—asynchronous and blocking—for the same reasons you have a choice between operation modes in many other network operations. As we describe in Chapter 5, "Operation Modes," there are tradeoffs and advantages to either choice you make, and they affect your overall application design.

All of the name and address resolution functions are flexible by design, to accommodate different address families. The input parameters for address functions, and the `hostent` structure used for output of both name and address resolution functions, can handle addresses of any length. We concentrate on Internet protocol (IP) addresses here, but this flexibility allows WinSock to adapt to the address scheme used by any address family.

hostent Structure

All the WinSock version 1.1 name and address resolution functions return their results in a `hostent` data structure, which contains all there is to know about an individual host—at least all there is to know in a single address family.

One limitation with `hostent` and the Berkeley Sockets–compatible name resolution functions is that they can report only on a single address family for each query. For example, you get IP address information only when you specify AF_INET for *h_addrtype*. You would need to make a second function call with a different *h_addrtype* value to get interface address information for other address families (assuming the WinSock version in use supported any other address families). As we describe in Chapter 17, WinSock version 2 has new functions that provide protocol-independent network interface information that can enumerate multiple address families.

The v1.1 WINSOCK.H file defines the `hostent` data structure as follows:

```
struct hostent {
   char  FAR * h_name;              /* official name of host */
   char  FAR * FAR * h_aliases;     /* alias list */
   short h_addrtype;                /* address family */
   short h_length;                  /* length of address */
   char  FAR * FAR * h_addr_list;  /* list of addresses */
};
typedef struct hostent HOSTENT;
typedef struct hostent *PHOSTENT;
typedef struct hostent FAR *LPHOSTENT;
```

h_name: contains the official name of a host. For TCP/IP, which primarily uses the Domain Name Service (DNS) protocol for hostname and address resolution, the "official name" is the DNS "canonical name." In a DNS database, each canonical name has an address (A) record.

h_aliases: points to an array of string pointers (terminated by a NULL pointer value). Each string points to an alias, which is an alternate host name for the same host, a synonym for the official name. In a DNS database, each alias has a canonical name (CNAME) record that specifies the corresponding canonical name. When you resolve an alias, first you retrieve the canonical name and then you use it to retrieve the address.

h_addrtype: denotes the type of address to which the *h_addr_list* field points. For TCP/IP, currently the only value you will find here is AF_INET or PF_INET (see "Protocol and Address Families" at the end of this chapter for a description of these macros). Notice that this is the same value that goes into the *sa_family* field in a `sockaddr` structure (the *sin_family* value in the `sockaddr_in` structure). This value differs for other protocol suites and addresses; for instance, you use AF_APPLETALK for an AppleTalk address, or AF_IPX for a Novell IPX/SPX address.

h_length: contains the length in bytes of each address to which the *h_addr_list* field points. This value differs according to the address type specified in the *h_addrtype* field. For TCP/IP (*h_addrtype*=AF_INET), *h_length* is always 4.

h_addr_list: points to an array of pointers to network addresses in network byte order (yes, some hosts have more than one address, since they may have more than one network interface). The last pointer entry in the array is followed by a NULL pointer value to mark the end of the array. The *h_length* field specifies the length of each address. Note: To simplify access to the primary address (the first in this array), the macro h_addr is available for h_addr_list[0].

Hostname Resolution

An application must have the network address of a host in order to communicate with it. The WinSock functions that listen, connect, send, and receive all use a network address rather than a host name. Since most people use host names instead of network addresses, you will need to perform hostname resolution to initiate communications from your client application. Again, hostname resolution is the process of translating a host name into a network address.

You need to choose between two functions that do hostname resolution. The main difference between them is their operation modes, but they also differ significantly in their use of buffers:

- `gethostbyname( )`: blocks until the name resolution completes; WinSock stores the results in a shared system buffer.
- `WSAAsyncGetHostByName( )`: returns immediately, and WinSock notifies the application asynchronously when name resolution completes; WinSock stores results in a buffer that the application provides.

Note: The WinSock specification dictates that these functions must not resolve address strings as host names. As a result, if you provided an IP address string like "128.127.50.1" as the *name* input argument to either function, then they should fail as they would with an unknown host (i.e., with WSAHOST_NOT_FOUND error).

All applications that prompt for a destination host should allow a user to input either an address or a host name. This means that applications must be able to distinguish between an address string or host name so they can act on them appropriately. As we describe in Chapter 7, the `GetAddr( )` function in our WinSockx sample library does precisely this.

gethostbyname( )

`gethostbyname( )` uses a host name to access a WinSock implementation's host database (which may be a host table, DNS, NIS, etc.), and returns complete host information, including official host name, all known aliases, and interface addresses.

```
struct hostent FAR * PASCAL FAR gethostbyname /* NULL on failure */
    (char FAR *name);       /* pointer to name of the host */
```

name: a null-terminated string containing the host name to resolve. The form for a host name is a standard domain name, as we describe a little later. Typically, this does not have to be a fully qualified domain name (FQDN), since most WinSocks will automatically append the domain portion of the local host's domain name to a host name that does not contain a period before trying to resolve it.

`gethostbyname( )` blocks until the hostname resolution operation completes (succeeds or fails). Upon completion, the return value is a pointer to a hostent structure, or a NULL on failure. On failure, you call `WSAGetLastError( )` to find the error value. The most common error value is WSAHOST_NOT_FOUND, which occurs when WinSock cannot resolve the host name.

On success, the return value points to the system buffer that contains the results. You need to use the contents of this buffer immediately since the WinSock DLL may reuse the buffer for the results of a call to `gethostbyname( )` by another process. If you do not copy the hostent contents immediately upon return from `gethostbyname( )`, subsequent calls may overwrite the results of your query (although this danger exists in 16-bit Windows more than in 32-bit Windows). The buffer is also read-only, so do not try to free it or change its contents, or a protection fault may result.

Code Example

The following code example shows how to use `gethostbyname( )`. We have written it to detect and redirect handling of an IP address string, in case the user does not type a host name (we show the network address resolution code example later in this chapter). The maximum number of addresses and aliases we have listed is optimistic. Berkeley Sockets version 4.3 only returns up to four of each, even when more are available.

```
#define MAX_ALIASES   8
#define MAX_ADDRS     8
/* RFC 1034 defines maximum hostname length of 255 characters */
#define MAXHOSTNAME   255
#define HOSTADDRSIZE  sizeof(struct in_addr)
extern void CopyHostent(LPSTR, LPSTR, LPSTR,
                        struct in_addr FAR*, struct in_addr FAR*)
char szHost[MAXHOSTNAME]          /* buffer for user input */
char szHostname[MAXHOSTNAME]      /* buffer for results: host name */
char aszAliases[MAX_ALIASES][MAXHOSTNAME];          /* aliases */
struct in_addr astAddrs[MAX_ADDRS][HOSTADDRSIZE];  /* addresses */
struct hostent FAR *lpstWSHostent; /* ptr to WinSock DLL hostent */
struct in_addr stHostAddr;         /* IP address */
struct in_addr FAR *alpAddrs;      /* array of IP addresses */
...
/* try host string as a dotted Internet address string */
stHostAddr.s_addr = inet_addr (szHost);
if ((stHostAddr.s_addr != INADDR_NONE) ||
    (!{_fstrcmp (szHost, "255.255.255.255"))) {
```

```
        /* inet_addr( ) returned a valid address value (0xFFFF return
         *  is acceptable if input was the limited broadcast address) */
           <do network address resolution (see later section)>

    } else {
        /* the string wasn't a dotted IP address, so try
         *  hostname resolution with the string */
        lpstWSHostent = gethostbyname(szHost);
        if (!lpstWSHostent) {          /* name resolution failed */
                <notify user of error>

        } else {                       /* else copy data immediately */
            /* This copies entire contents of hostent, although
             *  typically all you need is the primary IP address (which
             *  CopyHostent puts into stHostAddr) */
            CopyHostent(lpstWSHostent, szHostname, aszAliases,
                        &stHostAddr, alpAddrs);
        }
    } /* end hostname resolution */
```

The above code does name resolution of the string in *szHost* after checking to make sure the string is not an address in dotted Internet form. If `gethostbyname( )` returns a pointer to indicate success, we copy the contents of the hostent structure with the `CopyHostent( )` function shown next. Most applications do not need to copy the entire hostent structure contents, but we do so to demonstrate how to access all the fields in a hostent structure. Most applications only need the primary network address from the *h_addr_list[0]* field (also available with *h_addr* macro) in the hostent structure after a successful call to `gethostbyname( )`.

```
/*---------------------------------------------------------------------
 * Function: CopyHostent( )
 *
 * Description: Copy the contents of a hostent structure to
 *  specified buffers
 */
void CopyHostent(char FAR *lpWSHostent,
                 char FAR *szHostname,
                 char FAR *alpAliases[],
                 struct in_addr FAR *lpstHostAddr,
                 struct in_addr FAR *alpAddrs[])
{
```

```
    int i;

    /* copy official host name */
    _fstrcpy (szHostname,&(lpWSHostent->h_name));

    /* copy aliases */
    for (i=0;(lpWSHostent->h_aliases[i] && (i<MAX_ALIASES)); i++) {
        _fstrcpy (*alpAliases, *(lpWSHostent->h_aliases[i]));
                alpAliases++;
    }

    /* get primary interface address (the first in array
     *  h_addr_list[0], so we use h_addr macro to access it) */
    lpstHostAddr->s_addr = lpWSAHostent->h_addr;

    /* copy the other network addresses */
    for (i=1; (lpWSHostent->h_addr_list[i] && (i<MAX_ADDRS)); i++)
    {
        _fmemcpy (*alpAddrs, *(lpWSAHostent->h_addr_list[i]),
                  lpWSAHostent->h_length);
        alpAddrs++;
    }
} /* end CopyHostent( ) */
```

WSAAsyncGetHostByName( )

`WSAAsyncGetHostByName( )` uses a host name to access a WinSock implementation's host database (which may be a host table, DNS, NIS, etc.). It returns the same complete host information in a `hostent` structure that `gethostbyname( )` does (host name, aliases, and interface addresses).

```
HANDLE PASCAL FAR WSAAsyncGetHostByName           /* 0 on failure */
  (HWND hWnd,              /* window to rcv msg on completion */
   unsigned int wMsg,      /* message to be rcvd on completion */
   char FAR *name,         /* ptr to name of host to be resolved */
   char FAR *buf,          /* ptr to data area to rcv hostent data */
   int buflen);            /* size of data area buf above */
```

hWnd: handle of the window you want the asynchronous notification message posted to when the name resolution operation completes (succeeds or fails) *wMsg*: value for the user message you want WinSock to post to you when the name resolution operation completes. You should add to the predefined WM_USER base when creating your user message value to avoid conflicts with predefined system messages.

name: a null-terminated string containing the host name to resolve. The form for a host name is a standard domain name, as we describe a little later. Typically, this does not have to be a fully qualified domain name (FQDN), since most WinSocks will automatically append the domain portion to a host name that does not contain a period before trying to resolve it.

buf: a pointer to a buffer area into which WinSock can copy the results of a successful hostname resolution (the hostent structure, and all strings pointed to by the alias and address lists). The v1.1 WinSock specification recommends that the size of the buffer should be MAXGETHOSTSTRUCT bytes (see note below for more information).

buflen: the size of the buffer pointed to by the *buf* parameter

`WSAAsyncGetHostByName( )` always returns immediately, before the name resolution operation completes. The operation completes in the background and notifies the application with an asynchronous notification message upon completion. You can cancel the operation before completion with `WSACancelAsyncRequest( )`, as we describe in Chapter 5.

On failure, you call `WSAGetLastError( )` to find out the cause of the failure. The specification clearly indicates which errors you can expect to receive at this time (and which can occur later in the asynchronous notification message). One error the v1.1 WinSock specification does not list, however, is WSAEFAULT, which might occur if the buffer area is invalid. It is not clear whether WinSock will fail with this error immediately, or post it in an asynchronous notification message, so your application should be prepared for either possibility.

On success, `WSAAsyncGetHostByName( )` returns a nonzero *asynch query handle* that you can use to identify the subsequent asynchronous message response. This handle is helpful if you initiate more than one asynchronous operation simultaneously. You also use this handle if you need to cancel the asynchronous operation with `WSACancelAsyncRequest( )`. Success of the `WSAAsyncGetHostByName( )` function call indicates the successful *initiation* of the hostname resolution operation. It does not indicate success of the hostname resolution operation itself.

Note: The memory area you point to in *buf* must be valid when the name resolution process completes. As a result, you need to be sure to assign a persistent buffer that you can access after you call `WSAAsyncGetHostByName( )`.

This means you need to assign a globally allocated or static buffer, rather one that you create within the function that calls `WSAAsyncGetHostByName( )`.

Upon Completion

When WinSock completes the name resolution operation, it posts a message to the application. The notification message—which the application specifies in the *wMsg* parameter—contains the value of the asynch query handle originally returned by `WSAAsyncGetHostByName( )` in *wParam*, so you can match the response with the original query. You should use the WSAGETASYNCERROR( ) macro to check for an error in the upper word in *lParam* before you do anything else (the use of message crackers ensures portability of source code between 16-bit and 32-bit environments, where Window's procedure parameters differ significantly).

If the error value is nonzero, the operation failed. On failure, the error value indicates why the operation failed, and the buffer contents are indeterminate. If the error value is WSAENOBUFS, your buffer size was too small to accommodate the results. In this case the low word of *lParam* contains the buffer size you need; you should use the WSAGETASYNCBUFLEN( ) macro to retrieve this value. This should not be necessary, however, if you always allocate a buffer size of MAXGETHOSTSTRUCT (as defined in WINSOCK.H). The v1.1 WinSock specification recommends a buffer of the size MAXGETHOSTSTRUCT, although it does *not* guarantee that the results will never exceed this size.

If the error is zero, the operation succeeded. In this case you can use the WSAGETASYNCBUFLEN to extract the buffer length from the lower word in *lParam*, although most applications do not need to reference this value.

Sketch of Function Operation

We demonstrate the asynchronous hostname resolution process in detail in the following example code. For now, this quick sketch summarizes what occurs when an application calls `WSAAsyncGetHostByName( )`:

- The Windows Sockets application calls `WSAAsyncGetHostByName( )` with the value of the *wMsg* field (WM_USER+1 in our example, but this message could be any unique value the application chooses).
- The WinSock DLL returns a "query handle" (value 5, for example) that indicates the asynchronous request has been initiated successfully.
- The WinSock DLL then successfully resolves the host name, so it posts the WM_USER+1 message to the application without an error (to the window handle the application originally provided in the *hWnd* argument).

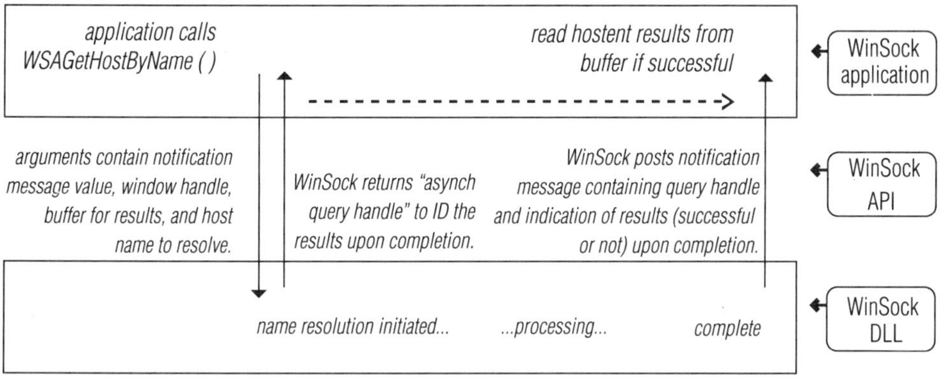

Figure 8-1 WinSock applications using asynchronous name resolution with WSAGetHostByName( ).

- The application's message handler receives the message, removes the query handle from `wParam`, and checks the upper word in `lParam` for an error. If no error, then the application knows that the buffer it pointed to when it originally called `WSAAsyncGetHostByName( )` now has the response from the query (the host information) in it. At this point the application can access the contents of the hostent structure from the application's buffer.

Code Example

Here is a pseudocode example of `WSAAsyncGetHostByName( )` in action, including the relevant portion of a message handler that responds to the asynchronous message when hostname resolution completes:

```
/* this asynchronous message can be any valid user message value */
#define HOST_CALLBACK  WM_USER+1
#define MAXHOSTNAME    255
extern HANDLE hWnd;
char szHost[MAXHOSTNAME]          /* buffer for user input */
static char achHostInfo[MAXGETHOSTSTRUCT]; /* buffer for results */
struct in_addr stHostAddr;        /* network address structure */
HANDLE hQuery;                    /* asynch query handle */
...
/* initiate hostname resolution with host name provided by user
 *  (this example assumes the application has already checked
```

```
 *  that the host string does not contain a dotted-IP address
*/
hQuery = WSAAsyncGetHostByName(hWnd, HOST_CALLBACK,
                szHost, achHostInfo, MAXGETHOSTSTRUCT);

if (!hQuery) {      /* returns zero for handle if asynch request
failed */
   <notify user of error>
}
```

And below is the section of a window procedure that handles the asynchronous notification message that WinSock posts upon completion of the hostname resolution operation. This example does not check the value of *wParam* for the "asynch query ID" value in the *hQuery* variable returned from `WSAAsyncGetHostByName( )` (in the code above), but it would if we had more than one query outstanding at a time. When successful, the WSAGETASYNCERROR( ) macro returns zero.

```
LONG FAR PASCAL __export SampleWndProc
   {HWND hwnd,
    UINT wMsg,
    WPARAM wParam,
    LPARAM lParam)
{
    int nAsyncError;
    struct in_addr stAddr;
        int i;

    switch (wMsg) {
         ...
         case (HOST_CALLBACK):
            /* check for an error */
            nAsyncError = WSAGETASYNCERROR(lParam);
            if (nAsyncError) {
                <report error to user>
            } else {
                /* get the primary interface address */
                stAddr.s_addr =
                   *((u_long FAR *)
                      (((struct hostent FAR *)achHostInfo)->h_addr));
```

```
            }
        }  /* end switch( ) */
    } /* end SampleWndProc( ) */
```

Address Resolution

Although applications do not need it as frequently, it is also possible to get complete host information—including the host name—from a network address. As mentioned earlier, two functions perform address resolution: `gethostbyaddr( )` and `WSAAsyncGetHostByAddr( )`. These functions are very similar to their name resolution counterparts, so we will highlight only the differences here.

gethostbyaddr( )

`gethostbyaddr( )` uses a network address to access a WinSock implementation's host database (which may be a host table, DNS, NIS, etc.) and returns complete host information, including official host name, all known aliases, and interface addresses.

```
struct hostent FAR * PASCAL FAR gethostbyaddr   /* NULL on failure */
     (char FAR *addr,          /* ptr to address in network byte order */
      int len,                 /* length of address (4 if af==AF_INET) */
     int type);                /* type of address (AF_INET==TCP/IP) */
```

addr: the network address to resolve. This should be in network byte order (as returned by `inet_addr( )`, or as stored in a `sockaddr` structure).

len: the length of the network address in bytes. For TCP/IP (type==AF_INET), *len* is always 4

type: denotes the type of the network address in *addr*. For TCP/IP, currently the only valid value is AF_INET (same value as PF_INET, as described in the "Protocols and Address Families" section later in this chapter).

As you can see, `gethostbyaddr( )` takes three input parameters. One parameter specifies the address value itself, and the other two indicate its size and type. The two address description parameters are necessary so WinSock can accommodate different address sizes and formats for different protocol suites.

Other than the fact that `gethostbyaddr( )` takes three input parameters for a network address and `gethostbyname( )` takes only one for a host name, there are no differences between these two functions. For details, see the description of `gethostbyname( )` earlier in this chapter.

Code Example

This code example is brief because of the similarities between `gethostbyaddr( )` and `gethostbyname( )`. For more details, you can refer to the code example for `gethostbyname( )` that appears earlier in this chapter.

```
struct in_addr stHostAddr;
LPHOSTENT lpstWSHostent;
...
<    this code example assumes that the application     >
<   assigned the value of a valid IP address in network  >
< order to stHostAddr before the call to gethostbyaddr( ) >
...
lpstWSHostent =
  gethostbyaddr(stHostAddr, AF_INET, sizeof(struct in_addr));

if (!lpstWSHostent) {  /* returns zero on failure */
   <notify user of error>
} else {
   <read results from hostent structure lpstWSHostent points to>
}
```

WSAAsyncGetHostByAddr( )

`WSAAsyncGetHostByAddr( )` uses a network address to access a WinSock implementation's host database (which may be a host table, DNS, NIS, etc.) and returns complete host information, including official host name, all known aliases, and interface addresses.

```
HANDLE PASCAL FAR WSAAsyncGetHostByAddr          /* 0 on failure */
      (HWND hWnd,                /* window to rcv msg on completion */
       unsigned int wMsg,        /* message to be rcvd on completion */
       char FAR *addr,           /* ptr to address of host */
       int len,                  /* length of address */
       int type,                 /* type of address (AF_INET) */
       char FAR *buf,            /* ptr to data area to rcv hostent data */
       int buflen);              /* size of data area buf above */
```

hWnd: handle of the window you want the asynchronous notification message posted to when the name resolution operation completes (succeeds or fails) *wMsg*: value for the user message you want WinSock to post to you when the name resolution operation completes. You should add to the predefined WM_USER base when creating your user message value to avoid conflicts with predefined system messages.

addr: the network address to resolve. This should be in network byte order (as returned by `inet_addr( )`, or as stored in a `sockaddr` structure).

len: the length of the network address in bytes. For TCP/IP (type==AF_INET), *len* is always 4.

type: denotes the type of the network address in *addr*. For TCP/IP, currently the only valid value is AF_INET (see the "Protocol and Address Families" section later in this chapter).

buf: a pointer to a buffer area into which WinSock can copy the results of a successful hostname resolution (the hostent structure, and all strings pointed to by the alias and address lists). The v1.1 WinSock specification recommends that the size of the buffer should be MAXGETHOSTSTRUCT bytes (also see note below for more information).

buflen: the size of the buffer pointed to by the *buf* parameter

The *addr* input parameter specifies the network address value to resolve, and *len* and *type* indicate the address size and type of the address, respectively. The two address description parameters are necessary so WinSock can accommodate different address sizes and formats for different protocol suites.

Other than the fact that `WSAAsyncGetHostByAddr( )` takes three input parameters for a network address and `WSAAsyncGetHostByName( )` takes only one for a host name, there are no differences between these two functions. For details about the `WSAAsyncGetHostByAddr( )` function, see the description of `WSAAsyncGetHostByName( )` earlier in this chapter.

Note: The memory area you point to in *buf* must be valid when the name resolution process completes. As a result, you need to be sure to assign a persistent buffer that you can access after you call `WSAAsyncGetHostByName( )`. This means you need to assign a globally allocated or static buffer, rather one that you create within the function that calls `WSAAsyncGetHostByName( )`.

Code Example

The following code example shows `WSAAsyncGetHostByAddr( )` in action. You can find the section of the window's procedure that handles the asynchronous notification message in the code example for `WSAAsyncGetHostByName( )` earlier in this chapter. The fact that both functions can share a single handler is further evidence of how similar they are.

```
#define MAXHOSTNAME    255
#define HOST_CALLBACK  WM_USER+1
extern HANDLE hWnd;
char szHost[MAXHOSTNAME]              /* buffer for user input */
static char achHostInfo[MAXGETHOSTSTRUCT]; /* buffer for results */
struct in_addr stHostAddr;            /* network address structure */
HANDLE hQuery;                        /* asynch query handle */
...
stHostAddr.s_addr = inet_addr (szHost); /* test for IP addr string */
if (stHostAddr.s_addr != INADDR_NONE) {
   /* network address provided by user, initiate address resolution */
    hQuery = WSAAsyncGetHostByName(hWnd, HOST_CALLBACK,
                     &stHostAddr,
                     sizeof(struct in_addr),
                     AF_INET,
                     achHostInfo,
                     MAXGETHOSTSTRUCT);
    if (!hQuery) {                  /* if asynch request failed */
        <notify user of error>
    }
} else {
       <do hostname resolution (see earlier section)>
}
```

Host Table, DNS, and NIS

The host database used to provide hostname and address resolution is transparent to an application using the Windows Sockets API. For the most part, a Windows Sockets application user or developer need never know how the WinSock DLL performs name or address resolution. The v1.1 Windows Sockets specification does not prescribe how resolution should be performed or configured, so there are differences between WinSock implementations. There are two basic types of host databases:

- *local:* a host table on the local system's disk
- *remote:* a shared database on a remote system

WinSock support of these two types varies. Most vendors support both, but some provide one type and not the other. If they support both, they may access the host table first, then the remote database, or vice versa. The access order is implementation specific and may be configurable. Of those with remote host database support, most use the Domain Name Service (DNS) Protocol to access the dynamic host database, but some also use Network Information Service (NIS).

It helps to know about these different host database types so that you are aware of their advantages and disadvantages. It also helps to know about the mechanisms behind them, so you can debug them if you run into problems. In most cases you will need to reference your WinSock vendor's documentation for details. We provide you with some general information here to provide a foundation and possibly fill in some areas the vendor's documentation does not describe.

Host Table

Many Windows Sockets vendors allow you to create a file that contains host names and their corresponding network addresses. This file is called a **host table**. Section B.4 in the v1.1 WinSock specification requires that the format of a host table *must* be the same format as the standard Berkeley UNIX /etc/hosts file. This can save you some typing since it allows you to take host database directly from a UNIX system. Where you should put this file on your local system is another question, however. The location for a host table file is very vendor specific.

Using a local host table has a few advantages:

- It makes the name resolution happen faster, since no network I/O is required. This is helpful if you are connected over a serial line or if your DNS servers are on a distant network, are busy (slow), or are unavailable for some reason.
- It allows you to maintain your own mapping (so you can add aliases, or add entries for hosts your name server does not know about).

But it also has disadvantages:

- On a typical network, you cannot possibly maintain a list of all hosts.
- Keeping up with changes on a network is difficult.
- Discrepancies between your host table and the correct network addresses can lead to confusion.

The bottom line is that host tables can be useful, but they must be used with caution.

Domain Name System (DNS)

In the mid-1980s, the Internet was small enough so that every host could fit in a single host table. The replacement for the static host table was a dynamic distributed database system called Domain Name System (DNS). The latest incarnation is described in RFCs 1034 and 1035. These documents describe the DNS hierarchical host name format and a method of distributing host information between different name servers throughout the Internet. The most important characteristic of DNS is that servers share host information. Servers update one another constantly, and if one server does not know the answer to your host query, it can ask others.

With DNS, hostname administration is decentralized on the Internet. Administration of the mapping between host names and addresses is delegated to different "domains." Inside a domain, there are subdomains. Each host name is unique in its (sub)domain, so its fully qualified domain name (FQDN) is guaranteed to be unique on the Internet.

The syntax for a host name can be described as follows:

```
{host name.}[subdomain.[subdomain.]...][domain][.]
```

An FQDN contains all portions, including the period at the end. Many TCP/IP implementations can resolve a host name by adding the missing components when an application does not provide an FQDN. In this regard, the capabilities vary widely between WinSock vendors: Typically, they simply assume that if there is no period anywhere in the name, they need to append a domain. RFC 1034 prescribes that each portion of a domain name (between each dot) may be 63 characters in length and that the total of all portions in an FQDN may be up to 255 characters.

With a WinSock configured to use DNS, any hostname or address resolution function call results in a query to a DNS server. WinSock sends the query via UDP to port 53 on the configured DNS server, formatted according to the DNS protocol. The WinSock specification does not prescribe what type of query to send, but typically WinSock sends a recursive query (DNS RD field set) and query types:

- an "IP address" query (A) with the host name (an FQDN) to request name resolution
- a "pointer record" query (PTR) with IP address bytes reversed and .in-addr.arpa appended to request address resolution
- or a request for all records (* or ANY)

If WinSock does not get a response, or a response indicates failure, follow-up behavior can vary. All implementations will retry a server that does not respond, since UDP is unreliable. Some allow configuration of more than one DNS server to try when the first one fails. For a WinSock name or address resolution function to succeed, the DNS query would need a response of the appropriate type. From an all records response, WinSock would typically use the information in address (A) or pointer (PTR) records for host and address resolution, and canonical name (CNAME) records for aliases. But it would ignore other records types: mail exchange (MX), host information (HINFO), start of authority (SOA), text information (TXT), and well-known services (WKS).

Two public domain WinSock utilities are available to help debug DNS problems when they arise. The WSHOST application by Andy Coates is handy for doing name and address resolution using WinSock. The NSLOOKUP application from Ashmount Research Ltd. implements its own DNS, so it uses WinSock to send and receive UDP DNS queries and responses. See Chapter 13, "Debugging," for more information on these utilities.

Version 2 of WinSock provides a mechanism for the addition of new name services (similar to the mechanism currently available in version 3.5 of Windows NT). Among other things, this may allow for lower-level access to DNS. There are untapped capabilities in the protocol that an implementation could make available to applications.

Network Information Service (NIS)

Sun Microsystem's Network Information Service (NIS)—known long ago as "yellow pages"—provides name resolution services similar to DNS and often provides its services alongside DNS. More accurately, NIS provides file synchronization of the /etc/hosts file between hosts on a network. It synchronizes other system files also, like /etc/services and /etc/protocols, among many others.

We will not describe NIS beyond this since so few WinSock implementations use NIS to do name and address resolution. We only mention it because in addition to resolving host names and addresses, it provides a mechanism for the other "database functions" that do service name and port number resolution, and protocol name and number resolution (see Chapter 10, "Support Routines").

Local Host Information

Oddly enough, the local IP address is not readily available from the Windows Sockets API. WinSock does not support the Berkeley Sockets `gethostid( )`

function or the `setsockopt( )` SIOGIFNETADDR command to return the local IP address. Whether or not to include an API to retrieve the local IP address was a controversial issue during the development of v1.1 of the WinSock specification. This is probably the most significant example of where the lowest common denominator ruled.

There was never any disagreement about whether or not such functionality was useful and necessary for many applications. The issue was whether or not to omit it, because some WinSock vendors did not have a way to retrieve the local IP address from their TCP/IP stack's native API. These vendors lobbied against being required to include this functionality in the WinSock API, and they won.

Without a `gethostid( )` equivalent in WinSock, there are only two ways for an application to find out its local IP address. Both are indirect and unreliable:

- Call `gethostname()`, then call `gethostbyname()` (or `WSAAsyncGetHostByName( )`).
- *On a connected socket*, you can call `getsockname( )`.

This is essentially a choice between two evils, since either method has faults. We recommend you use both in tandem to reduce the possibility of failure. We do this in our `GetHostID( )` function in the WinSockx sample library in Chapter 7. It may be ugly, but it works most of the time.

gethostname( )

The `gethostname( )` function copies the local host name to the buffer the application provides.

```
gethostname( ): Return the standard host name for local machine.
    int PASCAL FAR gethostname /* 0 on success, or SOCKET_ERROR */
        (char FAR *name,        /* buffer to receive host name */
         int namelen); /* length of name buffer */
```

name: buffer into which WinSock will copy the local host name

namelen: length in bytes of *name* buffer

Unfortunately, the v1.1 specification does not state what should happen if the local host does not have a host name configured. This might sound unusual, but it is actually quite common, especially among hosts that use PPP (Point-to-Point Protocol) or SLIP (Serial Line IP) on dial-up lines, which means they may have a different IP address every time they connect. Various v1.1 implementations exhibit a number of different behaviors in this circumstance:

- Some leave a NULL string and report success.
- Some fail and return the unlisted error WSAHOST_NOT_FOUND (none of the errors listed for `gethostname( )` is appropriate).
- Some return a special host name they subsequently recognize in `gethostbyname( )` as the local host name.

The last of these is the friendliest, since there is nothing you need to do to handle it. The first two possibilities are dead ends, unfortunately. If you do not have a local host name, you certainly cannot resolve it; and if you cannot resolve it, then this method will not provide the local IP address.

But even if you do get the local host name, the WinSock spec does not guarantee that you can resolve it to retrieve your local IP address. It is possible that `gethostbyname( )` or `WSAAsyncGetHostByName( )` will not even recognize its local host name, and the host table and DNS server fail, too. There are many ways to fail the `gethostname( )` and `gethostbyname( )` combination method to get the local host IP address, which is why we suggest you prepare with a backup plan using `getsockname( )`. See the `GetHostID( )` function in the WinSockx sample library in Chapter 7 for a code example.

Addresses and Formatting

A network address can have two forms: numeric and string. An IP address is a 32-bit unsigned integer in numeric form, such as 0x807F3201 (that's network order, which is big endian). In the standard string representation—called "Internet dot notation"—each of the 4-byte values is separated by a period, like 128.127.50.1. The hexadecimal representation is convenient for the numeric form (since you can identify each byte easily), and decimal is standard for the dot notation.

WinSock uses the data structure for an IP address—`struct in_addr`—wherever it references an IP address. You probably recognize it as one of the fields in the ubiquitous `sockaddr_in` data structure, which also contains a port number to describe a socket name.

WinSock has two functions for converting an IP address from numeric form to a string form, and vice versa: `inet_ntoa( )` and `inet_addr( )`. There are a number of macros for referencing common address values and parts of addresses. We describe all of these here.

in_addr structure

The Internet address structure contains a 32-bit Internet Protocol address in network byte order (big endian).

```
struct in_addr {
    union {
        struct { u_char s_b1,s_b2,s_b3,s_b4; } S_un_b;
        struct { u_short s_w1,s_w2; } S_un_w;
        u_long S_addr;
    } S_un;
};
```

The union allows access to individual fields, although applications typically use the `s_addr` field macro (see a description below) to access the S_addr definition of the structure, and treat the value as a long (an unsigned 32-bit integer). Applications rarely use the other union declarations, since there is seldom a need to pick apart an address. Since the current network mask is unavailable from the WinSock API—the `setsockopt( )` SIOCGIFNETMASK is not supported—the byte values in an address are ambiguous in respect to what portion of the address they represent (network, subnet, or host portion).

Address References

```
#define s_addr  S_un.S_addr      /* use this for most TCP and IP code */
#define s_host  S_un.S_un_b.s_b2 /* host on imp */
#define s_net   S_un.S_un_b.s_b1 /* network */
#define s_imp   S_un.S_un_w.s_w2 /* imp */
#define s_impno S_un.S_un_b.s_b4 /* imp # */
#define s_lh    S_un.S_un_b.s_b3 /* logical host */
```

These macros allow you to decompose an IP address by accessing specific portions:

- `s_addr`: the complete 32-bit IP address value in network order. Most applications that use an `in_addr` structure find it convenient to use this macro.
- `s_net`: the first byte in the network address, which denotes the IP address class (e.g., Class A: 0-127, Class B: 128-191, Class C: 192-223, Class D (multicast): 224-239, Class E (reserved): 240-255).
- `s_host, s_imp, s_impno, s_lh`: these are cruft left over from BSD; WinSock applications will never use these macros. They are used to

access an "interface message processor" (IMP), which is an intelligent packet-switching node on the ARPANET. WinSock does not support the AF_IMPLINK address family that uses these, as Berkeley Sockets does.

Address Classes

The WINSOCK.H file defines three IN_CLASSX macros, where "X" is "A," "B," or "C," to denote the IP address class (see Appendix B, "Quick Reference," for these and a new one defined for Class D, multicast addresses). You can use these macros to detect what address class an IP address is in. These are seldom needed even where IP classes are used, especially with RFC 1519's Classless Inter-Domain Routing (CIDR) in place.

Common Addresses

WINSOCK.H defines the values for a few commonly used IP addresses:

- INADDR_ANY: denotes an arbitrary IP address. Applications commonly use this macro to initialize the *sin_addr* field in a `sockaddr_in` structure before calling `bind( )` to request the network system to assign the default interface address.
- INADDR_NONE: denotes an invalid IP address. WinSock returns this from the `inet_addr( )` function to indicate failure.
- INADDR_BROADCAST: denotes 32-bit value for the standard IP limited broadcast address "255.255.255.255." Applications that need to send to or receive from the standard broadcast address typically use this macro.
- INADDR_LOOPBACK: denotes the standard IP loopback address, "127.0.0.1."

inet_addr( )

inet_addr( ) converts from a character string in standard Internet "dot notation" to a numeric value in network (big-endian) byte order.

```
unsigned long PASCAL FAR inet_addr   /* INADDR_NONE on failure */
      (char FAR *cp);  /* a char string in Internet "." format */
```

cp: IP address in standard dot notation, which is four decimal values from 0 to 255 separated by periods (e.g., "128.127.50.1").

There are not many ways for this function to fail: Either the string is not a valid IP address representation (bad format or values out of range), or the buffer pointed to is bogus (see note below about possible false failure indication). Note that the WinSock specification does not list any error values for this function, so `WSAGetLastError( )` will not give you the reason why it failed.

This function is fairly intelligent in that it will fill in the missing portions if you provide an incomplete dot-notation address string. Few applications or application users know how to take advantage of this capability, since it can be a little confusing. It is provided to retain compatibility with Berkeley Sockets. The way it works is as follows:

- If you provide three of the four address portions—like "a.b.c"— it interprets the last value as a 16-bit value. For example, if you specify the address string "128.127.6," `inet_ntoa( )` interprets it as the value for "128.127.0.6." Or if you specify "128.127.12866," the result is "128.127.50.66." The three-part notation is convenient for specifying Class B addresses xxx.net.host (where "xxx" is a value between 128 and 191, denoting a Class B IP address).
- If you provide two of the four portions—like "a.b"—it interprets the last part as a 24-bit value for the rightmost portions of the address. So, for example, it interprets "92.65" as "92.0.0.65," or "92.9876" as "92.0.38.148."
- If you provide one of the four portions, the value is stored directly into the address without any byte rearrangement. So, for instance, if you put in the value "65," the result is "0.0.0.65," or "2155819555" is "128.127.50.35."

Note: The `inet_addr( )` function is fairly stupid in another respect. If you pass the address string 255.255.255.255 (the limited broadcast address), then `inet_ntoa( )` will correctly return the 32-bit value 0xFFFFFFFF (INADDR_BROADCAST). Unfortunately, this value is the same as the INADDR_NONE value that `inet_addr( )` returns when it fails. As a result, if your application allows the limited broadcast address, you will need to check for the string explicitly, either before you call `inet_addr( )` or after it fails (as illustrated in the code example below).

Code Example

This code example shows the typical use of `inet_addr( )` to assign the destination address in a socket address structure. In addition, this example checks for a false failure from `inet_addr( )` caused by the limited broadcast address. We ignore the failure if we find the limited broadcast address string was used.

Note: This extra check for a broadcast address is only necessary in applications that use datagram (or raw) sockets—since stream sockets cannot use broadcast addresses—and only if the application allows the use of the broadcast address (which also means it would have to call `setsockopt( )` SO_BROADCAST at some point).

```
/* limited broadcast address string */
static char szHost[MAX_NAME_SIZE];  /* destination host */
struct sockaddr_in stDstAddr;       /* destination socket */
...
/* check if host string is a valid IP address */
stDstAddr.sin_addr.s_addr = inet_addr ((LPSTR)szHost);

/* did inet_addr( ) fail or process a broadcast address string? */
if ((stDstAddr.sin_addr.s_addr == INADDR_NONE) &&
    (_fstrcmp (szHost, "255.255.255.255")) {

     <address string not broadcast or any other valid address>
}
```

inet_ntoa( )

inet_ntoa( ) converts from a 32-bit numeric Internet address value to an ASCII string in Internet standard "dot notation" (e.g., 128.127.50.234).

```
char FAR * PASCAL FAR inet_ntoa /* NULL on failure */
      (struct in_addr in);      /* Internet address structure */
```

in: IP address value. Any 32-bit value is considered okay.

Virtually nothing can go wrong with this function since it will produce an IP dot-notation string for any 32-bit value. But it is a good idea to check for a NULL pointer return, nonetheless.

Note: The buffer pointed to by the return value is owned by the WinSock DLL and may be shared, so its contents may be highly volatile. You should copy the string immediately if you need to save it. Do not attempt to modify it or free this area of memory, or a protection fault may result.

Code Example

This code example shows how the `inet_ntoa( )` function reformats a numeric address in an `in_addr` IP address structure (in network order) into an address string in standard dotted Internet form.

```
#define MAX_ADDR_STRING_SIZE  16
static char szIPAddr[MAX_ADDR_STRING_SIZE]; /* addr string buffer */
LPSTR lpszIPAddr;                           /* addr string pointer */
struct in_addr stIPAddr;
...
/* contrived initialization for demonstration purposes
 *  (this IP address is in network order) */
stIPAddr.s_addr = 0x807F3242;
...
/* get string for an IP address */
lpszIPAddr = inet_ntoa(stIPAddr);

/* save the string retrieved from inet_ntoa( ) */
if (lpszIPAddr) {
      _fstrcpy ((LPSTR)szIPAddr, (LPSTR)lpszIPAddr);

      < szIPAddr now contains string "128.127.50.66" >
}
```

Protocol and Address Families

The *h_addrtype* field in a `hostent` structure corresponds to the *sin_family* field in a `sockaddr_in` Internet socket structure. Version 1.1 of WinSock specifies that the value in these fields should always have the value PF_INET, which identifies the "Internet protocol family." However, to be more precise, these fields should have the value AF_INET. Although the values for AF_INET and PF_INET are the same in WINSOCK.H, there is a subtle difference that history has blurred.

The values for AF_INET and PF_INET are the same in WinSock because they were the same in Berkeley Sockets. They should have differed since they are hierarchical. It should be possible to have more than one address format within a single protocol family, but it is not, because the protocol and address family labels are the same.

To preserve network source code compatibility and make updates easier, this mistake must be preserved. Many applications do not distinguish between AF_INET and PF_INET, so the latter two are used interchangeably in Berkeley Sockets (and WinSock v1.1) source code. The upshot is that when these applications are updated to use a new address scheme for the next version of the Internet Protocol, they will need to use a new protocol family macro with the same value as the one for the address family. Although IP version 6 addresses are in the same protocol family as IP version 4—the Internet family—they will use a different protocol family designator (e.g., AF_INET6 will have the same value as PF_INET6).

Fortunately, the architects of the version 2.0 WinSock specification have a plan for improving the API to deal with multiple address formats in a single protocol family. As we describe in Chapter 17, one of the major new features that WinSock 2 provides is protocol independence. WinSock 2 defines a protocol information structure that contains a detailed description of each protocol and address family. To allow for multiple address schemes within a protocol family, the protocol information structure includes a protocol version number.

9 Socket Information and Control

In This Chapter:

- Socket Control
- Socket Options
- Blocking Hooks
- Socket Names

The quieter you become, the more you can hear.

Baba Ram Dass

In this chapter we describe the functions that allow you to get or set socket attributes. Socket attributes affect the way sockets behave. Some attributes are of minor consequence, but others can alter a socket's behavior significantly. Many attributes are special purpose, though some are generically useful. A few attributes deal with socket state; we already discussed these, in Chapter 6, "Socket States." A few others are relevant to the socket operation mode, and we reference them in Chapter 5, "Operation Modes." We describe them all here and point you to other places in the text where we reference them. The purpose of this chapter is to tell you when, where, and how to use the socket information and control these functions provide.

Socket Control

The `ioctlsocket( )` "I/O control" socket function is the Windows Sockets counterpart of the Berkeley Sockets `ioctl( )` function. Like the `closesocket( )` function, `ioctlsocket( )` was renamed primarily to avoid link conflicts with the original function, which is common to C run-time libraries. However, it was renamed also because it has a fundamental functionality difference. The common `ioctl( )` function deals with file handles, and in the Windows Sockets API sockets are not (necessarily) equivalent to file handles.

Here is the prototype for the `ioctlsocket( )` function:

```
ioctlsocket( ): Set or Retrieve i/o mode(s) of a socket.
   int PASCAL FAR ioctlsocket /* 0 on success, or SOCKET_ERROR */
      (SOCKET s,            /* a valid socket */
       long cmd,            /* command to perform on socket s */
       u_long FAR *argp);   /* pointer to parameter for cmd */
```

s: socket handle for a valid socket, connected or not. Only the SIOCATMARK command restricts the socket type to stream.

cmd: I/O control command, one of three commands with each call: FIONBIO, FIONREAD, and SIOCATMARK. This is only a small subset of the commands that the Berkeley Sockets `ioctl( )` function supports.

argp: pointer to parameter for *cmd*

The return value is zero on success or `SOCKET_ERROR` on failure. The `ioctlsocket( )` function accepts any one of three commands: FIONBIO, FIONREAD, and SIOCATMARK. We will describe each of these commands individually and briefly discuss the commands that were left out.

FIONBIO

The `ioctlsocket( )` FIONBIO command allows an application to change the operation mode of a socket from (the default) blocking mode to nonblocking mode, or from nonblocking mode back to blocking mode. It is primarily intended for use in synchronous applications to change a socket from blocking operation mode (the default) to nonblocking. This is unnecessary in asynchronous applications, since the `WSAAsyncSelect( )` function automatically changes a socket to nonblocking mode.

When you call `ioctlsocket( )` with *cmd*=FIONBIO, the *argp* input argument operates as a Boolean value that enables or disables nonblocking operation mode, as follows:

- **argp*=TRUE (nonzero): Socket operates in nonblocking mode.
- **argp*=FALSE (zero): Socket operates in blocking mode.

It is rarely necessary to use the `ioctlsocket( )` FIONBIO command to change a socket from nonblocking back to (the default) blocking mode. The need to do so typically indicates a need to simplify your application design. There is little justification for switching socket operation modes more than once in the life of a socket. Doing so complicates your application and incurs unnecessary overhead.

One exception to the rule about switching operation modes from nonblocking back to blocking mode is if your application enables `setsockopt( )` SO_LINGER with a nonzero timeout. As we describe later in this chapter, the WinSock specification is unclear about how a close should occur on a nonblocking socket with a nonzero SO_LINGER timeout enabled, when `closesocket( )` fails with WSAEWOULDBLOCK. One way to avoid this gray area is to change your socket back to blocking mode before calling `closesocket( )`. However, the best way to avoid this potential problem is to leave SO_DONTLINGER enabled (the default setting), in which case the switch back to blocking mode is unnecessary.

Note that if the socket has asynchronous event notification enabled for any event (via `WSAAsyncSelect( )`), then this will be ineffective or will fail with WSAEINVAL. You must disable asynchronous notification by calling `WSAAsyncSelect( )` with zero for events before you can make the socket blocking again.

Code Example

Here is a code sample that shows how to use the FIONBIO command. We also discuss the use of `ioctlsocket( )` FIONBIO and show a code sample in Chapter 5, "Operation Modes":

```
int nRet;
u_long lOnOff = TRUE;
...
/* make our socket nonblocking */
nRet = ioctlsocket(nSock, FIONBIO, (u_long FAR *)&lOnOff);
if (nRet == SOCKET_ERROR) { /* returns 0 on success */
   WSAperror(hInst, hwnd, WSAGetLastError( ),
        (LPSTR)"ioctlsocket( )", TRUE);
   goto AppExit;
}
```

FIONREAD

The `ioctlsocket( )` FIONREAD command allows an application to "peek" at how many bytes of data are available to receive (i.e., pending in the network system's input buffers). The value it reports—in the buffer pointed to by *argp*—is slightly different for datagram and stream sockets. This reflects one fundamental difference between the two socket types and protocols: Datagram sockets preserve packet boundaries, and stream sockets do not.

- For a *datagram* socket, **argp* contains the number of bytes in the first datagram queued for the application to receive.
- For a *stream* socket, **argp* usually contains the total number of bytes queued for the application to receive, although this is not guaranteed. Some TCP/IP stacks may not report total bytes across network-system packet buffer boundaries, so you should not try to impose packet buffer boundaries by expecting to receive a certain number of bytes at any point in time.

An application typically uses `ioctlsocket()` FIONREAD to determine a buffer size to allocate, or perhaps to check for arrival of a specific amount of data. We recommend against either of these uses. They are unnecessary, and this operation represents an overhead your application can avoid, not to mention that it implicitly misuses system buffers.

Alternatively, we recommend that you simply preallocate the largest buffer your application will possibly need. Also, rather than peeking at the amount available, you should read data into your application buffers and check the return value from the `recv()` function. If you did not receive the expected amount, you can adjust your buffer pointer and call `recv()` again.

Note: Calling `ioctlsocket()` FIONREAD in response to an FD_READ data arrival notification message will *not* reenable FD_READ notification. You *must* call `recv()` or `recvfrom()` to receive any further FD_READ notification, which is yet another reason to use our recommended alternative.

Code Example

The following code sample shows how to use FIONREAD. In this code snippet, a datagram application allocates memory based on the size of the incoming datagram. Notice that the *argp* input argument points at the unsigned long where `ioctlsocket()` stores the result:

```
int nRet;
u_long lDgramSize;
SOCKET hSock;
...
hSock = socket (AF_INET, SOCK_DGRAM, 0);
if (hSock == INVALID_SOCKET) {
      <display windows sockets error value and exit>
}
...
/* get length of first datagram in system buffers */
nRet = ioctlsocket(nSock, FIONREAD, (u_long FAR*)&lDgramSize);
```

```
if (nRet == SOCKET_ERROR) {    /* 0 on success */
      <display windows sockets error value and exit>
} else {
      <allocate a buffer, then call recv( ) to read pending data>
}
```

SIOCATMARK

The `ioctlsocket( )` SIOCATMARK command determines whether there is any out-of-band data (i.e., "urgent data") to be read. This command is valid only for stream sockets, and only when the `setsockopt( )` SO_OOBINLINE option is *enabled* (SO_OOBINLINE is disabled by default).

When *cmd*=SIOCATMARK and `ioctlsocket( )` returns zero to indicate success, the *argp* input parameter contains the results. The value in *argp* operates as a Boolean value to indicate the presence or absence of urgent data, as follows:

- **argp*==TRUE (nonzero): No OOB data
- **argp*==FALSE (zero): OOB data available

Note that the value returned in *argp* is `FALSE` if urgent data *is* pending, and the value is `TRUE` if *not*. Not only is this counterintuitive, but it also contradicts the way `ioctl( )` SIOCATMARK works in Berkeley Sockets. There is no rhyme or reason for this change. It was a simple Boolean mistake that the WinSock architects overlooked because OOB is so seldom used.

We discuss the `ioctlsocket( )` SIOCATMARK command in more detail in Chapter 6, "Socket States." The SO_OOBINLINE socket option is described there also and later in this chapter as well.

Code Example

The following code example demonstrates a call to `ioctlsocket( )` SIOCATMARK:

```
int nRet;
u_long lUrgentUnFlag;
...
nRet = ioctlsocket(nSock, SIOCATMARK,
            (u_long FAR *)&lUrgentUnFlag);
if (nRet == SOCKET_ERROR) { /* 0 on success */
      <display windows sockets error value and exit>
```

```
} else if (lUrgentUnFlag == FALSE) { /* urgent data if FALSE */
      <call recv(MSG_OOB) to read urgent data>
}
```

Other Control Commands

The v1.1 Windows Sockets specification does not include many of the commands for the Berkeley Sockets `ioctl( )` function. The WinSock specification does not prescribe implementation of the following BSD commands:

`FIONASYNC:`	get or clear asynchronous I/O
`SIOCGIFADDR:`	get interface IP address
`SIOCGIFFLAGS:`	get interface flags (type, attributes, and status)
`SIOCGIFBRADDR:`	get broadcast address
`SIOCGIFNETMASK:`	get subnet mask
`SIOCSARP:`	set ARP entry
`SIOCGARP:`	get ARP entry
`SIODCDARP:`	delete ARP entry

Version 2.0 of the Windows Sockets specification does not support these APIs either, but it does provide mechanisms to retrieve the information that some of these commands provide. As we describe in Chapter 17, the `WSAIoctl( )` function can provide all of this interface information (except ARP entries) in INTERFACE_INFO structures.

Socket Options

getsockopt( ) and setsockopt( )

The Windows Sockets API supports many of the Berkeley Sockets–compatible options. There are two socket option functions: `setsockopt( )` changes an option setting, and `getsockopt( )` retrieves an option's current setting. You can use all options with `getsockopt( )`, but not all options are "settable" with `setsockopt( )`. Here are the prototypes for the `getsockopt( )` and `setsockopt( )` functions:

```
getsockopt( ): Retrieve option associated with a socket.
    int PASCAL FAR getsockopt  /* 0 on success, or SOCKET_ERROR */
        (SOCKET s,          /* a valid socket */
```

```
        int level,        /* SOL_SOCKET or IPPROTO_TCP */
        int optname,      /* socket option to be queried */
        char FAR *optval, /* buffer for option value retrieved */
        int FAR *optlen); /* pointer to size of optval buffer */
```

```
setsockopt( ): Set option associated with a socket.
    int PASCAL FAR setsockopt /* 0 on success, or SOCKET_ERROR */
       (SOCKET s,         /* a valid socket */
        int level,        /* SOL_SOCKET or IPPROTO_TCP */
        int optname,      /* socket option to be set */
        char FAR *optval, /* buffer for option value to be set */
        int optlen);      /* size of optval buffer */
```

As you can see, the prototypes for both are *almost* the same (note the different data types for the *optlen* parameter). The return value for both is zero on success and SOCKET_ERROR for failure. Here are descriptions of the function parameters:

socket: This is the handle for the socket you want to check or set. Theoretically, you can use any socket at any time for any option, but this is not universally true; there are differences between how WinSock implementations handle options. Some option values may be reset at connect time on stream sockets. Specifically, you should wait until you establish a connection before you set the SO_KEEPALIVE, SO_OOBINLINE, SO_RCVBUF, or SO_SNDBUF options on stream socket. For datagram sockets, this is not an issue.

level: The version 1.1 Windows Sockets specification supports only two option *levels:* SOL_SOCKET and IPPROTO_TCP. The *level* is related to the OSI model we introduced in Chapter 2, "Windows Sockets Concepts." The SOL_SOCKET *level* is the highest (application layer), and the IPPROTO_TCP is lower (transport layer). Berkeley Sockets supports IPPROTO_IP (network layer), which is, of course, below IPPROTO_TCP. The *level* categorizes different option types.

optname: This value identifies the option you want to get or set. It is an integer value, but you should always reference the manifest constant (macro) from the WINSOCK.H file. Each macro has a prefix that indicates the option level. So, for `SOL_SOCKET` level options the prefix is `SO_`, and for `IPPROTO_TCP` level options the prefix is `TCP_`. Later in this chapter, we describe each option in detail and show you how to use them.

optval: The `setsockopt( )` and `getsockopt( )` functions each use the "option value" parameter differently. For `setsockopt( )`, *optval* points to the input parameter value (i.e., the option setting you want to make). For `getsockopt( )`, *optval* points to the function results (i.e., the current value of the option) upon return.

optlen: The "option length" parameter is a different type for the `setsockopt( )` and `getsockopt( )` functions.

- for `setsockopt( )`, *optlen* is a *value*; it is the size of the optval buffer.
- for `getsockopt( )`, *optlen* is a *pointer*; it points to the size of the *optval* buffer on input and the size of the value retrieved in *optval* upon return.

To assure source code portability between 16-bit and 32-bit implementations, use `sizeof( )` to set the length value that *optlen* references.

Code Examples

Most option types are either Boolean or integer. The one exception is the `SO_LINGER` option, which references a linger structure. We have three code examples to illustrate the Boolean, integer, and linger structure options. The individual options we use are not important; we describe each of them later in this chapter. Each example is representative of other options of the same types.

We use `getsockopt( )` in one of these examples and `setsockopt( )` in the other two.

setsockopt( ) with Boolean Option

```
BOOL bOptVal = TRUE;     /* enable the Boolean option */
int nRet;
...
/* enable broadcasting on this socket */
nRet = setsockopt(nSock, SO_SOCKET, SO_BROADCAST,
       (char FAR *)&bOptVal, sizeof(BOOL));
if (wRet == SOCKET_ERROR) {
      <report the WinSock error value>
}
```

getsockopt( ) with Integer Option

```
int nOptVal;
int nOptLen = sizeof(int);
char achOutBuf[BUFSIZE];
int nRet;
...
/* retrieve the receive buffer size for this socket */
nRet = getsockopt(nSock, SO_SOCKET, SO_RCVBUF,
      (char FAR *)&nOptVal, (int FAR *)&nOptLen);
if (wRet == SOCKET_ERROR) {
      <report the WinSock error value>
} else {
      wsprintf (achOutBuf, "Receive Buffer Size: %d", nOptVal);
}
```

setsockopt( ) with struct linger Option

```
#define TIMEOUT 0
struct linger stLinger;
int nRet;
...
stLinger.l_onoff  = TRUE;
stLinger.l_linger = TIMEOUT;    /* seconds to linger */
/* set linger timeout for closesocket( ) on this socket */
nRet = setsockopt(nSock, SO_SOCKET, SO_LINGER,
      (char FAR *)&stLinger, sizeof(struct linger));
if (wRet == SOCKET_ERROR) {
      <report the WinSock error value>
}
```

SO_ACCEPTCONN

The SO_ACCEPTCONN option indicates whether a stream socket is currently listening. It works with the `getsockopt( )` function (not `setsockopt( )`) and returns `TRUE` in *optval* if the socket is currently listening, or `FALSE` if not. It is irrelevant to datagram sockets (a call will fail with WSAENOPROTOOPT).

Option name	*Data type*	*Default value*	*getsockopt( )*	*setsockopt( )*	*Socket type*	*Special notes*
SO_ACCEPTCONN	BOOL	FALSE	yes	no	DS	none

SO_ACCEPTCONN has little practical use. Applications typically do not need to check whether a socket is listening, since they already know if the `listen( )` function succeeds. We describe one (unlikely) use for SO_ACCEPTCONN in an application in Chapter 6, "Socket States." However, the chances are good that you'll never need to use this option.

SO_BROADCAST

The SO_BROADCAST option enables or disables the ability to send or receive datagrams addressed to the broadcast address (a call that references a stream socket will fail with WSAENOPROTOOPT). This option is a relic of Berkeley Sockets, where broadcasting is a privileged operation. Since most protocol stacks for Windows do not restrict broadcasting, this option is provided mostly for Berkeley Sockets compatibility. However, its use is *not* optional.

You *must* call `setsockopt( )` to enable SO_BROADCAST before any attempt to send or receive broadcast datagrams. Otherwise, a `sendto( )` or `recvfrom( )` with a broadcast address will fail with the WSAEACCESS ("permission denied") error.

Option name	*Data type*	*Default value*	*getsockopt( )*	*setsockopt( )*	*Socket type*	*Special notes*
SO_BROADCAST	BOOL	FALSE	yes	yes	DG	none

What Is a Broadcast Address?

There are a number of answers to this question. Here are all the broadcast addresses relevant to the TCP/IP suite.

Network-layer broadcast addresses

- *limited IP broadcast* (also called *local broadcast*): the classic 255.255.255.255 (INADDR_BROADCAST). They are "limited" because routers will never forward them beyond the local (sub)network.
- *net-directed IP broadcast:* an IP address comprised of a standard network address portion and host portion with all bits set. For example, the net-directed broadcast address for Class B network address 128.127 is 128.127.255.255. Routers optionally forward these.

- *subnet-directed IP broadcast:* an IP address comprised of a subnet address portion and host portion with all bits set. For example, if the subnet mask is 255.255.255.0 for Class B subnetwork address 128.127.126, then the subnet-directed broadcast address is 128.127.126.255. All routers forward these.
- *IP multicast:* a Class D IP address (range 224.0.0.0 to 239.255.255.255). To properly handle multicast addresses, a router must implement IGMP according to RFC 1112.

Link-layer broadcast addresses

- *hardware broadcast:* the media-specific "all-stations" address
- *multicast:* a media-specific software settable address (on Ethernet, a multicast address always has the low-order bit set in the high-order byte)

When you send a datagram to any of the broadcast IP (network-layer) addresses, the datagram addressing eventually occurs at the link layer (in the media access header) in addition to being set at the network layer. For example, when you send a packet to the limited broadcast address from a system with an Ethernet network interface, the destination address in the IP header is set to 255.255.255.255 and the (6-byte) destination address in the Ethernet header is set to 255:255:255:255:255:255 (all bits set). The mechanism for most other broadcast addresses is different but analogous to this.

Multicast addresses also have link-layer equivalents. The algorithms for converting multicast IP addresses into multicast hardware addresses are media specific, since hardware addresses are media specific also.

Multicast Addresses

Multicast addresses are beneficial. They allow groups of hosts to communicate without adverse effect to the rest of the network (aside from the network bandwidth they occupy). The Internet Engineering Task Force (IETF) multicasts real-time multimedia (sound, video, and data) coverage of its meetings on the Internet's "multicast backbone" (MBONE). Carl Malamud multicasts radio programming over the Internet. Multicasting offers some unique networking possibilities and has a bright future on the "yellow-brick information highway."

Note: The SO_BROADCAST option is *not* relevant to multicast addresses. Version 1.1 of Windows Sockets does not specify an API for multicast, although some Windows Sockets vendors do offer one. WinSock 2 includes the multicast API that Steve Deering defined for TCP/IP, but it also includes a protocol-independent API for multicast/multipoint. We describe how to use

Deering's multicast API in Chapter 16, "Optional Features," and we describe the WinSock 2 multipoint API in Chapter 17.

Proper Use of Broadcasts

You need to use broadcast addresses with caution. Every network interface picks up every packet it "sees" that has a broadcast destination address (multicast addresses are one exception). This incurs overhead on every host connected to the network, whether or not it has a network application to read the packet. One good way to make enemies quickly is to send a lot of broadcasts on a net (removing an Ethernet terminator is about the only thing better). Sending too many broadcast packets can effectively disable a network.

As long as you send them sparingly, there are two valid uses for broadcast packets:

- to elicit responses from hosts bound to the target port number
- to update information to all hosts bound to a target port number

For example, you could broadcast a probe to check for hosts running a particular datagram application, or periodically send information to the broadcast address to update simultaneously all the hosts running your datagram application. Just keep in mind that many routers do not forward broadcast packets, limiting access (as we mention above).

SO_DEBUG

The SO_DEBUG option enables or disables debug output from a Windows Sockets implementation. Support for SO_DEBUG is optional, however, and neither the v1.1 WinSock specification nor WinSock 2 defines how the mechanism works when it is implemented. You need to refer to your Windows Sockets supplier for availability and details on its use.

Option name	*Data type*	*Default value*	*getsockopt()*	*setsockopt()*	*Socket type*	*Special notes*
SO_DEBUG	BOOL	FALSE	yes	yes	DG or DS	optional in v1.1 WinSock

We recommend that you use a third-party application program for WinSock API debugging. In Chapter 13, "Debugging," we describe some application debuggers like WinScope or Trace Plus, which allow you to spy on the WinSock function calls, input parameter values, return values, and asynchronous notification messages. The beauty of such nonintrusive debuggers is that your debugging output remains the same over any WinSock implementation. The one advantage that implementation-specific SO_DEBUG output might offer is internal WinSock debugging information that the external debuggers cannot access.

SO_DONTLINGER

The SO_DONTLINGER option enables or disables immediate return from the `closesocket( )` function. When enabled (the default), any call to `closesocket( )` will return immediately, whether the socket is in blocking or nonblocking operation mode. Queued data will be sent, and the TCP/IP stack will attempt a graceful close in the background (a call with a datagram socket will fail with WSAENOPROTOOPT).

Option name	*Data type*	*Default value*	*getsockopt( )*	*setsockopt( )*	*Socket type*	*Special notes*
SO_DONTLINGER	BOOL	TRUE	yes	yes	DS	none

Disabling SO_DONTLINGER implicitly enables `SO_LINGER` with an indeterminate (zero or nonzero) timeout value. To avoid this ambiguity, you should enable SO_LINGER with a specific timeout value set in the linger structure. Enabling SO_LINGER with a nonzero value implicitly disables SO_DONTLINGER anyway.

When disabled, SO_DONTLINGER causes a blocking socket to block until the close attempt completes (successfully or not). We recommend that you do not use the SO_DONTLINGER option. Queued data is sent, and the TCP/IP stack attempts a graceful close of the virtual circuit. In effect, the close occurs in the foreground on a blocking socket.

When SO_DONTLINGER is disabled on a nonblocking socket, however, `closesocket( )` returns immediately with a WSAEWOULDBLOCK error failure. Unfortunately, there is more than one interpretation among WinSock vendors as to what the WSAEWOULDBLOCK error means in this case. Very different behaviors can result on different WinSocks (some close, and some don't), so you should avoid setting a nonzero timeout with SO_LINGER on a nonblocking socket. This is one case where changing the socket back to blocking with `ioctlsocket( )` FIONBIO is legitimate, but only if you have a valid reason for enabling SO_LINGER in the first place. See the "Avoiding Ambiguities" section under the SO_LINGER option description later in this chapter for more information.

SO_DONTROUTE

The SO_DONTROUTE option enables an application to bypass the standard routing mechanisms of the underlying protocol. Instead, the local protocol stack sends the packet to the appropriate network interface according to the network portion of the destination address.

Option name	*Data type*	*Default value*	*getsockopt( )*	*setsockopt( )*	*Socket type*	*Special notes*
SO_DONTROUTE	BOOL	FALSE	yes	yes	DG or DS	optional in v1.1 WinSock

Support for SO_DONTROUTE is optional since it is designed for multi-homed hosts (hosts with more than one network interface). Its purpose is to reroute packets internally (i.e., before they leave the local host machine) so that they use the interface card most local to the destination host. It has the effect of reducing some misguided network traffic and may allow you to utilize an underused network interface (to spread the workload). Its effect is benign on WinSock implementations that do not support it or do not have multiple interfaces installed. In both cases, calls to `setsockopt( )` SO_DONTROUTE are simply ignored.

SO_ERROR

The SO_ERROR option retrieves the current socket error value (a standard "WSA" error value) and then clears it. The task-based error—the one returned from `WSAGetLastError( )`–is not affected by this option. Conversely, one socket's error status is not affected by failures on another socket, although both will alter the task-based error (`WSAGetLastError( )` will report the most recent failure of the two). The failure of functions without a socket parameter will not change any individual socket error values either (only the task-based error).

Option name	*Data type*	*Default value*	*getsockopt( )*	*setsockopt( )*	*Socket type*	*Special notes*
SO_ERROR	int	FALSE	yes	no	DG or DS	none

The most common use of the SO_ERROR function is to retrieve the value of the error on a socket that is a member of an exception fd_set upon return from a call to `select( )`. In particular, SO_ERROR is often used to find out why a call to `connect( )` failed. In this instance, the following series of events would occur:

1. `connect( )` fails with the WSAEWOULDBLOCK error (after being called with a socket in nonblocking operation mode).
2. Nonblocking socket put in *exceptfds* and *writefds* with FD_SET, and `select( )` called.
3. `select( )` returns a value of 1, and FD_ISSET reveals that the connecting socket is a member of *exceptfds*.
4. `getsockopt( )` SO_ERROR returns the value of the WinSock error in *optval* (for example, WSAECONNREFUSED if the connection attempt was rejected, or WSAETIMEDOUT if the server never responded to the connect request).

Unfortunately, the v1.1 Windows Sockets specification is not very clear in its description of this option (fortunately, WinSock 2 clarifies things). As a result, there are many inconsistencies between v1.1 WinSock implementations. A number of WinSocks return the task-based error from `getsockopt( )` SO_ERROR rather than the socket-based error. If possible, you should use `WSAGetLastError( )` instead of SO_ERROR to ensure portability between WinSocks.

SO_KEEPALIVE

The SO_KEEPALIVE option enables or disables the keep-alive mechanism on a stream socket (a call with a datagram socket will fail with WSAENOPROTOOPT). In a nutshell, keep-alives detect a virtual circuit failure on an idle connection and report an error to the application. They are disabled by default.

Option name	*Data type*	*Default value*	*getsockopt()*	*setsockopt()*	*Socket type*	*Special notes*
SO_KEEPALIVE	BOOL	FALSE	yes	yes	DS	none

How Do Keep-Alives Work?

Typically, you need to send or receive data to detect a problem on a stream connection. If neither end of a connection is actively sending data, there is normally no network traffic between two connected hosts. With SO_KEEPALIVE enabled on an idle connection, the TCP/IP stack periodically sends an acknowledgment request called a keep-alive. A keep-alive TCP segment does not contain any data and identifies itself to the receiver by decrementing the last transmitted acknowledgment number. When a TCP/IP stack receives a keep-alive, it simply acknowledges it.

If a sender does not receive an acknowledgment for a keep-alive, it will attempt to retransmit the keep-alive packet (using its TCP data retransmission algorithm). If none of the retransmitted keep-alives receives an acknowledgment either, then the sender will reset the connection. Subsequently, any function call that references that socket will fail with WSAECONNABORTED. If you have the FD_CLOSE asynchronous event enabled, the WinSock DLL will post an FD_CLOSE message with the error. The `select( )` exception fd_set will also indicate failure after a keep-alive timeout.

When a host receives a keep-alive, it may respond with a TCP reset if it does not have a connection on the destination port number. In this case, the sender will stop sending keep-alives and will abort the connection locally. Subsequently, socket functions will fail with the WSAECONNRESET error (the WinSock DLL will notify the application of the error in an FD_CLOSE message if the application has FD_CLOSE asynch event notification enabled). The `select( )` exception fd_set will also indicate failure after a keep-alive elicits a TCP reset response.

Note: Enabling keep-alives on one side of a connection does not enable it on the other side. The other side will always respond to the keep-alives you send but will not send any of its own for your stack to acknowledge unless the application at the other end also explicitly enables keep-alives.

How Often Are Keep-Alives Sent?

The keep-alive mechanism is a required part of every TCP/IP implementation according to RFC 1122, "Hosts Requirements." RFC 1122 prescribes two hours as the default period a TCP/IP stack should wait between sending keep-alive packets. This makes the keep-alive mechanism less than ideal for most applications. In effect, this means that it may take up to two hours before an application with keep-alives enabled can detect that a connection has failed.

The authors of RFC 1122 prescribed two hours as the default in order to discourage the use of keep-alives. Keep-alives were the subject of a heated debate between two factions among those working on RFC 1122: One said keep-alives were evil no-ops that wasted bandwidth and should be handled at the application level, and the other faction said they simplify applications and enhance TCP connection reliability by adding error detection. The two factions compromised by leaving keep-alives in the Hosts Requirements RFC but making them less useful by assigning a long timeout.

In the end, many TCP/IP stack vendors ignored the RFC 1122 two-hour default recommendation, because too many of their customers wanted a shorter timeout. In other words, customers demanded that keep-alives should be more useful. As a result, most keep-alive timeout values are closer to two minutes than to two hours (but don't rely on this figure).

WinSock does not provide an API to check the keep-alive timeout value or to change it. RFC 1122 does stipulate that each TCP/IP stack must have a way to change the keep-alive timeout setting, so the timeout is usually available as a configuration option in TCP/IP stacks (so one setting affects all connections). WinSock does not address this implementation detail.

Implement Your Own Keep-Alive

Rather than using SO_KEEPALIVE, you should implement your own "keep-alive" mechanism at the application protocol level. This is only possible if you control the network source code for both the client and the server, but it is a relatively simple matter. You use a timer to send some special data periodically, and when the receiving end recognizes the data as a keep-alive packet, it should return a response.

In addition to having full control over how often you check the connection status, by sending data you benefit from the TCP retransmit logic, timeouts, and error reporting. With a TCP socket, the simple act of sending data is enough to detect a failed connection (e.g., the `send( )` function will fail with a WSAETIMEDOUT when the connection goes down without notification from the remote end).

SO_LINGER

The SO_LINGER option enables or disables immediate return from the `closesocket( )` function. It is disabled by default, and `closesocket( )` always returns immediately (with a blocking or nonblocking socket). Disabling SO_LINGER effectively enables the SO_DONTLINGER socket option.

In addition to changing the behavior of `closesocket( )`, with SO_LINGER enabled the timeout value setting also changes the behavior at the transport protocol level (TCP). SO_LINGER determines whether the underlying TCP/IP stack will close a virtual circuit gracefully, or forcefully (i.e., abort the connection). SO_LINGER is valid only on stream sockets (`getsockopt( )` or `setsockopt( )` will fail with WSAENOPROTOOPT on datagram sockets).

Option name	*Data type*	*Default value*	*getsockopt()*	*setsockopt()*	*Socket type*	*Special notes*
SO_LINGER	struct linger far *	SO_DONTLINGER enabled	yes	yes	DS	none

There are three settings for the SO_LINGER option:

- *Disabled (default):* `closesocket( )` attempts a graceful close until default timeout period expires, then does a forceful close. The close operation occurs in the background, since `closesocket( )` returns immediately on a socket in either blocking or nonblocking operation mode.
- *Enabled with nonzero timeout:* `closesocket( )` attempts a graceful close until timeout period expires, then does a forceful close. With a socket in blocking mode, the `closesocket( )` function blocks and calls the blocking hook function until the close operation completes (successfully or not). With a socket in nonblocking mode, `closesocket( )` may fail immediately with WSAEWOULDBLOCK. Unfortunately, the closure behavior on a nonblocking socket is ambiguous, as we describe later in the "Avoiding Ambiguities" section.
- *Enabled with zero timeout:* `closesocket( )` initiates a forceful close and returns immediately, whether the socket is in blocking or nonblocking operation mode.

When a TCP/IP stack completes the **graceful close** of a TCP connection,

1. It sends all data currently queued for sending from the system buffers (put there by application calls to `send( )` or `sendto( )`).
2. It waits for an acknowledgment of all data sent.
3. It performs "three-way handshake" to close the circuit (e.g., sends a TCP <FIN>, waits for an <ACK><FIN> from the other side, then sends an <ACK>).

When a graceful close does not complete within the timeout period you set or the default time period the stack uses, then a forceful close occurs.

When a TCP/IP stack performs a **forceful close** (i.e., a connection abort), it sends a TCP <RST>. If any data remains queued at that time (unacknowledged or unsent), the data is flushed from the system buffers.

We illustrate the TCP protocol mechanics of these two methods of closing in Appendix A, "TCP/IP Protocol Headers."

Avoiding Ambiguities

A number of ambiguities exist in the TCP connection close operation and process in general, and with SO_LINGER in particular. You should be aware of what these ambiguities are and how to avoid them:

- There may still be data pending that could prevent a graceful close, so you should always do a "half-close" with `shutdown( )` *how=1*, call `recv( )` until it returns zero or fails with any error, then call `closesocket( )`. The `CloseConn( )` function in the WinSockx sample library in Chapter 7 shows how this is done.
- The recommended "half-close" procedure will also avoid problems that can occur if you try to call `closesocket( )` immediately followed by `WSACleanup( )`. This can cause problems since some WinSock DLLs may close connections forcefully if they unload as an application exits, which can result in data loss.
- Disabling SO_DONTLINGER enables SO_LINGER with an indeterminate timeout value that can vary between WinSock implementations. You should enable SO_LINGER with a specific timeout instead, since it effectively disables SO_DONTLINGER. However, as we note below, a better way to avoid this ambiguity is to leave SO_DONTLINGER enabled.
- Do not enable SO_LINGER with a nonzero timeout on a nonblocking socket. There are differences in the close behavior if `closesocket( )` fails with WSAEWOULDBLOCK. Some WinSocks will complete the close in the background after WSAEWOULDBLOCK, but others require you to call `closesocket( )` again. To avoid this potential problem, you should use `ioctlsocket( )` FIONBIO to change the socket back to blocking before you call `closesocket( )`. Better yet, do not enable SO_LINGER (as we note below, it is rarely necessary).

Do You Need SO_LINGER?

Other than setting a zero timeout to initiate an abortive close, there are few instances you should need to enable SO_LINGER to set a nonzero timeout value. A TCP/IP stack calculates the default timeout period based on the round-trip time established during the life of a connection. As a result, the TCP/IP stack usually knows best what the timeout period for a close attempt should be. This timeout period differs on TCP connections between different hosts, connected by media with varying bandwidth capacities, and it is affected by network traffic loads. An application cannot predict what the ideal timeout period should be, and it should not try to. We recommend that you leave the default of SO_DONTLINGER enabled for most TCP connections.

linger Structure

The linger structure allows you to get the current SO_LINGER setting, or set it. The setting has two parts: a Boolean flag that indicates status, and—if enabled—a timeout value. Nothing else references the linger structure.

```
struct      linger {
      u_short l_onoff;          /* linger option on/off */
      u_short l_linger;         /* linger time in seconds */
};
typedef struct linger LINGER;
typedef struct linger *PLINGER;
typedef struct linger FAR *LPLINGER;
```

l_onoff: Boolean value to enable or disable the SO_LINGER option (TRUE: enables, FALSE: disables). Disabling SO_LINGER implicitly enables SO_DONTLINGER.

l_linger: timeout—in seconds—for graceful close on a stream socket connection. When timeout expires, the connection is aborted, and unsent or unacknowledged data may be lost.

Code Example

See the code example that appears earlier in this section under "Socket Options."

SO_OOBINLINE

The SO_OOBINLINE option enables or disables receipt of TCP urgent data within the normal stream. By default, this option is disabled so urgent data arrives "out of band." For more information, see Chapter 6, "Socket States."

Option name	*Data type*	*Default value*	*getsockopt( )*	*setsockopt( )*	*Socket type*	*Special notes*
SO_OOBINLINE	BOOL	FALSE	yes	yes	DS	none

When this option is disabled (the default), an application detects TCP urgent data with `select( )` exception fd_set, or with `WSAAsyncSelect( )` FD_OOB event. When these notifications occur, the application can read the OOB data by calling `recv( )` or `recvfrom( )` with the MSG_OOB flag set.

When this option is enabled, the application must scan each byte in the stream with `ioctlsocket( )` SIOCATMARK to detect OOB data. The data is a part of the normal stream so you read it without the MSG_OOB flag. If you must use expedited data, you should enable SO_OOBINLINE. Since there is less ambiguity about how it operates, you are more likely to guarantee portability between WinSock implementations.

See the description of `ioctlsocket( )` SIOCATMARK earlier in this chapter, or refer to Chapter 6, "Socket States," for more information.

SO_RCVBUF and SO_SNDBUF

The SO_RCVBUF and SO_SNDBUF options allow you to set the size of the buffers that the underlying TCP/IP stack uses for receiving and sending on the socket. These values have different meanings, depending what type of socket you have (datagram or stream).

Option name	*Data type*	*Default value*	*getsockopt( )*	*setsockopt( )*	*Socket type*	*Special notes*
SO_RCVBUF and SO_SNDBUF	int	implementation dependent	yes	yes	DG or DS	optional

For a stream socket, SO_RCVBUF is equivalent to the maximum TCP window size. In other words, the value you set will be advertised to the connection peer as the maximum amount of data it can send, until your TCP/IP stack tells it otherwise (with a window update).

These options can be *very* useful for datagram applications that receive bulk data or stream applications that send or receive bulk data. You can effectively increase the data throughput of applications that use either type of socket by increasing the buffer sizes with these options. Of course, the buffering capabilities of the WinSock implementation limit how much you can increase the buffer space. Also, since some stacks allocate static buffers to each socket, these options are optional. The SO_RCVBUF and SO_SNDBUF socket options are not available on all WinSock implementations (in which case `setsockopt( )` may fail with WSAENOPROTOOPT or WSAEINVAL).

Refer to the `GetBuf( )` function in our sample WinSockx library in Chapter 7 for an example of how to use `setsockopt( )` and `getsockopt( )` with SO_SDNBUF or SO_RCVBUF. The `GetBuf( )` function attempts to get as much receive or send buffer space as possible up to the limit in one of its input arguments.

SO_REUSEADDR

The SO_REUSEADDR option enables or disables the ability to reuse a local socket name on more than one socket. This option is usually used to avoid the

WSAEADDRINUSE error, although there are few legitimate needs for this option. This error may indicate a need to reexamine your application design. You should avoid using the SO_REUSEADDR option, if possible, since its use can have unexpected results.

Option name	*Data type*	*Default value*	*getsockopt( )*	*setsockopt( )*	*Socket type*	*Special notes*
SO_REUSEADDR	BOOL	FALSE	yes	yes	DG or DS	none

The combination of protocol, local IP address, and port number composes the socket name. If you have two sockets with the same name, as SO_REUSEADDR allows, things can get confusing for the underlying stack. For instance, with two stream sockets listening on the same port number, which one will get an incoming connection request to that port? It can only be one of the two. With two datagram sockets bound to the same port, you might expect both to receive data. However, the WinSock specification does not require this behavior, and not all WinSock implementations can deliver the same data to multiple sockets.

There are alternatives to the SO_REUSEADDR option, especially for client applications. Since most client applications can use an arbitrary local port, you should let `connect( )` assign a local port automatically. If your client application needs to use a range of local port numbers, you should use a randomize function to select an initial port number before calling `bind( )`, rather than using the same port number each time. You could design your application protocol to use a well-known port initially to tell the peer a different port number to use for the permanent connection (this is similar to how the "talk" application protocol works).

SO_TYPE

The SO_TYPE option retrieves the socket type. This value is set when you request a socket with the `socket( )` function. It cannot be set with `setsockopt( )`. The value retrieved indicates either SOCK_STREAM or SOCK_DGRAM for an PF_INET address family (i.e., TCP/IP) socket. It could report other values for other address families.

Option name	*Data type*	*Default value*	*getsockopt( )*	*setsockopt( )*	*Socket type*	*Special notes*
SO_TYPE	BOOL	none	yes	no	DG or DS	none

SO_TYPE is not a very useful option, since it tells you something you (should) already know. It is intended for servers that inherit sockets on startup. It could be used as a simple, innocuous test to see if a socket handle is valid.

TCP_NODELAY

The TCP_NODELAY option disables or enables the Nagle algorithm. When TCP_NODELAY is enabled, the Nagle algorithm is disabled.

Option name	*Data type*	*Default value*	*getsockopt( )*	*setsockopt( )*	*Socket type*	*Special notes*
TCP_NODELAY	BOOL	FALSE	yes	yes	DS	IPPROTO_TCP *level*, not SOL_SOCKET; no default setting

You should expect it will be *enabled* since the RFC 1122 "Host Requirements" says it *should* be (which is just short of requiring it); however, *no default* setting is prescribed by the v1.1 and 2.0 WinSock specifications for TCP_NODELAY. It may be enabled or disabled by default at the discretion of the WinSock implementor.

This default setting is optional for historical reasons. There is at least one widely deployed terminal emulator application that depends on having TCP_NODELAY disabled by default. If it is not disabled, it fails catastrophically when used to connect to some Hewlett-Packard HP-3000 mini-computers.

This optional default setting for TCP_NODELAY introduces an unfortunate ambiguity that allows for development of applications that inadvertently depend on TCP_NODELAY's being disabled. As a result, these applications may perform poorly on stacks that have TCP_NODELAY enabled by default. If you are developing a TCP application, you should ask your WinSock vendor what its default setting is and then enable it by default (if possible) in order to avoid this type of performance problem.

What Is the Nagle Algorithm?

The *Nagle algorithm* is the name given to the very simple and elegant solution that John Nagle presented in RFC 896, "Congestion Control in IP/TCP Internetworks." This was his answer to the congestion problem he experienced on his large and active internetwork at Ford Aerospace and Communications.

In brief, the algorithm stipulates that *TCP segments should not be sent until*

- All outstanding data is acknowledged.
- Or there's a maximum segment size (MSS) packet to send.

The net effect (pun intended) decreases network traffic, without decreasing data throughput. The effect is greater on slower and longer links, but in general the ratio of media, network, and transport protocol content to application data content is reduced, as the number of inefficient TCP segments is reduced. Instead of sending segments with only 1 byte of data and about 60 bytes of protocol header—like those that telnet produces with each user keystroke—the stack is allowed to coalesce data into multibyte segments.

The effect on most applications is negligible, and so most applications do not notice that the Nagle algorithm is enabled by default in most TCP/IP protocol stacks. However, there are some types of applications that are adversely affected by the delay that the Nagle algorithm introduces to data delivery.

Which Applications Need TCP_NODELAY?

Two types of applications can benefit by disabling the Nagle algorithm:

- an application that does two or more sends of small amounts of data and expects immediate responses from each
- an application that needs to receive a steady flow of data (this might be many small amounts, or large amounts that contain application-imposed message boundaries within the stream)

The classic example of an application that benefits by disabling the Nagle algorithm is an X-Server. It sends a constant stream of mouse movements and uses the response from each to track the mouse movements with the cursor. With the Nagle algorithm enabled, the mouse movements can appear jerky and intermittent since the data is not sent immediately after the X-Server application calls `send( )`.

You should reevaluate your application design if you find an increase in performance or usability with TCP_NODELAY enabled. Some applications, such as X-Servers, must have the TCP_NODELAY enabled because their dataflow is apparent to the user. But you can usually design your application protocol to eliminate any negative effects of the Nagle algorithm:

- Don't do writes and reads in lock-step, but allow some overlap between consecutive operations.
- Don't try to impose packet boundaries on the stream, but read whatever is available into system buffers.
- Build some flexibility into your data parser, so it can handle variable amounts of data in the application buffers.
- Think of how to deal with coalesced data.

It is possible to keep your network administrators happy by reducing wasteful network traffic and still keep your application users happy as well.

Note: The TCP_NODELAY is the only option in v1.1 that uses the IPPROTO_TCP value, rather than SOL_SOCKET, for the `setsockopt()` *level* parameter. The SO_DEBUG option is the same value as TCP_NODELAY, so if you are not careful to use the correct value for *level*, you may affect the SO_DEBUG setting rather than TCP_NODELAY. WinSock cannot detect this error, since both values are valid. Depending on how the WinSock implements SO_DEBUG, this could affect your application adversely, not to mention that it may fail to set the TCP_NODELAY option as you intended to.

Unsupported Options

A number of other Berkeley Sockets options are not supported by the Windows Sockets API. Specifically, the following options are not prescribed by the v1.1 Windows Sockets specification:

`IP_OPTIONS:`	set/get IP per-packet options (from <netinet/in.h>)
`IP_HDRINCL:`	header is included with data (raw)
`IP_TOS:`	IP type of service and precedence
`IP_TTL:`	IP time to live
`IP_RECVOPTS:`	receive all IP options with datagram
`IP_RECVRETOPTS:`	receive IP options for response
`IP_RECVDSTADDR:`	receive IP destination (source) address with datagram
`IP_RETOPTS:`	set/get IP per-packet options
`SO_RCVLOWAT:`	set/get size of receive "low-water" mark
`SO_RCVTIMEO:`	set/get receive timeout
`SO_SNDLOWAT:`	set/get size of send "low-water" mark
`SO_SNDTIMEO:`	set/get send timeout
`SO_USELOOPBACK:`	unused in BSD Sockets
`TCP_MAXSEG:`	set/get maximum TCP segment size

Future Options

At least one WinSock version, in Windows NT, currently supports the SO_SNDTIMEO and SO_RCVTIMEO options. The usefulness of these options is obvious: They allow an application to cause send or receive to fail with the WSAETIMEDOUT error after a set amount of time passes. (Note: SO_RCVTIMEO is relevant to both datagram and stream, but SO_SNDTIMEO is relevant only to stream sockets.) We describe these options in more detail, along with another new option that NT supports (SO_OPENTYPE) in Chapter 15, "Platforms." You can also refer to the Windows NT v3.5 SDK documentation for more information.

The IP_OPTIONS, IP_TOS, IP_TTL, and TCP_MAXSEG options are very useful to some applications (e.g., ping, or other diagnostic applications) and various media (e.g., wireless). As a result, version 2.0 of the Windows Sockets specification includes IP_OPTIONS, IP_TOS, and IP_TTL among its TCP/IP protocol-specific additions. We illustrate the use of the IP_TTL ("time-to-live") option in a sample traceroute application in Chapter 16, "Optional Features," and provide more information about these and other new options in Chapter 17, "WinSock 2." WinSock 2 of the Windows Sockets specification also supports quite a few new protocol-independent options.

Blocking Hooks

When an application initiates a blocking operation in 16-bit Windows, a WinSock DLL does not actually block all processing while the operation completes. To allow for multitasking in the nonpreemptive Windows environment, the WinSock specification requires WinSock implementations to "enter a loop in which it dispatches any Windows messages (yielding the processor to another thread if necessary) and check for the completion of the Windows Sockets function."[1] (Note: The reference to a "thread" in this quote is inappropriate, since 16-bit Windows yields between tasks, and threads are not supported.) This loop is in what is called a "blocking hook function."

The default blocking hook function that most WinSock implementations use is the same as the one provided in the documentation for the `WSASetBlockingHook( )` function. The `WSASetBlockingHook( )` function allows an application to replace the default blocking hook function with one of its own. The `WSAUnhookBlockingHook( )` function reinstalls the default blocking hook function.

WSASetBlockingHook( )

The `WSASetBlockingHook( )` function installs a custom blocking hook function.

```
FARPROC PASCAL FAR WSASetBlockingHook  /* NULL on failure */
        (FARPROC lpBlockFunc);     /* ptr to exported procedure of
                                      blocking hook to install */
```

[1] Section 3.1.1, v1.1 Windows Sockets specification (page 13, third paragraph)

lpBlockFunc: a pointer to an exported procedure you want to use as the blocking hook function that WinSock will call as a blocking operation waits for completion. You need not provide a procedure instance for the blocking hook function, but if the function is not exported properly, it can cause a general protection fault within a WinSock DLL when called during a blocking operation.

On failure, `WSASetBlockingHook( )` returns a NULL pointer. You can call `WSAGetLastError( )` to retrieve the specific error number. One possible error that the WinSock specification does not list is WSAEFAULT, which indicates that the function pointer you provided is invalid.

On success, `WSASetBlockingHook( )` returns a pointer to the current blocking hook function. You can always call `WSAUnhookBlockingHook( )` to restore the default blocking hook, but the pointer returned by `WSASetBlockingHook( )` allows you to save the current (custom) blocking hook, so you can replace it later. This allows "nesting" of blocking hooks within an application that needs to change them more than once during application execution. You need to be aware of race conditions if you attempt to change blocking hooks midstream in this manner, however. Be sure you know that the blocking hook you think is active is the one you are actually using.

Note: 32-bit Windows does not have default blocking hook functions, since blocking is real in the preemptive operating systems. Nonetheless, 32-bit Windows Sockets implementations will allow you to install a blocking hook function of your own and will call it as an operation blocks.

WSAUnhookBlockingHook( )

`WSAUnhookBlockingHook( )` replaces the current blocking hook function with the default blocking hook function.

```
/* 0 on success, SOCKET_ERROR on failure */
int PASCAL FAR WSAUnhookBlockingHook (void);
```

As you can see, `WSAUnhookBlockingHook( )` does not have any input parameters. The current task or thread is the implicit input parameter, since blocking hook functions are on a per-task basis.

On failure, `WSAUnhookBlockingHook( )` returns SOCKET_ERROR. You must call `WSAGetLastError( )` to get the cause of the failure. Although the v1.1 WinSock specification lists only one possible error (WSANOTINITIALISED), two others are possible: WSAENETDOWN and WSAEINPROGRESS.

On success, `WSAUnhookBlockingHook( )` reinstalls the default blocking hook function. Notice that it does not automatically "nest" blocking hooks. To do that, you need to save the return value from `WSASetBlockingHook( )` and then reinstall that blocking hook procedure with `WSASetBlockingHook( )` instead of calling `WSAUnhookBlockingHook( )`.

Blocking Hook Functions

There are many restrictions on what you can do within the blocking hook function. For example, the only legal WinSock call you can make within a blocking hook function is `WSACancelBlockingCall( )`. It is no coincidence that this is the only function that will not fail with WSAEINPROGRESS while a blocking operation is outstanding. This will cause the blocking hook function to fail with WSAEINTR to indicate the interrupted function call.

The legitimate reason for installing your own blocking hook function is to perform extra processing while the blocking operation is underway. For example, you could perform extra keyboard processing, or use the idle time to execute CPU-intensive operations such as data conversion or graphics functions.

The most common motivation to install a custom blocking hook function is to try to avoid reentrant messages. Although it is possible to do this on some WinSock implementations, it is not advisable. Other Windows Sockets implementations require the ability to process messages to complete function operation. If you install a blocking hook that prevents reentrant messages over any of these WinSock implementations, your application will fail (blocking operations may never complete).

To ensure WinSock portability, you should alter your application so it can handle reentrant messages gracefully instead of trying to avoid them (see Chapter 5, "Operation Modes," for more information).

You can justifiably install a blocking hook function that suppresses reentrant messages when you are creating a dynamic link library to run over WinSock and the applications calling your DLL cannot tolerate reentrant messages. Such a blocking hook function is justifiable in this case only because you cannot rewrite the applications that call your DLL. We discuss this in more detail and show such a blocking hook function in Chapter 11, "DLLs over WinSock."

Blocking Status

The blocking status is a Boolean indication of whether or not a socket has a blocking operation outstanding.

```
BOOL PASCAL FAR WSAIsBlocking          /* TRUE or FALSE */
        (void);
```

`WSAIsBlocking( )` does not take any input parameters; the implicit input parameter is the current task or thread. `WSAIsBlocking( )` cannot fail. It returns either

- TRUE if a blocking operation is outstanding in the current task or thread
- FALSE if no blocking operation is pending

You need `WSAIsBlocking( )` in any application that uses blocking operations. In the asynchronous Windows environment, it is likely that at some point you—or your application user—will attempt a WinSock function call while a blocking operation is outstanding. To avoid having the function fail with WSAEINPROGRESS, you should call `WSAIsBlocking( )` to check the blocking status first.

For more information, refer to Chapter 5, "Operation Modes."

Socket Names

Two functions allow you to retrieve both local and remote socket names after a socket has connected. The `getsockname( )` function returns the local socket name, and the `getpeername( )` function returns the remote socket name. Here are their prototypes:

```
getpeername( ): Retrieve socket name of peer connected to a socket.
    int PASCAL FAR getpeername /* 0 on success, or SOCKET_ERROR */
        (SOCKET s,             /* a connected socket */
         struct sockaddr FAR *name, /* structure for peer name */
         int FAR *namelen);    /* ptr to length of addr struct */

getsockname( ): Retrieve the (current) local name for a socket.
    int PASCAL FAR getsockname /* 0 on success, or SOCKET_ERROR */
        (SOCKET s,             /* a bound socket */
         struct sockaddr FAR *name, /* structure for local name */
         int FAR *namelen);    /* ptr to length of addr struct */
```

The input parameters for both functions are the same: *socket*, *address structure* (*struct sockaddr*), and *address structure length*. The two functions differ only in the contents of the address structure upon return from a successful call.

As we describe in Chapter 4, "Network Application Mechanics," every association is uniquely identified by this 5-tuple: protocol, local IP address, local port number, remote IP address, and remote port number. These represent the local socket name and the remote socket name. Complete socket names are not necessarily established for both ends until you establish the association itself.

Typically, client applications allow the network system to assign an arbitrary local port number, and server applications allow clients to connect from arbitrary remote port numbers. A client, however, does not have immediate access to its local port upon return from `connect( )`. A client application usually will not need this information, but the `getsockname( )` function can provide it if it does.

getsockname( )

The `getsockname( )` function returns the local socket name for a connected socket (i.e., after a successful call to `connect( )` or `accept( )`). It is valid for both stream and datagram sockets.

```
int PASCAL FAR getsockname /* 0 on success, SOCKET_ERROR on failure */
    (SOCKET s,                  /* a bound or connected socket */
     struct sockaddr FAR *name, /* structure to recv local name */
     int FAR *namelen);         /* length of address structure */
```

s:	handle of socket for which we want to retrieve the local name (which consists of the port number and IP address)
name:	socket address structure into which WinSock will put socket name info
namelen:	length in bytes of *name* buffer

You can call `getsockname( )` after `bind( )` to retrieve the local name of a socket, but you may retrieve only the local port number, not the IP address. You need to call `connect( )` before `getsockname( )` will reliably return the local IP address. The most common use of `getsockname( )` is in a client application after `connect( )` completes to retrieve the local port number WinSock assigned.

If you use a UDP socket, you can call `connect( )`, and you need not send anything from the host. The target address need not be local, or even a familiar IP address. This is the technique we use in our code example to try to retrieve the local IP address.

Code Example

The following code example shows an alternative to the `gethostname( )` /`gethostbyname( )` method demonstrated in Chapter 8, "Host Names and Addresses," for retrieving the local host address. There is still opportunity for problems trying to retrieve a local IP address with this method, but they are not as irrecoverable.

On a multihomed host—a system with more than one network interface—it is possible that the address you get back will not be the one you end up sending from (if another interface is closer to your target address). You should definitely avoid trying to `connect( )` to the loopback address (127.0.0.1), since `getsockname( )` could simply give that same address back to you as your own.

```
SOCKET s;
struct sockaddr_in stLclAddr;
struct sockaddr_in stRmtAddr;
int nRet;
...
s = socket(PF_INET, SOCK_DGRAM, 0);
if (s == INVALID_SOCKET) {
    <report WinSock error to user>
} else {
    /* the port and target address are arbitrary here; since we're
     *  using UDP, we're not actually sending anything on the net
     *  (not 127.0.0.1, so we don't get it back as our address) */
    stRmtAddr.sin_family      = PF_INET;
    stRmtAddr.sin_port        = IPPORT_ECHO;
    stRmtAddr.sin_addr.s_addr = inet_addr("128.127.50.1");
    nRet = connect(s,
                   (struct sockaddr FAR *)&stRmtAddr,
                   sizeof(struct sockaddr));

    if (nRet == SOCKET_ERROR) {
        <report WinSock error to user>
    } else {
        /* we now have a "connected" socket, so we can call
         *  getsockname( ) and should get back a local IP address */
        nRet = getsockname(s,
                   (struct sockaddr FAR *)&stLclAddr,
                   sizeof(struct sockaddr));
```

```
        if (nRet == SOCKET_ERROR) {
            <report WinSock error to user>
        } else {
            /* success!  We have retrieved our local address */
            DoPrintf ("Local IP Address: %s,
                    inet_ntoa(stLclAddr.sin_addr));
        }
    }
    closesocket(s);  /* we don't need this socket anymore */
}
```

getpeername( )

Usually a network application knows which remote host it is talking to, so there is no need to find out. You must know a remote address beforehand in order to `connect( )` or `sendto( )` a host, and both `accept( )` and `recvfrom( )` functions can tell you the remote address that responded. Nonetheless, there is a function that lets you check to whom you are connected: `getpeername( )`. The `getpeername( )` function returns the remote socket name on a connected socket (i.e., after a successful call to `connect( )` or `accept( )`). It is valid for both stream and datagram sockets.

```
int PASCAL FAR getpeername /*0 on success, SOCKET_ERROR on failure*/
    (SOCKET s,                  /* a connected socket */
     struct sockaddr FAR *name, /* structure to for peer */
     int FAR *namelen);         /* pointer to len of addr struct */
```

s: handle of socket for which we want to retrieve the remote name (which consists of the port number and IP address)

name: socket address structure into which WinSock will put socket name information

namelen: length in bytes of *name* buffer

Code Example

An application that inherits a connection is the most likely candidate for `getpeername( )`. Here's a code sketch that illustrates how to use it (although the context is unlikely). Note that this works with either a stream or datagram socket, but it is applicable only after a successful call to `connect( )` or `accept( )`. It does *not* work after a call to `sendto( )` or `recvfrom( )`:

```
int nRet;
SOCKET nListenSock, nConnSock;
struct sockaddr stRmtAddr, stLclAddr;
...
stLclAddr.sin_family = PF_INET;
stLclAddr.sin_port   = htons (IPPORT_ECHO);
stLclAddr.sin_addr   = INADDR_ANY;
nRet = bind(nListenSock,
      (struct sockaddr FAR *)&stLclAddr,
      sizeof(struct sockaddr);
if (nRet == SOCK_ERROR) {
      <report the WinSock error value>
      goto AppExit;
}
nRet = listen(nListenSock, 5);
if (nRet == SOCK_ERROR) {
      <report the WinSock error value>
      goto AppExit;
}
stConnSock = accept(nListenSock,
      (struct sockaddr FAR *)&stRmtAddr,
      sizeof(struct sockaddr);
if (nRet == SOCK_ERROR) {
      <report the WinSock error value>
      goto AppExit;
} else {
      /* accept( ) should have filled this info in already
       *  but we'll call getpeername to show how it's done */
      nRet = getpeername(nConnSock,
            (struct sockaddr FAR *)&stRmtAddr,
            sizeof(struct sockaddr));
      if (nRet == SOCK_ERROR) {
            <report the WinSock error value>
            goto AppExit;
      }
}
```

10 Support Routines

In This Chapter:

- Startup and Cleanup
- Byte Ordering
- Service Names and Ports
- Protocol Names and Numbers
- Error Reporting

The aspects of things that are most important to us are hidden because of their simplicity and familiarity.

Wittgenstein

Support routines do not provide network services but support other functions that do. Despite their secondary nature, they are some of the most common and necessary functions of all. At least two of them—for startup and cleanup—are required in every Windows Sockets application. The others are not required, but most applications use them. We show you the hows, whens, whys, and wherefores of these routines in this chapter.

Startup and Cleanup

Every WinSock application must initialize the WinSock DLL before it begins operation and notify the DLL to cleanup when it's done. WinSock applications must provide this explicit notification because 16-bit Windows does not notify a DLL as each application loads or unloads a DLL. While 32-bit Windows provides process and thread, attach and detach notification, 16-bit Windows notifies a DLL only of the first and last processes, with `LibMain( )` and `WEP( )`.

A WinSock DLL needs to know when every process comes and goes so it can allocate and deallocate process-specific resources. WinSock applications must call `WSAStartup( )` as they begin and `WSACleanup( )` as they end. Once is enough, but an application can call `WSAStartup( )` and `WSACleanup( )` any number of times as long as every successful call to startup has a matching successful call to cleanup also. It is rarely necessary to call `WSAStartup( )` more than once, but sometimes it is convenient with encapsulated functions in DLLs over WinSock, or class libraries. For instance, you could call `WSAStartup( )` along with each call to `socket( )` and call `WSACleanup( )` with every call to `closesocket( )`.

Internally, `WSAStartup( )` increments a reference count that starts at zero, and `WSACleanup( )` decrements it. The WinSock DLL only frees resources when cleanup makes the reference count go back to zero.

WSAStartup( )

`WSAStartup( )` must be the first WinSock function that a WinSock application uses. Otherwise, any other WinSock API function will fail with the error `WSAENOTINITIALISED` (note the British spelling of the error macro with an "s" instead of a "z"). A WinSock DLL uses this function call to register the calling task and allocate any necessary resources.

In addition to giving the WinSock DLL a chance to register the calling process, it gives the WinSock application a chance to learn about the WinSock implementation. The WinSock DLL provides information about itself in a WinSock API data structure called WSAData. Information is not extensive, since implementation specifics should be immaterial, but at the very least you need to check the version information.

Here is the prototype for the `WSAStartup( )` function:

```
int PASCAL FAR WSAStartup  /* 0 on success, or error value */
   (WORD wVersionRequired, /* highest version of WinSock API
                        required (hi-byte=minor, low-byte=major)*/
   LPWSADATA lpWSAData);   /* ptr to struct to receive details on
                              Windows Sockets implementation */
```

wVersionRequired: the major.minor version number your application requires. The LSB is the major version, and MSB is the minor version (revision number). You should request WinSock version 1.1 (0x0101) unless your application uses features unique to WinSock version 2.0 (0x0002). If your application uses WinSock 2 features, it should be equipped to "fall back" to 1.1, to guarantee compatibility with all WinSock implementations. WinSock 2 is fully "backward compatible" to WinSock 1.1.

lpWSAData: pointer to a buffer your WinSock application provides, and into which the WinSock DLL will fill in implementation specifics

Notice that `WSAStartup( )` returns 0 on success or an error value on failure. Many functions return a zero on success, but `WSAStartup( )` is the *only* function that returns a WinSock error value when it fails, as opposed to simply returning an error *indicator* like SOCKET_ERROR. You *cannot* use `WSAGetLastError( )` to retrieve the error if `WSAStartup( )` fails, since `WSAGetLastError( )` would fail with WSAENOTINITIALISED after `WSAStartup( )` failed. You must have at least one successful call to `WSAStartup( )` before any other WinSock function will succeed.

Even when `WSAStartup( )` succeeds, you should check the contents of the *wVersion* field in the WSAData structure pointed to by *lpWSAData*. `WSAStartup( )` provides for version negotiation, so it may succeed even when it does not support the version you request. We describe this process shortly and illustrate it in our code example.

When and Where?

`WSAStartup( )` must be the first WinSock function call an application makes, and `WSACleanup( )` should be the last. You already know that. So the next question is, "Where in your application should these function calls be located?" (Note: We deal with this issue in DLLs in Chapter 11, "DLLs over WinSock".)

It makes sense to match these routines with the startup and cleanup locations for the application itself. `WinMain( )` is the entry and exit point for all Windows applications, so it would seem to be the ideal location. As you can see, we have called `WSAStartup( )` and `WSACleanup( )` from `WinMain( )` in all of our sample applications. It is a convenient location for these calls, but it has its limitations.

By having `WSAStartup( )` in `WinMain( )` we have limited our applications so they will run only if a properly functioning WinSock DLL is available. If `WSAStartup( )` fails, we tell the user the error value and description and then exit the application. This works for us since we have nothing to do without a working WinSock DLL, but it would limit other multipurpose applications.

One option in `WinMain( )` is to continue application execution but set a variable to indicate `WSAStartup( )` failure so that the application either prohibits WinSock calls or notifies the user of the failure (again) when he or she tries network operations. Another option is to try `WSAStartup( )` after the application has started.

Another convenient location that matches with entries and exits is in the main window (or dialog) procedure in the WM_CREATE (or WM_INITDIALOG) and WM_CLOSE message handlers. This location is similar to `WinMain( )` but is further along in execution. If you want your application to continue execution even when `WSAStartup( )` fails, you could set the variable to avoid other WinSock calls (and errors) just as easily here too.

Some multipurpose applications use the network for transactions that have a distinct beginning and end. Such applications can call `WSAStartup( )` before beginning the network transaction and `WSACleanup( )` after the transaction is complete. The problem with this strategy is that your application will not "remember" that `WSAStartup( )` failed, so it will fail repeatedly.

The bottom line is that there are a number of times and locations in an application you can call `WSAStartup( )` and `WSACleanup( )`. You need to determine whether your application should run if WinSock is not available or not functioning. Also, give some thought to what to do when it fails, if you want to continue execution.

WSAStartup( ) Error Messages

A call to `WSAStartup( )` would seem to be the perfect way to check whether you have a WinSock DLL available and configured correctly as well as a functioning network connection. Unfortunately, however, it is not as perfect as it seems.

The first problem is if you statically linked with the WinSock library when you created your executable. If the WinSock DLL file is not available at run time, your application will not have the opportunity to call `WSAStartup( )`. Windows will not even run the application. We describe how to explicitly link a WinSock DLL to avoid this problem in Appendix D, "What You Need."

The second problem is that some WinSock implementations display a message box if a configuration or network problem exists with the WinSock DLL. Typically, WinSocks do not provide any way for an application to control or prevent the appearance of these message boxes. As a result, there is no way around this problem, no alternative ways to check for a proper WinSock configuration or network connection. Nonetheless, you may want to follow a `WSAStartup( )` failure with an error message of your own that suggests to the user what the problem is and how to correct it.

WSAData Structure

The Windows Sockets API data structure (struct WSAData) is for details about the WinSock DLL implementation. A WinSock application provides a buffer for this structure when it calls `WSAStartup( )`, and `WSAStartup( )` fills in version information, sockets available, datagram size, and other information. Here is the format of the `WSAData` structure and a description of each field:

```
typedef struct WSAData {
      WORD  wVersion;          /* version app expected to use */
      WORD  wHighVersion;      /* highest version available */
      char  szDescription[WSADESCRIPTION_LEN+1]; /* no format */
      char  szSystemStatus[WSASYS_STATUS_LEN+1]; /* no format */
      long  iMaxSockets;       /* max sockets available */
      long  iMaxUdpDg;         /* max datagram size */
      char FAR *lpVendorInfo; /* no format */
} WSADATA;
```

wVersion: the version of the Windows Sockets specification that the Windows Sockets DLL expects the caller to use. For example, if an application requested version 1.1 and the DLL supports version 1.1, then this field will have the value of 1.1.

The version number value is encoded the same as the *wVersionRequired* input parameter to `WSAStartup( )`: High-byte is minor version, and low-byte is major version. You can use the HIBYTE and LOBYTE macros to access them.

wHighVersion: the highest version of the Windows Sockets specification that this DLL can support (see the note below for encoding). For example, if a WinSock DLL supported both versions 1.1 and 2.0 of the specification, this field would have the value to indicate version 2.0 (in fact, this should be the case with all WinSock DLLs that support version 2.0, since it will be backward compatible to 1.1). The version number value is encoded the same as the *wVersion* field.

szDescription: a null-terminated string (maximum of 256 chars) into which a WinSock vendor can put any description. There is no predefined form or content for this text. Sometimes WinSock providers include an implementation version description, but typically they only state the manufacturer name and the WinSock version it supports.

The v1.1 WinSock specification does not specify a format for vendor descriptions or specific ID numbers for vendors, since without it there is no consistent way to identify each vendor. It does not provide a field for vendor version numbers, either. As a result, it is not possible to determine programmatically the vendor versions of particular implementations. True, this should not be necessary, but in fact it is needed sometimes to avoid incompatibility caused by bugs in particular vendor versions.

As we describe in Chapter 17, WinSock 2 addresses both of these issues with its protocol-independent features. Microsoft maintains a clearinghouse that assigns a unique ID to each service provider, and this ID number appears in the protocol information structure.

szSystemStatus: a null-terminated string (maximum of 128 chars) into which the WinSock DLL copies relevant status or configuration information. There is no predefined format or content, and both vary widely.

iMaxSockets: the maximum number of sockets a single process can potentially open. Unfortunately, there is no way to know whether or how this relates to the total number of sockets available in the system, or to which types of sockets (e.g., datagram or stream) this refers. A `socket( )` call *can* fail short of this number, depending on how many other sockets of various types are available or in use.

iMaxUdpDg: the size in bytes of the largest UDP datagram that can be sent or received by the WinSock implementation. If this value is 0, then the WinSock DLL can send or receive a datagram of any size (up to 32K signed, or 64K unsigned). You must also consider the capability of your receiver when sending datagrams. We recommend that you implement an application protocol for your sender and receiver to agree on a datagram size. Generally, the smaller the datagram—measured in terms of fragmentation and reassembly required—the better chance that your receiver will get it.

Datagram sockets are unreliable, so you cannot assume that a send will fail and return an error if WinSock cannot send. You should always use the value in *iMaxUdpDg* as the largest value for the *len* (length) field when you send on a datagram socket.

lpVendorInfo: a far pointer to vendor-specific data structure (just more miscellaneous stuff useless to a developer or end user)

Version Negotiation

The Windows Sockets specification uses the term "version negotiation" to describe the process where an application makes a request for a WinSock version and the WinSock DLL responds. Here's a sketch of the steps involved:

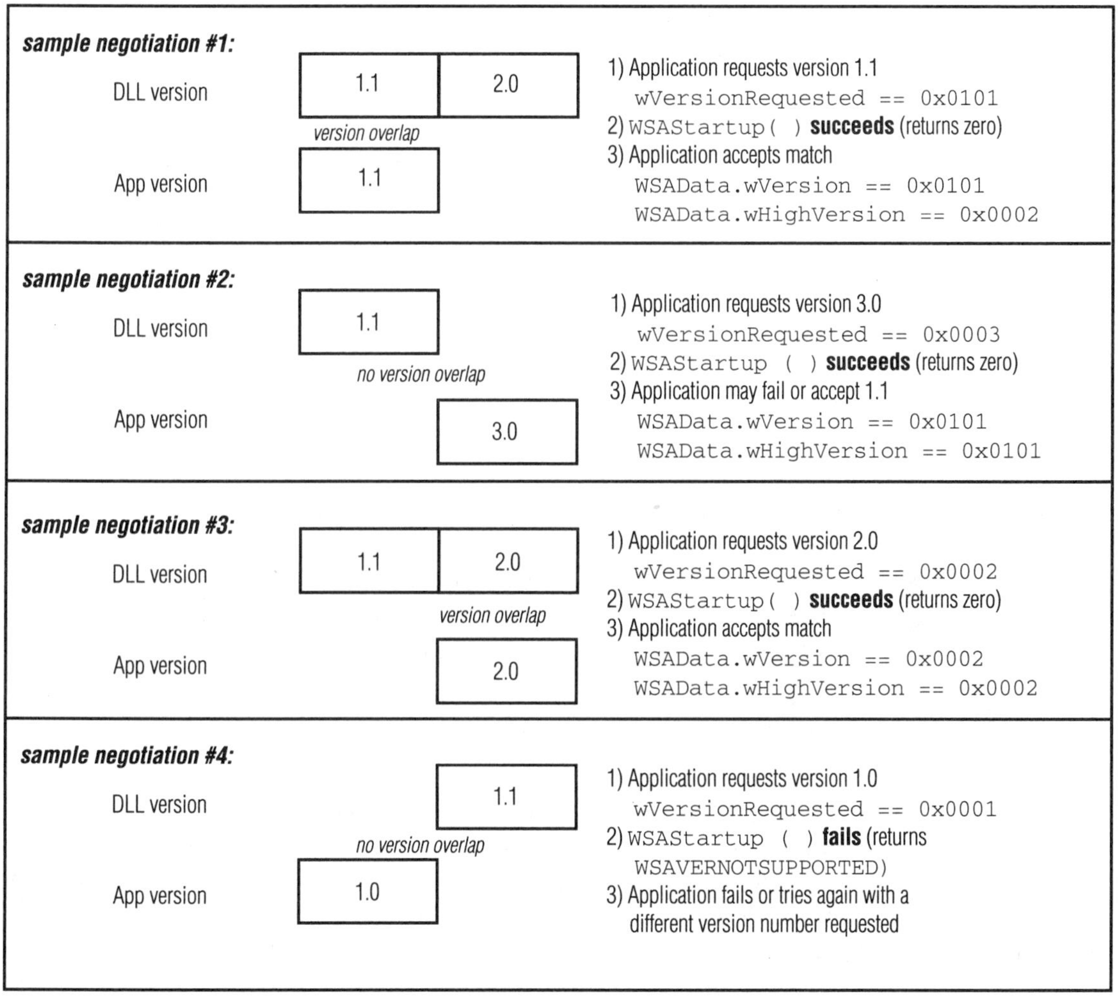

Figure 10-1 This shows a number of sample version negotiations. Notice that `WSAStartup( )` fails only when the DLL version is greater than the version the application requested.

- An application calls `WSAStartup( )`, requests a specific version, and provides a buffer.
- The WinSock DLL rejects the request—`WSAStartup( )` **fails**—if the version requested is *lower* than the version range the DLL supports. `WSAStartup( )` **succeeds** when the version required is equal to *or higher* than the version it supports. After both success and failure, `WSAStartup( )` returns version information in a WSAData structure it fills in the buffer the application provided.
- On failure, the application may try again with a *higher* version.
- On success, the application must compare the WSAData *wVersion* field value to *wVersionRequired* input to `WSAStartup( )` to verify it is the same version you requested. `WSAStartup( )` may have succeeded although the value in *wVersion*—the version the DLL expects your application to use—is higher than the value you requested.

The point of version negotiation is to allow either an application or a DLL to support more than one version of the WinSock API. The mechanism is not intuitive since `WSAStartup( )` fails only if you require a version lower than the version range a WinSock DLL provides. It does not fail if you request a higher version, even if there is not "version overlap."

Fortunately, version 2.0 of the Windows Sockets specification is fully "backward compatible" to version 1.1. Although version 2.0 has a number of significant new features (see Chapter 17 for details), it does not change the existing 1.1 API. Hence, even if your application requests and expects only 1.1, and does not check the *wVersion* field when `WSAStartup( )` succeeds, you will not have a problem. If 2.0 were *not* backward compatible with 1.1, your application could possibly fail later if you tried to use an unsupported feature.

Code Example

The following code example illustrates the "version negotiation" of an application that is capable of taking advantage of new features in a version 2.0 WinSock DLL but will use 1.1 if it needs to. You should not request 2.0 unless you need it, since some 1.1 WinSock DLLs may fail (in other words, don't test that every WinSock implementation supports the subtleties of version negotiation unless you have to).

```
#define MAKEWORD (low, high) \
      ((WORD)(((BYTE)(low)) | (((WORD)(BYTE)(high))<<8)))
#define WS_HI_MAJOR 0x02
```

```
#define WS_HI_MINOR 0x00
#define WS_LO_MAJOR 0x01
#define WS_LO_MINOR 0x01
...
WORD wVersionRequested =
    MAKEWORD(WS_HI_MAJOR, WS_HI_MINOR);
WSADATA stWSAData;
int nWSAErr;
BOOL bWSAVersion2 = FALSE;/* our Version 2.0 supported flag */

/*--------initialize Windows Sockets DLL-------*/
nWSAErr = WSAStartup(wVersionRequested, &stWSAData);

/* WSAStartup( ) returns error value if failed (0 on success) */
if (nWSAErr != 0) {
     if (nWSAErr == WSAVERNOTSUPPORTED) {
       /* DLL supports something higher than 2.0, but not
       * also 2.0, so we must quit */
       <report version mismatch error and quit>
     } else {
       <report error number contained in nWSAErr variable>
     }
     return;
}

/* inspect the version WinSock expects us to use to see if it
 *  is acceptable (we want 2.0, but we'll accept 1.1) */
if (wVersionRequested == stWSAData.wVersion){
    bWSAVersion2 = TRUE;  /* we can use version 2 features */
} else if (LOWORD(stWSAData.wHighestVersion) >= WS_LO_MAJOR) {
    if HIWORD(stWSAData.wHighestVersion) < WS_LO_MINOR)) {
        /*
         * major version supported by WinSock DLL is ok, but its
         * minor version is below our minimum requirement
         */
        <report version mismatch error and quit>
        WSACleanup( );
        return;
    }
} else {
    /*
```

```
      * major version supported by WinSock DLL
      *  is below our minimum requirement
      */
     <report version mismatch error and quit>
     WSACleanup( );
     return;
}
```

WSACleanup( )

For every successful call to WSAStartup( ), an application must have a matching successful call to WSACleanup( ). The only time a WinSock application does not need a call to WSACleanup( ) is if WSAStartup( ) failed. The WinSock DLL maintains a reference count for each process. It starts at zero, and each successful call to WSAStartup( ) increments the count, while each call to WSACleanup( ) decrements it. A WinSock DLL frees resources it allocated for a process only when the reference count goes back to zero with the last matching call to WSACleanup( )

```
int PASCAL FAR WSACleanup  /* 0 on success, or SOCKET_ERROR */
        (void);
```

WSACleanup( ) always returns immediately. On success, WSACleanup( ) returns zero. On failure, WSACleanup( ) returns SOCKET_ERROR. You call WSAGetLastError( ) to check the error value if it fails. The most likely error is WSAEINPROGRESS, which would occur if you called WSACleanup( ) while a blocking operation is still underway. You may get WSANOTINITIALISED if you call WSACleanup( ) too many times.

Although the purpose of WSACleanup( ) is to return resources that the WinSock DLL allocated for a task, it does not cancel blocking calls, and there is no guarantee that it will close all outstanding sockets. Before you call WSACleanup( ) you should

- Cancel any outstanding blocking operation with WSACancelBlockingCall( ), and wait until the blocking function fails with WSAEINTR.
- Cancel any pending calls to asynchronous database functions—like WSAAsyncGetHostByName( )—by calling WSACancelAsyncRequest( ).
- Close all open sockets with a successful call to closesocket( ).

Byte Ordering

A call to `connect( )` in a new or ported Sockets applications often fails with the WSAECONNREFUSED error. This happens when the client application—or the server application to which it is connecting—fails to convert the byte order of the port number from host order to network order before assigning it to the `sin_port` field in the `sockaddr_in` structure. The root cause of the problem is the different byte orders that various processors use to store values in memory.

Most systems running Windows have Intel processors, where the **host byte order** is little endian. However, the "Assigned Numbers" RFC stipulates the use of big endian for **network byte order** in multibyte values within TCP/IP protocol headers. Almost all WinSock data structures that contain multibyte values must store them in network order.

Section 2.3 in the v1.1 WinSock specification addresses the issue of byte ordering and singles out IP addresses and port numbers (`sin_addr` and `sin_port` in SOCKADDR_IN).

> *The rule of thumb:* Any multibyte input parameter value to a WinSock function and any multibyte field value in a WinSock structure should be in network order.

The only notable exceptions are the protocol number, which is always in host byte order in the protoent structure (`p_proto`), and the input parameter to either `getprotobynumber( )` or `WSAAsyncGetProtoByNumber( )`.

Note: It is entirely up to an application what byte order it uses in the application data it sends and receives. The byte ordering functions are intended for network-relevant WinSock data, not application data (although you are free to use them if you want).

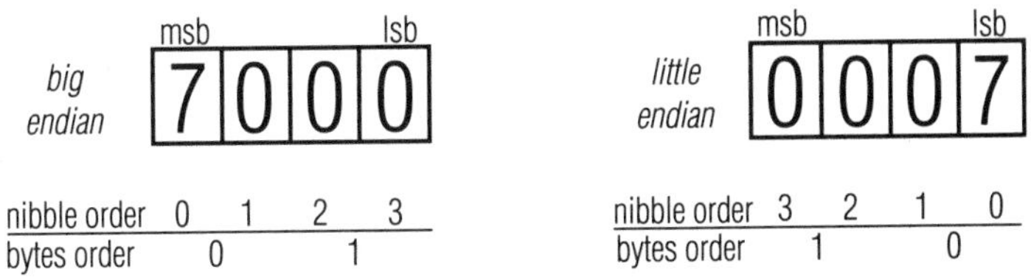

Figure 10-2 This illustrates how big-endian byte order compares to little endian. Big endian is network byte order, and little endian is host byte order on Intel processors (and others).

Byte Ordering Functions

WinSock has two pairs of functions to convert to and from network byte order:

- `htons( )` converts shorts (16-bit values) from host order to network order, and `ntohs( )` converts shorts from network to host byte order (little endian to big endian).
- `htonl( )` converts longs (32-bit values) from host order to network order, and `ntohl( )` converts longs from network byte order to host order (big endian to little endian)

```
u_short PASCAL FAR htons     /* 16-bit number in network order */
        (u_short hostshort); /* 16-bit number in host order */

u_short PASCAL FAR ntohs     /* 16-bit number in host order */
         (u_short netshort); /* 16-bit number in network order */

u_long PASCAL FAR ntohl      /* 32-bit number in host order */
         (u_long netlong);   /* 32-bit number in network order */

u_long PASCAL FAR htonl      /* 32-bit number in network order */
        (u_long hostlong);   /* 32-bit number in host order */
```

These functions cannot fail. All of them always return a value of the same size as the input value (16-bit or 32-bit). They do not always perform any byte reordering, however. If the native byte order for the current system is big endian, then these functions are no-ops.

To enhance the portability of your source code, you should always use the byte ordering functions where they are appropriate (according to the rule of thumb noted earlier). In other words, never make assumptions about the byte order of the computer system on which your application is running.

Code Example

Here is a code example that demonstrates the use of the `htonl( )`, `htons( )`, and `ntohs( )` functions in a server application:

```
struct sockaddr_in stLclAddr;
int nPort;
...
stLclAddr.sin_family      = PF_INET;
stLclAddr.sin_addr.s_addr = htonl(INADDR_ANY);
stLclAddr.sin_port = htons(IPPORT_ECHO);
...
nPort = ntohs(stLclAddr.sin_port);    /* get port for display */
```

Service Names and Ports

Every service has a port number, and many also have a name. Service names, like host names, provide a convenient way to refer to a well-known service. Also, like host names, they are more than a convenience. Although some well-known services have well-established port numbers associated with them (listed in the "Assigned Numbers" RFC, and maintained by IANA), others do not. Port numbers sometimes change. You can use the functions to resolve service names to find their respective port number.

Your application will be more robust and flexible if you use the WinSock functions to resolve a service name and use a hardcoded port number value only if that fails (WINSOCK.H has manifest constants for many well-known ports, like IPPORT_FTP for the File Transfer Protocol). Having a fallback to a hardcoded value allows your application to adapt when port numbers change or when the current WinSock configuration is incorrect (causing the service name resolution to fail).

The WinSock API has four service resolution functions: one pair for service name resolution, and the other pair for port number resolution. One function in each pair blocks until the operation completes, and the other notifies the application asynchronously upon completion. The functions are `getservbyname( )` and `WSAAsyncGetServByName( )`, `getservbyport( )` and `WSAAsyncGetServByPort( )`, respectively. These functions are similar to the other so-called database functions that provide protocol resolution (later in this chapter) and host resolution (in Chapter 8, "Host Names and Addresses").

The service resolution functions access a services database to retrieve service information (not to be confused with the Windows services registry). The WinSock specification does not prescribe the location, name, or format for the services database, since the WinSock API is supposed to hide this implementation detail. We describe the standard format WinSock adopted—the BSD UNIX */etc/services* file—later in this section, since it helps to know a little about the underlying mechanism in case of problems.

servent Structure

All of the service resolution functions return their results in a servent structure that contains information about a service. However, there is not much to tell: the official service name, a list of aliases, a port number (chances are we already had the protocol string). Here is what its definition looks like in WINSOCK.H:

```
struct      servent {
      char  FAR * s_name;           /* official service name */
      char  FAR * FAR * s_aliases;  /* alias list */
      short s_port;                 /* port # */
      char  FAR * s_proto;          /* protocol to use */
};
typedef struct servent SERVENT;
typedef struct servent *PSERVENT;
typedef struct servent FAR *LPSERVENT;
```

s_name: official name of the service. By convention, service names are all lowercase (e.g., "ftp," "gopher," "smtp," etc.).

s_aliases: array of null-terminated alias strings (i.e., alternate service names), terminated by a null pointer. To access the list of aliases, you need a simple while loop:

```
LPSERVENT lpstServ;
char achOutBuf[LARGEBUF];
int nStrLen=0, i;
...
while (lpstServ->s_aliases) {
   /* append service alias string to output buffer */
   i = wsprintf (&achOutBuf[nStrLen],
         "%s ", lpstServ->p_aliases);
   nStrLen += i;           /* update buffer index */
   lpstServ->s_aliases++;  /* point to next alias */
}
```

s_port: port number at which the service can be contacted (in network byte order, the same as you would assign to the `sockaddr_in` structure `sin_port` field, so byte reordering is unnecessary)

s_proto: null-terminated string with the name of the protocol. This is the same as the one you asked for, or the first one found if none is specified when you call the service resolution function.

Service Resolution

An application must have the port number in order to call `connect( )` or `bind( )`, `sendto( )` or `recvfrom( )`. Some port numbers are static, and some change (as defined by the "Assigned Numbers" RFC, maintained by IANA). To prepare your application for port numbers that may change, or simply to make your application more flexible, you can use one of the service name resolution functions. There are two functions to choose from, and each uses different operation modes:

- `getservbyname()` blocks until the service name resolution operation completes.
- `WSAAsyncGetServByName()` returns immediately and notifies the application asynchronously when the service name resolution operation completes.

getservbyname()

The `getservbyname()` function uses a service name and protocol name (if provided) to access a WinSock implementation's services database. It operates in blocking mode: It returns when the service name resolution operation completes (after it succeeds or fails).

```
struct servent FAR * PASCAL FAR getservbyname /* NULL on fail */
     (char FAR *name,      /* pointer to service name */
      char far *proto);    /* pointer to protocol name or NULL to
                              return first match of service name */
```

name: a null-terminated string containing the service name or alias to resolve. Some WinSock implementations are case sensitive, so use lower case for the service name, as found in a standard BSD UNIX */etc/services* file.

proto: a null-terminated string containing the protocol name for which you want the service. The protocol name is optional. It could be a NULL pointer to retrieve the first service matched. However, we recommend that you use the protocol name, since port numbers can vary between protocols. Furthermore, because some WinSock implementations are case sensitive, you should also use a lowercase protocol name, as found in a standard BSD UNIX */etc/services* file.

`getservbyname()` blocks until completion (and calls the blocking hook function). However, since the function typically accesses a local disk file for resolution (see the "Services Database" section later), it usually returns quickly.

On failure, `getservbyname()` returns zero. You can call `WSAGetLastError()` to find out why it failed. Typically, it fails with the WSANO_DATA error. This may mean the service name was not in the services database, or possibly the services database was not available (if the WinSock implementation is misconfigured).

On success, `getservbyname( )` returns a pointer to a `servent` structure. You need to read the contents of the servent structure immediately upon return from `getservbyname( )`, before another WinSock function call changes the contents. Do not attempt to free or change its contents, or a protection fault may result.

Code Example

The following code example shows a typical use of the blocking services database query function. Notice that if the query fails, we use a hardcoded value for the port number instead of failing. Also notice the use of the `htons( )` byte ordering function on the hardcoded value, but not on the value that comes from the `getservbyname( )` function call:

```
LPSERVENT lpstServ;
SOCKADDR_IN stRmtAddr;
...
lpstServ = getservbyname ("echo", "tcp");
if (!lpstServ) {    /* returns NULL pointer on failure */
      /* query failed, so use hardcoded port number */
      stRmtAddr.sin_port = htons(IPPORT_ECHO);
} else {
      /* query succeeded, so use port number returned */
      stRmtAddr.sin_port = lpstServ->s_port;
}
```

We could have copied the entire contents of the servent structure if we needed it. We demonstrate how in the code example for `WSAAsyncGetServByName( )`.

WSAAsyncGetServByName( )

```
WSAAsyncGetServByName( ):/* 0 on failure */
     (HWND hWnd,    /* handle of window to rcv msg on completion */
      unsigned int wMsg, /* message to be rcvd on completion */
      char FAR *name,    /* ptr to service name to be resolved */
      char FAR  *proto,  /* ptr to protocol name (may be NULL) */
      int type,          /* type of address (must be PF_INET) */
      int buflen);       /* size of data area buf above */
```

hWnd: handle of the window to which you want the asynchronous notification message posted when the asynch service by name database query completes *wMsg:* value for the user message you want to post. We recommend that you use the predefined WM_USER base when creating your user message value, to avoid conflicts with system messages.

name: a null-terminated string containing the service name or alias to resolve. Some WinSock implementations are case sensitive, so use lower case for the service name, as found in a standard BSD UNIX */etc/services* file.

proto: a null-terminated string containing the protocol name for which you want the service. The protocol name is optional. It could be a NULL pointer to retrieve the first service matched. However, we recommend that you use the protocol name, since port numbers can vary between protocols. Furthermore, because some WinSock implementations are case sensitive, you should also use a lowercase protocol name, as found in a standard BSD UNIX */etc/services* file.

buf: a pointer to a buffer area into which the WinSock DLL can copy the results of the query. The size of this area must accommodate a protoent structure, as well as the strings that the structure references (like the official protocol name and the array of aliases).

buflen: the size of the buffer area referenced by the *buf* parameter (the WinSock specification recommends at least MAXGETHOSTSTRUCT)

`WSAAsyncGetServByName()` always returns immediately, before the service name resolution operation completes. You can cancel the operation before completion with `WSACancelAsyncRequest()`, as we described in Chapter 5. However, because the function typically references a local database file, the operation happens quickly. As a result, it is doubtful that `WSACancelAsyncRequest()` would usually have time to be effective.

On failure, `WSAAsyncGetServByName()` returns zero, and you call `WSAGetLastError()` to get the cause of the failure. The specification clearly indicates which errors are likely to occur at this time. One error the v1.1 specification does not list that could occur if the buffer is invalid is WSAEFAULT. This may occur immediately, or in an asynchronous message, so you should be prepared for both.

On success, `WSAAsyncGetServByName()` returns a nonzero asynch query handle you can use to identify the response when the operation completes. This handle is helpful if you initiate more than one asynchronous operation simultaneously. You also need the handle to cancel the asynchronous operation with `WSACancelAsyncRequest()`. Success of the `WSAAsyncGetServByName()` function call indicates the successful initiation of the service name resolution operation. It does not indicate success of the service name resolution operation itself.

Note: Although you should be able to initiate multiple name resolution requests for simultaneous resolution, some WinSock implementations do not support this feature (i.e., they have bugs). As a result, to ensure compatibility with all WinSocks, you should try to serialize your requests so you initiate a new request after a previous request completes.

Upon Completion

When WinSock completes the service name resolution operation, it posts a message to the application. The notification message—which the application specifies in the *wMsg* parameter—contains the value of the asynch query handle originally returned by `WSAAsyncGetServByName( )` in *wParam*, so you can match the response with the original query. You should use the WSAGETASYNCERROR( ) macro to check for an error in the upper word in *lParam* before you do anything else (the use of macros ensures the portability of source code between 16-bit and 32-bit environments, where Windows procedure parameters differ significantly).

If the error value is nonzero, the operation failed. On failure, the error value indicates why the operation failed, and the buffer content is indeterminate. If the error value is WSAENOBUFS, your buffer size was too small to accommodate the results. In this case, the low word of *lParam* contains the buffer size you need; you should use the WSAGETASYNCBUFLEN( ) macro to retrieve this value. This problem should not occur if you always allocate a buffer size of at least MAXGETHOSTSTRUCT, as the WinSock specification recommends.

If the error is zero, the operation succeeded. In this case you can use the WSAGETASYNCBUFLEN( ) macro to extract the buffer length from the lower word in *lParam*, although most applications do not need to reference this value.

Code Example

Here is a pseudocode example of `WSAAsyncGetServByName( )` in action, including the relevant portion of a message handler that responds to the asynchronous message when hostname resolution completes:

```
#define MAXSERVNAME    64
#define SERV_CALLBACK  WM_USER+1
extern HANDLE hWnd;
char szServ[MAXHOST NAME]        /* buffer for user input */
char achServInfo[MAXGETHOSTSTRUCT]; /* buffer for results */
struct in_addr stHostAddr;       /* host address structure */
HANDLE hQuery;                   /* asynch query handle */
...
/* initiate asynchronous service name resolution */
```

```
hQuery = WSAAsyncGetServByName(hWnd, SERV_CALLBACK,
              "echo", "tcp", achServInfo, MAXGETHOSTSTRUCT);
if (!hQuery) {              /* if asynch request failed */
   <notify user of WinSock error>
}
```

And here is the section of a window procedure that handles the asynchronous notification message that WinSock posts upon completion of the service name resolution operation:

```
LONG FAR PASCAL SampleWndProc
   (HWND hwnd,
    UINT wMsg,
    WPARAM wParam,
    LPARAM lParam)
{
    int nAsyncError;
    struct servent FAR *lpstWSServent;
    int i;

    switch (wMsg) {
         ...
         case (SERV_CALLBACK):
            /* check for an error */
            nAsyncError = WSAGETASYNCERROR(lParam);
            if (nAsyncError) {
                <report error to user>
            } else {
                lpstWSServent =
                     (struct servent FAR *)achServInfo;

                /* display results (DoPrintf( ) is a fake function) */
                DoPrintf ("official service name: %s\n",
                          lpstWSServent->p_name);
                DoPrintf ("port number: %d\n",
                          lpstWSServent->s_port);
                DoPrintf ("protocol name: %s\n",
                          lpstWSServent->s_proto);

               for (i=0;lpWSServent->s_aliases[i]; i++) {
                    DoPrintf ("Alias %d: %s\n",
                              i+1, lpstWSServent->s_aliases[i]);
```

```
                    }
               }
            ...
         }  /* end switch( ) */
    }
```

Port Resolution

Applications do not need port number resolution as often as they need service name resolution, but it is also possible to get information about a service by referencing a port number. Two functions perform service port resolution: `getservbyport( )` and `WSAAsyncGetServByPort( )`. These functions are similar to their service name resolution counterparts, and other database routines, so we will highlight only the differences here.

getservbyport( )

The `getservbyport( )` function uses a port number to access the WinSock services database and retrieve the relevant service information. This function blocks until the port number resolution operation completes. It returns a pointer to a system buffer that contains a "service entry" (servent) structure. Since this system buffer may be altered by a subsequent WinSock call, you should reference the contents of the buffer immediately upon return.

```
struct servent FAR * PASCAL FAR getservbyport  /* NULL on fail */
       (int port,           /* port number, in network byte order */
        char FAR *proto);   /* pointer to protocol name or NULL to
                               return first match of service port */
```

port: port number of the service for which we want to retrieve service information.

proto: a null-terminated string containing the protocol name for which you want the service. This is optional (could be NULL), but we recommend you use it with a lowercase protocol name. You can use a protocol number resolution function to retrieve an appropriate string.

Other than the fact `getservbyport( )` takes a port number rather than a service name or alias, there are no other differences between this function and `getservbyname( )`. Both functions return a pointer to a servent structure. On failure, the pointer value is NULL. On success, the buffer—owned by the WinSock DLL—contains service information.

WSAAsyncGetServByPort( )

The `WSAAsyncGetServByPort( )` function uses a port number to access the WinSock services database and retrieve the relevant service information. This function returns immediately and notifies the application asynchronously when the port number resolution operation completes. The application provides a buffer into which the WinSock DLL copies service information.

```
WSAAsyncGetServByPort( ):
    HANDLE PASCAL FAR WSAAsyncGetServByPort   /* 0 on failure */
    (HWND hWnd,  /* handle of window to rcv msg on completion */
     unsigned int wMsg, /* message to be rcvd on completion */
     int port,    /* port number to be resolved (net byte order) */
     char FAR *proto,   /* ptr to protocol name (may be NULL) */
     char FAR *buf,     /* ptr to data area to rcv servent data */
     int buflen);       /* size of data area buf above */
```

hWnd: Handle of the window to which you want the asynchronous notification message posted when the asynch service by name database query completes

wMsg: Value for the user message you want to post. We recommend you use the predefined WM_USER base when creating your user message value, to avoid conflicts with system messages.

port: port number of the service for which we want to retrieve service information

proto: a null-terminated string containing the protocol name for which you want the service. The protocol name is optional. It could be a NULL pointer to retrieve the first service matched. However, we recommend that you use the protocol name, since port numbers can vary between protocols. Furthermore, because some WinSock implementations are case sensitive, you should also use a lowercase protocol name, as found in a standard BSD UNIX */etc/services* file. You can use a protocol number resolution function to retrieve an appropriate string.

buf: a pointer to a buffer area into which the WinSock DLL can copy the results of the query. The size of this area must accommodate a protoent structure, as well as the strings that the structure references (like the official protocol name and the array of aliases).

buflen: the size of the buffer area referenced by the *buf* parameter (the WinSock specification recommends at least MAXGETHOSTSTRUCT)

Other than the fact `WSAAsyncGetServByPort( )` takes a port number rather than a service name or alias, there are no other differences between this function and `WSAAsyncGetServByName( )`. Both operate asynchronously in the same fashion, return the same error values in the same circumstances, and provide the results—service information—in a servent structure in the application buffer.

Services Database

The services database used to provide service name and port number resolution is transparent to an application using the Windows Sockets API. For the most part, a WinSock application user or developer need never know how the WinSock DLL performs service resolution. The WinSock specification does not prescribe how resolution should be performed or configured, so there are differences between WinSock implementations.

Unlike host resolution, service resolution is not typically done via the network (à la DNS) but references a file on the local disk. However, a WinSock implementation that supports Network Information Service (NIS) may use the network to keep its services database file synchronized (for more information on NIS, see Chapter 8, "Host Names and Addresses").

In Berkeley Sockets, the "services database" is in the */etc/services* file, which is a formatted ASCII text file: easy to edit and view. "If the local files exist, the format of the files must be identical to that used in BSD UNIX, allowing for the differences in text file formats."[1] This is also the format used by the Internet Assigned Numbers Authority (IANA) in the "Assigned Numbers" RFC, which lists well-known port numbers and service names, among other things. Here is a partial listing of a standard BSD */etc/services* file to give you an idea of the contents and its simple format:

```
#name  port/protocol     aliases             comments
echo         7/tcp                           # Echo
echo         7/udp                           # Echo
discard      9/tcp       sink null           # Discard
discard      9/udp       sink null           # Discard
chargen      19/tcp      ttytest source      # Char Generator
```

[1] Section B.4 in the version 1.1 Windows Sockets specifications.

```
chargen    19/udp    ttytest source    # Char Generator
ftp        21/tcp                      # File Transfer
ftp        21/udp                      # File Transfer
telnet     23/tcp                      # Telnet
telnet     23/udp                      # Telnet
smtp       25/tcp    mail              # Mail Transfer
smtp       25/udp    mail              # Mail Transfer
finger     79/tcp    whois             # Finger
finger     79/udp    whois             # Finger
```

Each of the services resolution function returns all of this information for each service—except the comments—when they succeed. As we described above, this information is put into the servent structure upon completion.

Although the WinSock specification does not prescribe location of the services database, some WinSock implementations have their services file located in a directory named *etc* (although the *etc* directory is rarely located off the root directory, as it is in BSD UNIX). You should reference your WinSock vendor's documentation for details on the mechanism behind service resolution and on the configuration of the services database.

Protocol Names and Numbers

Every protocol has a number to represent it. These numbers are defined in the WINSOCK.H file as macros (e.g., IPPROTO_TCP, IPPROTO_UDP). There are only a few places an application might reference the protocol value:

- optionally in the *protocol* input parameter to the `socket()` function
- as the *level* parameter for the `setsockopt()` and `getsockopt()` functions for options that are not the common SOL_SOCKET level

However, the services resolution functions all take a protocol *name* as an input parameter. Some applications could use the protocol number resolution functions to retrieve the protocol name for use in a services resolution function call.

Protocol resolution is similar to service and host resolution, but many fewer applications use protocol resolution. The reason is simple: Protocol values do not change (like port numbers, protocol numbers are maintained by the IANA and listed in the "Assigned Numbers" RFC). As a result, we do a fairly quick survey of protocol resolution here. These functions are very similar to the host resolution functions (Chapter 8, "Host Names and Addresses), and especially to the services resolution functions (previous section in this chapter), so you should reference the documentation for these other functions for more information.

protoent Structure

All of the protocol resolution functions return their results in a protoent structure. Its definition looks like the following in WINSOCK.H:

```
struct      protoent {
      char  FAR * p_name;          /* official protocol name */
      char  FAR * FAR * p_aliases; /* alias list */
      short p_proto;              /* protocol number */
};
typedef struct protoent PROTOENT;
typedef struct protoent *PPROTOENT;
typedef struct protoent FAR *LPPROTOENT;
```

p_name: official name of the protocol. By convention, the official protocol name is lower case (e.g., "tcp," "udp," etc.) since it appears this way in the UNIX */etc/protocols* file. We recommend that you use lowercase for protocol names since some WinSocks may be case sensitive.

p_aliases: array of null-terminated alias strings, terminated by a null pointer. By convention (not by specification), the uppercase protocol name is an alias. The following code example demonstrates how to access all the entries in this field (this sample appends each alias string into a buffer, separated by spaces):

```
LPPROTOENT lpstProto;
char achOutBuf[LARGEBUF];
int nStrLen=0, i;
...
while (lpstProto->p_aliases) {
   /* append protocol alias string to output buffer */
   i = wsprintf (&achOutBuf[nStrLen],
         "%s ", lpstProto->p_aliases);
   nStrLen += i;                  /* update buffer index */
   lpstProto->p_aliases++;        /* point to next alias */
}
```

p_proto: the protocol number, in *host* byte order. This value is in host byte order for a few reasons. Most significantly, the value is only used locally by the `socket()` function. It can also be used by `getsockopt()` and `setsockopt()` as a *level* parameter value (e.g., IPPROTO_TCP). The value *is* in fact sent over the network; the standard values for the protocols database coincide with the standard values for the protocol field in an IP packet header. Since this is a byte-sized field, the `htons()` and `ntohs()` functions are clearly inappropriate.

Protocol Name Resolution

Protocol name resolution uses a protocol name to access the protocols database and retrieve protocol information. Few applications typically use these functions, since the flexibility provided is unnecessary; protocol values do not change the way service port numbers and (especially) host addresses do.

getprotobyname()

The `getprotobyname()` function uses the protocol name to access a WinSock's protocols database. It operates in blocking mode: It returns when the protocol name resolution operation completes (succeeds or fails).

```
/* returns NULL on failure */
struct protoent FAR * PASCAL FAR getprotobyname
      (char FAR *name);          /* pointer to protocol name */
```

name: a null-terminated string containing the protocol name or alias to resolve. Some WinSock implementations are case sensitive, so you should typically use lower case (uppercase protocols are aliases in the standard BSD UNIX */etc/protocols* file).

On failure, `getprotobyname()` returns zero (a NULL pointer). You call `WSAGetLastError()` to retrieve the error value that indicates why it failed. The most common error is WSANO_DATA, which could indicate either that the protocol name was not found or possibly that the protocol database itself was not found (due to a misconfigured WinSock).

On success, `getprotobyname()` returns a pointer to a `protoent` structure in a system buffer. You should reference the contents of the servent structure immediately upon return. Since WinSock owns the system buffer, it may overwrite the contents in subsequent function calls.

Code Example

The code example below illustrates usage of `getprotobyname( )`:

```
LPPROTOENT lpstProto;
SOCKADDR_IN lpstSockAddr;
SOCKET hSock;
int nProtocol;
...
/* we'll use the result for protocol parameter in socket( ) call */
lpstProto = getprotobyname("tcp");
if (!lpstProto) {    /* NULL pointer if getprotobyname( ) failed */
      nProtocol = IPPROTO_TCP;    /* macro defined in WINSOCK.H */
} else {
       nProtocol = lpstProto.p_proto;    /* save value retrieved */
}
...
hSock = socket(AF_INET, SOCK_STREAM, nProtocol);
```

WSAAsyncGetProtoByName( )

The `WSAAsyncGetProtoByName( )` function uses the protocol name to access a WinSock's protocols database `WSAAsyncGetProtoByName( )` operations in asynchronous operation mode: It returns immediately and notifies the application asynchronously when the protocol name resolution operation completes.

```
WSAAsyncGetProtoByName( ):
    HANDLE PASCAL FAR WSAAsyncGetProtoByName  /* 0 on failure */
    (HWND hWnd,    /* handle of window to rcv msg on completion */
     unsigned int wMsg,/* message to be rcvd on completion */
     char FAR *name,    /* ptr to protocol name to be resolved */
     char FAR *buf,     /* ptr to data area to rcv protoent data */
     int buflen);       /* size of data area buf above */
```

hWnd: handle of the window to which you want the asynchronous notification message posted when the asynch protocol by name database query completes

wMsg: value for the user message you want to post. We recommend that you use the predefined WM_USER base when creating your user message value, as with any user-defined message, to avoid message value conflicts.

name: a null-terminated string name of protocol to be resolved. By convention, these are lower case (e.g., "tcp"), although upper case will work as well (upper case is typically an alias in the BSD UNIX */etc/protocols* file).

buf: a pointer to a buffer area into which the WinSock DLL can copy the results of the query. The size of this area must accommodate a protoent structure, as well as the strings that the structure references (like the official protocol name and the array of aliases).

buflen: the size of the buffer area referenced by the *buf* parameter (the WinSock specification recommends at least MAXGETHOSTSTRUCT)

`WSAAsyncGetProtoByName( )` always returns immediately, before the service name resolution operation completes. You can cancel the operation before completion with `WSACancelAsyncRequest( )`, as we describe in Chapter 5. However, because the function typically references a local database file, the operation happens quickly. As a result, it is doubtful that `WSACancelAsyncRequest( )` would have time to be effective.

On failure, you call `WSAGetLastError( )` to get the cause of the failure. The specification clearly indicates which errors are likely to occur at this time. One error the v1.1 specification does not list that could occur if the buffer is invalid is WSAEFAULT. This may occur immediately, or in an asynchronous message, so you should be prepared for both.

On success, `WSAAsyncGetProtoByName( )` returns a nonzero asynch query handle you can use to identify the response when the operation completes. This handle is essential for differentiating responses when you initiate more than one asynchronous operation simultaneously. You would also need to reference the handle to cancel the asynchronous operation with `WSACancelAsyncRequest( )`. Success of the `WSAAsyncGetProtoByName( )` function call indicates successful initiation of the service name resolution operation. It does not indicate success of the service name resolution operation itself.

Code Example

This code example shows `WSAAsyncGetProtoByName( )` in action. First, here is the function call itself:

```
#define PROTO_CALLBACK  WM_USER+1
...
char achProtoBuf[MAXGETHOSTSTRUCT];
HANDLE hProtoQuery;
WORD wMsg = PROTO_CALLBACK;
...
hProtoQuery = WSAAsyncGetProtoByName (hWnd, PROTO_CALLBACK,
```

```
        "tcp",
        achProtoBuf,
        MAXGETHOSTSTRUCT);
if (!hProtoQuery) {
     /* Normally, we would probably not do anything about this
      *  error except use the hardcoded value IPPROTO_TCP (from
      *  WINSOCK.H file).  However, in this example we *need*
      *  this to succeed, since we're displaying the strings
      *  in the protocol structure (see asynch handler). */
     int nWSAErr = WSAGetLastError( );
     if (nWSAErr == WSAEWOULDBLOCK) {
          <schedule a retry (with timer) or tell user to retry>
     } else {
           <report WinSock error value>
     }
}
```

And here is the section of a window procedure that handles the asynchronous notification message:

```
LONG FAR PASCAL SampleWndProc
  (HWND hwnd,
   UINT wMsg,
   WPARAM wParam,
   LPARAM lParam)
{
  int nAsyncError, nStrLen, i;
  struct protoent FAR *lpstProto;
  extern char achProtoBuf[];
  extern char achOutput[];

  switch (wMsg) {
    ...
    case (PROTO_CALLBACK):
      /* WSAAsyncGetProtoByXXXX event notification */
      nAsyncError  = WSAGETASYNCERROR(lParam);
      if (nAsyncError) {
        <report WinSock error value>
      } else {
        /* the buffer contains the protoent
         *  structure filled-in by the WinSock
```

```
         *  DLL, followed by data it references
         *  (total length: WSAASYNCBUFLEN(lParam)).
         */
        lpstProto =
              (struct protoent FAR *)achProtoBuf;
        /* for illustration, we'll put the string
         *  contents of protoent into an output
         *  buffer for display.  Normally, you'd
         *  simply access the p_proto value. */
        wStrLen = wsprintf (achOutput,
              "official name: %s, aliases: ",
               lpstProto->p_name);
        while (lpstProto->p_aliases) {
          i = wsprintf (achOutput[wStrLen],
                 "%s ", lpstProto->p_aliases);

          wStrLen =+ i;  /* increment index */

          /* point to next alias string */
          lpstProto->p_aliases++;
        }  /* end while( ) */
      }  /* end else */
       ...
   }
}
```

Protocol Number Resolution

The functions `getprotobynumber( )` and `WSAAsyncGetProtoByNumber( )` take a protocol number as an input parameter and fill in the appropriate values in a protocol structure. Aside from this input parameter, there is no difference between these functions and their protocol name resolution counterparts (`getprotobyname( )` and `WSAAsyncGetProtoByName( )`). Please refer to their descriptions above for more detail.

```
/* returns NULL on failure */
struct protoent FAR * PASCAL FAR getprotobynumber
 (int number); /* protocol number, in host byte order */

WSAAsyncGetProtoByNumber( ):
 HANDLE PASCAL FAR WSAAsyncGetProtoByNumber /* 0 on failure */
```

```
(HWND hWnd, /* handle of window to rcv msg on completion */
unsigned int wMsg,/* message to be rcvd on completion */
int number, /* protocol number to be resolved */
char FAR *buf, /* ptr to data area to rcv protoent data */
int buflen); /* size of data area buf above */
```

number: The protocol number values coincide with the standard values for the protocol field in an IP packet header. The WINSOCK.H file has macros for the typical predefined values (e.g., IPPROTO_TCP, IPROTO_UDP).

Protocols Database

The protocols database WinSock uses to provide protocol name and number resolution is transparent to an application using the Windows Sockets API. For the most part, a WinSock application user or developer need never know how the WinSock DLL performs protocol resolution. The v1.1 WinSock specification does not prescribe how resolution should be performed or configured, so there are differences between WinSock implementations.

Similar to services resolution, but unlike host resolution, protocol resolution is not typically done via the network (á la DNS) but references a file on the local disk. However, a WinSock that supports Network Information Service (NIS) may use the network to keep its protocols database file updated (for more information, see Chapter 8, "Host Names and Addresses").

In Berkeley Sockets, the "protocols database" is in the */etc/protocol* file, which is a formatted ASCII text file: easy to edit and view. "If the local files exist, the format of the files must be identical to that used in BSD UNIX, allowing for the differences in text file formats."[2] This is also the format used by the Internet Assigned Numbers Authority (IANA) in the "Assigned Numbers" RFC, which lists well-known protocol numbers and protocol names, among other things. Here is a partial listing of a standard BSD */etc/protocol* file to give you an idea of the contents and its simple format:

```
# Internet (IP) protocols
#name number aliases comments
ip    0      IP     # internet protocol, pseudo protocol number
icmp  1      ICMP   # internet control message protocol
```

[2] Section B.4 in the version 1.1 Windows Sockets specification

```
tcp   6      TCP     # transmission control protocol
udp   17     UDP     # user datagram protocol
```

Each of the protocol resolution functions returns all of this information (excluding the comments). As we describe above, this information is put into the protoent structure upon completion.

Notice how little useful information this database contains. It only has identifiers for a protocol but nothing to describe the protocol attributes (like reliability, message boundary preservation, message sizes, etc.). As part of its multiple protocol support, WinSock version 2.0 provides new functions, structures, and mechanisms to supply much more information about the protocols available from a WinSock implementation. See Chapter 17 for more information.

Error Reporting

Berkeley Sockets provides a global error variable *errno*. This errno value is set by the operating system whenever a system call (e.g., any Sockets function) fails. However, Windows Sockets does not have an analogous errno variable. In its place, WinSock has the function `WSAGetLastError( )` to get the error value after a WinSock function fails. Windows Sockets also has the `WSASetLastError( )` function to set this error value when needed.

WSAGetLastError( )

In 32-bit Windows, it is possible to have a multithreaded application. To facilitate maintenance of an error variable on a per-thread basis, the Windows Sockets API created a function to return the error value, rather than supporting the global variable. This is more conducive to the Windows Sockets binary API, as provided by DLLs, since a DLL can maintain the socket state—including its error value—internally. The function is `WSAGetLastError( )`, and its prototype is as follows:

```
int PASCAL FAR WSAGetLastError  /* last error code (0 if none) */
        (void);
```

As you can see, it does not take an input parameter; the implicit input parameter is the current task or thread. `WSAGetLastError( )` returns the error value for the current task or thread; it does *not* return an error value for a particular socket. As a result, you must be sure to call

`WSAGetLastError( )` as soon as possible after a function fails, to have the relevant error value reported. Note that the value that `WSAGetLastError( )` reports is *not* reset to zero after a function succeeds (neither is the *errno* variable in Berkeley Sockets). The value is reset when the next WinSock function fails in a task or thread.

The function name `WSAGetLastError( )` gives a literal description of what the function reports: It returns the last error that occurred in a task or thread. It does *not* report the success or failure of the last Windows Sockets function call you made. It is also distinct from the socket-based error value returned from `getsockopt( )` SO_ERROR, although the two values may coincide at times. Note that `getsockopt( )` SO_ERROR does not reset the task-based error that `WSAGetLastError( )` returns.

You must rely on the return value of a function to detect the success or failure of that call. If you detect a failure, you should then call `WSAGetLastError( )` to retrieve the error value. The error value you retrieve will give you a clue about why the function failed. Some clues are more obvious than others. See Appendix C, "Error Reference," for a detailed description of the error, including suggestions for how to remedy the problem indicated.

The error values are defined as macros in the WINSOCK.H header file. Most of the macros are derived from Berkeley Sockets equivalents but have a "WSA" prefix attached. The error values themselves are also derived from their Berkeley Sockets equivalents, with a base value added. So, for example, the Berkeley Sockets error with the manifest constant WOULDBLOCK is defined in WINSOCK.H as WSAEWOULDBLOCK. The value for the Berkeley WOULDBLOCK error is 35, and this converts to the WinSock value 10035 when the WinSock "base value" WSABASEERR is added at compile time. Take a look at the definitions in WINSOCK.H for details.

WSASetLastError( )

In Windows Sockets applications, you can modify the error value that `WSAGetLastError( )` will return. This is the purpose of the `WSASetLastError( )` function:

```
void PASCAL FAR WSASetLastError
       (int iError);             /* error code to be returned */
```

iError: The value of the error code. This value typically is one of the standard WSA error values, as defined in WINSOCK.H; however, the specification does not prohibit you from using any other value. A subsequent call to `WSAGetLastError( )` will return any value you set, assuming no other function fails, thereby setting the task error to another value.

Note: The error value set with `WSASetLastError( )` does *not* affect the socket-based error value returned by `getsockopt( )` SO_ERROR.

Code Example

This function does not have many legitimate uses. If your application depends on it, you may be doing something wrong (like trying to use `WSAGetLastError( )` to report success or failure of functions, rather than relying on the return values of those functions). We recommend that you stay away from `WSASetLastError( )`.

For instance, here is an example of a *bad* design:

```
WSASetLastError(0);  /* reset task-based error to zero */
...
<do WinSock function calls>
...
if (WSAGetLastError != 0) {
   <handle error>
}
```

A minor problem with this is all the extra calls to `WSASetLastError( )` and `WSAGetLastError( )` that occur even when everything succeeds (i.e., no failures). The biggest problem with this design, however, is that there is no way to know which of the WinSock function calls may have failed. This will complicate debugging when you have a problem. Instead, you should always check the return value from each function call to determine success or failure. Return values are designed for that purpose. Use them, and your applications will be more robust and easier to maintain.

Error Text Display

The Windows Sockets API does not include a counterpart of the Berkeley Sockets `perror( )` function. However, we have created our own adaptation of `perror( )` called `WSAperror( )`, and we use it in all the sample applications in this book. The code for the WSAperror( ) function appears in the Sample Library in Chapter 7, along with the string resources it uses.

11
DLLs over WinSock

In This Chapter:

- Creating a New API
- DLL Issues
- Sample DLL

The less effort, the faster and more powerful you will be.

Bruce Lee

There is one fundamental reason to create a DLL that runs over the WinSock DLL: to put a different face on the Windows Sockets API. In other words, a DLL over WinSock provides a different application programming interface.

Since Windows Sockets is the great equalizer, you might wonder why anyone would want to create another API. There are as many good reasons as there are types of APIs you can create. All of them exist to add value to the network functionality WinSock provides. They do not reinvent the wheel, but they improve it.

A DLL over WinSock can allow existing applications written for another API and different protocols to run without change, or simplify development of applications that use standard application protocols, or simplify the WinSock API itself by hiding even more of the low-level details involved with network programming. The newly created API can be proprietary, or it can be a reincarnation of an existing API. Either way, it improves WinSock while it takes advantage of WinSock's ubiquitous presence and standardized API.

To further illustrate the motivation for DLLs over WinSock, this chapter describes the added values DLLs over WinSock provide. The task of creating DLLs over WinSock is very similar to creating a Windows Sockets application; therefore, most of what we've already covered for WinSock applications applies to DLLs over WinSock as well. However, there are some special considerations for a DLL. This chapter focuses on those special needs and describes approaches for dealing with them. We also show you how we dealt with them in our sample DLL, which addresses some of the common, troublesome problems we describe. Finally, C++ class libraries and Visual Basic custom controls (VBXs) provide nearly the same types of functionality as many DLLs and deal with many of the same issues, too. As a result, much of the information in this chapter is relevant to them as well.

Creating a New API

Just as WinSock can accommodate a vast array of network applications, it can also accommodate an infinite variety of network APIs. However countless the number of network APIs possible with a DLL over WinSock, all APIs fit into one of three basic types:

- emulated APIs
- application protocol APIs
- encapsulated WinSock APIs

Throughout this chapter we refer to the API that any DLL over WinSock provides as the **NewAPI**, and to the DLL itself as the **NewAPI DLL.** No matter what type of API a NewAPI DLL provides, it fits into the network scheme in the same general way. We illustrate this scheme in the NewAPI model in Figure 11-1.

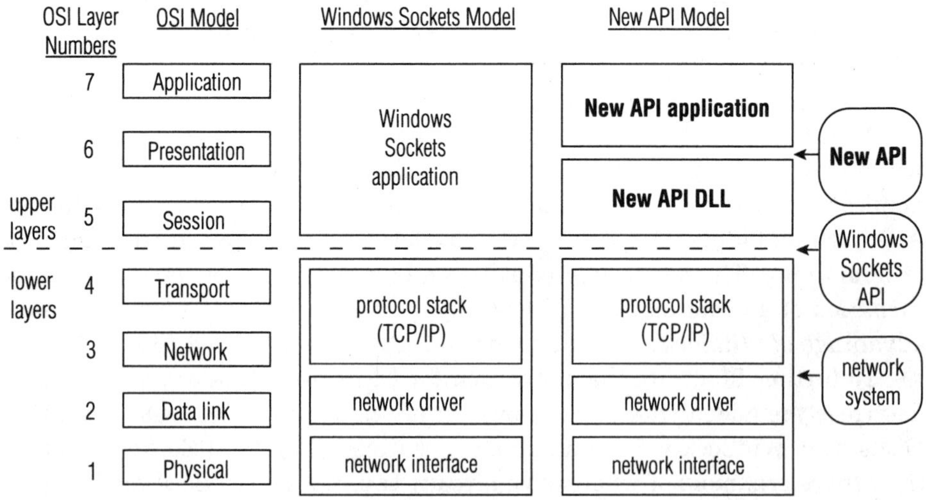

Figure 11-1 How the new API, its DLL, and applications compare to the Windows Sockets and OSI network reference models.

Notice in this figure that the NewAPI DLL could be a stack of DLLs, with each one using the API provided by the one beneath it. In this case, the NewAPI application would only be aware of the DLL at the top providing the API it uses. This "stackability" of DLLs is what makes a DLL over WinSock possible.

There are a few disadvantages to using the NewAPI provided by a DLL over WinSock. For one thing, an application that depends on such a proprietary API must always have the NewAPI DLL available in order to run. More importantly, if you use a NewAPI DLL you did not create, the source code may not be available. This means you cannot add functionality to take advantage of new or subtle application protocol features or utilize WinSock options. If you purchased the DLL, you may be obliged to pay royalties if you sell your application commercially. Worst of all, you are dependent on the DLL owner to fix bugs you encounter.

However, many of these problems are common to any DLL you use in Windows. Some of these concerns—such as being unable to fix bugs in a DLL you do not own—are endemic to operating systems themselves. Such problems typically represent a small price to pay for the many advantages that DLLs provide.

Emulated APIs

WinSock has gone a long way toward creating the universal network API, but many network applications that exist were written for the other network APIs WinSock made obsolete. You can emulate these legacy APIs in a DLL that runs over WinSock. This allows you and your customers to (re)use the installed base of existing applications that use these APIs over WinSock with little or no alteration. Thus, an emulated API lets you take advantage of the new technology WinSock offers, such as TCP/IP transport protocol and portability across vendors' implementations, without throwing away existing technology in working applications.

The similarities in functions between the emulated API and WinSock determine the amount of effort involved in creating the emulated API DLL and porting existing applications. If the two APIs are analogous, then the remapping should be relatively easy. If their paradigms differ greatly, you could have some difficulties. However, with the exception of APIs that offer lower-level services—network- and link-layer APIs—the WinSock API should be flexible enough to accommodate almost all other APIs you need to emulate.

Two examples of existing APIs that you could emulate in a DLL over WinSock are TLI Streams and OSI. Both TLI and OSI are transport-layer APIs like WinSock. They are both similar to Berkeley Sockets in numerous respects, and they have many applications written for them (especially for

TLI). The only downside is that you would have to adapt most existing source code to operate in Microsoft Windows.

There are a few examples of emulated API DLLs commercially available today. For instance, most database companies currently ship DLLs that emulate their standard structured query language (SQL) database-access API and run over WinSock. These provide a high-level (session- or presentation-layer) API that allows transparent network access to the database system. In addition to being an emulated API, these are also examples of our next type of DLL over WinSock: the application protocol API.

Application Protocol APIs

Application protocol APIs provide access to "high-level" protocols such as the File Transfer Protocol (FTP), telnet, the Simple Network Management Protocol (SNMP), SQL, and so on. They provide access to the application protocol services in a simplified API. The API is simple since it hides the application protocol details as well as the WinSock API details. The API may be as simple as the services the application protocol provides.

For example, you could create a DLL that provides simple mail transport protocol (SMTP) services. This would include a function to send a mail message. The input parameters to such a function call would have to include all the important fields in a mail message: server name, To:, From:, Subject:, Date:, Cc:, and the message content. When an application calls the NewAPI DLL with all of this information, the DLL

- gets a socket
- fills in the `sockaddr_in` structure
- connects to the server (maybe resolves the host name first)
- "speaks SMTP" with the server
- sends the message
- closes the socket
- returns the result to the calling application

Our sample FTP application in Chapter 7 provides another example of a potential application protocol API. The functions it employs to establish the control connection, send and receive FTP protocol commands, and use data connections for file transfer could easily be adapted for export in a DLL.

A few high-level API standards already exist for high-level protocols. For example, WinSNMP defines an API for creating applications that use the

Simple Network Management Protocol. The WinSNMP specification is already into its second version, a number of commercial WINSNMP.DLLs are available from different vendors, and quite a few powerful network management tools use it. RPC4WIN is another example. It provides an API for Sun's Open Network Computing (ONC) Remote Procedure Calls (RPC) Protocol. At least two commercial implementations are available.

Encapsulated WinSock APIs

Encapsulated WinSock APIs are simplified versions of the original WinSock API. They are not specialized for any application protocol in particular, but remain application protocol-independent.

Emulated APIs simplify the WinSock API by hiding low-level WinSock API details. They do not preclude low-level API access, but they do not require it either. The functions in an encapsulated WinSock API perform address resolution and byte ordering, initialize data structures, and process errors. They relieve the need to use many of the WinSock macros and data structures.

We present a sample DLL over WinSock later in this chapter. It implements an encapsulated WinSock API that we call WSASimpl. Among other things, it provides a connect routine that simplifies the process of establishing a TCP connection in a client application. Here is the prototype for `ConnectTCP()`:

```
SOCKET WINAPI ConnectTCP(   /* return socket or INVALID_SOCKET */
   LPSTR szDestination,     /* destination host name or address */
   LPSTR szService);        /* destination service or port # */
```

You provide a host name or address destination along with a port number or service name, and our WSASimpl `ConnectTCP()` function does the rest:

- It resolves the destination if it is a host name, or formats it if it is an address string.
- It resolves the service if it is a service name, or converts it to an integer in network order if it is a port number string.
- It requests a TCP socket.
- It initializes `sockaddr_in` structure with destination address and port number.
- It establishes the TCP connection.
- If any function fails, it interprets the error value and displays a message box with advice for the application user. Then it closes the socket.

- If it succeeds, it returns a socket handle for the application to reference as it sends and receives data, and closes the socket.

There are many significant advantages to encapsulated WinSock APIs. Besides being easier to use, they let you avoid bugs by reusing common functions. They also allow rapid prototyping of applications. You will appreciate these advantages when you see our sample DLL later in this chapter.

DLL Issues

If you are creating a brand-new API, you have the freedom to demand certain things from the application using the API. For example, you can have it call an equivalent of `WSAStartup()` and `WSACleanup()` to register and deregister, respectively, your DLL with the WinSock DLL. You could also have it provide a Window handle you could use for asynchronous messages and have it process asynchronous notification messages or provide your own notification messages. Creating an API from scratch is a luxury that is not often available, however.

Unfortunately, you are often limited in what you can expect of the application that is using your DLL. For most DLLs you must consider the requirements of the applications that will use your DLL, rather than the other way around. Many times these applications' requirements involve tricky issues you need to address in your DLL running over WinSock. Three of these problematic areas are

- reentrancy
- task management
- linking with the WinSock DLL

Reentrancy

Most network operations take time to complete. As we described in Chapter 5, the WinSock blocking hook function executes while a blocking operation is pending in 16-bit Windows. The default blocking hook function defined by the WinSock specification yields to other processes. In addition to allowing other applications to run, this also allows for reentrant message delivery. In other words, the calling application may get a Windows message as it waits for the call to your DLL to complete.

If your DLL emulates an API that does not create the possibility of reentrant messages, then you have a problem. Many applications that use such

APIs are not designed to handle reentrant messages. When such an application receives a "reentrant" message during a pending network operation, it often causes the application to fail.

Here's a scenario to illustrate the type of problem that can occur:

- A user performs a query in a database application that results in a call to your NewAPI DLL. The API that the application uses—and NewAPI provides—originally provided access to database files on disk and does not return until the operation completes (successfully, or not).
- NewAPI calls WinSock to perform the requested operation, which involves sending data (the query) and then receiving data (a response).
- WinSock performs the `send()` immediately and then blocks on the `recv()` call. As it blocks, it calls the default blocking hook function.
- Meanwhile, the bored application user is idly moving the mouse around and clicking on different things on the application. If this application were accessing disk files, the mouse messages would be ignored as the operation completes. Disk access in Windows is an exclusive operation (i.e., "unfriendly" in the 16-bit Windows multitasking sense), so the mouse messages are queued during disk access. But not this time.
- Because the default blocking hook calls `PeekMessage()`, the application yields to allow multitasking as the `recv()` operation blocks. As a result, the application gets a chance to process the mouse messages. Since the application did not expect to have this opportunity, it might attempt something that it should not do—such as initiate another database query, and the application could fail catastrophically as a result.

These types of applications cannot deal with reentrant messages, and typically you cannot access their source code to fix them. The only alternative is to prevent reentrant messages. There are a number of ways to do this, but only a few that respect the cooperative multitasking spirit of 16-bit Windows and work with all WinSock implementations. Let's examine one method of avoiding reentrant messages.

Setting the Blocking Hook

One simple way to implement a DLL to deal with the problem of reentrant messages is to use blocking sockets and call `WSASetBlockingHook( )` to replace the blocking hook function with one that does not allow the application to receive reentrant messages as you wait for a blocking function call to complete. It sounds good and easy, but unfortunately it does not always work.

Some WinSock implementations need to receive messages in order to complete network operations. This causes a problem since a blocking operation may never complete if the blocking hook function does not allow reentrant messages, or at least some normal message processing. There is no way for an application to know what messages a WinSock DLL needs, or its Window handle, so there is no way to avoid this problem with this design strategy.

Fortunately, most WinSocks do not have this limitation. In any case, this solution does not multitask well. There are other solutions available which are more elegant and flexible. For example, the sample DLL we present later in this chapter uses window subclassing to avoid reentrant messages.

Task Management

A DLL running over WinSock must satisfy the same requirements as any application that uses the WinSock DLL. Specifically, a DLL must call `WSAStartup()` in order to access WinSock, just like an application does. Since a DLL does not have a process or task ID of its own and `WSAStartup( )` works on a per-task basis, this requirement raises two questions:

- Which process will be registered with a WinSock DLL when a DLL calls `WSAStartup()`?
- How can the DLL be sure that process is active when it makes other WinSock calls?

There are basically two answers to the first question. The NewAPI DLL can either

- register the process of the application making the call, or
- register a "helper process"

There are a number of answers possible for the second question, all of which depend on the answer to the first question. We will detail each as we describe how to implement DLLs that register the application process, or register a "helper process."

Registering the Application Process

When an application calls a NewAPI DLL, the calling application is the active process. As a result, the NewAPI DLL can call `WSAStartup( )` at that time to register the application's process with the WinSock DLL (see Figure 11-2). It is the NewAPI DLL's responsibility to make sure that this task is active as it makes every subsequent call to WinSock using one of the sockets

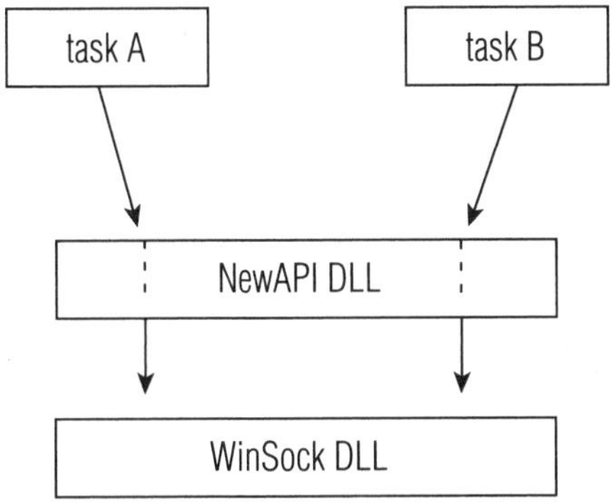

Figure 11-2 New API DLL uses the task ID of the calling application.

owned by this process. One easy way is to call `WSAStartup()` each time an application makes a function call that gets a new socket (so you only have to keep track of the outstanding sockets). You would then call `WSACleanup()` as each socket is closed.

You can make fewer calls to `WSAStartup()` if you also keep track of the task ID of each process you register and only call when a new one makes a call to NewAPI. In that case, you need to maintain a reference count with each task you recorded, to keep track of the number of sockets outstanding. As each socket is closed, you decrement the reference count, and when it reaches zero you call `WSACleanup()`.

Using this method works nicely with blocking sockets since the calling task remains active while the operation completes. With nonblocking sockets the task is also active whenever an application calls a DLL, which then calls WinSock. Asynchronous mode has a related problem: Since DLLs do not have windows of their own, you need to either use an existing window handle from your DLL—by subclassing, for example—or create a window of your own. For example, you could use a window in a helper process, which also works nicely with the other strategy for registering a task.

Registering a Helper Process

Another strategy for registering your DLL with the WinSock DLL involves initiating a helper process for the NewAPI DLL. This allows you to register the helper process's task with the WinSock DLL.

Your NewAPI DLL could initiate a helper process with `WinExec()` when the first application makes the first call to the new API (see Figure 11-3). First the helper process would call `WSAStartup()`. Then the helper task would make all the calls to WinSock in response to requests from applications

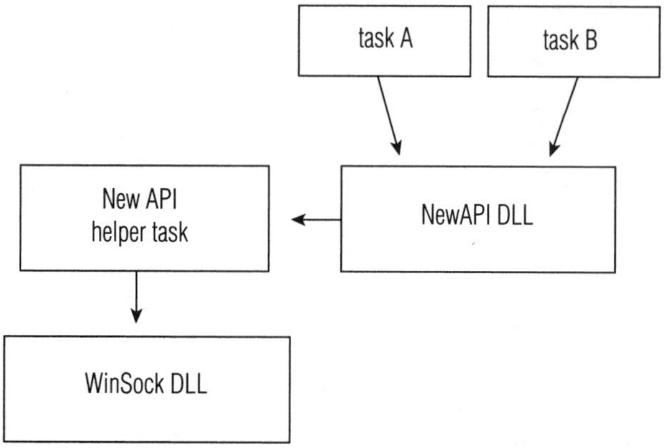

Figure 11-3 New API uses task ID of its own helper task.

calling NewAPI. This strategy would also allow you to use asynchronous operation mode since the helper task has its own window.

Unfortunately, this design is complicated by the question of how best to communicate between the NewAPI and the helper process. However you implement it, there will be overhead involved which can affect data throughput potential. Considering this performance compromise, the complicated nature of this design, and the system overhead involved in having a helper task for a DLL, the advantages of registering a single task are outweighed by its disadvantages.

Linking with the WinSock DLL

If you link with the winsock.lib or wsock32.lib import library when you create your DLL, Windows will automatically attempt to load the winsock.dll or wsock32.dll as it loads your DLL. This is called **implicit linking**, and it works very well. You need not do anything in your DLL to load the WinSock DLL at run time (when an application loads your DLL for execution).

However, if the WinSock DLL file is not available at run time, Windows won't load your DLL and will display an error message to indicate the missing WinSock DLL file. If the application using your NewAPI DLL is also implicitly linked with your NewAPI.lib—so it also attempts to load your DLL automatically at run time—then the application will not run when your DLL does not load. This is bad.

One way to avoid this problem is to use **explicit linking** to load the WinSock DLL from your NewAPI DLL. We show an example of how to do this with `LoadLibrary()` and `GetProcAddress()` in Appendix D. By explicitly linking, you allow Windows to load your DLL even when the WinSock DLL is not available. Obviously, you will not have WinSock access when the WinSock DLL won't load, but at least you will not prevent the application that implicitly (or explicitly) linked with your NewAPI.lib from running. This is good. This allows the application to handle a function failure from your NewAPI DLL gracefully, rather than have Windows prevent execution altogether.

The only trick to using explicit linking in a DLL is figuring out when to call `FreeLibrary()` to unload the WinSock DLL when you are done. The trick involves keeping track of the processes using your DLL, and when the last one finishes (i.e., closes the last socket in use), you can call `FreeLibrary()` to unload the WinSock DLL from memory.

Sample DLL

Our sample DLL provides an "encapsulated WinSock API" that allows a client application to establish a TCP connection to a server application, send and/or receive any amount of data, and then close the connection. We call the DLL WSASimpl to indicate the simplified WinSock API that it provides. There are only four exported functions. We already described the `ConnectTCP()` function used to initiate the TCP connection earlier in this chapter. Here are the prototypes of the other three functions:

```
/* Returns number of bytes sent, or SOCKET_ERROR on failure */
int WINAPI SendData(SOCKET,      /* connected TCP socket */
                    LPSTR,       /* buffer to send from */
                    int);        /* length to send */

/* Returns number of bytes received, or SOCKET_ERROR on failure */
int WINAPI RecvData(SOCKET,      /* connected TCP socket */
                    LPSTR,       /* buffer to receive data into */
                    int,         /* length to receive */
                    int);        /* timeout (in milliseconds) */

/* Returns 0 on success, or SOCKET_ERROR on failure */
int WINAPI CloseTCP(SOCKET,      /* connected TCP socket */
                    LPSTR,       /* buffer for any remaining data */
                     int);       /* size buffer for remaining data */
```

The functions in WSASimpl DLL all execute in blocking mode and yield to other processes to allow multitasking in 16-bit Windows, yet they also prevent reentrant messages. As described earlier, providing such an API is a requirement that many DLLs over WinSock must satisfy as they emulate existing APIs. Many existing applications expect network APIs to work like disk access: to block until the operation completes, and suspend message activity while underway. Such applications cannot tolerate reentrant messages.

WSASimpl uses blocking sockets throughout. The connect function returns a socket handle when the TCP connect operation completes. If this is the first socket this task has used, `ConnectTCP()` registers the task with WinSock by calling `WSAStartup()`. The send and receive functions return when they have transferred the amount requested. The receive function may also return when a timeout occurs. The close function returns when the connection is closed, and the socket is deallocated. `CloseTCP()` also decrements the reference count for the current task and calls `WSACleanup()` when the reference count reaches zero.

The WSASimpl DLL prevents reentrant messages by subclassing the active window of the calling application. In the subclass routine we capture keyboard and mouse messages so that they never reach the window. Figure 11-4 illustrates the task management and subclassing scheme that we use in our sample WSASimpl DLL.

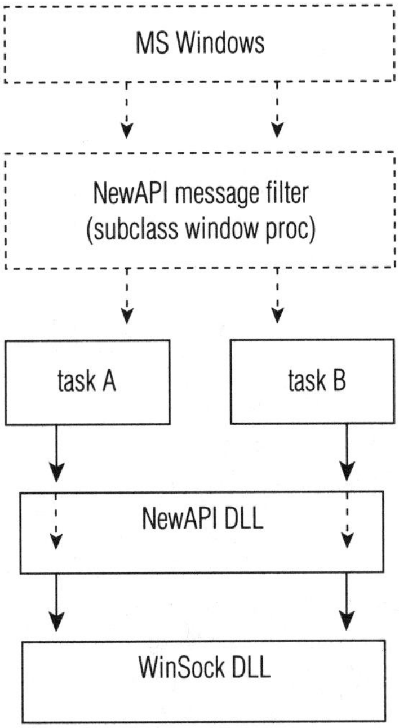

Figure 11-4 New API prevents reentrant messages by subclassing application window.

The architecture for the WSASimpl DLL is fairly simple. With each blocking function call, WSASimpl does the following:

- subclasses the active window
- sets a timer (in `RecvData()` only)
- makes the blocking WinSock function call
- unsubclasses the window

One significant limitation in our design is in our choice of windows to subclass. We note the active window and its window procedure when an application calls `ConnectTCP()`. This window is the one we subclass in `ConnectTCP()`, and we use this same window handle in all subsequent calls to `SendData()` and `RecvData()`. This helps allow cooperative multitasking in the 16-bit Windows environment, since it would not be practical to try to subclass the active window each time any of these functions was called. If the user were switching between tasks, however, all mouse and keyboard I/O in whatever application was currently active would be eliminated as we prevented reentrant messages by "eating" them in our subclass window procedure.

WSASimpl Application

Here is essentially all that is needed in an application that uses the simplified WinSock API in our WSASimpl DLL. This sample application connects to the echo port, sends a length of data, reads it back, and closes the connection. We do not need to display any error messages, since the WSASimpl DLL does that for us. Having a DLL display any type of message is not always desirable, but we do it knowingly in WSASimpl for the sake of simplicity in the applications that use the DLL.

```
SOCKET hSock;
char szHost[MAXHOST NAME];
char achOutBuf[BUFSIZE], achInBuf[BUFSIZE];

hSock = ConnectTCP ((LPSTR)szHost, (LPSTR)"echo");
if (hSock != INVALID_SOCKET) {
    SendData(hSock, achOutData, BUFSIZE);
    RecvData(hSock, achInBuf, BUFSIZE);
    CloseConn(hSock, 0, 0, hwnd);
}
```

WSASimpl DLL

```
/*---------------------------------------------------------------------
 *
 * Program: Simplified WinSock API DLL (for TCP Clients)
 *
 * file name: wsasimpl.c
 *
 * copyright by Bob Quinn, 1995
 *
 *  Description:
 *    This DLL provides an "encapsulated WinSock API," as described
 *    in Chapter 11 of _Windows Sockets Network Programming_.  It
 *    uses subclassing with blocking operation mode to provide basic
 *    functionality for TCP client applications.
 *
 --------------------------------------------------------------------*/
#define STRICT
#include "..\wsa_xtra.h"              /* see Chapter 7 */
#include <windows.h>
#include <windowsx.h>

#include <winsock.h>
#include "resource.h"
#include <string.h>    /* for _fmemcpy() */
#include <stdlib.h>    /* for atoi() */
#include "..\winsockx.h"              /* see Chapter 7 */

#define TIMEOUT_ID  WM_USER+1

/*------- important data structures ------*/
typedef struct TaskData {
  HTASK  hTask;                   /* task ID: primary key */
  int    nRefCount;               /* number of sockets owned by task */
  struct TaskData *lpstNext;      /* pointer to next entry in linked
list */
} TASKDATA, *PTASKDATA, FAR *LPTASKDATA;

typedef struct ConnData {
  SOCKET hSock;                   /* connection socket */
  LPTASKDATA lpstTask;            /* pointer to task structure */
  HWND   hwnd;                    /* handle of subclassed window */
  SOCKADDR_IN stRmtName;          /* remote host address and port */
```

```
  int   nTimeout;                /* timeout (in milliseconds) */
  DWORD lpfnWndProc;             /* task's window procedure */
  struct ConnData *lpstNext;     /* pointer to next entry in linked list
*/
} CONNDATA, *PCONNDATA, FAR *LPCONNDATA;

/*-------------- global data -------------*/
char szAppName[] = "wsasimpl";

HWND hWinMain;
HINSTANCE hInst;
WSADATA stWSAData;

LPCONNDATA lpstConnHead = 0L;    /* head of connection data list */
LPTASKDATA lpstTaskHead = 0L;    /* head of task data list */

/*-------- exported function prototypes ---------*/
int  WINAPI LibMain (HANDLE, WORD, WORD, LPSTR);
LONG CALLBACK SubclassProc (HWND, UINT, WPARAM, LPARAM);
SOCKET WINAPI ConnectTCP(LPSTR, LPSTR);
int WINAPI SendData(SOCKET, LPSTR, int);
int WINAPI RecvData(SOCKET, LPSTR, int, int);
int WINAPI CloseTCP(SOCKET, LPSTR, int);

/*-------- internal function prototypes ---------*/
int DoSend(SOCKET, LPSTR, int, LPCONNDATA);
int DoRecv(SOCKET, LPSTR, int, LPCONNDATA);
LPCONNDATA NewConn (SOCKET, PSOCKADDR_IN);
LPCONNDATA FindConn (SOCKET, HWND);
void      RemoveConn (LPCONNDATA);
LPTASKDATA NewTask (HTASK);
LPTASKDATA FindTask (HTASK);
void      RemoveTask (LPTASKDATA);

/*-----------------------------------------------------------------------
 *  Function: LibMain()
 *
 *  Description: DLL entry point (we do not have much to do here)
 *
 */
int PASCAL LibMain
  (HANDLE hInstance,
```

```
    WORD   wDataSeg,
    WORD   wHeapSize,
    LPSTR  lpszCmdLine)
{
    lpszCmdLine = lpszCmdLine; /* avoid warnings */
    wDataSeg    = wDataSeg;
    wHeapSize   = wHeapSize;

    hInst = hInstance;   /* save instance handle */

    return (1);
} /* end LibMain() */

/*---------------------------------------------------------------------
 * Function: SubclassProc()
 *
 * Description: Filter unwanted I/O messages from active window in
 *   each task while the blocking operation completes (to prevent
 *   reentrant messages)
 */
LONG FAR PASCAL EXPORT SubclassProc
  (HWND hwnd,
   UINT msg,
   WPARAM wParam,
   LPARAM lParam)
{
    LPCONNDATA lpstConn;             /* work pointer */

    lpstConn = FindConn(0, hwnd);    /* find our socket structure */

    switch (msg) {
      case WM_QUIT:
        /* close this connection */
        if (lpstConn) {
          CloseTCP(lpstConn->hSock, (LPSTR)0, INPUT_SIZE);
          RemoveConn(lpstConn);
          /* release timer (if it's active) */
          if (lpstConn->nTimeout)
            KillTimer(hwnd, TIMEOUT_ID);
        }
        break;
```

```
    case WM_CLOSE:
    case WM_TIMER:
      /* if timeout or close request, cancel pending operation */
      if(lpstConn && WSAIsBlocking())
          WSACancelBlockingCall();
      break;

    case WM_KEYDOWN:
    case WM_KEYUP:
    case WM_LBUTTONDBLCLK:
    case WM_LBUTTONDOWN:
    case WM_LBUTTONUP:
    case WM_MBUTTONDBLCLK:
    case WM_MBUTTONDOWN:
    case WM_MBUTTONUP:
    case WM_MOUSEACTIVATE:
    case WM_MOUSEMOVE:
    case WM_NCHITTEST:
    case WM_NCLBUTTONDBLCLK:
    case WM_NCLBUTTONDOWN:
    case WM_NCLBUTTONUP:
    case WM_NCMBUTTONDBLCLK:
    case WM_NCMBUTTONDOWN:
    case WM_NCMBUTTONUP:
    case WM_NCMOUSEMOVE:
    case WM_NCRBUTTONDBLCLK:
    case WM_NCRBUTTONDOWN:
    case WM_NCRBUTTONUP:
    case WM_NEXTDLGCTL:
    case WM_RBUTTONDBLCLK:
    case WM_RBUTTONDOWN:
    case WM_RBUTTONUP:
    case WM_SYSCHAR:
    case WM_SYSDEADCHAR:
    case WM_SYSKEYDOWN:
    case WM_SYSKEYUP:
      /* eat all mouse and keyboard messages */
      return (0L);

  default:
      break;
} /* end switch (msg) */
```

```
  if (lpstConn) {
    /* let original (pre-subclass) window handler process message */
    return (CallWindowProc ((WNDPROC)(lpstConn->lpfnWndProc),
         hwnd, msg, wParam, lParam));
  } else {
    return (0L);  /* this should never occur */
  }
} /* end SubClassProc() */
```

The `SubClassProc()` function above is the subclass procedure we install with a call to the WinAPI function `SetWindowLong()` GWL_WNDPROC within each of our blocking functions: `ConnectTCP()`, `RecvData()`, and `SendData()`. Its primary function is to capture and "eat" mouse and keyboard messages, but it also allows us to catch timer messages for `RecvData()` calls with timeout arguments.

This subclass routine can be customized to meet your needs. You can remove some of the messages we "eat" here, or add others as needed. Typically, the only type of messages that wreak havoc in an application that is not designed to handle reentrant messages are those that user I/O generate using the mouse and keyboard. Some applications may require you to capture other messages, and in some cases you may need to retain some state when messages are received (in other words, you cannot throw them away as we are doing with keyboard and mouse messages here). Notice that all messages we do not process are passed along to the original window procedure with a call to the WinAPI function `CallWindowProc()`.

```
/*--------------------------------------------------------------
 * Function: ConnectTCP()
 *
 * Description: Get a TCP socket and connect to server (along with
 *  other maintenance stuff, like subclassing window, and registering
 *  task)
 */
SOCKET WINAPI ConnectTCP(LPSTR szDestination, LPSTR szService)
{
  int nRet;
  HTASK hTask;
  SOCKET hSock;
  LPTASKDATA lpstTask;
  LPCONNDATA lpstConn;
```

```
SOCKADDR_IN stRmtName;

hTask = GetCurrentTask();      /* task handle: for our records */
lpstTask = FindTask (hTask);
if (!lpstTask) {
  /* register calling task (call WSAStartup()) */
  lpstTask = NewTask(hTask);
}
if (lpstTask) {
  /* get a TCP socket */
  hSock = socket (AF_INET, SOCK_STREAM, 0);
  if (hSock == INVALID_SOCKET)  {
    WSAperror(WSAGetLastError(), "socket()");
  } else {
    /* get destination address */
    stRmtName.sin_addr.s_addr = GetAddr(szDestination);

    if (stRmtName.sin_addr.s_addr != INADDR_NONE) {
      /* get destination port number */
      stRmtName.sin_port = GetPort(szService);

      if (stRmtName.sin_port) {
        /* create a new socket structure */
        lpstConn = NewConn(hSock, &stRmtName);

        if (lpstConn) {
          /* subclass the active window passed
           *  NOTE: This reveals one limitation in our API.
           *  This is the same window we will subclass during sends
           *  and receives, so we will not capture user I/O if the
           *  application calls SendData() or RecvData() with a
           *  different window active. */
          lpstConn->lpstTask = lpstTask;
          lpstConn->hwnd = GetActiveWindow();
          lpstConn->lpfnWndProc =
               GetWindowLong(lpstConn->hwnd,GWL_WNDPROC);
          SetWindowLong (lpstConn->hwnd, GWL_WNDPROC,
               (DWORD)SubclassProc);

          /* initiate nonblocking connect to server */
          stRmtName.sin_family = PF_INET;
```

```
          nRet = connect(hSock,(LPSOCKADDR)&stRmtName,SOCKADDR_LEN);

          if (nRet == SOCKET_ERROR) {
              int WSAErr = WSAGetLastError();

              if (WSAErr != WSAEINTR) {
                /* display all errors except "operation interrupted"
                 *  (unsubclass first so user can respond to error) */
                SetWindowLong(lpstConn->hwnd,GWL_WNDPROC,
                    (DWORD)lpstConn->lpfnWndProc);
                WSAperror(WSAErr, "connect()");
                  RemoveConn(lpstConn);
                closesocket(hSock);
                hSock = INVALID_SOCKET;
              }
          }
        } else {
          /* cannot create a connection structure */
          closesocket(hSock);
          hSock = INVALID_SOCKET;
        }
      } else {
        /* cannot resolve destination port number */
        closesocket(hSock);
        hSock = INVALID_SOCKET;
      }
    } else {
      /* cannot resolve destination address */
      closesocket(hSock);
      hSock = INVALID_SOCKET;
    }
  }
  /* if we failed, we need to clean up */
  if (hSock == INVALID_SOCKET) {
    RemoveTask(lpstTask);
  } else if (lpstConn) {
    /* unsubclass active window before we leave */
    SetWindowLong(lpstConn->hwnd,
        GWL_WNDPROC,
        (DWORD)lpstConn->lpfnWndProc);
  }
```

```
  }
  return (hSock);
} /* end ConnectTCP() */
```

The `ConnectTCP()` function above does all the initialization needed, in addition to resolving the host and the service, getting a socket, and calling `connect()`. Specifically, it creates a task structure and registers a new task with a call to `WSAStartup()`. It also creates a new connection structure to contain the vital connection components, such as remote socket name, socket handle, a pointer to our task structure, window handle, and original window procedure, for use when we pass along unprocessed messages from our subclass window procedure.

```
/*-----------------------------------------------------------------
 * Function: SendData()
 *
 * Description: Send data to socket from the buffer passed
 *  until the requested number of bytes is sent
 */
int WINAPI SendData(SOCKET hSock, LPSTR lpOutBuf, int cbTotalToSend)
{
  LPCONNDATA lpstConn;
  int cbTotalSent = 0, cbSent;
  int nRet = SOCKET_ERROR;    /* assume error */

  lpstConn = FindConn(hSock, 0);
  if (!lpstConn) {
    /* socket not found, so it's not valid */
    WSASetLastError(WSAENOTSOCK);

  } else {
    /* subclass the window provided at connnect to filter messages */
    SetWindowLong (lpstConn->hwnd, GWL_WNDPROC, (DWORD)SubclassProc);

    while  (((cbTotalToSend - cbTotalSent) > 0) &&
          (lpstConn->hSock != INVALID_SOCKET)) {
      cbSent = DoSend(hSock,
                      lpOutBuf+cbTotalSent,
                      cbTotalToSend - cbTotalSent,
                      lpstConn);
      if (cbSent != SOCKET_ERROR) {
```

```
        /* tally and quit the loop if we've sent amount requested */
        cbTotalSent += cbSent;
        if ((cbTotalToSend - cbTotalSent) <= 0)
          break;
      } else {
        /* if send failed, return an error */
        cbTotalSent = SOCKET_ERROR;
      }
    }
    /* unsubclass active window before we leave */
    SetWindowLong(lpstConn->hwnd, GWL_WNDPROC,
         (long)lpstConn->lpfnWndProc);
  }
  return (cbTotalSent);
} /* end SendData() */

/*------------------------------------------------------------------
 * Function: DoSend()
 *
 * Description: Loop to send data
 */
int DoSend(SOCKET hSock, LPSTR lpOutBuf, int cbTotalToSend,
  LPCONNDATA lpstConn)
{
  int cbTotalSent  = 0;
  int cbLeftToSend = cbTotalToSend;
  int nRet, WSAErr;
  /* send as much data as we can */
  while (cbLeftToSend > 0) {

    /* send data to client */
    nRet = send (hSock, lpOutBuf+cbTotalSent,
      cbLeftToSend < MTU_SIZE ? cbLeftToSend : MTU_SIZE, 0);

    if (nRet == SOCKET_ERROR) {
      WSAErr = WSAGetLastError();
      /* display all errors except "operation interrupted" */
      if (WSAErr != WSAEINTR) {
        /*  unsubclass first so user can respond to error */
        SetWindowLong(lpstConn->hwnd, GWL_WNDPROC,
        (DWORD)lpstConn->lpfnWndProc);
```

```
        WSAperror(WSAErr, (LPSTR)"send()");
      }
      break;
    } else {
      /* update byte counter, and display */
      cbTotalSent += nRet;
    }
    /* calculate what's left to send */
    cbLeftToSend = cbTotalSent - cbTotalToSend;
  }
  return (cbTotalSent);
} /* end DoSend() */

/*---------------------------------------------------------------
 * Function: RecvData()
 *
 * Description: Receive data from socket into buffer passed
 *  until the requested number of bytes is received or timeout
 *  period is exceeded
 */
int WINAPI RecvData(SOCKET hSock, LPSTR lpInBuf,
    int cbTotalToRecv, int nTimeout)
{
  LPCONNDATA lpstConn;
  int cbTotalRcvd = 0, cbRcvd;
  int nRet = SOCKET_ERROR;    /* assume error */

  lpstConn = FindConn(hSock, 0);
  if (!lpstConn) {
    /* socket not found, so it's not valid */
    WSASetLastError(WSAENOTSOCK);

  } else {
    /* subclass the active window to filter message traffic */
    SetWindowLong (lpstConn->hwnd, GWL_WNDPROC, (DWORD)SubclassProc);

    /* set a timer, if requested */
    if (nTimeout) {
      lpstConn->nTimeout = nTimeout;
      SetTimer(hWinMain, TIMEOUT_ID, nTimeout, 0L);
    }
```

```
    while (((cbTotalToRecv - cbTotalRcvd) > 0) &&
          (lpstConn->hSock != INVALID_SOCKET)) {
      cbRcvd = DoRecv(hSock,
                      lpInBuf+cbTotalRcvd,
                      cbTotalToRecv - cbTotalRcvd,
                      lpstConn);
      if (cbRcvd != SOCKET_ERROR) {
        /* tally and quit if we've received amount requested */
        cbTotalRcvd += cbRcvd;
        if ((cbTotalToRecv - cbTotalRcvd) <= 0) {
          if (lpstConn->nTimeout)
            /* release timer, if there is one */
            KillTimer (lpstConn->hwnd, TIMEOUT_ID);
          break;
        }
        if (lpstConn->nTimeout) {
          /* reset timer, if there is one */
          SetTimer(hWinMain, TIMEOUT_ID, lpstConn->nTimeout, 0L);
        }
      } else {
        /* if receive failed, return an error */
        cbTotalRcvd = SOCKET_ERROR;
      }
    }
    /* unsubclass active window before we leave */
    SetWindowLong(lpstConn->hwnd, GWL_WNDPROC,
       (long)lpstConn->lpfnWndProc);
    lpstConn->nTimeout = 0;  /* reset timer */
  }
  return (cbTotalRcvd);
} /* end RecvData() */

/*-----------------------------------------------------------------
 * Function: DoRecv()
 *
 * Description: Loop to receive data
 */
int DoRecv(SOCKET hSock, LPSTR lpInBuf, int cbTotalToRecv,
  LPCONNDATA lpstConn)
{
```

```
  int cbTotalRcvd = 0;
  int cbLeftToRecv = cbTotalToRecv;
  int nRet=0, WSAErr;

  /* read as much as we can buffer from client */
  while (cbLeftToRecv > 0) {

    nRet = recv (hSock,lpInBuf+cbTotalRcvd, cbLeftToRecv, 0);
    if (nRet == SOCKET_ERROR) {
      WSAErr = WSAGetLastError();
      /* display all errors except "operation interrupted" */
      if (WSAErr != WSAEINTR) {
        WSAperror(WSAErr, (LPSTR)"recv()");
        /* unsubclass first so user can respond to error */
        SetWindowLong(lpstConn->hwnd,GWL_WNDPROC,
         (DWORD)lpstConn->lpfnWndProc);
      }
      break;
    } else if (nRet == 0) { /* other side closed socket */
      /* quit if server closed connection */
      break;
    } else {
      /* update byte counter */
      cbTotalRcvd += nRet;
    }
    cbLeftToRecv = cbTotalToRecv - cbTotalRcvd;
  }
  return (cbTotalRcvd);
} /* end DoRecv() */
```

The `SendData()` and `RecvData()` functions above are essentially clones of each other. The obvious difference is that one sends data and the other receives it. The less obvious difference is that we have a timeout parameter for the `RecvData()` function.

There are times when a blocking send function could use a timeout, such as during a buffer deadlock, when you cannot send unless you clear the buffers with a receive first. But for the most part you can rely on the TCP/IP stack to time-out if it cannot send data. When you receive data, however, the TCP/IP stack will not time-out for you. Hence the timeout parameter for `RecvData()` that allows an application to instruct our DLL to cancel a pending receive when the timeout period expires.

Both SendData() and RecvData() provide loops that call DoSend() and DoRecv() functions that make the I/O calls to WinSock and provide the error messages in the event of failure.

```
/*---------------------------------------------------------------
 * Function: CloseTCP()
 *
 * Description: Execute a graceful close of a TCP connection unless
 *  there is a blocking operation pending (in which case we close the
 *  connection when the pending blocking operation fails)
 */
int WINAPI CloseTCP(SOCKET hSock, LPSTR lpInBuf, int len)
{
  int nRet = SOCKET_ERROR, cbBytesDone=0;
  LPCONNDATA lpstConn;

  lpstConn = FindConn(hSock, 0);
  if (!lpstConn) {
    /* socket not found, so it's not valid */
    WSASetLastError(WSAENOTSOCK);
  } else {
    if (WSAIsBlocking()) {
      /* cannot close socket now since blocking operation pending,
       *  so just cancel the blocking operation and we will close
       *  connection when pending operation fails with the WSAEINTR
       *  error value */
      WSACancelBlockingCall();
    } else {
      /* signal the end is near */
      lpstConn->hSock = INVALID_SOCKET;

      /* "half-close" the socket (and ignore any error) */
      nRet = shutdown (hSock, 1);

      /* read and discard remaining data (until EOF or any error) */
      nRet = 1;
      while (nRet && (nRet != SOCKET_ERROR)) {
          nRet = recv (hSock, lpInBuf, len-cbBytesDone, 0);
          if (nRet > 0)
            cbBytesDone += nRet;
      }
```

```
      /* close the socket, and ignore any error (since we cannot do much
       *  about them anyway) */
      nRet = closesocket (hSock);
    }
    RemoveConn(lpstConn);
  }
  return (nRet);
} /* end CloseTCP() */
```

The `CloseTCP()` routine above is the same as the `CloseConn()` function in the WinSockx sample library in Chapter 7. We use the standard method of closing a TCP connection gracefully: Call `shutdown()` with how = 1 to discontinue sends but still allow receives. We call `recv()` in a loop to read any remaining data from the connection. Notice that the `CloseTCP()` function takes a buffer pointer (and length) for our DLL to use as an input buffer for the application to retrieve this remaining data. Finally, when `recv()` either fails or returns zero to indicate a close request from the remote side, we call `closesocket()` to finalize the TCP connection close and deallocate the socket. The one difference from the version of `CloseTCP()` in Chapter 7 is that we call the WSASimpl `FindConn()` and `RemoveConn()` functions from this version of `CloseConn()`.

```
/*--------------------------------------------------------------
 * Function:NewConn()
 *
 * Description: Create a new socket structure and put in list
 */
LPCONNDATA NewConn (SOCKET hSock,PSOCKADDR_IN lpstRmtName) {
  int nAddrSize = sizeof(SOCKADDR);
  LPCONNDATA lpstConnTmp;
  LPCONNDATA lpstConn = (LPCONNDATA)0;
  HLOCAL hConnData;

  /* allocate memory for the new socket structure */
  hConnData = LocalAlloc (LMEM_ZEROINIT, sizeof(CONNDATA));

  if (hConnData) {
    /* lock it down and link it into the list */
    lpstConn = (LPCONNDATA) LocalLock(hConnData);

    if (!lpstConnHead) {
      lpstConnHead = lpstConn;
```

```
    } else {
      for (lpstConnTmp = lpstConnHead;
           lpstConnTmp && lpstConnTmp->lpstNext;
           lpstConnTmp = lpstConnTmp->lpstNext);
      lpstConnTmp->lpstNext = lpstConn;
    }
    /* initialize socket structure */
    lpstConn->hSock = hSock;
    _fmemcpy ((LPSTR)&(lpstConn->stRmtName),
              (LPSTR)lpstRmtName, sizeof(SOCKADDR));
  }
  return (lpstConn);
} /* end NewConn() */

/*-------------------------------------------------------------------
 * Function: FindConn()
 *
 * Description: Find socket structure for connection using
 *  either socket or subclassed window handle as search key
 */
LPCONNDATA FindConn (SOCKET hSock, HWND hwnd) {
  LPCONNDATA lpstConnTmp;

  for (lpstConnTmp = lpstConnHead;
       lpstConnTmp;
       lpstConnTmp = lpstConnTmp->lpstNext) {
    if (hSock) {
      if (lpstConnTmp->hSock == hSock)
        break;
    } else if (lpstConnTmp->hwnd == hwnd) {
      break;
    }
  }
  return (lpstConnTmp);
} /* end FindConn() */

/*-------------------------------------------------------------------
 * Function: RemoveConn()
 *
 * Description: Free the memory for socket structure, and free
 *  task structure also (or at least decrement reference count),
```

```
 *  and remove them from our linked list
 */
void RemoveConn (LPCONNDATA lpstConn) {
  LPCONNDATA lpstConnTmp;
  HLOCAL hConnTmp;

  if (lpstConn == lpstConnHead) {
    lpstConnHead = lpstConn->lpstNext;
  } else {
    for (lpstConnTmp = lpstConnHead;
         lpstConnTmp;
         lpstConnTmp = lpstConnTmp->lpstNext) {
      if (lpstConnTmp->lpstNext == lpstConn) {
        lpstConnTmp->lpstNext = lpstConn->lpstNext;
      }
    }
  }
  RemoveTask (lpstConn->lpstTask);
  hConnTmp = LocalHandle((void NEAR*)lpstConn);
  LocalUnlock (hConnTmp);
  LocalFree (hConnTmp);
} /* end RemoveConn() */
```

The three functions above—`NewConn()`, `FindConn()`, and `RemoveConn()` —provide for maintenance and search of our "database" of connection records within WSASimpl DLL. The database is a simple singly linked list of connection data records. Notice that there are two parameters in the `FindConn()` function, which allow us to use either a socket handle or window handle to find a connection record. We use the socket handle to search from our WSASimpl API functions to validate a socket and retrieve the connection's "vitals" before beginning an operation. We use the window handle to search from our subclass procedure primarily to retrieve the original window procedure, so we can pass along messages our subclass procedure does not process.

```
/*---------------------------------------------------------------
 * Function: NewTask()
 *
 * Description: Register current task with WinSock DLL by calling
 *  WSAStartup() and create a new task structure
 */
LPTASKDATA NewTask (HTASK hTask)
```

```
{
  HANDLE hTaskData;
  LPTASKDATA lpstTask = (LPTASKDATA)0;
  int nRet;

  /* register task with WinSock DLL */
  nRet = WSAStartup(WSA_VERSION, &stWSAData);
  if (nRet != 0) {
    hWinMain = GetActiveWindow();
    WSAperror(nRet, "WSAStartup()");
  } else {
    /* allocate memory for a window structure */
    hTaskData =
      LocalAlloc(LMEM_MOVEABLE|LMEM_ZEROINIT, sizeof(TASKDATA));
    if (hTaskData) {

      /* convert it to a pointer */
      lpstTask = (LPTASKDATA) LocalLock (hTaskData);
      if (lpstTask) {

        /* initialize structure */
        lpstTask->hTask = hTask;
        lpstTask->nRefCount = 1;

        /* link this new record into our linked list */
        if (!lpstTaskHead) {
          lpstTaskHead = lpstTask;
        } else {
          LPTASKDATA lpstTaskTmp;
          for (lpstTaskTmp = lpstTaskHead;
               lpstTaskTmp->lpstNext;
               lpstTaskTmp = lpstTaskTmp->lpstNext);
          lpstTaskTmp->lpstNext = lpstTask;
        }
      } else {
        /* set error to indicate memory problems, and free memory */
        WSASetLastError(WSAENOBUFS);
        LocalFree(hTaskData);
      }
    } else {
      /* set error to indicate we could not allocate memory */
```

```
      WSASetLastError(WSAENOBUFS);
    }
  }
  return (lpstTask);
} /* end NewTask() */

/*---------------------------------------------------------------
 * Function: FindTask()
 *
 * Description: Find task structure using task handle as key
 */
LPTASKDATA FindTask (HTASK hTask) {
  LPTASKDATA lpstTaskTmp;

  for (lpstTaskTmp = lpstTaskHead;
       lpstTaskTmp;
       lpstTaskTmp = lpstTaskTmp->lpstNext) {
    if (lpstTaskTmp->hTask == hTask)
      break;
  }
  return (lpstTaskTmp);
} /* end FindTask() */

/*---------------------------------------------------------------
 * Function: RemoveTask()
 *
 * Description: Decrement the task reference count, free
 *  the memory for task structure when ref count is zero, and
 *  call WSACleanup() to deregister with WinSock
 */
void RemoveTask (LPTASKDATA lpstTask) {
  LPTASKDATA lpstTaskTmp;
  HLOCAL hTaskTmp;

  lpstTask->nRefCount--;
  if (lpstTask->nRefCount <= 0) {
    /* reference count is zero, so free the task structure */
    if (lpstTask == lpstTaskHead) {
      lpstTaskHead = lpstTask->lpstNext;
    } else {
      for (lpstTaskTmp = lpstTaskHead;
```

```
            lpstTaskTmp;
            lpstTaskTmp = lpstTaskTmp->lpstNext) {
         if (lpstTaskTmp->lpstNext == lpstTask)
           lpstTaskTmp->lpstNext = lpstTask->lpstNext;
      }
    }
    hTaskTmp = LocalHandle((void NEAR*)lpstTask);
    LocalUnlock (hTaskTmp);
    LocalFree (hTaskTmp);

    /* lastly, call WSACleanup() to deregister task with WinSock */
    WSACleanup();
  }
} /* end RemoveTask() */
```

We use `NewTask()`, `FindTask()`, and `RemoveTask()` to maintain and search our database of tasks currently accessing the WSASimpl DLL. Similar to the connection database, we have a singly linked list of task structures. Each task structure contains nothing more than the task handle and pointer to the next record in the list. We have this database separate from the connection database, since a single task may have more than one connection, and having a single task structure allows us to conserve and register/deregister with WinSocks `WSAStartup()` and `WSACleanup()` only once per task.

12

Porting from BSD Sockets

In This Chapter:

- Differences to Consider
- Sixteen-bit Windows Considerations
- Incidentals
- Functions List

What is the truth? I do not know and I'm sorry I brought it up.

Edward Abbey

One of the many advantages of the Windows Sockets API is its strong tie to the legacy network API that was shipped with Berkeley Software Distribution version 4.3. Windows Sockets is not 100 percent compatible with the Berkeley Sockets API, but it supports a significant subset of functions. In theory, you can port Berkeley Sockets applications directly to WinSock. Unfortunately, reality does not support this theory.

Although the differences between Berkeley Sockets and Windows Sockets are relatively few in number, some are fundamental, and so are the changes they sometimes require. If you also consider the substantial interface code required for any Windows application, and the profound differences between the nonpreemptive 16-bit Windows "operating system" and UNIX, it becomes quite obvious why any port of an existing Berkeley Sockets application may require some significant time and effort.

In this chapter, we describe the differences between Windows Sockets and Berkeley Sockets applications. We focus on the Berkeley functions and features that are unavailable or changed in Windows Sockets and tell you how to recode in each case. We also point out a few significant 16-bit Windows operating-system differences and describe the types of code changes they require. We do not deal with user interface changes, since that topic is beyond the scope of this book.

Differences to Consider

To begin, Windows Sockets and Berkeley Sockets differ in basic architecture. Some Berkeley Sockets functions are native to the operating system (so-called system calls) and others reside in a static library and you link them in at program creation time. Berkeley Sockets source code is highly portable, but binary compatibility is limited to specific systems and to specific versions of operating systems.

WinSock, however, has all of its function calls available from a single dynamic link library (DLL). At program creation time you can link with an import library—a stub of sorts that does not contain any actual code but only a list of DLL entry points—and have Windows load the DLL automatically for you at run time, or you can load the DLL explicitly at run time (we describe these two methods in Appendix D). Every WinSock DLL from every vendor and on every platform is guaranteed to provide 100 percent binary compatibility, so executables are highly portable.

There are a number of implementation differences between Berkeley Sockets and Windows Sockets that affect your source code. To allow so many network-system vendors to create implementations of the Windows Sockets API, the Windows Sockets specification avoids prescribing implementation features. Some of these features have equivalents available in the WinSock or Windows API, but others do not.

Here's a summary of the most significant differences that will affect the port of an existing BSD Sockets application to WinSock:

- Sockets are not file handles.
- `select()` does not act as a timer.
- `signal()` is unavailable.
- Domain name is unavailable.
- Address information and manipulation are unavailable.
- `syslog()` is unavailable.
- `errno` variable is unavailable.
- `perror()` and `sterror()` are unavailable.
- Database file manipulation is unavailable.
- `bcmp()`, `bcopy()`, and `bzero()` are unavailable.
- Local IPC is unavailable.

- OOB API is different.
- `setsockopt()` SO_DEBUG is optional.

We describe each of these in detail in this section.

Sockets Are Not File Handles

In WinSock, socket handles are not equivalent to file handles. This nonequivalence is not mandated, but it should be assumed if you want to write a portable WinSock application. As Section 2.6.5.1 in the v1.1 WinSock specification states: "While nothing prevents an implementation from using regular file handles to identify sockets, nothing requires it either. Socket descriptors are not presumed to correspond to regular file handles."

This had a significant effect on the Windows Sockets API. Because sockets are not file handles, WinSock does not include a number of Berkeley Sockets functions, and it does not support some of the assumed features that go along with them. This has serious implications for many applications. As a result, they may require major design changes to port from UNIX. The following list summarizes the most important differences:

- You cannot `dup()` a socket.
- `close()` and `ioctl()` functions are renamed.
- `read()`, `write()`, and `fcntl()` functions are unavailable.
- Some `ioctlsocket()` FIO commands are unavailable.
- `select()'s fd_set` structure is opaque.
- `select()` does not act as a timer.

You Cannot dup() a Socket

The WinSock specification does not deal explicitly with sharing sockets between processes. It does not say it's possible to share sockets, nor does it say it's impossible. It implies an inability, however, by the fact that socket handles are not equivalent to file handles. This means you cannot duplicate a socket with `dup()` to use in another (child) process, as many UNIX applications allow (you can in 32-bit Windows, however, as we describe later).

Despite the absence of the topic in the WinSock specification, some 16-bit WinSock DLLs actually do allow tasks to share sockets, even if they do not provide sockets that are equivalent to file handles. No API allows them to do so explicitly—like `dup()`—but the sharing is implicit. You would need to ask your WinSock provider to see how it works. We recommend that you do not rely on socket sharing, since it limits the portability of your application between WinSock implementations.

close() and ioctl() Functions Are Renamed

The BSD Sockets functions `close()` and `ioctl()` are still available in WinSock, but their names were changed to avoid conflicts with their run-time library (file handle) counterparts. They were renamed to `closesocket()` and `ioctlsocket()`, respectively.

read(), write(), and fcntl() Functions Are Unavailable

Many consider the `read()` and `write()` functions as part of the Berkeley Sockets API, when in fact their use in network applications is only a side effect of socket and file handle equivalence in UNIX. All occurrences of `read()` and `write()` that reference socket handles must be replaced with `recv()` and `send()` to make your application portable to all WinSock implementations.

The `fcntl()` function is also used in some BSD Sockets applications and must be removed. Here are some notes on a few of the `fcntl()` commands. The others not listed are not supported mainly due to operating-system differences.

- The F_SETFL command with the FNDELAY flag (O_NDELAY in System V UNIX) to change a socket from blocking to nonblocking (and vice versa) is equivalent to `ioctlsocket()` FIONBIO, which is available in WinSock.
- You cannot duplicate a socket in WinSock, so there is no replacement for the F_DUPFD command.
- Signals are not available in WinSock, so the F_SETFL command with the FASYNC flag does not have an equivalent in WinSock, although you should consider using `WSAAsyncSelect()` for asynchronous notification as a replacement.

Some ioctlsocket() FIO Commands Are Unavailable

The `ioctlsocket()` function only supports the FIONBIO, FIONREAD, and SIOCATMARK commands. The other I/O control commands—including the file I/O commands FIOCLEX, FIONCLEX, FIOASYNC, FIOSETOWN, and FIOGETOWN—are not available in WinSock. Of these, only FIOASYNC has an alternative (see the discussion of signals in the next section).

select()'s fd_set Structure Is Opaque

Because the values of socket handles are indeterminate, the "file descriptor set" (fd_set structure) parameters cannot be treated as bit masks. You should always use the macros (FD_ZERO, FD_SET, FD_ISSET, and FD_CLR) to manipulate the fd_set contents. You cannot make any assumptions about the contents of an fd_set.

select() Does Not Act as a Timer

You cannot assume that `select()` with NULL fd_sets will provide a high-resolution timer as it does in UNIX. Since some WinSock implementations will fail with WSAEINVAL if you have NULL fd_sets, you should avoid using `select()` as a timer. Use the Windows timers instead.

signal( ) Is Unavailable

Signals are the software interrupt mechanism that UNIX uses to asynchronously notify applications of events or conditions. The resolution is crude: For each type of signal, there is only one signal per process. As a result, there is no way to differentiate between signals on different sockets. In this respect, the Windows Sockets asynchronous notification mechanism outshines UNIX. If you convert an application that uses signals to use `WSAAsyncSelect()`, you can gain functionality and simplify the application, too.

The following suggests how to replace some of the relevant signals. Replacements for other signals are not generally needed, and discussion of them is beyond the scope of this text (in 32-bit Windows structured exception handling is one alternative):

SIGALRM: Use a Windows timer to replace `alarm()` or `settimer()` function calls.

SIGIO: The `WSAAsyncSelect()` FD_READ and FD_WRITE events are ideal replacements to maintain asynchronous notification. In this case, you will receive a Windows message to notify of an event, rather than an upcall.

SIGURG: The `WSAAsyncSelect()` FD_OOB event is an ideal replacement.

Domain Name Is Unavailable

The `getdomainname()` and `setdomainname()` functions are not available in WinSock. The reasons for this are not clear but may relate to implementation specifics. Perhaps some of the Windows Sockets implementation vendors did not have an API to provide the domain easily, or they felt the format was too intimately tied to the Internet domain (and wanted to prepare for future support of other protocol suites).

The alternative for `getdomainname()` is not difficult to accomplish. You can resolve a host name to get the "official," canonical host name (you cannot be sure to get that from `gethostname()`). Then remove the hostname portion through string manipulation to end up with the domain name. There is no alternative for `setdomainname()`, however.

Address Information and Manipulation Are Unavailable

One of the most surprising inadequacies in the v1.1 Windows Sockets API is the lack of the `gethostid()` function or `ioctlsocket()` SIOCGIFNETADDR command. As we described in Chapter 8, the recommended way to get the local IP address is to use `gethostname()` followed by `gethostbyname()` (or `WSAAsyncGetHostByName()`). The alternative is to get a socket, `connect()` it, and use `getsockname()`; if it's a datagram socket, you do not even have to send anything. Both of these strategies have some limitations and potential for problems, however. The `GetHostID()` function in the sample library in Chapter 7 shows how this is done.

The following local address-related `ioctlsocket()` commands are not available either, and they do *not* have standard alternatives:

SIOCGIFADDR, SIOSIFADDR: Get and set interface address.

SIOCGIFFLAGS, SIOCSIFFLAGS: Get and set interface flags (e.g., supports broadcast, point-to-point, currently running, and so on).

SIOCGIFCONF: Get a list of interfaces and their configuration.

SIOCGIFDSTADDR, SIOCSIFDSTRADDR: Get and set point-to-point interface address.

SIOCGIFBRDADDR, SIOCSIFBRDADDR: Get and set broadcast address.

SIOCGIFNETMASK, SIOCSIFNETMASK: Get and set network (subnet) mask.

Most of these are inappropriate to WinSock because they are too low-level. WinSock claims to be only a transport-layer API.

However, the unavailability of the SIOCGIFNETMASK command is one exception. Some datagram applications have a legitimate need to send a subnet-directed broadcast. Without the SIOCGIFNETMASK capability, there is no accurate way to determine where the network portion of an address ends and the host portion begins. As a result, there is no way to determine a subnet broadcast address from an IP address.

Due to the lack of support for SIOCGIFNETMASK—and the fact that they are infrequently used—the address manipulation functions `inet_lnaof()` and `inet_network()` are not available. The `inet_makeaddr()` function is not available either, but you can easily replace it with some ASCII/integer conversion and string manipulation routines.

syslog( ) Is Unavailable

The syslog functions (`syslog()`, `openlog()`, `setlogmask()`, `closelog()`) are not supported in Windows. There is a "debugging terminal" common to both 16-bit and 32-bit Windows, and it is somewhat equivalent. You can send text strings to this device with the `OutputDebugString()` function, but you should be aware that the debugging terminal is not always available and there is not a good way to check if it is, and so it is not a good idea to leave `OutputDebugString()` calls enabled by default. You should either keep them out of production code altogether (with `#ifdef` statements), or enable them by setting variable flags on the fly (with user commands or configuration settings).

errno Variable Is Unavailable

Windows Sockets does not use the global *errno* variable to report WinSock error values. Part of the reason is that sockets are not equivalent to file handles (and the errno variable is used by files), but more responsible are architectural reasons. To retrieve the per-task or per-thread error value, use `WSAGetLastError()`; and to set it, use `WSASetLastError()`. You can also retrieve a per-socket error value with `getsockopt()` SO_ERROR, although this is not consistently implemented among all WinSocks.

The `h_errno` variable set by the host name resolution functions in Berkeley Sockets is also unavailable in WinSock. However, there is a predefined macro in WINSOCK.H that calls `WSAGetLastError()`.

perror( ) and strerror( ) Are Unavailable

WinSock does not have a function to print or return a text string to describe an error value. The WinSock specification authors wanted to avoid defining strings for different languages. However, the Berkeley error descriptions (in English) are already a de facto standard, so it did not take long for a Windows resource file (.RC) and function that provide the equivalent of `strerror()` to become widely available on the Internet. We use a similar version in the sample source code in this book (see the `WSAperror()` function in the sample library in Chapter 7).

Database File Manipulation Is Unavailable

Most WinSock implementations reference a local file for service/port and protocol resolution (as we describe in Chapter 10), and many provide a local host table for hostname resolution too (as we describe in Chapter 8). The WinSock specification requires that these local database files must be in standard Berkeley UNIX services, protocol, and hosts file format (although it does not prescribe a specific location).

The so-called database functions reference these files. However, a number of database file manipulation functions are missing from WinSock:

- `endprotoent()`, `getprotoent()`, `setprotoent()`
- `endservent()`, `getservent()`, `setservent()`

WinSock version 2.0 treats services in an entirely different way. It provides APIs for enumerating services available in a variety of ways. See Chapter 17 for more information.

bcmp( ), bcopy( ), and bzero( ) Are Unavailable

The UNIX byte-array manipulation functions are not available in WinSock or the typical run-time libraries. However, they map well to equivalent functions, so it is possible to create macros to replace them:

```
#define bcopy(s,d,n)      _fmemcpy((d),(s),(n))
#define bcmp(s1,s2,n)     _fmemcmp((s1),(s2),(n))
#define bzero(s,n)        _fmemset(((s),0,(n))
```

Local IPC Is Unavailable

Version 1.1 of the WinSock specification does not mention local interprocess communication (IPC) at all. WinSock does not include the `socketpair()` function or the UNIX communication domain. The specification does not even mandate local connection support on datagram or stream support to the local IP address or loopback IP address (127.0.0.1). As a result, local IPC support through WinSock is optional, so you should not create applications that depend on this feature (see Chapter 16, "Optional Features," for more information).

OOB API Is Different

The API for support of out-of-band (OOB) data (e.g., TCP "urgent data") does not map entirely well to Berkeley UNIX conventions. This is true in part because the v1.1 WinSock specification does not describe the API in detail or explain exactly how it maps to the underlying protocol. But it is also true because some of what is defined is almost the complete opposite of the Berkeley Sockets API.

With SO_OOBINLINE disabled (the default), the exceptfds for the `select()` function is set for sockets with urgent data pending, as in BSD. However, with the SO_OOBINLINE socket option enabled, the `ioctlsocket()` SIOCATMARK command returns FALSE if there *is* urgent data pending (see Chapter 6, "Socket States," for details).

As mentioned earlier, the FD_OOB event notification for `WSAAsyncSelect()` is a good replacement for the SIGURG signal.

setsockopt( ) SO_DEBUG Is Optional

The SO_DEBUG option for the `setsockopt()` function is optional in WinSock, and its implementation is not prescribed by the specification. In many cases you are better off using external debugging techniques that are compatible with all WinSock implementations, rather than relying on the implementation-specific methods (see Chapter 13, "Debugging," for more information).

Sixteen-bit Windows Considerations

32-bit Windows—running in Microsoft Windows NT and Windows 95—is very similar to UNIX in many respects, unlike 16-bit Windows. It even has a few advanced features, threading and overlapped I/O, for instance, that are unavailable in UNIX.

There is a long list of operating-system differences between 4.3BSD UNIX and 16-bit Windows. Since 16-bit Windows is the lowest common denominator in the Windows Sockets platforms, some of the WinSock characteristics we note here had an effect on the Windows Sockets API that 32-bit Windows also provides. Others in this list are not true for 32-bit Windows Sockets (as we describe shortly). But if you want your application to run on any WinSock implementation or platform, you must take the 16-bit Windows limitations into consideration:

- 16-bit Windows does not clean house.
- 16-bit Windows is nonpreemptive.
- 16-bit Windows file system is not secure.

- 16-bit Windows uses segmented addressing.
- `fork()` is unavailable.

Let's deal with each of these individually.

Sixteen-bit Windows Does Not Clean House

If you learn one thing from this book, we hope it is that to write a robust and portable network application, *you must not assume anything*. Among other things, you cannot assume that the operating system will clean up after your application when it completes. Windows does not automatically return all resources to the system when an application exits. This could mean trouble for many applications coming from UNIX, which is very accommodating in this regard.

In 16-bit Windows, your applications need to clean up on their own. This means you must free memory and any other system resources your application acquires during execution before you exit from your application. This also means you must close all open sockets.

`WSAStartup()` and `WSACleanup()` are new to Windows Sockets. As we described in Chapter 10, "Support Routines," you must call `WSACleanup()` once for each time your application calls `WSAStartup()` (typically applications call each one time). Do not assume that `WSACleanup()` will do everything for you. `WSACleanup()` returns resources that the WinSock DLL itself allocates on behalf of an application, but it does not promise to return resources that your application explicitly requests. In other words, `WSACleanup()` does not necessarily close your open sockets. You must be sure to do this on your own.

Sixteen-bit Windows Is Nonpreemptive

The fact that 16-bit Windows is nonpreemptive means that it is not a truly multitasking environment (32-bit Windows is fully preemptive, however, as we will discuss later). Each Windows task in the 16-bit Windows environment must yield to other processes to allow multitasking. This fundamental operating-system difference can be transparent to your application, but only if you prepare your application for it. As we described in Chapter 5, "Operation Modes":

- With blocking operations you need to be prepared for reentrant messages that can occur because of "fake blocking."
- With nonblocking operations you need actively to yield to avoid monopolizing the system.

While a blocking operation is pending, a WinSock DLL's blocking hook function must yield; as a result, it can receive Windows messages as it blocks. This means your applications must be coded to be reentered. Thus, you need to call `WSAIsBlocking()` to be sure you do not already have blocking operations pending before you process Windows messages, be prepared to encounter WSAEINPROGRESS errors occasionally, and know how to use `WSACancelBlockingCall()` when necessary.

The implications of "fake blocking" and having to deal with reentrant messages should not be a problem unless you are creating a DLL with an intermediate API of your own. In this case, you do not have control over the calling applications, so you cannot modify them to handle reentrant messages. However, there are strategies for dealing with this (see Chapter 11, "DLLs over WinSock").

With nonblocking operations the WinSock DLL does not automatically yield, so you need to yield in your application. This means that in any polling loop you should call a yield function similar to the one listed for the default blocking hook in the v1.1 Windows Sockets documentation for `WSASetBlockingHook()`. You also need to use a "busy flag" semaphore to prevent nesting that can occur as your application receives reentrant messages as you yield (see Chapter 5, "Operation Modes," for more information).

Sixteen-bit Windows File System Is Not Secure

In 16-bit Windows there is no concept of users or groups, and file attributes do not go much beyond read and write permissions. The 16-bit Windows file system is not secure (this is not true for the 32-bit Windows environment, however), so these are all foreign concepts. The assumption is that 16-bit Windows is a single-user system, a "personal computer." As a result, the functions that UNIX applications employ to get a user name to use to connect to another machine—`getlogin()` or `getuid()`—are unavailable (32-bit Windows does not support these either, but it has an alternative API for retrieving user ID).

When there is no user identifier available and you need one, you will have to prompt the user for a user ID, or use an application configuration file. The WinSock specification does not prescribe a standard API for user ID retrieval.

Sixteen-bit Windows Uses Segmented Addressing

Sixteen-bit applications running in Windows on an Intel processor use segmented addressing. This should be transparent to most applications, but to avoid problems you can simply use the large memory model when you compile your applications. This will automatically use far pointers where necessary, so you will not have to worry about casting or inadvertently causing a protection fault by mistakenly referencing a near pointer.

Do not worry about introducing incompatibilities for 32-bit Windows if you do choose to add "FAR *" declarations and casts. In 32-bit Windows, which supports "flat" 32-bit address space, the "FAR" macro is an empty #define.

fork( ) Is Unavailable

The `fork()` function is not really a sockets function, but we mention it here since so many UNIX server applications use it. There are a number of similar functions available in 32-bit Windows, but none in 16-bit Windows.

In any case, the main reason that applications use `fork()` is to avoid multiplexing multiple sockets within a single process. Asynchronous operation mode with the WinSock `WSAAsyncSelect()` function makes multiplexing relatively simple, and it fits the Windows message-driven paradigm well. We recommend you consider using `WSAAsyncSelect()` as you rewrite applications that currently use `fork()` (see Chapter 6, "Socket States," for more information on `WSAAsyncSelect()`).

Incidentals

This section describes other incidentals to consider as you port your BSD application to WinSock.

Include Files

In a Berkeley Sockets application there are many header files you need to include, and they vary depending on what socket functions you use in your application. Windows Sockets has consolidated all the relevant header file contents for you. All the macros, constants, structure definitions, and function prototypes are available in one header file: WINSOCK.H. That is all you need to include to use any API in WinSock.

Socket Domains

Berkeley Sockets is a generic interprocess communication (IPC) API; it supports a number of so-called communications domains. With the exception of the UNIX domain—which is for local IPC—a communication domain is another name for a protocol suite.

Windows Sockets implements the Berkeley model of protocol independence also, although version 1.1 of the Windows Sockets specification only focuses on TCP/IP support (PF_INET domain, also called AF_INET). WinSock version 2.0 describes support for other protocol suites. Indeed, v1.1-compliant versions of WinSock for Windows NT (32-bit Windows) supported IPX/SPX, AppleTalk, and DECNet prior to the work done for WinSock 2.0 (see Chapter 15, "Platforms," Chapter 16, "Optional Features," and Chapter 17, "WinSock 2" for more information).

Socket Types

Within the Internet domain, WinSock supports the standard socket types and default protocols: SOCK_DGRAM for the User Datagram Protocol (UDP) and SOCK_STREAM for the Transmission Control Protocol (TCP). However, the SOCK_RAW socket type is only optionally supported. Many Windows Sockets implementations do support it, however, and allow use of the IPPROTO_ICMP protocol (Internet Control Message Protocol). Although the WinSock specification does not describe how to use SOCK_RAW, the Berkeley paradigm is the de facto standard (for more information, refer to Chapter 16, "Optional Features").

Socket Handles

The values for socket handles are not defined by the v1.1 WinSock specification. As stated in Section 2.6.1, of the v1.1 specification, "Windows Sockets handles have no restrictions, other than that the value INVALID_SOCKET is not a valid socket."

As a result, you will need to alter any application that makes assumptions about socket handle values. You cannot assume they are small, nonnegative integers, and they may not even be restricted to a specific range (e.g., you cannot assume values 0 through NOFILE, which occur in UNIX).

Error Values

The Windows Sockets error values are direct descendants of the Berkeley Sockets error values, and so are the macros that represent them. There are only a few new WinSock-specific errors added. All the other errors are Berkeley error values, with a WinSock "base" value added. The base value is defined as the macro WSABASEERR in WINSOCK.H and has a value of 10,000. The macros for the error values are the same as those for Berkeley, with a prefix "WSA" added (for example, the BSD error ECONNRESET is WSAECONNRESET). Actually, the original BSD macros are redefined in

WINSOCK.H as their new WinSock counterparts, so it is not really necessary to change references to them in your Berkeley source code.

Functions List

The following table gives a one-for-one comparison of the functions in Berkeley Sockets and Windows Sockets. It shows at a glance where BSD and WinSock match and where they do not match. Note: Some of the functions listed here are not necessarily sockets functions, but we include them here because they are used in so many sockets applications.

4.3 BSD Sockets	*1.1 WinSock*	*Functional Description*
accept()	accept()	Accept an incoming connection attempt
bcmp()	_fmemcmp()	Compare each byte in a memory range
bcopy()	_fmemcpy()	Copy specified number of bytes from one specified memory location to another
bind()	bind()	Assign local name to unnamed socket
bzero()	_fmemset(buf,0,len);	Initialize a memory range with zeroes
close()	closesocket()	Close connection and return system resources
closelog()	*not available*	Close system log
connect()	connect()	Initiate a "connection" (datagram or stream)
fork()	CreateThread() and CreateProcess() (*not available in 16-bit Windows*)	Create a child process
getdomain()	*not available*	Get local domain name
gethostbyaddr()	gethostbyaddr() *or* WSAAsyncGetHostByAddr()	Given an IP address, get host information
gethostbyname()	gethostbyname() *or* WSAAsyncGetHostByName()	Given a host name, get host information

gethostid()	gethost name(), then gethostbyname() or connect(), then getsockname()	Get local IP address
getgid()	*not available*	Get group identifier
gethostname()	gethostname()	Get host name of local machine
getlogin()	*not available*	Get current login name
getpeername()	getpeername()	Get name of remote (connected) socket
getprotobyname()	getprotobyname() *or* WSAAsyncGetProtoByName()	Given protocol name, get protocol number
getprotobynumber()	getprotobynumber() *or* WSAAsyncGetProtoByNumber()	Given protocol number, get protocol name
getservbyname()	getservbyname() *or* WSAAsyncGetServByName()	Given service name and protocol name, get port number
getservbyport()	getservbyport() *or* WSAAsyncGetServByPort()	Given a service port number and protocol name, get service name
getsockname()	getsockname()	Get name for local socket
getsockopt()	getsockopt()	Given a socket option, return the value for that option on a given socket
getuid()	*not available*	Get user identifier
gettimeofday()	*not available*	Get or set the system date and time
herror()	*not available*	Display short error text on stderr device
htonl()	htonl()	Convert long from host to network byte order
htons()	htons()	Convert short from host to network byte order
inet_addr()	inet_addr()	Convert ASCII string in standard Internet '.' notation to 32-bit IP address value (net order)

`inet_lnaof()`	*not available*	Given an IP address, return local address part
`inet_makeaddr()`	*not available*	Given an Internet network number and local network address, construct an IP address
`inet_netof()`	*not available*	Given an IP address, return network number part
`inet_ntoa()`	`inet_ntoa()`	Convert an IP address value into ASCII string in standard Internet '.' notation
`inet_network()`	*not available*	Convert ASCII string in standard Internet '.' notation into network portion of IP address value
`ioctl()`	`ioctlsocket()`	Set or retrieve I/O modes of a socket
`listen()`	`listen()`	Listen for incoming connection requests
`openlog()`	*not available*	Open system log
`perror()`	*not available for WinSock error values*	Display short text description of current system error (errno) value on standard error device
`read()`	*not available**	Receive data from a "connected" socket
`readv()`	*not available***	Receive multiple buffers ("scatter read")
`recv()`	`recv()`	Receive data from a "connected" socket
`recvfrom()`	`recvfrom()`	Receive from a socket (datagram socket type may be unconnected, and receive from unicast, broadcast, or registered multicast address)
`recvmsg()`	*not available*	Return next message from a datagram socket

rresvport()	*not available*	Return a reserved port (range 512–1023)
select()	select() or WSAAsyncSelect()	Perform I/O multiplexing of specified sockets
send()	send()	Send data on a "connected" socket
sendto()	sendto()	Send on a socket (datagram socket type may be unconnected, and send to unicast, broadcast, or multicast address)
setdomainname()	*not available*	Set domain of host machine
sethostent()	*not available*	Open and rewind a "host database file"
sethostid()	*not available*	Assign primary local IP address
setlogmask()	*not available*	Set log priority mask and return previous mask
setsockopt()	setsockopt()	Set option associated with socket
signal()	*not available*	Notify a process when an event occurs
shutdown()	shutdown()	Shut down part of full-duplex TCP connection
socket()	socket()	Create an endpoint for communication, and return a socket handle for reference
socketpair()	*not available*	Create a pair of connected sockets
strerror()	*not available*	Return short description for error value
syslog()	*not available*	Log message in appropriate system log (among other places) if it has appropriate priority
write()	*not available**	Send data on a "connected" socket

writev()	*not available***	Send from multiple buffers ("gather write")
not available	WSACancelAysyncRequest()	Cancel an outstanding instance of a WSAAsyncGetXbyY() function
not available	WSACancelBlockingCall()	Cancel a blocking call currently in progress
not available	WSACleanup()	Sign off from Windows Sockets API
not available	WSAGetLastError()	Obtain last Windows Sockets API error
not available	WSAIsBlocking()	Determine if a blocking call is in progress
not available	WSASetBlockingHook()	Establish a blocking hook function
not available	WSASetLastError()	Set error to be returned by WSAGetLastError()
not available	WSAStartup()	Initialize the Windows Sockets API
not available	WSAUnhookBlockingHook()	Restore default blocking hook function

* These functions may be available in some WinSock implementations in which sockets are equivalent to file handles, but their use limits the portability of a WinSock application.

** WinSock version 2.0 implementations have scatter/gather functions (see Chapter 17 for details).

There is not always a specific reason why a Berkeley function is unavailable in WinSock. The general reason often applies: The original charter for WinSock required that the API would accommodate the needs of most network applications and could be implemented by all protocol stack vendors involved. In most cases the missing APIs did not meet these qualifications, although there are some cases where an API was dropped for simple reasons of expediency. Sometimes an API is unavailable because there is an existing equivalent in the WinAPI or Win32 API (and typically it does not map exactly to the BSD paradigm).

Here are some examples of functions that were not included and possible reasons for their exclusion:

- `readv()` and `writev()`: "scatter and gather" were left out mainly for reasons of expediency, not because they are not useful. In fact, the version 2.0 WinSock specification provides their functionality in new functions.
- `recvmsg()` and `sendmsg()`: There is simply no great need for these in applications (they are not different enough from `recv()` and `send()` on a datagram socket).
- `rresvport()`: They are not needed by many applications, and some vendors were unable to provide this functionality.
- `socketpair()`: It's for local IPC, for which other mechanisms are better suited to Windows.

13 Debugging

In This Chapter:

- Problem Types
- What Failed, and How?
- Problem Qualification
- Installation Debugging
- Network Debugging
- Application Debugging
- Debugging Tools

I've been waiting twenty years for someone to say to me: "You have to fight fire with fire," so that I could reply, "That's funny—I have always used water."

Howard Gossage

Every network application is bound to fail at some point in time. This does not necessarily reflect badly on the network application, but it does suggest the complicated and variable nature of networking itself. The network is a jungle. This is not to say it is wild and untamable, but rather that it is full of life and the unexpected can occur with so many variables involved. Many different problems can occur with network applications. Considering the number of things that have to go right with a network application, it is surprising that things work as well and as often as they do.

We loosely apply the term "debugging" to the process of dealing with a problem encountered during execution of a WinSock application. Our definition of a "bug" can mean more than just a mistake in an application. Our broad definition includes any unexpected and unwanted behavior that occurs during execution of a WinSock application. In this sense we consider any problem a bug, though the application itself is not necessarily at fault. "Trouble-shooting" might be a more accurate term to use, but the graphic analogy of chasing bugs is too appealing.

In this chapter we categorize several types of problems. We describe some simple debugging steps for each type, and we point you to the many debugging utilities that can help you figure out where your problem is, what your problem is, and how to fix it.

Problem Types

There are three basic types of problems that can cause unexpected and unwanted behavior in a WinSock application:

- installation problem
- network problem
- application problem

An application user or his or her system and network administrators can remedy installation and network problems. An application developer with access to the application source code is required to fix an application problem.

Installation Problem

An installation problem is the result of a misconfigured protocol stack or WinSock DLL. Examples include an invalid local IP address or subnet mask, a path that does not include the WinSock DLL file, an empty host table or incorrect name server address, and memory or interrupt conflicts with your network interface card.

Installation problems frequently cause application failures. This obviously occurs most often with new network-system installations, but it can occur in existing installations as well. As users install other software or hardware, they can introduce problems. The classic line that characterizes this type of problem is, "It stopped working for no reason; I have not changed a thing."

It's easy to forget about system and software changes, especially if they do not seem relevant. For example, the installation of a sound card on the same interrupt as your network card would suddenly cause (possibly intermittent) network-system failure. Something always changes. A persistent appeal to logic ("*some*thing had to change") and a quick review of system files (e.g., AUTOEXEC.BAT, CONFIG.SYS, and Windows.INI files) can help determine the cause.

Network Problem

A network problem occurs with a chronic or transient problem in the network system beyond the local system. Examples include an Ethernet segment failure due to a missing terminator, a misconfigured router, and a downed server system.

Network problems occur less often than configuration problems, but they are not uncommon. You can use some of the many network utilities available to help characterize this type of problem. Sometimes you or your application user can fix a network problem on the local system or network. Many times, however, they require assistance from your network or system administrators.

Application Problem

An application problem is a bug in the WinSock program, in the classic sense of the term. For example, it might be caused by an unanticipated nonfatal error (e.g., WSAEWOULDBLOCK), missing checks of the return values from `send()` or `recv()` to ensure complete data transfer, or calling `closesocket()` upon FD_CLOSE notification without reading any pending data first.

The frequency of application problems depends on the context. During the development stage, they are frequent. When an application problem is the likely cause, it does not hurt to do a few sanity checks to verify the network (like a ping), but you can often save time by using application debugging procedures before trying the complete and time-consuming network debugging procedure, such as looking at a network trace.

An application problem should be relatively rare in released applications. Assuming there was some quality assurance on the product, the most likely cause when a user encounters a real bug in a released application is that the user is using it over a WinSock implementation that the developer did not use to test. The first question to ask a user—after you ask for the error message—is the name of the WinSock vendor.

WinSock DLL Problem

There is also a fourth type of problem we have not considered: one caused by a bug in the WinSock implementation itself. Fortunately, these do not occur often, since most WinSock implementations have had a chance to mature. There are differences between WinSocks due to ambiguities in the specification, but these are not bugs in a WinSock DLL. The specification allows for these differences, and as we demonstrate throughout this book, you can create portable code that is not affected by differences among implementations. The key is not to expect anything that the specification does not explicitly promise.

When you encounter a problem, do not be too quick to blame the WinSock DLL. You should not assume that the WinSock DLL is at fault until you have ruled out every other possibility. Remember that there are many other WinSock applications out there that work just fine. It might help to try running some other WinSock applications, particularly if they are similar to yours, to do a quick check. You might also contact your WinSock vendor to see if an updated version is available.

If you think you have found a bona fide bug that you cannot code around without potentially breaking your application over other WinSocks, then the only thing to do is contact your WinSock vendor. In addition to a detailed description of the problem, they will want source code or an executable with which to recreate it. The easier you make it for them to zero in on the problem, the more likely you are to get it fixed promptly.

We do not recommend that you try to detect programmatically the WinSock vendor and use vendor-specific code. This approach defeats the purpose of vendor independence that WinSock provides, in addition to being unreliable because WinSock does not provide a standard means of vendor identification.

What Failed, and How Did It Fail?

When an application fails, the first thing to do is find out

- Which WinSock function failed (or what was the name of the asynchronous notification message that contained an error)?
- What was the WinSock error name (or value)?

Your application should have displayed these two items in an error message (as we recommend in Chapter 14, "Dos and Don'ts"). Look up the error in Appendix C, "Error Reference." In many cases, the WinSock function name and type of failure are enough to indicate the cause of a problem and its remedy.

Protection Faults

When an application fails without an error message (e.g., throws you out of Windows to the DOS prompt without notice), it usually indicates an installation problem (such as a memory conflict with your network interface card). In this case you need to refer to your network driver installation documentation (exclude the card's memory from your memory manager) or WinSock vendor installation instructions.

If the application failed with a general protection fault (GPF), then check the location of the failure. If it fails in a WinSock DLL, it may be a problem with the DLL, but most likely it is not. This may be a symptom of an invalid buffer pointer your application passed to the WinSock DLL. It can also occur if you have called `WSASetBlockingHook()` but have not exported your blocking hook function.

Problem Qualification

If you have not discovered the problem by doing the above, you need to look a little closer at the problem to determine your next step. In this section we present debugging tips for each of the three problem types: installation, network, and application. Our network debugging procedure has two procedures: host resolution debugging and generic network debugging. You need to qualify which type of problem you have in order to decide which type of debugging is appropriate.

As you qualify a problem, you often jump between debugging procedures. A problem often appears as one type until you reveal some characteristic that indicates another type. For instance, for a host resolution failure you may start with host resolution debugging, go to generic network debugging, and end up doing installation debugging.

If an application fails with any of the WinSock error values WSAHOST_NOT_FOUND, WSATRY_AGAIN, WSANO_RECOVERY, or WSANO_DATA, but you do not know what function failed, you know it was a "database routine" failure. One of the host, services, or protocols resolution functions (like `gethostbyname()`, `getservbyname()`, or `WSAAsyncGetProtoByNumber()`) has failed. If you do not know which function failed, then start with application debugging to figure it out. Most services or protocol resolution failures are due to installation problems. For host resolution function failures, see the host resolution debugging procedure.

If you are still not sure where to start, try this preliminary procedure to help determine whether you should start with the host resolution or generic network debugging procedure:

1. Ping the destination host name (i.e., the host name of the system the network application was trying to reach when it failed). If you can ping the host name, you know immediately that it is not a hostname resolution problem.
2. Ping the destination IP address.

   If step 1 fails but step 2 succeeds, then you probably have a hostname resolution problem.
3. Ping your local host name.
4. Ping your local IP address.

   If step 3 fails but step 4 succeeds, then you probably have a hostname resolution problem.
5. Otherwise, you should treat it as a generic TCP/IP problem.

Installation Debugging

We cannot tell you much about how to debug a WinSock vendor's installation, since their configurations vary tremendously. The WinSock specification does not prescribe WinSock architecture or configuration. For example, although Section B.4 in the v1.1 WinSock specification requires a uniform file format for the host, services, and protocols database files, their name and location may vary between WinSock vendors.

The best thing to do is to study the WinSock vendor's installation documentation and look for a trouble-shooting section. If that does not help, you can try to contact the vendor's technical support staff. If you still need assistance, you can try sending your problem description to mailing lists and USENET newsgroups on the Internet (see Appendix E, "Information Sources," for some good ones to try).

Network Debugging

Our term "network debugging" is not quite accurate, since application failures are rarely caused by network failures. We use the term in the broadest sense since we are trying to identify the problem we are having with a network application. In the final analysis, you may discover an application failure caused by a typographical error rather than any network operation or configuration. Since a WinSock application failure usually manifests itself as a network failure, you should always begin the trouble-shooting process by investigating—and trying to rule out—network failure.

Generic Network Debugging

This procedure is generic since it tests basic connectivity between TCP/IP hosts, without regard for the transport or application protocol your application uses. It should help to indicate whether you have an installation problem, network problem, or application problem.

To proceed you are likely to need the following information, in addition to the host name or address of the destination host in use when the WinSock application failed. If you are missing any of this information, you should look at your TCP/IP stack vendor's documentation for the information location, or refer to the network debugging utilities section that appears later in this chapter for hints about finding the information.

- local IP address
- subnet mask
- local router
- IP address of another host on local subnet
- IP address of a reliable host on the other side of the router

It is also helpful to know whether the destination address is on the local subnet (network and subnet portion of IP address same as in local IP address).

We recommend having a network analyzer on the local network to watch the packets (or to see if there are any). You should also pay close attention to any error messages you get from the test applications you use (ping, mostly). For more information on network analyzers and the test applications, see the "Debugging Tools" section later in this chapter.

Use the following debugging procedure after you qualify your WinSock application problem as a generic TCP/IP network problem (using the procedure in the "Problem Qualification" section that appears earlier in this chapter). The results of these steps will further qualify the type of network problem you are experiencing.

1. Ping the destination host. Use the IP address if you have it, or the host name if not. If this succeeds, then you know that you have basic end-to-end connectivity from your local host to the remote host and that the error that causes application failure was probably specific to the service being used. This points at either the local application or the application running on the destination host.
2. Ping your own IP address. If it succeeds, it simply verifies that your local network interface is configured with the IP address you thought. Note: This does not send any packets onto the network. If this fails, you have a network software installation or configuration problem (you probably have a different local IP address than you thought).
3. Ping another host on your subnet, or try a broadcast (255.255.255.255) if you do not know any local host addresses. If it succeeds, then you have local network connectivity (so chances are most of your local host's configuration is correct). If it fails, you probably have a hardware problem (either your network connection is unplugged, the local net is down, or your hardware configuration has a problem).
4. Ping your local router. If this succeeds, theoretically you should be able to communicate with any other host on your internet. If the destination host is off the local net and you could not ping it in step 1, then maybe the router you just pinged is not set as your default route in the local configuration. If this fails, then your router may be down.
5. Ping a reliable host on the other side of your router (or the interface on the other side of the router, if you know it). If this succeeds, then you know that you can accomplish the most difficult of basic connectivity tests. This hints that the problem is either on the destination system or

application, or in some router or network in between. If this fails, it could also be that your subnet mask is not set correctly (so you are trying to ARP locally instead of forwarding to a router, or vice versa).

6. Use the traceroute utility (which we describe later) and target the destination host. If this succeeds, then the problem is in the application at the other end. If this fails, the last router that reports its address may provide a clue as to where the failure is occurring.

7. If the destination application uses TCP, try using telnet to connect to the port number on which the application is listening at the server system. If this succeeds, then the application is apparently listening properly, so your application probably tried to connect to the wrong port or system. If this fails, then the server application either failed or is not listening on the right port. If you have an incorrect port on either the client or the server, check that you called `htons()` to convert to network byte order.

8. If connectivity appears correct, then you need to debug your application. Scrutinize your application; most likely you have a problem in your WinSock function calls, or you are not responding appropriately to an asynchronous notification or socket state. Are you expecting a behavior the WinSock specification does not explicitly promise?

Host Resolution Debugging

Use this procedure if a host resolution function failed with one of the WinSock error values WSAHOST_NOT_FOUND, WSATRY_AGAIN, WSANO_RECOVERY, or WSANO_DATA (see Appendix C, "Error Reference," for detailed descriptions of these errors).

Since host resolution functions often use the network to access the hosts database (DNS), it may be a network problem (see Chapter 8, "Host names and Addresses," for more information on the Domain Name System). Many host resolution failures are due to installation problems, because the configuration of host databases vary so much between WinSock implementations. It could be a simple problem of omission or formatting in your local database file (e.g., */etc/hosts*).

1. Check your WinSock configuration to see if it uses a hosts database file or a network server (DNS) to provide host resolution. If both, you should check whether WinSock references the hosts file or DNS first.

2. If you use a hosts database file, check whether destination (and local) host names are listed in the database file. Check if you can resolve any of the

other entries (to see if there is a formatting problem in the file). Try using the WSHOST application (see "Debugging Tools" section later for more information) or another application that calls `gethostbyname()` or `WSAAsyncGetHostByName()` to resolve a host name. Can you resolve any of the other host names in the host table? Does it stop resolving at some location in the file (where there might be an illegal character entry causing problems)? Maybe the host name is just wrong. You can check a host name mapping by e-mail:

- *To:* **resolve@cs.widiner.edu** *or* **dns@grasp.insa-lyon.fr**
- *Subject:* **help**
- *Body of the e-mail message:* **site <host name>**
- You will get the well-known Internet address back in an e-mail response, if there is one for that host name.

3. Ping DNS server (using IP address, of course). If this succeeds, then try to use the NSLOOKUP application to resolve the destination host name using the server. Try some other host names that you know the server should be able to resolve. If the others work but your destination does not, then you have the destination spelled incorrectly. If your DNS server does not work, then try another. If you are on the Internet, try rs.internic.net, for example (the Internet information center, which you should always be able to reach).

Application Debugging

The best thing to do to debug a WinSock application is watch the WinSock function calls the application makes. Look closely at the values of the input parameters, at the return codes and output parameters, and at Windows messages posted to your application (if it uses asynchronous WinSock functions). This may sound simple, but it is often very revealing.

Some WinSock implementations provide debugging tools to supply this information, and others produce this output when you enable the `setsockopt()` SO_DEBUG option. The best way to get this information, however, is by using a utility that captures the DLL calls and/or spies on Windows messages. These utilities provide information objectively, since they watch what occurs from outside the application and the WinSock DLL. Another major advantage is that you can get this information in a consistent format as your application runs over any WinSock implementation (another benefit of WinSock's binary compatibility).

It is possible to write your own utilities that intercept DLL calls and/or windows messages. The techniques have been documented in a number of articles and books (see the Finnegan reference in the articles list, and others in Appendix E, "Information Sources," for more information). But writing your own utilities is unnecessary, because at least two commercial utilities are available, as we describe in the next section.

Of course, you can always build standard debugging output into your application. Do not underestimate the value of `MessageBox()` or `assert()`. You can send strings to the Windows debug device with `OutputDebugString()`, although this has disadvantages (it tries to write to device AUX if a redirector like DBWIN is not running). You want to avoid trying to send debug output out over the network (à la SYSLOG), since using the network to debug a network application can confuse the problem. With any of these, be sure your finished application does not output debug information at undesired times (consider using `#ifdef` statements liberally, to avoid unwanted output in your production releases).

Debugging Tools

We describe a few different types of debugging tools in this section. Specifically, we have

- network debugging utilities
- application debugging utilities
- WinSock compliance and performance utilities
- other debugging tools

Network Debugging Utilities

In addition to some basic information you need when debugging, such as the router address and subnet mask, you will need to generate a lot of other information to zero in on a network application problem. There are many different utilities available to provide this information. Some of the utilities we describe are the UNIX versions, although the information is generic to TCP/IP and so typically is available from among the utilities in your particular TCP/IP implementation. You might need to dig through your documentation to find them. We also mention some of the public domain WinSock versions of these utilities and some that work over the packet driver interface.

There is a complete survey of (mostly UNIX-based) network debugging utilities in RFC 1147, "FYI on Network Management Tool Catalog: Tools for Monitoring and Debugging TCP/IP Internets and Interconnected Devices," edited by Robert H. Stine. Although published in 1990, most of its material is still valid and valuable. In particular, the abstracts and availability (which include hardware platforms) are very useful. If nothing else, at about 337K in size, the RFC gives a sense of the wealth of network management tools available.

ping

TCP/IP stacks always come with their own version of ping, which is the most basic and essential diagnostic tool available. The application name is an acronym for "Packet InterNet Groper," which is barely plausible. It is more likely that the application name came first—in reference to the sound submarine sonar makes—and the acronym's explanation was made up later. ping provides a way to reach out and gently touch another machine. It is the simplest way to check IP connectivity between two machines.

As just mentioned, it is called "ping" because it works like sonar in a submarine. You have probably heard sonar in movies where a submarine sends out a sound and you can hear the sound bounce back if another vessel is within range. The ping application does a "sounding" by sending an ICMP (Internet Control Message Protocol) echo request packet to a destination IP address. The TCP/IP stack at the destination address will respond—echo the sounding—by sending back an "echo reply" ICMP packet. TCP/IP stacks respond to "echo request" ICMP packets automatically (i.e., you do not need a server application running).

Note that the destination address can be a broadcast address as well as a unicast address. For a broadcast address, all stacks that see the echo request will respond. Your ping program may only show one response, but if you look at your ARP cache (see the "arp" command) or ICMP statistics, you will see evidence of the other replies. It can be a convenient way to find out what other machines are on the local subnet—the ARP cache will list their IP addresses—although your network neighbors and administrators will not look kindly on excessive use of a broadcast address.

In addition to simply testing whether another machine is up with its TCP/IP stack loaded and configured correctly, ping can provide a surprising amount of other information. For example, it verifies the routing between the source and destination hosts. It gives you a good idea about the round-trip time between here and there. Although it does not give definitive answers, it can provide important clues about packet loss (due to busy routers or misconfigured hosts). By varying the size of ping packets (usually possible with ping applications), you can detect any size sensitivity that may exist along the route between two hosts.

There are ping utilities available that run over WinSock. John Junod's WS_PING is widely available. However, because they rely on the v1.1 WinSock optional support of SOCK_RAW (IPPROTO_ICMP), they are not compatible with every Windows Sockets implementation (see Chapter 16, "Optional Features," for more information on SOCK_RAW support).

Beware that ping is not infallible. Firewall systems are gateways between networks that can filter out packets with specific protocols or port numbers. Often ICMP traffic, like ping's, is filtered, as are TCP packets other than those going to port 25 (the mail server). In other words, it is possible that a ping or finger can fail even though a system is up and running. In this case, you simply need to know that there is a firewall between you and the destination system to diagnose the problem.

traceroute

There is a variation of ping commonly available from TCP/IP vendors also. The **traceroute** facility is sometimes added (as an option) to an ICMP ping program, although the original traceroute application by Van Jacobson (found on Berkeley UNIX machines) used the UDP protocol. Rather than relying on the ICMP echo facility in TCP/IP stacks, it uses the time-to-live (TTL) mechanism in the Internet Protocol (IP). Here's how it works:

> Source host: sends out an IP packet (ICMP or UDP) with TTL=1.
>
> First router: decrements TTL by one, sees that it is zero, and sends an "TTL exceeded" ICMP error packet back to the source host. It contains the address of the router, so the source host can see where the error came from (hence, it finds out the address of a router along the route).
>
> Source host: sets TTL=2 and sends out another IP packet.
>
> First router: decrements TTL by one, forwards packet to next router on route to destination host.
>
> Second router: decrements TTL by one, sees that it is zero and sends an "TTL exceeded" ICMP error packet back to the source host.
>
> Source host: sets TTL=2, and so forth.

Here is an example of the output adapted from the traceroute "man page" (the help subsystem in BSD UNIX, invoked by typing "man traceroute"). Notice that some hops along the route do not respond with an "TTL exceeded" ICMP message (see the "***"). There are a number of possible explanations; for example, some network administrators intentionally configure routers to remain silent to protect their network address.

```
traceroute to nis.nsf.net (35.1.1.48), 30 hops max, 40 byte packet
     1  helios.ee.lbl.gov (128.3.112.1)  19 ms  19 ms  0 ms
     2  lilac-dmc.Berkeley.EDU (128.32.216.1)  39 ms  39 ms  19 ms
     3  ***
     4  ccngw-ner-cc.Berkeley.EDU (128.32.136.23) 39 ms  40 ms  39 ms
     5  ccn-nerif22.Berkeley.EDU (128.32.168.22) 39 ms  39 ms  39 ms
     6  128.32.197.4 (128.32.197.4)  40 ms  59 ms  59 ms
     7  131.119.2.5 (131.119.2.5)  59 ms  59 ms  59 ms
     8  129.140.70.13 (129.140.70.13)  99 ms  99 ms  80 ms
     9  129.140.71.6 (129.140.71.6)  139 ms  239 ms  319 ms
     10  129.140.81.7 (129.140.81.7)  220 ms  199 ms  199 ms
     11  nic.merit.edu (35.1.1.48)  239 ms  239 ms  239 ms
```

As its name implies, it shows you the route IP packets (ICMP or UDP) will take. The route it displays is not guaranteed to be accurate since it takes a number of different datagrams to complete, each of which could take a different route. But it gives you an idea of whether an application failure is caused by a routing problem. You can use traceroute to provide a clue about where on the route between hosts a packet is stopping.

Unfortunately, access to any fields in the IP header (like TTL) is not provided by v1.1 of the WinSock specification (it is in WinSock 2, however, as we describe in Chapter 17). By the BSD de facto standard, access to the IP TTL field would require SOCK_RAW IPPROTO_IP support or `setsockopt()` with *level*=IPPROTO_IP and *cmd*=IP_TTL. Most TCP/IP stacks have only a proprietary API to provide this low-level access, which means their version of the traceroute application is not usable on other WinSock implementations. An example of this is Peter Tattam's **hopchk** application (which only runs on the Trumpet WinSock DLL).

Note: traceroute is not infallible. As mentioned, the routes can vary between each datagram sent. Also, since it depends on datagrams, which are inherently unreliable, you may not always get the "TTL exceeded" ICMP responses. Furthermore, not all routers are configured to respond with "TTL exceeded" ICMP datagrams (to help conceal their identities).

nslookup

nslookup is a special-purpose utility, specifically designed to test the Domain Name Service (DNS). It allows interactive access to DNS servers, to send and receive specific types of queries and responses. You can use it to test your DNS servers, to get specific information about various hosts and domains, or to get a list of hosts in a domain. It helps to have some knowledge of the DNS protocol (RFC 1035, by Paul Mockapetris) to use it effectively.

A public domain utility called **dig** (domain information groper) is commonly installed on UNIX systems. It has similar capabilities to nslookup but is easier to use and is more flexible.

Ashmount Research created a public domain version of nslookup available for WinSock. The nice thing about it is that the DNS protocol is implemented within the application (which uses a UDP socket to send and transmit). It uses `gethostname()` and `WSAAsyncGetHostByName()` to resolve the DNS hostnames, but beyond that does not rely on the local hostname resolution capability. This makes it very useful for debugging DNS server problems.

There is also a public domain application that uses `gethostbyname()`, called **wshost** (from Andy H. Coates). It is not as sophisticated as nslookup, but it is also much simpler to use.

Standard UNIX Tools

The following three utilities are included with most UNIX operating systems. Your TCP/IP implementation may not have utilities by the same name, but it probably has the same information available from other utilities. At least these should give you an idea of the type of information that is commonly available from TCP/IP implementation support software.

- **arp:** displays and modifies the arp cache contents (the list of Internet-to-hardware address translation tables used by the address resolution protocol).
- **ifconfig:** primarily used to assign an address to a network interface (or configure parameters), you can also use it with the '-a' command line parameter to find out the local IP address(es), subnet mask, and subnet broadcast address.
- **netstat:** This utility is the general-purpose network information broker. It shows network statistics like the state of active sockets (including foreign address and port number), servers listening on a local system, and per-protocol statistics, which include counts of different packet types sent and received. It can display local interface information, such as the host name, IP address, hardware address, maximum transmittable unit (MTU) for the active media, and the current routing tables. The "netstat -ao" command is handy for listing servers running under inetd, which is the server application launcher in UNIX systems (it listens for connection requests on the appropriate port for each service, and launches the server application when a request arrives).

SNMP Tools

Many utilities designed for network debugging use the Simple Network Management Protocol (SNMP) to query SNMP-capable hosts for all kinds of information or to listen for SNMP problem reports, which are called "traps." There is even an open API specification called WinSNMP that provides many of the benefits that WinSock does, including a binary-compatible API for SNMP. WinSNMP DLLs are available from a number of TCP/IP vendors and run over WinSock DLLs. A number of vendors provide network management applications that are WinSNMP compatible.

Ad Hoc Tools

Many different utilities are available for debugging common TCP/IP application protocols. Some can help you in your everyday use of the network (for example, VRFY can help you find a correct e-mail address), and you can use them to locate application services as well as to debug problems. Here is a brief description of four such utilities:

- **telnet** is a great tool for checking on the availability of a TCP service, since you can specify a port number to connect to (if it succeeds, you know the server is listening, and if it fails, you know it's not).
- **vrfy** and **expn** check Simple Mail Transport Protocol (SMTP) servers.
- **nfsstat** debugs Network File System (NFS) problems (-s for server stats, -c for client stats).
- **rpcinfo** identifies and debugs NFS and remote procedure call (RPC) services.

Network Analyzers

Along with ping, **network analyzers** are a network application developer's best friend. Ask any network application developer who has had a network analyzer available for a while whether he or she would mind if you took it away, and you will get a look of fear and loathing. The closest analogy to developing a network application without a network analyzer is driving a car with your eyes closed.

Network analyzers allow you to capture and analyze the actual network packets that pass between network hosts. Many different versions are available, in hardware and software, but their function and purpose are the same. They have network interfaces run in promiscuous mode so they can capture any packet, whether or not the hardware address matches the interface's hardware address. They can capture an entire packet, including the media-specific data-link header (e.g., DIX Ethernet), to the application data, and everything in between. Various filters are available so that you can determine the packets you capture by specific contents (a specific TCP port number, for example). They are also capable of parsing each packet, so you can see the values throughout each header. The following is a sample output from a network analyzer:

```
Receive time:  85.154  (+0.015)    packet length:  64    received length:  64
Ethernet:    ( 3Com 3faeae - >3Com 3c4c83  type: IP(0x800)
Internet:    128.127.50.16 - >128.127.50.5        hl: 5   ver: 4   tos: 0x10
len: 40   id: 0x46e7 fragoff: 0   flags: 00 ttl: 60  prot: TCP(6)
 xsum: 0x33ca
TCP:          ftp(21 - >2189            seq: 69647890  ack: 0cf34d29
win: 7300   hl: 5   xsum: 0x4a8d urg: 0      flags: <ACK><FIN>
==================================================================
0000: 02 60 8c 3c 4c 83 02 60 - 8c 3f ae ae 08 00 45 10      |.`.<L..`.?... E.|
0010: 00 28 46 e7 00 00 3c 06 - 33 ca 01 01 01 09 01 01      | (F.  <.3.......|
0020: 01 05 00 15 08 8d 69 64 - 78 90 0c f3 4d 29 50 11      |.. ...idx...M)P.|
0030: 1c 84 4a 8d 00 00 32 32 - 31 20 47 6f 6f 64 62 79      |..J.  221 Goodby|
```

Notice all the valuable information it provides, including:

- Ethernet source and destination addresses, with the manufacturer code translated
- IP source and destination addresses
- TCP source and destination port numbers (with common FTP service identified)
- TCP sequence and acknowledgment numbers
- TCP window size
- TCP flags (notice that this packet is in the process of closing and acknowledging data)
- Application data (notice the "221 Goodbye" RFC 959 File Transfer Protocol application protocol text used while closing a connection)

Network analyzers provide an objective, third-party view of what is occurring between two network hosts. This provides empirical evidence to refute or support the results that utilities and applications display and imply. They provide a view into the black box that is the network. They are not always appropriate to every problem, but sometimes they are invaluable. If nothing else, they give you that warm fuzzy feeling that *something* is happening at times when you are not quite sure as you watch your application run.

It is possible to use them inappropriately, however. Sometimes having too much detail available is as bad as having too little. Analyzing a network trace when the WinSock error message can provide the answer is like using a sledgehammer to open a peanut. It will work, but it wastes energy and is messy, too.

Among the network analyzer products available, some ship with systems (like Etherfind on Sun Microsystems machines), others are commercial products, and some are freely available in the public domain. We have created a list of those we know about with some vital information about them.

- *Product name:* name of the LAN analyzer product
- *Type:* PD: Public Domain; Com: Commercial
- *Platform:* DOS, Windows, UNIX (usually many versions, although Etherfind is strictly for Sun systems), and hardware-based (a stand-alone dedicated unit)
- *Company name:* contact this company for more information

Product Name	*Type*	*Platform*	*Company Name*
DominoLAN	Com	Windows	Wandel and Golterman
Etherfind	Com	UNIX	Sun Microsystems
Etherload	PD	DOS	
LAN Traffic Monitor	Com	HW	Hewlett-Packard
LANAlert	Com	Windows	NCD, Inc.
LANalyzer	Com	Windows	Novell
LANDecoder	Com	Windows	Triticom
LANSight	Com	HW	Intel
LANVista	Com	Windows	Digilog
NetProbe	PD	DOS	
NetSight	Com	DOS	Intel
Netwatch	PD	DOS	Novell-sponsored
PacketView	Com	DOS	Klos Technologies

Sniffer	Com	HW	Network General
SpiderProbe	Com	HW	Spider Systems
TCPDump	PD	UNIX	
Trakker	Com	UNIX and Windows	Concord Systems

Table 13-1: LAN Analyzers available in the public domain and commercially for various hardware and operating system platforms

Application Debugging Utilities

As we mentioned earlier in our description of the application debugging procedure, you can reveal a lot about your application by simply logging the WinSock function calls that a WinSock application makes, the parameter values going in and out, and the return values as it executes. Building this capability into your application is unwieldy and unnecessary.

The same mechanism that provides binary compatibility to WinSock—dynamic linking—also allows applications to peek at WinSock calls and parameters. This section examines two commercial applications that allow you to log WinSock calls to a 16-bit WINSOCK.DLL (currently there aren't any similar tools available for the 32-bit WSOCK32.DLL), and includes some pointers to information that describe how to create your own WinSock function call watcher.

WinScope

WinScope is available from The Periscope Company, Inc., in Atlanta, Georgia (404-888-5335). To quote its documentation, "It's like Spy on steroids." This is a profound understatement. Like Spy (WinSight, Snoop, or Voyeur), WinScope is a nonintrusive debugger that allows you to watch Windows messages going to various windows. But unlike Spy, it also allows you to log the function calls to any DLL from any Windows application. It also allows you to set breakpoints. By default, it handles the complete WinAPI, but it supports a scripting language that lets you describe custom messages and functions to any DLL. This includes the WinSock DLL; Brent Stilley has made a script available for WinSock on Periscope's BBS system.

The information logged with each function call is complete. It includes all the input parameters' values, the return code, and the output parameters' values. For pointer arguments, it can display the contents of the buffer pointed to, including the values for individual fields within structures.

This utility is excellent for seeing what a Windows application does, because it shows *everything*. This is good, because often you can discover problems by seeing the WinSock function calls and messages in the context of your WinAPI function calls and messages (and it indents to show nesting that can occur when servicing reentrant messages). However, the information this utility logs by default is tremendous, which can be inconvenient if all you want are the WinSock functions. It is possible, however, to limit the functions and messages you log.

TracePlus/Winsock

TracePlus/Winsock is available from Systems Software Technology, Inc., in Woodland Hills, CA (818-346-2784). Like WinScope, it is a nonintrusive debugger that allows you to see all function calls made to a WinSock DLL with all of the vital information displayed. It is less powerful than WinScope—it handles only the WinSock API—but it is easier to use because of its focus. The one drawback is it does not log Windows messages, but the vendor promises it is adding this capability, and Spy accommodates nicely in the interim. (Note: they also promise a 32-bit version for WSOCK32.DLL.)

One minor annoyance is that it intrudes slightly when it calls `WSAGetLastError()` if there is a function failure (and it does not trace `WSAGetLastError()` calls from applications as a result). Another is that it displays the address structure contents in network order, so you see the Intel interpretation of the big-endian value. It also does not allow you to look at nonstandard options (like multicast).

Nonetheless, it's very convenient to use to get a consistent-format snapshot of a WinSock application in action over any WinSock implementation, and these drawbacks should disappear as the vendor updates the utility. It is a recommended addition to any WinSock application developer's toolbox.

Create Your Own WinSock Watcher

The tricks that WinScope and TracePlus/WinSock use to capture DLL calls and parameters as well as asynchronous notification messages are well documented with source code available to get you started if you are interested in creating your own "WinSock watcher" utility. Look for information on subclassing to capture window messages, and for watching DLL calls:

- Microsoft's Visual C++ v1.5 ships with "hooks" that you can adapt to WinSock.
- James Finnegan's article in the January 1994 issue of *Microsoft Systems Journal* describes his ProcHook utility.

- Timothy Adams describes a technique in "Intercepting DLL Function Calls," June 1992, *Windows/DOS Developer's Journal*.
- Schulman, Maxey, and Pietrek describe another technique in *Undocumented Windows*.

WinSock Compliance and Performance Utilities

Windows Sockets developers frequently lament the inability to test WinSock implementation conformance to the Windows Sockets specification. Such a WinSock tester might seem simple to create, but it is not, which is one reason why there is not one available.

The inherent flexibility of the WinSock API is a compliance-tester application's undoing. Consider the infinite variety of ways you can combine the many Windows Sockets functions and options to create an application. For a compliance tester to be valid, it would have to test all possible application variations. Also consider the many ambiguities and varying interpretations among WinSock vendors (all of which could be legitimate), and you get the idea of the difficulty in creating a comprehensive compliance tester.

The best compliance testers are existing WinSock applications. There are two others available, however, and one performance tester. Here's a quick description of them.

wsatest

The **wsatest** utility is a public domain application that first appeared at an FTP site in Sweden. The About box does not reveal who created it, which is a shame since someone deserves some credit for its design and creation. It is a handy little test tool that lets you make WinSock function calls interactively and displays the results. It is limited in some respects (e.g., it cannot do IPPROTO_ICMP) and has some bugs (e.g., some SO_ options are not implemented correctly), but overall it is an excellent way to make quick checks of what works in a WinSock DLL or to communicate with an application at the other end of a connection.

Windows Sockets API Tester (WSAT)

An ambitious Microsoft project, **WSAT** tries to be the ultimate WinSock API tester, but unfortunately it is huge and unwieldy. It is designed for WinSock implementors, not endusers or developers, not only because it is difficult to use, but also because its results are subject to interpretation. However, it can provide useful information to application developers. You can retrieve it from ftp://rhino.microsoft.com.

Socket Wrencher

Released by NetManage in May 1994, this application is a useful tool despite being a marketing gimmick. It can give you a good idea of how much throughput you can get using synchronous and asynchronous I/O with various buffer sizes on your network stack and interface card. Unfortunately, there is not much documentation to describe how it is written or on what equipment its own performance numbers are based. Comparing their numbers, which may have been with a 16-bit interface EISA bus NIC on a 100MHz Pentium machine, with your configuration's performance is not really meaningful. Nonetheless, it is a handy benchmarking tool.

Other Debugging Tools

- **WinSock implementation-specific tools:** Most WinSock implementations have their own method of outputting debug information, in their own format. Some have separate utilities, and others use the standard Windows debug output device (accessible from the COM port with a terminal attached, or with the DBWIN application). Their one advantage is they can show you some of the internal workings of the DLL as it services an application. Sometimes this can help when debugging.
- **Windows debuggers:** The value of standard code debuggers like Microsoft's codeview and (especially) NuMega's **SoftIce/W** hardly needs introduction. Sometimes they are overkill, and they can hide problems by their intrusive nature. But other times, nothing else will do.
- **Windows application auditors:** The debug version of Windows (from the Windows SDK) and NuMega's Bounds Checker can reveal bad WinAPI parameters, inefficient Windows resource usage, and a host of other things. These mistakes are made (and left) even in high-priced commercial applications. It is not uncommon for a working application to do things that are not obviously wrong and may not be harmful, but that are also not "legal" and could have been avoided. These tools help to identify subtle errors in an application.

14 Dos and Don'ts

In This Chapter:

- Characterizing Your Application
- Application Data Flow
- Stream Algorithms
- Datagram Algorithms
- Good-News Code
- Common Traps and Pitfalls

We do not err because the truth is difficult to see. It is visible at a glance. We err because this is more comfortable.

Alexander Solzhenitsyn

At this point we have covered everything you need to know to write any WinSock application. We have described the Winsock API from top to bottom, from application framework to a microscopic examination of each function call. We have also shown how to use it all in application samples.

Throughout the book, we offer suggestions for what to do and what not to do when designing and implementing a WinSock application. In this chapter we summarize many of the points we make in this text, to emphasize their importance and provide a single location for reference. We also fill in some missing details about important implementation considerations and give a few algorithms to deal with real-world application problems.

This chapter does not contain philosophies, but practical advice. Use what we tell you here, and your WinSock application will perform well; it will be robust and portable. As a result, you will have happy users and will spend less time debugging and fielding support calls.

Characterizing Your Application

This section presents a brief overview of the choices involved with application design, along with some criteria for how to make a choice, some pointers to more information, and a few recommendations. One choice we do not discuss here deals with what platform to use. For the choices available and the issues involved, please see Chapter 15, "Platforms."

- Will your application implement a standard application protocol, or will you design your own? As we mention in Chapter 2, the specifications for standard protocols like FTP and Telnet are available in RFCs. Even if you are planning to implement your own application protocol, you should consider using these proven protocols as models.
- Will you use stream or datagram transport protocols? Chapter 3 described the fundamental differences in the services these protocols provide. Unless you know you need datagram, you should stick with stream. Otherwise, you may find yourself trying to reinvent reliability.
- Will your application be a client, a server, or both (as a peer)? If you have any questions about which is which, look at Chapter 4. As a rule, your application protocol will determine which role your application will play.
- What operation mode will you use? As we suggest in Chapter 5, your choice of operation mode should be simple: Asynchronous can provide the best performance with the least effort and the most flexibility.
- How will you detect changes in socket state as the application progresses? As we describe in Chapter 6, asynchronous notification is the most efficient means of socket state detection. About the only time you should opt instead for blocking or nonblocking operation is if you are porting existing sockets code to 32-bit Windows (which provides preemptive multitasking).

These decisions define the architecture of your application. The implementation details of the network portions are your next consideration.

Application Data Flow

Every network application sends or receives data. Some applications transmit only small quantities of data for short periods, so data throughput is not a big concern. But most applications need to send or receive data in bulk, at least from time to time. For instance, even an interactive application like Telnet that typically sends and receives small quantities of data may occasionally need to transfer data in bulk. The question of how to maximize data flow is almost a universal concern among network applications.

The major issues involved in moving data quickly are similar for both datagram and stream sockets. There are significant differences between the two also, but they are not as substantial as their similarities.

The steps we identify in Figure 14-1 trace the data as it flows from creation to its network application destination. This illustration differs from figures in other chapters that show data traversal through the OSI layers. However, the OSI layers are still represented here: the upper layers by the sending and receiving applications, and the lower layers by the network-system.

Figure 14-1 illustrates a simplified view of the data flow, with the flow in only a single direction. The purpose of this simple illustration is to highlight the many "stops" along the data path. Each stop is a potential bottleneck that can slow a data flow and adversely affect your application's performance. To create a network application that performs well, the solution is simple:

> **The rule of thumb:** *Make big pipes, and keep the data pumping through them.*

Use Big Buffers

As Figure 14-1 illustrates, there are two I/O buffers in every network application: the application buffer and the network-system buffer. You have full control over the size of the application buffer, and in many instances you can control the network-system buffer too. In general, *the bigger the buffer the better.*

Actually, the size of the application buffer does not affect data throughput dramatically. As long as your application buffers are big enough to hold the largest block of data you will send or receive at any time, it should be adequate. The point is that you want to allow your application to send and receive sufficient amounts of data (which we define in a moment). You should minimize the number of calls you need to send or receive data.

On the other hand, the size of the network-system buffer available to your application can make a big difference in data throughput. If your application moves bulk data, you should try to get as much network buffer space

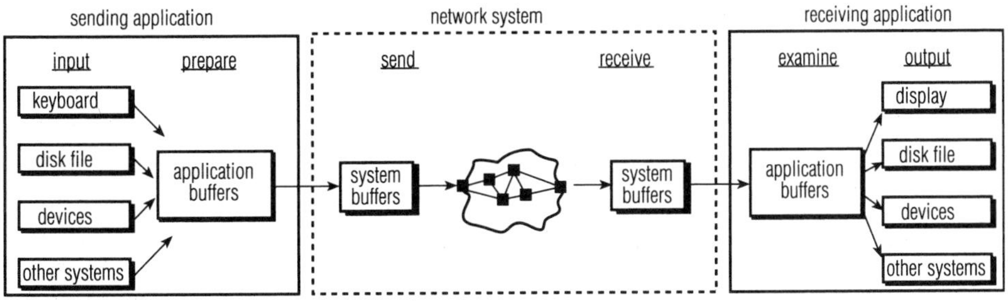

Figure 14-1 Data flow between two network applications.

as you can by calling `setsockopt( )` SO_SNDBUF and SO_RCVBUF. Unfortunately these socket options, which we describe in Chapter 9, "Socket Information and Control," are optional in WinSock, so you may not always be able to increase buffer space. But it is worth the try.

Think MTU

Each type of network media—Ethernet, PPP, X.25, Token Ring—have different "maximum transmittable units" (MTU). The MTU is the largest packet size they can handle, including the media header, network header (IP), transport (TCP or UDP), and application data. As a large IP packet traverses a router to a media with a smaller MTU, the router fragments the IP packet. When the packet reaches the final destination, the TCP/IP stack reassembles the IP packet. In general, you should do what you can to reduce fragmentation and reassembly to reduce system overhead and increase the data flow.

On TCP this is not as much of an issue, since the size of outgoing packets is often determined by "maximum segment size" (MSS) negotiation. If the MSS negotiation does not occur when a TCP connect occurs, each stack will use the default MSS of 536 bytes if the destination address is off the local network (which means it's going through a router). That means that no matter how much you ask to send or receive, the stack only sends 536 bytes of data in any TCP packet.

On UDP, it is possible to send any size datagram, and IP handles fragmentation and reassembly. This is not advisable, however, for a number of reasons. It incurs extra network-system overhead by forcing fragmentation and reassembly, and it misuses network-system buffers at the receiving end, where the entire datagram must be reassembled before delivery (packet boundary preserved; see Figure 14-2). Worst of all, if the local or remote

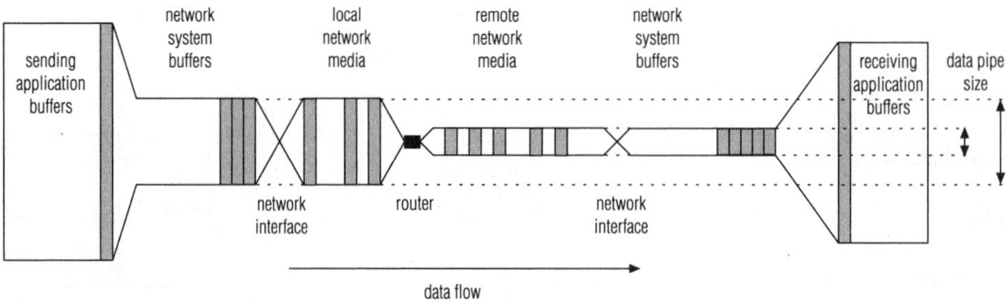

Figure 14-2 Illustrates use of network-system buffers and fragmentation and reassembly of a datagram when transmitted through a router.

network-systems do not have adequate buffer space available the operation may fail *without an error,* since datagrams are unreliable.

The point is that although it may seem that trying to transfer large amounts of data in each I/O would be better, it is not. You should stick to something closer to the MSS of about 536 to minimize system overhead, although you can go a bit larger as a compromise. After all, system buffer sizes tend to be around the MTU size, so going with a number closer to a likely MTU may use system buffers more efficiently. This will also increase data flow between hosts on local networks (i.e., not going through routers).

We recommend using no more than 1460 for TCP and 1472 for UDP. These match the MTU sizes of the ubiquitous DIX Ethernet media, and they are a common value for the negotiated MSS. This maximizes efficiency for the common case.

Consider the Maxim

You should always consider the robustness principle when doing network I/O:

> *Be conservative in what you do, be liberal in what you accept from others.*[1]

This rule has two important corollaries that prescribe how much data to send and receive:

- send moderate amounts
- receive large amounts

Send Moderate Amounts

As a rule, you should avoid specifying a small value for *len* each time you call `send( )` or `sendto( )`. Consider the protocol overhead involved with each data transmission, and try to fill each TCP or UDP packet with as much data as possible, without causing fragmentation.

Because a datagram socket preserves message boundaries, sending a single byte of data literally means sending 1 byte of data, plus 8 bytes of UDP header, plus 20 bytes of IP header (at least), plus the media header (e.g., 14 bytes in DIX Ethernet). So, that is a 1:42 data-to-overhead ratio — not good. But then again, if you are not trying to send bulk data and your application protocol requires it, then it is acceptable.

[1] RFC 793, "Transmission Control Protocol," J. Postel.

The overhead in stream sockets is even greater, since the TCP header is at least 20 bytes long, so the ratio of data to overhead with a single byte of data is 1:54. However, most stacks implement the Nagle algorithm to protect the network from this by coalescing data before sending it. We discuss this in more detail ahead; we mention it here to point out that typically sending a single byte on a TCP socket is not as bad as with a UDP socket.

Receive Large Amounts

The rule against receiving small amounts of data is much stricter than the rule against sending small amounts. You should always avoid specifying a small value for *len* when you call `recv( )` or `recvfrom( )`. You should always read as much as you can buffer.

On a datagram socket, specifying a small length does not affect data throughput but can cause you to lose data. If you specify a length that is less than the number of bytes available in the next queued datagram, the datagram is truncated, and `recv( )` or `recvfrom( )` will fail with WSAEMSGSIZE. The remaining data is irrecoverable; the TCP/IP stack discards it as the datagram is truncated (WinSock version 2 allows partial datagram reads with the MSG_PARTIAL I/O flag for the new `WSARecv( )` function).

On a stream socket you will never lose any data, but specifying a small length decreases data throughput dramatically. While data remains in the receiver's network-system buffers, the TCP window is reduced, which effectively slows the data flow from the sending end. The TCP window advertises the network-system buffer availability to the sender, so read operations throttle send operations. The net effect is that the faster you get your data out of the network-system buffers with larger receive lengths, the faster the other end can send data.

Do Not Peek

As we mention in Chapter 6, you should avoid the data peek operation provided by the MSG_PEEK I/O flag and `ioctlsocket( )` FIONREAD command. It is always a wasteful operation that misuses network-system buffers and is sometimes a dangerous one with the potential for deadlock if the data for a stream socket straddles a buffer boundary.

You can increase your data flow by simply reading data without peeking first. This frees the network-system buffers to receive more data. On a datagram socket, this means that fewer datagrams will be dropped when network-system buffers are unavailable. On a stream socket, it means the TCP window can open up faster.

Receive Before You Send

In applications that use asynchronous operation mode (as they should), the order of network I/O operations is not an issue. The system notifies your application with FD_READ when data arrives, and you read it. If a send fails because buffers are unavailable—perhaps they are full of incoming data—the system notifies the application with FD_WRITE when the buffers are free again.

However, in blocking and nonblocking applications, you determine the order of network I/O operations. In applications that send and receive data on the same socket simultaneously, it is critical that they always receive data before trying to send it. On a blocking socket, a deadlock situation can occur if you try to send when local network-system buffers are full of incoming data. On a nonblocking socket, you should always try to receive data if a send fails with WSAEWOULDBLOCK.

Stream Algorithms

As we describe in Chapter 3, stream sockets provide reliable data delivery. But reliable data delivery is a qualified term, and some applications need to deal with a number of side effects of this promise. In this section we provide a few strategies for dealing with the limitations of a stream socket:

- sending structured data
- sending interactive data
- detecting a dead connection
- verifying data delivery

Sending Structured Data

Many applications send structured data on a stream connection. However, the WinSock API does not provide a way to preserve message boundaries on stream sockets, since TCP does not provide a record service. The elemental data unit in a stream is a byte, and there is no way to preserve message boundaries.

To overcome this limitation, an application can impose record boundaries on data once it has been received. The trick is to read the data into the application buffers and parse it there. If your application sends fixed-length records, this is very easy to do, but this is not a problem even if you send variable-length data records (see Figure 14-3).

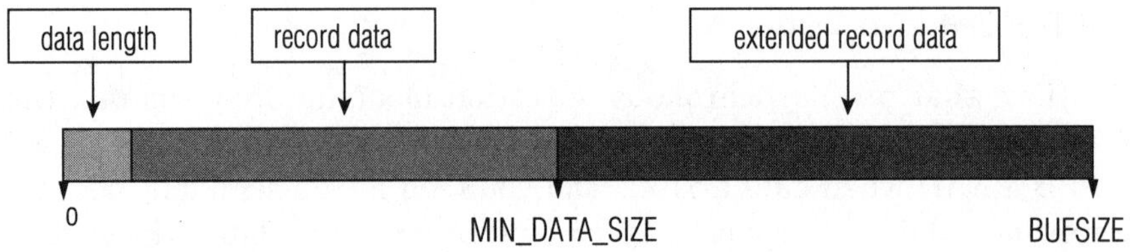

Figure 14-3 Illustrates buffer layout for variable-length record handling on a stream socket.

The algorithm to read variable-length data on a stream socket boils down to these steps:

1. Read the minimum amount of data.
2. Retrieve the data (record) length from the beginning of the buffer.
3. Process if we have already received enough (the minimum record size), or receive and append more data into buffer until we get the total amount specified in the data length field.

In our algorithm, the data records have the record length field in the first few bytes of the data record, but this is not a requirement. You can adapt this algorithm quite easily to read the length field from another location in the data record.

Code Example

Here is a pseudocode example that implements the algorithm to read variable-length records on a stream socket. You can also refer to the sample FTP client in Chapter 7 for another example. Notice that we use application state to keep track of whether we are currently reading the data length or the actual record data.

```
#define STATE_GETTING_LENGTH  1
#define STATE_GETTING_DATA    2
#define DATALEN      2
#define MINDATASIZE  510
#define MAXDATASIZE  2046
...
static int nAppState   = STATE_GETTING_LENGTH; /* bit flags for state */
static int nDataToRead = MINDATASIZE+DATALEN;
static int nDataLen = 0;
```

```
int nDataRecvd;
static char achDataIn[MAXDATASIZE+DATALEN];
static char FAR *lpDataPtr = achDataIn;
 ...
   case FD_READ:
     ...
     <check for error in FD_READ msg>
     ...
     <if you were to ignore extra messages, here's where to do it>
     ...
     nDataRecvd = recv(s, lpDataPtr, nDataToRead, 0);
     if (nDataRecvd == SOCKET_ERROR) {
        if (WSAGetLastError == WSAEWOULDBLOCK) {
           break;    /* handle gracefully */
        } else {
           <handle error>
        }
     } else if (!nDataRecvd) {
       /* If recv( ) returns 0, then the other end closed connection.
        *  This is unlikely to occur if your application protocol is
        *  well defined, and unnecessary if you have registered for
        *  FD_CLOSE, but nonetheless you might want to handle it.
        */
     } else {
       if (nAppState & STATE_GETTING_LENGTH) {
         nDataLen += nDataRecvd;
         if (nDataLen >= DATALEN) {  /* we got the data length */
           nDataToRead = ((int)*(achDataIn))-DATALEN-nDataRecvd;
           nAppState = STATE_GETTING_DATA;
           nDataLen = 0;
        } else {
           nDataToRead -= nDataRecvd; /* update bytes to read */
        }
     } else if (nAppState & STATE_GETTING_DATA) {
        nDataToRead -= nDataRecvd;   /* update bytes to read */
     }
     if (nDataToRead <= 0) { /* we got it all! */
       nDataToRead = MINDATASIZE + DATALEN;   /* reset things */
       nAppState = STATE_GETTING_LENGTH;
       lpDataIn = (char FAR *)achDataIn;
```

```
        <deal with data; remember it starts after length in buffer>
      }
    }

      } else {           /* we still have more data to read */
         lpDataIn += nDataRecvd;      /* update pointer into buffer */
      }
   }
```

Sending Interactive Data

An application that uses "interactive data" sends data in real time and expects the responses in real time also. Applications of this type are sensitive to the latency introduced by congestion avoidance algorithms in TCP, like the Nagle algorithm. As we describe in Chapter 9, "Socket Information and Control," the classic example of such an application is an X-Server. X-Servers send mouse movements and use the response from the X-Client to update the mouse cursor in the X-Server display.

As a rule, you should not disable the Nagle algorithm with `setsockopt( )` TCP_NODELAY. It is rarely necessary to do so, and it does *not* increase data throughput. The beauty of the Nagle algorithm is that it only delays inefficient TCP segments, so in effect it causes more efficient use of the local and remote network-system buffers, as it also reduces network overhead.

Detecting a Dead Connection

One of the most common questions on TCP applications is how to detect when a connection has expired. The classic test case involves physically disconnecting a system's network interface while the connection sits idle. Unfortunately, when an application is not sending or receiving, the network-system will not detect that you have unplugged the computer from the network. The application will never know. Network I/O is required to detect a dead connection.

There are basically two strategies to choose from:

- use TCP keep-alives
- use an application-level keep-alive

As we describe in Chapter 9, "Socket Information and Control," enabling TCP keep-alives with the `setsockopt( )` SO_KEEPALIVE option has many disadvantages. In particular, you do not know the timeout value, and there is no way to change it.

The advantage to implementing an application-level keep-alive mechanism is that you get full control over detection. The downside is that it complicates your application. It is not a complicated algorithm, however:

1. Set a timer.
2. When the timer goes off, send a no-op "keep-alive" packet that your application peer will recognize and respond to.
3. If the attempt to send the keep-alive fails, you know the connection is dead.
4. If you do not receive the response by the time the timeout period expires, you know the connection is dead.
5. If you receive the response and read it successfully, you know the connection is alive.

Verifying Data Delivery

Another classic test of TCP reliability involves physically disconnecting a system from the network as an application sends data. Surprisingly, the send operation succeeds since the network-system can successfully copy the data to be sent from the application buffer to the network-system buffers. A successful send does not have any relation to the packet transmission or receipt of an acknowledgment from the receiver.

In this instance the network-system will attempt to retransmit the packet, and when the retransmission eventually times out, it aborts the connection. For an application to find out, it would either have to perform an I/O operation, which would fail, or have registered for FD_CLOSE notification with `WSAAsyncSelect( )`, which would contain an error value. The error would be WSAECONNABORTED.

When a connection terminates abnormally like this, or any other way,

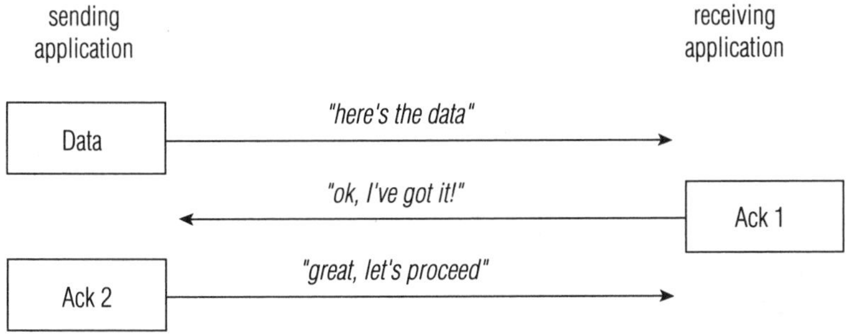

Figure 14-4 Illustrates three-way handshake between two applications as they synchronize to verify data delivery.

there is no way for the sender to know what data the receiver actually got. The receiver may have read data and acknowledged it, but the sender never saw the acknowledgment. If an application was in the middle of a very large data transfer, it would be necessary to start again from the beginning, without knowing where you left off. If this were important data—like financial transactions, for example—not knowing which ones were actually received could be disastrous.

The only way for a sending application to know exactly what data has been read by the receiver is if you implement a session-layer protocol between the applications in which the receiver acknowledges receipt of data at regular intervals, and the sender acknowledges receipt of the acknowledgment. A "three-way handshake" like this is the only way to verify data receipt between two systems (see Figure 14-4).

This algorithm uses the reliability of TCP to guarantee delivery of the acknowledgments, as well as the data. Both ends will eventually detect a connection failure since they both will be doing network I/O. If the sender does not get an acknowledgment (ack1), it should assume the data since the previous "synch point" was lost (and save it). If the receiver does not get an acknowledgment (ack2), it should assume data since the previous synch point is incomplete (and discard it). When a new connection is established, the sending and receiving applications can pick up where they left off.

Datagram Algorithms

Datagram sockets are unreliable. The most significant implication of this unreliability is that the protocol stack is not obliged to report any error conditions when you use a datagram socket. There are fewer errors that can occur on a datagram socket, but there are some. Some WinSock implementations report errors, so you should be able to handle them gracefully. However, most WinSocks fail silently with datagram sockets.

For example, you may never know when

- The local system does not have network-system buffers available, so a `send( )` or `sendto( )` succeeds although the data is not sent.
- An intermediate router rejects the datagram and returns an ICMP destination unreachable error packet.
- The destination host drops an incoming datagram silently if there are no network-system buffers available to buffer data.
- A destination host returns an ICMP Port Unreachable error packet if no socket is listening on the destination port.

To adapt an application to datagram unreliability, you must provide reliability yourself. All the challenges you face relate to the lack of services in UDP, many of which TCP provides:

- implementing a timeout
- sequencing datagrams
- throttling sends
- synchronizing sender and receiver

Implementing a Timeout

In datagram applications that expect a response to a datagram, you need to implement a timeout period after which to give up or try again. In other words, when the response you expect within a reasonable time period does not arrive, your application must take appropriate action.

In UDP, the "reasonable time period" is a tricky call, just as it is in TCP. The biggest problem is adjusting your timeout period to the variable round-trip time that can occur on different media, and different routes between source and destination hosts, and how quickly the receiver responds (which can be affected by how busy it is at the time).

The easiest answer to this is to use the longest timeout value possible. This is your best strategy if you are sending only one or a few datagrams. However, there is always the danger you might pick a timeout period that is too short, in which case you will fail too soon. Be generous with the timeout period so your application can handle long delays that often occur over long distances or slow media (like serial lines or satellite links).

The more difficult strategy of implementing a timeout involves making the timeout period adaptive. This is essential, however, if your application retransmits data, and maintaining fast data throughput is important. You can derive a reasonable timeout by recording the response time from queries sent to the remote host, averaging a good number of them (the more, the better), and doubling it.

Sequencing Datagrams

Since IP can reroute datagrams, the datagrams may sometimes arrive in a different order than you sent them. Since they do not contain sequence numbers, you must provide sequence numbers in the datagram data if sequence is important to your application, or if you retransmit datagrams.

When the receiver detects an out-of-sequence datagram, the easiest thing to do is discard it. But if your application needs to preserve the data it receives, you need to reorder datagrams as they arrive. (Remember: datagrams often arrive in a different order than they were sent after traversing different routes through an internetwork.)

There are a few different ways to sequence incoming data: by datagram, by time, or by byte count. Sequencing by datagram or time is possible if you send fixed-length data, but messages that vary in size require sequencing by byte count. Even with fixed-length data, the main advantage to using byte count method of datagram sequencing is that it makes it easier to detect packet loss.

Throttling Sends

In many cases bulk data input occurs in spurts. UDP does not provide data acknowledgment or a window mechanism like TCP does, so it is possible to overrun the receiver's buffers—or any place along the route between hosts—and lose datagrams by sending too much data at one time. The sending application may also be using a high-bandwidth media or running on a fast machine with a fast network interface, whereas the receiver may be on a slower link or slower machine. To avoid overflowing the receiver's buffers, the sender should be aware of the application's buffering capacity and assume the media link is low bandwidth. In other words, code for the worst case scenario.

Synchronizing Sender and Receiver

Applications that send and receive real-time data can get out of synch with each other due to inconsistent network delays. The sender may send well-spaced datagrams, but network anomalies can delay some datagrams and result in datagrams being "bunched up" at the receiver. The simplest way to deal with this is to include timing information in each datagram. The receiver may also try to estimate the timing by averaging the arrival rate of incoming packets. The problem with averaging is that an accurate calculation must account for packet loss.

Good-News Code

*Good-news code** assumes that all news will be good news. Good-news code does not check the return value from function calls, because it assumes that success and failure are absolutes. It does not display error messages or let users cancel when they want to. Good-news code is eternally optimistic. Good-news code is bad news.

* Michael S. Greenberg deserves credit for originating the concept of "Good News Code".

Optimism is a good thing, but not when it's blind. The primary directive burned into every computer programmer's brain should be "*don't assume anything*." Assumption is the root of all application bugs. The robustness principle is as relevant to WinSock applications as they "talk" to the WinSock API as it is to WinSock implementations as they talk to other protocol stacks. Once again the robustness maxim applies and is worth repeating:

Be conservative in what you do, be liberal in what you accept from others.[2]

Well-adjusted code hopes for the best but expects the worst. This cautious attitude and thorough testing produce applications that work well when things go right and do not stumble and choke when things go wrong. Writing such robust network applications is not difficult, but it does take extra effort. The short-term pain the effort inflicts is nothing compared to the long-term pain it can avoid. A stitch in time, saves nine. Trite but true.

Here is a summary of the requirements of any robust network application that also provides user friendliness (which translates into supportability for any application):

- check returns
- check for partial success
- expect any error at any time
- check for nonfatal errors
- handle errors gracefully
- tell the user everything
- leave an out
- do not ignore warnings

Check Returns

There are a few functions that cannot fail—like `htons( )` and its ilk, `WSAIsBlocking( )` and `WSAGetLastError( )`—but most functions are not infallible. Their return value indicates whether they succeed or fail, and you should *always* check it upon return from a function.

Again this should go without saying, but it *needs* to be said. Coding a return check and handling an error condition take extra effort, so it requires

[2] RFC 793, "Transmission Control Protocol." J. Postel.

discipline on the part of the application developer. But there is nothing else that does more to ensure a bug-free application.

Check for Partial Success

Checking return values from every function is essential, but it is just a first step an application should take after a function returns. Applications must also take the second step and qualify the success or failure. In some cases, functions can have partial successes, or nonfatal failures.

An example of a *partial success* is when an I/O function (`recv( )`, `send( )`, etc.) transfers *some* of the data requested, but *not all*. As we mention in Chapter 5, "Operation Modes," it is very common—especially, although not exclusively, on a nonblocking socket—for a `send( )` or `recv( )` function to transfer fewer bytes than the "length" parameter requested. In this case, an application should simply adjust the buffer pointer and length parameter and retry the operation.

Do not assume that all the data in the "length" parameter was transferred if an I/O operation did not fail. If your application requests the transfer of any value more than 1, you should check the return value to make sure that all the data was transferred.

Expect Any Error at Any Time

There is one word to describe when an application should expect errors: *always*. You need to code defensively to create a robust network application; to do so, *do not assume anything* at any time. Do not assume the only errors you will encounter are the ones listed with each function in the WinSock specification. Section 3.3.4, "Error Handling," in the v1.1 Windows Sockets specification warns against this:

> Note that this specification defines a recommended set of error codes, and lists the possible errors which may be returned as a result of each function. It may be the case in some implementations that other Windows Sockets error codes will be returned in addition to those listed, and applications should be prepared to handle errors other than those enumerated under each API description.

The specification is a common denominator among WinSock implementations. The errors it lists do not provide "fine resolution" in all cases, which means it does not account for certain conditions that some network-systems can detect. Finer resolution in error reporting is a double-edged sword: More accurate error values make it easier to diagnose problems when they occur but also more difficult to write an application that can handle all contingencies.

Check for Nonfatal Errors

A *nonfatal failure* occurs when a function fails of a temporary error condition. If a function fails, you need to check why it failed rather than assume that the failure should be fatal to the application. Check why it failed by retrieving and examining the error value that resulted from the failure (e.g., call `WSAGetLastError( )`).

The most common example of a nonfatal error is WSAEWOULDBLOCK. This error typically indicates a transient condition, so in effect it means "try again later." It can also mean that the requested operation is initiated but is not yet complete. If your application has a nonblocking socket, you should expect to see this error from any function that takes a socket as an input parameter. You should also expect it with the other WinSock functions (that do not take a socket as an input parameter) that have WSAEWOULDBLOCK listed as possible errors.

Similarly, in applications that use blocking sockets or blocking functions, WinSock function calls should be prepared to handle the nonfatal WSAEINPROGRESS error. This error indicates that a blocking operation is in progress. In effect, this also means to try again later, although you can handle it in other ways (e.g., cancelling the outstanding blocking operation).

See Appendix C, "Error Reference," for more information on functions and errors and how to retrieve and deal with them.

Handle Errors Gracefully

There are two basic kinds of errors: those an application *user* must remedy, and those an application *developer* must remedy (we have a list of each type in Appendix C). A user must fix errors that are due to network-system problems. A developer must fix errors that an application does not handle gracefully (e.g., those that needlessly cause the application to fail, or report a nonfatal error condition).

The user-fixable errors can result from misconfigurations of the local system, from anomalies on the network, or from problems on server systems. An application is not at fault for these errors, but it is responsible for reporting them to the application user.

An application developer must correct an application that cannot gracefully handle error conditions during execution. A user should never see an error value that is not user fixable. Error conditions are a frequent and normal part of network operation. Many errors are nonfatal or are so trivial they do not warrant an error display to the user interface. Application developers need to code defensively, so that their applications expect errors and can handle them appropriately. Networks are nasty places; only armored applications are happy applications.

Tell the User Everything

At a minimum, the error information your application reports to the user should include the name of the WinSock function that failed, the WinSock error number or manifest constant, and a short description of the error. It would also behoove you to make suggestions to the user, if there is any possibility the user can remedy the problem (we provide some of these to you in the detailed descriptions in Appendix C).

In our sample application in Chapter 7 we describe a common error value to a string function that you can use.

Leave an Out

Always leave some way for your application to exit in case an unexpected condition occurs. For example, you should always impose a limit on "for loops" and allow a manual (user-initiated) or timer-based break in "while loops" or blocking operations.

Although WSAEWOULDBLOCK errors often occur, and you should expect them, they can indicate a fatal error condition if you get too many of them. Blocking `recv( )` calls may never be satisfied, and since the WinSock API does not provide a timeout mechanism, you should consider implementing your own. At the very least, you should allow your application users to abort an operation if and when they think there is a problem. Users should never have to resort to using a "three-finger salute" (CTRL-ALT-DELETE) to kill an application that has encountered something unanticipated from which no escape is provided.

Do Not Ignore Warnings

This is another one of those things that should go without saying, but given the number of production applications that ignore this rule, *it needs to be said*. During development of an application you should eliminate all compiler warnings, or at the very least you should understand what they mean. A warning is an application bug waiting to occur. If you want your application to be extra robust, eliminate all the warnings with the compiler set to the highest warning level.

Common Traps and Pitfalls

Network application development provides many opportunities to make mistakes. In this section we spotlight some common traps and pitfalls and provide suggestions for avoiding them or recovering from them. We categorize the issues into the following application areas in which they occur:

- opening and naming a socket
- connecting
- listening and accepting
- sending and receiving
- closing a socket
- using host names and addresses
- using `WSAAsyncSelect( )`
- using blocking sockets
- exiting an application
- miscellaneous areas

Opening and Naming a Socket

- **Expect any handle value except INVALID_SOCKET:** You should never make any assumptions about the value of a socket handle returned from `socket( )`. The only guarantee is that it will not have the value of INVALID_SOCKET, so it could be zero and it could be a large value (any value that 16-bits or 32-bits can handle).
- **Expect the WSAEADDRINUSE error:** If your application is a server and is not causing this error itself, then your user is. This error usually means you are trying to run two versions of a server application on the machine at the same time. Do not assume you can prevent this from happening by simply limiting your application to one instance. There are other possible causes of this error. The user may be trying to run someone else's version of the same server application, or another application may have used the same port local number. It is also possible that some Windows problem could leave an orphan socket from a previous run of your application. If your application calls bind, you should prepare your application to encounter the WSAEADDRINUSE error. When this occurs in most applications, you should simply tell your user the error description and let him or her figure out which application is wrongly running the server.
- **Avoid the WSAEADDRINUSE error**: One way to avoid the WSAEADDRINUSE error is to set the SO_REUSEADDR option in your application. This is not a good idea, because it can have unexpected

results (e.g., you do not know which of the listening sockets will answer a connection request). It is rarely justifiable.

In server applications you cannot really (and will not want to) avoid the WSAEADDRINUSE error. Client applications are another story, however! Calling `bind( )` is what causes this error. Since very few client applications need to `bind( )` to a specific socket name, it is easy to avoid if you are writing a client application.

- **Avoid bind( ) in client applications:** As just stated, the WSAEADDRINUSE error is often encountered in client applications that call the `bind( )` function. There are a few application protocols that require clients to have source port numbers in specific ranges—like the UNIX remote shell and printing applications, `rsh` and `lpr`—but overall, specific local port numbers are rarely needed in client applications. If you do need to use `bind( )` with some specific port values in your client application, you probably want to use some randomize function to try to avoid port conflicts that can result in the WSAEADDRINUSE error.

Connecting

There are many reasons why a call to `connect( )` will fail, as evidenced by the many error codes the v1.1 specification lists for the function. Many of the errors are self-explanatory and commonly expected. A few of them seem to cause problems unnecessarily time and time again.

- **Expect the WSAEWOULDBLOCK error:** On a nonblocking socket, your application should expect the `connect( )` function to fail with the WSAEWOULDBLOCK error. How fast the stream connection completes or the fact that a socket might use a (connectionless) datagram protocol does not matter. A nonfatal WSAEWOULDBLOCK error should be expected and ignored.

  To detect a successful connection attempt, you need to prepare ahead of time or to check after the fact, depending on whether your application operates asynchronously or synchronously. For asynchronous operation, you would call `WSAAsyncSelect( )` before calling `connect( )` to register for FD_CONNECT. For synchronous operation, you would call `select( )` with the *writefds* and *exceptfds* input arguments set to detect completion of the connect operation on the socket(s) of interest, or you could simply use one of the I/O functions (`send( )` or `recv( )`). We discussed these options in detail in Chapter 6, "Socket States."

- **Do not loop on connect( ) to detect connection completion**: As we also described in Chapter 6, "Socket States," you cannot count on specific error values to indicate operation success or completion. Some WinSocks do not allow more than one call to `connect( )`, so all calls after the first fail with WSAEINVAL.
- **Avoid the WSAEISCONN error on UDP sockets:** In Berkeley Sockets, you need to disconnect a UDP socket by calling `connect( )` with the address family (AF_INET), port 0, and an invalid IP address (0.0.0.0) before you can call `connect( )` to "reconnect" the socket to another address and/or port. The WinSock specification does not specifically state this requirement, and not all Windows Sockets implementations enforce it, but because BSD compliance is (at least) optional, you should disconnect a UDP socket before you try to reconnect to another socket to avoid failing with the WSAEISCONN error.

Listening and Accepting

There are a few ways to go astray as you accept connection requests or prepare to accept them. The bad news is that both of the functions involved — `listen( )` and `accept( )`—can pose problems. The good news is that there are ways to deal with any of these problems.

- **Do not expect listen( )'s backlog to limit simultaneous connections:** The meaning of the backlog input parameter for the `listen( )` function is often confused. It does not limit the number of simultaneous connections an application can have. Rather, it simply limits the number of *pending* connections a listening socket can have. In other words, it determines the maximum number of back-to-back calls to `accept( )` that could possibly succeed without any new connection requests having arrived.

  If you want to limit your server to handle a certain number of connections at any one time, and to reject all connection attempts while it handles those, you must close the listening socket. Then, when you are ready to accept new connections, you can get a new socket and call `bind( )` and `listen( )` again.
- **Expect accept( ) to fail:** The `accept( )` function could fail even if you have a pending connection. Any of the errors WSAEMFILE, WSAENOBUFS, or even WSAEWOULDBLOCK could occur after FD_ACCEPT notification or after `select( )` *writefds* indicated `accept( )` should succeed. This is unlikely but possible, so your application should be prepared to handle it.

- The best thing to do is either to set some internal application state so that you can retry the operation later (perhaps when you close one of the other sockets) or to use a timer to retry the operation again later. You should not have to abort the application; that would be undesirable since other sockets may be connected and functioning perfectly well.

Sending and Receiving

Sending and receiving data is the raison d'être for network applications. If they fail at that, then they obviously have a serious problem. It's amazing, but easy to see why, so many network applications have such serious problems. Luckily, the problems are easy to avoid.

- **Always check the number of bytes transferred:** We described this problem earlier, under the rule *"Qualify success and failure!"* but it occurs so frequently that it's worth mentioning again. Without question, the most common problem among network applications is (apparent) loss of data, or data corruption. Either of these problems results from wrongly assuming that the number of bytes requested in an I/O function (send or receive) is the number of bytes actually transferred if the function returns without an error.

  After any successful call to `send( )`, `sendto( )`, `recv( )`, or `recvfrom( )`, you should check the return value to see if it is what you expected (e.g., equal to the "length" parameter). If not, adjust both the "length" amount and the pointer into your buffer, and recall the I/O function.

- **Always read before you write:** If your application sends and receives data, you should always try to clear the buffers by calling `recv( )` or `recvfrom( )` before you attempt to send data if there is any chance of pending data. In a worst-case scenario, trying to send without clearing system buffers can result in a buffer deadlock. At a minimum trying to send without clearing system buffers can decrease data throughput by wasting valuable system buffer space.

- **Do not assume send success means data was sent:** When `send( )` or `sendto( )` succeeds, this means the network-system copied the data from the application buffers into the network-system buffers. It does *not* mean that the receiver has acknowledged the data (on the receiving end), or that the stack has even sent the data. See the "Stream Algorithms" section earlier in this chapter for more information.

- **Never lie about buffer length:** The *len* parameter for `recv()` and `recvfrom()` is literally the length of the buffer pointed to by the *buf* parameter. Do not ask for more data than you can possibly buffer, even if you know you will not receive more than you can handle. Some WinSock implementations will check that all buffer space is writable, so your `recv()` or `recvfrom()` will fail unexpectedly. It is not clear what error will be returned in this case. WSAEFAULT is the standard BSD derivative to indicate an invalid pointer, but WSAEINVAL is the standard for a invalid parameter. However, neither of these is listed in the v1.1 specification for `recv()` or `recvfrom()`.

- **Never pass a NULL pointer:** The WinSock specification does not require WinSock implementations to validate buffer space, and many do not. If you inadvertently pass a bogus pointer, you are likely to cause a protection fault in the WinSock DLL.

- **Read data as it arrives:** Do not use the system buffers as your own by waiting until you have a certain amount of data to read before reading it. Always read data into your own buffers as it arrives. Stream connections do not preserve packet boundaries, and you should not try to make them do it artificially. If violating the spirit of data streams is not enough to encourage you to do the right thing, consider that your data throughput can suffer if you do not read data as it arrives, and you can cause buffer starvation of other applications or of other sockets in your application.

- **Avoid WSAEMSGSIZE:** Stream sockets give you as much data as you have space for in your buffer, even if more data is pending. However, because datagram sockets preserve packet boundaries, they give you precisely as much data as you have specified (i.e., the buffer "length" you specify on a `recv()` or `recvfrom()`). If you do not provide enough buffer space for a pending message, then a call to `recv()` or `recvfrom()` will fail with the WSAEMSGSIZE error.

  Typically, it is very easy to avoid this error, since you usually know the maximum size of any datagram you are likely to receive. For the unlikely application where you could receive datagrams of any (unknown) size, the best thing to do is prepare for the worst by calling `getsockopt()` SO_RCVBUF to get the maximum datagram size the WinSock implementation can handle. Otherwise, you could simply allocate the largest sized buffer you are willing to handle.

- **Expect WSAEWOULDBLOCK *anytime*:** Even after you get proof positive there is data pending to read (i.e., FD_READ notification, or `recv()` with MSG_PEEK succeeds, or `ioctlsocket()` FIONREAD succeeds, or `select( )` *readfds* is set), a receive call can still fail with WSAEWOULDBLOCK. Be prepared to handle the error.

Closing a Socket

Many potential problems are associated with closing a socket. The close operation on a stream socket involves closing the virtual circuit as well as freeing the socket resources, so it's no surprise that most closing problems occur with stream sockets. Most of these problems can be avoided by applying the "divide-and-conquer" strategy to the closing procedure. In other words, you need to handle the close of the virtual circuit separately from the close of the socket. Here is how to accomplish that. (Note: This is the algorithm we use in the `CloseConn( )` function in our sample WinSockx library described in Chapter 7.)

How to close a stream connection gracefully:

1. Continue to send data until you are done sending.
2. Call `shutdown( )` with *how=1* to notify your peer that you are done sending.
3. Loop on `recv( )` until it returns zero (to indicate EOF) or fails with any error. Note: If you are registered for FD_READ asynch notification, this loop could generate extra FD_READ messages if there is still data to read. There are different ways to deal with these, but the easiest is simply to set an application or socket state flag so you ignore them when they arrive.
4. You can call `setsockopt( )` SO_LINGER if you want to set a timeout on the close (or set it to zero if you want to abort the connection).
5. Call `closesocket( )`.

Actually, the close procedure listed here is not just for use when an FD_CLOSE notification message arrives—it is universally applicable. Whenever you finish sending in a stream connection (step 1), you can use steps 2 through 5 to close the connection.

Using Host Names and Addresses

- **Always copy results from gethostbyname( ) immediately:** The system buffer pointed to by the return from this and other synchronous database functions is liable to change if other Windows Sockets applications are running simultaneously. You should copy the contents from the buffer immediately upon return from the function.

- **Expect gethostname( ) to return a NULL string:** The WinSock specification does not mandate that a local host must have a host name. As a result, some hosts can potentially return a NULL string from a call to `gethostname( )` to get the local host name, since there may not be one assigned. This is not surprising if you consider the fact that many hosts on the Internet do not have (consistent) identities, as they might be dialing into PPP connections, where their identity (IP address) changes with each call. Be prepared to handle it.

Using WSAAsyncSelect

Nothing in the WinSock API inspires such fear and loathing through misunderstanding as the `WSAAsyncSelect( )` function. It is really not so mysterious and problematic once you get to know it. The best way to get to know this beast's friendly side is simply to avoid its nasty side. Here's what you want to do:

- **Expect extra FD_READ messages after the recv( ) loop call:** If you have registered for FD_READ notification, then every time you call `recv( )` with data pending, the WinSock DLL will post an FD_READ message to your application. This means it posts messages even if you do not read the data (i.e., you "peek" at it).
- **Avoid calling recv(MSG_PEEK) in response to FD_READ**: It generates an extra FD_READ message, and the operation is redundant anyway (since you already know data is waiting to be read). These things generate unnecessary system overhead and slow down your application. In any case, you should not be trying to check for a certain amount of data, since TCP sockets are data streams (where packet boundaries are not preserved). And you should not try to use them as your own (which could cause buffer starvation for other sockets). Just read data into your own (application) buffers. It will clear the stack buffers and reduce system overhead, and you can parse the data just as well there.
- **Expect data pending even after FD_CLOSE message has been received:** Receipt of an FD_CLOSE event notification message means that a close request has been received from the remote host (the peer to which that socket is connected). The WinSock DLL posts an FD_CLOSE message when the close request arrives from the remote host, regardless of the current state of the local socket. You should always check for data pending before you close a socket in response to an FD_CLOSE message. See the next pointer for the best way to close a connection.
- **Expect FD_CLOSE message to arrive early**: The arrival of an FD_CLOSE message is in effect a message from the connected peer saying it

has finished sending data. This does not mean your application has necessarily read all the data yet (as we just mentioned), nor does it mean that you need to stop sending yet. You can continue to send data, even after receiving an FD_CLOSE notification message. With all this in mind, here's a sketch of what you should do to close a connection: When an FD_CLOSE message arrives, you should set a state flag in your application to indicate that you need to close the connection. Then use the five-step procedure described earlier to close the connection gracefully.

- **Always yield during bulk data transfers:** Even though the `WSAAsyncSelect( )` asynchronous notification mechanism uses Windows messaging to keep data moving during a send or receive, an application can still effectively lockup the nonpreemptive 16-bit Windows system. As a result, you should still have a call to a blocking hooklike function (one that yields and handles messages properly by calling `PeekMessage( )`, `DispatchMessage( )`, and `TranslateMessage( )`) in your send and receive routines. Be careful to prevent nesting, which can occur if you try processing one of your own messages when you yield.
- **Avoid calling WSAAsyncSelect( ) frequently:** One common misconception is that an application needs to call `WSAAsyncSelect( )` each time it receives an FD_ asynch notification message. Such explicit reenabling of event notification is not necessary. Your application reenables the asynch notification mechanism implicitly by calling an event's respective reenabling routine (e.g., calling `recv( )` or `recvfrom( )` after you receive an FD_READ message will reenable FD_READ notification).
- **Always call reenabling function whenever notification received:** Each FD_ asynch notification message can contain an error. Some of these errors are nonfatal, so you should not assume the socket is not usable whenever an error is received (e.g., if you use a datagram socket to `sendto( )` many different hosts, you might receive WSAENETUNREACH or WSAECONNRESET errors from some). You should still call the reenabling function to ensure further notification (which may or may not fail with the same error, or another different error).
- **Avoid calling WSAGetLastError( ) when message contains error:** The return value from `WSAGetLastError( )` may or may not be the same as the error contained in an asynchronous notification message, depending on what transpired on the socket in the meantime. As indicated by the previous description, in most cases you should handle messages that contain errors in a somewhat normal fashion after handling the error condition (i.e., call the reenabling function).

- **Expect messages after WSAAsyncSelect( ) called to cancel:** If you call `WSAAsyncSelect( )` with no events selected (i.e., 0 for "event" parameter), this cancels the asynchronous notification. However, there could be notification messages in your application's message queue already that have yet to be processed by your window procedure. You need to be ready to handle them when they arrive.

  The best way for an application to be prepared if you do not want to service an event message after cancellation is to keep some application state. If you set an application internal flag that in effect says "ignore async messages" when you call `WSAAsyncSelect( )` to cancel notification, you can check the application state flags before you service messages that arrive.

- **Expect messages after closesocket( ) call:** Just as you can still receive messages after you cancelled asynch notification any messages still remain in your message queue, you can also receive messages after `closesocket( )` (see previous description for more information).

Using Blocking Sockets

- **Expect reentrant messages:** And do not try to prevent them. One fact of life in 16-bit Windows is that an application can get a "reentrant" message while waiting for a blocking operation to complete. You cannot prevent this by using `WSASetBlockingHook( )` to install a blocking hook function that does not yield (i.e., that does not call `PeekMessage( )`). This will cause your application to fail on some WinSock implementations (the blocking operations will never complete). See comments below describing how to handle reentrant messages.

- **Avoid returning TRUE all the time:** As described in the v1.1 WinSock specification in the documentation for `WSASetBlockingHook( )`, the return of a blocking hook function is a Boolean value that is supposed to indicate whether there is a message to process. If your blocking hook function returns TRUE all the time, it can cause some WinSock implementations to continue calling your blocking hook function endlessly.

- **Always export your blocking hook function:** Be sure to export your blocking hook function, or your application may cause a GPF in the WinSock DLL when it calls your blocking hook function.

- **Expect blocking hook no-op in 32-bit Windows:** Do not expect the blocking hook function to be called; it's a nonoperation. Blocking operations do not call a blocking hook function, even if you call `WSASetBlockingHook( )` to install your own.

- **Expect the WSAEINPROGRESS error:** If you have a blocking socket, or call any of the blocking functions, then you should handle the WSAEINPROGRESS error throughout your application. Actually, you can usually avoid the error if your application does not respond to asynchronous events (e.g., a user menu selection, or data arrival, etc.) by blindly making WinSock function calls. If instead you call `WSAIsBlocking( )` to check for outstanding blocking operations, or if you keep track of the socket state in your application, you are less likely to make inappropriate WinSock function calls.
- However, despite any precautions, if you do any blocking operations, at some time or other your WinSock functions are likely to fail with WSAEINPROGRESS. This error is easy to handle, since it is nonfatal. You can choose to simply ignore it or to queue the request (by saving it in some socket state you maintain in your application). You could also warn the user that the requested operation could not be performed and ask if he or she would like to cancel it, or go ahead and cancel it on the assumption that the user does want to cancel it (e.g., when the user has asked to quit the application).
- **Always wait for the WSAEINTR error:** The `WSACancelBlockingCall()` function cancels any pending blocking operation, causing the blocking function to fail with WSAEINTR. As we describe in detail in Chapter 5, "Operation Modes," after you cancel a blocking operation by calling `WSACancelBlockingCall( )`—perhaps setting a state flag in your application to indicate the cancellation—*you need to wait for the blocking function to fail with the WSAEINTR error* before doing anything else.

  Any function that can block should handle the WSAEINTR error. The Windows Sockets specification warns that using `WSACancelBlockingCall( )` to cancel anything other than `accept( )` or `select( )` can leave a socket in an indeterminate state. For example, after a blocking `recv( )` call fails with WSAEINTR, the `WSAIsBlocking( )` function may still return TRUE.

  As a result, "the only operation that the application can depend on being able to perform on a socket is a call to `closesocket( )`." Furthermore, for maximum portability we recommend that you reset the connection after any function other than `accept( )` or `select( )` fails with WSAEINTR error, since the integrity of the stream may be compromised (which would make a graceful close of the connection impossible).

- **Avoid aborting stream connections:** TCP/IP systems are supposed to be able to handle an aborted connection (receipt of a TCP reset) without any problem, but some cannot. If that's not enough reason, you are much less likely to lose data at either end if you do not abort every connection. As a result, you should try to close gracefully when possible.

  It's easy enough to do since it is the default. Remember that SO_LINGER with 0 timeout sends a reset immediately. Also remember that a reset is sent when the SO_LINGER timeout period expires, so you should avoid setting short timeout periods, since these are likely to send a reset inadvertently on slow links (e.g., PPP or SLIP connections).

- **Expect the WSAEWOULDBLOCK error from closesocket( ) (SO_LINGER enabled):** After you call SO_LINGER to set a nonzero timeout value on a nonblocking socket, `closesocket( )` may fail with the WSAEWOULDBLOCK error (it blocks on a blocking socket until timeout or graceful close). When `closesocket( )` fails with the WSAEWOULDBLOCK, some WinSock implementations close the socket in the background, but *others do not*. As we described in Chapter 9, "Socket Information and Control," the best way to avoid this ambiguity is to avoid enabling SO_LINGER with a nonzero timeout on a nonblocking socket.

- **Always wait for close to complete before calling WSACleanup:** Another `closesocket( )` subtlety is the default behavior. Since SO_DONTLINGER is enabled by default, `closesocket( )` returns immediately whether you pass a blocking socket or a nonblocking socket. This means that if your application has not closed the socket prior to calling `closesocket( )`, your application may cause a connection reset if you call `WSACleanup( )` and exit the application too soon. There is no way to monitor how a close proceeds after you have called `closesocket( )`, since the socket is invalid and the WinSock DLL will not post any more asynchronous events. This is another important reason why you should use the recommended close procedure (with `shutdown( )` prior to `closesocket( )`). See the `CloseConn( )` function in the sample WinSockx library in Chapter 7 for an example.

Exiting an Application

- **Always call closesocket( ):** If your application calls `socket( )` and the function succeeds (i.e., does not return INVALID_SOCKET), then you must always call `closesocket( )` to close the socket before your application exits. It does not matter if any socket functions fail during program execution; the socket is not automatically closed by the WinSock implementation. Your application must call `closesocket( )` whether or not you have established a connection to a remote socket or a connection was aborted prematurely. Whether or not an association ever existed, you must call `closesocket( )` to release socket resources for reuse by the WinSock implementation.

- **Always call WSACleanup( ):** Every WinSock application is required to call `WSAStartup( )` at least once to register its task with the WinSock implementation before it calls any other Windows Sockets functions (or they will fail with the WSANOTINITIALISED error). Just as WinSock applications are required to close any socket they open, so must an application deregister any task it registers.

  An application is allowed to call `WSAStartup( )` any number of times, but for every successful call to `WSAStartup( )`, an application must also make a matching successful call to the `WSACleanup( )` function. Only the last `WSACleanup( )` function will deregister the task and return any allocated resources to the WinSock implementation (after which any other WinSock functions the application makes will again fail with WSANOTINITIALISED). See Chapter 10, "Support Routines," for more information.

- **Avoid calling WSACancelAsyncRequest( ) unnecessarily:** The `WSACancelAsyncRequest( )` function cancels an asynchronous operation initiated with one of the `WSAAsyncGetXByY( )` "database" functions. Note that `WSACancelAsyncRequest( )` is *not* necessary if you call `WSAAsyncSelect( )`, but only if you made a request to resolve a host, protocol, or service asynchronously and have not yet received a response.

- **Always wait after WSACancelBlockingCall( ):** Do not close a socket or call `WSACleanup( )` immediately after you call `WSACancelBlockingCall( )`. Instead, you should always wait until the cancelled blocking operation fails with WSAEINTR. Only then should you call `closesocket( )` and `WSACleanup( )`. (Note: We discuss this in a bit more detail above under "Always wait for the WSAEINTR error" pointer.)

Miscellaneous Areas

- **Expect WSAEINTR if you use WSACancelBlockingCall( ) anywhere:** If you call `WSACancelBlockingCall( )` anywhere in your application, then you should be prepared to handle the WSAEINTR error from any function call that initiates a blocking operation. Since the socket may be in an indeterminate state after a blocking call is cancelled, you may want to handle the WSAEINTR error after any function using a blocking socket by closing the socket.

- **Always convert to network order:** The contents of any WinSock structure are in network order, so you need to be sure to convert values before assigning them. For example, be sure to convert the value of the port number from host order to network order by using the `htons( )` function before you assign the value to the `sin_port` field of the `sockaddr_in` structure. Conversely, remember that structures filled in by WinSock functions will be in network order, so you should convert them to host order (e.g., with `ntohs( )`) before displaying them or using them locally.

- **bind( ) does not report socket name immediately:** It is possible for an application to call `bind( )` with INADDR_ANY for an address and/or 0 for a port number if the application wants the local network-system to select the appropriate interface (address) and/or port number (e.g., socket name). However, upon return from a successful call to `bind( )`, there is no guarantee that the `sockaddr_in` structure will not contain the local address and/or port number assigned by the system. To get this information, you need to call the `getsockname( )` function, although that also has limitations before a connection is established (see next note).

- **getsockname( ) does not report socket name without connection established:** Unless an application made a call to `bind( )` with a local interface address specified, the `getsockname( )` function may not reliably report the local IP address assigned by the network-system. To do so, an application needs to establish connection (i.e., with a call to `connect( )`, *not* `sendto( )` or `recvfrom( )`) to a remote socket. The only reliable way to get the local IP address before a socket is connected is by using the functions `gethostname( )` and `gethostbyname( )` (or `WSAAsyncGetHostByName( )`).

  Note that the specification does not say whether `getsockname( )` will fail to report the local port number assigned if an application calls `bind( )` with a port number 0 (so the system assigns the port number). It is probably safer (i.e., more portable between WinSock implementations) to assume that you *cannot* reliably retrieve the local port until a connection is established on the socket.

- **Do not call WSAGetLastError( ) after WSAStartup( ):** The `WSAStartup( )` function is the first function call a WinSock application must make to register its task with the WinSock implementation. Any other function call, such as `WSAGetLastError( )`, will fail with the WSANOTINITIALISED error until an application makes a successful call to `WSAStartup( )`. As a result, if `WSAStartup( )` fails, it returns the actual error value to describe its failure (it returns zero on success). Do not call `WSAGetLastError( )` if `WSAStartup( )` fails.

- **Avoid system modal boxes in asynch mode:** One of the major benefits of using asynchronous operation mode (`WSAAsyncSelect( )`) in your application is that you can do more multitasking in asynchronous mode than in synchronous mode (blocking or nonblocking). When your application is executing in synchronous mode, the `send( )` or `recv( )` loop is not executing when a window or dialog procedure is executing. However, this is not true in an asynchronous (message-driven) application. Windows and dialogs process asynchronous notification messages so you can send and receive as your user works in the foreground. However, system modal boxes are one significant exception to this. When system modal boxes are active, your application will not receive FD_ event notification messages.

15
Platforms

In This Chapter:

- The WOSA Network Model
- Thirty-two-bit WinSock
- Other Platforms

Sacred cows make great hamburgers.

Robert Reisner

They say "it takes money to make money." Similarly, it takes an installed base for an operating system to attract application developers. With estimates of about 100 million copies of Win 3.x, Windows for Workgroups, and Windows NT shipped by June of 1995, and 50 million copies of Windows 95 expected to ship within the first year. Microsoft Windows is rich and is getting richer. As a result, Windows has an impressive number and variety of applications written for it. This self-feeding popularity has had other interesting results as well.

In an effort to tap the large and diverse application base, vendors of other operating systems have created binary-compatible versions of the Microsoft Windows API for their systems. These Windows emulators allow users to run Windows applications on these other platforms without modification. Similarly, operating-system vendors have also created binary-compatible versions of the Windows Sockets API to make the many WinSock applications available also.

Microsoft has built bridges from Windows to other operating systems as well. The development of the "Windows Open Systems Architecture" (WOSA) includes Windows Sockets, among other APIs. WOSA appears to be Microsoft's embrace of open systems, although Microsoft still maintains proprietary APIs as well (even in WinSock).

In this chapter we describe how Windows Sockets fits into Microsoft's WOSA in terms of the OSI network reference model. We describe all the platforms on which Windows Sockets is now available (at least those we know about at this time). The other platforms we mention in this chapter provide a standard nonpreemptive 16-bit Windows emulation. All except for Windows NT and Windows 95.

Windows NT introduced the 32-bit Windows environment, and Windows 95 also supports it. They are preemptive operating systems, with threads and native support of 32-bit code. In addition to extending the Win16 API, they also extended their WinSock API. In this chapter we describe the additions they made, most of which version 2.0 of the Windows Sockets specification incorporates.

The WOSA Network Model

The Internet is the ultimate open system. Many say that open systems invite anarchy and point to the structure of the Internet as evidence. Ironically, although the Internet is unstructured to the point of anarchy, its success shows that open systems promote cooperative conformity. The Internet owes its success entirely to the open systems standards that define its communications protocols. Without these independent standards, the heterogeneous Internet system could never have evolved.

Surely, the desire to tap into the phenomenal growth of the Internet played a part in Microsoft's recognition of the natural advantages that open systems have over proprietary systems. Its development of WOSA is a manifestation of this recognition. There are nine APIs in three groups currently under the WOSA umbrella: Here's a quote from Microsoft's "WOSA Backgrounder," a white paper of sorts.

> Microsoft is committed to providing an open platform that delivers all the benefits of open systems. The specifications for all WOSA components have been developed through an open process in which independent software vendors and industry groups work together to create the best possible design. WOSA incorporates existing standards whenever available, and through the open process new groups have been formed to define standards where they are needed.[1]

The description of WOSA catalogs a long list of benefits, all of which WinSock can claim also. We mention many of these in Chapter 1, "Introduction to Windows Sockets." Windows Sockets is a significant part of the communications services component in WOSA. It is no accident that Microsoft representatives played a major role in the development of the Windows Sockets specification.

[1] "WOSA Backgrounder: Delivering Enterprise Services to the Windows-based Desktop," (c) 1992, 1993 Microsoft (from the Microsoft Development Library)

In parallel to the development of the WinSock specification, Microsoft developed its Windows Sockets APIs for WFW, and both 16-bit and 32-bit versions for Windows NT. Since then, it was added to Windows 95. Microsoft built upon the standard WinSock API to take advantage of new features in its new Windows versions. In particular, it created a 32-bit WinSock API (see Figure 15-1).

Thirty-two-bit WinSock

Windows Sockets is the predominant API for the Internet protocol suite (TCP/IP) in Windows NT. Streams and TLI are also available, but mainly for portability. Microsoft recommends the use of WinSock for TCP/IP network programming on Windows NT and has added support for other protocols to WinSock as well (namely AppleTalk, IPX/SPX, ISO TP4, and NetBEUI).

WinSock applications inherit some benefits from the improvements in Windows NT itself. Unlike its 16-bit predecessor, Windows NT is a preemptive operating system (more on this in a moment). NT also supports threading, 32-bit addressing, and a new 32-bit Windows API (Win32), all of which we discuss later in this chapter. Windows NT also has a new 32-bit Windows Sockets API. The 16-bit function prototypes and data types all look the same in the 32-bit API, but the integer and boolean data types are widened from 16 to 32 bits in size. The standard WINSOCK.H file is polymorphic, so the width of the parameters changes automatically in each environment.

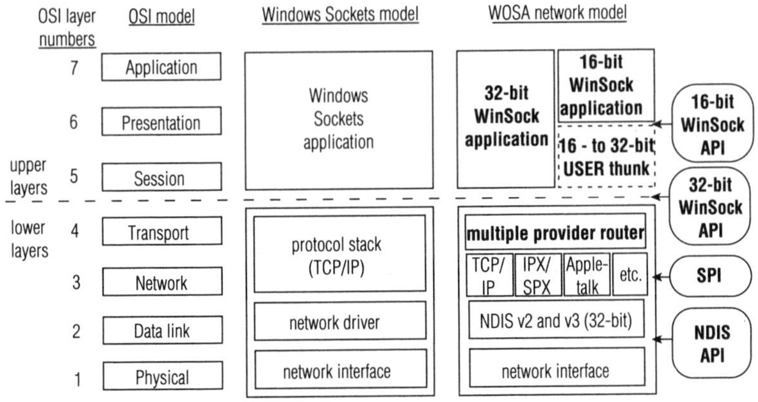

Figure 15-1 Windows Open Systems Architecture WinSock network model in 32-bit Windows showing multiple WinSocks implemented with Service Provider Interfaces (SPIs) under a common WinSock API.

It is possible to run 16-bit WinSock applications in the 32-bit Windows NT environment, however. In order for NT to support both 16-bit and 32-bit WinSock applications, NT has the 32-bit WinSock API in a separate DLL with a different name. This allows NT to provide two WinSock APIs simultaneously. The 32-bit WinSock is available from WSOCK32.DLL, and the 16-bit standard is (still) available from WINSOCK.DLL.

To create an application that uses the 32-bit Windows Sockets API, you need to

- `#include` the same WINSOCK.H file
- compile with a 32-bit compiler
- link with the wsock32.lib import library rather than winsock.lib (or explicitly load the wsock32.lib at run-time)

You can create a single source code version of your application that you can compile for either the 16-bit or 32-bit API. You need to write CPU integer size-independent code. This is not difficult, and because the rules are well documented in Win32 application development books and manuals, we will not repeat them here. All of the sample code in this book may be compiled with 16-bit or 32-bit compilers.

Windows 95

Almost everything we have said or will say about NT also holds true for Windows 95. We note exceptions where they occur. The most significant difference between NT's and 95's Windows Sockets implementations is completely transparent: The Windows 95 16-bit WinSock DLL does not thunk down to the 32-bit WSOCK32 as it does in Windows NT (hence the dotted box around the thunk layer in Figure 15-1).

Cross-Execution

The 32-bit WinSock API is also available for the 16-bit Windows environment. A WSOCK32.DLL ships with Win32s, the Win32 API emulator for 16-bit Windows. This provides a "thunk layer" that allows you to run 32-bit WinSock applications over a 16-bit WinSock DLL. The same limitations in effect 32-bit applications running over Win32s also hold true for 32-bit WinSock applications: Your application cannot use any 32-bit operating-system features that are unavailable in 16-bit Windows (like threading or security).

Thirty-two-bit WinSock Features

To take advantage of operating-system features in NT, the 32-bit WinSock includes new socket options. It also has some entirely new functions that provide for creation of UNIX-like network services (daemons) and for multiple protocol and name resolution support.

New Socket Options

Windows NT and Windows 95 support a number of new socket options that v1.1 of the Windows Socket specification does not include. The options we describe here are unique to Windows Sockets on Windows NT (and 95). Although WinNT and Win95 support the options relevant to multicast, we wait until Chapter 16, "Optional Features," to describe them since they are available on other WinSock implementations as well.

In addition to the `setsockopt()` and `getsockopt()` socket options we document here—**SO_OPENTYPE**, **SO_RCVTIMEO**, and **SO_SNDTIMEO**—NT's WINSOCK.H header file also contains a few other new additions that remain undocumented:

- **TCP_BSDURGENT:** a IPPROTO_TCP *level* option, to determine whether the TCP urgent data (i.e., "out-of-band data") offset should be interpreted RFC 1122 style or BSD style (we describe the differences in Chapter 6, "Socket States")
- **SO_MAXDG:** a SOL_SOCKET *level* option that apparently provides the opportunity to get and set the maximum datagram size (the optional SO_RCVBUF and SO_SNDBUF options are not supported)
- **SO_MAXPATHDG:** remains a mystery

SO_OPENTYPE

The `SO_OPEN_TYPE` option allows an application to open socket handles for nonoverlapped (synchronous) I/O.

Option name	*Data type*	*Default*	*getsockopt()*	*setsockopt()*	*Socket type*	*Special notes*
SO_OPENTYPE	int	0 (overlapped)	yes	yes	DG or DS	see text

Win32 enables new sockets for overlapped I/O by default. As a result, you can use the sockets for asynchronous I/O with `ReadFile()`, `WriteFile()`, and `WaitCommEvent()` functions, among others. However, because you cannot use C run-time libraries, or use the socket as a standard I/O handle on an overlapped socket, you may prefer to have nonoverlapped socket handles in many instances. You must use the SO_OPENTYPE option to request nonoverlapped sockets.

As we describe in Chapter 17, WinSock 2 includes overlapped I/O support. Unlike Win32, in WinSock 2 sockets are not enabled for overlapped I/O by default. You must call `WSASocket()` with the WSA_OVERLAPPED_FLAG set to get an overlapped I/O-capable socket handle.

Overlapped sockets provide a significant advantage over nonoverlapped sockets because they avoid an extra copy of data. The WinSock implementation copies the data directly to and from the application buffer, rather than using an intermediate system buffer. This can obviously offer performance advantages, but it does mean the application cannot disturb the buffer until the data transfer is complete (or cancelled). Overlapped sockets will be added to version 2.0 of the WinSock specification but without this option (there is a new `WSASocket()` function call, with a bit flag to request overlapped I/O).

There are some special things you should note about the SO_OPENTYPE option:

- The option is on a per-thread, not per socket, basis and it is preserved throughout the life of a thread (so you do not have to reset it before you get each socket).
- You must set it *before* you open any socket in a thread (`setsockopt()` ignores any value in the *socket*, so INVALID_SOCKET is the standard value to use).
- It affects socket handles generated by either `socket()` or `accept()`.
- Once it is set, you cannot use `WSAAsyncSelect()` (fails with WSAEINVAL) or the SO_RCVTIMEO or SO_SNDTIMEO option (`getsockopt()` or `setsockopt()` will fail with WSAENOPROTOOPT).

A number of option values are possible for the SO_OPENTYPE option. Either nonzero option causes a thread to generate sockets for nonoverlapped I/O. If you have a single thread with multiple sockets that require different settings, you should do a `getsockopt()` before you set the new option value, then call `setsockopt()` again afterward to reset the original value. It is possible to have a thread that uses both overlapped and nonoverlapped sockets simultaneously.

The valid values for *optval* are

- *zero:* sets the default option value (which requests overlapped I/O sockets)
- SO_SYNCHRONOUS_ALERT: requests nonoverlapped sockets and

allows operations performed on the socket handle to be alerted by an asynchronous procedure call (APC)

- SO_SYNCHRONOUS_NONALERT: requests nonoverlapped sockets and prevents APC delivery to a thread waiting on a socket I/O request

This code example shows a call to set SO_OPENTYPE on a thread; it changes the socket from the default of overlapped to nonoverlapped with no APC delivery:

```
int nOptVal = SO_SYNCHRONOUS_NONALERT;
int nRet;
...
nRet = setsockopt(INVALID_SOCKET, SOL_SOCKET, SO_OPENTYPE,
    (char FAR *)nOptVal, sizeof(int));
if (nRet == SOCKET_ERROR) {
    <report WinSock error>
} else {
    <call socket( ) to get non-overlapped socket>
}
```

SO_RCVTIMEO and SO_SNDTIMEO

The SO_RCVTIMEO and SO_SNDTIMEO options allow you to set the timeout value for receive or send operations, respectively (with `recv( )`, `recvfrom( )`, `send( )`, or `sendto( )`).

Option name	*Data type*	*Default*	*getsockopt( )*	*setsockopt( )*	*Socket type*	*Special notes*
SO_RCVTIMEO and SO_SNDTIMEO	int	0 (infinite timeout)	yes	yes	DG or DS	only available on overlapped sockets

The SO_RCVTIMEO and SO_SNDTIMEO timeout values offer a distinct performance advantage over the timeout mechanism available in the `select( )` function. They avoid kernel transitions and other overhead that the `select( )` function incurs, so you should use them instead of `select( )` when possible.

The *optval* parameter contains the timeout value, which is in units of milliseconds. The default timeout is none (zero), which means they will not time out (the timeout value is infinite). Any timeout value between 500 to 2,147,483,647 is valid (it's a signed 32-bit integer). WinSock accepts any value less than 500 ms as 500 ms. After you set a nonzero timeout value, any I/O function will fail with WSAETIMEDOUT when the requested I/O operation fails to complete within the timeout period.

Service Features

The Service Control Manager in 32-bit Windows provides a number of extended features for WinSock server applications. For instance, the Service Manager can allow your service to start up automatically when a client makes a connection request, and it will start up any dependent services as well. It also allows management of access control lists, which facilitate security.

In an effort to support multiple protocols and multiple service resolution mechanisms, Microsoft implemented the new RnR (Registration and Resolution) APIs. For instance, you can register your service with a number of different protocols and "name spaces." Microsoft also independently developed the "Service Registration and Resolution APIs" specification and implemented it in Version 3.5 Windows NT.

Version 2.0 of the WinSock specification incorporates APIs derived from version 1.0 of RnR. We describe the WinSock 2 version in Chapter 17. We will briefly describe the v1.0 RnR API here:

- **`CloseEnum( )`**: ends a network resource enumeration started by a call to the `OpenEnum( )` function, which you use to enumerate resources (like the service you could provide in a server application). This function is only relevant to services, not to protocols or resources.
- **`EnumProtocols( )`**: returns the number and types of protocols available from the WinSock implementation in the current system configuration.
- **`EnumResource( )`**: continues a network-resource enumeration started by the `OpenEnum( )` function.
- **`GetAddressByName( )`**: returns address information about a specific service. It is analogous to the current WinSock (and BSD 4.3 Sockets) `gethostbyname( )` but is a much richer and more powerful interface capable of working over multiple name services.
- **`GetNameByType( )`**: get a service name and information if you input a valid DCE (Distributed Computer Environment) service GUID (Globally Unique Identifier). Note: There are macros available for translation between standard TCP/IP service port numbers and GUIDs.
- **`GetService( )`**: get service description if you input a valid service name.

- `GetTypeByName( )`: get service type if you input a valid service name.
- `OpenEnum( )`: starts to return information about resources available. You can continue the enumeration with `EnumResource( )` and should complete the query by calling `CloseEnum( )`. The `OpenEnum( )` function builds on the existing Win32 `WNetOpenEnum( )` function. This function is relevant only to services, not to protocols or resources.
- `SetService( )`: registers or deregisters a service within one or more name spaces.

Other Protocol Suites

In 32-bit Windows, you can use the WinSock API to access protocol stacks other than the standard Internet protocol suite (TCP/IP). Although the v1.1 specification focuses on TCP/IP, WinSock is protocol independent like its Berkeley Sockets predecessor. Windows NT supports IPX/SPX, AppleTalk, ISO TP4, and NetBEUI with WinSock as well. A number of new header files contain the requisite address structures and socket types:

- ATALKWSH.H: AppleTalk
- WSHISOTP.H: ISO TP4
- WSIPX.H and WSNWLINK.H: IPX/SPX (generic and NT-specific)
- WSNETBS.H: NetBEUI (NetBIOS)

To provide for multiple WinSock implementations—each of which may support different protocol suites—Microsoft created a service provider interface (SPI) for stacks to "talk to." It documented this API—which amounts to an extension of WOSA—and pointed out some problematic areas. Microsoft presents this information in a surprisingly understated and short, unformatted text specification titled "Windows Sockets Transport Independence for Windows NT." It uses helper DLLs and the NT Registry to extend WOSA's Transport Device Interface (TDI), so they could map the Windows Sockets API onto it. (We illustrate this layer and its API in Figure 15-1.)

This multiple provider router architecture is essentially the same that version 2.0 of the Windows Sockets specification implements to support for multiple WinSock implementations simultaneously. In addition to protocol suites previously mentioned, Digital Equipment Corporation uses this architecture to provide a WinSock API for the DECNet protocol suite in its DEC Pathworks product for NT.

Thirty-two-bit Operating System Advantages

WinSock applications using the Win32 API can take advantage of a number of Win32 operating-system features that are not available in 16-bit Windows. As we describe in Chapter 12, "Porting from BSD Sockets," many of these features make it easier to port existing network application code from Berkeley Sockets to Windows Sockets. It can also make it easier for you to write an application from scratch for the NT environment. The only problem with creating an application that relies on these features, however, is that you may not be able to run your application in the 16-bit Windows environment.

Blocking Is Real!

Surely one of the most welcome benefits of preemptive multitasking that 32-bit Windows provides for Windows Sockets is that blocking is *real*. In other words, when you call a function like `connect()` with a blocking socket, your process does not yield to others in the system as you wait for the operation to complete. There is no need to, since the operating system automatically allocates processing time between different processes currently executing. Hence, there is no default blocking hook function that executes while a blocking operation pends, nor is there any chance of receiving reentrant messages.

This makes it possible to write simple network applications, but with this new feature comes some responsibility. You need to keep in mind that your process is *truly blocking*. By default, within a thread your users cannot interact with your application interface while the blocking operation is pending, so there is no way they can cancel a blocking operation. By utilizing separate threads for each blocking socket, you can overcome this limitation.

Although there is no default blocking hook function in 32-bit Windows, you *can* use `WSASetBlockingHook()` to install a blocking hook function of your own, and the WinSock will call it for you as a blocking operation pends. A blocking hook is another way to allow users to interact with an application while a blocking operation pends and allow them to cancel the blocking operation if they need to.

As we described earlier, you also have the option of setting a timeout on I/O operations with the SO_RCVTIMEO and SO_SNDTIMEO socket options (assuming you are using an overlapped socket).

Threading

In UNIX, many network applications spawn multiple processes, especially server applications. In 32-bit Windows (both WinNT and Win95), you can also create new processes, but threads are a preferred variation that is much less demanding of system resources. They have their limits, too, and excessive context switches between threads should be avoided, but they can greatly enhance performance in a network application if used properly. In using overlapped I/O, the operating system creates threads as required by the demands of pending I/O requests.

Sockets Are File Handles

As in BSD Sockets, WinNT and Win95 socket handles are equivalent to file handles. As a result, you can manipulate them in many ways that can provide some added flexibility to your network applications. For example, you can use `DuplicateHandle( )` on a socket handle so that one process can "share" the socket handle owned by another process.

Console Interface

It seems ironic that the same people who gave us Windows should herald the fact they provide a text-based console interface, but they do. Many of the Microsoft sample applications—in fact, all of their WinSock samples—use the text-based interface, rather than Windows. The reason is simple: They avoid the extra code that tends to distract from the central illustrative purpose of an application sample. It is also easier to write.

As a result, you can use the console to write quick-and-dirty test applications, just like in the days before Windows. You can even use the asynchronous operating mode by creating a message loop with `GetModuleHandle(NULL)` to get your HINSTANCE. This is very convenient when you want to test some network code and not bother with all the fancy trimmings. For that matter, even some finished applications—like servers—can do without a fancy graphical interface.

Other Platforms

As mentioned earlier, it's possible to run WinSock applications on operating platforms other than Microsoft's Windows 3.0 or 3.1, Windows for Workgroups, Windows NT, or Windows 95. To capitalize on the many Windows applications available, many operating-system vendors created Windows emulators that could run Windows applications. And with the advent of WinSock, they extended the emulators to provide Windows Sockets compatibility for the same reasons.

Sun Microsystem's WABI and OS/2 running Windows NextStep are just two of the systems that currently advertise WinSock availability for their

Microsoft Windows emulators. A number of operating systems have Windows emulation systems but do not yet have WinSock implementations. These include Linux, QNX, and SCO UNIX. Watch for more. Windows Sockets means portability: across stacks, across Windows systems, across operating systems, and provides for universal network applications.

16 Optional Features

When you are at sea, keep clear of the land.

Publilius Syrus

In This Chapter:

- Optional Standard Is an Oxymoron
- Should You Use Optional Features?
- Raw Sockets
- Multicast
- Loopback
- Sharing Sockets
- Optional Options
- Sockets as File Handles
- Expect Any Error Anywhere
- Other Optional Features

The primary goal of the Windows Sockets specification is to provide a single API across all TCP/IP protocol stacks. To this end, the many TCP/IP stack vendors who cooperated in its development agreed to compromise a few features that were not available from all TCP/IP stacks. Rather than leave some of these features out of the specification altogether, they made them optional. They defined the syntax and semantics for most of these optional features, but not for all of them.

Optional features were not always intentional, however. The v1.1 WinSock specification does not prescribe the proper API behavior for some circumstances, which leaves it open to interpretation. Fortunately, most of these ambiguities are corner cases that applications can usually avoid.

In this chapter we survey the optional features of the Windows Sockets API. We describe the options and, where possible, show you how to use them. As mentioned, many of these features are optional by intent, but we described others that were optional because of ambiguities in the specification. One of the features we described in detail—multicast—was not even considered at the time the specification was being created. Since that time, however, there has been more demand for a multicast API, and multicast support is now available in some WinSock implementations.

Optional Standard Is an Oxymoron

In an API specification as large as WinSock, which supports a protocol suite as rich and flexible as TCP/IP, with so many WinSock providers trying to agree on a single standard, it is difficult to satisfy everyone's requirements and limitations. In the name of progress, those involved must occasionally compromise by using words like "should" and "may" rather than "must" when describing the proper API and behavior. With these words, they introduce optional features.

Defining a specification involves making some features optional in order to satisfy the common denominator among WinSock providers. Allowing different behavior in a specification designed to describe *The Way* is indeed a contradiction, but it is a necessary evil that is executed in the name of the greater good. The main goal remains the focus: agreement on the core API, the one on which the majority of network applications will rely. Ultimately, those who use the specification—WinSock application developers and users—will determine how standard the optional features are.

Among the intentional options in the WinSock specification, the degree to which WinSock or other relevant standards describe the API and behavior can vary greatly. For example, the method and format of debug output from the SO_DEBUG option are completely arbitrary. By contrast, the use of raw sockets (SOCK_RAW socket type) for access to ICMP is well defined by Berkeley Sockets and RFC 1122, "Hosts Requirements."

In a large specification like WinSock, unintentional options—caused by ambiguities and omissions—are also inevitable. We describe the most prominent of these in this chapter, along with intentional options. We describe when, why, and how to use them.

Should You Use Optional Features?

The immediate answer to the question of whether or not you should use optional features is definitively *yes, you should!* (Just do not depend on them.) Most optional features can enhance the performance and capabilities of your application. However, your application should not fail if and when the optional features are not available. For example, you can generally get better bulk data throughput if you increase your input and output buffer sizes with SO_RCVBUF and SO_SNDBUF, respectively. However, your application should still be able to function with the default buffer sizes if your attempts to change the buffer sizes fail (with the WSAENOPROTOOPT or WSAEINVAL error).

You can (and should) avoid dependence on some optional features by redesigning your application. For example, you should not require a specific amount of receive buffer space for your application to function. The v1.1 WinSock specification does not require WinSocks to support the SO_RCVBUF socket option, so you may not be able to specify the system buffer space you get. For stream sockets, you can (and should) always allocate this buffer space in your application instead of relying on system buffers. For datagram sockets, you would have to redesign your application protocol to use smaller datagrams.

Of course, some applications cannot possibly function when a Windows Sockets implementation does not support a particular optional feature. For example, raw sockets support is essential to many network monitoring type applications that use ICMP pings.

Options to Avoid

You should avoid using options that do not have standard API and behavior definitions, such as sharing sockets. The v1.1 specification does not mention the possibility of sharing sockets between two different processes, so socket sharing is an optional feature by implication. (Note: WinSock 2 does provide a mechanism for socket sharing.) The problem is that each v1.1 WinSock implementation that allows sharing may have different requirements. The SO_DEBUG socket option is another optional feature without a description. The WinSock specification does not describe raw sockets or multicast support either, but fortunately we can refer to the de facto standards defined by Berkeley Sockets.

Using a proprietary API extension like socket sharing is a step backward. You limit your application and complicate it as well. The v1.1 WinSock does not define a standard way to identify individual WinSock implementations. There is no standards committee to assign specific manufacturer identifiers like the IEEE does for Ethernet and Token Ring network interface manufacturers. The `WSAData` structure returned by `WSAStartup()` provides a location for vendor-specific information but does not prescribe the format. (Note: As we describe in Chapter 17, WinSock 2 provides vendor-specific IDs and a different mechanism for their retrieval.)

In any case, the programming convenience of application reliance on optional features does not justify the incompatibility your application will suffer on different WinSock implementations. For instance, an application that uses socket sharing will not function on WinSocks that do not allow socket sharing, and may not function on different WinSocks that do allow it. Since it is possible to write any type of application without relying on proprietary features, we recommend that you avoid proprietary features altogether for the benefit of portability. After all, the main reason to use WinSock is to avoid proprietary APIs and take advantage of the standard.

Raw Sockets

SOCK_RAW is a type of socket that denotes a "raw socket" in the same way that SOCK_STREAM denotes a stream socket and SOCK_DGRAM denotes a datagram socket. It's a manifest constant (defined in WINSOCK.H) that you use as the value for the *type* parameter in the `socket()` function. As Section 2.6.10 of the v1.1 Windows Socket specification states, the support of SOCK_RAW is not mandated. However, it is encouraged, so many WinSock implementations do provide support (notable exceptions are the TCP/IP stacks from Microsoft).

Unfortunately, the WinSock specification does not describe the acceptable syntax. There are many variations of raw sockets, and they correspond to different levels of support. True raw sockets allow free reign of the network and transport protocol headers.

Fortunately, few applications need low-level raw sockets support. Most applications require the common variation that allows access to the ICMP protocol to provide the ping facility, and this is what most WinSock implementations provide. The Berkeley sockets API model for this "raw ICMP" API is well defined.

The ICMP ping Application

As we described in Chapter 13, "Debugging," the ICMP ping facility provides a way to reach out and gently touch another machine. All TCP/IP hosts are required to reply to an ICMP echo request. Sending an echo request and reading the echo reply is the simplest way to check IP connectivity between two network hosts, and by implication it can provide a surprising amount of other information.

The ICMP ping capability is essential for any network management application designed to run over WinSock, but many average applications can benefit also. By embedding ICMP ping, an application can perform simple diagnostics automatically. This can help application users and provide essential information to support personnel.

To create an ICMP ping application, a WinSock `socket()` function must support the "raw ICMP" socket type (*af*=AF_INET, *type*=SOCK_RAW, *protocol*=IPPROTO_ICMP). The following code example shows you how.

Code Example

The following code example illustrates the essentials that go into a ping application. There are a few things to notice in this example:

- You can use this code in any operation mode (blocking, nonblocking, or asynchronous).
- The ID and sequence numbers in the ICMP header (`nIcmpId` and `nIcmpSeq`) allow an application to match echo requests with replies. At least one WinSock implementation uses the ID field for their own, so we recommend using the sequence field for portability.
- You can expect the echo reply to contain a copy of the data you send.
- The syntax for sends and receives are asymmetric. As in Berkeley Sockets, you provide the ICMP header and data when you send, but when you receive you get the IP header as well as the ICMP header and data.
- In implementations that support the IP_TTL socket option (which we describe next), you could alter the IP time to live before sending the ICMP echo and read the destination address from the ICMP error packet response and trace the route of the datagram.

```
/* ICMP types */
#define ICMP_ECHOREPLY  0    /* ICMP type: echo reply */
#define ICMP_ECHOREQ    8    /* ICMP type: echo request */

/* definition of ICMP header as per RFC 792 */
typedef struct icmp_hdr {
      u_char   icmp_type;    /* type of message */
      u_char   icmp_code;    /* type sub code */
      u_short  icmp_cksum;   /* one's complement cksum */
      u_short  icmp_id;      /* identifier */
      u_short  icmp_seq;     /* sequence number */
      char  icmp_data[1];    /* data */
} ICMP_HDR, *PICMPHDR, FAR *LPICMPHDR;
#define ICMP_HDR_LEN  sizeof(ICMP_HDR)

/* definition of IP header version 4 as per RFC 791 */
#define     IPVERSION   4
typedef struct ip_hdr {
      u_char      ip_hl;      /* header length */
      u_char      ip_v;       /* version */
      u_char      ip_tos;     /* type of service */
      short       ip_len;     /* total length */
      u_short     ip_id;      /* identification */
      short       ip_off;     /* fragment offset field */
```

```
      u_char      ip_ttl;      /* time to live */
      u_char      ip_p;        /* protocol */
      u_short     ip_cksum;    /* checksum */
      struct      in_addr ip_src;    /* source address */
      struct      in_addr ip_dst;    /* destination address */
} IP_HDR, *PIP_HDR, *LPIP_HDR;
#define IP_HDR_LEN sizeof(IP_HDR)

#define PNGBUFSIZE 8192+ICMP_HDR_LEN+IP_HDR_LEN

/* external functions */
extern void  WSAErrMsg(LPSTR);

/* private data */
static ICMP_HDR FAR *lpIcmpHdr; /* pointers into our I/O buffer */
static IP_HDR    FAR *lpIpHdr;
static char achIOBuf[PNGBUFSIZE];
static SOCKADDR_IN stFromAddr;
static DWORD lCurrentTime, lRoundTripTime;

/*---------------------------------------------------------------
 * Function icmp_open()
 *
 * Description: opens an ICMP "raw" socket
SOCKET icmp_open(void) {
  SOCKET s;
  s = socket (AF_INET, SOCK_RAW, IPPROTO_ICMP);
  if (s == SOCKET_ERROR) {
    WSAErrMsg("socket(type=SOCK_RAW, protocol=IPPROTO_ICMP)");
    return (INVALID_SOCKET);
  }
  return (s);
} /* end icmp_open() */

/*---------------------------------------------------------------
 * Function: icmp_sendto()
 *
 * Description: Initializes an ICMP header, inserts the current
 *  time in the ICMP data and initializes the data, then sends
 *  the ICMP Echo Request to destination address.
 */
```

```
int icmp_sendto (SOCKET s,
    HWND hwnd,
    LPSOCKADDR_IN lpstToAddr,
    int nIcmpId,
    int nIcmpSeq,
    int nEchoDataLen) {
  int nAddrLen = sizeof(SOCKADDR_IN);
  int nRet;
  u_short i;
  char c;
  /*---------------------- init ICMP header ----------------------*/
  lpIcmpHdr = (ICMP_HDR FAR *)achIOBuf;
  lpIcmpHdr->icmp_type  = ICMP_ECHOREQ;
  lpIcmpHdr->icmp_code  = 0;
  lpIcmpHdr->icmp_cksum = 0;
  lpIcmpHdr->icmp_id = nIcmpId++;
  lpIcmpHdr->icmp_seq   = nIcmpSeq++;
  /*----------------------put data into packet----------------------
   * insert the current time, so we can calculate round-trip time
   *  upon receipt of echo reply (which will echo data we sent) */
  lCurrentTime = GetCurrentTime();
  _fmemcpy (&(achIOBuf[ICMP_HDR_LEN]),&lCurrentTime,sizeof(long));

  /* data length includes the time (but not icmp header) */
  c=' ';   /* first char: space, right after the time */
  for (i=ICMP_HDR_LEN+sizeof(long);
       ((i < (nEchoDataLen+ICMP_HDR_LEN)) && (i < PNGBUFSIZE));
       i++) {
    achIOBuf[i] = c;
    c++;
    if (c > '~')  /* go up to ASCII 126, then back to 32 */
      c= ' ';
  }
  /*----------------------assign ICMP checksum----------------------
   * ICMP checksum includes ICMP header and data, and assumes current
   *  checksum value of zero in header */
  lpIcmpHdr->icmp_cksum = cksum((u_short FAR *)lpIcmpHdr,
      nEchoDataLen+ICMP_HDR_LEN);

  /*---------------------send ICMP echo request--------------------*/
```

```
  nRet = sendto (s,          /* socket */
    (LPSTR)lpIcmpHdr,        /* buffer */
    nEchoDataLen+ICMP_HDR_LEN+sizeof(long),  /* length */
    0,                       /* flags */
    (LPSOCKADDR)lpstToAddr, /* destination */
    sizeof(SOCKADDR_IN));    /* address length */

  if (nRet == SOCKET_ERROR) {
    WSAErrMsg("sendto()");
  }
  return (nRet);
} /* end icmp_sendto() */

/*-----------------------------------------------------------------
 * Function: icmp_recvfrom()
 *
 * Description: Receive icmp echo reply, parse the reply packet
 *  to remove the send time from the ICMP data
 */
u_long icmp_recvfrom(SOCKET s,
    LPINT lpnIcmpId,
    LPINT lpnIcmpSeq,
    LPSOCKADDR_IN lpstFromAddr) {
  u_long lSendTime;
  int nAddrLen = sizeof(struct sockaddr_in);
  int nRet, i;

  /*--------------------receive ICMP echo reply--------------------*/
  stFromAddr.sin_family = AF_INET;
  stFromAddr.sin_addr.s_addr = INADDR_ANY; /* not used on input
  anyway */
  stFromAddr.sin_port = 0;   /* port not used in ICMP */
  nRet = recvfrom (s,              /* socket */
      (LPSTR)achIOBuf,             /* buffer */
      PNGBUFSIZE+ICMP_HDR_LEN+sizeof(long)+IP_HDR_LEN,  /* length */
      0,                           /* flags */
      (LPSOCKADDR)lpstFromAddr,    /* source */
      &nAddrLen);                  /* addrlen*/

  if (nRet == SOCKET_ERROR) {
    WSAErrMsg("recvfrom()");
```

```
  }
  /*---------------------- parse data ----------------------
   * remove the time from data for return.
   *  NOTE: the data received and sent may be asymmetric, as they
   *  are in Berkeley Sockets. As a result, we may receive
   *  the IP header, although we did not send it. This subtlety is
   *  not often implemented, so we do a quick check of the data
   *  received to see if it includes the IP header (we look for 0x45
   *  value in first byte of buffer to check if IP header present).
   */
  /* figure out the offset to data */
  if (achIOBuf[0] == 0x45) {  /* IP header present? */
    i = IP_HDR_LEN + ICMP_HDR_LEN;
    lpIcmpHdr = (LPICMPHDR) &(achIOBuf[IP_HDR_LEN]);
  } else {
    i = ICMP_HDR_LEN;
    lpIcmpHdr = (LPICMPHDR) achIOBuf;
  }

  /* pull out the ICMP ID and sequence numbers */
  *lpnIcmpId  = lpIcmpHdr->icmp_id;
  *lpnIcmpSeq = lpIcmpHdr->icmp_seq;

  /* remove the send time from the ICMP data */
  _fmemcpy (&lSendTime, (&achIOBuf[i]), sizeof(u_long));

  return (lSendTime);
} /* end icmp_recvfrom( ) */

/*-----------------------------------------------------------------
 * Function: cksum( )
 *
 * Description: Calculate Internet checksum for data buffer and
 *  length (one's complement sum of 16-bit words). Used in IP,
 *  ICMP, UDP, IGMP.
 */
u_short cksum (u_short FAR*lpBuf, int nLen) {
  register long lSum = 0L;  /* work variables */

  /* Note: To handle odd number of bytes, last (even) byte in
   *  buffer has a value of 0 (we assume that it does) */
```

```
  while (nLen > 0) {
    lSum += *(lpBuf++); /* add word value to sum */
    nLen -= 2;          /* decrement byte count by 2 */
  }
  /* put 32-bit sum into 16-bits */
  lSum = (lSum & 0xffff) + (lSum>>16);
  lSum += (lSum >> 16);

  /* return Internet checksum. Note: Integral type
   * conversion warning is expected here. It's ok. */
  return (~lSum);
} /* end cksum( ) */
```

IP_TTL traceroute

The traceroute utility reports the IP addresses of all router "hops" between you and a destination host. It uses the time-to-live (TTL) mechanism in the Internet Protocol (IP) to elicit a response from each intermediate router. All routers decrement the TTL in each IP header they receive, and they typically respond to a TTL of 0 by returning an ICMP "TTL exceeded" error packet to the sender. It can work with UDP or ICMP datagrams (see the illustration of this in Chapter 13, "Debugging").

Unfortunately, v1.1 of the WinSock specification does not provide API access to the contents of an IP header (like TTL). By the BSD de facto standard, access to the IP TTL field would require SOCK_RAW IPPROTO_IP support *or* the `setsockopt()` (*level*=IPPROTO_IP, *cmd*=IP_TTL) support.

Many WinSock-compliant TCP/IP implementations come with a traceroute utility. However, they access a proprietary API to provide this low-level IP header access. As a result, their traceroute application will not run over other WinSock implementations. Fortunately, WinSock version 2.0 prescribes support for the BSD-style IP_TTL option. The following code sample shows how to use it. Note: the value we use for IP_TTL is compatible with Berkeley sockets, however it conflicts with Steve Deering's multicast value (which we describe next). This macro value may change in WinSock version 2.0.

Code Example

```
#define IP_TTL    4    /* level=IPPROTO_IP option, time-to-live */
#define MAX_TTL  255   /* maximum IP time-to-live value */
/*
 * Function set_IP_TTL()
```

```
 *
 * Description: Attempts to set the IP time-to-live value using the
 *  IP_TTL socket option (which is rarely supported). This is necessary
 *  to implement a traceroute application.
 */
int set_ttl (SOCKET s, int nTimeToLive) {
  int nRet;
  nRet = setsockopt (s,
            IPPROTO_IP,
            IP_TTL,
            (LPSTR)&nTimeToLive,
            sizeof(int));
  if (nRet==SOCKET_ERROR) {
    WSAErrMsg("setsockopt(level=IPPROTO_IP, option=IP_TTL)");
  }
  return (nRet);
} /* end set_IP_TTL( ) */
```

Multicast

In RFC-1112, "Host Extensions for IP Multicasting," Steve Deering details the extensions that TCP/IP protocol stacks use to support multicasting (RFC-1122, "Hosts Requirements," has a few additions and clarifications). He describes the mechanics of multicast and focuses on the Internet Group Management Protocol (IGMP). The main purpose of IGMP is to allow IP hosts to report group memberships to any local "multicast routers" (routers that support IGMP). In effect, IGMP is the muscle behind multicast. By keeping routers informed about multicast hosts, it allows multicast datagrams to traverse an internetwork and reach many hosts simultaneously. The ability to traverse an internetwork and reach an unlimited number of "member" hosts simultaneously without affecting others adversely is the linchpin of multicast.

In an effort to create a multicast test bed despite the lack of multicast-capable routers on the Internet, the IETF established the multicast backbone (MBONE). The MBONE is a virtual network that allows multicast datagrams to traverse the Internet across nonmulticast routers in an IP "tunnel." A special router encapsulates multicast datagrams and sends them as unicast IP datagrams to other special routers, which deencapsulate them and send them on the local network as standard multicast datagrams. As demonstrated by the live MBONE multicast of the Rolling Stones rock concert on November 18, 1994, from Dallas, Texas, even this limited capability has impressive potential.

The video was choppy and the audio was low fidelity, but like early radio and TV broadcasts, it got everyone excited. It was a harbinger of what's to come.

A Class D IP address in the range 224.0.0.0 to 239.255.255.255 is a "multicast address." Each is also known as a "host group address," since datagrams with a multicast destination address can be received by all hosts that have joined the group that an address represents. The address 224.0.0.0 is reserved, and 224.0.0.1 is assigned to the permanent group of all IP hosts. The "Assigned Numbers" RFC publishes other permanent host group addresses.

A host with a TCP/IP stack must support IGMP to join a multicast group in order to receive multicast datagrams. Any host can send a multicast datagram without being a group member. Multicast datagrams can only traverse routers that are IGMP capable (i.e., multicast routers), unless "tunneled" as described earlier.

Why Use Multicast?

Multicast addresses provide limited broadcasting, but without the problems and limitations of traditional broadcasts. Since they do not use a broadcast hardware address, only those hosts that have joined a group "read" the packet off the net. As a result, multicast datagrams do not incur the extra overhead that traditional broadcast packets do.

Sending datagrams to a multicast address is analogous to transmitting radio signals on a particular frequency. Just as you must tune a radio receiver to the particular frequency to receive the radio signal, you must join a multicast group to receive the multicast packets. Unlike a radio transmission, however, you need not be in range to receive the signal. Provided the route between you and the sender has properly configured multicast routers (or MBONE), you can receive multicast datagrams from anywhere.

The downside of multicast is that multicast-capable routers are still relatively rare. And multicasts must be coordinated between networked hosts to avoid conflicts, make sure someone is listening, and conserve limited network bandwidth.

Multicast API

Steve Deering also wrote "IP Multicast Extensions for 4.3BSD and Related Systems" which describes the extensions to the Sockets API for support of multicasting. We will describe this API in the remainder of this section and show you how to use it. The v1.1 Windows Sockets specification does not reference any of this, and very few Windows Sockets implementations currently provide support, but there are bound to be more. Version 2.0 of the Windows Sockets specification includes this API.

The multicast API uses a number of new socket options. As with the other socket options we describe in Chapter 10, "Socket Information and Control," you set and retrieve the values for these options with `setsockopt()` and `getsockopt()`. The value of the `getsockopt()` and `setsockopt()` *level* parameter for all of these options is `IPPROTO_IP`. Only two of the five new options use an integer type for the option value. Two of them use a new multicast structure (`struct im_req`), and another uses an `in_addr` structure.

As with any option, if a WinSock implementation does not support it, the call to either `setsockopt()` or `getsockopt()` will fail with WSAENOPROTOOPT.

IP_ADD_MEMBERSHIP

The `IP_ADD_MEMBERSHIP` option allows you to join a multicast group specified by the host group address in the multicast address structure. You must join a group to receive multicast datagrams. You do not need to join a group to send multicast datagrams.

Option name	*Data type*	*Default*	*getsockopt()*	*setsockopt()*	*Socket type*	*Special notes*
IP_ADD_MEMBERSHIP	struct ip_mreq	<none>	no	yes	DG or RAW	level IPPROTO_IP

You can join multiple host groups on a single socket. The maximum number of memberships is typically 20, although this value may differ on different WinSock implementations. This value can also vary over a single WinSock implementation since (link-layer) network drivers have their own limits. You can also join the same host group address on multiple interfaces.

The multicast address structure is defined as follows:

```
struct ip_mreq {
      struct in_addr imr_multiaddr; /* multicast group to join */
      struct in_addr imr_interface; /* interface to join on */
}
```

imr_multiaddr: The multicast host group to join. By joining, you implicitly notify your local multicast router of your membership (the TCP/IP stack sends an IGMP), and you enable your local interface (network driver) to receive multicast datagrams destined for this multicast address.

imr_interface: This is the IP address of the local network interface on which you wish to receive multicast datagrams. Typically, you will specify INADDR_ANY for this value to use the default interface. You can specify any multicast-capable interface on your system.

You can have multiple sockets join the same group address on different ports. Be careful, though. You may run into problems if the underlying protocol stack does not use the multicast address along with the port number to demultiplex the packet at the UDP (transport) level.

It is also possible to have multiple sockets join the same or different groups on the *same* port number. To do so, you need to call `setsockopt( )` SO_REUSEADDR to allow duplicate socket names. However, the same caveats in the description of SO_REUSEADDR in Chapter 9 apply here. You need to be careful and test this over different WinSocks, since demultiplexing multicast data to multiple sockets can have varying results.

When successful, this option will cause your TCP/IP protocol stack to send an IGMP Host Membership Report to 224.0.0.1 (the "all-hosts" multicast group). See the "Multicast Mechanics" section later.

IP_DROP_MEMBERSHIP

The IP_DROP_MEMBERSHIP option allows you to drop the host membership in a multicast group.

Option name	*Data type*	*Default*	*getsockopt( )*	*setsockopt( )*	*Socket type*	*Special notes*
IP_DROP_ MEMBERSHIP	struct ip_mreq	<none>	no	yes	DG or RAW	level IPPROTO_IP

The underlying TCP/IP stack keeps a reference count of the number of requests to join a particular host group. When you set the IP_DROP_MEMBERSHIP option for a particular group, the underlying stack decrements the reference count by one. The stack sends notification to drop a multicast group membership to the (data-link) network driver only when the reference count is zero. This option does not generate any IGMP activity.

IP_MULTICAST_IF

The IP_MULTICAST_IF option allows you to specify a default local interface from which to send multicast packets. This option is relevant only on hosts with more than one interface.

Option name	Data type	Default	getsockopt()	setsockopt()	Socket type	Special notes
IP_ MULTICAST_IF	struct in_addr	FALSE	no	yes	DG or RAW	level IPPROTO_IP

All multicast-capable hosts must have a default multicast interface, so you are not required to use this option. You may override the default and IP_MULTICAST_IF selection by specifying an interface when you join a group (with `setsockopt()` IP_ADD_MEMBERSHIP).

IP_MULTICAST_LOOP

The IP_MULTICAST_LOOP option enables or disables the receipt of multicast packets you send to a multicast group you are a member of.

Option name	Data type	Default	getsockopt()	setsockopt()	Socket type	Special notes
IP_ MULTICAST_ LOOP	BOOL	TRUE	yes	yes	DG or RAW	level IPPROTO_IP

This option is enabled by default. In other words, by default you will get a copy of all multicast packets you send, from each of the interfaces that you have joined as a group member.

IP_MULTICAST_TTL

The IP_MULTICAST_TTL option allows you to change the IP "time-to-live" (TTL) value in the multicast packets you send. You need to use this option if you want to send multicast packets beyond the local network, since the default TTL for multicast packets is one.

Option name	Data type	Default	getsockopt()	setsockopt()	Socket type	Special notes
IP_ MULTICAST_ TTL	int	1	yes	yes	DG or RAW	level IPPROTO_IP

To send multicast packets beyond the local network, your local router and any other routers between you and the hosts you want to send to must be multicast capable (i.e., they must be "multicast routers," with support for IGMP).

You can check whether there are any host group members currently available, with an "expanding ring search." You start with a TTL value of zero and then larger TTL values for each subsequent send to the multicast address, until you get a response (the suggested TTL value sequence is 0, 1, 2, 4, 8, 16, 32). Eventually, you will elicit a response from one or more group members "listening" on the same UDP port number to which you are sending.

You can use any valid host group address as a destination address in an expanding ring search. You cannot use the "all-hosts" group (224.0.0.1), however, since multicast routers never forward packets destined for that group beyond the local network (this limitation is similar to the limitation on packets sent to the IP broadcast address).

Multicast Mechanics

You do not need to know a lot about the mechanics of multicast support since the WinSock API insulates you from the low-level details. But as with anything else, it helps to know something so that you know what to look for when you encounter problems. For the most part, you need a network analyzer to put this information to practical use, since it all has to do with the Internet Group Management Protocol (IGMP) that TCP/IP stacks use to provide multicast support. The following information is from RFC 1112, "Host Extensions for IP Multicasting," August 1989, by Steve Deering.

When a TCP/IP host starts, it sends a host membership report to the all-hosts group (224.0.0.1) from each network interfaces to notify the multicast routers. Every host remains a member of the all-hosts group for as long as the host is active.

When you join a specific multicast group with `setsockopt` (IPPROTO_IP, IP_ADD_MEMBERSHIP), your TCP/IP stack notifies the driver so it can create a hardware multicast address (for example, low-order 23-bits of multicast address become low-order 23-bits of Ethernet address). If this is the first membership request for this group, it also sends an IGMP "host membership report" packet immediately, then sends another at a random timeout period up to 10 seconds later to cover the possibility of the initial report's being lost or damaged (datagrams are unreliable, after all).

Multicast routers send IGMP "host membership queries" to the all-hosts group periodically to refresh their knowledge of memberships present on a particular network. If it does not receive any reports for a particular group after some number of queries, then the routers assume that that group has no local members and that they need not forward remotely originated multicasts for that group onto the local network.

When a host sees a "host membership query" (which only multicast routers send, never multicast hosts), it does not send reports immediately. Instead it starts a random delay timer for each of its group memberships on the network interface of the incoming query. When a timer expires, it sends the host membership report to the all-hosts address (so other hosts on the local net see it), but *only* if it has not seen a report for the same group from some other host. As a result, each host membership query typically generates only one report for each group present on a network. Multicast routers need not know which hosts belong to a group, only that (at least) one host belongs to a group on a particular network.

Hosts never send a host membership report for the all-hosts group in response to a host membership query, since the all-hosts group's membership is a given. A multicast host sends a host membership report for the all-hosts group only when it initializes each multicast interface at boot time.

Code Example

The following macros may already be defined in your WINSOCK.H file, and they may or may not be the same. Unfortunately, there is some confusion about the socket option values. The original values Steve Deering defined in his document "IP Multicast Extensions for 4.3BSD UNIX Related Systems (MULTICAST 1.2 Release)" had IP_MULTICAST_IF defined with a value of two. However, Berkeley Sockets already had the IPPROTO_IP level socket option of value two assigned to IP_TTL. There were other conflicts with other values, so Berkeley changed all the values by adding 7. The multicast socket options defined in the WINSOCK.H file that comes with the v3.5 Windows NT SDK have the original Steve Deering values (not the BSD-compatible values). WinSock version 2 will probably adopt the Berkeley values.

As mentioned, you can use any UDP socket to send to a multicast address. You do not need to use any of the multicast options. In addition to `sendto()` (which we use in this example), you could use `connect()` to set a default destination port and address and then `send()`. As always, if you use `connect()` and `send()`, you will need to call `connect()` again with the destination port and address both set to 0 to reset the socket before you can change the destination port and address.

```
#ifndef IP_MULTICAST_IF
/*
 * The following constants are taken from include/netinet/in.h
 *  in Berkeley Software Distribution version 4.4. Note that these
```

```
 *  values *DIFFER* from the original values defined by Steve
Deering
 *  as described in "IP Multicast Extensions for 4.3BSD UNIX
Related
 *  Systems (MULTICAST 1.2 Release)."  It describes the extensions
 *  to BSD, SunOS, and Ultrix to support multicasting, as specified
 *  by RFC 1112.
*/
#define IP_MULTICAST_IF    9   /* set/get IP multicast interface */
#define IP_MULTICAST_TTL   10  /* set/get IP multicast TTL */
#define IP_MULTICAST_LOOP  11  /* set/get IP multicast loopback */
#define IP_ADD_MEMBERSHIP  12  /* add  (set) IP group membership */
#define IP_DROP_MEMBERSHIP 13  /* drop (set) IP group membership */

#define IP_DEFAULT_MULTICAST_TTL       1
#define IP_DEFAULT_MULTICAST_LOOP      1
#define IP_MAX_MEMBERSHIPS             20

/* the structure used to add and drop multicast addresses */
typedef struct ip_mreq {
   struct in_addr imr_multiaddr; /* multicast group to join */
   struct in_addr imr_interface; /* interface to join on */
}IP_MREQ;
#endif
...
#define DESTINATION_MCAST"234.5.6.7"
#define DESTINATION_PORT 4567
...
int nRet, nSize, nOptVal;
SOCKET hSock;
achInBuf[BUFSIZE];
struct sockaddr_in stSourceAddr, stDestAddr;
u_short nSourcePort;
struct ip_mreq stIpMreq;
...
/* get a datagram (UDP) socket */
hSock = socket(PF_INET, SOCK_DGRAM, 0);
if (hSock == INVALID_SOCKET) {
  <notify user of WinSock error>
}
...
```

```
/*---------------------- to send ----------------------
/* Theoretically, you do not need any special preparation to
 *  send to a multicast address. However, you may want a few
 *  things to overcome the limits of the default behavior. */
...
/* init source address structure */
stSourceAddr.sin_family      = PF_INET;
stSourceAddr.sin_port        = htons(nSourcePort);
stSourceAddr.sin_addr.s_addr = INADDR_ANY;
/*
 * calling bind() is not required, but some implementations need it
 *  before you can reference any multicast socket options
 */
nRet = bind (hSock,
   (struct sockaddr FAR *)&stSourceAddr,
   sizeof(struct sockaddr));
if (nRet == SOCKET_ERROR) {
  <notify user of WinSock error>
}
...
/* disable loopback of multicast datagrams we send, since the
 *  default—according to Steve Deering—is to loopback all
 *  datagrams sent on any interface that is a member of the
 *  destination group address of that datagram */
nOptVal = FALSE;
nRet = setsockopt (hSock, IPPROTO_IP, IP_MULTICAST_LOOP,
   (char FAR *)nOptVal, sizeof(int));
if (nRet == SOCKET_ERROR) {
   /* Rather than notifying the user, we make note that this option
    *  failed. Some WinSocks do not support this option, and default
    *  with loopback disabled, so this failure is of no consequence.
    *  However, if we *do* get loop-backed data, we will know why. */
   bLoopFailed = TRUE;
}
...
/* increase the IP TTL from the default of 1 to 64, so our
 *  multicast datagrams can get off of the local network */
nOptVal = 64;
nRet = setsockopt (hSock, IPPROTO_IP, IP_MULTICAST_TTL,
     (char FAR *)nOptVal, sizeof(int));
if (nRet == SOCKET_ERROR) {
  <notify user of WinSock error>
}
...
```

```
/* initialize the destination address structure */
stDestAddr.sin_family         = PF_INET;
stDestAddr.sin_addr.s_addr    = inet_addr (DESTINATION_MCAST);
stDestAddr.sin_port           = htons (DESTINATION_PORT);
...
nRet = sendto (hSock, (char FAR *)achOutBuf,
   lstrlen(achOutBuf), 0,
   (struct sockaddr FAR *) &stDestAddr,
   sizeof(struct sockaddr));
if (nRet == SOCKET_ERROR) {
  <notify user of WinSock error>
}
...
/*----------------------- to receive -----------------------
 * register for FD_READ events (any operation mode will work, but
 *  we happened to use asynchronous mode in this example) */
nRet = WSAAsyncSelect (hSock, hwnd, WM_READ_DATA, FD_READ);
if (nRet == SOCKET_ERROR) {
  <notify user of WinSock error>
}
...
/* join the multicast group we want to receive datagrams from */
stIpMreq.imr_multiaddr.s_addr = DESTINATION_MCAST; /* group addr */
stIpMreq.imr_interface.s_addr = INADDR_ANY;        /* use default */
nRet = setsockopt (hSock, IPPROTO_IP, IP_ADD_MEMBERSHIP,
   (char FAR *)&stIpMreq, sizeof (struct ip_mreq));
if (nRet == SOCKET_ERROR) {
  <notify user of WinSock error>
}
...
/* multicast datagram receive routine from our window procedure */
case WM_READ_DATA:
   if (WSAGETSELECTERROR (lParam)) {
         <notify user of WinSock Error>
   }
   switch (WSAGETSELECTEVENT (lParam)) {
         case FD_READ:
               /* Recv the available data */
               nSize = sizeof(struct sockaddr);
               nRet = recvfrom (hSock, (char FAR *)achInBuf,
                     BUFSIZE, 0,
```

```
                (struct sockaddr *) &stSockAddr, &nSize);
            if (nRet == SOCKET_ERROR) {
                <notify user of WinSock error>
            }
            break;
    }
```

Loopback

Loopback is the ability to send data on a virtual circuit between two stream sockets or two datagram sockets in the same or different processes. One common use is for development and testing network applications, without a network (on a stand-alone computer). Another is to allow one application to access the services of another, even if it is located on the same machine. These expectations are perfectly reasonable, but the v1.1 Windows Sockets specification does not guarantee the availability of these capabilities (including 127.0.0.1, the de facto standard loopback address on TCP/IP hosts). Since 16-bit Windows is not a true multitasking environment, this is not really surprising.

Although a number of WinSock implementations can loop back successfully, to ensure compatibility with all WinSock implementations you should not design an application that depends on its availability.

Sharing Sockets

By "sharing sockets" we are talking about allowing two or more tasks to use a single socket handle. In other words, task A gets a socket descriptor from a successful call to `socket()`, and task B uses that descriptor in socket calls. The v1.1 WinSock spec does not say it's illegal, but it does not say that it's legal either, so you should not assume you can do it.

You might be tempted to do it if you wanted to create an application that spawned other applications. For example, an "inet daemon" in UNIX keeps sockets listening on different ports for various servers, and when a connection request comes in it spawns the application and hands off the connected socket.

As we described in Chapter 11, "DLLs over WinSock," socket sharing can simplify intermediate DLL design. Since DLLs do not have task ids of their own, they inherit the id of the task currently active. It would be convenient if a DLL could access a socket no matter which task was currently active (assuming the DLL made sure to call `WSAStartup()` to register the task with the WinSock DLL).

Is Socket Sharing Possible?

Some WinSock implementations allow socket sharing between any task that has successfully called `WSAStartup()` to register with the WinSock DLL. We call this implicit sharing, since it is automatic. The task that "owns" the socket—the active task when the socket was created—does not have to "export" it actively, nor do the other tasks need to "import" it either. Typically, the only limitation is that only the "owner" task can close the socket.

WinSock version 1.1 does not have a standard API for explicit socket sharing, but WinSock version 2.0 does. This new API is modeled after the BSD UNIX model and is currently supported in 32-bit WinSock. You share sockets explicitly by calling `DuplicateHandle()` (see Chapter 17 for more information).

The bottom line is that to ensure compatibility among 1.1 WinSock implementations, you should not attempt to share sockets between different applications.

Optional Options

A number of `setsockopt()` and `getsockopt()` options are optional. In some cases, Berkeley (or another) precedent defines their function well. However, in other cases, the precedent is either inadequate or is not well established. In Chapter 9, "Socket Information and Control," we describe all the socket options, including the optional ones in the v1.1 WinSock specification. They are SO_DEBUG, SO_DONTROUTE, SO_RCVBUF, and SO_SNDBUF.

The specification states that all Windows Sockets implementations should recognize all options and return plausible values for each. An implementation may silently ignore an optional option on `setsockopt()` and return a constant value for `getsockopt()`. The `getsockopt()` function may even return the value set by `setsockopt()`, without using the value at all. On some WinSock implementations that do not support the option named, `getsockopt()` or `setsockopt()` will fail with WSAENOPROTOOPT.

The Microsoft 32-bit Windows Sockets interface (WSOCK32.DLL) also has a number of options not found in the v1.1 Windows Sockets specification. The SO_SNDTIMEO and SO_RCVTIMEO options are compatible with their counterparts in Berkeley Sockets. The SO_OPENTYPE option is new to the Win32 API and deals with what Microsoft calls "overlapped I/O." We describe these options in detail in Chapter 15, "Platforms."

Sockets as File Handles

"In Berkeley Sockets, sockets are represented by standard file descriptors. While nothing in the Windows Sockets API prevents an implementation from using regular file handles to identify sockets, nothing requires it either."[1] In other words, you cannot assume that a socket is equivalent to a file handle.

In addition to causing the WinSock specification writers to rename the `close()` and `ioctl()` functions to `closesocket()` and `ioctlsocket()`, and avoiding support of `fcntl()`, `read()`, and `write()`, the fact that file handles and sockets are not required to be equivalent caused the authors to create the macros for access to the fd_set structures of the `select()` function. Related to the changes necessary in `select()` is the fact that—unlike with file handles—you can never make any assumptions about the value of a socket handle. We discuss this difference between sockets and file handles in detail in Chapter 12, "Porting from BSD Sockets."

Expect Any Error Anywhere

Note that this specification defines a recommended set of error codes, and lists the possible errors which may be returned as a result of each function. It may be the case in some implementations that other Windows Sockets error codes will be returned in addition to those listed, and applications should be prepared to handle errors other than those enumerated under each API description.[2]

In effect, this paragraph puts the onus of responsibility on applications. WinSock implementations are not relieved of responsibility entirely, since they must return the listed errors for the listed conditions. This quote states that implementations can return any other WinSock errors they want under any conditions not listed by the specification.

Each additional error is an optional feature. These are not bad, since they provide additional information that can help you debug a problem when it arises. They should not require any extra coding if your application is designed to handle errors properly. Unlike other optional features, you *must* be prepared to deal with these to ensure maximum portability for your application.

Other Optional Features

The most significant other optional feature is support of protocol suites—or in Sockets parlance, "domains"—other than TCP/IP (the Internet domain). Most significantly, the WinSock DLL for Windows NT provides support for AppleTalk, Novell IPX/SPX, ISO TP4, and NetBEUI. Version 2.0 of the Windows Sockets

[1] v1.1 Windows Sockets specification, Section 2.6.5.1, `close()` and `closesocket()`

[2] v1.1 Windows Sockets specification, Section 3.3.4, Error Handling, paragraph 3

specification endorses most of the NT APIs as the de facto standard for these protocol suites (see Chapters 15 and 17 for more information).

There are a number of other optional features throughout the v1.1 WinSock API. Most of the remainder result from ambiguities. For example, as mentioned in Chapter 6, "Socket States," the specification does not say you cannot use `select()` with NULL *readfds*, *writefds*, and *exceptfds* input arguments as a timer, but it does not say you can either. In this case, as with other similar cases, if the Windows Sockets specification does not specifically make a statement one way or the other, then you should assume the feature is not widely supported.

As we said earlier: You should use optional features when they are available, since they add value to the WinSock API. However, you should not design your applications to depend on them, since this will limit the number of WinSock implementations your application can use. Although with some optional features—like SOCK_RAW and multicast—you do not have much choice; the only way your application can work is if the WinSock implementation provides the optional feature support in the de facto standard fashion.

17 WinSock 2

As we acquire more knowledge, things do not become more comprehensible, but more mysterious.

Will Durant

In This Chapter:

- Do You Need WinSock 2?
- Overview of Features
- Multiple Protocol Support
- Overlapped I/O
- Scatter and Gather
- Quality of Service
- Socket Groups
- Multipoint and Multicast
- Conditional Acceptance
- Connect and Disconnect Data
- Socket Sharing
- Protocol-specific Additions

WinSock version 1.1 has met, if not exceeded, its authors' original intent to provide a powerful and flexible API for creating universal TCP/IP applications. You can create any type of client or server TCP/IP application with an implementation of Windows Sockets based on the version 1.1 Windows Sockets specification. You can port Berkeley Sockets applications and take advantage of the message-based Microsoft Windows programming environment and paradigm. But that's not to say that WinSock cannot provide more.

The authors of Windows Sockets version 1.1 intentionally limited its scope to expedite the process and ensure its success. WinSock 1.1 deals primarily with TCP/IP because the software vendors involved sold TCP/IP network software, but it also conveniently allowed them to ignore the difficult issue of how to provide a single API for multiple vendors simultaneously. This focus on TCP/IP did not preclude the possibility that WinSock—like its Berkeley Sockets Model—could support other protocol suites at some point in the future. The future is now.

Windows Sockets version 2.0 (WinSock 2) formalizes the API for a number of other protocol suites—DecNet, IPX/SPX, and OSI—and allows them to coexist simultaneously. WinSock 2 also adds substantial new functionality. Most importantly, it does all this and still retains full backward compatibility with the existing 1.1—some of which is clarified further—so all existing WinSock applications can continue to run without modification.

WinSock 2 goes beyond simply allowing the coexistence of multiple protocol stacks; it also allows the creation of applications that are network-protocol independent. A WinSock 2 application can transparently select a protocol based on its service needs. The application can adapt to differences in network names and addresses using the mechanisms WinSock 2 provides.

WinSock 2 also clarifies existing ambiguities in the 1.1 WinSock specification and adds new extensions that take advantage of operating-system features and enhance application performance and efficiency. Finally, WinSock 2 includes a number of new protocol-specific extensions. These extensions, such as the multicast socket options described in Chapter 16, are relegated to a separate annex, since the main WinSock 2 protocol specification is protocol-independent.

In this chapter we describe the major features of Windows Sockets version 2.0 and tell to some extent when and how to use them. We tell you about what to look for, and why you might want it, and we provide a brief sketch of how to use it. You will need to refer to the actual WinSock 2 specification for more details.

Do You Need WinSock 2?

If you have to ask whether you need WinSock 2 features, then the chances are good that you do not need them. As the saying goes: "If it (your application) isn't broken, then don't fix it."

Many of WinSock 2's new features are designed for cutting-edge network applications, not the average workhorse applications in existence today. WinSock 2 can improve performance and provide broader connectivity for common applications, but if your application runs well now and provides the connectivity you need, then you can benefit only incrementally. Since your 1.1-compatible application will run on any WinSock 2 installation without change, unless you see a distinct need for a WinSock 2 feature, then we recommend that you do not modify your existing applications.

WinSock 2 is a superset of the version 1.1 WinSock API. WinSock 2 implementations are guaranteed to be 100 percent backward compatible to WinSock version 1.1, with one exception. You can run WinSock 1.1 applications over a WinSock 2 implementation without changing a thing, unless your application uses blocking hooks. The familiar 16-bit WINSOCK.DLL and 32-bit WSOCK32.DLL are still available as a front end to WinSock 2 implementations, but if you use blocking hooks, you will need to rewrite your application so it will function without them.

Without changing any WinSock function calls in your existing source code, you can adapt your application to WinSock 2 by including the new **<winsock2.h>** header file and relinking with the new 32-bit WinSock 2 **WS2_-32.DLL** (a 16-bit WinSock 2 API is not available). To take full advantage of the many new WinSock 2 features—to provide protocol independence or enhance performance—you will have to make significant changes to most WinSock applications. If you do, we recommend you try to allow your application to "fall back" to use the v1.1 API if a WinSock 2 installation is not available. That way you can take advantage of WinSock 2 features but still allow execution over WinSock 1.1 installations.

Overview of Features

The list of new features in WinSock 2 is impressive. The new offerings vary widely, so they are difficult to summarize without simply listing them. Here are the categories we describe in this chapter, with short descriptions of each:

- *Multiple protocol support:* protocol independence to allow generic network services
- *Scatter and gather:* multiple buffers support for sends and receives
- *Overlapped I/O:* asynchronous I/O using event objects to enhance performance
- *Quality of service:* set flow specifications, and receive notification of changes
- *Socket groups:* group sockets by attribute, and assign priorities within the group
- *Multipoint and multicast:* selectively send data to multiple targets
- *Conditional acceptance:* examine attributes of a remote socket, and reject or accept the request before the connection completes at the transport level
- *Connect and disconnect data:* send and receive data outside the normal data channel during connection or disconnection exchange in some protocols
- *Socket sharing:* share sockets between one or more processes
- *Protocol-specific additions:* these vary

The version 2 WinSock API has almost twice as many functions as version 1.1. Many of these new functions are specific to the new features they support, but many others are primarily less protocol-specific versions of 1.1 APIs. Here is a brief list of the new functions that add support for new features to existing functions:

WinSock 1.1	*WinSock 2.0*	*Features added*
`accept()`	`WSAAccept()`	overlapped I/O
		conditional acceptance

		connect data quality of service socket groups
connect()	WSAConnect()	overlapped I/O connect data quality of service
htonl()	WSAHtonl()	protocol independence
htons()	WSAHtons()	protocol independence
inet_addr()	WSAAddressToString()	protocol independence
inet_ntoa()	WSAStringToAddress()	protocol independence
ioctlsocket()	WSAIoctl()	overlapped I/O quality of service socket groups multicast and multipoint *protocol-specific additions*
recv()	WSARecv()	overlapped I/O
recvfrom()	WSARecvFrom()	overlapped I/O
send()	WSASend()	overlapped I/O
sendto()	WSASendTo()	overlapped I/O
socket()	WSASocket()	protocol independence socket groups multicast and multipoint
WSAAsyncSelect()	WSALookupServiceBegin()	overlapped I/O socket groups quality of service
gethostbyname() getservbyname()	WSALookupServiceBegin() WSALookupServiceNext()	protocol independence

```
WSAAsyncGetHostByName()

WSAAsyncGetServByName() WSALookupServiceEnd()
```

Multiple Protocol Support

As we mentioned earlier, the authors of WinSock version 1.1 deliberately limited its scope in the name of expediency. One result of this is the simple architecture of WinSock 1.1. A single WINSOCK.DLL (or WSOCK32.DLL) provides the WinSock API, and this DLL "talks" to the underlying protocol stack via a proprietary programming interface. This works fairly well since v1.1 of WinSock only supports one protocol suite—TCP/IP—and most computers running Windows have only a single network interface.

However, this architecture limits a system to only one WinSock DLL active in the system path at a time. As a result, it is not easy to have more than one WinSock implementation on a machine at one time. There are legitimate reasons to want multiple WinSock implementations. For example, one might want a protocol stack from one vendor over the Ethernet connection and a different vendor's stack over the Serial Line.

WinSock 2 has an all-new architecture that provides much more flexibility. The new WinSock 2 architecture allows for simultaneous support of multiple protocol stacks, interfaces, and service providers. There is still one DLL on top, but there is another layer below, and a standard service provider interface, both of which add flexibility.

WinSock 2 Architecture

WinSock 2 adopts the Windows Open Systems Architecture (WOSA) model, which separates the API from the protocol service provider. In this model the WinSock DLL provides the standard API, and each vendor installs its own service provider layer underneath. The API layer "talks" to a service provider via a standardized Service Provider Interface (SPI), and it is capable of multiplexing between multiple service providers simultaneously. Figure 17-1 illustrates the WinSock 2 architecture

Note that the WinSock 2 specification has two distinct parts: the API for application developers, and the SPI for protocol stack and namespace service providers. Notice also that the intermediate DLL layers are independent of both the application developers and service providers. These DLLs are provided and maintained by Microsoft and Intel.

Ideally, the intermediate layer is virtually transparent and does little more than maintain the registry of service providers.

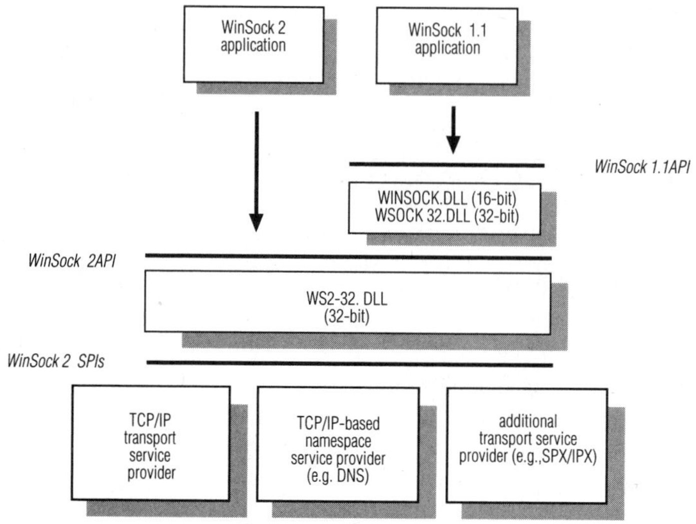

Figure 17-1 WinSock 2 WOSA architecture, with WinSock 1.1 binary compatibility and support for multiple transport and namespace service providers.

Protocol Independence

The WOSA architecture in WinSock 2 allows simultaneous support of multiple protocol stacks from one or more vendors. In addition, the WinSock 2 API provides a number of new functions that allow an application to be protocol independent, so it can take full advantage of the multiple protocol support.

WinSock 2 provides an API for listing the protocols available and vital information to describe them. Multiple protocol support highlights the differences between protocols, and addressing and naming conventions are the two most significant among them. Since WinSock 1.1 has a number of TCP/IP-specific address functions, WinSock 2 has added a number of protocol-independent renditions. We provide a brief description of each of these now. WinSock 2 has also added namespace-independent versions to DNS-specific name functions, and we describe these in the next section.

- `WSAEnumProtocols()`: This is the keystone for protocol independence in the WinSock 2 API. You call this to query about the availability of specific protocols, or simply to ask for a list of all protocols available. The WinSock 2 DLL has a registry of installed protocols and service providers and fills the buffer you provide with an array of WSAPROTOCOL_INFO structures that describe each protocol available in detail and returns the number of protocols reported on.

The most important fields in the WSAPROTOCOL_INFO structure contain the "service flags." These bitmasks indicate whether the protocol supports services such as *guaranteed delivery, guaranteed order, expedited data, quality of service, broadcast, multipoint (multicast)*, and so forth.

```
typedef struct _WSAPROTOCOL_INFO {
  DWORD dwServiceFlags1;           /* bitmask of services provided */
  DWORD dwServiceFlags2;           /* additional protocol attributes */
  DWORD dwServiceFlags3;           /*      "          "          "     */
  DWORD dwServiceFlags4;           /*      "          "          "     */
  DWORD dwProviderFlags;           /* vendor-specific bitmask */
  GUID ProviderID;                 /* unique service provider ID # */
  DWORD dwCatalogEntryId;          /* Catalog of Protocols */
  WSAPROTOCOLCHAIN ProtocolChain; /* Layered Service Providers */
  INT iVersion;                    /* protocol version number */
  INT iAddressFamily;              /* address family (e.g., AF_INET) */
  INT iMaxSockAddr;                /* maximum address length */
  INT iMinSockAddr;                /* minimum address length */
  INT iSocketType;                 /* socket type (e.g., SOCK_DGRAM) */
  INT iProtocol;                   /* protocol (e.g., IPPROTO_TCP) */
  INT iProtocolMaxOffset;          /* maximum protocol argument */
  INT iNetworkByteOrder;           /* net byte order (0==big endian) */
  INT iSecurityScheme;             /* type of security (if any) */
  DWORD dwMessageSize;             /* max datagram (0 for stream) */
  CHAR lpProtocol[WSAPROTOCOL_LEN+1];    /* protocol
  string (e.g., "tcp")             */
} WSAPROTOCOL_INFO, FAR *LPWSAPROTOCOL_INFO;
```

- `WSAHtonl()`, `WSAHtons()`, `WSANtohl()`, `WSANtohs()`: These are extensions of the WinSock 1.1 (and Berkeley Sockets) `htonl()`, `htons()`, `ntohl()` and `ntohs()` functions for converting short and long integers between network and host order. These functions now take a socket descriptor parameter so that the WinSock DLL can determine the proper byte ordering scheme. Currently only big endian and little endian are in use (big endian is the network order on TCP/IP networks), but this technique allows for definition of others in the future.
- `getsockopt()` SO_MAX_MSG_SIZE option: maximum size of a message for message-oriented socket types (meaningless for stream sockets). This option is the WinSock 2 replacement for the *iMaxUdpDg* field returned

in the WSAData structure from `WSAStartup()` in WinSock 1.1. Note that it is also the same size as provided in the *dwMessageSize* field of the WSAPROTOCOL_INFO structure for this protocol.

- `getsockopt()` SO_PROTOCOL_INFO option: describes the protocol bound to this socket. The information is returned in a WSAPROTOCOL_INFO structure and is the same as that returned from `WSAEnumProtocols()`.
- `getsockopt()` and `setsockopt()` PVD_CONFIG: allows two-way "communication" with a service provider implementation by reference to an opaque data structure that the service provider defines. In a sense, it's a proprietary API within the standard API that each service provider can define and use as needed.

Namespace Independence

In WinSock 2 parlance, a *namespace* incorporates host names, service names, and protocol names, as well as the protocols and mechanisms used to satisfy queries. For example, in the TCP/IP realm the namespace involves use of the Domain Name Service (DNS) to resolve host names and references a service and protocol database—usually a standard */etc/services* and */etc/protocol* file—to resolve services and protocols (see Chapters 8 and 10 for more information). All of this, and the APIs to place queries, make up the WinSock 1.1 namespace.

WinSock 2 can support multiple namespaces simultaneously. So, for example, the TCP/IP (WinSock 1.1) namespace can coexist with the Network Information Service (NIS) and the NetWare namespace that uses the NetWare Directory Service (NDS), or the Service Advertisement Protocol (SAP), or scans the NetWare Bindery to resolve service addresses. WinSock 2 allows applications to be selective about the namespace they use.

The mechanism WinSock2 provides to implement namespace independence is similar to the one that provides protocol independence. Basically, you make a query and select which response suits your application best.

The primary WinSock2 function for name resolution is `WSALookupServiceNext()`, which—framed by calls to `WSALookupServiceBegin()` and `WSALookupServiceEnd()`—fills in an array of generic address information structures (CSADDR_INFO). The WinSock 2 interface has redefined the concept of a namespace to include protocols and services, as well as host names. The `WSALookupServiceNext()` function is not like the familiar WinSock 1.1 `gethostbyname()`: It is much more powerful and flexible.

In addition to providing address information, `WSAGetAddressByName()` also provides services and protocol information about each host it reports on. The information returned in the CSADDR_INFO structure even includes the local port number and address for the service in addition to the remote port number and address. `WSALookupServiceNext()` returns everything you need for a server application to do a `bind()` and `listen()`, and for a client application to `connect()`, without having known anything but a host name to start. But wait, there is more!

```
typedef struct _SOCKET_ADDRESS {
      LPSOCKADDR  lpSockaddr;    /* Note the lowercase 'a' */
      INT iSockaddrLength;
} SOCKET_ADDRESS, FAR *LPSOCKET_ADDRESS;

typedef struct _CSADDR_INFO {
      SOCKET_ADDRESS    LocalAddr;      /* local socket name */
      SOCKET_ADDRESS    RemoteAddr;     /* remote socket name */
      INT               iSocketType; /* stream, datagram, etc. */
      INT               iProtocol;      /* e.g. IPPROTO_TCP */
} CSADDR_INFO, FAR *LPCSADDR_INFO;
```

Instead of providing a host name, you could provide a protocol, a service, any combination, *or nothing at all*. By default, `WSALookupServiceNext()` stops searching for service addresses as soon as it finds the first match. However, it has input parameters that allow you to request multiple responses with a quick and simple search, or request a more exhaustive (and expensive) search to find all services available.

- `WSALookupServiceNext()`: powerful function that combines the functionality of `gethostbyname()`, `getservbyname()`, `WSAAsyncGetHostByName()`, and `WSAAsyncGetServByName()` to provide flexible, powerful, and easy-to-use host name resolution and service location

You can also search the namespace for a service with `WSALookupServiceNext()` referencing a "service type." This argument takes what is called a "globally unique identifier" (GUID), as we describe next.

Globally Unique Identifiers

The concept of a "globally unique identifier" (GUID) is borrowed from the distributed computing environment (DCE) model from the Open Software Foundation (OSF). A 128-bit GUID uniquely identifies a service without having to rely on registration with a central authority. It can do this because GUIDs can be locally generated that are statistically certain to be unique across both space and time. There are a number of preassigned GUIDs for well-known services, and WinSock 2 provides a GUID generator for new services.

- `WSAGetServiceClassInfo()`: retrieve all information about a service classówhich is analogous to a well-known service—and the service provider
- `WSAGetServiceClassNameByClassId()`: retrieve the name of the service associated with a GUID
- Macros SVCID_TCP(port number) and SVCID_UDP(port number): convert from a well-known port number for the respective protocol, into a previously defined (well-known) GUID
- Macros PORT_FROM_TCP(GUID) and PORT_FROM_UDP(GUID): convert from a well-known GUID to the equivalent port number for the respective protocol

For services that are not well known, the vendor of the service will provide a service name and/or GUID for you to use so your client application can locate the service (the server application).

Generic Address Formatting

In order to handle the variety of address formats in a protocol-independent manner, WinSock 2 defines two new functions for address-to-string and string-to-address conversion: `WSAAddressToString()` and `WSAStringToAddress()`. The functionality these two new functions provide was formerly done in a TCP/IP-specific manner with `inet_ntoa()` and `inet_addr()`, respectively.

- `WSAAddressToString()`: converts a SOCKADDR structure into a formatted string representation of the address
- `WSAStringToAddress()`: converts a formatted string representation of an address into the formal numeric form acceptable for programmatic use

Parametric Service Searches

WinSock 2 allows you to make more explicit searches for services than `WSALookupServiceNext()` provides. With the `WSALookupServiceBegin()`, `WSALookupServiceNext()`, and `WSALookupServiceEnd()` functions and their helper functions, it is possible to search a hierarchical namespace for services based on specific service properties. Some properties are universally recognized and canonical, whereas others may be very specific and proprietary. As we describe in the next section, WinSock 2 provides an API for installation of new services and properties.

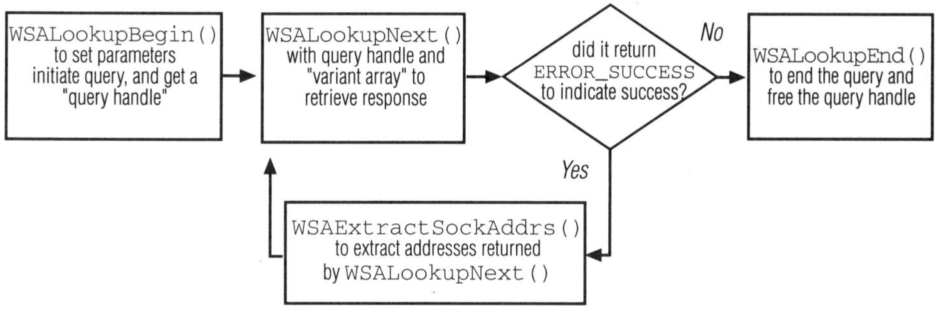

Figure 17-2 Algorithm for searching a hierarchical namespace for services.

Figure 17-2 illustrates how to use the WinSock 2 functions to query for one or more services in a hierarchical namespace. Note that this query could be an exhaustive enumeration of all services available or very specific in nature, depending on the input parameters you use. For example, you can specify the default context in the namespace hierarchy, or start at the top of the "tree."

- `WSALookupServiceBegin()`: initiates the service query of hierarchical namespace using the properties provided as search parameters, and returns a "query handle" for reference.
- `WSALookupServiceNext()`: takes query handle from `WSALookupServiceBegin()` as input argument, and retrieves results into buffers provided. As Figure 17.2 illustrates, typically, you would call `WSALookupServiceNext()` until it fails. At that point, the error value would be WSA_E_NOMORE to indicate there is no more data available.
- `WSALookupServiceEnd()`: frees the query handle after a query is complete (regardless of whether the query succeeds or fails).

Service Installation and Registration

WinSock 2 has adopted the Microsoft Service-Address Registration and Resolution, known as the RnR API, as its own and has given it some new names. The service query algorithm described above is derived from the RnR API and is similar to the "resolution" API currently available in Windows NT version 3.51. WinSock 2 also has analogs for the "registration" API that allows installation of new services (server applications) and adds them to the namespace.

The `WSASetService()` function is part of the RnR API and allows an application to register or deregister a service within one or more namespaces. These namespaces can be very specific in nature, including specific contexts within a namespace hierarchy. A service class is analogous to a well-known service in Internet parlance—for example, the FTP service class—and a service instance is simply an individual instance of a service class (e.g. "Engineering's FTP Server").

The `WSASetService()` function also allows for mapping between a service class and a GUID.

- `WSASetService()`: registers or deregisters a service in one or more namespaces. (Note that this function may be used synchronously, or asynchronously with a callback function.)
- `WSAInstallServiceClass()`: registers a service class schema with a name space. A schema contains the characteristics that all class instances have in common, such as class name and ID (a GUID).
- `WSARemoveServiceClass()`: deregisters a service class shema from a name space.
- `WSAGetServiceClassInfo()`: retrieves all the class information (schemas) in a namespace, by class ID, or vendor ID.
- `WSAGetServiceClassNameByClassId()`: retrieves the service class name associated with a service class ID (GUID).

Overlapped I/O

WinSock 2 brings the overlapped I/O model in the Win32 API into the fold. It uses exactly the same constructs and mechanisms, although it utilizes different names. For example, the WSAOVERLAPPED structure (shown below) is the same as the Win32 OVERLAPPED structure, and the `WSASetEvent()` and `WSAResetEvent()` functions act the same as the Win32 `SetEvent()` and `ResetEvent()` functions.

Overlapped I/O allows an application to request asynchronous network I/O unlike that provided by `WSAAsyncSelect()`. The main advantage of overlapped I/O is the potential for enhanced data throughput by avoiding an extra data copy during sends and receives. In a sense, overlapped I/O cuts out the service provider middle-layer and short-circuits the data route from the network to the application.

The asynchronous nature of overlapped I/O also allows more flexibility in the timing relationships between applications and the network. For example, a multimedia application that generates an audio stream will generally have a fixed amount of new data to send at regular intervals. Networks, however, provide inconsistent bandwidth capacity, so they cannot always accept the stream when a multimedia application is ready to send it. With overlapped I/O an application can post a buffer and leave, rather than hang around and wait for the network to consume the buffer contents. Similar advantages can also be realized on the receiving end. Thus, asynchronous operation mode with overlapped I/O can help to smooth out the timing differences between bursty networks and constant-rate media streams.

To use overlapped I/O, an application must first open an overlapped I/O-capable socket by calling `WSASocket()` with the WSA_FLAG_OVERLAPPED flag set (note, however, that for backward compatibility, the `socket()` function also returns an overlapped-capable socket by default). Subsequently, the application must provide a pointer to a WSA_OVERLAPPED structure as it sends data with `WSASend()` or `WSASendTo()` or receives data with `WSARecv()` or `WSARecvFrom()`. The service provider will then copy data directly between the user buffer and the low-level network interface whenever possible. Thus, it avoids an extra data copy by foregoing the intermediate network-system buffers whenever possible.

There are two ways to use the overlapped I/O functions: with "event objects" (WSAEVENT) or "completion routines." The `WSASend()`, `WSASendTo()`, `WSARecv()`, and `WSARecvFrom()` functions can take an event object in the WSAOVERLAPPED structure provided as an input argument (notice the *hEvent* field in the structure below), or you can specify the address of a completion routine that WinSock will invoke upon completion.

Event objects are a primitive form of a synchronization object in comparison to mutexes and semaphores. You create an event object with a call to `WSACreateEvent()`. Callback routines are simply exported functions in which you can make any network I/O function calls. You should be aware, however, that you can call only a limited subset of non-WinSock functions from the upcall context (in the 32-bit environment, completion routines can only be invoked when a process is in an alertable state, for example, after a call to `WSAWaitForMultipleEvents()`).

```
typedef struct _WSAOVERLAPPED {
      DWORD         Internal;       /* reserved */
      DWORD         InternalHigh;   /* reserved */
      DWORD         Offset;         /* not used for network I/O */
      DWORD         OffsetHigh;     /* not used for network I/O */
      WSAEVENT      hEvent;         /* a valid event object */
} WSAOVERLAPPED, FAR *WSAOVERLAPPED;
```

Figure 17-3 illustrates three ways of using event objects that are compatible with the Win32 API. These are analogous to the three operation modes we described in Chapter 5: blocking, nonblocking, and asynchronous. However,

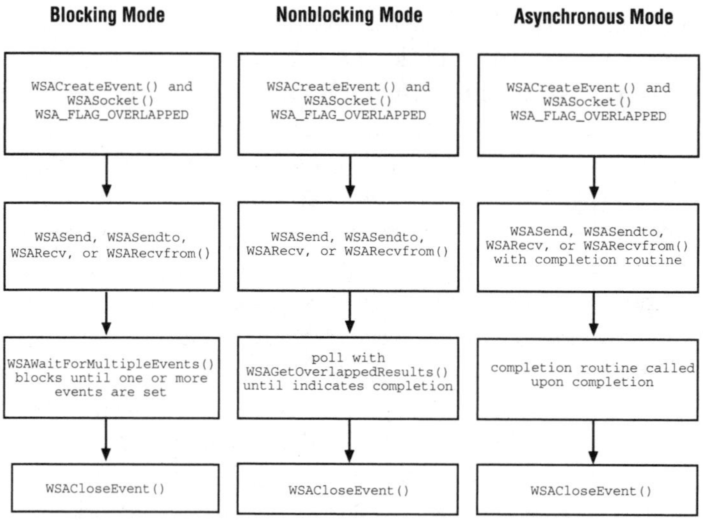

Figure 17-3 Various operation modes possible to detect operation completion with event objects when performing overlapped I/O.

there is another new way in WinSock 2 that builds upon the asynchronous `WSAAsyncSelect()` model with event objects. The WinSock 2 `WSAEventSelect()` function allows you to associate any FD_ event (FD_READ, FD_WRITE, FD_CONNECT, etc.) with an event object. When an event occurs, WinSock 2 sets the specified event object. You then use `WSAEnumNetworkEvents()` to determine which of the network events have occurred on a socket since the last time this function was called. Note that the `WSAEventSelect()` function allows a WinSock 2 application to use event objects to detect connection completion, connection requests, and connection closure, in addition to network I/O.

As in the Win32 API, WinSock 2 also includes two functions that allow the manual setting and resetting of event objects. The `WSASetEvent()` function sets an event object, and the `WSAResetEvent()` clears it.

There are a few important things to remember when using overlapped I/O. You cannot cancel a pending overlapped I/O request. Data always arrives in order, but event notification may not. An application must be sure not to disturb the data buffer provided until completion notification is received.

- `WSACreateEvent()`: creates a new event object (which is cleared upon creation)
- `WSASocket()` (with WSA_FLAG_OVERLAPPED flag): creates an overlapped I/O capable socket

- `WSAEnumNetworkEvents()`: allows an application to detect which events have occurred since the last time this function was called; primarily designed for use when a `WSAEventSelect()` FD_event occurs
- `WSAEventSelect()`: requests a WinSock 2 implementation to set an event object when a particular FD_ event occurs
- `WSAGetOverlappedResult()`: allows polling of an event object, and provides status and error information about a completed operation
- `WSARecv()`, `WSARecvFrom()`, `WSASend()`, `WSASendTo()`: I/O functions that can support overlapped I/O with event objects or completion routines
- `WSAResetEvent()`: clears an event object (resets to an unsignaled state)
- `WSASetEvent()`: sets an event object (set to a signaled state)
- `WSAWaitForMultipleEvents()`: blocks until one or more of the event objects are set
- `WSACloseEvent()`: frees an event object

Scatter and Gather

The scatter and gather support in WinSock 2 is analogous to "vectored I/O," as supported by the Berkeley Sockets `readv()` and `writev()` functions. This functionality is useful for applications that send and receive formatted data such as one or more fixed headers, followed by data, and perhaps followed by a fixed trailer. These functions allow you to "scatter" the data received to a number of different buffers upon receipt, or "gather" the various outgoing data portions from a number of different buffers for sending. The WinSock 2 I/O functions `WSASend()` and `WSASendTo()` allow "gather," and `WSARecv()` and `WSARecvFrom()` allow "scatter."

- `WSARecv()`, `WSARecvFrom()`: used to receive into one or more buffers (i.e., "scatter").
- `WSASend()`, `WSASendTo()`: used to send from one or more buffers (i.e., "gather").

These functions take an array of WSABUF structures for one input argument, and another argument indicates the number of WSABUF structures in the array.

```
typedef struct _WSABUF {
      int          len;      /* length of the buffer */
      char FAR *  buf;      /* pointer to the buffer */
} WSABUF, FAR *LPWSABUF;
```

For stream sockets, each buffer is filled, but `WSARecv()` or `WSARecvFrom()` may return before all buffers are full.

For datagram sockets, each call to `WSARecv()` or `WSARecvFrom()` receives a single message up to the buffer size, which may be truncated, in which case the function fails with WSAEMSGSIZE to indicate data loss. With some message-oriented protocols, you can use the MSG_PARTIAL flag to avoid data loss due to truncation and receive the remainder in subsequent receives (the MSG_PARTIAL flag is unset when you have read the complete message).

Quality of Service

WinSock has always been as media independent as the underlying network drivers and TCP/IP protocol implementations. However, some topologies or carrier systems—like wireless, phone connections, and ATM—require special consideration, and WinSock 2 has quality of service APIs to address their needs. Quality of service does not address RSVP-style reservation for TCP/IP networks, due to its special requirements; RSVP has its own APIs, as described in the *WinSock 2 Protocol-Specific Annex*.

The quality-of-service support in WinSock 2 is useful regardless of the media and transport in use, since it also addresses the special needs of applications that send time-critical data such as video and audio.

To specify quality of service (QOS), an application indicates its QOS requirements when it initiates a connection with `WSAConnect()`, or `WSAIoctl()` SIO_SET_QOS or SIO_SET_GROUP_QOS if it is a connectionless socket (more on socket groups in the next section). These functions can take a QOS argument that contains flow specifications for sending and receiving. As shown in the type definition below, the FLOWSPEC structure allows an application to provide detailed parameters. An application also requests a level of guarantee from the service provider, which the provider may or may not accept. WinSock 2 provides a number of predefined QOS "templates" that an application can request by name with `WSAGetQOSByName()` to avoid having to set all the parameters.

The service provider may respond to the request from `WSAIoctl()` by failing with the WSANOPROTOOPT error if QOS is not supported. Otherwise, it may fail the `WSAConnect()` function call with WSAEOPNOTSUP if the specified level of service requested cannot be met. The application can choose to scale back its parameters and call the function again to attempt to "renegotiate" QOS, or close the socket to give up. (Note: The QOS specified in a call to `WSAConnect()` overrides a default set by `WSAIoctl()`, but does not reset it.)

```
typedef enum {
      BestEffortService,      /* no guarantees of reliability */
      PredictiveService,      /* generally highly reliable */
      GuaranteedService       /* highest level of reliability */
      GUARANTEE;

typedef struct _flowspec {
      int32       TokenRate;          /* bytes/sec expected */
      int32       TokenBucketSize;    /* max bucket size (bytes) */
      int32       PeakBandwidth;      /* max bytes/sec */
      int32       Latency;            /* max acceptable delay (us)*/
      int32       DelayVariation;     /* max-min difference (ms) */
      GUARANTEE   LevelOfGuarantee;   /* reliability expected */
      int32       CostOfCall;         /* reserved (must be 0) */
      int32       NetworkAvailability; /* indicates network up when
      set*/
} FLOWSPEC, FAR * LPFLOWSPEC;

typedef struct _QualityOfService {
      FLOWSPEC    SendingFlowspec;
      FLOWSPEC    ReceivingFlowspec;
      WSABUF      ProviderSpecific;
} QOS, FAR * LPQOS;
```

WinSock 2 also provides new network events that can notify an application of a change in QOS while a connection is active. A service provider triggers the FD_QOS and FD_GROUP_QOS events for `WSAAsyncSelect()` and `WSAEventSelect()` when any field in the flow specification changes. At that time, the application can call `WSAIoctl()` SIO_GET_QOS or SIO_GET_GROUP_QOS to get the current QOS for a socket or socket group.

- `WSAAccept()`: retrieves the associated QOS requirement along with a connection request, and may reject the connection on the basis of the QOS requested
- `WSAConnect()`: has QOS input parameters that allow an application to specify the send and receive flow specifications for a socket or socket group

- `WSAGetQOSByName()`: retrieves a predefined QOS "template," and automatically sets the values in a QOS structure
- `WSAEventSelect()` and `WSAAsyncSelect()` FD_QOS and FD_GROUP_QOS events: provide notification when flow specifications change for a socket or socket group
- `WSAIoctl()` SIO_SET_QOS, SIO_SET_GROUP_QOS: sets the default QOS for a socket or socket group, or renegotiates QOS on an existing connection
- `WSAIoctl()` SIO_GET_QOS, SIO_GET_GROUP_QOS: retrieves the current QOS available for a socket or socket group

Socket Groups

WinSock 2 allows an application or cooperating set of applications to define a set of sockets as a socket group. These are especially valuable for applications that transmit multiple streams of time-sensitive data, like video and audio. The classic example is a video conference application that can sacrifice video data during times of lower bandwidth in order to ensure that audio streams continue to get through.

The `WSASocket()` and `WSAAccept()` functions provide a mechanism that allows an application to assign a new socket to a socket group as it is created. Two types of groups are possible; constrained and unconstrained. A **constrained group** can only include connection-oriented sockets that are connected to the same host, and an **unconstrained group** can contain sockets of any type. All the sockets in either type of group must come from the same transport service provider.

Once a group is created, an application retrieves the socket group ID by calling `getsockopt()` SO_GROUP_ID. Subsequent calls to the `WSAAccept()` "condition function" and `WSASocket()` can reference this group ID to add the new socket to the existing group. An application can assign attributes to the group at the time of creation, or after it creates the group. For example, an application can specify the default group QOS settings with `WSAConnect()` or `WSAIoctl()`.

The most valuable aspect of socket groups is the ability to specify different priorities to individual group members with `setsockopt()` SO_GROUP_PRIORITY. This capability allows an application to indicate to the service provider how bandwidth and other resources should best be divided among a socket group's members. Some media experience variations in reliability and throughput, and even the most reliable media experience bandwidth variations due to network traffic variations. By assigning priorities to individual sockets in a group, an application can provide reasonable assurance that the higher-priority data will get through at the expense of the lower-priority data when bandwidth is reduced.

In conjunction with individual or group QOS change notification (FD_QOS or FD_GROUP_QOS with `WSAEventSelect()` or `WSAAsyncSelect()`), group priorities allow creation of very sophisticated network applications.

- `WSASocket()`, `WSAAccept()`: create a new (constrained or unconstrained) socket group, or add new sockets to an existing group
- `WSAConnect()`: assigns default QOS attributes to a group
- `WSAIoctl()` SIO_GET_GROUP_QOS, SIO_SET_GROUP_QOS: get or set the group's QOS setting
- `getsockopt()` SO_GROUP_ID, SO_GROUP_PRIORITY: retrieve the group ID or priority within a group for an individual socket
- `setsockopt()` SO_GROUP_PRIORITY: assigns the priority within a socket group to an individual socket

Multipoint and Multicast

WinSock 2 defines new APIs for support of protocol-independent multipoint and multicast datagram transmission (referred to as "multipoint," for simplicity). There are basically three types of multipoint implementations currently available, and WinSock 2 provides APIs to address the needs of all of them. In the following list, "control plane" refers to how a multipoint session is established, and "data plane" refers to how data is transmitted between multipoint session participants:

- rooted control plane and rooted data plane: *ATM, ST-II*
- rooted control plane and nonrooted data plane: *T.120*
- nonrooted control plane and nonrooted data plane: *IP Multicast, H.320 (MCU)*

In a rooted control plane, a single socket acts as a "server" of sorts and allows participants to join. This so-called c-root controls the multipoint session, and when it goes away (i.e., when an application closes the socket), the session goes away with it.

In a rooted data plane, a single socket is the source and/or destination of all multipoint data. When it goes away, data transmission ceases in a multipoint session. Obviously, in most rooted multipoint sessions with rooted data and control planes, the control and data roots are usually the same socket, although this is not necessarily true.

In nonrooted control planes, any multipoint participant can join or leave without any interaction with other participants. In nonrooted data planes, any multipoint participant can send or receive multipoint data.

To initiate or join a multipoint session, an application must create a socket with a protocol that supports multipoint. The WSAPROTOCOL_INFO structure indicates multipoint support if the attribute bitflags include XP1_SUPPORT_MULTIPOINT. Additionally, it may indicate a rooted control plane with XP1_MULTIPOINT_CONTROL_PLANE and/or a rooted data plane with XP1_MULTIPOINT_DATA_PLANE (if not set, these are non-rooted when XP1_SUPPORT_MULTIPOINT attribute is set).

In addition to specifying a protocol that supports multipoint, an application must also indicate whether the socket will be a "root" or "leaf" in the control plane and in the data plane. The *dwflags* input argument must be bitwise-or would with a combination of one "C"ontrol flag and one "D"ata flag from the following:

- WSA_FLAG_MULTIPOINT_C_ROOT: a root on the control plane
- WSA_FLAG_MULTIPOINT_C_LEAF: a leaf on the control plane
- WSA_FLAG_MULTIPOINT_D_ROOT: a root on the data plane
- WSA_FLAG_MULTIPOINT_D_LEAF: a leaf on the data plane

For example, for IP multicast support, you would specify

```
WSA_FLAG_MULTIPOINT_C_LEAF | WSA_FLAG_MULTIPOINT_D_LEAF
```

For T.120, you could specify either

```
WSA_FLAG_MULTIPOINT_C_ROOT | WSA_FLAG_MULTIPOINT_D_LEAF
```

or

```
WSA_FLAG_MULTIPOINT_C_LEAF | WSA_FLAG_MULTIPOINT_D_LEAF
```

In a rooted control plane, a leaf may request admission from a root with a call to `WSAJoinLeaf()`. A root can detect a request from a leaf if it calls `listen()` and receives FD_ACCEPT asynchronous event notification. To admit the leaf, the root calls `accept()` or `WSAAccept()` in the standard manner. The leaf can detect acceptance from the root by FD_CONNECT asynchronous notification.

In a rooted control plane a root may also send an invitation to a leaf. In this case the root calls `WSAJoinLeaf()`, and the leaf must call `listen()` and detect FD_ACCEPT event notification. The leaf accepts the invitation to join by calling `accept()` or `WSAAccept()`, and the root receives acceptance notification with FD_CONNECT.

In a nonrooted control plane (such as IP multicast), every application must call `WSAJoinLeaf()` to join the multipoint session. The service provider posts an FD_CONNECT event notification to indicate completion.

The protocol-independent multipoint APIs do not provide an equivalent API for the `get/setsockopt()` IP_MULTICAST_IF option we describe in Chapter 16. The new protocol-independent APIs do not preclude the use of existing protocol-specific APIs such as these or others. You can use protocol-specific APIs with or without also using the protocol-independent APIs.

- `accept() or WSAAccept()`: From a root accept a request to join a multipoint session from a leaf, and from a leaf acknowledge the acceptance from the root
- `WSAJoinLeaf()`: From a root invite leaf nodes to join a multipoint session, and from a leaf request admittance to a multipoint session
- `listen()`: Passively await a request (in a root) or an invitation (in a leaf) in a rooted control plane multipoint protocol
- `WSAIoctl()` SIO_MULTIPOINT_LOOPBACK: Specify whether a multipoint participant should receive each datagram it sends (for IP multicast, loopback is typically enabled by default)
- `WSAIoctl()` SIO_MULTICAST_SCOPE: Specify the "time to live" for a multicast transmission. This is the number of router "hops" the datagram can make, which is equivalent to the number of internetwork segments it can traverse

Conditional Acceptance

With `WSAAccept()` WinSock 2 allows an application to examine the attributes of a connection request from a remote host before it accepts the request rather than rejecting it after the connection is established, as an application must do with `accept()`. To enable this capability, an application must specify a pointer to a function in the *lpfnCondition* input parameter. Here is the prototype for the condition function:

```
int CALLBACK ConditionFunc(
     LPWSABUF lpCallerId,     /* address of connecting entity */
     LPWSABUF lpCallerData,   /* connect data (if any) */
     LPQOS    lpSQOS,         /* caller's socket QOS (if any) */
     LPQOS lpGQOS,            /* caller's group QOS (if any) */
     LPWSABUF lpCalleeId,     /* local address of socket */
     LPWSABUF lpCalleeData,   /* connection data for caller */
     GROUP FAR *g,            /* group id or type (if any) */
     DWORD dwCallbackData);   /* result from condition function */
```

The job of the condition function is to decide whether the connection request will be accepted, rejected, or deferred (indicated by the return values CF_ACCEPT, CF_REJECT, or CF_DEFER). When a connection request is accepted, the condition function may also assign the newly created socket to a socket group.

Deferring a connection request can be useful in instances where the application wishes to alert the user of the incoming connection request and allow them to decide whether or not to accept the connection. For example, servers may do a "reverse lookup" to retrieve the hostname associated with the connecting host's address, to verify the host. Deferring the result is necessary, since this lookup may take some time to complete. On the first pass through `WSAAccept()`, the condition function captures the caller's address, QOS information, and any connect data. It defers processing of the connection request until the user has made a decision based on these parameters. Once the decision is made, the application calls `WSAAccept()` again, and the condition function signals the decision (acceptance or rejection).

After the service provider calls the condition function, it returns a result value in the *dwCallbackData* argument upon return from `WSAAccept()` to indicate either acceptance (CF_ACCEPT), rejection (CF_REJECT), or indecision (CF_DEFER). If no decision is made (CF_DEFER), the service provider does not complete or reject the connection request. In this case, the application must call `WSAAccept()` again until the condition function returns a definitive answer (CF_ACCEPT or CF_REJECT).

- `WSAAccept()`: This function has an input argument for a pointer to a condition function.

Connect and Disconnect Data

When a socket uses a protocol that supports connect and disconnect data, WinSock 2 allows an application to send or receive a small amount of data as it initiates a connection with `WSAConnect()` or accepts an incoming connection request with `WSAAccept()`. Protocols that support connect data have the XP1_CONNECT_DATA attribute flag set, and those that support disconnect data have the XP1_DISCONNECT_DATA attribute flag set.

Connect data may accompany an incoming connection request. In such a case, *lpCallerData* contains a pointer to a buffer. For a server (callee) application to read the data, it must specify a "condition function" when it calls `WSAAccept()` (as we describe in the "Conditional Acceptance" section above). The condition function receives a pointer to a buffer that contains the caller's connect data as an input argument, and it may use the data to determine whether to accept or reject the connection request. The condition function may then also return its own connect data to the caller. The client (caller) may read the connect data from the server (callee) buffer specified in the *lpCalleeData* when it receives a connection completion indication.

The method for sending and receiving disconnect data is similar to the method used for connect data but requires an existing connection. Either end of a connection can call `WSASendDisconnect()` to initiate the close of a connection at any time. This function call is similar to the `shutdown()` function with respect to the way it does a "half-close" of an existing connection without deallocating the socket (as `closesocket()` does). It differs from `shutdown()` since it can send data along with the close request.

When a socket receives a close request, it can read the disconnect data with a call to `WSARecvDisconnect()`. It can then call `WSASendDisconnect()` to return disconnect data of its own before deallocating the socket with `closesocket()`. When the socket that originally initiated the close receives a close indication from the remote end, it can read the disconnect data with a call to `WSARecvDisconnect()` before deallocating the socket with `closesocket()`.

- `WSAAccept()`: The condition function reads the connect data from a caller from a buffer pointed to by the *lpCallerData* input argument, then may optionally return data to the caller in the *lpCalleeData* buffer.
- `WSAConnect()`: After it receives a connection completion indication, the client (caller) may read the connect data from the callee in the buffer pointed to by the *lpCallerData* input argument.
- `WSASendDisconnect()`: This function initiates a half-close and sends disconnect data, or sends disconnect data in response to a close request.
- `WSARecvDisconnect()`: After it receives a close indication from the remote end, this function reads disconnect data.

Socket Sharing

WinSock 2 provides a mechanism for one or more processes to access an existing socket owned by another process. (Note: This is not necessary for sharing sockets between threads.) An application uses existing interprocess communication mechanisms, such as DDE or OLE, to get the handle of a target process that needs to share an existing socket. The application then calls `WSADuplicateSocket()` to get a WSAPROTOCOL_INFO that can be passed back to the target process. The target process must then reference the WSAPROTOCOL_INFO structure in a call to `WSASocket()` to get a duplicate of the original socket handle. This sequence can be repeated multiple times with the same process or other processes (the target process can only use each WSAPROTOCOL_INFO structure only once).

During the life of the socket, any of the processes with access to the socket can affect the socket state and set socket attributes. For example, any process can call `connect()`, `WSAConnect`, `bind()`, `listen()`, `accept()`, or `WSAAccept()` to affect a socket connection. If one process uses `setsockopt()`, `ioctlsocket()`, `WSAIoctl()`, `WSAEventSelect()`, or `WSAAsyncSelect()` to alter socket attributes, all other processes are affected by the change.

If a process uses `WSAAsyncSelect()` or `WSAEventSelect()` to request asynchronous notification of socket events, then only that process receives notification. However, it is important to note that

- *Incoming data is not duplicated between processes.* If one process reads data from a socket, this data is not available to other processes. However, only one such event object (from any process) may be associated with a socket at one time.
- *Event objects are not duplicated between processes.* Each process must use `WSACreateEvent()` to create its own event objects associated with a socket.

Any of the processes accessing a duplicated socket handle can call `shutdown()` to close a connection or `closesocket()` to end access to the socket. However, the socket itself is not deallocated until all processes with handles to the socket call `closesocket()`.

- `WSADuplicateSocket()`: returns a pointer to a WSAPROTOCOL_INFO structure with which a different process can create a duplicate of an existing socket with a call to `WSASocket()`.

Protocol-specific Additions

In addition to the many new options already mentioned, there are also a number of new protocol-specific additions. The WinSock 2 specification describes these and other protocol-specific additions in the **Windows Sockets 2 Protocol-specific Annex** that is part and parcel of the WinSock 2 specification proper.

This annex includes specifics for newly supported protocols like Novell SPX/IPX, DECNet, and OSI. In addition, it will contain a number of new TCP/IP protocol-specific additions. We describe the new TCP/IP-specific raw sockets and multicast options in Chapter 16. Some of the others that the annex describes are listed in this section.

WSAIoctl()

WinSock 2 `WSAIoctl()` function's SIO_GET_INTERFACE_LIST opcode is not necessarily TCP/IP protocol-specific, but it addresses the needs of most TCP/IP service providers.

- INTERFACE_LIST: provides an array of INTERFACE_INFO structures that describe each network interface and/or driver status, attributes, and capabilities (defined in the protocol-specific WS2TCPIP.H header file):

```
typedef struct _INTERFACE_INFO {
      u_long iiFlags:            /* bitmask of interface
      attributes */
      struct sockaddr iiAddress; /* IP address of interface */
      struct sockaddr iiBroadcastAddress; /* broadcast address
      for interface */
      struct sockaddr iiNetmask;          /* subnet bitmask
      used by interface */
} INTERFACE_INFO, *PINTERFACE_INFO, FAR *LPINTERFACE_INFO;
```

The bitflags for the *iiFlags* bitmask field may have the following values:

- IFF_UP: Network interface is up and ready for use.
- IFF_BROADCAST: This interface supports broadcast.
- IFF_LOOPBACK: This is a loopback interface.

- IFF_POINTTOPOINT: This is a point-to-point link.
- IFF_MULTICAST: This interface supports multicast.

get/setsockopt()

WinSock 2 includes two completely new options:

- UDP_NOCHECKSUM (*level*=SOL_SOCKET): This function disables checksum in outgoing UDP datagrams (so the checksum value is set to zero).
- TCP_EXPEDITED_1122 (*level*=IPPROTO_TCP): If set, it indicates the TCP/IP service provider implements expedited data (also called out-of-band or urgent data) as described by RFC 1122. This means the urgent offset points to the byte of urgent data. If not set, it indicates that expedited data is implemented in the Berkeley Sockets fashion (as described by RFC 793), so the urgent offset points to the byte *after* urgent data.

WinSock 2 includes a number of socket options that affect or describe the IP header (all *level*=IPPROTO_IP). Most of these are not new, since they have always been available in Berkeley Sockets implementations. In all cases, the values used are the same as those described by RFC 791:

- IP_OPTIONS: specifies the IP options for outgoing datagrams
- IP_TOS: specifies type of service for outgoing datagrams
- IP_TTL: specifies time-to-live value for outgoing datagrams
- IP_HDRINCL: indicates whether an application must provide the IP header along with data for outgoing SOCK_RAW datagrams

As noted earlier, the IP multicast options we describe in Chapter 16 are also included in WinSock 2.

A

TCP/IP Protocol Headers

In This Appendix:

- Layering within TCP/IP Packets
- ARP Header
- IP Header
- ICMP Header
- IGMP Header
- TCP Header
- UDP Header
- Sample Dialogs

This appendix contains illustrations and short descriptions of the network and transport protocols in the Internet Protocol suite (TCP/IP). Typically, you will not need these since the WinSock API insulates you from the low-level details of protocol headers or their explicit behaviors. However, you may find a need to reference them if you ever use a network analyzer when trying to debug an application. These can come in handy.

In fact, we strongly recommend that you leave a network analyzer on your net during development, or at least during the final testing of your application. Software-based network analyzers are available from a number of vendors, and a number of free ones are available on the Internet also (see Chapter 13, "Debugging," for more information). Having one can make your job easier, since it provides immediate empirical evidence of your network application's operation. Those who have them depend on them and have trouble imagining life without them. Mention taking it away, and the immediate analogy that comes to mind is of going blind.

Layering within TCP/IP Packets

Network packets reflect the OSI network layers. Another way to "stack" the protocols as we do in the OSI network reference model is to illustrate how each

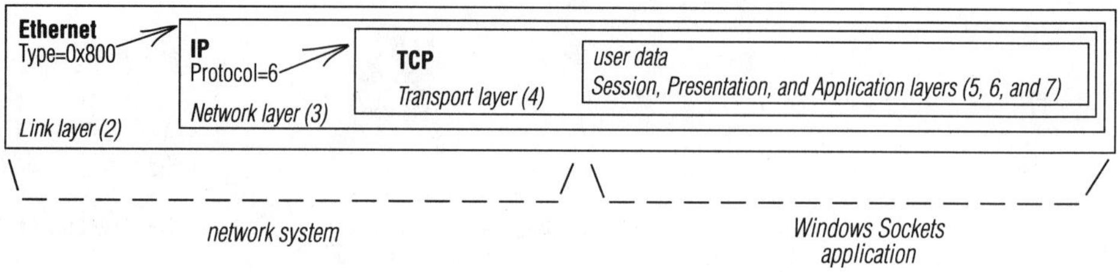

Figure A-1 Protocols often have fields in their header that indicate what they contain.

layer "encapsulates" the layer above it. As Figure A-1 shows, the format of each protocol header includes a field that indicates what type of protocol it encapsulates, so one layer interfaces with the next layer by indicating its protocol type.

For example, assuming the correct hardware and IP address in Figure A-1,

- The network driver finds that the type value (0x800) is registered, so it "upcalls" the registered address—IP protocol stack—and passes up the packet.
- The IP protocol stack checks the protocol value and passes the packet to the TCP handler in the TCP/IP protocol stack.
- The TCP handler checks whether there is an active socket receiving on the target port number and notifies the application of "readability" if there is one.

The "Assigned Numbers" RFC (updated regularly) contains the values for network and transport protocol types, as well as the port numbers for many well-known services.

ARP Header

- *hardware type:* type of hardware address

  value=1: Ethernet (10 MB)

  value=2: Ethernet (3 Mb)

  value=3: Amateur Radio AX.25

  value=4: Proteon ProNet Rings

  value=5: CHAOSnet

  value=6: IEEE 802

  value=7: ARCNET
- *protocol type:* type of protocol address being mapped (0x800 for Internet Protocol)
- *hardware length:* size in bytes of hardware address (6 for Ethernet and Token Ring)

- *protocol length:* size in bytes of protocol address (4 for IP)
- *operation code:*

  value=1: ARP request value=3: RARP request

  value=2: ARP reply value=4: RARP reply
- *source hardware address:* hardware address of sender
- *source protocol address:* protocol address of sender
- *destination hardware address:* hardware address of receiver (broadcast if unknown)
- *destination protocol address:* hardware address of receiver (0 if unknown)

IP Header

- *IP version:* current version is 4
- *IP header length:* packet length (20 bytes without options), plus all the data it contains (which usually includes a transport header, like TCP)
- *type of service:* three bit fields to determine precedence, and one each to indicate delay, throughput, and reliability

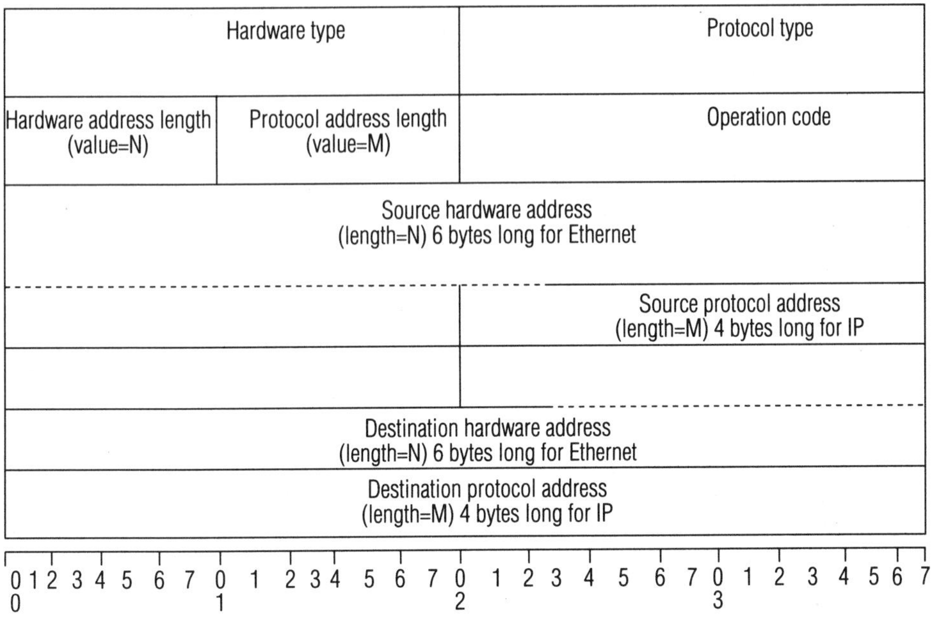

Figure A-2 Address Resolution Protocol (ARP), as described by RFCs 826 and 1256.

- *IP packet ID:* the serial number of an IP packet (same for all fragments)
- *fragment bit flags (3 bits):*

  bit 0: reserved
  bit 1: value=0, may fragment   value=1, do not fragment
  bit 2: value=0, last fragment   value=1, more fragments

- *IP fragment offset:* location of this fragment in original packet in 8-byte units
- *time to live:* number of router "hops" possible
- *transport protocol:*

ip	0	IP	# internet protocol, pseudo protocol number
icmp	1	ICMP	# internet control message protocol
igmp	2	IGMP	# internet group management protocol
tcp	6	TCP	# transmission control protocol
udp	17	UDP	# user datagram protocol

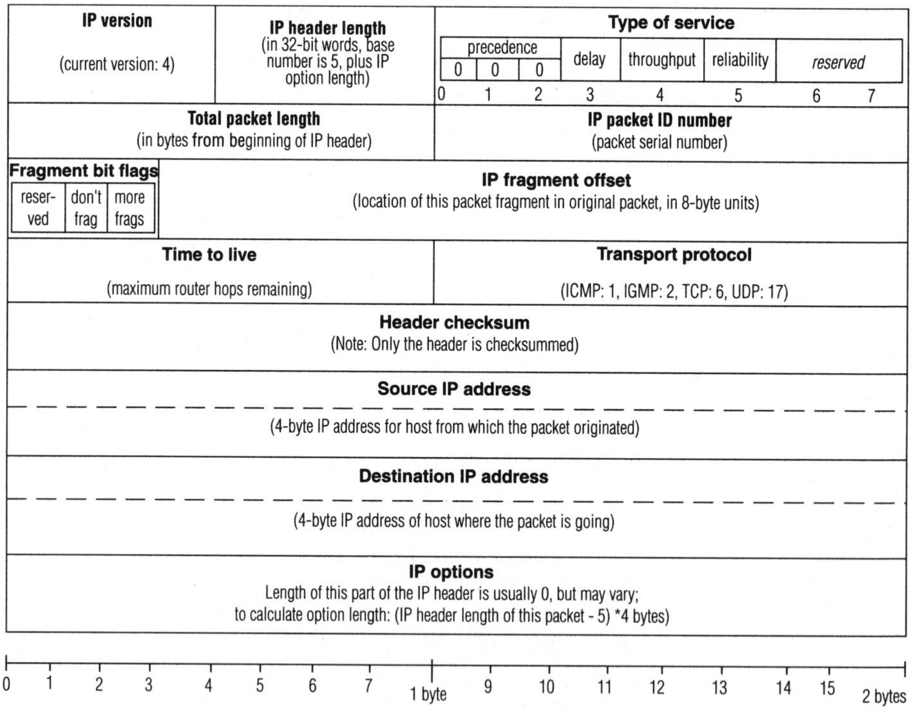

Figure A-3 Internet Protocol (IP), as described by RFC 791

These values came right out of the standard BSD UNIX protocols database file */etc/protocols*. They would be the same values returned by protocol database functions. As gaps indicate, this list is not complete.

- *header checksum:* one's complement sum of 16-bit words (not bytes) in the header (does not include data). For computing the checksum, the checksum field is zeroed. For implementation details, see ping code sample in Chapter 16, "Optional Features" (ICMP, TCP, UDP, and IGMP use the same algorithm).
- *destination and source IP addresses:* 32-bit Internet addresses in network byte order
- *IP options (length varies):*

bit 0:	value=0: do not copy to fragments	value=1: copy to fragments
bits 1-2:	value=0: control class	value=1: debug and measurement class
bits 3-8:	value=0: end of list	value=1: NOP
	value=2: security	value=3: loose source routing
	value=4: internet timestamp	value=7: record route
	value=8: stream ID	value=9: strict source routing

ICMP Header

- *type* and *code:*

type=0: echo reply (code=0, unused; data is returned from echo request)

type=3: destination unreachable

code=0: network unreachable	code=1: host unreachable
code=2: protocol unreachable	code=3: port unreachable
code=4: frag needed but IP df set	code=5: source route failed

type=4: source quench (code=0, unused)

type=5: redirect

code=0: network redirect	code=1: host redirect
code=2: type of service net redirect	code=3: type of service host redirect

type=8: echo request (code=0, unused)

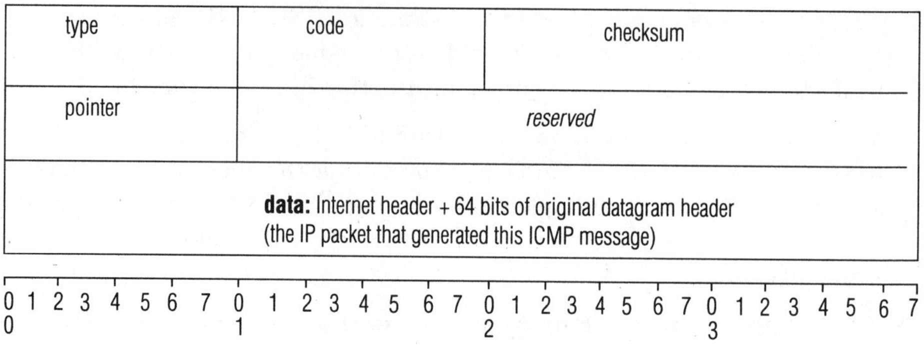

Figure A-4 Internet Control Message Protocol (ICMP), as described by RFC 792.

type=9: router solicitation (code=0, unused)

type=10: router advertisement (code=0, unused)

type=11: time exceeded

code=0: IP time-to-live exceeded   code=1: frag reassembly timeout

type=12: parameter problem

code=0: pointer field in ICMP header indicates error

type=13: request time (code=0, unused)

type=14: reply time (code=0, unused)

type=15: information request (code=0, unused)

type=16: information reply (code=0, unused)

type=17: address mask request (code=0, unused)

type=18: address mask reply (code=0, unused)

- *checksum (of header and data):* standard IP checksum of ICMP header and data (see IP header checksum for more information)
- *pointer:* number of first incorrect octet (for type 12, parameter problem)
- *reserved:* <unused>
- *data:* depends on ICMP type

IGMP Header

- *version:* RFC 1112 describes version 1 of IGMP (RFC 988 specifies version 0, now obsolete).

- *type:* There are two types of IGMP messages of concern to hosts (more for routers):

  value=1: host membership query value=2: host membership report

- *reserved:* This is zeroed when sent, ignored when received.
- *checksum (of header only):* This is the standard IP checksum of 8-octet IGMP message (see IP header for details).
- *group address:* A class D IP address, that is in the range 224.0.0.1 (all-hosts group address) through 239.255.255.255 (224.0.0.0 never used).

See Chapter 16, "Optional Features," for more information on multicast addresses and IGMP protocol mechanics.

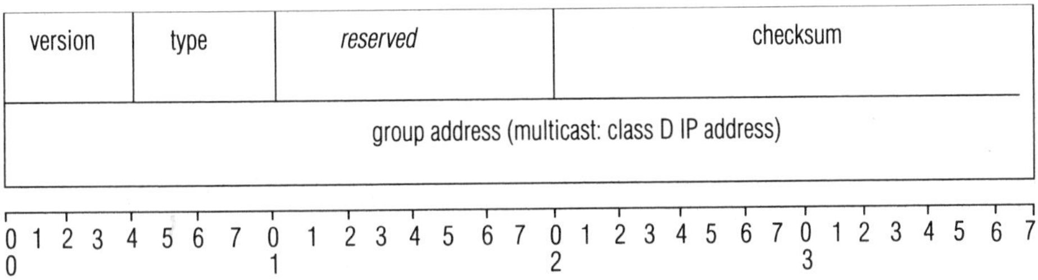

Figure A-5 Internet Group Management Protocol (IGMP), as described by RFC 1112.

TCP Header

- *source port:* port number of the sender (see Appendix B, "Quick Reference," Macros section, for a list of well-known port numbers)
- *destination port:* port number of the receiver
- *sequence number:* octet sequence number (starts with clock-driven random value)
- *acknowledgment number:* sequence number of last octet received (and implicitly acknowledges all prior octets)
- *offset:* number of 32-bit words in TCP header (5, unless TCP options present)
- *bit flags:*

  bit 6: urgent (or out-of-band) bit 7: acknowledgment

  bit 8: push bit 9: reset (abort connection)

  bit 10: synchronize (establish connection) bit 11: finish (close connection)

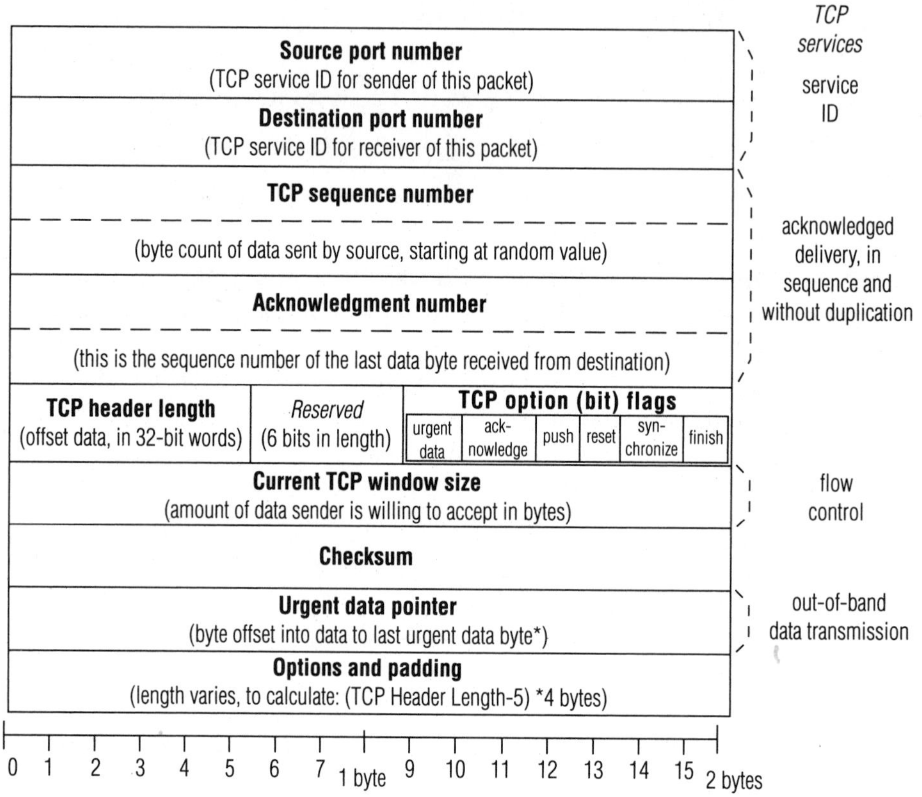

Figure A-6 Transport Control Protocol (TCP), as described by RFCs 793 and 1122.

- *window size:* amount of buffer space available for data on sender
- *checksum (of header and data):* standard IP checksum of TCP header and data (see IP header for more information)
- *urgent pointer:* valid when urgent bit flag set in TCP header; there are two different and incompatible ways to interpret it:

  RFC 1122 style: points to last urgent byte

  RFC 793 style (also called BSD style): points to byte *after* last urgent byte
- *options:* options are in 32-bit words, formatted as follows:

  byte 1: option   byte 2: size   byte 3 and beyond: data

  option value=0: end of options

  option value=1: padding byte

option value=2: maximum segment size (MSS=2 bytes data)

UDP Header

- *source port:* port number of the sender (see Appendix B, "Quick Reference," Macros section for a list of well-known port numbers)
- *destination port:* port number of the receiver
- *packet length:* length in bytes of UDP header and data
- *checksum (of header and data):* standard IP checksum algorithm applied to UDP header and data; optional, but typically enabled (see IP header checksum for more information)

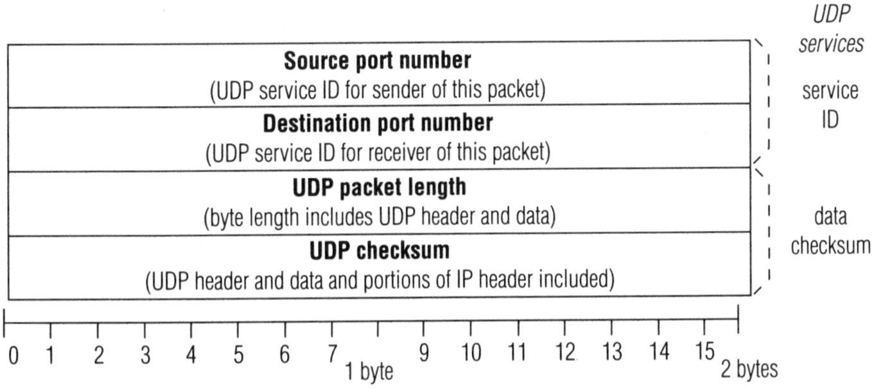

Figure A-7 User Datagram Protocol (UDP), as described by RFC 768.

Sample Dialogs

Here we illustrate two sample protocol dialogs between clients and servers. One shows a TCP client connecting to a TCP server on the same subnet. The other describes a UDP client sending to a UDP server on a different subnet.

We do not deal at all with specific network media in this text. Aside from hardware address resolution (which does not exist on serial connections), all the issues and techniques we cover are essentially the same for any network media. In other words, the subnets referenced could be Ethernet, Token Ring, FDDI, or Serial (PPP or SLIP), and our scenarios (and later our debugging procedures) are applicable to all of them.

We do not attempt to be comprehensive in these examples, only to sketch some key protocol elements in each exchange and relate them to API events. These descriptions provide a few reference points to use if you ever need to debug an application. They highlight the most relevant portions of the protocols involved. For more complete information, please reference the protocol specifications themselves (RFCs) or, better yet, get one of the many great reference books available.

Server on Same Subnet

In this scenario, we are using TCP, the stream (connection-oriented) transport protocol, to establish a connection between two hosts. Both of the hosts are located on the same subnet. In other words, the network traffic between the two is not going through a router, although it may go through one or more bridges (which are transparent to the IP layer).

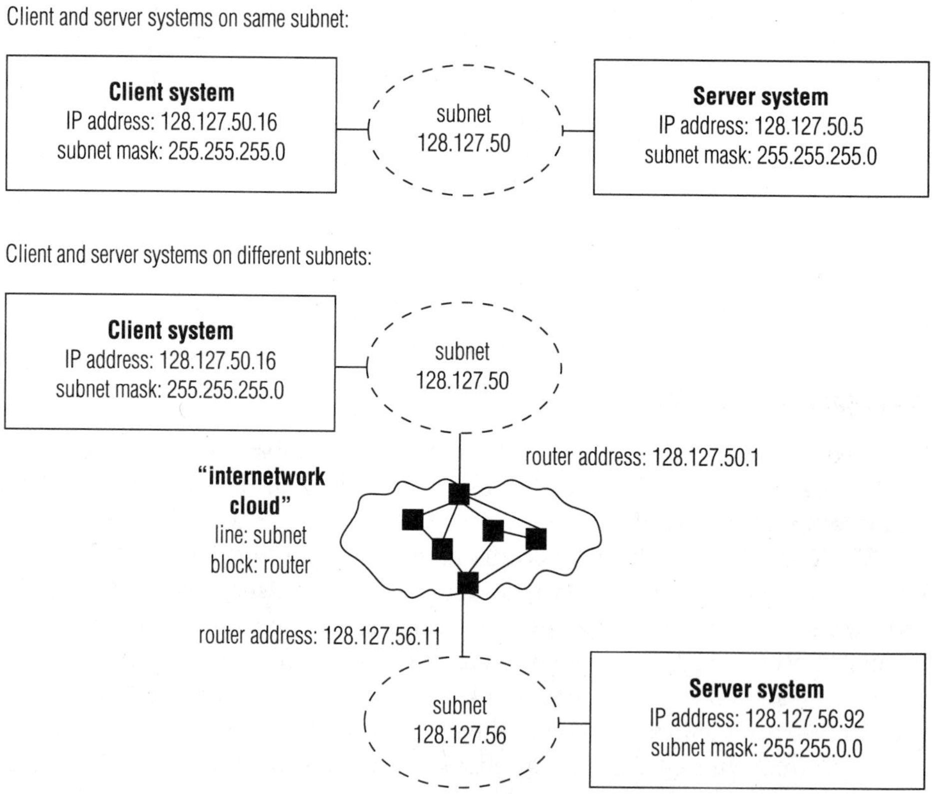

Figure A-8 Local and remote client and server configurations.

Here is a description of each event that occurs in this scenario. Notice the major application phases: *connecting* (which also includes resolving hardware addresses), *sending and receiving data*, and *closing*. We relate the significant WinSock functions and events. The illustrations are incomplete; they only include relevant portions of the TCP headers (compare these to the TCP header description that appears earlier in this appendix).

connecting

1. To start the connection operation, an application calls the WinSock `connect( )` function to initiate the connection at the transport level. This is a client application, by definition, and in this sample it is using a SOCK_STREAM (TCP) socket.
2. When the TCP/IP protocol stack (network system) receives the request to connect, it checks whether it knows the hardware address for the target IP interface/host. If it does, or if it is using a serial protocol—like PPP or SLIP—in which case there is no hardware address, skip to step 6. If not, it broadcasts an ARP request.

begin resolving hardware address

3. All hosts on the local network see the ARP request packet, which is sent to the hardware broadcast address (e.g., on Ethernet, all bits set in the 6-byte address). Upon receipt, the data-link layer (driver) hands it up to the TCP/IP stack.
4. If the destination IP address in the ARP request matches the receiver's IP address, then the stack updates the ARP cache with the hardware address of the client interface and its IP address. It then puts its hardware address into an ARP reply packet and sends it back to the system (hardware address) that sent the ARP request.
5. When the stack on the client system receives the ARP reply from the server, it puts the entry into its ARP cache. This maps the server's IP address to its hardware address.

done resolving hardware address

6. The client system then sends a connection request packet to the server system. This consists of an IP packet with the server system's IP address as the destination and the client system as the source. The IP packet contains a TCP segment with the <SYN> flag set and the destination port number for the server application to which the client is trying to connect.

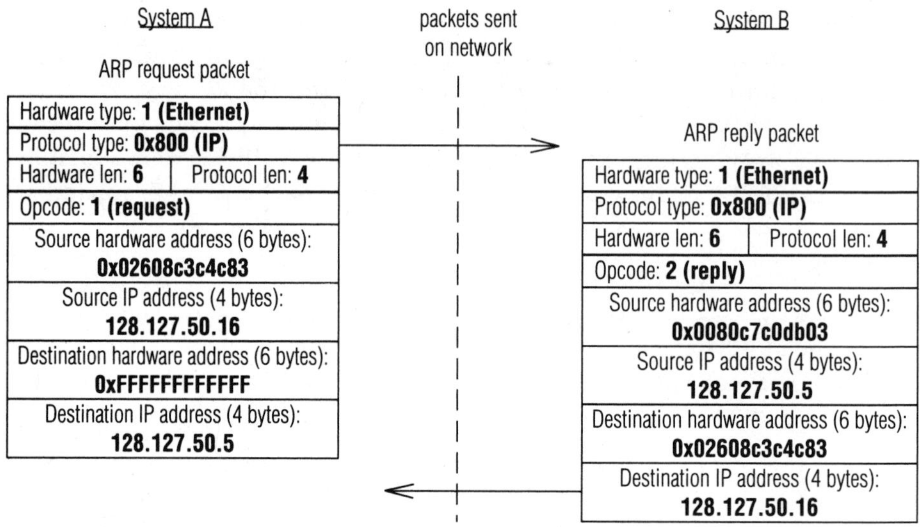

Figure A-9 ARP request, and response containing hardware address that corresponds to IP address sent.

7. When a TCP/IP protocol stack receives the TCP <SYN> packet, it checks whether it has a TCP socket listening on the destination port. If so, it responds with a TCP segment with the <ACK><SYN> flags set to accept the connection request at the transport protocol layer (if not, it responds with a TCP <RST> to refuse the request). At this point, WinSock posts an FD_ACCEPT for `WSAAsyncSelect()` to notify the server application of the pending connection, or indicates "readability" for `select()`. The application must call `accept()` to establish the connection at the application layer and must get a new socket handle with which to communicate with the client.

8. When the client receives the TCP <ACK><SYN>, it responds with a TCP <ACK> (if it received a TCP <RST>, `connect()` would fail with WSAECONNREFUSED). At that point, a blocking `connect()` call will return successfully to indicate connection completion, or `select()` indicates "writability," or WinSock posts FD_CONNECT (and FD_WRITE) event notification messages for `WSAAsyncSelect()`.

sending and receiving

1. The TCP bidirectional stream "pipe" is open at this point, so either the client or server can send data. As system A sends data, it updates the sequence number in the TCP header to reflect the data sent so far (the sequence number references the first byte of data in the TCP packet). Any TCP segment containing data might have the <PSH> flag set.

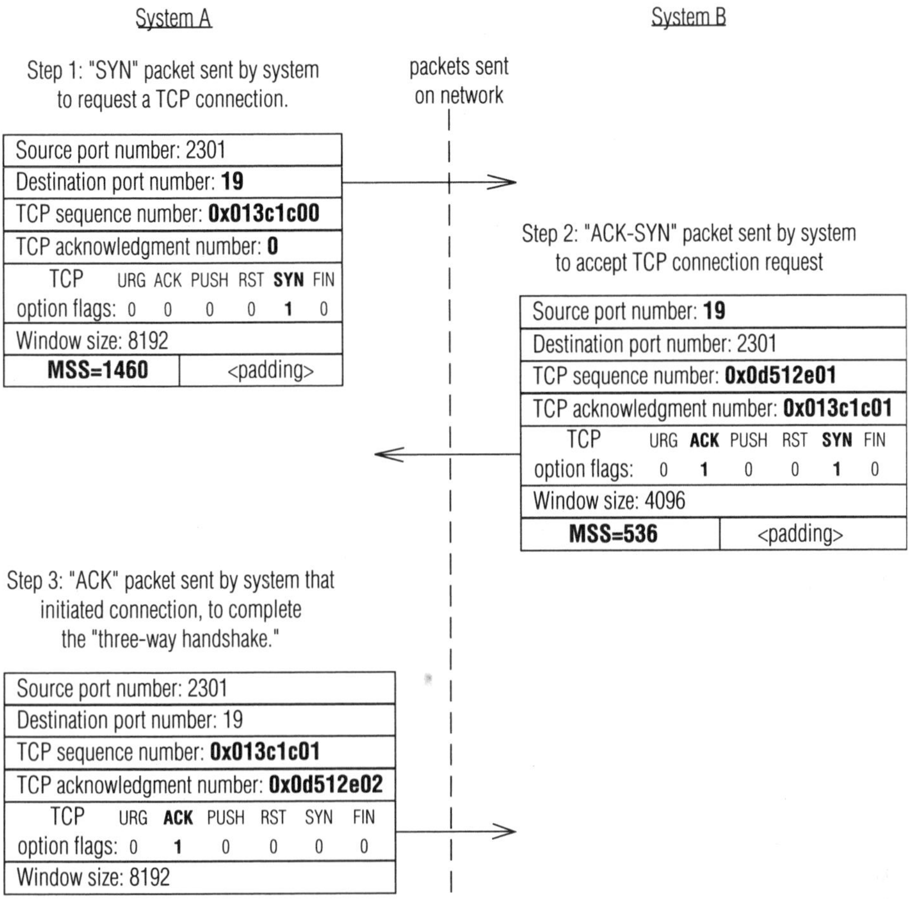

Figure A-10 Significant fields in TCP headers as they appear in TCP packets exchanged to establish a connection.

2. When system B receives a TCP data segment, WinSock notifies an application of data receipt by posting an FD_READ for `WSAAsyncSelect( )`, or indicating "readability" for `select( )`. System B responds to data receipt by sending a TCP <ACK> and an acknowledgment number calculated by adding the number of data bytes received to the sender's sequence number. The TCP window size may also be decremented by the amount received if the application has yet to read the data. If the TCP window is zero, attempts by system A to `send( )` will fail with WSAEWOULDBLOCK.

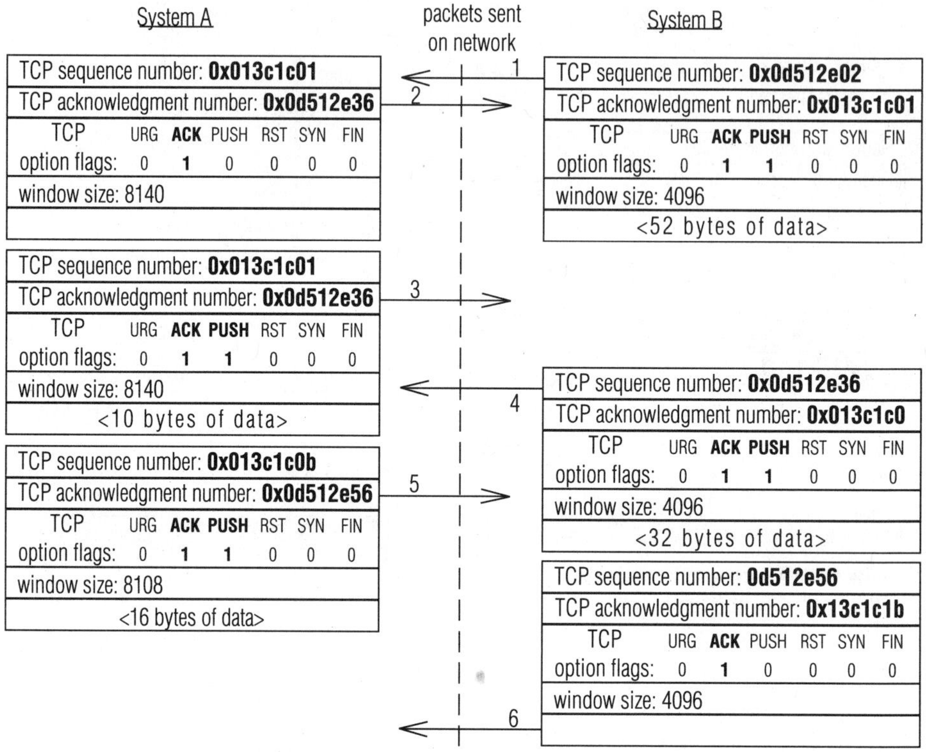

Figure A-11 Significant fields in TCP headers as they appear in TCP packets exchanging data.

3. As the application on System B calls `recv( )`, WinSock copies the data from stack buffers to the application buffers (if data is still remaining, WinSock posts another FD_READ or indicates "readability" for `select( )`). After the application reads a significant portion, system B may send a TCP segment with an updated window that reflects the amount read.
4. Upon receipt of a window update on system A, if an attempt to `send( )` had failed with WSAEWOULDBLOCK, WinSock posts an FD_WRITE to an application so it may call `send( )` again.

aborting

1. A client or server can abort a connection at any time by sending a TCP <RST>.

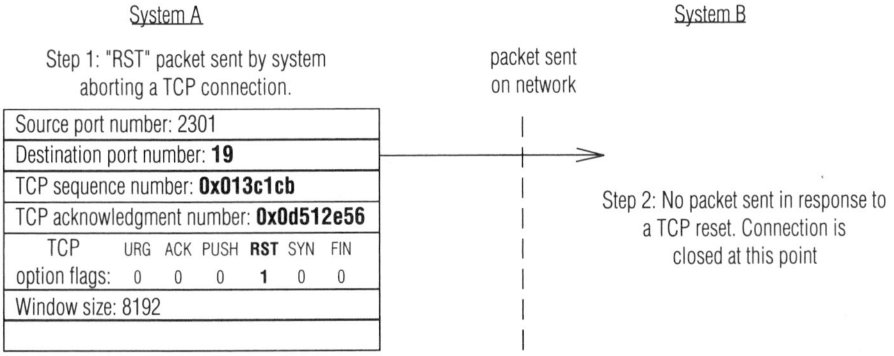

Figure A-12 Significant fields in TCP headers as they appear in TCP packet sent to "hard-close" a TCP connection.

2. Upon receipt, no protocol response is necessary. WinSock will post an FD_CLOSE containing a WSAECONNRESET error for `WSAAsyncSelect( )`, or indicate an "exception" for `select( )`. Any other function calls that reference the connected socket will fail, and `WSAGetLastError( )` will return WSAECONNRESET.

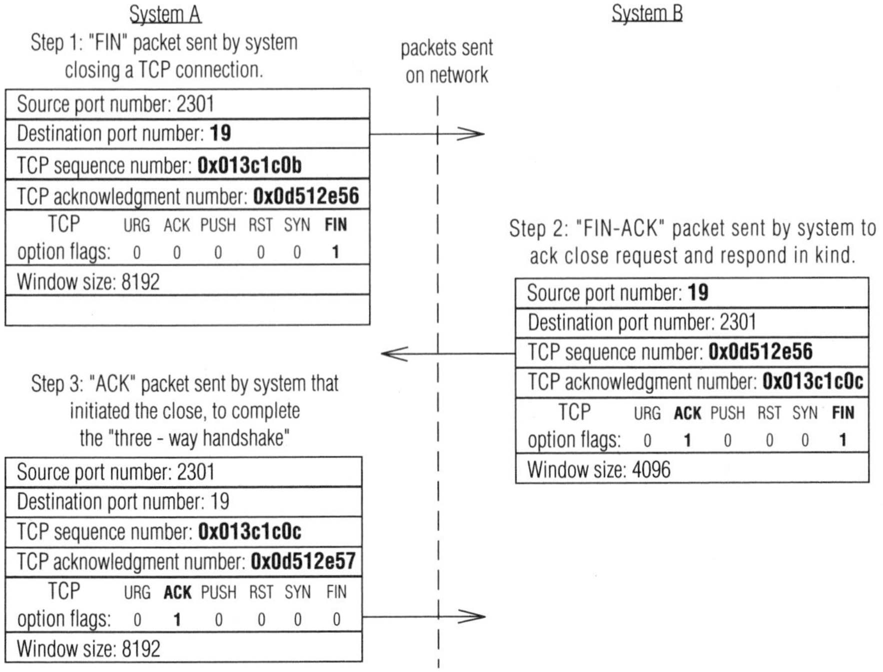

Figure A-13 Significant fields in TCP headers as they appear in TCP packets exchanged to close a connection gracefully.

closing gracefully

1. Either end can initiate a graceful close by sending a TCP packet with the <FIN> (finish) flag set. If the application on system A sends a <FIN> by calling `shutdown( )` or `closesocket( )` (with SO_DONTLINGER or a nonzero LINGER), this effectively notifies the other end that the application is done sending any more data.
2. After a host receives a TCP <FIN>, WinSock posts FD_CLOSE notification for `WSAAsyncSelect( )`. Although a <FIN> indicates the other side is done sending, it does not necessarily mean you have read all the data it already sent. Nor does it mean you must stop sending data. Whether you will have any more data to send or receive will depend on your application.
3. To complete the graceful close, the application on system B must eventually call `shutdown( )` or `closesocket( )`. System B will then send a TCP <FIN>.
4. When system A receives the <FIN>, it will respond with an <ACK>. At this point, a blocking `closesocket( )` on system A (SO_LINGER enabled with nonzero timeout on a blocking socket) will return indicating success. If a nonzero SO_LINGER timeout had expired before the close completed, system A would have sent a TCP <RST>.

Server on Different Subnet

In this second scenario we describe an application pair—client and server—that are located on different subnets. The behavior is essentially the same between IP hosts on subnets with one, two, or more routers and subnets of any network media types between them.

In this sample the applications use SOCK_DGRAM sockets and the UDP protocol to communicate. If we were using the stream transport protocol between these hosts, the TCP dialog would be the same as that described above. The lower-layer (ARP) traffic would be the same as we describe here.

Since the datagram protocol is connectionless (stateless), the application phases we illustrated in the TCP scenario—connection, sending and receiving, closing—are abstract here. An application may not always establish a virtual connection at that session layer within the application protocol. There is no concept of graceful closes or aborts unless the application defines one.

connecting

1. When the application user requests communication with the server, our sample datagram (UDP) client application calls `connect( )` to establish a default destination IP address and port (many UDP applications do not use `connect( )`). With a datagram socket, the `connect( )` function does not attempt to send anything on the network, so ARP is not necessary yet either. Many UDP applications also call `bind( )` to receive on a specific port.

sending and receiving

2. The client application calls `send( )` to initiate communication with the server (applications that do not use `connect( )` call `sendto( )`). The TCP/IP protocol stack (network system) inspects the destination address and sees that it is not local to this subnet. It then checks whether it knows the hardware address for the local router. If not, it resolves the hardware address of the local router using ARP in the same manner in which it resolved the address of a local host (as described in the previous scenario with a host on the same subnet).
3. The protocol stack sends a media packet (e.g., Ethernet) with the (hardware) destination address of the router. This contains an IP packet with the destination address of the server system, and the IP packet contains a UDP packet with the destination (server) port number.
4. The local router—which may have more than one interface connected to different subnets—checks which subnet the destination IP address is on. If it's on one that is directly connected to one of its interfaces, it resolves the hardware address of the host (using ARP) and forwards the UDP packet. If not, it forwards the datagram to the next router.
5. Upon receipt of the UDP packet, the server's TCP/IP protocol stack checks that it has a UDP socket ready to receive on the destination port. If so, it buffers the data, and WinSock notifies the server application with FD_READ for `WSAAsyncSelect( )` or indicates "readability" for `select( )`. UDP does not acknowledge the data upon receipt, nor would it return an error if it could not buffer the packet. If the receiver did not have a UDP socket ready to receive on that port, it would respond with a "port unreachable" ICMP error message. WinSock might fail a subsequent `send( )` or `recv( )` with WSAECONNRESET to indicate receipt of the "port unreachable" ICMP message, but typically there is no indication of this error.

6. When the server gets "readability" notification, it must call `recvfrom()` to read the message. To send data, the server application could `connect()` to the source address and port number returned in `recvfrom()`'s *from* parameter (followed by `send()`) or just `sendto()` that address and port number.

closing

7. Either the client or the server can call `closesocket()` at any time to close the datagram socket and free its resources. The TCP/IP stack does not send anything on the net to indicate closure when it closes a datagram socket.

B Quick Reference

In This Appendix:

- Structures
- Functions
- Macros

This appendix contains an inventory of everything in the version 1.1 WinSock API. It has a comprehensive list of data structures, functions, and macros, with descriptions, cross references, and related information. This list includes some things that are not officially part of the v1.1 Windows Sockets specification. Either these additions were left out of the original specification by oversight, or they are optional features. Most of them are included in version 2 of the WinSock specification.

Structures

The WinSock functions reference the following structures. Other than **im_req**, they are all defined in the WINSOCK.H file. We list them in alphabetical order, give a short description of each, cross-reference them with the functions that use them, and point to the chapter that describes them in detail. The *extended types* list for most of them are macros from the WINSOCK.H file that you can use as aliases for the types defined.

fd_set: "file descriptor set structure" contains a set of sockets (set with the FD_ macros). The `select()` function takes three fd_sets—read, write, and exception—as input parameters to denote the sockets of interest. See Chapter 6, "Socket States."

```
struct fd_set {
     u_short fd_count;                  /* how many are SET */
     SOCKET      fd_array[FD_SETSIZE]; /* an array of SOCKETs */
} fd_set;
```

extended types:

```
typedef struct fd_set FD_SET;
typedef struct fd_set *PFD_SET;
typedef struct fd_set FAR *LPFD_SET;
```

functions: `select()`

hostent: "host structure" contains the results of a host name or address query. Note the common usage of the `h_addr` field macro to reference the first address in the address list. The `MAXGETHOSTSTRUCT` macro refers to the largest hostent structure any gethost function can return (including the information pointed to in the structure). See Chapter 8, "Host Names and Addresses."

```
struct      hostent {
      char  FAR * h_name;           /* official name of host */
      char  FAR * FAR * h_aliases; /* alias list */
      short h_addrtype;             /* address type (PF_INET) */
      short h_length;               /* length of address */
      char  FAR * FAR * h_addr_list;     /* list of addresses */
#define h_addr    h_addr_list[0]    /* address */
};
```

extended types:

```
typedef struct hostent HOSTENT;
typedef struct hostent *PHOSTENT;
typedef struct hostent FAR *LPHOSTENT;
```

functions: `gethostbyaddr()`, `gethostbyname()`, `WSAAsyncGetHostByAddr()`, `WSAAsyncGetHostByName()`

im_req: "multicast address structure" contains an IP multicast group (a class D IP address) and optionally also the local interface address. This structure is used by WinSocks that have optional multicast support (see Chapter 16, "Optional Features," for more information).

```
struct ip_mreq {
      struct  in_addr imr_multiaddr;  /*IP multicast address of group*/
      struct  in_addr imr_interface;  /*local IP address of interface*/
};
```

functions: `setsockopt()` `IP_ADD_MEMBERSHIP` and `IP_DROP_MEMBERSHIP`

in_addr: "Internet address structure" contains a 32-bit Internet Protocol address. The union allows access to individual fields, although typically applications use the `s_addr` field macro to treat the value as a long. The `INADDR_ANY` macro is commonly used to initialize to the default address. `INADDR_BROADCAST` and `INADDR_LOOPBACK` denote other common addresses. There are also a number of `IN_CLASS` macros you can use to decompose network and host address portions according to their IP address class. See Chapter 8, "Host Names and Addresses."

```
struct in_addr {
      union {
            struct { u_char s_b1,s_b2,s_b3,s_b4; } S_un_b;
            struct { u_short s_w1,s_w2; } S_un_w;
            u_long S_addr;
      } S_un;
#define s_addr    S_un.S_addr       /* use this for IP address references */
#define s_host    S_un.S_un_b.s_b2  /* host on imp */
#define s_net     S_un.S_un_b.s_b1  /* network */
#define s_imp     S_un.S_un_w.s_w2  /* imp */
#define s_impno   S_un.S_un_b.s_b4  /* imp # */
#define s_lh      S_un.S_un_b.s_b3  /* logical host */
};
```

extended types:

```
typedef struct in_addr IN_ADDR;
typedef struct in_addr *PIN_ADDR;
typedef struct in_addr FAR *LPIN_ADDR;
```

functions: `inet_ntoa()`

also see: `struct sockaddr_in` (which has one field of type `struct in_addr`) and `struct ip_mreq` (which has two fields of type `struct in_addr`)

linger: "close timeout structure" used to set (or get) a time limit (in seconds) for a graceful close of a TCP socket connection (normally unnecessary). See Chapter 9, "Socket Information and Control."

```
struct      linger {
      u_short l_onoff;        /* linger option on/off */
      u_short l_linger;       /* linger time in seconds */
};
```

extended types:

```
      typedef struct linger LINGER;
      typedef struct linger *PLINGER;
      typedef struct linger FAR *LPLINGER;
```

functions: getsockopt() and setsockopt() with SO_LINGER

protoent: "protocols structure" contains the results of a protocol (name or number) database query. It contains everything there is to know (from an application standpoint) about a protocol. See Chapter 10, "Support Routines."

```
struct      protoent {
      char  FAR * p_name;            /* official protocol name */
      char  FAR * FAR * p_aliases; /* alias list */
      short p_proto;                 /* protocol number */
};
```

extended types:

```
      typedef struct protoent PROTOENT;
      typedef struct protoent *PPROTOENT;
      typedef struct protoent FAR *LPPROTOENT;
```

functions: getprotobyname(), getprotobynumber(), WSAAsyncGetProtoByName(), WSAAsyncGetProtoByNumber()

servent: "services structure" contains the results of a service (name or port number) database query. It contains everything there is to know (from an application standpoint) about a service. See Chapter 10, "Support Routines."

```
struct      servent {
      char  FAR * s_name;            /* official service name */
      char  FAR * FAR * s_aliases; /* alias list */
      short s_port;                  /* port # */
      char  FAR * s_proto;           /* protocol to use */
};
```

extended types:

```
typedef struct servent SERVENT;
typedef struct servent *PSERVENT;
typedef struct servent FAR *LPSERVENT;
```

functions: `getservbyname()`, `getservbyport()`, `WSAAsyncGetServByName()`, `WSAAsyncGetServByPort()`

sockaddr: "generic address structure." Although many functions reference this structure type explicitly, the implicit reference is to another specific address structure. Typically, the pointer to a generic address structure is cast from a specific address family structure (e.g., `struct sockaddr_in` for TCP/IP). See Chapter 4, "Network Application Mechanics."

```
struct sockaddr {
    u_short sa_family;    /* address family (e.g., PF_INET) */
    char    sa_data[14]; /* up to 14 bytes of direct address */
}
```

extended types:

```
typedef struct sockaddr SOCKADDR;
typedef struct sockaddr *PSOCKADDR;
typedef struct sockaddr FAR *LPSOCKADDR;
```

functions: `accept()`, `bind()`, `connect()`, `getpeername()`, `getsockname()`, `recvfrom()`, `sendto()`.

sockaddr_in: "Internet address structure." This is the address structure specific to the Internet Protocol suite (TCP/IP). Typically, an application declares a variable of this type, then casts its pointer to the generic address structure type (struct sockaddr) for input to functions. See Chapter 4, "Network Application Mechanics."

```
struct sockaddr_in {
      short        sin_family;       /* protocol family (PF_INET) */
      u_short      sin_port;         /* port number (network order) */
      struct       in_addr sin_addr; /* IP address */
      char         sin_zero[8];      /* <unused filler> */
};
```

extended types:

```
typedef struct sockaddr_in SOCKADDR_IN;
typedef struct sockaddr_in *PSOCKADDR_IN;
typedef struct sockaddr_in FAR *LPSOCKADDR_IN;
```

functions: None explicitly, many implicitly. See `struct sockaddr` for more information.

timeval: "timeout structure" sets the timeout value for the `select()` function (which blocks, even when nonblocking socket(s) are referenced in the file descriptor set). See Chapter 6, "Socket States."

```
struct timeval {
      long  tv_sec;    /* seconds */
      long  tv_usec;   /* and microseconds */
};
```

extended types:

```
typedef struct timeval TIMEVAL;
typedef struct timeval *PTIMEVAL;
typedef struct timeval FAR *LPTIMEVAL;
```

functions: `select()`

WSAData: "WinSock DLL data structure" contains all there is to know about a specific WinSock implementation, after the DLL initialization. See Chapter 10, "Support Routines."

```
typedef struct WSAData {
      WORD          wVersion;      /* version app to use */
      WORD          wHighVersion;  /* highest ver supported */
      char          szDescription[WSADESCRIPTION_LEN+1];
      char          szSystemStatus[WSASYS_STATUS_LEN+1];
      long          iMaxSockets;   /* max sockets provided */
      long          iMaxUdpDg;     /* max UDP datagram data */
      char FAR *    lpVendorInfo;  /* <for WinSock use> */
}WSAData;
```

functions: `WSAStartup()`

Functions

Here are the prototypes of all the functions in the v1.1 Windows Sockets API, along with short descriptions.

accept(): An incoming connection is acknowledged and associated with an immediately created socket. The original socket returns to listening state, and the new socket inherits properties of listening socket (like blocking or nonblocking, and asynchronous events registered with `WSAAsyncSelect()`). See Chapter 4, "Network Application Mechanics."

```
SOCKET PASCAL FAR accept  /* value INVALID_SOCKET on failure */
    (SOCKET s,                  /* a listening socket */
     struct sockaddr FAR *addr, /* address of connecting entity */
     int FAR *addrlen);         /* pointer to len of addr struct */
```

bind(): Assign a local name to an unnamed socket (associate a local address and port with a socket). Required before you can call `listen()`. See Chapter 4.

```
int PASCAL FAR bind       /* 0 on success, SOCKET_ERROR on failure */
    (SOCKET s,                  /* an unbound socket */
     const struct sockaddr FAR *name,  /* address to bind to socket*/
     int namelen);              /* length of address struct */
```

closesocket(): Remove a socket from the per-process object reference table (close any connection, release the socket descriptor). See Chapter 4. Note: The function behavior is affected by `setsockopt()` SO_LINGER. See Chapter 9.

```
int PASCAL FAR closesocket /*0 on success, SOCKET_ERROR on failure*/
    (SOCKET s);                 /* a valid socket */
```

connect(): Initiate a "connection" on the specified socket. On datagram sockets, a connection is just a default destination address, and on stream a connection is an actual virtual circuit. See Chapter 4.

```
int PASCAL FAR connect    /*0 on success, SOCKET_ERROR on failure*/
    (SOCKET s,                  /* an unconnected socket */
     const struct sockaddr FAR *name, /* address to connect to */
     int namelen);              /* length of address structure */
```

gethostbyaddr(): Retrieve the host information (name(s) and address) corresponding to a network address. See Chapter 8.

```
struct hostent FAR * PASCAL FAR gethostbyaddr  /* NULL on failure */
    (const char FAR *addr,  /* ptr to addr (network byte order) */
     int len,           /* length of address (4 if af==PF_INET) */
     int type);         /* type of address (must be PF_INET) */
```

gethostbyname(): Retrieve the host information (name(s) and address(es)) corresponding to a host name. See Chapter 8.

```
struct hostent FAR * PASCAL FAR gethostbyname  /* NULL on failure */
    (const char FAR *name);       /* name of the host to resolve */
```

gethostname(): Return the standard host name for the local machine. Note: Be sure to check for a NULL string in *name* when successful, in case no host name is configured. See Chapter 8.

```
int PASCAL FAR gethostname /*0 on success, SOCKET_ERROR on failure*/
    (char FAR *name,             /* buffer to receive host name */
     int namelen);               /* length of name buffer */
```

getpeername(): Retrieve the current name of the peer connected to a socket. See Chapter 10.

```
int PASCAL FAR getpeername /*0 on success, SOCKET_ERROR on failure*/
    (SOCKET s,                   /* a connected socket */
     struct sockaddr FAR *name, /* peer address and port number */
     int FAR *namelen);          /* pointer to len of addr struct */
```

getprotobyname(): Retrieve the protocol name and number corresponding to a protocol name. See Chapter 10.

```
struct protoent FAR * PASCAL FAR getprotobyname  /*NULL on failure*/
    (const char FAR *name);     /* pointer to protocol name */
```

getprotobynumber(): Retrieve the protocol name and port corresponding to a service name. See Chapter 10.

```
struct protoent FAR *PASCAL FAR getprotobynumber /*NULL on failure*/
    (int number);        /* protocol number, in host byte order */
```

getservbyname(): Retrieve the service name and port corresponding to a service name. See Chapter 10.

```
struct servent FAR * PASCAL FAR getservbyname  /* NULL on failure */
    (const char FAR *name,    /* pointer to service name */
     const char far *proto); /* pointer to protocol name or NULL
                             to return first match of service name */
```

getservbyport(): Retrieve the service name(s) corresponding to a port number. See Chapter 10.

```
struct servent FAR * PASCAL FAR getservbyport /* NULL on failure */
    (int port,                /* port number, in network byte order */
     const char FAR *proto); /* pointer to protocol name or NULL
                            to return first match of service port */
```

getsockname(): Retrieve the local name for a socket. Note: The local interface address may not be returned until a connection is established. See Chapter 8.

```
int PASCAL FAR getsockname /*0 on success, SOCKET_ERROR on failure*/
    (SOCKET s,                  /* a bound socket */
     struct sockaddr FAR *name, /* structure to recv local name */
     int FAR *namelen);         /* length of address structure */
```

getsockopt(): Retrieve option associated with a socket. See options summary under `setsockopt()` later in this appendix. Also see Chapter 9.

```
int PASCAL FAR getsockopt  /*0 on success, SOCKET_ERROR on failure*/
    (SOCKET s,             /* a valid socket */
     int level,            /* only SOL_SOCKET level supported */
     int optname,          /* socket option being queried */
     char FAR *optval,     /* buffer for option value retrieved */
     int FAR *optlen);     /* pointer to size of optval buffer */
```

htonl(): Convert a 32-bit number from host byte order to network byte order (big endian). See Chapter 10.

```
u_long PASCAL FAR htonl  /* 32-bit number in network byte order */
    (u_long hostlong);   /* 32-bit number in host byte order */
```

htons(): Convert a 16-bit number from host byte order to network byte order (big endian). See Chapter 10.

```
u_short PASCAL FAR htons /* 16-bit number in network byte order */
    (u_short hostshort); /* 16-bit number in host byte order */
```

inet_addr(): Converts a character string representing a number in the Internet standard (dot) notation to an Internet address value (32-bit big endian). See Chapter 8.

```
unsigned long PASCAL FAR inet_addr  /* INADDR_NONE on failure */
    (const char FAR *cp);   /* a char string in Internet "." format */
```

inet_ntoa(): Converts an Internet address value to an ASCII string in the Internet standard dot notation (e.g., "a.b.c.d"). See Chapter 8.

```
char FAR * PASCAL FAR inet_ntoa /* NULL on failure */
    (struct in_addr in);      /* Internet host address structure */
```

ioctlsocket(): Set or retrieve I/O mode(s) of a socket. Commands available are FIONBIO, FIONREAD, and SIOCATMARK. See Chapter 9.

```
int PASCAL FAR ioctlsocket /*0 on success, SOCKET_ERROR on failure*/
    (SOCKET s,                /* a valid socket */
     long cmd,                /* command to perform on socket s */
     u_long FAR *argp);       /* pointer to parameter for cmd */
```

listen(): Listen for incoming connections on a specified socket. The SOMAXCONN macro indicates the maximum value possible for backlog; it's good practice to use it as the input value for the *backlog* parameter. See Chapter 4.

```
int PASCAL FAR listen      /* 0 on success, SOCKET_ERROR on failure */
    (SOCKET s,             /* a bound, unconnected socket */
     int backlog);         /* max len of pending connection queue */
```

ntohl(): Convert a 32-bit value from network byte order to host byte order. See Chapter 10.

```
u_long PASCAL FAR ntohl  /* 32-bit number in host byte order */
    (u_long netlong);    /* 32-bit number in network byte order */
```

ntohs(): Convert a 16-bit value from network byte order to host byte order. See Chapter 10.

```
u_short PASCAL FAR ntohs /* 16-bit number in host byte order */
    (u_short netshort);  /* 16-bit number in network byte order */
```

recv(): Receive data from a connected socket. See Chapter 4. Valid values for the *flags* parameter are MSG_OOB and MSG_PEEK. See Chapter 6.

```
int PASCAL FAR recv    /* # bytes recv would, SOCKET_ERROR on failure */
    (SOCKET s,                /* a connected socket */
     char FAR *buf,           /* buffer for incoming data */
     int len,                 /* length of buf */
     int flags);              /* option flags */
```

recvfrom(): Receive datagram from either a connected or unconnected socket. See Chapter 4. Valid values for the *flags* parameter are MSG_OOB and MSG_PEEK. See Chapter 6.

```
int PASCAL FAR recvfrom    /* # bytes recv would, SOCKET_ERROR on failure */
    (SOCKET s,                /* a bound socket */
     char FAR *buf,           /* buffer for incoming data */
     int len,                 /* length of buf */
     int flags,               /* option flags */
     struct sockaddr FAR *from, /* buffer for source addr on return */
     int FAR *fromlen);       /* pointer to length of addr struct */
```

select(): Perform synchronous I/O multiplexing (determine status of one or more sockets in each socket set, blocking if timeout nonzero). There are a number of macros for manipulation of the fd_set structure arguments (for use on input and upon return). See Chapter 6.

```
int PASCAL FAR select /*# sockets ready,0 on timeout,SOCKET_ERROR */
    (int nfds,            /* not used, included for compatibility */
     struct fd_set FAR *readfds,      /* check for readability */
     struct fd_set FAR *writefds,     /* check for writability */
     struct fd_set FAR *exceptfds,    /* check for errors */
     const struct timeval FAR *timeout);    /* time to wait */
```

send(): Send data on a connected socket. MSG_DONTROUTE is the only defined value for the *flags* parameter. See Chapter 4.

```
int PASCAL FAR send    /* # bytes sent, SOCKET_ERROR on failure */
    (SOCKET s,            /* a connected socket */
```

```
        const char FAR *buf, /* buffer containing outgoing data */
        int len,             /* length of data to send from buf */
        int flags);          /* option flags */
```

sendto(): Send datagram to either a connected or unconnected socket. MSG_DONTROUTE is the only defined value for the *flags* parameter. See Chapter 4

```
int PASCAL FAR sendto  /* # bytes sent, SOCKET_ERROR on failure */
    (SOCKET s,             /* a valid socket */
     const char FAR *buf, /* buffer containing outgoing data */
     int len,              /* length of data to send from buf */
     int flags,            /* option flags */
     const struct sockaddr FAR *to,  /* ptr to target address */
     int tolen);           /* length of address structure */
```

setsockopt(): Set option associated with a socket. See Chapter 9.

```
int PASCAL FAR setsockopt  /*0 on success, SOCKET_ERROR on failure*/
    (SOCKET s,                 /* a valid socket */
     int level,                /* SOL_SOCKET or IPPROTO_TCP */
     int optname,              /* socket option to set */
     const char FAR *optval,/* buffer for option value to be set */
     int optlen);              /* size of optval buffer */
```

Value	*Data type*	*Meaning*	*Default*	*1*	*2*	*3*	*4*	*5*
SO_ACCEPTCONN	BOOL	Socket is listening.	FALSE unless listen() performed	•		•		
SO_BROADCAST	BOOL	Socket is configured for the transmission of broadcast messages.	FALSE	•	•		•	
SO_DEBUG	BOOL	Debugging is enabled.	FALSE	•	•	•	•	•
SO_DONTLINGER	BOOL	If true, the SO_LINGER option is disabled.	TRUE	•	•	•		
SO_DONTROUTE	BOOL	Routing is disabled.	FALSE	•	•	•	•	•
SO_ERROR	int	Retrieve error status and clear.	0	•		•	•	

Value	*Data type*	*Meaning*	*Default*	*1*	*2*	*3*	*4*	*5*
SO_KEEPALIVE	BOOL	Keep-alives are being sent.	FALSE	•	•	•		
SO_LINGER	struct linger FAR *	Returns the current linger options.	*l_onoff* is 0	•	•	•		
SO_OOBINLINE	BOOL	Out-of-band data is being received in the normal data stream.	FALSE	•	•	•		
SO_RCVBUF	int	Buffer size for receives	Implementation-dependent	•	•	•	•	•
SO_REUSEADDR	BOOL	The address to which this socket is bound can be used by others.	FALSE	•	•	•	•	
SO_SNDBUF	int	Buffer size for sends	Implementation-dependent	•	•	•	•	•
SO_TYPE	int	The type of the socket (e.g., SOCK_STREAM)	As created via socket()	•		•	•	
TCP_NODELAY*	BOOL	Disables the Nagle algorithm for send coalescing.	Implementation-dependent	•	•	•		

Table B-1: Socket options for getsockopt() and setsockopt().

Notes:
1: getsockopt() option
2: setsockopt() option
3: stream socket option
4: datagram socket option
5: This option is optional. An implementation may
- silently ignore this option with setsockopt() and return a constant value from getsockopt()
- or accept a value from setsockopt() and return it from getsockopt() without using it at all

*: This option level is IPPROTO_TCP (all others are SOL_SOCKET).

shutdown(): Shutdown part of a full-duplex stream connection (disable sends and/or receives). Note: We recommend *how*=1 (disable sends), followed by recv() and closesocket() for graceful close of a TCP connection. See Chapter 4.

```
int PASCAL FAR shutdown  /*0 on success, SOCKET_ERROR on failure */
   (SOCKET s,            /* a valid datagram socket or a connected stream socket */
   int how);             /* flag describing shutdown */
```

socket(): Create an endpoint for communication and return a socket. See Chapter 4.

```
SOCKET PASCAL FAR socket /* INVALID_SOCKET on failure */
   (int af,              /* address format: PF_INET or AF_UNSPEC */
    int type,            /* type spec: SOCK_STREAM or SOCK_DGRAM */
    int protocol);       /* protocol to use (if af==AF_UNSPEC) */
```

WSAAsyncGetHostByAddr(): Retrieve the IP address and aliases corresponding to a host's IP address. The size of *buf* must be large enough to accommodate the hostent structure and strings that it points to. The v1.1 WinSock specification recommends that the buffer size should be at least MAXGETHOSTSTRUCT. See Chapter 8.

```
HANDLE PASCAL FAR WSAAsyncGetHostByAddr     /* 0 on failure */
   (HWND hWnd,  /* handle of window to receive msg on completion */
    u_int wMsg, /* message to be received on completion */
    const char FAR *addr, /* ptr to address of host */
    int len,        /* length of address */
    int type,       /* type of address (must be PF_INET) */
    char FAR *buf,  /* ptr to data area to receive hostent data */
    int buflen);    /* size of data area buf above */
```

WSAAsyncGetHostByName(): Retrieve the IP address and aliases corresponding to a host name. The size of *buf* must be large enough to accommodate the hostent structure and strings that it points to. The v1.1 WinSock specification recommends that the buffer size should be at least MAXGETHOSTSTRUCT. See Chapter 8.

```
HANDLE PASCAL FAR WSAAsyncGetHostByName     /* 0 on failure */
   (HWND hWnd,  /* handle of window to receive msg on completion */
    u_int wMsg, /* message to be received on completion */
    const char FAR *name, /* host name to be resolved */
    char FAR *buf,  /* ptr to data area to receive hostent data */
    int buflen);    /* size of data area buf above */
```

WSAAsyncGetProtoByName(): Retrieve the protocol name and port corresponding to a service name. The v1.1 WinSock specification recommends that the buffer size should be at least MAXGETHOSTSTRUCT. See Chapter 10.

```
HANDLE PASCAL FAR WSAAsyncGetProtoByName    /* 0 on failure */
   (HWND hWnd,  /* handle of window to receive msg on completion */
    u_int wMsg,      /* message to be received on completion */
    const char FAR *name,  /* protocol name to resolve */
    char FAR *buf,   /* ptr to data area to receive protoent data */
    int buflen);     /* size of data area buf above */
```

WSAAsyncGetProtoByNumber(): Retrieve the protocol name and aliases corresponding to a service number (port). The v1.1 WinSock specification recommends that the buffer size should be at least MAXGETHOSTSTRUCT. See Chapter 10.

```
HANDLE PASCAL FAR WSAAsyncGetProtoByNumber  /* 0 on failure */
   (HWND hWnd,  /* handle of window to receive msg on completion */
    u_int wMsg,      /* message to be received on completion */
    int number,      /* protocol number to resolve */
    char FAR *buf,   /* ptr to data area to receive protoent data */
    int buflen);     /* size of data area buf above */
```

WSAAsyncGetServByName(): Retrieve the service port number and aliases corresponding to a service name. The v1.1 WinSock specification recommends that the buffer size should be at least MAXGETHOSTSTRUCT. See Chapter 10.

```
HANDLE PASCAL FAR WSAAsyncGetServByName  /* 0 on failure */
       (HWND hWnd,  /* handle of window to receive msg on completion */
        u_int wMsg, /* message to be received on completion */
        const char FAR *name,  /* service name to resolve */
        const char FAR *proto, /* protocol name (may be NULL) */
        char FAR *buf,         /* buffer to receive servent data */
        int buflen);           /* size of data area buf above */
```

WSAAsyncGetServByPort(): Retrieve the service name and aliases corresponding to a service number (port). The v1.1 WinSock specification recommends that the buffer size should be at least MAXGETHOSTSTRUCT. See Chapter 10.

```
HANDLE PASCAL FAR WSAAsyncGetServByPort      /* 0 on failure */
    (HWND hWnd,  /* handle of window to receive msg on completion */
     u_int wMsg, /* message to be received on completion */
     int port,        /* port number to resolve (network order) */
     const char FAR *proto, /* protocol name (may be NULL) */
     char FAR *buf,   /* ptr to data area to receive servent data */
     int buflen);     /* size of data area buf above */
```

WSAAsyncSelect(): Request notification of significant network events via a message to application window procedure; it is an asynchronous version of `select()`. *lEvent* notification flags include: FD_CLOSE, FD_CONNECT, FD_OOB, FD_READ, and FD_WRITE. See Chapter 6.

```
int PASCAL FAR WSAAsyncSelect /* 0 on success, or SOCKET_ERROR */
    (SOCKET s,      /* socket for which event notification needed */
     HWND hWnd,     /* handle for window to receive event messages */
     u_int wMsg,    /* message to receive when any event occurs */
     long lEvent); /* bitmask of network events to be reported */
```

WSACancelAsyncRequest(): Cancel an outstanding instance of an asynchronous database function (e.g., `WSAAsyncGetHostByName()`). See Chapter 10.

```
int PASCAL FAR WSACancelAsyncRequest /* 0 on success, or
                                        SOCKET_ERROR on failure */
    (HANDLE hAsyncTaskHandle);  /* asynch operation to cancel */
```

WSACancelBlockingCall(): Cancel a blocking call currently in progress. See Chapter 5

```
int PASCAL FAR WSACancelBlockingCall /* 0 on success,
                                        SOCKET_ERROR on failure */
    (void);
```

WSACleanup(): Sign off from the underlying Windows Sockets API. For each successful call to `WSAStartup()`, there must always be a matching call to `WSACleanup()` to reduce the useage count on the WinSock DLL and release system resources. See Chapter 10.

```
int PASCAL FAR WSACleanup  /*0 on success, SOCKET_ERROR */
    (void);
```

WSAGetLastError(): Obtain the value of the last Windows Sockets API Error. This is a task- (or thread-) based error (for socket-based error, use `getsockopt()` SO_ERROR). The error value is *not* reset to zero by successful function calls. See Chapter 10.

```
int PASCAL FAR WSAGetLastError  /* last error code (0 if none) */
    (void);
```

WSAIsBlocking(): Determine if a blocking call is in progress. See Chapters 5 and 9.

```
BOOL PASCAL FAR WSAIsBlocking               /* TRUE or FALSE */
    (void);
```

WSASetBlockingHook(): Establish an application-specific blocking hook function. This returns a pointer to the current blocking hook function. See Chapter 9.

```
FARPROC PASCAL FAR WSASetBlockingHook       /* NULL on failure */
    (FARPROC lpBlockFunc);    /* ptr to procedure instance address
                                 of exported function to install */
```

WSASetLastError(): Set the task- (or thread-) based error to be returned by subsequent calls to `WSAGetLastError()`. See Chapter 10.

```
void PASCAL FAR WSASetLastError
    (int iError);               /* error code to be returned */
```

WSAStartup(): Initialize the underlying Windows Sockets DLL. Note: Every WinSock application must make a successful call to `WSAStartup()` or all WinSock function calls will fail with the WSANOTINITIALISED error. Each successful call to `WSAStartup()` must be matched by a call to `WSACleanup()`. See Chapter 10.

```
int PASCAL FAR WSAStartup     /* 0 on success */
    (WORD wVersionRequired,   /* highest version of Windows Sockets
                                 API required (high-byte=minor version,
                                 low-byte=major version)*/
     LPWSADATA lpWSAData);    /* ptr to struct to receive details on
                                 Windows Sockets implementation */
```

WSAUnhookBlockingHook(): Restore the default blocking hook function. See Chapter 9.

```
int PASCAL FAR WSAUnhookBlockingHook  /* 0 on success, or SOCKET_ERROR
     (void);
```

Macros

We have two sections of macros: those not in WINSOCK.H (dubbed "optional"), and those that are in WINSOCK.H.

Optional Macros

We explicitly provide the definition for the following macros since the current v1.1 WINSOCK.H file does not include their definition.

The v1.1 WinSock specification refers to the `MAKEWORD` macro in a code example shown in the documentation for `WSAAsyncSelect()`, but this macro is not included in the WINSOCK.H file (or anywhere in the specification, either). A simple oversight. Here it is now (as derived from `MAKELONG` in WINDOWS.H).

```
#define MAKEWORD (low, high) \
       ((WORD)(((BYTE)(low)) | (((WORD)(BYTE)(high)) << 8)))
```

These macros create equivalents for commonly used memory copy, compare, and initialize functions that are part of the C runtime library on UNIX systems. These are simple conveniences to ease porting, and for reasons of good coding practices you should not use them in code you write from scratch.

```
#define bcopy(s,d,n)    _fmemcpy((d),(s),(n))
#define bcmp(s1,s2,n)   _fmemcmp((s1),(s2),(n))
#define bzero(s,n)      _fmemset(((s),0,(n))
```

Multicast (class D Internet protocol) address check (range from 224.0.0.0 through 239.255.255.255):

```
#define  IN_CLASSD(i)     (((long)(i) & 0xf0000000) == 0xe0000000)
#define  IN_MULTICAST(i) IN_CLASSD(i)
```

Options for use with get/setsockopt( ) at the IP level. First word of comment is data type; bool is stored in int. Note: The option values 9–13 were values 2–7 in the v3.5 WinNT WSOCK32.DLL.

```
#define IP_HDRINCL           2  /* int; header is included with data */
#define IP_TOS               3  /* int; IP type of service and preced. */
#define IP_TTL               4  /* int; IP time to live */
#define IP_RECVOPTS          5  /* bool; receive all IP opts w/dgram */
#define IP_RECVRETOPTS       6  /* bool; receive IP opts for response */
#define IP_RECVDSTADDR       7  /* bool; receive IP dst addr w/dgram */
#define IP_RETOPTS           8  /* ip_opts; set/get IP options */
/* Note: the following are BSD compatible but WinNT differs (by 7) */
#define IP_MULTICAST_IF      9  /* u_char; set/get IP multicast i/f  */
#define IP_MULTICAST_TTL     10 /* u_char; set/get IP multicast ttl */
#define IP_MULTICAST_LOOP    11 /* u_char; set/get IP multicast loopback*/
#define IP_ADD_MEMBERSHIP    12 /* ip_mreq; add an IP group membership */
#define IP_DROP_MEMBERSHIP 13 /* ip_mreq; drop an IP group membership */
```

Defaults and limits for multicast options:

```
#define IP_DEFAULT_MULTICAST_TTL   1    /* default TTL is one hop  */
#define IP_DEFAULT_MULTICAST_LOOP  1    /* default loopback enabled  */
#define IP_MAX_MEMBERSHIPS         20   /* max memberships per socket */
```

Special multicast addresses:

```
/* Unspecified multicast address (not used) 224.0.0.0 */
#define INADDR_UNSPEC_GROUP      (u_long)0xe0000000
/* All-hosts group address */
#define INADDR_ALLHOSTS_GROUP    (u_long)0xe0000001
```

Additional protocol families supported by 32-bit Windows (WinNT and Win95):

```
#define AF_IPX    6                  /* IPX and SPX */
#define PF_IPX    AF_IPX
```

These options are exclusive to 32-bit Windows (WinNT and Win95). Used with `setsockopt()` and `INVALID_SOCKET` for the socket parameter, it changes the default thread-based option, so subsequent calls to `socket()` by the current thread will return sockets that will not do overlapping I/O (see Chapter 15, "Platforms," for more information).

```
#define SO_OPENTYPE      0x7008
#define SO_SYNCHRONOUS_ALERT     0x10
#define SO_SYNCHRONOUS_NONALERT 0x20
```

Options for connect and disconnect data and options (supported by WinNT and Win95). Used only by non-TCP/IP transports such as DECNet, OSI TP4, and so forth.

```
#define SO_CONNDATA      0x7000
#define SO_CONNOPT       0x7001
#define SO_DISCDATA      0x7002
#define SO_DISCOPT       0x7003
#define SO_CONNDATALEN   0x7004
#define SO_CONNOPTLEN    0x7005
#define SO_DISCDATALEN   0x7006
#define SO_DISCOPTLEN    0x7007
```

Other NT-specific options (undocumented):

```
#define SO_MAXDG         0x7009
#define SO_MAXPATHDG     0x700A
```

New NT-specific I/O flag (undocumented):

```
#define MSG_PARTIAL  0x8000  /* partial send or recv
                                  for message xport*/
```

New NT-specific error value (undocumented):

```
#define WSAEDISCON    (WSABASEERR+101)
```

Macros in WINSOCK.H

All of the following macros are in the v1.1 WINSOCK.H file. In most cases, we do not show you the values for these macros, since part of the reason for macros is that there is no need to know the values (so you therefore do not code to depend on them). We have also left out a few macro categories:

- The socket option macros are covered in the table along with the `setsockopt()` function above.

- The error value macros are covered in Appendix C, "Error Reference."
- The extended data types are referenced along with their respective structures at the beginning of this appendix.

Standard function failure indicator. You should use this macro instead of "–1" to facilitate portable source code.

```
#define SOCKET_ERROR -1
```

This value is guaranteed as an invalid socket handle value (Note: Any other value—including 0—is valid), and indicates failure for the `socket()` and `accept()` functions.

```
#define INVALID_SOCKET (SOCKET)(~0)
```

The opaque socket type used in all instances that refer to a socket descriptor:

```
typedef u_int SOCKET;
```

The manifest constant to indicate a "socket level" option for `setsockopt()` or `getsockopt()`:

```
#define SOL_SOCKET  0xFFFF
```

The maximum lengths for the *szDescription* and *szSystemStatus* fields in the `WSAData` structure (filled in by the `WSAStartup()` function):

```
#define WSADESCRIPTION_LEN 256 /* max length of szDescription field */
#define WSASYS_STATUS_LEN  128 /* max length of szSystemStatus field */
```

Macros used to manipulate the read, write, and exception `fd_set` structure input parameters for the `select()` function:

```
FD_SETSIZE          /* maximum number of sockets possible in an fdset */
FD_CLR (fd, set)    /* removes a socket from an fd_set */
FD_SET (fd, set)    /* adds a socket to an fd_set */
FD_ZERO (set)       /* clears the contents of an fd_set */
FD_ISSET (fd, set) /* checks if a socket is a member of a set */
```

These are for setting and checking the time in the timeout structure (`struct timeval`) used in `select()` function calls. The timerisset and timercmp macros would be useful if the `select()` function guaranteed to return the time remaining after the `select()` function returns. However, in WinSock, as in BSD Sockets, this is *not* guaranteed.

```
timerclear (tvp)  /* sets timeout value to zero */
timerisset (tvp)  /* boolean indicates if timeout value is nonzero */
timercmp (tvp, uvp, cmp) /* boolean indicates if timeout value tvp is
                          * greater or less than uvp (cmp must be either
                          * '<' or '>' and not '=<' or '=>') */
```

Commands for the `ioctlsocket()` function. Only `FIONREAD`, `FIONBIO`, and `SIOCATMARK` are explicitly supported by the v1.1 WinSock specification (the others are likely to cause `ioctlsocket()` to fail with `WSAEINVAL`, although the function may also fail silently to avoid incompatibilities).

```
FIONREAD   /* get number of bytes available to read */
FIONBIO    /* set/clear nonblocking operation mode */
FIOASYNC   /* set/clear async I/O */
SIOCSHIWAT /* set socket high-water mark */
SIOCGHIWAT /* get   "      "      "     "   */
SIOCSLOWAT /* set socket low-water mark */
SIOCGLOWAT /* get   "      "     "      "  */
SIOCATMARK /* boolean: FALSE if at OOB data mark (opposite of BSD) */
```

Protocols (values in IP header, returned from `getprotobyname()`, etc.), used as *level* parameter in `setsockopt()` and (optionally) as *protocol* input parameter for `socket()`. Found in */etc/protocols* file in BSD systems (values from "Assigned Numbers" RFC):

```
#define IPPROTO_IP    0     /* dummy for IP */
#define IPPROTO_ICMP  1     /* control message protocol */
#define IPPROTO_GGP   2     /* gateway^2 (deprecated) */
#define IPPROTO_TCP   6     /* tcp */
#define IPPROTO_PUP   12    /* pup */
#define IPPROTO_UDP   17    /* user datagram protocol */
#define IPPROTO_IDP   22    /* xns idp */
#define IPPROTO_ND    77    /* UNOFFICIAL net disk proto */
#define IPPROTO_RAW   255   /* raw IP packet */
#define IPPROTO_MAX   256   /*it's a single byte value */
```

Macros for port numbers that correspond to standard network services (found in */etc/services* file on BSD systems. Note: These are in host order (so if you use them to initialize the sin_port field in a sockaddr_in structure, you will still need to convert to network order with htons()). The values are from "Assigned Numbers" RFC.

```
#define IPPORT_ECHO    7  /* TCP and UDP service echoes data sent */
#define IPPORT_DISCARD 9  /* TCP and UDP service "eats" data sent */
#define IPPORT_SYSTAT  11 /* TCP service returns system status */
#define IPPORT_DAYTIME 13 /* TCP and UDP service returns formatted d/t
                           *  string (e.g. "Mon Dec  5 12:17:33 1994" */
#define IPPORT_NETSTAT 15 /* TCP system net status service */
#define IPPORT_FTP     21 /* TCP file transfer service */
#define IPPORT_TELNET  23 /* TCP remote login service */
#define IPPORT_SMTP    25 /* TCP simple mail transport service */
#define IPPORT_TIMESERVER 37 /* TCP and UDP time service */
#define IPPORT_NAMESERVER 42 /**OBSOLETE** 42 is *not* DNS, 53 is */
#define IPPORT_WHOIS   43 /* TCP and UDP "whois" for user/system info */
#define IPPORT_MTP     57 /* TCP and UDP any private terminal access */
#define IPPORT_TFTP    69 /* TCP and UDP trivial file transfer service */
#define IPPORT_RJE     77 /* TCP and UDP "remote job entry" */
#define IPPORT_FINGER  79 /* TCP and UDP "finger" user and system info */
#define IPPORT_TTYLINK 87 /* TCP and UDP any private terminal link */
#define IPPORT_SUPDUP  95 /* TCP and UDP "supdup" application service */
#define IPPORT_EXECSERVER  512 /* TCP remote execution (rexec) */
#define IPPORT_LOGINSERVER 513 /* TCP remote login (rlogin) */
#define IPPORT_CMDSERVER 514   /* TCP shell service (alias "rcmd") */
#define IPPORT_EFSSERVER 520   /* TCP extended file name server */
#define IPPORT_BIFFUDP   512   /* UDP "biff" to notify user of mail */
#define IPPORT_WHOSERVER 513   /* UDP remote who's who (rwho) service */
#define IPPORT_ROUTESERVER 520 /* UDP local routing process */
#define IPPORT_RESERVED  1024  /**RESERVED** last privileged port */
```

Link numbers: For Interface Message Protocol family (AF_IMPLINK), which WinSock does not support and almost no one uses in BSD. It is for communication via raw sockets to point-to-point intelligent packet-switching nodes, found on original ARPANET.

```
#define IMPLINK_IP  155
#define IMPLINK_LOWEXPER    156
#define IMPLINK_HIGHEXPER   158
```

The following macros deal with the bits in internet address integers. Some of them are limited somewhat, since they do not take subnet masks into account (on subnets, the decomposition of addresses to host and net parts is done according to subnet mask, not the masks here). Note: IN_CLASSD appears in "Optional Macros" section.

```
IN_CLASSA(i)            (((long)(i) & 0x80000000) == 0)
IN_CLASSA_NET           0xff000000
IN_CLASSA_NSHIFT        24
IN_CLASSA_HOST          0x00ffffff
IN_CLASSA_MAX           128
IN_CLASSB(i)            (((long)(i) & 0xc0000000) == 0x80000000)
IN_CLASSB_NET           0xffff0000
IN_CLASSB_NSHIFT        16
IN_CLASSB_HOST          0x0000ffff
IN_CLASSB_MAX           65536
IN_CLASSC(i)            (((long)(i) & 0xc0000000) == 0xc0000000)
IN_CLASSC_NET           0xffffff00
IN_CLASSC_NSHIFT        8
IN_CLASSC_HOST          0x000000ff
```

Special IP addresses:

```
#define INADDR_ANY      (u_long)0x00000000 /* denotes system default */
#define INADDR_LOOPBACK   0x7f000001    /* loopback address 127.0.0.1 */
#define INADDR_BROADCAST (u_long)0xffffffff /* limited broadcast addr */
#define INADDR_NONE       0xffffffff    /* denotes invalid IP address */
```

Address families, for use as sin_family value in (any variation of the) `sockaddr` structure. The v1.1 specification supports only AF_INET and AF_UNSPEC (values from "Assigned Numbers" RFC).

```
#define AF_UNSPEC  0      /* unspecified */
#define AF_UNIX    1      /* local to host (pipes, portals) */
#define AF_INET    2      /* internetwork: UDP, TCP, etc. */
#define AF_IMPLINK 3      /* arpanet interface message processor */
#define AF_PUP     4      /* pup protocols (e.g., BSP) */
#define AF_CHAOS   5      /* mit CHAOS protocols */
#define AF_NS      6      /* XEROX NS protocols */
#define AF_ISO     7      /* ISO protocols */
#define AF_OSI   AF_ISO   /* OSI is ISO */
#define AF_ECMA    8      /* European computer manufacturers */
#define AF_DATAKIT 9      /* datakit protocols */
#define AF_CCITT   10     /* CCITT protocols, X.25, etc., */
```

```
#define AF_SNA       11   /* IBM SNA */
#define AF_DECnet    12   /* DECnet */
#define AF_DLI       13   /* Direct data-link interface */
#define AF_LAT       14   /* LAT */
#define AF_HYLINK    15   /* NSC Hyperchannel */
#define AF_APPLETALK 16 /* AppleTalk */
#define AF_NETBIOS   17 /* NetBios-style addresses */
#define AF_MAX       18
```

Socket types, as used in *type* parameter for `socket()` function. `SOCK_STREAM` and `SOCK_DGRAM` are the only (`PF_INET`) socket types guaranteed by the v1.1 Windows Sockets specification. `SOCK_RAW` is optionally available. The other types are available on Windows NT and may be available in version 2.0 of WinSock (also see "Optional Macros" section for other NT types).

```
#define SOCK_STREAM     1  /* stream socket */
#define SOCK_DGRAM      2  /* datagram socket */
#define SOCK_RAW        3  /* raw-protocol interface */
#define SOCK_RDM        4  /* reliably-delivered message */
#define SOCK_SEQPACKET  5  /* sequenced packet stream */
```

Maximum *backlog* queue length parameter for `listen()`:.

```
#define SOMAXCONN   5
```

Flags to affect I/O operation accordingly:

```
#define MSG_OOB        1  /* recv()/recvfrom(): process urgent data */
#define MSG_PEEK       2  /* recv()/recvfrom(): peek at incoming data */
#define MSG_DONTROUTE 4  /* send()/sendto(): do not use routing tables */
```

This is the maximum sized buffer filled by `WSAAsyncGetXByY()` functions. It represents not only the size of the structure (hostent, servent, or protoent) but also the memory used by all the strings pointed to by fields in the structure (this constant value is based on RFC 883).

```
#define MAXGETHOSTSTRUCT  1024
```

Bit flags used as input parameters to the `WSAAsyncSelect()` function in the *lEvent* input parameter to denote the events you would like the WinSock DLL to notify your application by sending a Windows message (the message in the *wMsg* parameter). You can use a bitwise-OR operator to combine any of these flags in a single call to `WSAAsyncSelect()`.

```
#define FD_READ    0x1   /* data availability */
#define FD_WRITE   0x2   /* write buffer availability */
#define FD_OOB     0x4   /* OOB data availability */
#define FD_ACCEPT  0x8   /* incoming connect request */
#define FD_CONNECT 0x10  /* outgoing connect completion */
#define FD_CLOSE   0x20  /* virtual circuit closed by remote */
```

This macro is provided purely to allow convenient porting of existing BSD Sockets code (`h_errno` contains the error values for `gethostbyname()` and `gethostbyaddr()` in BSD Sockets), so as a rule we do not recommend using it.

```
#define h_errno  WSAGetLastError()
```

`WSAAsync()` function message parameter composition and decomposition macros. Their use is recommended to facilitate portable source code.

```
/*
 * WSAGETASYNCBUFLEN is intended for use by the Windows Sockets
 *  application to extract the buffer length from the lParam in the
 *  response to a WSAAsyncGetXByY().
 */
#define WSAGETASYNCBUFLEN(lParam)  LOWORD(lParam)
/*
 * WSAGETASYNCERROR is intended for use by the Windows Sockets
 *  application to extract the error code from the lParam in the
 *  response to a WSAAsyncGetXByY().
 */
#define WSAGETASYNCERROR(lParam)   HIWORD(lParam)
/*
 * WSAGETSELECTEVENT is intended for use by the Windows Sockets
 *  application to extract the event code from the lParam in the
 *  response to a WSAAsyncSelect().
 */
#define WSAGETSELECTEVENT(lParam)  LOWORD(lParam)
/*
 * WSAGETSELECTERROR is intended for use by the Windows Sockets
 *  application to extract the error code from the lParam in the
 *  response to a WSAAsyncSelect().
 */
#define WSAGETSELECTERROR(lParam)   HIWORD(lParam)
```

C Error Reference

In This Appendix:

- Where to Get Error Values
- What Errors to Expect
- User-fixable Errors
- Detailed Error Descriptions
- Errors in Numerical Order

The WinSock "WSA" error values are a significant part of the Windows Sockets API. Although there are a few exceptions, most WinSock functions can fail at times. A robust application will always verify the return value from a function call to check for failure. When a WinSock function fails, the resulting error value is the key to why it failed. And knowing why it failed is the key to finding a remedy or a way to work around the problem.

In Chapter 14, "Dos and Don'ts," we describe when to expect errors (anytime), which errors to expect (any error), and how an application should handle them (tell the application user as much as you know). In Chapter 10, "Support Routines," we tell you how to retrieve and report errors using `WSAGetLastError()`. We also show you one way to display error strings with our own `WSAperror()` in the sample WinSockx library in Chapter 7. In this appendix we tell you everything there is to know about the errors themselves.

After a quick review of where to get errors and which errors to expect, we list user-fixable errors (the only ones a user should ever see). The bulk of this appendix provides a detailed description of each WinSock error: what each error means, what causes them, and how an application should deal with them. We finish with a cross-reference list to use in case you have only the numeric value of the error, not the text name.

Where to Get Error Values

There are two kinds of errors in Windows Sockets: task-based (or thread-based) and socket-based. An application can retrieve the task-based error by calling `WSAGetLastError()` immediately after a WinSock function fails (see Chapter 10, "Support Routines," for more information). The socket-based error is

- reported in a `WSAAsyncSelect()` asynchronous FD_ event notification message (which you can extract with the platform-independent "message cracker" macro **WSAGETSELECTERROR(lParam)**). See Chapter 6, "Socket States," for more information.
- retrieved by a call to `getsockopt()` **SO_ERROR** (which also resets the error value to zero). See Chapter 9, "Socket Information and Control," for more information.

`WSAStartup()` is the only function that returns an actual error value, rather than simply indicating an error condition (function failure). This makes sense, since you cannot call `WSAGetLastError()` to retrieve the error value until `WSAStartup()` succeeds; otherwise it will fail with WSAENOTINITIALISED (see Chapter 10, "Support Routines," for more information).

Windows Sockets does not support the Berkeley Sockets error variables *errno* or *h_errno* because these per-process global variables do not allow for per-thread error information. The WINSOCK.H header file provides a macro for *h_errno* for Berkeley source code compatibility (it simply calls `WSAGetLastError()`). The equivalent macro for *errno* was not included since some applications use *errno* for nonsocket (e.g., file handle) errors.

Most of the error values and their manifest constants (macros) are derived from Berkeley Sockets. The WinSock error values are the BSD error values with a "WinSock API base" error (WSABASEERR) value added to each of them. The macro for each WinSock API error is the equivalent BSD error's macro, with the three letter "WSA" prepended to it. So, for instance, the BSD manifest constant for the "would block" error is defined in the Berkeley Sockets ERRNO.H header file as

```
#define EWOULDBLOCK 35
```

and WINSOCK.H redefines it as

```
#define WSAEWOULDBLOCK (WSABASEERR+35)
```

A few (lower-value) WinSock error macro definitions refer to Microsoft C constants. In some cases, these redefine file-access errors since Windows NT can treat a socket like a file handle. A few other (higher-value) macros are entirely new to Windows Sockets. They refer to error conditions unique to Windows Sockets, such as invalid WinSock version requests, uninitialized WinSock DLL access, or failed hostname resolution attempts.

All of the Windows Sockets error values have macros defined for them in the WINSOCK.H header file. They all have a "WSA" prefix, and their values are all biased by the WinSock API base error WSABASEERR (10000) value. The value for WSABASEERR is fairly arbitrary. It's high simply because error values in the Windows API are high by convention. There is a benefit, though: The unique bias creates identifiable WinSock error values.

What Errors to Expect

Do not assume the only errors you will encounter are the ones listed with each function in the WinSock specification. Section 3.3.4, "Error Handling," in the v1.1 Windows Sockets specification warns against this:

> Note that this specification defines a recommended set of error codes, and lists the possible errors which may be returned as a result of each function. It may be the case in some implementations that other Windows Sockets error codes will be returned in addition to those listed, and applications should be prepared to handle errors other than those enumerated under each API description.

The specification is a common denominator among WinSock implementations. The errors it lists do not provide "fine resolution" in all cases, which means it does not account for some conditions that some network systems can detect. Finer resolution in error reporting is a double-edged sword: With more accurate error values it is easier to diagnose problems when they occur, but it is also more difficult to write an application that can handle all contingencies. The better prepared your application is for any error, the more gracefully you will handle it, and the easier you will make your job and the job of your support staff.

User-fixable Errors

There are two basic types of errors: those an application user can remedy, and those he or she cannot. As we describe in Chapter 14, "Dos and Don'ts," a user should never see an error that is not user-fixable. If your user does, then you need to fix your application to handle the error gracefully. Here is a list of user-fixable errors:

WSAEADDRINUSE	(10048)	Address already in use
WSAECONNABORTED	(10053)	Software caused connection abort
WSAECONNREFUSED	(10061)	Connection refused
WSAECONNRESET	(10054)	Connection reset by peer
WSAEDESTADDRREQ	(10039)	Destination address required
WSAEHOSTUNREACH	(10065)	No route to host
WSAEMFILE	(10024)	Too many open files
WSAENETDOWN	(10050)	Network is down
WSAENETRESET	(10052)	Network dropped connection
WSAENOBUFS	(10055)	No buffer space available
WSAENETUNREACH	(10051)	Network is unreachable
WSAETIMEDOUT	(10060)	Connection timed out
WSAHOST_NOT_FOUND	(11001)	Host not found
WSASYSNOTREADY	(10091)	Network subsystem is unavailable
WSANOTINITIALISED	(10093)	WSAStartup() not performed
WSANO_DATA	(11004)	Valid name, no data of that type
WSANO_RECOVERY	(11003)	Non-recoverable query error
WSATRY_AGAIN	(11002)	Non-authoritative host found
WSAVERNOTSUPPORTED	(10092)	Wrong WinSock DLL version

Each of these "user-fixable" errors have user suggestions in the detailed error list in the next section. To help your users fix these errors themselves as much as possible, pass on some of these suggestions in your error messages. This will avoid support calls. To help yourself when you do get a support call, be sure to include the context of the error in every error message, along with the error value and description (i.e., include the name of the function that caused the error).

Detailed Error Descriptions

The Windows Sockets specification describes error definitions for each function, but it does not provide any short error text for an application to use at run time to describe a problem to a user. The Windows Sockets API does not have analogs for the Berkeley `perror()` and `herror()` functions that take the error value as input and output the (short) text of each error value (we show the code for an alternative in Chapter 10, "Support Routines"). Since Windows Sockets is practically a clone of Berkeley Sockets, and the rule of thumb is "*When in doubt, defer to Berkeley,*" we can adopt the Berkeley Software Distribution error text as our own.

Among other things, that is exactly what we have done here. We took the text of the *errno* manual page in BSD 4.3, filled in gaps, and embellished, completing the information. The Windows Sockets errors are listed in alphabetical order below (they are cross-referenced in a list in numerical order at the end of this appendix). Every error description contains at least the following elements:

- *Summary Information*:
  - Error macro: manifest constant, as defined in WINSOCK.H
  - Error value: as defined in v1.1 WINSOCK.H
  - Short description
- *Berkeley description:* This text describes the equivalent BSD 4.3 error value (with some input from other UNIX *errno* values as well). Most of the text comes from the output from the "man errno" command in UNIX.
- *WinSock description:* This contains a quick comparison to the Berkeley counterpart and a long description of the WinSock error.
- *WinSock functions:* These are the functions that explicitly list this error in the v1.1 Windows Sockets specification.

Other information varies between different errors. Some of the additional information includes these items:

- *Microsoft C description:* The first few WinSock errors are carryovers from the standard C run-time library. Typically their descriptions are similar.
- *Detailed descriptions:* These give the specific meanings that some WinSock functions have for some errors.
- *TCP/IP scenario:* This is a description of the TCP/IP suite network traffic (i.e., TCP, UDP, ICMP, ARP, DNS) that typically causes the error.

- *Developer suggestions:* These suggest what an application developer can do to avoid the error.
- *User suggestions:* These offer advice about what an application user can do to diagnose the error condition further and possibly remedy it.
- *Additional functions:* These provide a generic description of the type of functions that can return this error, which may include functions other than those listed by the WinSock specification. It may also make explicit mention of other functions that can fail with this error.
- *See also:* These point to other errors that are similar. Developers should consider handling the referenced errors similarly.

Although most of this appendix is for application developers, the user suggestions contain information that users and application support personnel might also find useful when an application fails. We suggest local configuration changes that might remedy the problem and network and server conditions that might be the cause. The errors that have user suggestions all appear in the "User-fixable errors" list given earlier.

The WinSock description and TCP/IP scenario elements contain detailed descriptions of the errors, which also describe possible causes and offer a potential remedy. For more information on debugging problems, see Chapter 13, "Debugging."

Errorless Functions

Eight of the forty-six functions in the Windows Sockets API are not referenced in any of the "WinSock function" lists in the following detailed descriptions. The v1.1 WinSock specification does not list any errors for these functions. Specifically, these errorless functions are the byte order functions (`htonl()`, `htons()`, `ntohl()`, and `ntohs()`), the address manipulation functions (`inet_addr()` and `inet_ntoa`), `WSAGetLastError()`, and `WSAIsBlocking()`.

Some of these functions cannot fail, which explains their absence from the error list that follows. Of the two that can fail, neither of them sets an error value you can retrieve from `WSAGetLastError()` (refer to Chapter 10, "Support Routines," for more information on any of these errorless functions).

- the byte order functions—`htonl()`, `htons()`, `ntohl()`, and `ntohl()`—cannot fail.
- `WSAGetLastError()` and `WSAIsBlocking()` cannot fail.

- The address manipulation functions, `inet_ntoa()` and `inet_addr()`, *can* fail. However, they do not need to set the WinSock error value, because there is only one reason for their failure: The input parameter was invalid. For `inet_addr()`, this could mean the content of the buffer passed or the buffer itself is invalid.

Functionless Errors

There are a total of 50 unique WinSock error values. The values for WSANO_DATA and WSANO_ADDRESS (11004) are duplicates, so we only count one of them. The v1.1 WinSock specification ascribes only 33 of the 50 errors to any of the WinSock functions in the v1.1 Windows Sockets specification. Thirteen errors have "<none>" next to the list of WinSock functions that can produce them. That's about one-quarter of all the error values.

Some of these neglected error values are among those mentioned earlier that provide "finer resolution" on different WinSock implementations. In some cases, these errors are platform dependent. For instance, you might get WSAEBADF in place of WSAENOTSOCK on a system that provides some socket and file handle equivalency. But most of these functionless errors are simply out of place; they are inappropriate to the Windows Sockets API as it exists in the v1.1 specification. You are unlikely to encounter them. But that is *not* to say you should not be prepared.

As we pointed out earlier, your application should be ready to encounter any error at any time. Although the specification does not list an error for a function, it does allow for it. In fact, on occasion you can benefit if the WinSock implementation returns these other errors. The occurrence of an unlisted error can provide extra detail. This can help you (or your support staff) to zero in on the cause when your application runs into a problem.

Some WinSock implementations use these errors inappropriately, but they have a particular meaning. They signal unusual error conditions for which there is no WinSock error equivalent. Unfortunately, to find out what these errors mean, you need to contact that WinSock provider.

Error Description List

What follows is the complete list of WinSock errors and descriptions:

<no macro available> (0) *No error*

WSABASEERR (10000) *No error*

Berkeley Description: no equivalent

WinSock description: No error

Detailed description: At least one WinSock implementation will occasionally fail a function and report this as the error value even though the function *succeeded.* You should simply ignore this error when it occurs.

WinSock functions: <none>

WSAEACCES (10013) *Permission denied*

Berkeley description: An attempt was made to access a file in a way forbidden by its file access permissions.

Microsoft C description: Permission denied. The file's permission setting does not allow the specified access. This error signifies that an attempt was made to access a file (or, in some cases, a directory) in a way that is incompatible with the file's attributes. For example, the error can occur when an attempt is made to read from a file that is not open, to open an existing read-only file for writing, or to open a directory instead of a file. Under MS-DOS versions 3.0 and later, EACCES may also indicate a locking or sharing violation. The error can also occur in an attempt to rename a file or directory or to remove an existing directory.

WinSock description: Same as Berkeley

Detailed description:

send() and sendto(): The requested address is a broadcast address, but the appropriate flag was not set (i.e., you did not call `setsockopt()` SO_BROADCAST).

WinSock functions: `send()`, `sendto()`

Additional functions: `setsockopt()` and any function that takes a socket (or file handle) as an input parameter.

WSAEADDRINUSE (10048) *Address already in use*

Berkeley description: Only one usage of each address is normally permitted.

WinSock description: Same as Berkeley. The "address" the error refers to is typically the local socket name, which made up of the 3-tuple: protocol, port number, and IP address.

Developer suggestions: Do not call `bind()` in a client application. Instead, let the network system assign the local port; very few application protocols require a client to bind to a specific port number or port number range. Alternately, you could call `setsockopt()` SO_REUSEADDR to allow duplicate local addresses in a single application, but we don't recommend this approach.

User suggestions: Do not try running two of the same types of server applications on the same machine. For instance, this error will occur if you try to run two applications that have FTP servers. In this case, the second application will fail with WSAEADDRINUSE.

Winsock functions: bind(), connect(), listen(), FD_CONNECT

WSAEADDRNOTAVAIL (10049) *Cannot assign requested address*

Berkeley description: This normally results from an attempt to create a socket with an address not on this machine.

WinSock description: Partly the same as Berkeley. The "address" the error refers to is the remote socket name, which is made up of the 3-tuple: protocol, port, and address. This error occurs when the sin_port value is zero in a sockaddr_in structure for connect() or sendto().

In Berkeley, this error also occurs when you are trying to name the local socket (assign local address and port number) with bind(), but Windows Sockets does not ascribe this error to bind(), for some unknown reason.

Developer suggestions: Assume bind() will fail with this error. Let the network-system assign the default local IP address by referencing INADDR_ANY in the sin_addr field of a sockaddr_in structure input to bind().

WinSock functions: connect(), sendto(), FD_CONNECT

Additional functions: The v1.1 specification does not ascribe this error to the function bind(), but this may have been an oversight.

WSAEAFNOSUPPORT (10047) *Address family not supported by protocol family*

Berkeley description: An address incompatible with the requested protocol was used. For example, you should not necessarily expect to be able to use NS addresses with ARPA Internet protocols.

WinSock description: Same as Berkeley, and then some. The error occurs with the socket() function, which takes the socket type, protocol, and address family as input parameters.

It also occurs with functions that take a socket handle and a sockaddr structure as input parameters. A socket already has a type (a protocol), and each sockaddr structure has an address family field to define its format. A function fails with WSAEAFNOSUPPORT if the address family referenced in sockaddr is not compatible with the referenced socket's protocol.

This error apparently also takes the place of WSAEPFNOSUPPORT (which means "protocol family not supported"), since that error is not listed for socket() in the v1.1 WinSock specification.

WinSock functions: bind(), connect(), sendto(), socket(), FD_CONNECT

See also: WSAEPROTOTYPE

WSAEALREADY (10037) *Operation already in progress*

Berkeley description: An operation was attempted on a nonblocking object that already had an operation in progress.

WinSock description: Unlike Berkeley Sockets, in WinSock WSAEALREADY means that the asynchronous operation you attempted to cancel has already been cancelled. However, there is little distinction between WSAEALREADY and WSAEINVAL, since a WinSock DLL cannot tell the difference between an asynchronous operation that has been cancelled and one that was never valid.

WinSock functions: `WSACancelAsyncRequest()`

Additional functions: Berkeley Sockets' `connect()` returns this error on subsequent calls, after an initial call on a nonblocking socket, and before the connection is established (at which time `connect()` fails with WSAEISCONN). Note: Some WinSocks fail with WSAEINVAL when you call `connect()` a second time (or subsequent) on a nonblocking socket, regardless of the socket state.

WSAEBADF (10009) *Bad file descriptor*

Berkeley description: A file descriptor argument was out of range or referred to no open file, or a read (write) request was made to a file that was only open for writing (reading).

Microsoft C description: Bad file number. The specified file handle is not a valid file handle value or does not refer to an open file; or an attempt was made to write to a file or device opened for read-only access (or vice versa).

WinSock description: No equivalent in WinSock. However, because a BSD socket is equivalent to a file handle, some Windows Sockets platforms provide some file handle and socket equivalency. In this case, the WSAEBADF error might mean the same as a WSAENOTSOCK error.

WinSock functions: <none>

Additional functions: any function that takes a socket (or file handle) as an input parameter

See also: WSAENOTSOCK

WSAECONNABORTED (10053) *Software caused connection abort*

Berkeley description: A connection abort was caused internal to your host machine. The software caused a connection abort because there is no space on the socket's queue and the socket cannot receive further connections.

WinSock description: Partly the same as Berkeley. The error can occur when the local network system aborts a connection. This would occur if WinSock aborts an established connection after data retransmission fails (receiver never acknowledges data sent on a stream socket).

TCP/IP scenario: A connection will time out if the local system does not receive an (ACK)nowledgment for data sent. It would also time out if a (FIN)ish TCP packet is not ACK'd (and even if the FIN is ACK'd, it will eventually time out if a FIN is not returned).

User suggestions: There are a number of things to check that might help to identify the reason(s) for the failure. Basically, you want to identify where the problem occurred.

- Ping the remote host to which you were connected. If it does not respond, it might be off-line or there may be a network problem along the way. If it does respond, then this problem might have been a transient one (so you can reconnect now), or the server application you were connected to might have terminated (so you might not be able to connect again).
- Ping a local host to verify that your local network is still functioning (if on a serial connection, see next step).
- Ping your local router address. If you are on a serial connection, your local router is the IP address of the host you initially logged onto with SLIP or PPP.
- Ping a host on the same subnet as the host you were connected to (if you know one). This will verify that the destination network is functioning.
- Try a "traceroute" to the host to which you were connected. This will not reveal too much unless you know the router addresses at the remote end, but it might help to identify if the problem is somewhere along the way.

WinSock functions: `recv()`, `recvfrom()`, `sendto()`, FD_CLOSE

Additional functions: `send()` can also fail with WSAECONNABORTED. Any function that takes a socket as an input parameter—except `closesocket()`—could potentially fail with this error.

See also: WSAECONNRESET, WSAENETRESET, WSAETIMEDOUT

WSAECONNREFUSED (10061) *Connection refused*

Berkeley description: No connection could be made because the target machine actively refused it. This usually results from trying to connect to a service that is inactive on the foreign host.

WinSock description: Same as Berkeley

TCP/IP scenario: In TCP terms (stream sockets), it means an attempt to connect (by sending a TCP SYN packet) caused the destination host to respond to the host by returning a reset (a TCP RST packet). If an application sends a UDP packet to a host/port that does not have a datagram socket "listening," the network system may respond by sending back a "port unreachable" ICMP packet.

User suggestions: Either you went to the wrong host, or the server application you are trying to contact is not executing. Check the destination address you are using. If you used a host name, did it resolve to the correct address? If the hostname resolution uses a local host table, it's possible you resolved to an old, obsolete address. It's also possible that the local services file has an incorrect port number (although this is unlikely).

You can verify that the remote system is rejecting your connection attempt by checking the network statistics locally. Check that your network system (WinSock implementation) has a utility that shows network statistics. You could use this to verify that you are receiving TCP resets or "port unreachable" ICMP packets each time you attempt to connect.

Developer suggestions: If you have a network analyzer available, you can quickly check if the destination port number and host address are what you expect. On the server end, you could use a network system utility similar to BSD's "netstat -a" command to check that your server is running and also listening on the right port number.

This is one of the most frequent errors and one of the best to encounter, since it's also one of the least ambiguous. There are only a few possible causes for this error:

- *You tried to connect to the wrong port.* This is a common problem. You need to call `htons()` to translate a constant value to network byte order before assigning it to the sin_port field in the `sockaddr` structure.
- *You tried to connect to the wrong destination host address.*
- *The server application is not running on the destination host.*
- *The server application is not listening on the right port.* The server application might need to call `htons()` to translate the port to network byte order in the `sockaddr` structure.

WinSock functions: With a stream socket: `connect()` and FD_CONNECT `WSAAsyncSelect()` notification message

Additional functions: With a datagram socket: `send()` or `sendto()`, or FD_READ

WSAECONNRESET (10054) *Connection reset by peer*

Berkeley description: A connection was forcibly closed by a peer. This normally results from a loss of the connection on the remote socket due to a timeout or a reboot.

WinSock description: Same as Berkeley. On a stream socket, the connection was reset. This reset could be generated locally by the network system when it detects a connection failure, or it might be received from the remote host (in TCP terms, the remote host sent a RST packet). This error is also possible on a datagram socket; for instance, this error could result if your application sends a UDP datagram to a host, which rejects it by responding with a "port unreachable" ICMP message.

User suggestions: Some network systems have commands to report statistics. In this case, it might be possible to check the count of TCP RST packets, or "port unreachable" ICMP packets received. See other suggestions under WSAECONNABORTED.

WinSock functions: `recv()`, `recvfrom()`, `send()`, `sendto()`, FD_CLOSE

Additional functions: Any function that does I/O on the network could generate this error. Two functions that are conspicuously absent from the current function list above are `shutdown()` and `closesocket()`.

See also: WSAECONNABORTED, WSAENETRESET, WSAETIMEDOUT

WSAEDESTADDRREQ (10039) *Destination address required*

Berkeley description: A required address was omitted from an operation on a socket.

WinSock description: Same as Berkeley. The explanation is simple and obvious: In order to connect to or send to a destination address, you need to provide the destination address. This error occurs if the `sin_addr` is INADDR_ANY (i.e., a long zero) in the `sockaddr_in` structure passed to `sendto()`. Note: Although `connect()` and FD_CONNECT also have this error listed, the documentation specifically states that WSAEADDRNOTAVAIL is appropriate if INADDR_ANY is passed as a destination address.

User suggestions: Did you enter a destination host name? If so, then the application might have had a problem resolving the name (see suggestions at WSATRY_AGAIN for more information).

Developer suggestions: If you do not detect it beforehand (e.g., after failed calls to `inet_addr()` or `gethostbyname()`), then simply test your address value for zero before you pass it to `sendto()`.

WinSock functions: `connect()`, `sendto()`, FD_CONNECT

WSAEDQUOT (10069) *Disk quota exceeded*

Berkeley description: A write to an ordinary file, the creation of a directory or symbolic link, or the creation of a directory entry failed because the user's quota of disk blocks was exhausted; or the allocation of an inode for a newly created file failed because the user's quota of inodes was exhausted.

WinSock description: No equivalent. This has no network-relevant analog (although the "inode" reference could refer to a network file system entry).

WinSock functions: <none>

WSAEFAULT (10014) *Bad address*

Berkeley description: The system detected an invalid address in attempting to use an argument of a call.

WinSock description: Same as Berkeley, and then some. Specifically, the v1.1 WinSock specification notes that this error occurs if the length of the buffer is too small; for instance, if the length of a struct `sockaddr` is not equivalent to the `sizeof(struct sockaddr)`. However, it also occurs when an application passes an invalid pointer value.

Developer suggestions: Always check the return value from a memory allocation to be sure it succeeded. Always be sure to allocate enough space.

WinSock functions: `accept()`, `bind()`, `connect()`, `gethostname()`, `getpeername()`, `getsockname()`, `getsockopt()`, `recvfrom()`, `send()`, `sendto()`, `setsockopt()` if buffer length is too small

Additional functions: Any function that takes a pointer as an input parameter: `inet_addr()`, `inet_ntoa()`, `ioctlsocket()`, `gethostbyaddr()`, `gethostbyname()`, `getservbyname()`, `getservbyport()`, `WSAAsyncGetHostByName()`, `WSAAsyncGetHostByAddr()`, `WSAAsyncGetProtoByName()`, `WSAAsyncGetProtoByNumber`, `WSAAsyncGetServByName()`, `WSAAsyncGetServByPort()`, `WSASetBlockingHook()`

WSAEHOSTDOWN (10064) *Host is down*

Berkeley description: A socket operation failed because the destination host was down. A socket operation encountered a dead host. Networking activity on the local host has not been initiated.

WinSock description: No equivalent. The only time a WinSock might use this error—at least with a TCP/IP implementation of WinSock—it fails a function with other errors (for example, WSAETIMEDOUT).

WinSock functions: <none>

See also: WSAECONNABORTED, WSAECONNRESET, WSAENETRESET, WSAETIMEDOUT

WSAEHOSTUNREACH (10065) *No route to host*

Berkeley description: A socket operation was attempted to an unreachable host.

WinSock description: Same as Berkeley. Unlike Berkeley, however, WinSock v1.1 does not ascribe this error to any functions. In its place, WinSock uses the error WSAENETUNREACH exclusively.

TCP/IP scenario: In BSD-compatible implementations, the local network system generates this error if no default route is configured. Typically, though, WinSock generates WSAENETUNREACH when it receives a "host unreachable" ICMP message from a router instead of WSAEHOSTUNREACH. The ICMP message means that the router cannot forward the IP datagram, possibly because it did not get a response to the ARP request (which might mean the destination host is down).

User suggestions: See WSAENETUNREACH for details

WinSock functions: <none>

Additional functions: Any function that does network I/O
See also: WSAENETUNREACH

WSAEINPROGRESS (10036) *Operation now in progress*

Berkeley description: An operation that takes a long time to complete (such as a `connect()`) was attempted on a nonblocking socket (see `ioctl()`).

WinSock description: The Windows Sockets definition of this error is *very different* from Berkeley. WinSock only allows a single blocking operation to be outstanding per task (or thread), and if you make any other function call (whether or not it references that or any other socket) the function fails with the WSAEINPROGRESS error. It means that there is a blocking operation outstanding.

It is also possible that WinSock might return this error after an application calls `connect()` a second time on a nonblocking socket while the connection is pending (i.e., after the first failed with WSAEWOULDBLOCK). This is what occurs in Berkeley Sockets.

Developer suggestions: Handle this as a nonfatal error. Any application that uses a blocking socket or calls any blocking functions must handle this error. You can attempt to avoid the error by calling `WSAIsBlocking()` before making any WinSock function calls, or keep some application state.

WinSock functions: `accept()`, `bind()`, `closesocket()`, `connect()`, `gethostbyaddr()`, `gethostbyname()`, `gethostname()`, `getpeername()`, `getprotobyname()`, `getprotobynumber()`, `getservbyname()`, `getservbyport()`, `getsockname()`, `getsockopt()`, `ioctlsocket()`, `listen()`, `recv()`, `recvfrom()`, `select()`, `send()`, `sendto()`, `setsockopt()`, `shutdown()`, `socket()`, `WSAAsyncGetHostByAddr()`, `WSAAsyncGetHostByName()`, `WSAAsyncGetProtoByName()`, `WSAAsyncGetProtoByNumber()`, `WSAAsyncGetServByName()`, `WSAAsyncGetServByPort()`, `WSAAsyncSelect()`, `WSACancelAsyncRequest()`, `WSACleanup()`, `WSASetBlockingHook()`

Additional functions: Any WinSock function except `WSACancel BlockingCall()` (in particular, `WSAStartup()` and `WSAUnhook BlockingHook()`)

WSAEINTR (10004) *Interrupted function call*

Berkeley description: An asynchronous signal (such as SIGINTor SIGQUIT) was caught by the process during the execution of an interruptible function. If the signal handler performs a normal return, the interrupted function call will seem to have returned the error condition.

WinSock description: Not the same as Berkeley, but analogous. In WinSock it means a blocking operation was interrupted by a call to `WSACancelBlockingCall()`.

Developer suggestions: You need to be prepared to handle this error on any functions that reference blocking sockets, or any calls to blocking functions if you allow the user to cancel a blocking call. Whether to handle it as a fatal or nonfatal error depends on the application and the context, so it's entirely up to you to decide.

WinSock functions: Any function capable of a blocking operation can return this error: `accept()`, `closesocket()`, `connect()`, `gethostbyname()`, `gethostbyaddr()`, `getprotobyname()`, `getprotobynumber()`, `getservbyname()`, `getservbyport()`, `recv()`, `recvfrom()`, `select()`, `send()`, `sendto()`.

Additional functions: Any of the `WSAAsyncGetXByY()` database functions may return this error in the asynchronous notification message to indicate that the previous call was cancelled with a call to `WSACancelAsyncRequest()`.

WSAEINVAL (10022) *Invalid argument*

Berkeley description: Some invalid argument was supplied (for example, specifying an invalid level to the `setsockopt()` function).

Microsoft C description: Invalid argument. An invalid value was given for one of the arguments to a function. For example, the value given for the origin when positioning a file pointer (by means of a call to `fseek`) is before the beginning of the file.

WinSock description: Similar to Berkeley and Microsoft C, the generic meaning is that an application passed an invalid input parameter in a function call. The error refers to content as well as value (e.g., it may occur when a pointer to a structure is invalid or when a value in a structure field is invalid). In some instances, it also refers to the current state of the socket input parameter.

Detailed descriptions (relevant to socket states):

accept():	`listen()` was not invoked prior to `accept()`
bind():	socket already bound to an address
getsockname():	socket not bound with `bind()`
listen():	socket not bound with `bind()` *or* already connected
recv() and recvfrom():	socket not bound (for a datagram socket) *or* not yet connected (for a stream socket), or the requested length is zero (whether a length > 32K is acceptable as a nonnegative value is unclear, so do not use them)
send() and sendto():	socket not bound (for a datagram) *or* not yet connected (for a stream socket)

The v1.1 specification also has a detailed description for the `connect()` function; it says: "Socket not already bound to an address." This text is a typo that makes no sense. Ignore it. The standard meaning for WSAEINVAL applies to `connect()` (invalid argument).

WinSock functions: `accept()`, `bind()`, `getsockname()`, `ioctlsocket()`, `listen()`, `recv()`, `recvfrom()`, `select()`, `send()`, `setsockopt()`, `shutdown()`, `WSAStartup()`, `WSAAsyncSelect()`, `WSACancelAsyncRequest()`, `WSACancelBlockingCall()`, FD_CONNECT

Additional functions: Any WinSock function that takes input parameters that could be invalid (i.e., have bounds, or specific values) might return this error.

WSAEISCONN (10056) *Socket is already connected*

Berkeley description: A connect request was made on an already connected socket; or a `sendto()` or `sendmsg()` request on a connected socket specified a destination when already connected.

WinSock description: Same as Berkeley, except WinSock does not support the `sendmsg()` function, and some WinSock implementations do not require an application with a datagram socket to "disconnect" (by calling `connect()` with a AF_INET NULL destination address: INADDR_ANY (0.0.0.0), and port 0) before redirecting datagrams with `sendto()` or `connect()`. On a stream socket, some applications use this error with a nonblocking socket calling `connect()` to detect when a connection attempt has completed. However, this is not recommended since some WinSocks fail with WSAEINVAL on subsequent `connect()` calls.

Developer suggestions: To make your application more portable: With a datagram socket, do not use `connect()` and `sendto()` on the same socket in an application, and always "disconnect" before calling `connect()` more than once; with a stream socket, do not call `connect()` more than once (use `select()` or `WSAAsyncSelect()` to detect connection completion).

WinSock functions: `listen()`, FD_CONNECT

Additional functions: `connect()`, `sendto()`

WSAELOOP (10062) *Too many levels of symbolic links*

Berkeley description: A pathname lookup involved more than eight symbolic links. Too many links were encountered in translating a path name.

WinSock description: No equivalent

WinSock functions: <none>

WSAEMFILE (10024) *Too many open files*

Berkeley description: Too many open files. No process may have more than a system-defined number of file descriptors open at one time.

Microsoft C description: Too many open files. No more file handles are available, so no more files can be opened.

WinSock description: Similar to Berkeley and Microsoft C, but in reference to sockets rather than file handles (although the descriptions in the v1.1 specification say "no more file descriptors available"). Generically, the error means the network system has run out of socket handles.

User suggestions: It may indicate that there are too many WinSock applications running simultaneously, but this is unlikely since most network systems have many socket handles available. It could also occur if an application opens and closes sockets often but does not properly close the sockets (which leaves them open, as "orphans"). To recover the orphaned sockets, you may need to force an unload of the WinSock DLL. To do this, you can try closing the application and restarting it to recover the open sockets; but you may have to end all WinSock applications, or exit from Windows.

WinSock functions: Any function that allocates a new descriptor: `accept()`, `listen()`, and `socket()`. The v1.1 specification also lists `connect()`, although it does not allocate a descriptor.

WSAEMSGSIZE (10040) *Message too long*

Berkeley description: A message sent on a socket was larger than the internal message buffer or some other network limit.

WinSock description: Similar to Berkeley.

Detailed description:

recv() and *recvfrom():* If the datagram you read is larger than the buffer you supplied, then WinSock truncates the datagram (i.e., copies what it can into your buffer) and fails the function.

send() and *sendto():* You cannot send a datagram as large as you have requested. Note that the v1.1 WinSock specification does *not* explicitly state that this error occurs if the value you request is larger than the value of the `iMaxUdpDg` field in the `WSAData` structure (filled-in by `WSAStartup()`). Since the buffering requirements for sending are less than those for receiving datagrams, it's conceivable that you can send a datagram larger than you can receive.

WinSock functions: `recv()`, `recvfrom()`, `send()`, `sendto()`

WSAENAMETOOLONG (10063) *File name too long*

Berkeley description: A component of a path name exceeded 255 (MAXNAMELEN) characters, or an entire path name exceeded 1023 (MAXPATHLEN-1) characters.

WinSock description: No equivalent.

WinSock functions: <none>

WSAENETDOWN (10050) *Network is down*

Berkeley description: A socket operation encountered a dead network.

WinSock description: Same as Berkeley. As you can see from the comprehensive list of WinSock functions, this error is the catch-all. When it occurs, it could indicate a serious failure of your network system (i.e., the protocol stack that the WinSock DLL uses runs over).

User suggestions: Check your WinSock, protocol stack, network driver, and network interface card configuration. Note that this error occurs rarely, since a WinSock implementation cannot reliably detect hardware problems.

WinSock functions: `accept()`, `bind()`, `closesocket()`, `connect()`, `gethostbyaddr()`, `gethostbyname()`, `gethostname()`, `getpeername()`, `getprotobyname()`, `getprotobynumber()`, `getservbyname()`, `getservbyport()`, `getsockname()`, `getsockopt()`, `ioctlsocket()`, `listen()`, `recv()`, `recvfrom()`, `select()`, `send()`, `sendto()`, `setsockopt()`, `shutdown()`, `socket()`, `WSAAsyncGetHostByAddr()`, `WSAAsyncGetHostByName()`, `WSAAsyncGetProtoByName()`, `WSAAsyncGetProtoByNumber()`, `WSAAsyncGetServByName()`, `WSAAsyncGetServByPort()`, `WSAAsyncSelect()`, `WSACancelAsyncRequest()`, `WSACancelBlockingCall()`, `WSACleanup()`, `WSASetBlockingHook()`, FD_ACCEPT, FD_CLOSE, FD_OOB, FD_READ, FD_WRITE

Additional functions: All functions capable of failing can fail with this error. The v1.1 specification forgot to include `WSASetLastError()` and `WSAUnhookBlockingHook()`.

WSAENETRESET (10052) *Network dropped connection on reset*

Berkeley description: The host you were connected to crashed and rebooted.

WinSock description: Same as Berkeley.

Detailed description:

setsockopt(): WinSock generates this error if you try to set SO_KEEPALIVE on a connection that has already timed out.

User suggestions: See WSAECONNABORTED for details.

WinSock functions: `send()`, `sendto()`, `setsockopt()`

Additional functions: Any function that does network I/O: `recv()`, `recvfrom()`, FD_READ, FD_WRITE

See also: WSAECONNABORTED, WSAECONNRESET, WSAETIMEDOUT

WSAENETUNREACH (10051) *Network is unreachable*

Berkeley description: A socket operation was attempted to an unreachable network.

WinSock description: Almost the same as Berkeley. For WinSock, this error is equivalent to Berkeley's EHOSTUNREACH error, the catch-all error for unreachable hosts: "You cannot get there from here."

TCP/IP scenario: The local network system could generate this error if no default route is configured. Typically, though, WinSock generates this error when it receives a "host unreachable" ICMP message from a router. The ICMP message means that a router cannot forward the IP datagram, possibly because it did not get a response to the ARP request (which might mean the destination host is down). Note: This error may also result if you are trying to send a multicast packet and the default gateway does not support multicast (check your interface configuration).

User suggestions: Try to ping the destination host to see if you get the same results (chances are, you will). Check the destination address itself; is it the one you wanted to go to? Check whether you have a router configured in your network system (your WinSock implementation). Do a traceroute to try to determine where the failure occurs along the route between your host and the destination host.

WinSock functions: `connect()`, `sendto()`, FD_CONNECT

Additional functions: Any function that does network I/O: `recv()`, `recvfrom()`, `send()`, FD_READ, FD_WRITE

See also: WSAEHOSTUNREACH

WSAENOBUFS (10055) *No buffer space available*

Berkeley description: An operation on a socket or pipe was not performed because the system lacked sufficient buffer space or because a queue was full.

WinSock description: Same as Berkeley. The WinSock implementation was unable to allocate additional memory to accommodate the function request.

User suggestions: This error indicates a shortage of resources on your system. It can occur if you are trying to run too many applications (of any kind) simultaneously on your machine. If this tends to occur after running certain applications for a while, it might be a symptom of an application that does not return system resources (like memory) properly. It may also indicate you are not closing the applications properly. If it persists, exit Windows or reboot your machine to remedy the problem. You can monitor available memory with the Program Manager's "Help/About..." command.

WinSock functions: `accept()`, `bind()`, `connect()`, `listen()`, `send()`, `sendto()`, `socket()`, `WSAAsyncGetHostByAddr()`, `WSAAsyncGetHostByName()`, `WSAAsyncGetProtoByName()`, `WSAAsyncGetProtoByNumber()`, `WSAAsyncGetServByName()`, `WSAAsyncGetServByPort()`, FD_CONNECT

Additional functions: Any other functions that use network system buffer space, like the "database functions," `setsockopt()` with SO_RCVBUF or SO_SNDBUF options

WSAENOPROTOOPT (10042) *Bad protocol option*

Berkeley description: A bad option or level was specified in a `getsockopt()` or `setsockopt()` call.

WinSock description: Same as Berkeley: the value in the *level* or *optname* input arguments to `getsockopt()` or `setsockopt()` is unknown or unsupported.

Detailed description:

> SO_BROADCAST is not supported on sockets of type SOCK_STREAM.
>
> SO_ACCEPTCONN, SO_DONTLINGER, SO_KEEPALIVE, SO_LINGER, SO_OOBINLINE, and TCP_NODELAY are not supported on sockets of type SOCK_DGRAM.
>
> SO_DEBUG, SO_DONTROUTE, SO_RCVBUF, SO_SNDBUF, and TCP_NODELAY are optional socket options.
>
> SO_ACCEPTCONN, SO_ERROR, and SO_TYPE are read-only options, so they work with `getsockopt()`, but *not* with `setsockopt()`.

Developer suggestions: Check the parameters. Are you using an optional *level* or *optname* value that may not be supported on all WinSock implementations? If so, treat this as a nonfatal error and ignore it, if possible.

WinSock functions: `getsockopt()`, `setsockopt()`

Additional functions: Bad IP headers can cause routers and remote hosts to issue "parameter problem" ICMP messages, which result in an ENOPROTOOPT error on Berkeley-derived systems. These errors might be reported on any function that does network I/O (e.g., `connect()`, `send()`, `recv()`, etc.).

See also: WSAEINVAL

WSAENOTCONN (10057) *Socket is not connected*

Berkeley description: A request to send or receive data was disallowed because the socket is not connected and (when sending on a datagram socket) no address was supplied.

WinSock description: Same as Berkeley, and then some. An application attempted an input/output network function call before establishing an association with a remote socket (i.e., before calling `connect()` or `accept()`). It also has a specific meaning for `setsockopt()`.

Detailed description:

setsockopt(): WinSock generates this error if you try to set SO_KEEPALIVE but the connection has already been aborted (e.g., a TCP reset received from remote host).

Developer suggestions: If you encounter this error, most likely your application ignored the failure of some previous function. Although some WinSock implementations might not issue other errors if a connection fails, you can handle this error as you would handle others that indicate connection failure.

WinSock functions: `getpeername()`, `recv()`, `recvfrom()`, `send()`, `sendto()`, `setsockopt()`, `shutdown()`, FD_CONNECT

See also: WSAECONNABORTED, WSAECONNRESET, WSAENETRESET, WSAETIMEDOUT

WSAENOTEMPTY (10066) *Directory not empty*

Berkeley description: A directory with entries other than "." and ".." was supplied to a remove directory or rename call.

WinSock description: No equivalent

WinSock functions: <none>

WSAENOTSOCK (10038) *Socket operation on nonsocket*

Berkeley description: An operation was attempted on something that is not a socket. The specified socket parameter refers to a file, not a socket.

WinSock description: Same as Berkeley. The socket input parameter is not a valid socket handle (either it never was valid, it is a file handle (not a socket handle), or if it was a socket handle, it has been closed).

Detailed description:

select(): fails with WSAENOTSOCK if any socket in any of the three `fd_set` input arguments is an invalid socket handle

Developer suggestions: Did you close a socket inadvertently in one part of an application without keeping another part notified? Use socket state in an application and/or handle this error gracefully as a nonfatal error.

WinSock functions: Any function that takes a socket as an input parameter: `accept()`, `bind()`, `closesocket()`, `connect()`, `getpeername()`, `getsockname()`, `getsockopt()`, `ioctlsocket()`, `listen()`, `recv()`, `recvfrom()`, `select()`, `send()`, `sendto()`, `setsockopt()`, `shutdown()`, FD_CONNECT

Additional functions: The v1.1 WinSock specification has this error listed for the FD_CONNECT event, but since this error condition can be detected when `WSAAsyncSelect()` is called, it could be listed for the function itself.

WSAEOPNOTSUPP (10045) *Operation not supported*

Berkeley description: The attempted operation is not supported for the type of object referenced. Usually this occurs when a file descriptor refers to a file or socket that cannot support this operation, for example, trying to accept a connection on a datagram socket.

WinSock description: Same as Berkeley. "You cannot make a silk purse from a sow's ear."

Detailed descriptions:
accept(), listen(): The socket is not of the type that supports connection-oriented service.
recv(), recvfrom(), send(), sendto(): MSG_OOB was specified, but the socket is not of type SOCK_STREAM.
Developer suggestions: Don't do that.
WinSock functions: `accept()`, `listen()`, `recv()`, `recvfrom()`, `send()`, `sendto()`

WSAEPFNOSUPPORT (10046) *Protocol family not supported*

Berkeley description: The protocol family has not been configured into the system, or no implementation for it exists.

WinSock description: Same as Berkeley. Apparently, the Windows Sockets specification left this out by oversight. The WSAEAFNOSUPPORT is the likely substitute error for this in WinSock, although its Berkeley meaning is slightly different. However, the WSAEPROTONOSUPPORT is another possible equivalent for WinSock to use in place of this error.

WinSock functions: <none>

Additional functions: For Berkeley compatibility, the `socket()` function should fail with this error if an unsupported address family is requested.

See also: WSAEAFNOSUPPORT

WSAEPROCLIM (10067) *Too many processes*

Berkeley description: No equivalent in 4.3 BSD or compatible operating systems

WinSock description: No equivalent

WinSock functions: <none>

Additional functions: If a WinSock implementation has an upper limit to the number of simultaneous tasks it can handle, an application's initial call to `WSAStartup()` could fail with this error.

WSAEPROTONOSUPPORT (10043) *Protocol not supported*

Berkeley description: The protocol has not been configured into the system, or no implementation for it exists.

WinSock description: Same as Berkeley. So, for example, if a WinSock implementation does not support SOCK_RAW with IPPROTO_IP (or any other protocol), then the `socket()` call would fail with WSAEPROTONOSUPPORT (however, if the WinSock implementation does not support SOCK_RAW at all, you should expect `socket()` to fail with the WSAESOCKTNOSUPPORT error).

Developer suggestion: Are you trying to use an optional feature? Handle the request as a nonfatal error (if possible), since some WinSocks can legally fail the request.

WinSock functions: `socket()`
See also: WSAESOCKTNOSUPPORT

WSAEPROTOTYPE (10041) *Protocol wrong type for socket*

Berkeley description: A protocol was specified that does not support the semantics of the socket type requested. For example, you cannot use the ARPA Internet UDP protocol with type SOCK_STREAM.

WinSock description: Same as Berkeley. This error occurs if you specifically reference a protocol that is not part of the address family you also reference. The only function that takes these two explicit parameters is `socket()`.

Developer suggestions: Since there is only one corresponding protocol for each of the datagram and stream socket types in the Internet address family, you should simply leave the value in the *protocol* input parameter to `socket()`. Alternately, you could call `getprotobyname()` or `WSAAsyncGetProtoByName()` to get the appropriate protocol value from the network system.

WinSock functions: `socket()`
See also: WSAEAFNOSUPPORT, WSAEAPNOSUPPORT

WSAEREMOTE (10071) *Too many levels of remote in path*

Berkeley description: Item is not local to the host. A server has attempted to handle an NFS request by generating a request to another NFS server, which is not allowed.

WinSock description: No equivalent. The WinSock API does not provide access to the Network File System application protocol, so this error is irrelevant to WinSock.

WinSock functions: <none>

WSAESHUTDOWN (10058) *Cannot send after socket shutdown*

Berkeley description: A request to send data was disallowed because the socket had already been shut down with a previous `shutdown()` call.

WinSock description: Same as Berkeley. By calling `shutdown()` you do a partial close of a socket, which means you have discontinued sending. The WinSock implementation will not allow you to send after this.

TCP/IP scenario: Calling `shutdown()` with *how*=1 or *how*=2 sends a TCP FIN packet to the remote address, which literally means "I'm done sending." If the local host sent any more data after that point, it would be in clear violation of the TCP specification (RFCs 793 and 1122).

Developer suggestion: The simple suggestion is "Don't do that." No matter what value you use for the *how* parameter to the `shutdown()` function, you cannot send afterwards. To avoid the mistake of trying to send on a socket after you have initiated a close, keep track of the socket state in your application (and check it before you attempt I/O).

WinSock functions: `recv()`, `recvfrom()`, `send()`, `sendto()`, with stream sockets only

WSAESOCKTNOSUPPORT (10044) *Socket type not supported*

Berkeley description: The support for the socket type has not been configured into the system, or no implementation for it exists.

WinSock description: Similar to Berkeley. The WinSock description for this error is "The specified socket type is not supported in this address family," which qualifies the error condition a bit more than the Berkeley explanation does. So, for example, you can expect this error after `socket()` fails if a WinSock implementation does not support *type*=SOCK_RAW within the Internet address family (AF_INET).

Developer suggestion: Are you trying to use an optional feature? Handle the request as a nonfatal error (if possible), since some WinSocks can legally fail the request.

WinSock functions: `socket()`

See also: WSAEPROTOTYPE, WSAEPROTONOSUPPORT

WSAESTALE (10070) *Stale NFS file handle*

Berkeley description: An attempt was made to access an open file on a Network File System (NFS) that is now unavailable as referenced by the file descriptor. This may indicate that the file was deleted on the NFS server or that some other catastrophic event occurred.

WinSock description: No equivalent. NFS is "network-related" in the strictest sense, but the Network File System Protocol is an application protocol (i.e., a "high-level" protocol). The Windows Sockets API provides access to "low-level" APIs (like the transport protocols TCP and UDP), so this error is irrelevant to WinSock.

WinSock functions: <none>

WSAETIMEDOUT (10060) *Connection timed out*

Berkeley description: A `connect()` or `send()` request failed because the connected party did not properly respond after a period of time. (The timeout period depends on the communication protocol.)

WinSock description: Same as Berkeley, but less applicable. This error is relevant to `connect()`, but not to `send()` or `sendto()` as it is in Berkeley Sockets.

User suggestions: Check the obvious first: Check that the destination address is a valid IP address. If you used a host name, did it resolve to the correct address? If the hostname resolution uses a local host table, it's possible you resolved to an obsolete address. Can you ping that host name?

Do you have a router configured? Is the router up and running (check by pinging it, and then ping an address on the other side of it)? Try a traceroute to the destination address to check that all the routers are functioning.

Check your subnet mask. If you do not have the proper subnet mask, your network system may treat a local address as a remote address (so it forwards addresses on the local subnet to the router, rather than broadcasting an ARP request locally), or vice versa.

WinSock functions: `connect()`, FD_CONNECT

Additional functions: Any function that does I/O on the network could generate this error, as could the `WSAAsyncSelect()` events FD_OOB, FD_READ, and FD_WRITE.

See also: WSAECONNABORTED, WSAECONNRESET, WSAENETRESET

WSAETOOMANYREFS (10059) *Too many references; cannot splice*

Berkeley description: There are too many references to some kernel-level object; the associated resource has run out.

WinSock description: No equivalent

WinSock functions: <none>

WSAEUSERS (10068) *Too many users*

Berkeley description: The quota system ran out of table entries.

WinSock description: No equivalent

WinSock functions: <none>

WSAEWOULDBLOCK (10035) *Resource temporarily unavailable*

Berkeley description: This is a temporary condition, and later calls to the same routine may complete normally (also known as EAGAIN error in BSD version 4.3).

WinSock description: Same as Berkeley. The socket is marked as nonblocking (nonblocking operation mode), and the requested operation is not complete at this time.

Detailed descriptions:

connect(): The operation is underway but as yet is incomplete.

closesocket(): This occurs on a nonblocking socket with nonzero timeout set with `setsockopt()` SO_LINGER. The behavior may vary: Some WinSocks might complete in the background, and others may require another call to `closesocket` to complete. To avoid this ambiguity, do not set nonzero timeout on nonblocking sockets (see Chapter 9 for more information).

send() or *sendto():* The network system is out of buffer space, so try again later or wait until FD_WRITE notification (`WSAAsyncSelect()`) or `select()` *writefds* is set.

all other functions: Retry the operation again later since it cannot be satisfied at this time.

Developer suggestions: Every application that uses nonblocking sockets must be prepared for this error on *any* call to the functions mentioned below. For instance, even if you request to `send()` a few bytes of data on a newly created TCP connection, `send()` could fail with WSAEWOULDBLOCK (if, say, the network system has a TCP slow-start algorithm implemented). The `WSAAsyncSelect()` FD_WRITE event is specifically designed to notify an application after a WSAEWOULDBLOCK error when buffer space is available again so `send()` or `sendto()` should succeed.

WinSock functions: `accept()`, `closesocket()`, `connect()`, `recv()`, `recvfrom()`, `send()`, `sendto()`, `WSAAsyncGetHostByAddr()`, `WSAAsyncGetHostByName()`, `WSAAsyncGetProtoByName()`, `WSAAsyncGetProtoByNumber()`, `WSAAsyncGetServByName()`, `WSAAsyncGetServByPort()`

WSAHOST_NOT_FOUND (11001) *Host not found*

Berkeley description: No such host is known. The name you have used is not an official host name or alias, however, another type of name server request may be successful.

WinSock description: Same as Berkeley. Any of the WinSock name resolution functions can fail with this error. The WinSock API does not provide any way to select specific name resolution protocols, server address, or record type.

TCP/IP scenario: Most WinSock implementations use the Domain Name System (DNS) Protocol for host name to address resolution, although a few use the Network Information System (NIS). Assuming you have a name server configured instead of or as well as a host table, a hostname resolution request causes a WinSock DLL to send a DNS "A" record query (address query) to the configured DNS query. If you have more than one server configured, the hostname query fails only after the WinSock DLL has queried all servers.

User suggestions: Check that you have a name server(s) and/or host table configured. If you are using a name server(s), check whether the server host(s) is up (e.g., try to ping the server(s)). You could also try to resolve another host name you know should work, to check that the name resolution server application is running.

If you are using a host table exclusively, you will need to update it to add the destination host name and address.

Developer suggestions: For protocols and services, consider using a hard-coded value for the protocol number or service port number in case your resolution attempt fails.

WinSock functions: `gethostbyaddr()`, `gethostbyname()`, `WSAAsyncGetHostByAddr()`, `WSAAsyncGetHostByName()`, `WSAAsyncGetProtoByName()`,

WSAAsyncGetProtoByNumber(), WSAAsyncGetServByName(), WSAAsyncGetServByPort()

Additional functions: It is strange that the asynchronous protocol and services functions can fail with this error but the synchronous functions cannot. The missing functions are getprotobyname(), getprotobynumber(), getservbyname(), and getservbyport().

See also: WSANO_DATA, WSANO_RECOVERY, WSATRY_AGAIN

WSANOTINITIALISED (10093) *Successful WSAStartup() not yet performed*

Berkeley description: No equivalent

WinSock description: Either your application has not called WSAStartup(), or WSAStartup() failed, or—possibly—you are accessing a socket that the current active task does not own (i.e., you are trying to share a socket between tasks). Note the British spelling (with an "S" instead of a "Z").

User suggestions: Chances are the network subsystem is misconfigured or inactive. See WSASYSNOTREADY for details.

Developer suggestions: WSAStartup() failed, and you did not detect it, or it was not called for the current task at all, or you called WSACleanup() too many times.

WinSock functions: accept(), bind(), closesocket(), connect(), gethostbyaddr(), gethostbyname(), gethostname(), getpeername(), getprotobyname(), getprotobynumber(), getservbyname(), getservbyport(), getsockname(), getsockopt(), ioctlsocket(), listen(), recv(), recvfrom(), select(), send(), sendto(), setsockopt(), shutdown(), socket(), WSAAsyncGetHostByAddr(), WSAAsyncGetHostByName(), WSAAsyncGetProtoByName(), WSAAsyncGetProtoByNumber(), WSAAsyncGetServByName(), WSAAsyncGetServByPort(), WSAAsyncSelect(), WSACancelAsyncRequest(), WSACancelBlockingCall(), WSACleanup(), WSASetBlockingHook(), WSAUnhookBlockingHook()

Additional functions: The only function capable of failing with a WinSock error that does not list the error is WSAUnhookBlockingHook(). Clearly, this oversight was not intentional.

WSANO_DATA (11004) *Valid name, no data record of requested type*

Berkeley description: The requested name is valid, but does not have an Internet IP address at the name server. This is not a temporary error. This means another type of request to the name server will result in an answer.

WinSock description: Same as Berkeley for host resolution. For protocol and services resolution, the name or number was not found in the respective database.

User suggestions: See WSAHOST_NOT_FOUND for details.

WinSock functions: `gethostbyaddr()`, `gethostbyname()`, `getprotobyname()`, `getprotobynumber()`, `getservbyname()`, `getservbyport()`, `WSAAsyncGetProtoByName()`, `WSAAsyncGetProtoByNumber()`, `WSAAsyncGetServByName()`, `WSAAsyncGetServByPort()`, `WSAAsyncGetHostByAddr()`, `WSAAsyncGetHostByName()`

See also: WSAHOST_NOT_FOUND, WSANO_RECOVERY, WSATRY_AGAIN

WSANO_RECOVERY (11003) *This is a nonrecoverable error*

Berkeley description: This is a nonrecoverable error.

WinSock description: Same as Berkeley. Specifically, the v1.1 Windows Sockets specification notes the Domain Name System (DNS) errors FORMERR, REFUSED, and NOTIMP. For protocols and services resolution, it means the respective database was not located.

Detailed description (from RFC 1035, "Domain Names," by P. Mockapetris):

Format error: The name server was unable to interpret the query.

Request refused: The name server refuses to satisfy your query for policy reasons.

Not implemented: The name server does not perform specified operation.

User suggestions: See WSAHOST_NOT_FOUND for details.

WinSock functions: `gethostbyaddr()`, `gethostbyname()`, `getprotobyname()`, `getprotobynumber()`, `getservbyname()`, `getservbyport()`, `WSAAsyncGetProtoByName()`, `WSAAsyncGetProtoByNumber()`, `WSAAsyncGetServByNumber()`, `WSAAsyncGetServByPort()`, `WSAAsyncGetServByAddr()`, `WSAAsyncGetHostByName()`

See also: WSAHOST_NOT_FOUND, WSANO_DATA, WSATRY_AGAIN

WSASYSNOTREADY (10091) *Network subsystem is unavailable*

Berkeley description: No equivalent

WinSock description: The WinSock implementation cannot function at this time because the underlying system it uses to provide network services is currently unavailable.

User suggestions:

- Check that the WINSOCK.DLL file is in the current path.
- Check that the WINSOCK.DLL file is from the same vendor as your underlying protocol stack. You cannot mix and match (WINSOCK DLLs must be supplied by the same vendor that provided your underlying protocol stack).
- You cannot use more than one WinSock implementation simultaneously. If you have more than one WINSOCK DLL on your system, be sure the

first one in the path is appropriate for the network subsystem currently loaded, and may not match the network system loaded.

- Check your WinSock implementation documentation to be sure all necessary components are currently installed and configured correctly.

WinSock function: `WSAStartup()`

WSATRY_AGAIN (11002) *Nonauthoritative host not found*

Berkeley description: This is usually a temporary error and means that the local server did not receive a response from an authoritative server. A retry at some time later may be successful.

WinSock description: Same as Berkeley. Notice that asynchronous service and protocols functions are listed below, in addition to the hostname resolution functions.

User suggestions: See WSAHOST_NOT_FOUND for details.

WinSock functions: `gethostbyaddr()`, `gethostbyname()`, `WSAAsyncGetHostByAddr()`, `WSAAsyncGetHostByName()`, `WSAAsyncGetProtoByName()`, `WSAAsyncGetProtoByNumber()`, `WSAAsyncGetServByName()`, `WSAAsyncGetServByPort()`

See also: WSANO_DATA, WSANO_RECOVERY, WSATRY_AGAIN

WSAVERNOTSUPPORTED (10092) *WINSOCK.DLL version out of range*

Berkeley description: No equivalent

WinSock description: The current WinSock implementation does not support the Windows Sockets specification version requested by the application.

User suggestions: Do you have the WinSock DLL that supports the version of the WinSock specification required by the application? If so, is there an older DLL in a directory in the path ahead of the directory containing the newer DLL? If not, check with your WinSock vendor to see if it has a newer WinSock available.

Developer suggestion: Use the sample code fragment in the `WSAStartup()` documentation in the v1.1 specification, which demonstrates how an application negotiates a Windows Sockets specification version.

Note: The MAKEWORD macro referenced in the code fragment is *not* available in the WINSOCK.H header file or in any standard header files. Here is a usable macro:

```
#define MAKEWORD(low, high) ((WORD)(((BYTE)(low)) | (((WORD)((BYTE)(high))) << 8)))
```

WinSock function: `WSAStartup()`

Errors in Numerical Order

WSABASEERR	(0)	No error
WSAEINTR	(10004)	Interrupted system call
WSAEBADF	(10009)	Bad file number
WSAEACCES	(10013)	Permission denied
WSAEFAULT	(10014)	Bad address
WSAEINVAL	(10022)	Invalid argument
WSAEMFILE	(10024)	Too many open files
WSAEWOULDBLOCK	(10035)	Operation would block
WSAEINPROGRESS	(10036)	Operation now in progress
WSAEALREADY	(10037)	Operation already in progress
WSAENOTSOCK	(10038)	Socket operation on nonsocket
WSAEDESTADDRREQ	(10039)	Destination address required
WSAEMSGSIZE	(10040)	Message too long
WSAEPROTOTYPE	(10041)	Protocol wrong type for socket
WSAENOPROTOOPT	(10042)	Bad protocol option
WSAEPROTONOSUPPORT	(10043)	Protocol not supported
WSAESOCKTNOSUPPORT	(10044)	Socket type not supported
WSAEOPNOTSUPP	(10045)	Operation not supported on socket
WSAEPFNOSUPPORT	(10046)	Protocol family not supported
WSAEAFNOSUPPORT	(10047)	Address family not supported by protocol family
WSAEADDRINUSE	(10048)	Address already in use
WSAEADDRNOTAVAIL	(10049)	Cannot assign requested address
WSAENETDOWN	(10050)	Network is down
WSAENETUNREACH	(10051)	Network is unreachable
WSAENETRESET	(10052)	Net dropped connection or reset

WSAECONNABORTED	(10053)	Software caused connection abort
WSAECONNRESET	(10054)	Connection reset by peer
WSAENOBUFS	(10055)	No buffer space available
WSAEISCONN	(10056)	Socket is already connected
WSAENOTCONN	(10057)	Socket is not connected
WSAESHUTDOWN	(10058)	Cannot send after socket shutdown
WSAETOOMANYREFS	(10059)	Too many references, cannot splice
WSAETIMEDOUT	(10060)	Connection timed out
WSAECONNREFUSED	(10061)	Connection refused
WSAELOOP	(10062)	Too many levels of symbolic links
WSAENAMETOOLONG	(10063)	File name too long
WSAEHOSTDOWN	(10064)	Host is down
WSAEHOSTUNREACH	(10065)	No route to host
WSAENOTEMPTY	(10066)	Directory not empty
WSAEPROCLIM	(10067)	Too many processes
WSAEUSERS	(10068)	Too many users
WSAEDQUOT	(10069)	Disk quota exceeded
WSAESTALE	(10070)	Stale NFS file handle
WSASYSNOTREADY	(10091)	Network subsystem is unavailable
WSAVERNOTSUPPORTED	(10092)	WINSOCK DLL version out of range
WSANOTINITIALISED	(10093)	Successful WSASTARTUP not yet performed
WSAEREMOTE	(10071)	Too many levels of remote in path
WSAHOST_NOT_FOUND	(11001)	Host not found
WSATRY_AGAIN	(11002)	Nonauthoritative host not found
WSANO_RECOVERY	(11003)	Nonrecoverable errors: FORMERR, REFUSED, NOTIMP

WSANO_DATA	(11004)*	Valid name, no data record of requested type
WSANO_ADDRESS	(11004)*	No address, look for MX record

* Note that these are same value (typically, only WSANO_DATA is reported).

D What You Need

In This Appendix:

- Essential Files
- Compile and Link Mechanics
- Using Different WinSocks
- Using Different Languages

This appendix summarizes what you need to create a WinSock application and maintain a test environment. We tell you what files you need, where to get them, or how to create them yourself. We consider the mechanics of application creation and execution. We describe how to switch between different WinSock implementations, and we mention the use of languages other than C.

Essential Files

The most essential file of all is a copy of the Windows Sockets version 1.1 specification itself (dated 20 January 1993). This is the definitive reference for WinSock by Martin Hall, Mark Towfiq, Geoff Arnold, David Treadwell, and Henry Sanders. The original work is in Microsoft Word version 2.0 format (**winsock.doc**), although it is also available in straight text (winsock.txt), postscript (winsock.ps), Windows help (winsock.hlp), and hypertext markup language (winsock.htm) formats.

The essential file for WinSock development is the **winsock.h** header file. This contains all the structure definitions, macro definitions, and function prototypes for the WinSock API. You need to `#include` this file in your WinSock source code files.

In most cases you'll also need a **winsock.lib** import library file for the 16-bit WinSock API, or **wsock32.lib** for the 32-bit WinSock API. You can link with either library in order to load the WinSock dynamic link library—winsock.dll or wsock32.dll, respectively—at run time.

Of course, you'll also need a **winsock.dll** in order to run your 16-bit WinSock applications (or **wsock32.dll** for 32-bit applications). And these dynamic link libraries require a properly installed TCP/IP protocol stack and a network interface (Ethernet, SLIP, PPP, etc.).

Section A.2.1 (Appendix A) of the version 1.1 WinSock specification lists a number of other header files and indicates that any WinSock development kit must provide them. However, there is no need for them. The other header files are listed for backward compatibility with Berkeley source code. They are superfluous for a number of reasons: Their essential contents are already included in the WinSock.h file; you need to make some changes to most Berkeley Sockets source code to port them to WinSock anyway; and it's easy enough to `#ifdef` out the files if they are unavailable.

Where to Get Them

The Windows Sockets specification (**winsock.doc**) and standard **winsock.h** and 16-bit **winsock.lib** files are available at many FTP sites on the Internet, including

ftp://ftp.sockets.com/winsock

ftp://sunsite.unc.edu/pub/micro/pc-stuff/ms-windows/winsock

ftp://ftp.microsoft.com/busys/winsock

If you already have a winsock.dll file, you can create your own copy of the 16-bit import library (winsock.lib) with the *implib.exe* utility that ships with Microsoft C and Borland C. Just type

```
implib winsock.lib winsock.dll
```

Many TCP/IP stack vendors can provide a winsock.dll, including the shareware Trumpet WinSock version available from Peter Tattam. It's important to remember that you must have a winsock.dll from the same vendor that provided your TCP/IP stack.

The 32-bit wsock32.dll ships with Windows NT and Windows 95 and runs over the Microsoft TCP/IP stack. These 32-bit environments also have a winsock.dll file that acts as a "thunk-layer" to allow 16-bit WinSock applications to run over the 32-bit wsock32.dll. Conversely, Microsoft's Win32s installs a 32-bit wsock32.dll thunk layer in 16-bit Windows environments (Windows version 3.1 and Windows for Workgroups 3.11) over any vendor's WinSock DLL currently in use. We describe this architecture in Chapter 15, "Platforms."

The 32-bit **wsock32.lib** Microsoft ships with Microsoft Visual C++ version 2.0 (there's also a nonstandard version of winsock.h that contains Microsoft's own extensions).

Compile and Link Mechanics

You do not need to do anything special to compile WinSock source code. The only important consideration is that you include the winsock.h file in any source module that uses WinSock functions, macros, or structures.

Most applications link *implicitly* with a WinSock DLL (winsock.dll or wsock32.dll) at run time. Implicit linking is easy, since no extra code is needed. Implicit linking occurs automatically if you link with either the **winsock.lib** or **wsock32.lib** import libraries when you create your executable. The disadvantage is that your application will not run at all if the Windows subsystem cannot find the WinSock DLL at run time.

Not being able to run the application when the winsock.dll file is unavailable is okay for most WinSock applications, since you can't do much without a WinSock DLL anyway. However, there are times when you'd like your application to run whether or not the winsock.dll file is available. For example, your application may not require network access to be useful, or perhaps you want to provide your own explanation to your application user about the missing winsock.dll file.

To allow your application to run without a winsock.dll file available, you need to link with the winsock.dll *explicitly*. To do this, you use the Win API function `LoadLibrary( )`, followed by `GetProcAddress( )`, to initialize a pointer to each function your application uses. You also want to check for the existence of the DLL before you call `LoadLibrary( )` since Windows automatically displays a message box indicating the DLL cannot be found if `LoadLibrary( )` fails. The following code example shows how to do this:

```
#include <winsock.h>
. . .
int (PASCAL FAR * lpfn_recv)(SOCKET, char FAR *, int, int);
int (PASCAL FAR * lpfn_send)(SOCKET, char FAR *, int, int);
int (PASCAL FAR * lpfn_WSAStartup)(WORD, LPWSADATA);
int (PASCAL FAR * lpfn_WSACleanup)(void);
int (PASCAL FAR * lpfn_WSAGetLastError)(void);
```

```
OFSTRUCT  stFile;
HFILE     hFile;
HINSTANCE hWinSockDLL = 0;
. . .
#ifdef WIN32
hFile = OpenFile("wsock32.dll", (OFSTRUCT FAR*)&stFile, OF_EXIST);
if (hFile != HFILE_ERROR)
   hWinSockDLL = LoadLibrary ("wsock32.dll");
#else
hFile = OpenFile("winsock.dll", (OFSTRUCT FAR*)&stFile, OF_EXIST);
if (hFile != HFILE_ERROR)
   hWinSockDLL = LoadLibrary ("winsock.dll");
#endif
if (hWinsockDLL >= 32) {
   (FARPROC)lpfn_recv  = GetProcAddress (hWinsockDLL,"recv");
   (FARPROC)lpfn_send  = GetProcAddress (hWinsockDLL,"send");
   (FARPROC)lpfn_WSAStartup =
         GetProcAddress(hWinSockDLL,"WSAStartup");
   (FARPROC)lpfn_WSACleanup =
         GetProcAddress(hWinSockDLL,"WSACleanup");
   (FARPROC)lpfn_WSAGetLastError =
         GetProcAddress(hWinsockDLL,"WSAGetLastError");
   /* Check for any null pointers in case GetProcAddress failed */
   if (!lpfn_recv | !lpfn_send | !lpfn_WSAStartup |
       !lpfn_WSACleanup | !lpfn_WSAGetLastError) {
         FreeLibrary (hWinSockDLL);
         hWinSockDLL = 0;
   }
}
if (!hWinSockDLL) {
   MessageBox (hwnd, "Unable to load winsock.dll", "Error");
}
```

Also, do not forget to call `FreeLibrary(hWinSockDLL)` after you call `WSACleanup( )` to free the instance resource and unload the DLL from memory.

Using Different WinSocks

One of the limitations of WinSock version 1.1 is that you can only have one active winsock.dll on your system at a time. This would be fine if all WinSock implementations were created equal, but as we have described, they are not.

Part of the process of WinSock application development involves testing an application over different WinSock implementations. As a result, it is not unusual for an application developer to need to switch between various vendors' WinSocks and TCP/IP protocol stacks. This is tricky but not too difficult.

A significant variety of WinSock and TCP/IP stack architectures are available for Windows, and each one has its own requirements when you want to switch between them. There are differences in the network interface drivers they use, in whether they have a terminate-and-stay-resident (TSR) portion that must be loaded before running Windows, and in whether they load as a virtual device drivers (VxD) when Windows loads.

It's not difficult to create a batch file for each protocol stack you have, which will allow you to switch quickly to that stack for testing. In the best case, it's simply a matter of exiting from Windows and running the batch file. In the worst case, you'll need to execute the batch file and reboot the PC before you run Windows again.

To create a batch file for a vendor's stack, do the following:

1. Before you install the vendor's stack, make a copy of your existing **autoexec.bat, config.sys,** and **system.ini** files.
2. Install the vendor's protocol stack using its installation program, and allow it to modify any files it requests.
3. Note whether any of the files listed in step 1 have been modified, and copy them into the directory where you installed the new stack vendor's software. The simplest thing to look for is the path where you installed the WinSock software.
4. Create a batch file that copies these key configuration files to their respective locations.

Here are the types of changes you can expect most WinSock protocol stack installation applications make to these configuration files:

autoexec.bat: It will have changes to the path, and possibly a terminate-and-stay-resident (TSR) program load that may be related to the network driver in use. If the stack uses an NDIS driver, it runs netbind.

config.sys: It will have device drivers, including protman.dos if the stack uses an NDIS driver.

system.ini: It will have virtual device drivers lines added (file names with .386 extensions).

Using Different Languages

The WinSock specification was originally designed with the C programming language in mind, so its constructs are very C-centric. However, since the API is provided in a dynamic link library, it is possible to access WinSock from any language capable of utilizing a DLL. This includes most languages, including PASCAL, C++, and even Visual Basic.

The WinSock programming community has produced a number of public domain and shareware files available at many Internet sites that address the needs of other languages. This includes a Pascal-compatible version of the winsock.h file, Visual Basic versions of the winsock.h file, Visual Basic Custom Controls for WinSock, and C++ WinSock class libraries. Numerous commercial products are also available, many of which implement application protocols and provide high-level APIs to simplify application development. The main reason to purchase a commercial development kit is to get support as you develop applications.

For up-to-date links to many network sites that contain this type of WinSock programming information, you can refer to http://www.sockets.com.

E Information Sources

In This Appendix:

- Internet Sources
- Bibliography

This appendix contains recommended information sources of all types. It's split into two sections: Internet sources and a Bibliography. The Internet sources are newsgroups, mail lists, FTP sites, and World Wide Web pages. The bibliography contains magazine and journal articles, textbooks, frequently asked question (FAQ) listings, and Internet requests for comments (RFCs).

Internet Sources

This section contains the "dynamic" information sources available on the Internet:

- URLs and URIs
- FTP Sites
- List Servers
- Mail Lists
- Newsgroups
- Web Pages

There are many places where you can get pointers to new sources of information. The best way to find out about them as they appear is by reading relevant newsgroups and mail lists. FAQs can point you to them after the fact, and many Internet books have pointers.

URLs and URIs

To access various resources on the Internet, you need a destination host, the name of a resource, and an indication of what protocol to use to access the resource. Meet the universal resource locator (URL). URLs tell you where to go, what to see, and what to do. URLs are a subset of universal resource identifiers (URIs), and Tim Berners-Lee—the father of World Wide Web—describes both in a pair of draft RFCs available on www.cern.ch, the home of the World Wide Web. Here we paraphrase from those documents:

- *URI:* encodes the names and addresses of objects on the Internet. They encapsulate a name in any registered namespace, and label it with the namespace, to produce a member of the universal set of objects.
- *URL:* encodes the physical addresses of objects that are retrievable using application protocols already deployed on the Internet. It is a form of URI that expresses an address that maps onto a specific access algorithm.

You won't typically use URIs, but you will often use URLs. Here's a simple high-level description of the **URL syntax**. The draft RFC details the complete syntax in Bakus-Naur form, but here is a simpler description of the URL form in common notation (**{}** surround required parameters, **[ ]** surround optional parameters, and other characters are mandatory separators).

```
{service}://{host}[:port]/[path/.../][file name]
```

- *service* (required field): The service is a standard service name that indicates the protocol to use; Berners-Lee calls them "URL schemes." The standard URL syntax currently recognizes file, ftp, gopher, and http (Note: "file" requires local disk access, rather than a network access).
- *host* (required field): The host is the host name or IP address of the network destination on which to access the service.
- *port* (optional field): The port number is not frequently used, but may be specified if the service is available on a nonstandard port number.
- *path* (optional field): This specifies the path name to the destination directory on the target host. Note: A path without a file after it always ends with a forward slash character ("/").

We use URLs throughout the remainder of this appendix to denote resource locations, where appropriate.

FTP Sites

The File Transfer Protocol (FTP) provides the most fundamental means of transferring files on the Internet. Here is a list of WinSock-related or networking-related sites you may find helpful. Almost all network software vendors maintain FTP sites, although we don't list them here. These sites are worth exploring since they sometimes have interesting files you would otherwise not know about.

ftp://ftp.sockets.com

FTP site for this book. All source code, errata, and other new information about this book are available. Additional WinSock information is also available.

ftp://ftp.stardust.com/pub/winsock

This site hosts many WinSock files including documentation, public domain and shareware applications, and a description of the WinSock application development consulting and educational services they offer.

ftp://ftp.cica.indiana.edu/pub/pc/win3/winsock	(United States)
ftp://wuarchive.wustl.edu/systems/ibmpc/simtel/win3/winsock	
ftp://mirrors.aol.com/pub/cica/pc/win3/winsock	
ftp://ftp.tu-clausthal.de/pub/windows/winsock	(Germany)
ftp://ftp.sunet.se/pub/pc/windows	(Sweden)
ftp://info.nic.surfnet.nl/mirror-archive/software/winsock	(The Netherlands)
ftp://ftp.monash.edu.au/pub/win3/winsock	(Australia)
ftp://ftp.hk.super.net/pub/windows	(Hong Kong)
ftp://ftp.iij.ad.jp/pub/win3/winsock	(Japan)
ftp://ftp.demon.co.uk/pub/ibmpc/winsock	(United Kingdom)

These are some of the best sites from which to get public domain and shareware Windows Socket applications, including development and debugging tools. A few of the public domain applications have source code available.

ftp://rtfm.mit.edu

This site has a complete database of USENET FAQs, with a useful text search tool to find exactly the FAQ you need (see the "FAQs" section in this appendix for more information).

ftp://ftp.rahul.net/pub/mitch/YABL

This site contains an annotated bibliography of C and UNIX books.

ftp://cs.washington.edu/pub/cstyle.tar.Z
ftp://ftp.cs.utoronto.ca/doc/programming
ftp://ftp.cs.umd.edu

Indian Hill Style Guide, and other useful C-programming documents can be found here.

ftp://ftp.csd.uwm.edu/pub/inet.services.txt

Scott Yanoff's great list of Internet services pointers resides here; although it is not WinSock specific, it is a great resource for Internet newcomers.

ftp://ftp.isi.edu/in–notes/iana/assignments

This site has the latest from the Internet Assigned Numbers Authority (IANA), like standard port numbers, and multicast addresses. IANA regularly updates the "Assigned Numbers" RFC.

ftp://ftp.internic.net

This is the Internet Network Information Center, the primary repository for RFCs.

ftp://ftp.trumpet.com.au/ftp/pub/winsock

This is Peter Tattam's home site for his shareware Trumpet WinSock implementation and applications.

ftp://ftp.uu.net

/networking/bsd-net2: Berkeley Software Distribution (BSD) source code
/usenet/news.answers: FAQs from USENET newsgroups
/published/books: Addison-Wesley has source code from published books
ftp://gatekeeper.dec.com

You can find all kinds of useful stuff here, like RFCs and BSD source code. This site has a good keyword search utility that helps locate what you need.

ftp://ftp.intel.com/pub/winsock2

Information on Winsock version 2.

List Servers

Some e-mail locations have list servers that automatically send requested information. To send a request, you specify your query in the "Subject:" field in the message header, or in the main body of your message, or in a combination of both. Different list servers and queries require different formats. We describe the format with each entry below.

info@lcs.com: subject: "faq" for Windows Sockets application FAQ

resolve@cs.widener.edu or **dns@grasp.insa-lyon.fr:** subject: "help"; message body: "site *domain name or address*"; it mails back the domain name information (i.e., it provides DNS name resolution via e-mail)

mail-server@nisc.sri.com: nothing in the subject field; message body: "send rfcnnnn.txt" to have an RFC text file sent to you

Mail Lists

Here are a few mail lists to which you can subscribe. Be sure to note how to get off the list in case you get tired of the e-mail traffic.

winnews: Microsoft WinNews Electronic newsletter, created by Microsoft's Personal Operating System's Division (POSD) to include the latest announcement and resource pointers for MS Windows. Currently this is read-only for announcements. To subscribe, mail to enews@microsoft.nwnet.com with "subscribe winnews" in the message body.

winsock-hackers: Not heavily trafficked, but the best place to expose your WinSock development question to many of the WinSock heavies. It is well read by most of the WinSock implementors, so this is the place where many WinSock specification ambiguities are discussed. Subscribe by mailing to listserv@sunsite.unc.edu with a subject and body of "subscribe winsock-hackers."

winsock-l: Good place for WinSock application users, also for developers but not many development issues are discussed. Not as heavily trafficked as the alt.winsock newsgroup, but useful. To join, mail to list–admin@papa.indstate.edu with nothing in Subject:, and "subscribe winsock-l" as the (only) textual body of the message. List members have access to WinSock applications at ftp://papa.indstate.edu/winsock-l, which is regularly updated.

Newsgroups

USENET newsgroup access is available from any Internet service provider. There are interest groups for everything under the sun including a lot of network-programming-related traffic. The rules of courtesy dictate that you should always refer to the "frequently asked questions" for answers before you post a question (see FAQs section in this appendix for more information).

alt.winsock: deals with everything related to Windows Sockets. There are occasional messages dealing with programming, but it tends to stay crowded with messages about the shareware WinSock implementations and the latest WinSock applications (problems or praises).

alt.winsock.programming: a good place to ask questions, or simply lurk watching for information. There's a manageable amount of traffic here.

comp.os.ms-windows.networking.tcp-ip: This is a bit redundant of alt.winsock, but without the volume of message traffic.

comp.os.ms-windows.networking.windows: Many people send the same WinSock-related messages here as well as to alt.winsock and tcp-ip.

comp.os.ms-windows.programmer.win32: This deals with generic Win32 programming questions, but there are some specific to WSOCK32 and others dealing with UNIX-to-Win32 porting issues.

Web Pages

World Wide Web traffic has surpassed FTP traffic on the Internet. The web is everywhere, and growing daily. There are countless useful sites for WinSock-related information, although only a few specialize in WinSock programming. Many of the FTP sites listed in the FTP section of this appendix also have web pages. There are many search engines for finding information anywhere on the Internet. Here are some pointers you may find helpful.

http://www.sockets.com/

The home site for this book. All source code, errata, and other new information about this book are available. Lots of additional WinSock information is also available.

http://www.stardust.com/

This is home site for Stardust Technologies WinSock Resource Center, which maintains a comprehensive repository of WinSock development information, including documentation, articles, software, sample code and more for WinSock versions 1.1 and 2.

http://www.yahoo.com

This web hub has a database of links to many useful web sites, including other web search engines. It's a user-friendly and effective way to find web sites with answers to your WinSock, networking, and protocol standards questions.

http://www.tucows.com
The ultimate collection of WinSock software.

http://cwsapps.texas.net
http://cws.wilmington.net
Here you'll find "The Consummate WinSock Applications List," which has Forest Stroud's annotated list of popular shareware and public domain WinSock applications.

http://www.primenet.com/~larsenc/
This site has a WinSock programming and application FAQ.

http://www.webcrawler.com/WebCrawler/WebQuery.html
This has hundreds of thousands of web documents indexed for keyword searches.

http://www.cmpcmm.com/cc/standards.html
This is an excellent jump point when looking for any standards documents of any kind, but those dealing with network-related standards in particular.

http://www.internic.net
The Internet Network Information Center (NIC) is the primary repository of RFCs, as well as other helpful information (like a comprehensive list of Internet Service Providers).

http://www.lycos.com/lycosinc/
Lycos is another helpful web search system.

http://www.eit.com/techinfo/mbone/mbone.html

http://www.research.att.com/mbone–faq.html
These are Internet multicast backbone (MBONE) references.

http://www.eecs.nwu.edu/unix.html
This site provides a "reference desk" for UNIX.

http://www.NeoSoft.com/internet/paml

Here is a list of publicly accessible mailing lists.

http://www.uwm.edu/Mirror/inet.services.html

This site has a great list of Internet services pointers; they are not WinSock specific, but they're helpful for Internet newcomers.

Bibliography

This section contains the "static" information sources:

- RFCs
- FAQs
- Magazine and Journal Articles
- Textbooks

RFCs

Requests for Comments (RFCs) are the official specifications for Internet standards, surprisingly enough. They started out informally, but the IAB (Internet Activities Board) and IETF (Internet Engineering Task Force) now have a well-established standards review process for RFCs. The central site for RFCs is **ds.internic.net** (ftp://ftp.internic.net or http://www.internic.net), though RFCs are widely available. Many of these RFCs get updated regularly. You can check the latest RFC index for the current version.

Berners-Lee, Tim. draft-bernerslee-www-uri-00, "Universal Resource Identifiers in WWW," March 12, 1994, and draft-ietf-uri-uri-03, "Uniform Resource Locators," March 21, 1994. These describe URIs and URLs (see earlier section in this appendix) used to address World Wide Web pages (for WWW browsers like NetScape and Mosaic).

Braden, R., Borman, D., and Partridge, C. "Computing the Internet Checksum," Sept. 1988, summarizes techniques and algorithms for efficiently computing the Internet checksum used in IP, TCP, UDP, and ICMP headers.

Cohen, David. IEN 137, "On Holy Wars and a Plea for Peace," 1 April 1980. As the date implies, this is a funny IEN ("Internet Experiment Notes," which were the precursors to RFCs), but it's also very informative. It gives the derivation of the terms "big endian" and "little endian," which are based on Jonathan Swift's Lilliputians and Blefuscians. They had a holy war about which end of the egg to break, analogous to the holy war about whether to transmit MSB or LSB first.

Deering, Steve. RFC 1112, "Host Extensions for IP Multicasting," Aug. 1989, describes the TCP/IP protocol stack extensions required of a host to support multicasting and provides mechanics of the Internet Group Management Protocol (IGMP) used for multicasting.

Deering, Steve. RFC 1256, "ICMP Router Discovery Messages," Sept. 1991, describes the ICMP router discovery mechanism (router solicitation and router advertisements).

Stine, Robert H. RFC 1175, "FYI on Network Management Tool Catalog: Tools for Monitoring and Debugging TCP/IP Internets and Interconnected Devices," 1990. The title says it all. Although dated 1990, it is still relevant.

Mockapetris, P.

RFC 1034, "Domain Names—Concepts and Facilities," Nov. 1987, is an introduction to DNS.

RFC 1035, "Domain Names—Implementation and Specification," Nov. 1987, describes the details of the domain name system and protocol.

Plummer, David C. RFC 826, "An Ethernet Address Resolution Protocol," Nov. 1982, describes ARP over Ethernet. It contains this great quote: "The world is a jungle in general, and the networking game contributes many animals."

Postel, Jonathan B.

RFC 768, "User Datagram Protocol," Aug. 1980, describes UDP.

RFC 791, "Internet Protocol," Sept. 1981, describes IP.

RFC 792, "Internet Control Message Protocol," Sept. 1981, describes ICMP.

RFC 793, "Transmission Control Protocol," Sept. 1981, describes TCP.

RFC 821, "Simple Mail Transfer Protocol," Aug. 1982, describes SMTP.

RFC 862, "Echo Protocol," May 1983, describes TCP and UDP echo service.

RFC 863, "Discard Protocol," May 1983, describes TCP and UDP discard service.

RFC 864, "Character Generator Protocol," May 1983, describes TCP and UDP chargen.

Postel, J. B. and Reynolds, J. K.

RFC 854, "Telnet Protocol Specification," May 1983, describes basic telnet.

RFC 959, "File Transfer Protocol (FTP)," Oct. 1985, describes FTP.

Reynolds, J. K. and Postel, J. B. RFC 1700, "Assigned Numbers," Oct. 1994, describes network byte ordering (big endian) and lists all standard numbers on the Internet: protocols, well-known ports, multicast addresses, Sun RPC numbers, and so forth.

Romao, Artur, RFC 1713, "Tools for DNS Debugging," Nov. 1994, is an informational RFC that catalogs and describes tools for detection and correction of anomalies in a DNS configuration (describes host, dnswalk, lamers, DOC, DDT, and BIND checker code).

FAQs

Frequently Asked Questions (FAQs) answer common questions. Each USENET newsgroup usually has at least one FAQ. There are a few sites for USENET FAQs, but two of the best are ftp://**ftp.uu.net/usenet/news.answers** and ftp://**rtfm.mit.edu**. Whenever you start reading a newsgroup and a question occurs to you, you should check the FAQ for an answer before asking. They are not called "frequently asked questions" for nothing.

Adoba, Bernard <adoba@internaut.com>, "Frequently Asked Questions (and answers) about TCP/IP on PC-Compatible Computers"
http://www.cis.ohio–state.edu/hypertext/faq/usenet/ibmpc–tcp–ip–faq/part1/faq.html
http://www.zilker.net/users/internaut/update.html

Kriz, Harry M. <hmkriz@vt.edu>, "Windows and TCP/IP for Internet Access"
ftp://nebula.lib.vt.edu/pub/windows/winsock/wtcpip0?.asc ('?' varies by version)
http://learning.lib.vt.edu/wintcpip/wintcpip.html

Larsen, C. <larsenc@lcs.com>, "WinSock Application FAQ"
Very comprehensive. Available by mailing to info@lcs.com, Subject: faq.

Sinkovits, Ed <edsink@mbnet.mb.ca> or Compuserve: 73003,3065, "Winsock Client Software Packages"
Very comprehensive. Available on CICA and mirror sites:
ftp://ftp.cica.indiana.edu/pub/pc/win3/winsock/winter??.zip ('?' varies by version)

Summit, Steve <scs@eskimo.com>, "C-faq"
A syntax and semantics discussion that covers things like null pointers, arrays, pointers, C-style, and use of the lint utility.
ftp://mirrors.aol.com/pub/rtfm/usenet/comp.lang.c
ftp://ftp.seas.gwu.edu/pub/rtfm/comp/lang/c

Magazine and Journal Articles

The articles collected here are from various magazines, with a number of them from the Microsoft Developers' Network CD (MSDN CD). This subscription service available from Microsoft provides you with a new CD-ROM quarterly that contains articles from *Microsoft Systems Journal*, some Microsoft Press texts (like Petzold), Technical Education seminars, white papers, specifications, and so forth, and any sample source code that accompany these. It is a gold mine with an easy-to-use, effective, and fast search utility, and is definitely recommended.

Adams, Timothy. "Intercepting DLL Function Calls," *Windows/DOS Developer's Journal*, June 1992, describes how to write a utility that intercepts calls from any application to any DLL. It could be used as a model for a generic WinSock application debugging utility like TracePlus or WinScope (as described in Chapter 13, "Debugging").

Allard, J. (Keith Moore and David Treadwell). "Plug into Serious Network Programming with the Windows Sockets API," *Microsoft Systems Journal*, July 1993, is an introductory description of the Windows Sockets API, which includes a sample asynchronous application called WORMHOLE (source code is available from ftp://ftp.microsoft.com and on *Microsoft Developer Network* CD-ROM).

Chan, Chuck (Margaret K. Johnson, Keith Moore, and David Treadwell). "Write an NT WinSock Service," *Byte Magazine*, Dec. 1994, describes how to take advantage of Windows NT features to write a secure server in a design akin to a UNIX daemon (i.e., the operating system spawns the service process when it receives a connection request). Although somewhat high level, it has many useful pointers.

Collyer, Geoff (and Henry Spencer). "News Need Not Be Slow," is a short and sweet collection of sensible rules of thumb for optimizing any application. It uses the optimization of the BSD USENET news server application as a practical example of what can be accomplished. It says things like "prepare for the worst, but optimize for the typical case," and "buying in bulk is often cheaper... the law of diminishing returns does apply to buying in bulk." Highly recommended.

Dolenc, A. (A. Lemmke, D. Keppel, G. V. Reilly). "Notes on Writing Portable Programs in C," describes the behavior of different C-preprocessors, compilers and environments, with some references to ANSI C.

Dreyer, Lori (John Miller and Al Dunn). "Porting a UNIX/XWindows Application to Windows Using Win32s," USENET comp.os.ms-windows.programmer.win32, September 12, 1994. This is a telling saga of the pain suffered during a comprehensive code port that illuminates some fundamental programming differences between the UNIX and Windows worlds. It deals mostly with non-Sockets issues.

Edson, Dave. "Dave's Top Ten List of Tricks, Hints, and Techniques for Programming in Windows," *Microsoft Systems Journal*, Oct. 1992, includes suggestions for Windows application development that are still valid and helpful.

Finnegan, James. "Hook and Monitor any 16-bit Windows Function with Our ProcHook DLL," *Microsoft Systems Journal*, Jan. 1994, shows you how to write your own WinSock DLL debugging tool that will show all the function calls any WinSock application makes to any WinSock implementation. WinScope and TracePlus use similar techniques, as described in Chapter 13, "Debugging."

Jablon, David P. "Windows Sockets," *UNIX Review*, Oct. 1994. This is a good "heads up" for anyone familiar with BSD Sockets (in the UNIX environment) and new to Windows Sockets. It lists many of the issues we cover in Chapter 12, "Porting Applications from BSD Sockets."

Long, David. "Designing DLLs for Multiple Client Applications, Part 1: Strategy" and "Part 2: Implementation," April 21, 1993, Technical Articles: Kernels and Drivers for Windows (16-bit) on *Microsoft Developer Network* CD-ROM.

Long, David (and Dan Ruder). "Mechanics of Dynamic Linking," Jan. 1993, *Microsoft Developer Network* CD-ROM, provides a good explanation of how the mechanism that makes WinSock's binary computability is possible.

Microsoft. "Windows Sockets Transport Independence for Windows NT," from *Microsoft Developer Network* CD-ROM, explains how to use Windows NT's "Transport Device Interface," generically known as the Service Provider Interface (SPI) in WOSA. This mechanism is the basis for WinSock 2's multiple protocol, although details have changed (for the better).

Microsoft. "WOSA Backgrounder: Delivering Enterprise Services to the Windows-based Desktop," created July 1993, from *Microsoft Developer Network* CD-ROM.

Schulzrinne, Henning. "Voice Communication across the Internet: A Network Voice Terminal," describes the UNIX-based "network voice terminal" he calls nevot and thoroughly explores the issues involved in voice transmission in particular, and real-time data transmission in general.

Sparling, Chip. "Plugging into TCP/IP with Windows Sockets," *Data Communications*, Oct. 1993, provides an introduction to Windows Sockets API with comparisons to existing de facto standard APIs.

Spencer, Henry (David Keppel and Mark Brader). "Recommended C Style and Coding Standards." The scope is coding style, not functional organization. Available with other C-related articles from:
ftp://cs.washington.edu/pub/cstyle.tar.Z
ftp://ftp.cs.toronto.edu/doc/programming
ftp://ftp.cs.umd.edu/pub/style-guide

Treadwell, David. "Developing Transport-Independent Applications Using the Windows Sockets Interface," Tech Ed 1994 Windows NT, Microsoft Development Library, from *Microsoft Developer Network* CD-ROM, introduces programming with WinSock, with some emphasis on NT, its multiple transport support, and how to use it.

Textbooks

Brown, Ralf (and Jim Kyle). *Network Interrupts: A Programmer's Reference to Network APIs*, Addison-Wesley, Reading, MA, 1994, ISBN: 0-201-62664-6. This is a conglomerate of quick references for just about every network API in existence (including WinSock and BSD 4.x Sockets). The Windows Sockets API has obsoleted many, but it's a convenient, all-in-one reference for the driver APIs (ODI, NDIS, and Packet Driver).

Carl-Mitchell, Smoot (and John S. Quarterman). *Practical Internetworking with TCP/IP and UNIX*, Addison-Wesley, Reading, MA, 1993, ISBN: 0-201-58629-0. This contains practical descriptions of all aspects of TCP/IP in UNIX systems, with discussion of MAC and PC integration. It's a great quick reference that answers many questions, or at least gets you pointed in a direction so you can answer it yourself.

Cole, Gerald D. *Computer Networking for Systems Programmers*, John Wiley and Sons, New York, NY, 1990, ISBN: 0-471-51057-2. A comprehensive survey of networking layers and protocols, it makes a good "quick reference" book: very readable but not in-depth.

Comer, Douglas. *Internetworking with TCP/IP, Volume I*, Prentice-Hall, Englewood Cliffs, NJ, 1991, ISBN: 0-13-468505-9. This beginner's-level introduction (undergraduate text book) to the structure of the TCP/IP protocol suite makes the transition to advanced texts like RFCs, Stevens Volume I, or Stallings Volume III relatively painless.

Dumas, Arthur. *Programming WinSock*, Sams Publishing, Indianapolis, IN, 1995, ISBN: 0-672-30594-1. This provides a good tutorial for using WinSock with C++; it doesn't cover many of the intricacies of WinSock, but includes source code that illustrates many of the basics.

Estrada, Susan. *Connecting to the Internet*, O'Reilly & Associates, Sebastopol, CA, 1993, ISBN: 1-56592-061-9. An excellent introduction to Internet service providers, and what you need to know to get connected. This book gives a quick overview of what's available on the Internet, and lots of information about the different types of Internet access available. It is best at providing practical advice about how to choose what's best for you or your business.

Hunt, Craig. *TCP/IP Network Administration*, O'Reilly & Associates, Sebastopol, CA, 1992, ISBN: 0-937175-82-X. This is battle armor for anyone in the trenches. It is detailed, yet readable, like anything edited by Mike Loukides.

Krol, Ed. *The Whole Internet: User's Guide & Catalog*, O'Reilly & Associates, Sebastopol, CA, 1992, ISBN: 1-56592-025-2. There are a *lot* of Internet guide books available these days, but this is still one of the best. This isn't surprising, since Ed wrote the original Internet guide in 1989 (RFC 1118, "Hitchhiker's Guide to the Internet").

Myers, Brian (and Eric Hamer). *Mastering Windows NT Programming*, Sybex, Alameda, CA, 1993, ISBN: 0-7821-1264-1. This is a comprehensive, detailed, and readable programming guide and reference for Windows NT. It is similar to Petzold's for Windows 3.1.

Petzold, Charles. *Programming Windows 3.1. (3rd ed.)*, Microsoft Press, Redmond, WA, 1992, ISBN: 1-55615-395-3. The definitive Windows 3.1 programming guide and reference, this text contains lots of sample code (includes disk).

Pietrek, Matt. *Windows Internals*, Addison-Wesley, Reading, MA, 1993, ISBN: 0-201-62217-3. This is a companion to *Undocumented Windows* that exposes components in the black box that is Windows. It helps you to understand what you should and shouldn't do in your 16-bit Windows applications (and why). Also, it can provide guidance when you need some hint as to which way a bug scurried.

Raymond, Eric. *The New Hacker's Dictionary*, MIT Press, Cambridge, MA, 1991, ISBN: 0-262-68069-6. This is not an average (lame) computer dictionary. Hackerspeak is obfuscated English, and this text defines the grammar and vocabulary. It will help you with USENET messages, RFCs, as well as encounters with hacknoids. Besides being useful, it's pretty entertaining, too. Note: This text is also available in electronic form on the Internet from the Gutenberg Project.

Richter, Jeffrey. *Advanced Windows Programming*, Microsoft Press, Redmond, WA, 1995, ISBN: 1-55615-677-4. This is a very useful tutorial and reference for Win32 programming.

Schulman, Andrew. *Unauthorized Windows 95: Developers Resource Kit*, IDG Books, San Mateo, CA, 1994, ISBN: 1-56884-305-4. A glimpse at the internals Windows 95 before its release, it reveals the "new" operating system's MS-DOS foundation.

Schulman, Andrew (David Maxey and Matt Pietrek). *Undocumented Windows*, Addison-Wesley, Reading, MA, 1992, ISBN: 0-201-60834-0. This is full of information about the mechanics of Microsoft Windows 3.x. and includes useful source code for exploring Windows and debugging application problems.

Stallings, William, *Networking Standards: A Guide to OSI, ISDN, LAN and MAN*, Addison-Wesley, Reading, MA, 1993, ISBN: 0-201-56357-6. If you need to delve into the low-level "network access" layers (layers 1 and 2 in the OSI network reference model), then you want a copy of this book. It focuses on OSI, but it deals with details in many medias: Broadband, ISDN, Ethernet, IEEE 802.5, FDDI, ATM, and Frame Relay.

Stevens, W. Richard. *Advanced Programming in the UNIX Environment*, Addison-Wesley, Reading, MA, 1992, ISBN: 0-201-56317-7. This comprehensive reference for programming with the run-time library of the (any) UNIX environment contains excellent descriptions of concepts with code illustrations in C. It describes programming standards: ANSI, IEEE POSIX, and X/Open, and references specifics in a variety of UNIX platforms ("vanilla SVR4." 4.3+BSD, BSD/386, and SunOS 4.1.1 and 4.1.2). It is edited by Brian Kernighan.

Stevens, W. Richard. *TCP/IP Illustrated, Volume I*, Addison-Wesley, Reading, MA, 1994, ISBN: 0-201-63346-9. It doesn't get any better than this comprehensive, in-depth, and readable book. If you need to program or debug a TCP/IP network, you should have a copy of this book.

Stevens, W. Richard. *UNIX Network Programming*, Prentice-Hall, Englewood Cliffs, NJ, 1990, ISBN: 0-13-949876-1. This is the definitive reference for Berkeley Sockets and System V TLI. It describes all the various UNIX interprocess communication paradigms. It provides many examples of common TCP/IP application protocols, including ping, TFTP, LPR, and BSD "r" (remote) utilities such as rsh. We highly recommend this book.

Tannenbaum, Andrew S. *Computer Networks*, Prentice-Hall, Englewood Cliffs, NJ, 1989, ISBN: 0-13-162959-X. This standard network reference has a comprehensive survey of every layer in the OSI network reference model.

Umar, Amjad. *Distributed Computing: A Practical Synthesis*, Prentice-Hall, Englewood Cliffs, NJ, 1993, ISBN: 0-13-036252-2. An excellent introduction to network hardware and software architecture, with descriptions of many open standards, this text contains a nice mix of high-level management discussions and down-and-dirty technical applications and integration (with case studies).

Index

D

E

P